Official Rules of Sports & Games

1988–89

Official Rules of Sports & Games

1988–89

EDITED BY
REGINALD MOORE

THE KINGSWOOD PRESS

The Kingswood Press
an imprint of William Heinemann Ltd
10 Upper Grosvenor Street, London W1X 9PA

LONDON   MELBOURNE
JOHANNESBURG   AUCKLAND

First published 1949
Seventeenth edition 1987

0 434 98062 5

Photoset by Wilmaset, Birkenhead, Wirral
Printed in Great Britain by Butler & Tanner Ltd, Frome

CONTENTS

ACKNOWLEDGEMENTS

The publishers wish to acknowledge with thanks the very helpful co-operation which they have received from the following associations, who should be consulted over any queries about the games concerned. Without the assistance which these associations and their officials have given, which includes the permission to reproduce these copyright rules and laws and a great deal of help over the illustrations, the publication of this book would not have been possible.

Grand National Archery Society,
7th Street, National Agriculture Centre, Stoneleigh, Kenilworth, Warwicks., CV8 2LG.

Amateur Athletic Association,
Francis House, Francis Street, London, SW1P 1DE.

The Badminton Association of England,
Bradwell Road, Loughton Lodge, Milton Keynes, MK8 9LA.

English Basket Ball Association,
Calomax House, Lupton Avenue, Leeds, LS9 7EE.

English Bowling Association,
2A Iddesleigh Road, Bournemouth, BH3 7JR.

Marylebone Cricket Club,
Lord's Ground, London, NW8 8QN.

The Croquet Association,
The Hurlingham Club, Ranelagh Gardens, London, SW6 3PR.

The Eton Fives Association,
The Moor House, Lane End, High Wycombe, Bucks.

Rugby Fives Association,
32 Dulwich Common, London SE21.

The Football Association,
16 Lancaster Gate, London, W2 3LW.

The British American Football League,
Amway House, Michigan Drive, Tangwell, Milton Keynes, Bucks., MK15 8HD.

Rugby Football Union,
Twickenham, TW2 7RQ.

Rugby Football League,
180 Chapeltown Road, Leeds, LS7 4HT.

The Royal and Ancient Golf Club of St. Andrews,
Fife, KY16 9JD.

Hockey Rules Board,
26 Stompond Lane, Walton-on-Thames, Surrey, KT12 1HB.

British Ice Hockey Association,
48 Barmouth Road, Shirley, Croydon, Surrey, CR0 5EQ.

All England Women's Lacrosse Association,
16 Upper Woburn Place, London, WC1H 0QP.

English Lacrosse Union,
'Lynton', 70 High Road, Rayleigh, Essex, SS6 7AP.

All England Netball Association,
Francis House, Francis Street, London, SW1P 1DE.

National Rounders Association,
4 Gloucester Close, Desford, Leics.

Squash Rackets Association,
Francis House, Francis Street, London, SW1P 1DE.

Tennis and Rackets Association,
c/o The Queen's Club, Palliser Road, London, W14 9EQ.

The International Tennis Federation,
Church Road, Wimbledon, London, SW19 5TF.

The International Table Tennis Federation,
53 London Road, St. Leonards-on-Sea, E. Sussex, TN37 6AY.

Amateur Swimming Association,
Water Polo Committee,
Harold Fern House, Derby Square, Loughborough, Leicestershire.

English Volleyball Association,
128 Melton Road, West Bridgford, Nottingham, NG2 6EP.

The Rules of
Archery

Archery
RULES OF SHOOTING
FITA Article numbers quoted are those used in FITA Constitution and Rules

INTRODUCTION

(*See Note* on p. 57)

G.N.A.S. Laws

3. The shooting regulations as prescribed in its Rules of Shooting shall be accepted as governing the relevant branches of the sport of archery throughout the area under the Society's jurisdiction. The Rules of Shooting are the responsibility of the National Council.

4. No Regional Society, County Association, archery club or similar organisation recognised by the Society shall include in its Constitution or Shooting Regulations any provisions which conflict with those of the Society. A copy of each County Association's and Regional Society's Constitution shall be deposited with National Council.

12. All members, affiliated clubs, associated organisations, associations, county associations and regional societies shall accept the jurisdiction of the Society and shall conform to such conditions, shooting rules and regulations as may be determined from time to time.

14. (*a*) No archer, other than a member of the Society or one whose national society is affiliated to the Federation Internationale de Tir a l'Arc may compete or officiate at any of the Society's meetings or at any meeting of a Regional Society or a County Association or at a Club or Association affiliated to a Regional Society. This clause does not apply to Ladies Paramount.

(*b*) No archer, other than a British National of the United Kingdom may be the holder of a British National Championship or of any of the challenge trophies offered at the British

National Target Championship Meetings and the Grand National Archery meeting.

(*c*) A professional archer may not hold a Championship title or challenge trophy nor may he receive any prize in connection with any tournament organised by or held under the auspices of the Grand National Archery Society or any affiliated body unless specifically offered for competition for professional archers only, not shooting in competition with amateurs.

A professional archer is one who uses his skill in shooting with the bow and arrow as a means of making his living.

Declaration of professionalism or reinstatement of amateur status shall be dealt with by the national Council at its discretion. (N.B. For purposes of international competition the attention of members is drawn to the Rules of Amateur Status laid down from time to time by the Federation Internationale de Tir a l'Arc.)

Amateur Status

An amateur in archery practises the sport in all or one of the various branches as a leisure pursuit.

1. He shall observe the rules of the IOC, his International Federation and his National Federation.

2. He shall not have received any financial rewards or material benefits in connection with his sport participation except:

(*a*) He may be a physical education or sport teacher giving elementary instruction.

(*b*) Accept, subject to certain limitation:

(i) assistance administered through his National Olympic Committee or National Federation.

(ii) compensation authorised by his NOC or National Federation, in case of necessity, to cover financial loss resulting from his absence from work.

(*c*) Accept prizes or trophies not to exceed 700 Swiss francs in value. Cash prizes are not allowed.

(*d*) Accept academic and technical scholarships.

3. Full details of amateur status and the IOC Eligibility Articles 201–205 inclusive.

I. TARGET ARCHERY

100. Target Faces

(a) The Standard British target face is circular, 122 cm (4 ft) in diameter. This British target face is composed as follows:

A circle in the centre 24.4 cm diameter, ringed by four concentric bands the breadth of each, measured radially, being 12.2 cm.

The colours of the target face are: (from the centre outwards) gold, red, blue, black, and white.

The centre of the gold is termed the "pinhole".

The standard FITA face is as above but each colour is divided into two zones of equal width by a line not exceeding 2 mm in width.

(b) Any dividing line which may be used between colours shall be made entirely within the higher scoring zone.

(c) Any line marking the outermost edge of the white shall be made entirely within the scoring zone.

(d) Tolerances on British faces are permitted as follows:

4 mm on the full 122 cm diameter

3 mm in any one zone of 12.2 cm

3 mm on the 24.4 cm diameter of the Gold.

101. Range Layout

(a) The targets shall be set up at one end of the ground. They shall be inclined at an angle of about 15 degrees, with the pinholes 130 cm (4 ft 3 in) above the ground.

(b) Minimum spacing of target centres shall be:

Archers shooting singly			2.44 m	(8 ft)
,,	,,	in pairs	3.05 m	(10 ft)
,,	,,	in threes	3.66 m	(12 ft)

(c) Each target shall be securely anchored so that it cannot blow off its stand. Likewise stands shall be anchored to prevent them from blowing over.

(d) All targets shall be clearly numbered.

(e) The shooting line (over which the archers shall take up their shooting positions) shall be measured from points vertically below the pinholes.

(f) Shooting marks, consisting of discs or other flat markers, shall be positioned opposite the targets at the appropriate distances. The shooting marks are to bear the number of the target opposite to which they are placed.

(g) Lines at right angles to the shooting line and extending from the shooting line to the target line making lanes containing one, two or three bosses may be laid down.

(h) A waiting line shall be placed at least five yards behind the shooting line.

(i) On grounds where the public have right of access an area shall be roped off to indicate that no one can pass behind the targets within 50 yards of them. Where an efficient backstop netting, a bank or other similar device (not a hedge or penetrable fence) high enough for the top of the stop as seen from the shooting line to be at least as far above the top of the target as the gold is below the top of the target, then this distance may be reduced to 25 yards. The area to be roped shall extend from the ends of the "safety line" so that no one can pass within 20 yards of the ends of the target line, 10 yards of the shooting line and 15 yards behind the shooting line.

102. Equipment

Three types of bow are recognised:

(a) Bows and their accessories which conform in all respects to the following:

(i) A bow of any type may be used provided it subscribes to the accepted principle and meaning of the word bow as used in Target Archery; e.g. an article consisting of a handle (grip), riser and two flexible limbs each ending in a tip with a string nock.

The bow is braced for use by a single bowstring attached directly between the two string nocks only and, in operation, is held in one hand by its handle (grip) while the fingers of the other hand draw, hold back and release the string.

(ii) A bowstring may be made up of any number of strands of the material chosen for the purpose, with a centre serving to accommodate the drawing fingers, a nocking point to which may be added serving(s) to fit the arrow nock as necessary, and to locate this point one or two nock locators may be positioned and in each of the two ends of the bowstring a loop to be placed in the string nocks of the bow when braced.

In addition, one attachment which may not exceed a diameter of one centimetre in any direction is permitted on the string to serve as nose or lip mark.

The serving on the string must not end within the archer's vision at full draw. A bowstring must not in any way offer aid in aiming through "peephole", marking or any other means.

(iii) An arrowrest, which can be adjustable, any movable pressure button, pressure point or arrowplate and draw check indicator may all be used on the bow provided they are not electric or electronic and do not offer an additional aid in aiming.

(iv) A bowsight, a bowmark or a point of aim on the ground for aiming is permitted, but at no time may more than one such device be used.

(1) A bowsight as attached to the bow for the purpose of aiming may allow for windage adjustment as well as elevation setting but it is subject to the following provision:

it shall not incorporate a prism or lens or other magnifying device, levelling or electric devices nor shall it provide for more than one sighting point.

An attachment to which the bowsight is fixed is permitted.

The length of any sight (ring, barrel, conical, etc.) shall not exceed the minimum inside diameter of the aperture. A hood is not to exceed a length of 1 cm irrespective of shape.

(2) A bowmark is a single mark made on the bow for the purpose of aiming. Such mark may be made in pencil, tape or any other suitable marking material.

A plate or tape with distance markings may be mounted on the bow as a guide but must not in any way offer any additional aid.

(3) A point of aim on the ground is a marker placed in the shooting lane between the shooting line and the target. Such marker may not exceed a diameter of 7.5 cm and must not protrude above the ground more than 15 cm.

(v) Stabilisers and torque flight compensators on the bow

are permitted provided they do not:

(1) serve as a string guide
(2) touch anything but the bow
(3) represent any obstacle to other archers as far as place on the shooting line is concerned.

(vi) Arrows of any type may be used provided they subscribe to the accepted principle and meaning of the word arrow as used in Target Archery, and that such arrows do not cause undue damage to target faces and buttresses.

An arrow consists of a shaft with head (point), nock, fletching and, if desired, cresting and/or numbers. The arrows of each archer shall be marked with the archer's name, initials or insignia and all arrows used for the same end of 3 or 6 arrows shall carry the same pattern and colour(s) of fletching, nocks and cresting (if any).

(vii) Finger protection in the form of finger stalls or tips, gloves, shooting tab or tape (plaster) to draw, hold back and release the string is permitted, provided they are smooth and with no device to help to hold and/or release the string.

Shooting tabs may be built up of several layers of any materials suitable for their use and allow for the part of the tab behind that used for drawing the string to be stiff using different materials for this build-up (the latter can be leather, plastic, metal, etc.). No shapes have been specified and no limitations in respect of size.

A separator between the fingers to prevent pinching the arrow may be used.

On the bow hand an ordinary glove, mitten or similar may be worn.

(viii) Field glasses, telescopes and other visual aids may be used for spotting arrows.

Ordinary spectacles as necessary or shooting spectacles provided they are fitted with the same lenses normally worn by the archer, and sun glasses may be worn.

None may be fitted with microhole lenses, glasses or similar marked in any way which can assist aiming.

(ix) Accessories are permitted such as bracers, dress shield, bowsling, belt or ground quiver, tassel and foot markers not protruding above the ground more than one centimetre.

(*b*) Crossbows which conform to the Rules and Conditions stated in Part V.

(*c*) Compound and other bows and their accessories which do not meet the requirements of para. 102 (a).

103. Separate Styles and Conditions

(*a*) Bows conforming to 102 (*a*).

(i) Free Style: As 102 (*a*).

(ii) Barebow:

(1) As 102 (*a*) (i) and the bow must be free from any protrusions, marks or blemishes or laminated pieces which could be used in aiming. The inside of the upper limb shall be without trade marks.

(2) As 102 (*a*) (ii), except that there shall be no attachment to the string to act as a nose or lip mark, or other marks to aid finger position selection.

(3) An arrowrest, arrowplate and pressure button are allowed. These may be adjustable.

(4) As 102 (*a*) (vi) except that in Field Archery the arrows need be numbered by rings only to be plainly visible, and at least 3 mm wide and approximately 3 mm spacing.

(5) As 102 (*a*) (vii).

(6) As 102 (*a*) (ix) except footmarkers.

(7) As 102 (*a*) (viii) except that field glasses and other visual aids may not be used when shooting Field Rounds with unmarked distances.

(8) The following are not permitted:

> Any aid for estimating distances
> Any memoranda that assist in improving scores
> Sights, draw check indicator and mounted stabilisers—the bow must be bare.

(iii) Traditional—As barebow except that (1) the arrows shall be made of wood except for the fletchings, and they may be fitted with metallic piles and plastic nocks; (2) the archers draw position, and the relationship of the arrow to the drawing fingers must not change, i.e. face walking and string-walking are not permitted; (3) an arrowrest is permitted, but may not be adjustable: a pressure button is not permitted.

(*b*) Crossbows (see Part V).

(*c*) Bows conforming to 102 (*c*).

(i) Unlimited – No restrictions as to accessories, but the bow must be free and held in the hand.

(ii) Limited – The bow must be held in the hand and the string must be drawn, held back and released by the fingers of the other hand. A level, peepsight and pressure button are permitted but a scope is not allowed. A cable guard may be fitted.

(iii) Bowhunter – The bow must be held in the hand and the string must be drawn, held back and released by the fingers of the other hand. No marking or attachment may appear on the bow or string which may be used as an aid to aiming. A cable guard, one stabiliser not longer than 30.5 cm (12 in.), a pressure button, and an adjustable arrowrest and plate are permitted.

(*a*) Shooting, except in the case of permanently or semi-permanently disabled archers, shall be from an unsupported standing position, placing one foot on each side of the shooting line.

(*b*) (i) The order in which archers shall shoot at their respective targets shall be the order in which they appear on the target list and the drawing up of the target list shall be a matter for arrangement by the Tournament Organisers. Unless otherwise directed, No. 3 on each target shall be the Target Captain, and No. 4 the Lieutenant. The Captain shall be responsible for the orderly conduct of shooting in accordance with the Rules of Shooting.

(ii) The order of shooting in all Tournaments of Record Status shall rotate. For other Tournaments, including Club Target Days, rotation shall be optional. (This rule does not apply to the Worcester Round.)

(*c*) Six arrows shall be shot at an end. Each archer shall shoot three arrows and immediately retire and, when all on a target have shot, shall shoot three more. If an archer persists in shooting more than three arrows consecutively he may be disqualified by the Judge.

(*d*) In the event of an archer shooting more than six arrows at an end, the archer shall be penalised by losing the value of his best arrow(s) in the target, and such arrow(s) shall not be measured for a Gold prize.

(e) An arrow shall be deemed not to have been shot, if the archer can touch it with his bow without moving his feet from their normal position in relation to the shooting line. In which case another arrow may be shot in its place. If another arrow is not available he may only retrieve his misnocked arrow with the Judge's permission.

(f) If from any cause an archer is not prepared to shoot before all have shot, such archer shall lose the benefit of that end.

(g) Archers arriving late shall not be allowed to make up any ends that they have missed.

(h) An archer shall retire from the shooting line as soon as his last arrow has been shot. The last archer on a target may, however, remain on the shooting line to keep company with another archer still shooting.

(i) Two and half minutes shall be the maximum time for an archer to shoot three arrows, the time to start from when the archer steps on to the shooting line.

(j) Whilst an archer is on the shooting line, he shall receive no information by word or otherwise from anyone except the Judge or Field Captain(s).

(k) At any Meeting no practice is allowed on the ground the same day, except that one end of six arrows may be shot as sighters before the beginning of each day's shooting, but only after competitors have come under the Judge's orders at the Assembly. Such sighters shall not be recorded.

(l) If for any reason an archer is alone on a target he must notify the Judge who shall arrange for him to be transferred to another target or another archer to be transferred to join him.

(m) The maximum number of archers on a target shall be six.

105. Control of Shooting

(a) The Lady Paramount shall be the supreme arbitrator on all matters connected with the Tournament at which she officiates.

(b) At all times, whenever shooting takes place, it must be under the control of a Field Captain.

At larger meetings a Judge shall be appointed to take charge of the shooting. Field Captains, to whom the Judge may delegate his authority, may be appointed as necessary. If a Field Captain has not been appointed previously, the Judge may appoint any experienced archer to act in this capacity.

At Tournaments the Judge and Field Captains shall be non-shooting.

(*c*) The Judge shall be in sole control of the shooting and shall resolve all disputes (subject to the supreme authority of the Lady Paramount) in accordance with the Rules of Shooting.

106. Scoring

(*a*) The scoring points for hits on the target face for G.N.A.S. Rounds are:

Gold 9, Red 7, Blue 5, Black 3, White 1.

The scoring points for hits on the target face for F.I.T.A. Rounds are:

Inner Gold 10, Outer Gold 9, Inner Red 8, Outer Red 7, Inner Blue 6, Outer Blue 5, Inner Black 4, Outer Black 3, Inner White 2, Outer White 1.

The value shall be determined by the position of the arrow shaft.

(*b*) Archers shall identify their arrows by pointing at the nocks. Neither the arrow nor the target face shall be touched until the final decision as to score has been given and any such interference with the target or arrow shall disqualify the archer from scoring the higher value.

The Lieutenant will identify the arrows with the score called and will assist the Captain in any way that may be required. No. 1 on the target shall identify the Lieutenant's score.

The duty of entering the scores on the score sheet may be shared by the archers on each target, but the Target Captain shall remain responsible for ensuring that scores are correctly recorded. The Target Captain and Lieutenant will check the score sheet and the Target Captain and the archer shall sign it as correct. The Lieutenant shall sign the Target Captain's score sheet. The attention of archers is drawn to their responsibility for ensuring that when signing score sheets the score, etc., that they sign for is correct.

(*c*) If an arrow touches two colours or any dividing line it shall be scored as being of that of the higher value.

(*d*) If any doubt or dispute shall arise it shall be decided by the Target Captain subject to appeal to the Judge.

(*e*) No alteration shall be made in the value of any arrow as entered on the score sheet, to the advantage of its owner, after such arrow has been drawn from the target.

Any alteration to the recorded score must be initialled by the Judge in a differing coloured ink prior to the withdrawal of the arrow from the target. No arrows shall be withdrawn from the target (without the express direction of the Captain) until all the archers' scores have been entered on the score sheet and the Captain is satisfied that they are correctly entered.

(*f*) If an arrow is observed to rebound from a target, the archer concerned shall draw the attention of the Judge to the fact after having shot his sixth arrow (or third if shooting in ends of 3 only) by retiring two paces from the shooting line and holding his bow above his head.

Upon the Judge satisfying himself that the claim is justified, the archer shall be permitted to shoot another arrow separately in the same end after all archers on that target have completed their normal shooting, such arrow to be numbered or preferably marked by the Judge.

To prevent frivolous bouncer claims, the archer is to be warned individually that if six original arrows were shot not including a bouncer, then his highest scoring arrow may, at the discretion of the Judge on repetition of a false claim, be deducted from that end's score. The Judge shall take part in that competitor's scoring to ensure that only the correct number of arrows are scored, and that the bouncer was not caused by striking another arrow already in the target. An arrow passing through a target cannot be scored.

(*g*) An arrow passing through the target face but remaining in the boss shall be withdrawn by the Captain or Lieutenant and shall be inserted from the back in the same place and at the assumed angle of original penetration until the pile is visible in the target face, when the score shall be determined.

(*h*) An arrow hitting and remaining embedded in another arrow shall be scored the same as the arrow struck.

(*i*) An arrow in the target, which has or may have been deflected by another arrow already in the target, shall be scored according to the position of its shaft in the target face.

(*j*) An arrow on the ground believed to have hit and rebounded from another arrow shall be scored the value of the struck arrow, if the latter is found in the target with its nock damaged in a compatible manner.

(*k*) If an arrow fails to enter the buttress and is hanging in the target face it shall be pushed in by the Judge or shall be removed and the Judge will ensure that the appropriate score is recorded when scoring takes place.

(*l*) The F.I.T.A. Rule that bouncers shall only be scored if arrow holes on the target face are marked applies to all F.I.T.A. Rounds shot including those shot at Club Target Days, inter-county matches, etc.

(*m*) An archer may delegate another archer on the same target to record his score and pick up his arrows.

(*n*) An incapacitated archer may nominate an assistant, who shall be under the control and discipline of the Judge, to record his score and pick up his arrows.

(*o*) In the event of a tie for a score prize the winner shall be the one of those who tie who has the greatest number of hits. Should this result in a tie the prize shall be awarded to the archer among those who tie who has the greatest number of Golds. Should this number also be the same the archers shall be declared joint winners. Where the prize is for (i) most hits, or (ii) most Golds, ties shall be resolved on the above principle in the following order (i) highest score, most Golds, (ii) highest score, most hits.

(*p*) When a shoot (other than the annual Grand National Archery Meeting) is abandoned due to adverse weather conditions, the placings and prizes shall be awarded on the cumulative score at the conclusion of the last full end shot by the competitors, by instruction of the Judge.

(*q*) Bows which are recognised in Rule 102 (*b*) and (*c*) MAY NOT BE USED IN DIRECT COMPETITION with bows recognised in Rule 102 (*a*). Archers using bows recognised in Rule 102 (*b*) and (*c*) shall not be eligible for any prize, medal, trophy or other award, classification, handicap or other distinction which has not been specifically devised or designated for archers using such bows.

The allocation of any prize, medal, trophy or other award shall be a matter for each individual tournament organiser. Classification, handicap or other distinction shall remain the sole prerogative of the Grand National Archery Society.

107. Dress Regulations

(*a*) At all Tournaments with National Record Status members of the Society shooting and officiating are required to wear the accepted dress.

(*b*) (i) Ladies are required to wear a dress or skirt or trousers (slacks) with suitable blouse.

(ii) Gentlemen are required to wear full length trousers and long or short sleeved shirts.

(iii) Sweaters/cardigans/blazers may be worn.

Each garment shall be plain dark green or white. There is no objection to wearing green and white garments together.

Waterproof clothing worn only during inclement weather is not subject to these regulations, but both white and green waterproofs are available and are recommended.

(*c*) Footwear must be worn by all competitors at all times during the Tournament.

(*d*) Advertising material must not be carried or worn. The name/emblem of an archer's Country, Regional or County Association or Club may be worn on the uniform or shooting clothes.

(*e*) Any archer not conforming to the above regulations shall be requested by the Judge and Organiser to leave the shooting line and will not be permitted to shoot.

108. Recognised Rounds for Record and Classification Purposes

(*a*) The following Rounds are recognised by the Society:

York: 6 dozen arrows at 100 yd.; 4 dozen arrows at 80 yd.; 2 dozen arrows at 60 yd.

Western: 4 dozen arrows at 60 yd.; 4 dozen arrows at 50 yd.

St. George: 3 dozen arrows at 100 yd.; 3 dozen arrows at 80 yd.; 3 dozen arrows at 60 yd.

National: 4 dozen arrows at 60 yd.; 2 dozen arrows at 50 yd.

New Western: 4 dozen arrows at 100 yd.; 4 dozen arrows at 80 yd.

Windsor: 3 dozen arrows at 60 yd.; 3 dozen arrows at 50 yd.; 3 dozen arrows at 40 yd.

New National: 4 dozen arrows at 100 yd.; 2 dozen arrows at 80 yd.

American: 30 arrows at 60 yd.; 30 arrows at 50 yd.; 30 arrows at 40 yd.

Hereford: 6 dozen arrows at 80 yd.; 4 dozen arrows at 60 yd.; 2 dozen arrows at 50 yd.

Albion: 3 dozen arrows at 80 yd.; 3 dozen arrows at 60 yd.; 3 dozen arrows at 50 yd.

Long Western: 4 dozen arrows at 80 yd.; 4 dozen arrows at 60 yd.

Long National: 4 dozen arrows at 80 yd.; 2 dozen arrows at 60 yd.

Long Metric (Gentlemen)**:** 3 dozen arrows at 90 m.; 3 dozen arrows at 70 m.

F.I.T.A. (Gentlemen)**:** 3 dozen arrows at 90 m., 3 dozen arrows at 70 m., 3 dozen arrows at 50 m., 3 dozen arrows at 30 m.

F.I.T.A. (Ladies)**:** 3 dozen arrows at 70 m., 3 dozen arrows at 60 m., 3 dozen arrows at 50 m., 3 dozen arrows at 30 m.

Short Metric: 3 dozen arrows at 50 m., 3 dozen arrows at 30 m.

Long Metric (Ladies)**:** 3 dozen arrows at 70 m., 3 dozen arrows at 60 m.

(*b*) in every round the longer, or longest distance is shot first, and the shorter, or shortest distance last.

(*c*) When F.I.T.A. and Metric Rounds are shot, F.I.T.A. Rules apply.

(*d*) (i) A F.I.T.A. Round may be shot in one day or over two consecutive days under F.I.T.A. Rules.

(ii) All other Rounds to be shot in one day. (Except in accordance with Rule for Championships of more than one day's duration.)

(*e*) In addition any "local" round made up of other numbers of arrows at specified distances may be used in Clubs and Tournaments provided the Rules of Shooting are adhered to in all respects and subjects to their non-recognition by the

G.N.A.S. for Record, Classification or Handicap purposes.

109. Club Events

(a) Club Target Day

(i) A Target Day is any day and time appointed under the Rules of the Club and previously announced to the Members.

(ii) There is no statutory limit to the number of officially appointed Target Days in any one week.

(iii) All scores made must be entered in the Club Record Book.

(iv) Target Days should commence punctually at the announced time.

(v) All shooting shall be in accordance with G.N.A.S. Rules of Shooting.

(vi) On any Club Target Day there shall be a minimum of two archers shooting, not necessarily on the same Target, each recording the other's scores in order that these scores may be recognised. An archer shooting alone may claim his score provided that it has been recorded throughout by a non-shooting archer.

(b) Open Meeting

An Open Meeting is an event run as a competition open to all Members of G.N.A.S. and F.I.T.A. Affiliated Members, with all the necessary organisation, advertising of the event, judging, etc., run under G.N.A.S. Rules of Shooting.

(c) Tournament

A Tournament is an Event at which awards are given. This may be an Open or Closed Meeting.

110. Six Gold Badge

(a) The award, which is for six consecutive arrows shot at one end into the gold, is open to Members of the Society.

(b) The shortest distances at which it may be gained are:
Gentlemen – 80 yd.   Ladies – 60 yd.

(c) In the F.I.T.A. Round the badge will be awarded for six consecutive arrows at one end shot into the Gold zone at:
Gentlemen – 90 or 70 metres   Ladies – 70 or 60 metres

(d) The Six Gold End must be made at a Meeting organised

by the Society or by any of its associated bodies, or in competition at an Associated Club's Target Day, under G.N.A.S. Rules of Shooting.

(*e*) Claims for the award must be submitted to the G.N.A.S. Secretary on the appropriate form, accompanied by the original score sheet duly signed by the Club Secretary or Meeting Organiser.

111. F.I.T.A. Star Badge

The award is open to Members of the Society according to qualifications and applications as laid down in F.I.T.A. Rules. Claims for the award must be submitted to the G.N.A.S. Secretary on the appropriate form.

120. Regulations for the Grand National Archery Meeting

(*a*) The meeting shall consist of not less than three days' shooting, weather permitting, during which a Handicap Meeting may be held.

(*b*) A lady shall be invited to officiate as Lady Paramount by the Secretary after consultation with the National Council.

(*c*) The Judges shall be appointed by National Council.

121. Rounds

(*a*) The Ladies' Meeting shall consist of: Two Hereford Rounds. Ladies may enter for the National Round only.

(*b*) The Gentlemen's Meeting shall consist of: Two York Rounds.

122. Winners

The winner shall be those Archers obtaining the greatest scores over the Double Hereford and York Rounds respectively.

In the event of a tie the archer making the greatest number of hits amongst those who have ties shall be the winner. In the event of this resulting in a tie the winner shall be the one of those who tie who has the greatest number of Golds. Should this number also be the same the archers shall be declared joint winners.

123. Shooting

If, owing to the state of the weather, the full number of arrows is not shot on the first or second day, the remaining arrows shall, if possible, be shot on the next day, providing that not more than eighteen dozen arrows are shot in any one day. The Judge in consultation with the Secretary (Organiser) and Field Captain shall decide whether any other Competitions shall be cancelled.

124. Challenge Trophies and Prizes

(*a*) The Challenge Trophies are open only to British Nationals of the United Kingdom. Unless the winner is permanently resident in the United Kingdom the trophy shall remain in the custody of the Society. Any question as to the residence of the winner shall be decided by the National Council, whose decision shall be final.

(*b*) No awards shall be made unless one complete Round is shot, and if the Double Round be incomplete, the prizes and Challenge Trophies shall be awarded on the one round only that has been completed.

(*c*) Certain Challenge Trophies, i.e. those of the original National Round Championships, will be awarded on the two National Rounds. All Ladies will be competing for these.

(*d*) (i) The County Challenge Trophies shall be awarded to the County Teams making the highest aggregate scores at the Championship Meeting. The archer making the highest score in a winning team shall be entitled to hold the Trophy until the next meeting.

(ii) Each County's teams score shall consist of the four, or fewer, highest scores made by the Ladies and Gentlemen respectively competing at the Championship Meeting.

(iii) Archers competing who are affiliated to the Society through one of its Affiliated Clubs (Associate Member) shall shoot for the County through which their G.N.A.S. Affiliation Fees are paid.

Archers competing who are Ordinary Members of the Society, or whose G.N.A.S. Affiliation Fees are paid through an Associated Organisation of G.N.A.S. shall notify the

G.N.A.S. Secretary and the Secretary of the County concerned by 1st January in each year of the County for which they wish to shoot.

140. Regulations for the British National Target Championship

(*a*) The Annual Championship shall consist of not less than two days shooting, weather permitting.

(*b*) A lady shall be invited to officiate as Lady Paramount by the Secretary after consultation with the National Council.

(*c*) The Judges shall be appointed by National Council.

141. Rounds

(*a*) The Ladies' Championship shall consist of two Hereford Rounds.

(*b*) The Gentlemen's Championship shall consist of two York Rounds.

142. Titles

The Championship Titles are open only to British Nationals of the United Kingdom and shall be awarded to the archers obtaining the greatest scores over the Double Hereford and York Rounds respectively. In the event of a tie the archer making the greatest number of hits amongst those who have ties shall be the Champion. In the event of this resulting in a tie the Champion shall be the one of those who tie who has the greatest number of Golds. Should this number also be the same the archers shall be declared joint Champions.

143. Shooting

If, owing to the state of the weather, the full number of arrows is not shot on the first day, the remaining arrows, shall, if possible, be shot on the second day, If, owing to the state of the weather, a full Round cannot be shot the Judge in consultation with the Tournament Organiser and Field Captain shall determine at which point the Champions shall be declared.

144. Challenge Trophies

(*a*) The Challenge Trophies are open only to British Nationals of the United Kingdom.

(b) The Regional and County Challenge Trophies and/or medals shall be awarded to the respective teams making the highest aggregate scores at the Championship Meeting. The archer making the highest score in a winning team shall be entitled to hold the trophy until the next meeting.

Each team's score shall consist of the four, or fewer, highest scores made by Ladies and/or Gentlemen competing at the Championship Meeting.

(c) The County and Region for which an archer shall shoot shall be determined by applying Rule 124 (d) (iii).

160. Regulations for the UK Masters' Tournament

The UK Masters' Tournament is held annually, usually during the second weekend in June. The Tournament is by invitation only to:

(a) All Grand Master Bowmen, Master Bowmen and Junior Master Bowmen.

(b) Archers from F.I.T.A. Member Associations.

(c) Archers nominated by the G.N.A.S. Target Selection Committee.

161. Rounds

A single F.I.T.A. Round shall be shot over two consecutive days under F.I.T.A. Target Archery Rules.

162. Titles

No titles are awarded.

163. Challenge Trophies

The Challenge Trophies are open to all competitors under the conditions stated in 124 (a).

180. Indoor Target Archery

181. Recognised Rounds

The following Rounds are recognised by the Society:

(a) **Stafford Round:** 6 dozen arrows at 30 metres at an 80 cm target face.

(*b*) **Portsmouth Round:** 5 dozen arrows at 20 yards at a 60 cm target face.

(*c*) **Worcester Round:** 5 dozen arrows at 20 yards at a 40.64 cm (16 in) target face.

(*d*) **F.I.T.A. Round I:** 30 arrows at 18 metres at a 40 cm target face.

(*e*) **F.I.T.A. Round II:** 30 arrows at 25 metres at a 60 cm target face.

(*f*) In addition any "local" round made up of other numbers of arrows at specified distances may be used in Clubs and Tournaments provided the Rules of Shooting are adhered to in all respects and subject to their non-recognition by the G.N.A.S. for record, classification or handicap purposes.

182. Regulations for the Stafford and Portsmouth Rounds

The Rules of Target Archery shall apply with the following exceptions.

(*a*) **Target Faces.** The target faces used shall be:

(i) Stafford Round: 80 cm diameter 10 zone at a distance of 30 metres (standard F.I.T.A. target face).

(ii) Portsmouth Round: 60 cm diameter 10 zone at a distance of 20 yards (standard coloured and zoned).

(iii) Tolerances on 80 cm and 60 cm target faces shall not exceed 2 mm on any one zone and 3 mm on the diameter of each target face.

(*b*) **Range Layout.** Target centres shall be placed so as to allow archers to stand at a minimum of 0.91 m (3 ft) intervals while shooting.

(*c*) **Shooting**

(i) Archers may shoot singly or in pairs provided that Rule 182(*b*) is complied with. Archers shall rotate the order of shooting when shooting singly, and alternate when shooting in pairs.

(ii) An end shall consist of 3 arrows.

(iii) 3 Sighter arrows shall be shot.

(*d*) **Scoring**

The scoring points for hits on the target, reading from the inner Gold to the outer White are 10, 9, 8, 7, 6, 5, 4, 3, 2, 1.

183. Regulations for the Worcester Round

The Rules of Target Archery shall apply with the following exceptions:

(a) **Target Faces**

(i) The target faces used shall be circular 40.64 cm (16 in) in diameter.

This target face is composed as follows:

A circle in the centre 8.13 cm (3¼ in) diameter ringed by four concentric bands, the breadth of each measured radially being 4.064 cm (1⅝ in).

The centre circle shall be coloured white and the four concentric bands black. The concentric bands shall be divided by white lines. Each of the white dividing lines shall be of no greater width than 1 mm (0.04 in).

(ii) Tolerances on target faces are permitted as follows:

2 mm (0.08 in) on each zone and 2 mm (0.08 in) on full 40.64 cm (16 in) diameter.

(b) **Range Layout**

(i) The centres of the target bosses on which the target faces are affixed shall be placed so as to allow archers to stand at a minimum of 0.91 m (3 ft) intervals while shooting.

(ii) The shooting line (over which the archers shall take up their shooting positions) shall be measured from points vertically below the centre of the target boss on which target faces are affixed.

(c) **Shooting**

(i) Five arrows shall be shot at an end. Each archer will shoot his five arrows before retiring from the shooting line.

(ii) In the event of an archer shooting more than five arrows at an end the archer shall be penalised by losing the value of his best arrow(s) in the target.

(iii) At any meeting no practice is allowed except that one end of five arrows may be shot as sighters.

(iv) The maximum number of archers on a target boss shall be four.

(v) Five minutes shall be the maximum time for an archer to shoot an end. The time to start from when the archer steps on to the shooting line.

(*d*) **Scoring**

The scoring points for hits on the target face are: 5, 4, 3, 2, 1, reading from the centre white circle.

(*e*) **Recognised Round**

(i) The Round shall consist of 12 ends (60 arrows).

(ii) The distance to be shot is twenty yards.

(iii) Each boss shall hold four target faces.

(iv) Target faces shall be arranged thus:

      1   2

      3   4

(v) Two archers of a group shall shoot five arrows when the second group shall then shoot their five arrows.

(vi) The first group of two archers shall shoot at the higher targets; the second group at the lower targets.

(vii) When all archers have shot 30 arrows those who have been shooting at the lower targets shall change to the higher targets and those who have been shooting at the higher targets shall shoot at the lower targets, thus:

Those who have been shooting on targets 1 and 2 shall shoot the remaining 30 arrows on targets 3 and 4 retaining their same shooting positions.

184. Regulations for the F.I.T.A. Rounds I and II

(*a*) F.I.T.A. Rules 950–954 will apply.

(*b*) **Shooting and Scoring**

(i) Each archer shall shoot his arrows in ends of three.

(ii) Two ends of sighter arrows are permitted each day preceding the commencement of shooting.

(iii) Scoring shall take place after each end of three arrows.

(*c*) **Other Rules and Regulations**

In all other aspects the rules of Target Archery shall apply except that the two and a half minute time limit for shooting three arrows may not be extended.

If space does not permit a waiting line may be omitted.

185. Regulations for the National Indoor Championship Meeting

(*a*) A Double F.I.T.A. II Round shall be shot at the National Championship Meeting.

(*b*) Regulations for National Championship Meetings, Rules 140–144 apply as appropriate.

(*c*) National Records may be established according to Part VIII.

II. FIELD ARCHERY

200. Regulations

(*a*) G.N.A.S. Rules of Shooting 102, 103, 201–206 shall apply to G.N.A.S. recognised Rounds and any other traditional or local round run under the G.N.A.S. Rules of Shooting.

(*b*) At National Record Status and F.I.T.A. Round events at and above County Championship level there shall be an initial equipment inspection. At such meetings an archer's equipment shall be liable to inspection at any time.

201. General Field Archery Rules

(*a*) Judges shall be appointed, working under a Field Captain to be in control of the shoot.

(*b*) The duties of the Field Captain and Judges shall be:

(i) to ensure that adequate safety precautions have been observed in the lay-out of the course and practice area (if any).

(ii) to address the assembled competitors before the shoot commences on safety precautions and any other appropriate matter including method of starting the event, the starting points of each group, etc.

(iii) to ensure that all competitors are conversant with the rules of the competition and the method of scoring.

(iv) to resolve disputes or queries that may arise in interpretation of the rules or other matters.

(*c*) Each shooting group shall consist of not more than six and not less than three archers, one of whom shall be designated Target Captain and two others as scorers.

(*d*) The Target Captain shall be responsible for the orderly conduct of shooting within the group, and have the ultimate responsibility for scoring the arrows.

(*e*) Each scorer shall be supplied with and complete a separate set of score cards for the shooting group and the duties of scorers shall be as follows:

(i) to write down the score of each competitor in the group.

(ii) to complete the score card at the end of the shooting.

(iii) to be responsible for deciding the value of each arrow, in the case of a dispute a Judge shall make the final decision.

(*f*) The score cards shall be signed by the scorer at the end of shooting, and by the archer as an acceptance of the final score.

(*g*) Should the two score cards not agree, then the lower score shall be taken as the result.

(*h*) The use of binoculars and other visual aids is not permitted in G.N.A.S. Field Archery and F.I.T.A. unmarked rounds.

(*i*) The archer's more forward foot must be in contact and behind the shooting post while shooting, except in the F.I.T.A. Hunter, Field and Combination Rounds when the archer shall stand with both feet behind the relevant shooting line, which is an imaginary line parallel to the target through the shooting post.

(*j*) If, in competitions where the targets have not been marked, an arrow is observed to bounce from, or is believed to have passed through, the target face, the Field Captain or a member of the Technical Commission, shall be called prior to any other arrows being shot at the target. One or other shall check it and if it appears that the arrow has bounced from or passed through the target face then another arrow may be shot at that target from the same position as the bouncing or passing through arrow was shot.

(*k*) Archers waiting their turn to shoot shall stand well back behind the archers who are shooting.

202. Specific Rules Relating to the G.N.A.S. "Recognised" Rounds

(*a*) Foresters Round

The standard Unit shall consist of the following 14 shots:

Three 24″ diameter faces at a distance of up to 70 yd.

Four 18″ diameter faces at a distance of up to 50 yd.

Four 12″ diameter faces at a distance of up to 40 yd.

Three 6″ diameter faces at a distance of up to 20 yd.

Targets. The target faces shall be of animal or bird design, and shall have inscribed on them an outer circle of fixed diameter, an inner circle of half that diameter, and a spot of one-sixth that diameter.

Thus: | 24″ Face | 12″ Inner Circle. | 4″ Spot |
|---|---|---|
| 18″ Face | 9″ Inner Circle. | 3″ Spot |
| 12″ Face | 6″ Inner Circle. | 2″ Spot |
| 6″ Face | 3″ Inner Circle. | 1″ Spot |

Shooting Rules. At a 24″ Target, four arrows are shot, one from each of four posts. At an 18″ Target, three arrows are shot, one from each of three posts. At a 12″ Target, two arrows are shot, one from each of two posts. At a 6″ Target, only one arrow is shot from one post. Multi-post shots may be equidistant from the target or 'walk-up' or 'walk-away'.

Scoring	Aiming spot	15 points
	Inner circle	10 points
	Outer circle	5 points

Range Marking. In either Marked or Unmarked distances.

(*b*) **Four Shot Foresters Round**

Shooting:	On Forester animal faces, over unmarked Forester distances.
Shots:	Four walk-up shots at each face.
Scoring:	15, 10, and 5 for spot, inner and outer respectively.
Unit:	Fourteen faces in each unit ($3 \times 24''$; $4 \times 18''$; $4 \times 12''$; $3 \times 6''$)—112 shots, maximum possible score 1680.
Dimensions of Scoring Zones:	Spot: one-sixth of the outer diameter. Inner: half the outer diameter.

(*c*) **Big Game Round**

The standard Unit shall consist of the following 14 shots, at the suggested ranges:

Three group 1 Targets at a distance of 70 to 40 yd.

Three group 2 Targets at a distance of 50 to 30 yd.

Four group 3 Targets at a distance of 40 to 20 yd.

Four group 4 Targets at a distance of 30 to 10 yd.

Targets. The target faces shall be of animal or bird design, with the scoring area divided into two parts. The high-scoring area, is the smaller area, situated in the "heart/lung" region of the animal, and is known as the "kill" zone. The low-scoring area, is the remainder of the animal within the marked perimeter, and is known as the "wound" zone.

Targets are classed into groups one, two, three and four, according to size.

Group 1. $40'' \times 28''$—Bear, deer, moose, elk, caribou.

Group 2. $28'' \times 22''$—Antelope, small deer, wolf, mountain lion.

Group 3. $22'' \times 14''$—Coyote, javelina, turkey, fox, goose, wildcat, pheasant.

Group 4. $14'' \times 11''$—Turtle, duck, grouse, crow, skunk, jackrabbit, wood-chuck.

Any animal or bird consistent in size with a particular group may be used.

Shooting Rules. Three shots are permitted at each target, one from each of three posts, each successive post being closer to the target than the previous pone.

Arrows shall be identifiable as to order of shooting. The archer shall stop shooting as soon as a hit is considered to have been made.

Scoring. The score is decided by the position of the arrow in the Target (i.e. in the "kill" or "wound" zone) and the number of arrows shot.

	kill	*wound*
1st arrow score	20	16
2nd arrow score	14	10
3rd arrow score	8	4

Only the score of the first "scoring" arrow counts.

Range Marking. In either Marked or Unmarked distances.

(*d*) **The National Animal Round**

The standard unit shall consist of 16 targets, and two units, mixed so that all the targets of one unit are not consecutive, shall comprise the round. The distances shall not be marked.

Targets. The target faces shall be of an animal or bird design, and shall have described upon them a circle of either 30, 22.5, 15 or 7.5 cm diameter according to the size of the animal picture and in the heart/lung region. The higher scoring area (the kill zone) shall be within the circle and the remainder of the animal shall be the lower scoring area (the wound zone).

The course shall be laid out so that each unit shall consist of the following targets set within the prescribed range, and the aggregate distance shot at each target face size shall be within the prescribed distances.

Number of faces	Kill zone diameter	Distance range	Aggregate distance	Allowance (plus or minus)
4	30 cm	55–30 m	320 m	16 m
4	22.5 cm	45–20 cm	240 m	12 m
4	15 cm	35–10 m	160 m	8 m
4	7.5 cm	20–5 m	80 cm	4 m

The total distance shot shall be 800 m plus or minus 20 m for the whole unit.

Shooting. Two arrows shall be shot at each target, one from each of two posts set within the prescribed range.

Scoring. Kill zone—10 points; wound zone—5 points.

N.B. Swedish Big Game round faces fulfil the requirements set out above, and shall be used at National Record Status events.

203. Other Rounds

Traditional or local rounds involving differing targets and methods of scoring may be shot in either Club or Open Competition providing that the G.N.A.S. rules affecting safety are observed and that the rules are made known to all competitors before shooting starts.

204. Separate Classes and Styles

(a) There shall be separate classes for Ladies, Gentlemen and Juniors (see Rule 704).

(b) Styles as defined in Rule 103.

205. Juniors

Where Juniors under 15 years of age shoot in a group containing archers above this age, the Juniors shall shoot last. *For other Junior Rules see Part VII and 806 (c) in G.N.A.S. Rules.*

206. Regulations for the National Field Archery Championship Meeting

(*a*) The Championship shall be be held annually and shall consist of one Hunter round and one Field round shot over two days.

(*b*) The Championship shall be shot according to G.N.A.S. rule 202 (*e*).

(*c*) The National Championship Titles and awards shall be open to members of the G.N.A.S. only.

(*d*) The Open Championship Titles and awards shall be open to all competitors from F.I.T.A. Member Associations.

(*e*) Unless the winner of any trophy is permanently resident in the U.K., the trophies shall remain in the custody of the Society at its Headquarters.

(*f*) The Judges for the event shall be appointed by National Council.

III. FLIGHT SHOOTING

300. Basis

(*a*) The three classes for which competitions may take place are:

    A. Target Bows.

    B. Flight Bows.

    C. Free-style.

Ladies, Gentlemen and Juniors may compete equally in each class.

(*b*) The Classes may be subdivided into bow weights, as follows:

    1—16 kg (35 lb).

    2—23 kg (50 lb).

    3—Unlimited.

Except for the target bow and unlimited classes flight bows shall be weighed as follows:

(i) Bows shall be weighed just prior to commencement of shooting. Weight of bow, length of arrow, and the class for which this combination is eligible, shall be recorded on a label affixed to the face of the bow.

(ii) The weight of the bow shall be taken at two inches less than the length of the longest arrow, and again at one inch less than the length of this arrow. The difference in these weights shall be added to the last weight of the bow at full draw.

Weighing bows at full draw is optional with the competitor. When an overdraw device is used and permits a draw in excess of one inch from the back of the bow, this excess shall be considered a portion of the arrow length for bow weighing purposes.

(c) For classes A and B only hand bows may be used and the bow must be held in the unsupported hand.

(d) If competitions for both Target and Flight Bows are being held on the same occasion, all shooting with Target Bows must be completed first.

301. Range Layout

(a) The Range Line, at right angles to the shooting line shall be clearly marked at 150 yards then at 50 yard intervals to at least 50 yards beyond the existing distance shot in the U.K.

(b) Red warning flags shall be placed at each side of the range at 75 yards from the line of distance markers at a distance of 150 yards from the shooting line.

302. Equipment

(a) A Target Bow is any bow with which the user has shot at least two standard Target or Field Rounds. In the event of a breakage, a similar bow may be used as replacement.

(b) Any type of bow, other than a cross-bow, may be entered for Classes B and C.

(c) In the Target Bow class competitors must use their own length standard Target arrows and normal tab or shooting glove.

(d) In Classes B and C any type of arrow may be used.

(e) Sipurs are not permitted in Class A.

(f) Mechanical releases, inter-moving drawing and/or re-lease aids are prohibited.

The following may be used in Classes B and C:

Six-gold ring, Flipper or Strap (single or double), block sipur, and angle measuring device.

(g) In the event of a breakage a substitute bow or limb may be used providing it is checked for conforming to its class. In the event of this not being done the archer will automatically be transferred to the unlimited class.

303. Shooting

(a) Competitors should be at least six feet apart, and must not advance their leading foot over the shooting line.

(b) Each competitor may have one assistant or adviser, who must keep at least one yard behind the shooting line.

(c) (i) At least four ends, each of three arrows, will be shot.

(ii) After all classes have shot the first end competitors and officials will go forward. Competitors will stand by their furthest arrow. A marker with a label attached bearing the name of the competitor and class will then be placed at the pile end of the furthest arrow in each class.

(iii) Arrows will then be withdrawn.

(iv) Succeeding ends will then be shot and markers adjusted where necessary.

304. Control of Shooting

There shall be a Range Captain in charge who will act as Referee and Judge. His decision shall be final. He will also be responsible for the safety of spectators, who must at all times, when shooting is in progress, be not less than 10 yards behind the shooting line.

305. Measurements

Measurement of distances shall be made with a steel tape along the range line. The distances shot shall be measured to that point on the range line at which a line at right angles to the range line passes the point where the arrow enters the ground. If the arrow is lying on the ground the line should pass through the pile end of the arrow.

IV. CLOUT SHOOTING

400. Regulations

The Rules of Target Archery shall apply except as enumerated in the following paragraphs.

The Organisers shall take all reasonable steps to ensure that there be no risk occasioned to people, animals or property from arrows that miss the target area by overshot or to either side (N.B. a distance of 75 yards from the Clout centre to the boundary of any land to which the public has access is deemed reasonable).

401. Targets

The centre of the Target shall be marked by a brightly coloured distinctive flag 12″ square, set as close as practicable to ground level on a smooth vertical stick. The stick should not project above the flag.

402. Shooting

(*a*) Shooting may be either "two way" or "one way".

(*b*) Six sighter arrows shall be shot in each direction when shooting two ways.

(*c*) The Organiser, after considering general safety, archers' comfort and the duties of scorers, shall use his discretion as to the number of archers allocated to each target.

403. Scoring

(*a*) Scores shall be determined according to the distance of arrows at point of entry in ground from centre of flag stick.

> Within a radius of 18 inches—5 points
> 3 feet—4 points
> 6 feet—3 points
> 9 feet—2 points
> 12 feet—1 point.

Arrows which have hit and remain embedded in the Clout shall score 5 provided they are not embedded in a lower scoring ring whereupon they shall score according to the ring in which they are embedded.

(*b*) Rings of the above radii may be marked on the ground,

the lines drawn being wholly within each circle.

(*c*) Where it is not practical to draw lines on the ground, scores shall be determined with a non-stretch cord or tape looped round the centre stick and clearly marked to measure the various radii.

(*d*) No person other than the appointed scorers shall enter the target area until all arrows have been withdrawn and placed in their respective scoring groups. An arrow withdrawn by any other than an appointed scorer shall not be scored.

404. Round

(*a*) A Clout Round consists of 36 arrows.

(*b*) Distances to be shot shall be determined by the organisers. These would normally be:

> for Gentlemen—9 score yards
> for Ladies   —7 score yards

405. National Championship Round

The National Championship shall be decided over a Double Clout Round.

V. CROSSBOW ARCHERY

500. Regulations

The Rules of Target Archery shall apply with the following exceptions:

(*a*) Crossbowmen shall shoot on separate targets from other archers and not compete with them.

(*b*) No person under 16 years of age may shoot unless in adult care and no person less than 12 years of age may shoot or manipulate a crossbow.

501. Equipment

(*a*) A crossbow stock and mechanism may be made from any material. No mechanical aids or rests are permitted. Prods may be made of any other material except metal. The length measured along the curves shall not exceed 36 inches.

(*b*) The draw-length shall be measured from the back of the prod to the string latch. Draw-weight shall not exceed 1280 lb/

in with a maximum draw of 18 inches. (To determine the lb/in multiply the draw-length by the draw-weight.) The draw-weight shall be marked on the prod, e.g. 70 lb @ 18".

(c) A string may be made of any non-metallic material.

(d) Bolts may be made of any material and of such design as not to cause unreasonable damage to the target. Bolt length is minimum 12 inches, maximum 15 inches. Three fletchings, feather or plastic, shall be fitted.

(e) Telescopic or magnifying sights are not allowed.

(f) Stirrups attached to the stock or ground are permitted, provided that Rule 501 (b) is complied with.

(g) Pistol crossbows are not permitted.

(h) The use of safety catches is recommended and will become mandatory in 1983.

502. Recognised Rounds

(a) Windsor Round shot on a 60 cm F.I.T.A. face scoring 9, 7, 5, 3, 1. The Championship Round shall be a Double Windsor.

(b) American Round shot on a 60 cm F.I.T.A. face scoring 10, 9, 8, 7, 6, 5, 4, 3, 2,1.

(c) Western Round shot on an 80 cm F.I.T.A. face scoring 10, 9, 8, 7, 6, 5, 4, 3, 2, 1.

(d) Any recognised G.N.A.S. or F.I.T.A. Round.

503. Field Archery

(a) Current Field Archery Rules shall apply with those exceptions detailed in 500 (a) and (b).

(b) Targets shall be fixed below skyline.

(c) Field Rounds as recognised by G.N.A.S. or F.I.T.A. shall be shot.

504. The Crossbow and the Law

When travelling on public transport or walking in a public thoroughfare it is essential that the prod be removed and the stock and prod be carried in a case or cover.

505. Safety Rules

If shooting is interrupted for any reason, crossbows shall be lowered immediately so that they are directed at the ground immediately in front of the shooting line and the bolt removed. Safety catches, where fitted, shall be applied.

VI. OTHER FORMS OF ARCHERY

600. Popinjay Shooting

Set-up for Popinjay

(*a*) The full complement of a Popinjay "roost" shall consist of:

> One Cock Bird
> Four Hens
> Minimum of twenty-four Chicks.

(*b*) Body size of all birds shall be $1\frac{1}{2}''$ long $\frac{3}{4}''$ in diameter—only the plumage shall differ:

> —that of the Cock Bird being most resplendent and $10''$–$12''$ high.

> —that of the Hen Birds being shorter $6''$–$8''$ high and less colourful.

> —that of the Chicks being shortest $3''$–$4''$ high.

(*c*) The Chicks shall be perched on spikes $6''$ long, not less than $4''$ apart, in three rows, the vertical height between rows being not less than 3 feet. The Hen Birds shall be perched on spikes $18''$ above the top row and shall be spaced not less than $8''$ apart.

The Cock Bird shall be perched on a central spike not less than $30''$ above the top row.

(*d*) The perches may be attached to, or hauled up, a mast or wall to a height of 90 feet (measured to the Cock Bird).

Arrangements must be made to ensure that when in position the perches are firmly held against movement by wind.

(*e*) All obstructions on and within the framework of perches must be softened with rubber or sponge rubber (or similar resilient material) to lessen the risk of arrow breakage.

(*f*) No hard and fast shooting position is dictated, although

ARCHERY

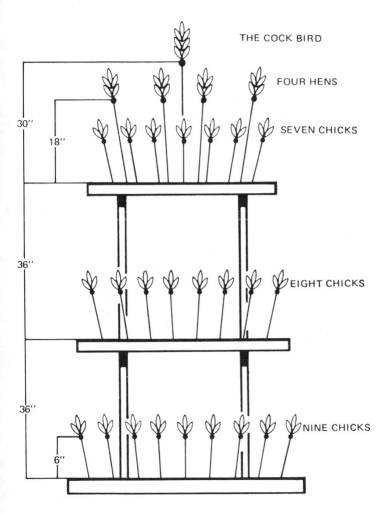

Typical Popinjay "roost" showing minimum complement.

it should be pointed out to all competitors that a near vertical, close to mast attitude will offer a better target to the archer, inasmuch as a greater number of birds will be in line of the arrow flight path.

(g) Each and every part of the Popinjay Mast and Framework of Perches must be made to be safe from breakage and/or dislodgement by arrow or the elements.

(h) Whenever possible a shelter should be provided for competitors, a temporary structure approx. 7′ 6″ high covered on top with $\frac{1}{2}$″ wire mesh is sufficient for this purpose. If no shelter is available competitors waiting to shoot must be made to wait outside the arrow fall-out area.

601. Arrows
Only arrows with blunts $\frac{3}{4}$″ to 1″ in diameter shall be used.

602. Shooting
(a) Archers will draw for order of shooting.

(b) Only one archer shall shoot at a time.

(c) Archers must shoot in rotation—only one arrow being shot per end.

(d) Disabled archers may shoot with the aid of a prop.

603. Mast Captain
A Mast Captain shall be appointed to ensure that shooting is conducted in a safe and proper manner.

604. Scoring
(a) The scoring points for hits are:

    Cock Bird—5 points
    Hen Bird —3 points
    Chick   —1 point

(b) Birds must be struck with the arrow and be dislodged and fall to the ground to score.

605. "Round"
Results may be determined by time limit or by a declared number of arrows.

606. Regulations for Tournaments

Popinjay Tournament Schedules shall bear the following information:

(*a*) Whether competition is determined by time limit or by number of arrows shot per person.

(*b*) Maximum number of archers that will be accepted.

Note: The G.N.A.S. Insurance Scheme does not cover for risks attendant on the erection and dismantling of Popinjay Masts.

620. Archery Golf

Regulations

(*a*) Only one bow shall be used throughout a round. In case of breakage it may be replaced.

(*b*) Any arrows may be used.

(*c*) The archer shall "hole out" by hitting a white cardboard disc 4″ in diameter, placed on the ground at least one yard within the edge of the green level with the hole.

(*d*) An arrow landing off the fairway or in a bunker shall incur one extra stroke.

(*e*) The archer must stand immediately behind where his arrow lands to shoot the next arrow.

(*f*) A lost arrow incurs the normal penalty (as in golf) for stroke play but loses the hole in match play.

(*g*) The winner of the previous "hole" takes the first shot for the next hole.

(*h*) The current Golf Rules and local Course Regulations shall apply in all cases not covered by the foregoing rules.

640. Archery Darts

Regulations

The Rules of Target Archery shall apply with the following exceptions:

Target Faces

Archery Darts Faces 76.2 cm (2′ 6″) in diameter shall be used.

General Rules

(*a*) The Targets shall be set up so that the centre of the Bull is at the centre of a 122 cm minimum diameter boss 130 cm from the ground.

(*b*) The minimum shooting distance shall be 13.7 m (15 yds).

(*c*) An End shall consist of three arrows unless a game is finished in less.

(*d*) The order of starting shall be determined by the toss of a coin.

(*e*) Each match must start and finish on a Double (the narrow outer ring). The inner ring counts treble; the inner Bull counts 50; and the outer Bull 25.

(*f*) A practice end of three arrows must be shot at the Bull.

(*g*) The value of an arrow shall be determined by the position of the greater part of the shaft.

(*h*) Scoring shall be by the subtraction method, so that the score required for the completion of each game is always shown.

(*i*) If the score required to complete the game is exceeded in the course of an End, then that End ceases, and no account is taken of the score obtained during that End.

Note: Local variations may be used.

VIII. RECORDS

800. National Record

A National Record may be established and submitted to National Council for ratification at:

(*a*) Any Meeting organised by F.I.T.A., F.I.T.A. Members, G.N.A.S., Regional Societies.

(*b*) Any Meeting which has applied to National Council by 31st December in respect of target archery, and before 31st October of the preceding year in respect of field archery, for prior recognition and has been granted such status. It shall be a condition that such meeting shall be open to all members of G.N.A.S.

801. Submission of Claims

Claims for National Records shall be submitted to the G.N.A.S. Secretary on the appropriate form except for National Championships and U.K. Masters Tournament when the Secretary will submit claims to National Council.

The claim forms must be completed prior to the dispersal of the Meetings at which the record has been made, one copy shall be handed to the archer and one copy retained by the Tournament Organiser. Both copies must be sent to the Secretary within 28 days of the date on which the record was made.

The claim form sent by the Tournament Organiser shall be accompanied by the original score sheet (or a photo copy) and the results sheet as circulated.

802. Target Archery

(a) A world record may be established for the F.I.T.A. Round and each distance of the F.I.T.A. Round according to qualifications laid down in F.I.T.A. Rules.

Claims for World Records shall be submitted to the G.N.A.S. Secretary supported by the necessary documents for onward transmission to F.I.T.A. for ratification.

(b) National Records may be claimed for any single or double round shot at recognised Record Status Meetings but where a Double Round is shot on the one day the second Round will not be accepted for Record purposes.

803. Field Archery

(a) Record Rounds are restricted to National Animal, Unmarked Hunter, Marked Field and F.I.T.A. Combination Rounds.

(b) National Records are to be maintained for all classes and styles of Compound Bow Field archery. Initial claims for records will be entertained only if the scores submitted are equal or greater than the corresponding record score for the conventional recurve bow class on style.

(c) National Records may be claimed by and granted to Junior Field Archers (both under 12 and under 15 years of age) if the round shot was that appropriate to the age of the claimant or if the claimant has shot a more difficult round than his age demanded. The record granted being that for the age group of the claimant and not for the difficult round if that had been shot.

804. Flight Shooting

(*a*) National records may be claimed in all classes. The measurements must be checked and witnessed by the Range Captain and one other responsible person. In addition the Range Captain must certify that the ground over which the shot was made was reasonably flat and level.

(*b*) A new record may be established when the measurement is at least one yard longer than an existing record.

805. Clout Shooting

National records may be established for "one way" and "two way" when shooting is at the following distances:

> Gentlemen—9 score yards
> Ladies   —7 score yards

IX. CLASSIFICATION AND HANDICAP SCHEMES

900. Classification Regulations for all Disciplines

(*a*) The use of the Classification Scheme by Clubs is optional and the administration of it shall be in the hands of Club officials.

(*b*) Initial grading or subsequent upgrading occurs immediately the necessary scores have been made in the calendar year.

(*c*) The qualification holds for one year immediately following that in which it is gained. If it is not maintained during that year, reclassification shall be on the scores made during the year.

(*d*) The scheme shall apply only to those archers using equipment defined in Clause 102 (*a*) and for compound bows, Clause 102 (*c*).

901. Target Archery

(*a*) To gain Class I, II or III a member must shoot during the calendar year and under G.N.A.S. Rules of Shooting, three Rounds of, or better than, the scores set out in Table A at a meeting organised by G.N.A.S. or a body affiliated to G.N.A.S. or at an Associated Club Target Day when a minimum of two archers are shooting together (see Rule 109 (*a*) (vi).

(*b*) **Master Bowman**

(i) Qualifying Rounds: York, F.I.T.A. (Gentlemen); Hereford, F.I.T.A. (Ladies).

(ii) Number of Rounds: Four, including at least one York/Hereford and one F.I.T.A.

(iii) Any two of the Rounds must be shot at a meeting organised by F.I.T.A., F.I.T.A. Members, G.N.A.S., a Regional Society or County Association. The remainder may be shot at any of the above or at any Associated Club Tournament or Target Day when a minimum of two archers are shooting together on the same target.

(*c*) **Grand Master Bowman**

(i) Qualifying Rounds: York, F.I.T.A. (Gentlemen); Hereford, F.I.T.A. (Ladies).

(ii) Number of Rounds: 2 F.I.T.A., 1 York/Hereford.

(iii) All Rounds must be shot at Meetings organised by F.I.T.A., F.I.T.A. Members, G.N.A.S. or a Regional Society, including Regional Inter-County Tournaments whether such meetings are open or closed.

(*d*) **Junior Master Bowman**

(i) Qualifying Rounds: York, Men's F.I.T.A., (Boys); Hereford, Ladies' F.I.T.A., Metric I, (Girls).

(ii) Number of Rounds: Four of the Rounds must be shot, with a minimum of one and a maximum of three F.I.T.A./Rounds.

(iii) One Round must be shot at a meeting organised by F.I.T.A., F.I.T.A. Members, G.N.A.S., a Regional Society or County Association. The other three Rounds may be shot at the above or at a Club Tournament or Target Day with a minimum of two archers shooting supervised by a Senior (see Rule 109 (*a*) (vi).

902. Field Archery

(*a*) Qualifying Rounds: F.I.T.A. Hunter, F.I.T.A. Field and F.I.T.A. Combination.

(*b*) Qualifying scores: As in Table on p. 52.

(*c*) **Grand Master Bowman**

(i) Number of Rounds (each Round must be of the required

standard):

> 2 Hunter, 2 Field
> 2 Hunter, 1 Field, 1 Combination
> 1 Hunter, 2 Field, 1 Combination

TABLE A   Qualifying Scores—Senior

	GMB	MB	1st Class	2nd Class	3rd Class
Gentlemen:					
York	1085	1000	798	560	342
F.I.T.A.	1223	1153	980	753	512
St. George			646	475	304
New Western			512	347	202
New National			368	243	139
Long Metric			431	302	181
Short Metric				451	331
Hereford				760	519
Albion				614	436
Long Western				494	330
Long National				351	228
Western					455
National					330
Windsor					568
American					473
Ladies:					
Hereford	1112	1033	843	606	378
F.I.T.A	1198	1121	933	688	439
Albion			672	502	325
Long Western			551	389	236
Long National			395	272	161
Long Metric			443	312	187
Short Metric				376	253
Western				516	348
National				375	249
Windsor				631	450
American				525	375

(ii) All Rounds must be shot at Meetings organised by F.I.T.A., F.I.T.A. Members, G.N.A.S., a Regional Championship Meeting, a Regional Inter-Counties Meeting, County Championship or any competition granted National Record Status (only two scores shot at the same venue may be used for this qualification).

(*d*) **Master Bowman**

(i) Number of Rounds (each Round must be of the required standard):

> 3 Hunter, 1 Field
> 2 Hunter, 2 Field
> 1 Hunter, 3 Field
> 2 Hunter, 1 Field, 1 F.I.T.A. Combination
> 1 Hunter, 2 Field, 1 F.I.T.A. Combination

(ii) Two Rounds must be shot at Meetings detailed in (*c*)(ii) above. The remainder may be shot at any of the above or at any Associated Club Open Tournament when a minimum of three archers are shooting together on one target.

(*e*) **Classes I, II & III**

N.B. Qualifying scores may be obtained by shooting the same Unit twice.

(i) Number of Rounds:

1st Class:	As for Master Bowman
2nd & 3rd Class:	Two Rounds, each of which must be of the required standard

(ii) Rounds must be shot at any of the Meetings detailed in (*d*)(ii) above or at a Classification Shoot when a minimum of three archers are shooting together on the same target.

TABLE C Qualifying score tables for Recurve Bow Styles

	GMB	MB	1st CLASS	2nd CLASS	3rd CLASS
Freestyle:					
Ladies	400	350	300	230	160
Gentlemen	440	400	350	270	180
Girls		300	250	180	100
Boys		350	300	230	150

	GMB	MB	1st CLASS	2nd CLASS	3rd CLASS
Barebow:					
Ladies	350	300	230	160	110
Gentlemen	400	350	300	230	160
Girls		230	180	110	60
Boys		300	250	180	100
Traditional:					
Ladies	300	230	160	110	60
Gentlemen	350	300	230	160	110
Girls		180	110	60	40
Boys		230	180	110	60

TABLE D Qualifying score tables for Compound Bow Styles

	GMB	MB	1st CLASS	2nd CLASS	3rd CLASS
Unlimited:					
Ladies	440	385	330	255	180
Gentlemen	490	440	385	300	200
Girls		330	275	200	110
Boys		385	330	255	165
Limited:	As for Freestyle recurve bow styles				
Bowhunter:	As for Barebow recurve bow styles				

(There is no separate scheme for those under 15 years of age. Should such Juniors wish to enter the classification scheme they must shoot the full distance.)

903. Flight Shooting

(*a*) Archers can qualify as Master Flight Shot or 1st Class Flight Shot at any Flight Shoot organised by G.N.A.S., a Regional Society or County Association under G.N.A.S. Rules of Shooting.

(*b*) Archers can qualify as Grand Master Flight Shot at any of the above except that the County Association Meeting must be the County Championships.

(*c*) Minimum distances:

	Ladies	Gentlemen
Grand Master Flight Shot	450 yards	550 yards

| Master Flight Shot | 340 yards | 440 yards |
| 1st Class Flight Shot | 275 yards | 375 yards |

904. Crossbow Shooting

Using the Windsor Round.

Qualifying Scores

Master Arbalist	780	3 scores	(2 and 1)	
Arbalist 1st Class	630	3 scores	(1 and 2)	see
Arbalist 2nd Class	480	3 scores	(1 and 2)	below

Qualifying Meetings

For the Master Arbalist 2 and for the 1st and 2nd Class Arbalist 1, scores must be made at a Meeting organised by F.I.T.A., F.I.T.A. Members, G.N.A.S., a Regional Society, or County Association. The remainder may be shot at any of the above or at any Associated Club Tournament or Target Day when a minimum of two archers are shooting together on the same Target.

905. Submission of Claim

(*a*) Claims for the title of Grand Master and Master in all disciplines shall be submitted to the G.N.A.S. Secretary on the appropriate form. The Secretary will, on behalf of the National Council:

(i) Satisfy himself as to the validity of the claim.

(ii) Notify the claimant and send him the appropriate badge.

(iii) Publicise the award.

(*b*) It shall be the responsibility of the archer concerned to submit the claim together with the following documents of proof.

(i) **Rounds shot at Club Meetings.** The original score sheet endorsed by an Officer of the Club to the effect that the Round was shot at a Club Tournament or Target Day.

(ii) **Rounds shot at any other Meeting.** The official Result Sheet sent out by the Organiser(s) of the Meeting.

(*c*) Any such claim shall also include a certificate that the archer was using a bow recognised as in Rule 102 (*a*).

920. Handicap Scheme

Copies of the G.N.A.S. Handicap Tables, which include the Rules for the operation of the Scheme, can be obtained from the G.N.A.S. Secretary.

921. Handicap Improvement Medal

(*a*) The medals are Challenge Trophies and remain the property of the G.N.A.S.

(*b*) One medal will be loaned on application to any Club having not less than ten shooting members, which has been an Associated Club of the Society for at least twelve months.

(*c*) In the event of a Club ceasing to function, the Secretary thereof will be personally responsible for returning the medal to the Society.

(*d*) The Club will notify to the Secretary the name and address of the winner of the medal each year immediately it has been awarded (giving old and new handicap figures) or, if it has not been duly competed for, will return it to the Society.

(*e*) (i) The medal is to be awarded to the member, lady or gentleman, who having been a member of the Club for not less than six months prior to January 1st attains the greatest improvement in handicap during the following calendar year provided that he or she shall have shot not fewer than twelve rounds on his or her own Club Target Days during that period, in addition to any eligible rounds shot elsewhere. If owing to adverse weather, no member has shot twelve rounds on Club Target Days during the period, the Club Committee has discretion to make the award on a slightly lesser number of rounds.

(ii) In the event of a tie, those who tied shall shoot it off on a day and round to be decided by the Club, or, at the Club's discretion, the medal may be awarded to the member with the greatest number of attendances during the period amongst those who have tied.

(*f*) The G.N.A.S. Handicap Regulations and Tables must be used for assessing all handicaps in connection with the award of these medals.

(*g*) The holder of the medal should wear it on all Club Target

Days at which he or she is present. It is left to each Club to impose any penalty in this connection.

Printed by permission of the Grand National Archery Society. Many of the Rules have here been abbreviated for reasons of space. Copies of the complete Rules and Regulations, including those for Junior Archery, can be obtained from the Society.

The Rules of
Athletics

Athletics

These are extracts from the official Rules for Competitions under the Laws of the A.A.A. (see Note on p. 84). The following terms, used throughout, have the following meanings:

Area Association: Northern Counties A.A., Midland Counties A.A.A., Southern Counties A.A.A., Welsh A.A.A., and such other 'Area' Associations as may be formed by the A.A.A. from time to time.

"District": A District of the N.C.A.A., a group of Counties or similar geographical sub-divisions of an "Area" having a separate Committee for administrative purposes.

"Club": Affiliated Club, Business House Club, University, College, School, Service Unit, Pre-Service Unit or other Society or Association of Amateur Athletes.

AMATEUR DEFINITION

1. All competitions held under the Laws of the Association are confined to amateurs under the following definitions:

(1) An amateur is a person of the male sex who abides by the eligibility rules of the A.A.A.

(2) Competition under A.A.A. Laws is restricted to amateur athletes who are under the jurisdiction of a Member of the I.A.A.F. and who are eligible to compete under the rules laid down by the A.A.A. (But see Rules 107 (b) and (c).)

(3) Persons ineligible to take part in competitions under A.A.A. Rules *are listed in detail under this heading in "A.A.A. Rules for Competition".*

An athlete who is a qualified teacher of Physical Education recognised by the Department of Education and Science does not lose his amateur status by being so employed.

The *expenses* of any athlete may be paid by the body responsible for the entry, *subject to the detailed provisions set out in "A.A.A. Rules for Competition" under this heading.*

GENERAL CONDITIONS

2. (1) In these Rules the term "14 years of age" on a given date refers to an athlete whose 14th birthday falls on or before the given date, but who has not reached his 15th birthday on that date. Similarly for "15 years of age", etc.

(2) Open Competitions:

(*A*) Individual:

(i) An Open Competition is one which is open to all athletes who have reached the age of 18 years (including those in a particular district or area) and which is not confined to members of Closed Clubs.

(ii) To compete in County, District, Area and National Championships, League competition, Road Relays and Road Races up to and including 5 km, and all Track and Field Competitions, an athlete over the age of 18 must be a member of a Club or Association affiliated directly or indirectly to the A.A.A.

(iii) (*a*) A competitor taking part in an Open Competition must have reached the age of 18 years on the day of competition. (*b*) Competitors who are under 18 may compete in certain Open Competitions, as specified in Rules 20, 21 and 22. (*c*) Competitors who are 18, 19 and 20, taking part in Cross Country, Road Running and Road Relay Running, are governed by Rule 21 (2) and (3). (*d*) Competitors who are 15 and 16 may compete in certain Open Competitions, as specified in Rule 20 (1) (*c*), (*d*).

(*B*) Team:

(i) Open Team Competitions, Team Contests, Relay Races, Team Races and Tugs-of-War are competitions open to all clubs (including all clubs in a particular district or area) and not confined to Closed Clubs.

(ii) Invitation inter-club competitions are not Open Competitions unless more than 6 teams are invited. The promoters of a team competition other than an Open Team Competition may make such qualifying conditions as they think fit, including the right to stipulate that the competition is for first-claim members only.

(3) The following are *not* Open Competitions: events

confined to H.M. Services; events confined to employees of a particular trade or occupation; events promoted in rural areas and confined to residents within 10 miles radius from the ground.

(4) Every Club, Society and Managing Body promoting an athletic meeting under A.A.A. Laws, and every person tendering an entry, shall be deemed to have submitted to the jurisdiction of the Association on all questions which may arise.

3. No club or member under the jurisdiction of the A.A.A. may compete outside the United Kingdom, and no foreign club or member may compete within England and Wales, without the permission of the General Committee, except in the International Cross-Country Race.

No British athlete resident in England and Wales may compete under A.A.A. Laws as a member of a foreign athletic club.

REGISTRATION

5. Anyone competing in any open athletic competition in England or Wales promoted by a Club, Association or Managing Body which is not in possession of a permit for that particular competition, shall thereby disqualify himself from competing under A.A.A. Laws.

The following do not require registration: events confined to members of any particular club or firm; events promoted by and confined to H.M. Services; events confined to employees of a County or Local Authority; events open to pre-Service Organisations, combinations of Schools, Boy Scouts, Youth Clubs and other Juvenile Organisations.

Open Cross-Country Races and Tug-of-War competitions may be held only by organisations holding permits from those sports associations.

ENTRIES

6. Every entry shall be made to the Secretary of the promoting body, who has the right to refuse an entry without giving a reason.

7. No entry either for individual or team events may be made except upon the form of entry issued or approved by the A.A.A., which must be dated and completed with all the particulars required.

8. Every entry must be made in the real name of the competitor, which shall appear on the programme.

9. Every individual entry shall be signed by the intending competitor himself, who shall be responsible for all statements therein.

10. Every entry for a Colts', Boys', Youths', Juniors' or Veterans' race shall state the date of birth and present age in years and months of the intending competitor.

11. Every entry for a team competition shall be signed by the Secretary or other authorised official of the club on whose behalf the entry is made.

12. No entry may be accepted unless accompanied by the stipulated entrance fee.

14. When an athlete is a member of two or more Clubs, the Club he has belonged to for the longest unbroken period shall have first claim upon his services. While at school an athlete remains first claim to his school.

15. An Open Club is a Club whose membership is not confined to persons in a particular occupation or business organisation. All other Clubs, societies and organisations affiliated directly or indirectly to an Area Association shall be deemed Closed Clubs.

16. Ineligibility of a competitor in an Inter-Club or Inter-Team competition does not necessarily disqualify the club he represents and in such a case the competition shall be decided as if the ineligible competitor had not taken part.

17. In open team competitions, consisting of several events, the total entry of each competing club shall not exceed twice the number allowed to compete. All entrants are eligible to compete in any of the events comprising the competition.

In an open relay race, clubs shall not be allowed to enter more than three times the number entitled to compete. A club entering more than one team in a race shall be allowed to select their teams from the Club Entry for that event. Teams must be declared before the start of the race.

No one shall be allowed to compete in a team unless his name appears on the programme in the Club Entry. If it is impracticable to issue a programme, it is recommended that a complete list of the entries should be provided for the information of the Referee.

RULES FOR COMPETITIONS
CONFINED TO PARTICULAR
CLASSES

18. Colts:

(1) Track (excluding Track Walking) and Field Events for Colts shall be confined to competitors who have reached their 11th but not their 13th birthdays by midnight August 31st/ September 1st in the year of competition. Colts shall not be allowed to compete in more than three individual events on one day. This rule does not apply to Pentathlon competitions. Colts may compete in events up to 3,000 m. (but not the steeplechase). Colts may not compete against Youth/Juniors or Seniors in any events.

(2) Road running and Road Relay running for Colts shall be confined to competitors who are 12 and 13 years of age on April 1st for competitions held between April 1st and August 31st, or on August 31st for competitions held between September 1st and March 31st. The distance shall not exceed 5,000 metres.

(3) Cross Country running for Colts shall be confined to competitors who are 11 or 12 years of age on September 1st prior to the competition. The distance shall not exceed $2\frac{1}{2}$ miles.

19. Boys:

(1) Track (excluding Track Walking) and Field events for Boys shall be confined to competitors who have reached their 13th but not their 15th birthdays by midnight August 31st/ September 1st in the year of competition. Boys shall not be allowed to compete in more than three individual events on one day. This rule does not apply to Pentathlon competitions. Boys may not compete in steeplechases.

(2) Road running and Road Relay running for Boys shall be confined to competitors who are 14 and 15 on April 1st (for

competitions held between April 1st and August 31st) or August 31st (for competitions between September 1st and March 31st). The distance shall not exceed 6,500 metres.

(3) Cross Country running for Boys shall be confined to competitors who are 13 or 14 on September 1st prior to the competition. The distance shall not exceed 3 miles.

(4) Track and Road Walking for Colts shall be confined to competitors who have reached their 11th but not their 13th birthday by midnight August 31st/September 1st immediately prior to the competition. The distance shall not exceed 5,000 metres.

(5) Track and Road Walking for Boys shall be confined to competitors who have reached their 13th but not their 15th birthdays on August 31st in the year of competition. The distance shall not exceed 10,000 metres.

20. Youths:

(1) Track and Field events for Youths shall be confined to competitors who have reached their 15th but not their 17th birthdays by midnight August 31st/September 1st in the year of competition. They shall not be allowed to compete in more than three individual events on any one day. This rule does not apply to Combined Events competitions.

(2) Road Running and Road Relay Running for Youths shall be confined to competitors who are 16 and 17 on April 1st (for competitions held between April 1st and August 31st) or August 31st (for competitions between September 1st and March 31st). The distance shall not exceed 8,000 metres.

(3) Cross Country Running for Youths shall be confined to competitors who are 15 or 16 on September 1st prior to the competition. The distance shall not exceed 4 miles.

(4) Track and Road Walking for Youths shall be confined to competitors who have reached their 15th but not their 17th birthdays on August 31st in the year of competition. The distance should not exceed 15 km for first year Youths nor 20 km for second year Youths.

21. Juniors:

(1) Track and Field events for Juniors shall be confined to competitors who have reached their 17th birthdays by midnight August 31st/September 1st but not their 20th birthdays by

midnight December 31st in the year of competition. They shall not be allowed to compete in more than three individual events on any one day. This rule does not apply to Combined Events competitions.

(2) Road Running and Road Relay Running for Juniors shall be confined to competitors aged 18 and 19 on April 1st (for competitions held between April 1st and August 31st) or August 31st (for competitions between September 1st and March 31st). The distance shall not exceed 6 miles.

(3) Cross Country running for Juniors shall be confined to competitors who are 17, 18 or 19 on September 1st prior to competition. The distance shall not exceed 6 miles.

(4) Track and Road Walking for Juniors shall be confined to competitors who have reached their 17th birthdays by midnight August 31st/September 1st but not their 20th birthdays by midnight/December 31st in the calendar year of competition. The distance shall not exceed 35 km for the first year Juniors and it shall not exceed 50 km for the second and third year Juniors.

22. Seniors:

(1) In Track and Field events a Senior is a competitor aged at least 19 on September 1st in the year of competition. A competitor aged at least 18 on the day of competition may be allowed to take part in any Senior event.

(2) A competitor in a Senior Road Race or Senior Road Relay Race where the Race or Section does not exceed 15 km ($9\frac{1}{2}$ miles) must be at least 16 on the day of competition. Where the Race or Section exceeds 15 km but does not exceed 25 km, he must be at least 17. Where the distance exceeds 25 km but does not exceed 50 km he must be at least 18. For a Race or Section exceeding 50 km he must be 20 years of age on the day of the competition.

23. Veterans:

Events for Veterans shall be confined to competitors aged at least 40 on the day of competition.

RULES FOR PROMOTING BODIES

33. Any Club or Association desirous of obtaining a permit for a Sports Meeting must make application to the Hon. Sec. of the County Association or District Committee in whose area the event is to be held. Applications for the registration of Cross-Country races must be made to the Hon. Sec., E.C.C.U.

Where any open event for women or girls is included, a permit must be obtained from the W.A.A.A.

No Club, Association or Managing Body shall permit any athletic event to be televised, either live or subsequently, without prior permission of the A.A.A.

34. All advertisements, programmes, etc. shall state that the Meeting is held "under A.A.A. Laws". This does not apply to International Meetings.

35. If an open team event is included, full particulars shall be clearly stated. In the case of a relay race, the distance of each section, and the order in which the sections are to be run, must be similarly stated.

36. Every club or committee to which a permit has been granted must exhibit it in a conspicuous place.

37. Every programme shall state the value of each prize offered for competition except in the case of any events in which cups and/or medals only are awarded.

38. Within seven days after the competition, a programme marked with the names of the winners, etc., shall be sent to the Hon. Sec. of the Area Association, who shall keep it for reference.

39. No individual or team shall be allowed to compete in any event unless a properly completed entry form has been accepted *or* evidence is produced that a properly completed entry form was sent to the organisers in accordance with their instructions and the Referee is of the opinion that it would be just and reasonable to give permission.

40. In competitions where the composition of heats is printed in the programme, no competitor shall be allowed to compete in any heat other than that in which his name appears; but the Referee shall have power, if he thinks the circumstances justify it, to permit a departure from this rule.

PRIZES

41. Money, saving certificates, bonds, stamps or cheques *must not* be offered as prizes; nor may vouchers or orders on tradesmen, except for book or record tokens and athletic clothing or equipment.

42. No prize of a greater value than the equivalent of US $250 (dollars) shall be offered, except as a Challenge Prize which cannot be won outright in a single competition.

43. The amount actually paid (after deducting any discount) shall be considered the value of the prize.

44. Every objection by a competitor to the value of a prize shall be made within 14 days.

45. Every prize at a meeting where open events are decided shall be publicly presented on the ground on the day of the meeting.

46. Any competitor who receives a prize to which he is not entitled shall return it forthwith on being asked to do so.

47. A Challenge Prize belongs to the promoting body until won outright and must be returned by the holder on request.

48. A Challenge Prize holder who is in all respects eligible to compete has an interest in the trophy and the right to enter the next competition.

49. If properly entered according to the governing conditions, the accidental omission of the holder's name from the programme does not debar him from competing.

DRESSING ACCOMMODATION

50. (*a*) Every promoting body shall provide sufficient and convenient accommodation for the competitors.

(*b*) Where a competition for colts or boys is included, separate dressing accommodation shall whenever possible be provided.

BETTING

51. Open betting is prohibited and must be rigorously suppressed.

COMPETITION RULES

Clothing and Footwear

52. In all events competitors must wear at least a vest and shorts which are clean and so designed and worn as not to be objectionable.

53. Competitors may compete in bare feet or with shoes on one or both feet. The purpose of shoes is to give protection and stability to the feet and a firm grip of the ground; they must not be constructed so as to give the competitor any additional assistance.

Numbers

54. Every competitor shall be supplied with and wear during competition a distinctive number corresponding with his number in the programme.

Assistance

55. A competitor shall not receive any assistance, except as provided in these Rules.

Tracks and Measurements

56. The inner edge of all tracks must be distinctly marked, cinder and other permanent tracks preferably by a raised border of concrete or other suitable material 2 in (5 cm) high, otherwise by a chalk line or white tape.

Races up to 110 m must be run on a straight course, in lanes, so as to allow a separate course for each competitor. The width between the lanes must be not less than 1.22 m.

Stations

57. In races, stations for competitors shall be drawn, the competitor drawing No. 1 taking, in straight sprint races, the station on the left facing the winning post and, in races on a circular track, the station nearest the centre of the ground.

58. Starting blocks are permissible in races up to and including 400 m. They must be approved by the Starter.

The Start

59. The start of a race shall be denoted by a line 5 cm wide at right angles to the inner edge of the track. In all races not run in lanes the starting line shall be curved, so that all competitors cover the same distance.

60. All questions concerning the start shall be in the absolute discretion of the Starter, whose decision shall be final.

61. Competitors must be placed in their respective stations by marksmen. An assembly line shall be drawn 3 m behind the starting line. Marksmen shall place competitors on the assembly lines and signal to the Starter when all is ready. A competitor must not touch either the startline or the ground in front of it with his hands or his feet when on his mark.

62. All races except Time handicaps shall be started by the report of a pistol or any similar apparatus. The pistol shall be fired upwards into the air and it is essential that it should give a satisfactory flash which can be seen clearly by the Timekeepers. The time will be taken from the flash.

63. When the Starter has received the signal from the marksman, he shall give the competitors the following commands:

(i) For competitors running a distance up to and including 400 m:

(a) "On your marks";

(b) "Set",

and when all competitors are Set, i.e. motionless on mark, the pistol shall be fired.

(ii) For competitors running, or walking, a distance greater than 400 m:

"On your marks"

and when all competitors are steady the pistol shall be fired.

If for any reason the Starter has to speak to any competitor after the order "On your marks" and before the pistol is fired, he shall order all competitors to stand up and the marksman shall place them on the assembly line again.

If a competitor leaves his mark with hand or foot before the pistol is fired, it shall be considered a false start. Any competitor making a false start shall be warned; if responsible for two false starts, he shall be disqualified.

Winners of Preliminary Heats

65. In the preliminary rounds of races, at least the winner, and preferably the winner and second should qualify for the next round or final. Any other competitors to qualify shall be decided either according to their places or their times.

66. The following minimum rest must be allowed between the last heat of the round and the first heat of the subsequent round or final:

Up to 100 m	20 min.
100–200 m	40 min.
200–400 m	60 min.
400–800 m	80 min.
Over 800 m	100 min.

The Race

67. Any competitor jostling, running across or obstructing another so as to impede his progress shall be liable to disqualification. The Referee shall have power, in such cases, to order the race to be re-run.

In all races run in lanes, each competitor should keep in his allotted lane from start to finish.

68. A competitor after voluntarily leaving the track shall not be allowed to continue in the race. A competitor who leaves the course of a road race shall not be allowed to continue if by going off course he lessens the distance to be covered.

69. (a) No attendant shall accompany any competitor on the mark or in the race, nor shall any competitor be allowed to receive assistance or refreshment from anyone during a race of 10 km or less.

(b) No official or other person within the arena, except an official timekeeper appointed to do so, shall indicate intermediate times to competitors.

The Finish

70. The finish shall be a line 2 in (5 cm) wide drawn across the track at right angles to the inner edge. The competitors shall be placed in the order in which any part of the body (i.e. 'torso', as distinguished from neck, head, arms, legs, hands or feet)

reaches the vertical plane of the nearer edge of the Finish Line.

71. Any protest or objection must be made to the Referee or Judges immediately after the competition. *Protests are governed by the regulations set out in detail in Rules 71 to 74 of "A.A.A. Rules for Competition".*

75. Doping before or during competition is forbidden.

FIELD EVENTS

Competition Rules

General

76. A draw shall be made to decide the order in which competitors shall take their trials and this order should be printed on the programme. The Judges shall have power to alter this order.

A competitor cannot hold over any of his trials to a subsequent round, except in the High Jump and Pole Vault. A competitor in a field event who unreasonably delays making a trial renders himself liable to disqualification after warning.

77. (1) Ties in scratch events shall be decided as follows:

(*a*) In jumping or vaulting for height: the competitor with the lowest number of jumps at the height *at which the tie occurs* shall be awarded the higher place; if the tie still remains, the competitor with the lowest total of failures throughout the competition up to the height last cleared shall be awarded the higher place; if the tie still remains, the competitors tying shall have one more jump at the lower height at which they failed, and if no decision is reached the bar should be lowered or raised 1 cm at a time—8 cm in the pole vault—with one jump at each height until the tie is decided.

(*b*) In throwing or jumping for distance: the second best performance of the competitors tying shall decide the tie; if the tie remains, the third best and so on. If the tie still remains and it concerns the first place, the competitors shall have such additional number of extra trials as is required.

High Jump

78. (*a*) The uprights or posts shall not be moved during the competition unless the Judges consider the take-off or landing ground has become unsuitable. Such a change shall be made only after a round is completed.

(*b*) Unless such details are specified on the programme, the Judges shall decide the height at which the competition shall start, and the different heights to which the bar will be raised at the end of each round. The competitors shall be informed of the details before the competition begins.

(*c*) A competitor may commence jumping at any height above the minimum height and may jump at his own discretion at any subsequent height. Three consecutive failures, regardless of the height at which any of them occurs, disqualify from further jumping.

N.B. The effect of this Rule is that a competitor may forgo his second and third jumps or vaults at a particular height (after failing once or twice) and still jump at a subsequent height.

(*d*) Even after all the other competitors have failed, a competitor is entitled to continue jumping until he has forfeited his right to compete further and his best jump shall be recorded as the winning height.

(*e*) A competitor may place marks to assist him in his run up and take-off and a handkerchief on the cross-bar for sighting purposes. The distance of the run is unlimited.

(*f*) All measurements shall be made perpendicularly from the ground to the upper side of the cross-bar where it is lowest. A steel or fibre-glass measure should be used. Any measurements of a new height should be made before competitors attempt that height. In the case of records the officials must check the measurement after the height has been cleared. The height shall be recorded to the nearest 1 cm below the height measured; i.e. fractions less than 1 cm must be ignored.

N.B. Judges should ensure, before commencing the competition, that the under-side and front of the cross-bar are distinguishable, and that the bar is always replaced in a similar manner.

(*g*) A competitor fails if he: (i) in the course of a jump

dislodges the bar so that it falls from the pegs; or (ii) touches the ground or landing area beyond the plane of the uprights without clearing the bar (if a jumper when he jumps touches the landing area and in the opinion of the judges no advantage is gained, the jump should not for that reason be considered a failure); or (iii) takes off from both feet.

79. Any style of uprights or posts may be used provided they are rigid. *See further details under this Rule in "A.A.A. Rules for Competition".*

80. Ties in High Jump and Pole Vault: *see details in "A.A.A. Rules".*

Pole Vault

81. No marks shall be placed on the runway, but a competitor may place marks alongside the runway. Any competitor may have the uprights moved in either direction, but they must not be moved more than 80 cm from the prolongation of the inside edge of the top of the stop-board. If the uprights are moved, the Judges should make a remeasurement to ensure there is no variation in the height.

The take-off for the pole shall be from a wooden or metal box.

A competitor fails if he: (i) in the course of a vault dislodges the bar so that it falls from the pegs; (ii) touches the ground, including the standing area beyond the vertical plane of the upper part of the stopboard, with any part of his body or with his pole, without first clearing the bar (iii) at the moment he makes a vault, or after leaving the ground, places his lower hand above the upper one or moves the upper hand higher up on the pole.

82. Any style of uprights or posts may be used provided they are rigid. *Details of specifications are given in "A.A.A. Rules".*

Long Jump

83. (*a*) The competition may be decided *either* by each competitor being allowed from 3 to 6 trials *or* by each being allowed 3 trials and the three to eight best competitors allowed 3 more.

(*b*) Each competitor shall be credited with the best of all his trials.

(c) The take-off shall be from a board the edge of which nearer the landing area shall be called the "scratch line". If a competitor takes off before reaching the board, it shall not for that reason be counted as a failure.

(d) The distance of the run is unlimited. No marks shall be placed on the runway, but a competitor may place marks alongside the runway. No competitor may place, or cause to be placed, any mark beyond the scratch line.

(e) If any competitor touches the ground beyond the scratch line or scratch line extended, with any part of his body, whether running up without jumping or in the act of jumping, it shall be counted as a failure.

(f) It shall be counted as a failure if a competitor, after completing a jump, walks back through the landing area.

(g) The measurement of the jumps shall be made at right angles from the nearest break in the ground in the landing area made by any part of the competitor's body to the scratch line. If, in the course of landing, a competitor touches the ground outside the landing area nearer to the scratch line than the break in the ground to which the measurement of the jump would have been made, such jump shall not be measured but shall count as a failure. The distance shall be measured to the nearest 1 cm below the distance covered.

Details of Long Jump Specifications are given in Rules 84 and 85 in "A.A.A. Rules".

Triple Jump

86. The *hop* shall be made so that the competitor first lands upon the foot with which he took off, in the *step* he shall land on the other foot, from which subsequently the *jump* is performed. If the competitor while jumping touches the ground with the "sleeping" leg, it shall be considered as a failure.

87. *Details of Triple Jump Specifications are given in "A.A.A. Rules".*

Putting the Shot

88. In order to avoid accidents, competitors must be given instructions that implements must be thrown during practice

only from the circles or scratch line or the immediate vicinity, and must be returned during practice or competition by hand and not thrown back to the starting area.

No competitor may place, or cause to be placed, any mark within the throwing sector.

Gloves may not be worn.

No device of any kind—e.g. the taping of fingers—which in any way assists a competitor when making a throw shall be allowed. But the use of tape to cover hand injury will be allowed if the Referee is satisfied on medical or other evidence that it is necessary.

A competitor must commence the throw from a stationary position within the circle.

It shall be a foul throw if the competitor, after he has stepped into the circle and started to make the throw, touches with part of his body the ground outside the circle, the top of the stop-board or the top of the circle. When leaving the circle, the first contact with the top of the circle or the ground outside the circle must be completely behind the white line drawn outside the circle and the rear edge of which runs theoretically through the centre of the circle.

A foul throw or letting go of the implement in an attempt shall be reckoned as a trial.

The circle must be clearly marked on the ground by chalk, or otherwise, and all measurements must be made from the nearer edge of the mark first made in the ground by the implement to the inner edge of the circle along a line drawn from the mark to the centre of the circle.

In making his puts the competitor may rest his feet against but not on top of the stop-board.

The shot shall be put from the shoulder with one hand only. At the time the competitor takes a stance in the ring, the shot shall touch or be in close proximity to the chin and the hand shall not be dropped below this position during the action of putting. The shot must not be brought behind the line of the shoulders.

For a valid put, the shot must fall so that the point from which measurement is to be made is within the inner edges of lines marking a sector of 40° set out on the ground so that the radii lines cross at the centre of the circle.

All measurements should be made immediately after each put.

Details of Putting the Shot Specifications are given in Rules 89 and 90 in "A.A.A. Rules".

Throwing the Hammer

91. All hammer throws shall be made from an enclosure or cage.

The competitor in his starting position prior to the preliminary swings or turns is allowed to put the head of the hammer on the ground inside or outside the circle.

It shall not be considered a foul throw if the head of the hammer touches the ground when the competitor makes the preliminary swings or turns. But if, after having so touched the ground, he stops throwing so as to begin the trial again, this shall count as a failure.

Details of Throwing the Hammer Specifications are given in Rules 92 and 93 in "A.A.A. Rules".

Throwing the Discus

94. All discus throws shall be made from an enclosure or cage.

For a valid throw the discus must fall so that the point from which measurement is to be made is within the inner edges of lines marking a sector of 40° set out on the ground so that the radii lines cross at the centre of the circle.

95. *Throwing the Discus Specifications are detailed in "A.A.A. Rules".*

Throwing the Javelin

96. The length of the runway shall be not more than 36.5 m but not less than 30 m and shall be marked by 2 parallel lines 5 cm wide and 4 m apart.

The throw shall be made from behind an arc of a circle drawn with a radius of 8 m; such arc shall consist of a strip made of wood or metal 7 cm wide, painted white and sunk flush with the ground. Lines shall be drawn from the extremities of the arc at right angles to the parallel lines marking the runway. These lines shall be 1.5 m long and 7 cm wide.

ATHLETICS

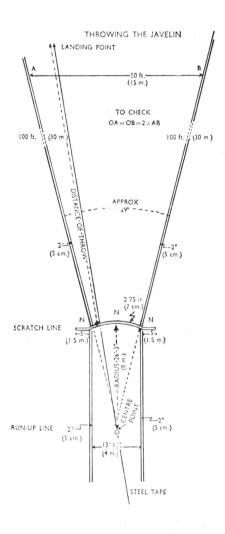

THROWING THE JAVELIN

LANDING POINT

A
B

50 ft.
(15 m.)

TO CHECK
OA = OB = 2 × AB

100 ft. (30 m.)
100 ft. (30 m.)

DISTANCE OF THROW

APPROX
29°

2"
(5 cm.)
2"
(5 cm.)

2.75 in.
(7 cm.)

SCRATCH LINE

N N N N

5'
(1.5 m.)
5'
(1.5 m.)

RADIUS 26'3"
(8 m.)

CENTRE POINT

RUN-UP LINE
2"
(5 cm.)
2"
(5 cm.)

O

13' 1½"
(4 m.)

STEEL TAPE

All throws to be valid must fall within the inner edge of lines marking the sector set out on the ground by extending for a distance of 90 m the lines from the centre of the circle, of which the arc is a part, through the points at which the arc joins the lines marking the runway. A competitor's throw must not be marked and measured if he steps on the arc or extended scratch lines, or if he crosses the scratch line on the ground marked N (*see diagram*) at any time, before a fair throw has been indicated by the judge at the throwing end. He is allowed to run on or outside the run-up lines provided that at the moment of throwing he is behind the arc and between the run-up lines.

The javelin must be held with one hand only, and at the grip, so that the little finger is nearest to the point. The javelin shall be thrown over the shoulder or upper part of the throwing arm, and must not be slung or hurled. *Non-orthodox styles are not permitted.*

In throwing the javelin no marks shall be placed on the runway but competitors may place marks at the side of the runway.

No throw shall be valid in which the tip of the metal head does not strike the ground before any other part of the javelin, or if the competitor crosses the scratch line or its extension. The competitor must not place his foot or feet upon the scratch line or board.

Javelin Specifications are detailed in Rule 97 of "A.A.A. Rules". Rules 98–100 are spare.

RULES FOR PARTICULAR EVENTS

Hurdle Races

101. A hurdle should consist of two uprights, or standards, supporting a rectangular frame or gate and should have a level top rail. The hurdle may be adjustable in height, but must be rigidly fastened at the required height for each event.

102. All races shall be run in lanes and each competitor shall run in his own lane throughout. He shall be disqualified if he trails his foot or leg alongside any hurdle, or jumps any hurdle not in his own lane, or deliberately knocks down any hurdle by

hand or foot.

Hurdle races for Seniors should be over 10 flights of hurdles as follows:

Distance of Race	Height of Hurdles	From Start to First Hurdle	Between Hurdles	From Last Hurdle to Finish
110 m	106.7 cm	13.72 m	9.14 m	14.02 m
400 m	91.4 cm	45 m	35 m	40 m

In Women's 100 m hurdles, over 10 flights, height of hurdles should be 84 cm, 13 m from start to first hurdle, 8.5 m between hurdles, and 10.5 m from last hurdle to finish.

Steeplechases

103. (*a*) The standard distances shall be: (i) 3,000 m. There shall be 28 hurdles and 7 water jumps. (ii) 2,000 m. There shall be 18 hurdles and 5 water jumps. (iii) 1,500 m. There shall be 13 hurdles and 3 water jumps.

(*b*) The hurdles shall be 91.4 cm high. Each flight shall be at least 3.66 m in total width. The water jump shall be 3.66 m in width and length, the water being 70 cm deep at the hurdle end and sloping to field level at the farther end.

(*c*) Every competitor must go over or through the water. He shall be disqualified if he jumps to the right or left of the water jump or trails his leg or foot alongside any obstacle. He may jump or vault over each hurdle and may place a foot on each hurdle and on the hurdle at the water jump.

Combined Events

104. The Pentathlon (men) consists of 5 events in the following order: Long Jump, Throwing the Javelin, 200 Metres, Throwing the Discus, and 1,500 Metres. The Heptathlon (women). First day: 100 Metres Hurdles, High Jump, Putting the Shot, 200 Metres. Second day: Long Jump, Javelin, 800 Metres. The Decathlon consists of 10 events in the following order: 100 Metres, Long Jump, Putting the Shot, High Jump and 400 Metres on the first day; 110 Metres Hurdles, Throwing the

Discus, Pole Vault, Throwing the Javelin and 1,500 Metres on the following day. It is permissible to decide all the events on the same day and in that case the order may be varied. Any athlete failing to take part in any of the events shall be considered to have abandoned the competition.

Relay Races

105. (a) Lines shall be drawn across the track to mark the distance of the stages and to denote the scratch line.

(b) Lines shall also be drawn 10 m before and after the scratch line to denote the take-over zone.

(c) The positions of the teams at the start of the race shall be drawn and shall be retained at each take-over zone, except that in races where lanes are not used, or have ceased to operate, waiting runners can move to the inside position as incoming team-mates arrive, provided this can be done without fouling.

(d) When relay races up to 400 m are contested on a circular track, each team should, if possible, have a separate lane and each lane must be the full distance.

(e) Except for the first runner, where the stage to be run does not exceed 200 m the outgoing runner may commence his run not more than 10 m outside the take-over zone: where the stage exceeds 200 m the outgoing runner must commence his run within the take-over zone. Additional lines in a different colour from that used for the take-over zone markings should be drawn to indicate the additional 10 m zone at all change-over points.

(f) In events where the first lap only is run in lanes, outgoing competitors after leaving the take-over zone are free to take up any positions on the track.

(g) In sprint relay races up and down a track, the take-over is by touch, contact being made within a clearly defined area of 1 m beyond, and at each end of, the relay distance.

(h) The baton must be carried in the hand throughout the race, and if dropped must be recovered by the athlete who dropped it. The baton must be passed only within the take-over zone. At the finish the baton is to be passed to an official by the last runner.

(i) Competitors after handing over the baton should

remain in their lanes or zones until the course is clear. Should any competitor wilfully impede a member of another team, he is liable to cause his own team to be disqualified.

(*j*) Assistance by pushing-off or any other method will cause disqualification.

(*k*) When a relay race is being run in lanes, a competitor may place a check mark on the track within his own lane but may not place, or cause to be placed, any marking object on or alongside the track.

(*l*) Once a team has competed in the preliminary round(s) of an event its composition must not be altered, except in the case of injury or illness.

(*m*) It is permissible for the order of running to be changed between heats and succeeding round or final.

(*n*) No competitor may run two sections for a team.

(*o*) The baton shall be a smooth hollow tube circular in section made of any rigid material in one piece, not more than 30 cm and not less than 28 cm long. The circumference shall be 12–13 cm and the weight not less than 50 gm.

Team Races

106. The composition of a team must not be changed after a heat has been run, except through injury or illness. Only competitors finishing the full distance are eligible to compete in the final.

The team scoring the least number of points, according to the positions in which the members of the team finish whose positions are to count, shall be the winner. In the case of a tie on points, the team whose last scoring member finished nearest the first place shall be the winner.

Road Running

107. Road races, including Marathon races, shall be run on roads. Runners must follow the traffic rules of the road, especially at roundabouts; when traffic makes it unsuitable, the course may be on a bicycle path or footpath alongside the road, but should not be on soft ground such as verges. The start and finish may be in an enclosed ground or arena.

The term 'Marathon Race' shall only be applied to a race of 26 miles 385 yd (42,195 m).

Walking Races

108. Walking is progression by steps so taken that unbroken contact with the ground is maintained, i.e. the advancing foot must make contact with the ground before the rear foot leaves it. Any competitor disqualified by a walking Judge must at once retire from the competition.

Tug-of-War Rules

The complete rules for Tug-of-War are included in the Tug-of-War Association Handbook.

109. Teams shall consist of an equal number of pulling members with a maximum of 8 per team. In Senior competitions no pulling member shall be under 17. All heats shall be won by two pulls out of three.

The rope shall not be less than 10 cm and not more than 12.5 cm in circumference, and the minimum length not less than 32 m.

The rope shall have a coloured tape or marking at the centre; two white ones each 2 m on either side of the centre marking; and two additional coloured ones each 5 m on either side of the centre marking. Ground markings shall consist of three lines parallel to each other, the distance between the centre line and each of the others being 2 m.

A Pull shall be won when one of the side markings on the rope is pulled over the side ground line farthest from it.

Printed by permission of the A.A.A. It should be noted that many of the Rules given above have here been abbreviated for reasons of space. Copies of the current edition of the A.A.A. Handbook, containing the complete A.A.A. Rules for Competitions, are available from the Association.

NOTE. *These Rules relate to competitions involving male athletes. The W.A.A.A. have their own set of competitive Rules.*

The Laws of
Badminton

DIAGRAM (A).

| | 1'6''
0.46 | 17' 0''
5.18 | 1'6''
0.46 |

Back Boundary Line,

2'6''
0.76 — also Long Service Line for Singles

Long Service Line for Doubles

13'0''
3.96

Right Service Court — Centre Line — Left Service Court

6'6''
1.98 — Short Service Line

Side Line for Doubles — for Singles — for Singles — Side Line for Doubles

POST — for Singles — N E T — for Singles — POST

6'6''
1.98
Side Line — Side Line — Side Line

Short Service Line

13'0''
3.96

Left Service Court — Centre Line — Right Service Court

Long Service Line for Doubles

2'6''
0.76 — Back Boundary Line;

also Long Service Line for Singles

| 20' 0''
6.10 |

44' 0''
13.40

Diagonal Measurement of full Court: 48ft. 4in. or 14.723 Metres.
Diagonal Measurement of half Court 29ft. 8¼in. or 9.061 Metres.
(from post to back boundary line).

Measurements are quoted in Feet (') and Inches ('') and in Metres.

DIAGRAM (B). Singles Court.

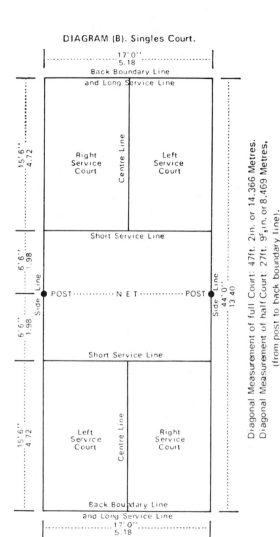

Measurements are quoted in Feet (') and Inches ('') and in Metres.

Badminton

Court

1. (*a*) The Court shall be a rectangle and laid out as in Diagram "A" (except in the case provided for in paragraph (*d*) of this Law) and to the measurements there shown, and shall be defined preferably by white or yellow lines or, if this is not possible, by other equally distinguishable lines, $1\frac{1}{2}$ in (40 mm) wide.

(*b*) To show the zone in which a shuttle of correct pace lands when tested (see Law 4*d*), an additional four marks $1\frac{1}{2}$ in by $1\frac{1}{2}$ in (40 mm by 40 mm) may be made as follows: inside each sideline for singles of the right service court, 1 ft 9 in (530 mm) and 3 ft 3 in (990 mm) from the back boundary line. In making these marks, their width shall be within the measurement given, i.e. the marks will be from 530 mm to 570 mm and from 950 mm to 990 mm from the outside of the back boundary line.

(*c*) (i) The width, $1\frac{1}{2}$ in (40 mm) of the centre lines shall be equally divided between between the right and left service courts.

(ii) The width, $1\frac{1}{2}$ in (40 mm) of each of the short service line and the doubles long service line shall fall within the 13 ft (3.960 m) measurement given as the length of the service court.

(iii) The width, $1\frac{1}{2}$ in (40 mm) of all other lines shall fall within the measurements given.

(*d*) Where space does not permit of the marking out of a court for doubles, a court may be marked out for singles only as shown in Diagram "B". The back boundary lines become also the long service lines, and the posts, or the strips of material representing them as referred to in Law 2, shall be placed on the side lines.

Posts

2. The posts shall be 5 ft 1 in (1.55 m) in height from the surface of the court. They shall be sufficiently firm to keep the net

strained as provided in Law 3, and shall be placed on the side boundary lines of the court. Where this is not practicable, some method must be employed for indicating the position of the side boundary line where it passes under the net, e.g. by the use of a thin post or strip of material, not less than $1\frac{1}{2}$ in (40 mm) in width, fixed to the side boundary line and rising vertically to the net cord. Where this is in use on a court marked for doubles it shall be placed on the boundary line of the doubles court irrespective of whether single or doubles are being played.

Net

3. The net shall be made of fine natural cord or artificial fibre of a dark colour and even thickness with not less than $\frac{5}{8}$ in (15 mm) and not more than $\frac{3}{4}$ in (20 mm) mesh. It shall be firmly stretched from post to post, and shall be 2 ft 6 in (0.76 m) in depth. The top of the net shall be 5 ft (1.524 m) in height from the floor at the centre, and 5 ft 1 in (1.55 in) at the posts, and shall be edged with a 3 in (75 mm) white tape doubled and supported by a cord or cable run through the tape and strained over and flush with the top of the posts.

Shuttle and Racket
Shuttle

Principles

4. The shuttle may be made from natural, synthetic or other manufactured product or any of those combinations.

The feel on the racket and the flight characteristics, generally, should be similar to those produced by the natural feathered shuttle, which has a cork base covered by a thin layer of leather.

Having Regard to the Principles:

(*a*) *General Design*:

(i) The shuttle shall have 14 to 16 feathers fixed in the base.

(ii) The feathers can have a variable length from $2\frac{1}{2}$ to $2\frac{3}{4}$ in (64 mm to 70 mm), but in each shuttle they shall be the same length when measured from the tip to the top of the base.

(iii) The tips of the feathers shall form a circle with a diameter within the range of $2\frac{1}{4}$ to $2\frac{5}{8}$ in (58 mm to 68 mm).

(iv) The feathers shall be fastened firmly with thread or other suitable material.

(v) The base shall be:

— 1 inch to 1⅛ in (25 mm to 28 mm) in diameter

—rounded on the bottom.

(*b*) *Weight*:

The shuttle shall weigh from 73 to 85 grains (4.74 to 5.50 grammes).

(*c*) *Non-feathered Shuttles*:

(i) The skirt, or simulation of feathers in synthetic or other manufactured materials, replaces natural feathers.

(ii) The base is described in paragraph 4(a)(v).

(iii) Measurements shall be the same as in paragraph 4(a)(i)-(iv). However, because of the difference in the specific gravity and behaviour of synthetic and manufactured materials in comparison with feathers, a variation of up to ten per cent in the stated measurements is acceptable.

(*d*) *Pace and Flight*:

A shuttle shall be deemed to be of correct pace when it is hit by a player with a full underhand stroke from a spot immediately above one back boundary line in a direction parallel to the sidelines and at an upward angle, to fall not less than 1 ft 9 in (530 mm) and not more than 3 ft 3 in (990 mm) short of the other back boundary line.

(*e*) *Modifications*:

Subject to there being no variation in the general design, pace and flight of the shuttle, modifications in the above specification may be made, with the approval of the national organisation concerned:

(i) in places where atmospheric conditions due either to altitude or climate make the standard shuttle unsuitable; or

(ii) if special circumstances exist which make it otherwise necessary in the interests of the game.

Racket

(*f*) (i) The hitting surface of the racket shall be flat and consist of a pattern of crossed strings connected to a frame and alternatively interlaced or bonded where they cross— and the stringing pattern shall be generally uniform and, in particular, not less dense in the centre than in any other area.

(ii) The frame of the racket, including the handle, shall not exceed 680 mm in overall length and 230 mm in overall width.

(iii) The overall length of the head shall not exceed 290 mm.

(iv) The strung surface shall not exceed 280 mm in overall length and 220 mm in overall width.

(v) The frame, including the handle, and the strings:

— shall be free of attached objects and protrusions, other than those utilised solely and specifically to limit or prevent wear and tear, or vibration, or to distribute weight, or to secure the handle by cord to the player's hand, and which are reasonable in size and placement for such purposes; and

— shall be free of any device which makes it possible for a player to change materially the shape of the racket.

The International Badminton Federation shall rule on the question of whether any racket or prototype complies with the above specifications or is otherwise approved or not approved for play. Such ruling may be undertaken on its own initiative or upon application by any party with a bona fide interest therein, including any player, equipment manufacturer or National Association or member thereof.

Players

5. (*a*) The word "Player" applies to all those taking part in a game.

(*b*) The game shall be played, in the case of the doubles game, by two players a side, and in the case of the singles game, by one player a side.

(*c*) The side for the time being having the right to serve shall be called the "In" side, and the opposing side shall be called the "Out" side.

The Toss

6. Before commencing play the opposing sides shall toss, and the side winning the toss shall have the option of: (*a*) Serving first; or (*b*) Not serving first; or (*c*) Choosing Ends.

The side losing the toss shall then have choice of any alternative remaining.

Scoring

7. (*a*) The doubles and men's singles game consists of 15 points. Provided that when the score is 13-all, the side which first reached 13 has the option of "Setting" the game to 5, and that when the score is 14-all, the side which first reached 14 has the option of "Setting" the game to 3. After a game has been "Set" the score is called "Love-All", and the side which first scores 5 or 3 points, according as the game has been "Set" at 13 or 14-all, wins the game. In either case the claim to "Set" the game must be made before the next service is delivered after the score has reached 13-all or 14-all.

(*b*) The ladies' singles game consists of 11 points. Provided that when the score is 9-all the player who first reached 9 has the option of "Setting" the game to 3, and when the score is 10-all the player who first reached 10 has the option of "Setting" the game to 2.

(*c*) A side rejecting the option of "Setting" at the first opportunity shall not be thereby barred from "Setting" if a second opportunity arises.

(*d*) Notwithstanding para. (*a*) above, it is permissible by prior arrangement for only one game to be played and also for this to consist of 21 points, in which case "Setting" shall be as for the game of 15 points with scores of 19 and 20 being substituted for 13 and 14 respectively.

(*e*) In handicap games, "Setting" is not permitted.

8. The opposing sides shall contest the best of three games, unless otherwise agreed. The players shall change ends at the commencement of the second game and also of the third game (if any). In the third game the players shall change ends when the leading score reaches:

(*a*) 8 in a game of 15 points;

(*b*) 6 in a game of 11 points.

Or, in handicap events, when one of the sides has scored half the total number of points required to win the game (the next highest number being taken in case of fractions). When it has been agreed to play only one game the players shall change ends as provided above for the third game.

In a game of 21 points, the players shall change ends when the leading score reaches 11 or in handicap games as indicated above.

If, inadvertently, the players omit to change ends as provided in this Law at the score indicated, the ends shall be changed immediately the mistake is discovered, and the existing score shall stand.

Doubles Play

9. (*a*) It having been decided which side is to have the first service, the player in the right-hand service court of that side commences the game by serving to the player in the service court diagonally opposite. If the latter player returns the shuttle before it touches the ground it is to be returned by one of the "In" side, and then returned by one of the "Out" side, and so on, till a fault is made or the shuttle ceases to be "In Play" (*vide* paragraph (*b*)). If a fault is made by the "In" side, its right to continue serving is lost, as only one player on the side beginning a game is entitled to do so (*vide* Law 11), and the opponent in the right-hand service court then becomes the server; but if the service is not returned, or the fault is made by the "Out" side, the "In" side scores a point. The "In" side players then change from one service court to the other, the service now being from the left-hand service court to the player in the service court diagonally opposite. So long as a side remains "In", service is delivered alternately from each service court into the one diagonally opposite, the change being made by the "In" side when, and only when, a point is added to its score.

(*b*) The first service of a side in each innings shall be made from the right-hand service court. A "Service" is delivered as soon as the shuttle is struck by the server's racket. The shuttle is thereafter "In Play" until it touches the ground, or until a fault or "Let" occurs, or except as provided in Law 18. After the service is delivered, the server and the player served to may take up any positions they choose on their side of the net, irrespective of any boundary lines.

10. The player served to may alone receive the service, but

should the shuttle touch, or be struck by, his partner, the "In" side scores a point. No player may receive two consecutive services in the same game, except as provided in Law 12.

11. Only one player of the side beginning a game shall be entitled to serve in its first innings. In all subsequent innings each partner shall have the right, and they shall serve consecutively. The side winning a game shall always serve first in the next game, but either of the winners may serve and either of the losers may receive the service.

12. If a player serves out of turn, or from the wrong service court (owing to a mistake as to the service court from which service is at the time being in order), *and his side wins the rally*, it shall be a "Let", provided that such "Let" be claimed and allowed, or ordered by the umpire, before the next succeeding service is delivered.

If a player of the "Out" side standing in the wrong service court is prepared to receive the service when it is delivered, *and his side wins the rally*, it shall be a "Let", provided that such "Let" be claimed and allowed, or ordered by the umpire, before the next succeeding service is delivered.

If in either of the above cases the side at fault *loses the rally*, the mistake shall stand and the players' positions shall not be corrected.

Should a player inadvertently change sides when he should not do so, and the mistake not be discovered until after the next succeeding service has been delivered, the mistake shall stand, and a "Let" cannot be claimed or allowed, and the players' positions shall not be corrected.

Singles Play

13. In singles, Laws 9 and 12 hold good, except that:

(*a*) The players shall serve from and receive service in their respective right-hand service courts only when the server's score is 0 or an even number of points in the game, the service being delivered from and received in their respective left-hand service courts when the server's score is an odd number of points. Setting does not affect this sequence.

(*b*) Both players shall change service courts after each point has been scored.

Faults

14. A fault made by a player of the side which is "In" puts the server out; if made by a player whose side is "Out", it counts a point to the "In" side.

It is a fault:

(*a*) If, in serving, (i) the initial point of contact with the shuttle is not on the base of the shuttle, or (ii) any part of the shuttle at the instant of being struck be higher than the server's waist, or (iii) if at the instant of the shuttle being struck the shaft of the racket be not pointing in a downward direction to such an extent that the whole of the head of the racket is discernibly below the whole of the server's hand holding the racket.

(*b*) If, in serving, the shuttle does not pass over the net, or falls into the wrong service court (i.e., into the one not diagonally opposite to the server), or falls short of the short service line or beyond the long service line, or outside the side boundary lines of the service court into which service is in order.

(*c*) If the server's feet are not in the service court from which service is at the time being in order, or if the feet of the player receiving the service are not in the service court diagonally opposite until the service is delivered. (*Vide* Law 16.)

(*d*) If, once the service has started, any player makes preliminary feints or otherwise intentionally baulks his opponent, or if any player deliberately delays serving the shuttle or in getting ready to receive it so as to obtain an unfair advantage. (When the server and receiver have taken up their respective positions to serve and to receive, the first forward movement of the server's racket constitutes the start of the service and such must be continuous thereafter.)

(*e*) If, either in service or play, the shuttle falls outside the boundaries of the court, or passes through or under the net, or fails to pass the net, or touches the roof or side walls, or the person or dress of a player. (A shuttle falling on a line shall be deemed to have fallen in the court or service court of which such line is a boundary.)

(*f*) If, when in play, the initial point of contact with the shuttle is not on the striker's side of the net. (The striker may, however, follow the shuttle over the net with his racket in the course of his stroke.)

(*g*) If, when the shuttle is "In Play", a player touches the net or its supports with racket, person or dress.

(*h*) If the shuttle be caught and held on the racket and then slung during the execution of a stroke; or if the shuttle be hit twice in succession by the same player with two strokes; or if the shuttle be hit by a player and his partner successively.

(*i*) If, in play, a player strikes the shuttle (unless he thereby makes a good return) or is struck by it, whether he is standing within or outside the boundaries of the court.

(*j*) If a player obstructs an opponent.

(*k*) If Law 16 be transgressed.

(*l*) If a player is guilty of flagrant, repeated or persistent offences under Law 21.

(*m*) If the server, in attempting to serve, misses the shuttle.

GENERAL

15. The server may not serve till his opponent is ready, but the opponent shall be deemed to be ready if a return of the service be attempted.

16. The server and the player served to must stand within the limits of their respective service courts (as bounded by the short and long service, the centre, and side lines), and some part of both feet of these players must remain in contact with the surface of the court in a stationary position until the service is delivered. A foot on or touching a line in the case of either the server or the receiver shall be held to be outside his service court. (*Vide* Law 14 (*c*).) The respective partners may take up any position, provided they do not unsight or otherwise obstruct an apponent.

17. (*a*) If, in the course of service or rally, the shuttle touches and passes over the net, the stroke is not invalidated thereby. It is a good return if the shuttle having passed outside either post drops on or within the boundary lines of the opposite court. A "Let" may be given by the umpire for any unforeseen or accidental hindrance.

(*b*) If, in service, or during a rally, a shuttle, *after passing over the net*, is caught in or on the net, it is a "Let".

(*c*) If the receiver is faulted for moving before the service is delivered, or for not being within the correct service court, in accordance with Laws 14 (*c*) or 16, and at the same time the server is also faulted for a service infringement, it shall be a "Let".

(*d*) When a "Let" occurs, the play since the last service shall not count, and the player who served shall serve again, except when Law 12 is applicable.

18. If, when in play, the shuttle strikes the net and remains suspended there, or strikes the net and falls towards the surface of the court on the striker's side of the net, or hits the surface outside the court and an opponent then touches the net or shuttle with his racket or person, there is no penalty, as the shuttle is not *then* in play.

19. If a player has a chance of striking the shuttle in a downward direction when quite near the net, his opponent must not put up his racket near the net on the chance of the shuttle rebounding from it. This is obstruction within the meaning of Law 14 (*j*).

A player may, however, hold up his racket to protect his face from being hit if he does not thereby baulk his opponent.

20. It shall be the duty of the umpire to call "Fault" or "Let" should either occur, without appeal being made by the players, and to give his decision on any appeal regarding a point in dispute, if made before the next service; and also to appoint linesmen and service judges at his discretion. An umpire's decision shall be final, but he shall uphold the decision of a linesman or service judge. This shall not preclude the umpire also from faulting the server or receiver. Where, however, a referee is appointed, an appeal shall lie to him from the decision of an umpire on questions of law only.

Continuous Play

21. (*a*) Play shall be continuous from the first service till the match be concluded; except that (i) in international competi-

tive events there shall be allowed an interval not exceeding five minutes between the second and third games of a match; (ii) in countries where conditions render it desirable, there shall be allowed, subject to the previously published approval of the national organisation concerned, an interval not exceeding five minutes between the second and third games of a match, in singles or doubles, or both; and (iii) when necessitated by circumstances not within the control of the players, the umpire may suspend play for such a period as he may consider necessary. If play be suspended, the existing score shall stand and play be resumed from that point.

(*b*) Under no circumstances shall play be suspended to enable a player to recover his strength or wind, or to receive instruction or advice.

(*c*) Except in the case of an interval provided for above, no player shall be allowed to receive advice during a match or to leave the court until the match be concluded without the umpire's consent.

(*d*) The umpire shall be the sole judge of any suspension of play.

Copyright by the Badminton Association of England. The Laws are as revised in 1939 and adopted by the International Badminton Federation. Subsequently revised up to date.

The Rules of
Basketball

REGULATION SIZE COURT

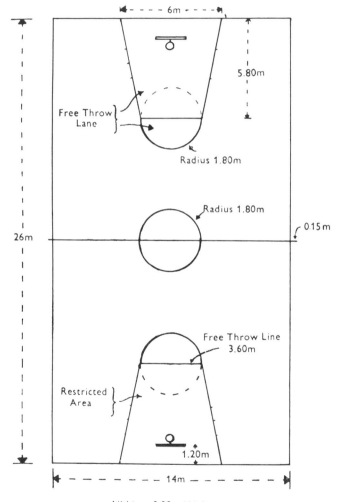

All Lines 0.05m Wide

Basketball

RULE 1

The Game

1. Definition

Basketball is played by two teams of five players each. The purpose of each team is to throw the ball into the opponents' basket and to prevent the other team from securing the ball or scoring. The ball may be passed, thrown, tapped, rolled or dribbled in any direction, subject to the restrictions laid down in the following Rules.

RULE 2

Equipment

2. Court—Dimensions

The playing court shall be a rectangular hard surface free from obstructions and shall have dimensions of 26 m in length by 14 m in width, measured from the inside edge of the boundary lines.

The following variations in the dimensions are permitted: plus or minus 2 m on the length and plus or minus 1 m on the width, the variations being proportional to each other.

The height of the ceiling should be at least 7 m. The playing surface should be uniformly and adequately lighted. The light units should be placed where they will not hinder the vision of players.

3. Boundary lines

The playing court shall be marked by well defined lines, which shall be at every point at least 2 m from any obstruction. The lines of the long sides of the court shall be termed the Side Lines, those of the short sides, the End Lines. The distance between these lines and the spectators should be at least 2 m.

REGULATION FREE THROW LANE

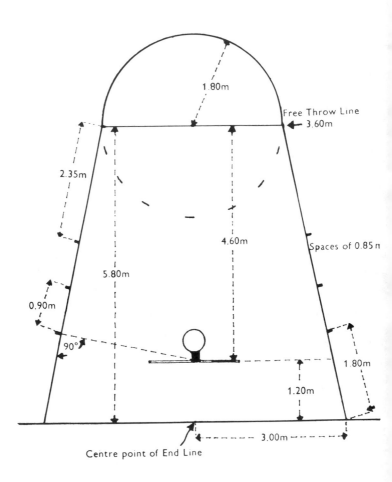

1.80m

Free Throw Line
3.60m

2.35m

4.60m

Spaces of 0.85m

5.80m

0.90m

90°

1.80m

1.20m

3.00m

Centre point of End Line

The lines mentioned in this article and in the following must be drawn so as to be perfectly visible and be 5 cm in width.

4. Centre Circle

The centre circle shall have a radius of 1.80 m and it shall be marked in the centre of the court. The radius shall be measured to the outer edge of the circumference.

5. Centre Line—Front Court, Back Court

A Centre Line shall be drawn, parallel to the end lines, from the mid-points of the side lines and shall extend 15 cm beyond each side line.

A team's Front Court is that part of the court between the end line behind the opponents' basket and the nearer edge of the Centre Line. The other part of the court, including the Centre Line, is the team's Back Court.

6. Free Throw Lines

A free throw line shall be drawn parallel to each end line. It shall have its further edge 5.80 m from the inner edge of the end line, and it shall be 3.60 m long and its mid-point shall lie on the line joining the mid-points of the two end lines.

7. Restricted Areas and Free Throw Lanes

The restricted areas shall be spaces marked in the court which are limited by the end lines, the free throw lines and by lines which originate at the end lines, their outer edges being 3 m from the mid-points of the end lines, and terminate at the ends of the free throw lines.

The free throw lanes are the restricted areas extended in the playing court by semi-circles with a radius of 1.80 m, their centres at the mid-points of the free throw lines. Similar semi-circles shall be drawn with a broken line within the restricted areas.

Spaces along the free throw lanes, to be used by players during free throws, shall be marked as follows:

The first space shall be situated 1.80 m from the inside edge of the end line, measured along the line at the side of the free throw lane, and shall be 85 cm in width. The second space shall be adjacent to the first and shall also be 85 cm in width. The lines used to mark these spaces shall be 10 cm long and be perpendicular to the side line of the free throw lane and shall be drawn outside the space they are delimiting.

8. Backboards—Size, Material and Position

Each of the two backboards shall be made of hard wood, 3 cm thick, or of a suitable transparent material (made in one piece and of the same degree of rigidity as those made of wood), and their dimensions shall be 1.80 m horizontally and 1.20 m vertically. The front surface shall be flat and unless it is transparent, it shall be white. This surface shall be marked as follows: a rectangle shall be drawn behind the ring and marked by a line 5 cm wide. The rectangle shall have outside dimensions of 59 cm horizontally and 45 cm vertically. The top edge of its base line shall be level with the ring.

Borders of the backboards shall be marked with a line, 5 cm wide. These lines shall be of a colour contrasting with the background. Normally, if the backboard is transparent, it shall be marked in white; in other cases in black. The edges of the backboards and the rectangles marked on them should be of the same colour.

The backboards shall be rigidly mounted in a position at each end of the court at right-angles to the floor, parallel to the end lines, and with their lower edges 2.75 m above the floor. Their centres shall lie in the perpendiculars erected at the points in the court 1.20 m from the mid-points of the end lines. The uprights supporting the backboards shall be at a distance of at least 1 m from the outer edge of the end lines and shall be of a bright colour in contrast with the background in such a manner that they will be clearly visible to the players. Both the backboards and supports shall be suitably padded to prevent injury.

9. Baskets

The basket shall comprise the rings and the nets. The rings shall be constructed from solid iron, 45 cm in inside diameter, painted orange. The metal of the rings shall be 20 mm in diameter, with the possible addition of small-gauge loops on the under-edge or similar device for attaching the nets. They should be rigidly attached to the backboards and should lie in a horizontal plane 3.05 m above the floor, equidistant from the two vertical edges of the backboard. The nearest point of the inside edge of the rings shall be 15 cm from the faces of the backboards.

The nets shall be of white cord suspended from the rings and constructed so as to check the ball momentarily as it passes through the basket. They shall be 40 cm in length.

10. Ball—Material, Size and Weight

The ball shall be spherical; it shall be made with an outer surface of leather, rubber or synthetic material; it shall be not less than 75 cm nor more than 78 cm in circumference; it shall weigh not less than 600 gm nor more than 650 gm; and it shall be inflated to an air pressure such that when it is dropped on to a solid wooden floor or the playing surface from a height of about 1.80 m measured to the bottom of the ball, it will rebound to a height, measured to the top of the ball, of not less than about 1.20 m nor more than about 1.40 m.

The home team shall provide at least one used ball that meets the above specifications. The Referee shall be the sole judge of the legality of the ball and he may select for use a ball provided by the visiting team.

11. Technical Equipment

The following Technical Equipment shall be provided by the home team and shall be at the disposal of the Officials and their assistants:

(a) The Game Clock and the time-out watch. The Time-keeper shall be provided with at least a game clock and a stopwatch. The clock, used for timing periods of play and the intervals between them, and the stop-watch, used for timing time-outs, shall be placed so that they may be clearly seen by both the Timekeeper and the Scorer.

(b) A suitable device, visible to players and spectators, shall be provided for the administration of the 30-seconds Rule and shall be operated by the 30-seconds Operator.

(*c*) The official Score Sheet shall be the one approved by the International Amateur Basketball Federation, and it shall be filled in by the Scorer before and during the game as provided for in these Rules.

(*d*) There shall be suitable equipment for all signals provided for in these Rules, including a Score Board visible to players, spectators and the Scorer's Table.

(*e*) Markers numbered 1 to 5 shall be at the disposal of the Scorer. Every time a player commits a foul, the Scorer shall raise in a manner visible to both Coaches the marker with the number corresponding to the number of fouls committed by that player. The markers shall be white with numbers, a minimum size of 20 cm by 10 cm, from 1 to 4 in black and 5 in red.

(*f*) The Scorer shall be provided with two Team Foul Markers. These shall be red constructed in such a way that when positioned on the Scorer's Table, they are easily visible to players, Coaches and Officials. The moment the ball goes into play following the seventh player foul by a team, a marker shall be positioned on the Scorer's Table at the end nearer the bench of the team that has committed the seventh player foul.

RULE 3

Players, Substitutes and Coaches

12. Teams

Each team shall consist of not more than ten players, one of whom shall be the captain, and of a Coach who may be seconded by an Assistant Coach. (See also art. 15.) In tournaments where a team has to play more than five games the number of players in each team may be increased to twelve.

Five players from each team shall be on the court during playing time (for exceptions see art. 33) and may be substituted within the provisions contained in these Rules.

Each player shall be numbered on the front and back of his shirt with plain numbers of solid colour contrasting with the colour of his shirt, and made of material not less than 2 cm wide. The numbers on the back shall be at least 20 cm high and those on the front at least 10 cm high. Teams shall use numbers from 4 to 15. Players on the same team shall not wear duplicate numbers. Shirts of the same colour, on both the back and front, shall be worn by all players of the same team.

13. Player leaving Court

A player may not leave the playing court to gain an unfair advantage. For penalty see art. 77.

14. Captain—Duties and Powers

The Captain shall be the representative of his team and shall control its play. (See also art. 89.) The Captain may address an Official on matters of interpretation or to obtain essential information when necessary, if it is done in a courteous manner.

Before leaving the playing court for any valid reason, the Captain shall inform the Referee regarding the player who will replace him during his absence.

15. Coaches

At least 20 minutes before the game is scheduled to begin, the Coaches shall furnish the Scorer with names and numbers of players who are to play in the game, as well as the names of the Captain of the team, the Coach and the Assistant Coach. At least 10 minutes before the game the Coaches will confirm their agreement with the names and numbers of their players and Coaches inscribed by signing the scoresheet; and at the same time indicate the five players who are to start the game. The Coach of Team "A" will be the first to provide this information. If a player changes his number during the game he shall report the change to the Scorer and Referee. Requests for charged time-outs shall be made by the Coach. When a Coach decides to request a substitution, he shall instruct the substitute to report to the Scorer. The player must be ready to play immediately. (See art. 12, 41, 46 and Procedure before the game.)

If there is an Assistant Coach, his name must be inscribed on the Score Sheet before the beginning of the game. He shall assume the responsibilities of the Coach if for any reason the Coach is unable to continue.

The team captain may act as Coach. If he must leave the playing court for any valid reason, he may continue to act as Coach. However, if he must leave following a disqualifying foul, or if he is unable to act as Coach owing to severe injury, his substitute as Captain shall also replace him as Coach.

RULE 4

Officials and their Duties

16. Officials and their Assistants

The Officials shall be a Referee and an Umpire, who shall be assisted by a Timekeeper, a Scorer and a 30-seconds Operator.

It cannot be too strongly emphasised that the Referee and the Umpire of a given game should not be connected in any way with either of the organisations represented on the court, and that they should be thoroughly competent and impartial. The Officials have no authority to agree to changes in the Rules. They shall wear a uniform consisting of basketball shoes, long grey trousers and grey shirt.

17. Duties and Powers of Referee

The Referee shall inspect and approve all equipment, including all the signals used by the Officials and their Assistants. He shall designate the official timepiece and recognise its operator, and shall also recognise the Scorer and the 30-seconds Operator. He shall not permit any player to wear objects which in his judgment are dangerous to other players.

The Referee shall toss the ball at the centre to start the game. He shall decide whether a goal shall count if the Officials disagree. He shall have power to forfeit a game when conditions warrant. He shall decide matters upon which the Timekeeper and the Scorer disagree. At the end of each half and of each extra period, or at any time he feels necessary, he shall carefully examine the Scoresheet, approve the score and confirm the time that remains to be played. His approval at the end of the game terminates the connection of the Officials with the game.

The Referee shall have power to make decisions on any point not specifically covered in the Rules.

18. Duties of Officials—Referee and Umpire

The Officials shall conduct the game in accordance with the Rules. This includes: putting the ball in play, determining when the ball becomes dead, administering penalties, ordering time-out, beckoning substitutes to come on the court, handing the ball to a player when such player is to make a throw-in from out-of-bounds whenever this is provided for in these Rules (see art. 68 and 80), and silently counting seconds to administer provisions contained in art. 31, 58, 59, 60, 68 and 72.

Before the beginning of the game, the Officials shall agree upon a division of the playing court, to be covered by each of them. After each foul or jump-ball decision, the Officials shall exchange their positions.

The Officials shall blow their whistles and simultaneously give the signal to stop the clock (signal 5 or 12), followed by all the signals, to make clear their decision.

The Officials shall not whistle after a goal from the field or resulting from a free throw, but shall clearly indicate that a goal has been scored by using signal 1 or 3.

If verbal communication is necessary to make a decision clear, this must be done in English for all international games.

19. Time and Place for Decisions

The Officials shall have powers to make decisions for infractions of the rules committed either within or outside the boundary lines; these powers shall start when they arrive on the court, which shall be 20 minutes before the game is scheduled to begin and shall terminate with the expiration of playing time as approved by the Referee.

Penalties for fouls committed before the game or during intervals of play shall be administered as described in article 74.

If during the period between the end of playing time and the signing of the Score Sheet there is any unsportsmanlike behaviour by players, Coaches, Assistant Coaches or team followers, the Referee must record on the Score Sheet that an incident has occurred and ensure that a detailed report is submitted to the responsible authority which shall deal with the matter with appropriate severity.

Neither Official shall have authority to set aside or question decisions made by the other within the limits of his respective duties as outlined in these Rules.

If the Officials make approximately simultaneous decisions on the same play and the infractions involve different penalties, the more severe penalty shall be imposed, except in the case of a double foul as defined in article 83.

However, in other situations where simultaneous fouls are called against both teams, the foul carrying the more serious free throw penalty shall be considered the more severe and shall be administered last, with possession of the ball for a throw-in as a penalty cancelled.

20. Calling of Fouls

When a personal foul has been committed the Official shall blow his whistle and simultaneously give the signal (no. 12) to stop the clock. He shall then indicate to the offender that a foul has been committed, the nature of the foul and, if necessary, the number of the player. The offending player is required to acknowledge this by raising his hand in the air. The Official shall then move into position to establish clearly visual contact with the Scorer and signal the number of the offender, the nature of the offence and the penalty that is to follow. When the foul has been acknowledged by the Scorer, inscribed on the score-sheet and the foul marker raised, the Officials shall exchange positions. The game shall be resumed by one of the Officials handing the ball to the player who is to take the throw-in from out-of-bounds at the side line or end line, or take the free throw(s) from the free-throw line. Exceptions: art. 83.

The Officials shall also penalise unsportsmanlike conduct by any player, Coach, Assistant Coach, substitute or team follower. If there is a flagrant case of such conduct, the Officials shall penalise it by disqualifying the offender from the game and banishing any offending substitute, Coach, attendant or team follower.

21. Duties of Scorer

The Scorer shall keep a chronological running summary of the points scored; he shall record the field goals made and the free throws made or missed. He shall record the personal and technical fouls called on each player and shall notify the Referee immediately when the fifth foul is called on any player. He shall record the time-outs charged to each team, and shall notify a Coach through an Official when he has taken a second time-out in each half. He shall also indicate the number of fouls committed by each player by using the numbered markers as provided in article 11 (*e*).

The Scorer shall keep a record of the names and numbers of players who are to start the game and of all substitutes who enter the game. When there is an infraction of the Rules pertaining to submission of line-up, substitutions or numbers of players, he shall notify the nearer Official as soon as possible when the infraction is discovered.

The sounding of the Scorer's signal does not stop the game. He should be careful to sound his signal only when the ball is dead and the game watch is stopped, and before the ball is again in play.

It is essential that the Scorer's signal be different from that of the Timekeeper and of the Officials.

22. Duties of Timekeeper

The Timekeeper shall note when each half is to start and shall notify the Referee more than three minutes before this time so that he may notify the teams, or cause them to be notified, at least three minutes before the half is to start. He shall keep record of playing time and time of stoppage as provided in these Rules.

For a charged time-out the Timekeeper shall start a timeout watch and shall direct the Scorer to signal the Referee when it is time to resume play.

The Timekeeper shall indicate with a gong, pistol or bell the expiration of playing time in each half, or extra period. This signal terminates actual playing time in each period. If the Timekeeper's signal fails to sound, or if it is not heard, the Timekeeper shall go on the court or use other means to notify the Referee immediately. If, in the meantime, a goal has been made or a foul has occurred, the Referee shall consult the Timekeeper and the Scorer. If they agree that the time was up before the ball was in the air on its way to the basket or before the foul was committed, the Referee shall rule that the goal does not count, or in the case of a foul, that it shall be disregarded, but if they disagree, the goal shall count or the foul be penalised unless the Referee has knowledge that would alter this ruling.

23. Duties of 30-seconds Operator

The 30-seconds Operator shall operate the 30-seconds device or watch (see art. 11(b)) as provided in article 62 in these rules.

The signal of the 30-second Operator causes the ball to become a dead ball.

RULE 5

Playing Regulations

24. Playing Time

The game shall consist of two halves of 20 minutes each, with normally an interval of 10 minutes between halves.

25. Beginning of Game

The game shall be started by a jump-ball in the centre circle. The Referee shall make the toss between any two opponents. The same procedure shall be followed at the beginning of the second half and, if necessary, of each extra period.

The visiting team shall have choice of baskets in the first

half; on neutral courts teams shall toss for baskets. For the second half the teams shall change baskets.

The game cannot begin if one of the teams is not on the court with five players ready to play. If 15 minutes after the starting time the defaulting team is not present, the other team wins the game by forfeit.

26. Jump-Ball

A jump-ball takes place when the Official tosses the ball between two opposing players.

During a jump-ball the two jumpers shall stand with their feet inside that half of the circle which is nearer to their own baskets, with one foot near the centre of the line that is between them. The Official shall then toss the ball upward (vertically) between the jumpers, to a height greater than either of them can reach by jumping and so that it will drop between them. The ball must be tapped by one or both of the jumpers *after* it reaches its highest point. If it touches the floor without being tapped by at least one of the jumpers, the jump-ball shall be re-taken.

Neither jumper shall tap the ball before it reaches its highest point, nor leave their positions until the ball has been tapped. Either jumper may tap the ball twice only. After the second tap by a jumper, he shall not touch the ball again until it has touched one of the eight non-jumpers, the floor, the basket, or the backboard. Under this provision, four taps are possible, two by each jumper. When a jump-ball takes place, the eight non-jumpers shall remain outside the circle (cylinder) until the ball has been tapped. Team-mates may not occupy adjacent positions around the circle if an opponent desires one of the positions.

During a jump-ball the Officials shall see that the other players are in such positions that they do not interfere with the jumpers.

27. Violation during Jump-Ball

A player shall not violate provisions governing jump-ball. If, before the ball is tapped, a jumper leaves the jumping position or if a non-jumper enters the circle (cylinder), it is a violation which shall be called immediately by one of the Officials. If either of these occurs, the violation is disregarded. If there is a violation by both teams or if the Official make a bad toss, the jump-ball shall be re-taken.

Penalty. See article 66.

28. Goal—When Made and its Value

A goal is made when a live ball enters the basket from above and remains in or passes through.

A goal from the field counts 2 points unless attempted from beyond the 3-point line when it counts 3 points; a goal from a free throw counts 1 point. A goal from the field counts for the team attacking the basket into which the ball is thrown.

If the ball accidentally enters the basket from below, it shall become dead and play shall be resumed by a jump-ball at the nearest free throw line.

If, however, a player deliberately causes the ball to enter the basket from below, it is a violation and play shall be resumed by an opponent throwing the ball in from the side line out-of-bounds at the point nearest to where the violation occurred.

29. Interfere with Ball in Offence

An offensive player may not touch the ball when it is in its downward flight above the level of the ring and is directly above the restricted area, whether it is a shot for goal or a pass. This restriction applies only until the ball touches the ring.

An offensive player shall not touch his opponent's basket or backboard while the ball is on the ring during a shot for goal.

Penalty. No point can be scored and the ball is awarded to opponents for a throw-in from out-of-bounds at a position on the side line nearest the point where the violation occurred (see art. 66).

30. Interfere with Ball in Defence

A defensive player shall not touch the ball after it has started its downward flight during an opponent's shot for goal and while the ball is above the level of the ring. This restriction applies only until the ball touches the ring or until it is apparent it will not touch it.

A defensive player shall not touch his own basket or backboard while the ball is on the ring during a shot for goal, or touch the ball or basket while the ball is within such basket.

Penalty. The ball becomes dead when violation occurs. The shooter is awarded the point if during a free throw as in article 73, and 2 or 3 points if during a shot for goal from the field according to the place from where the shot for goal was attempted. Ball is awarded out-of-bounds from behind the end line as though the shot had been successful and there had been no violation.

31. Throw-in after Field Goal or Successful Last Free Throw

After a field goal or successful last free throw, any opponent of the team credited with the score shall be entitled to throw the ball in from any point out-of-bounds at the end of the court where the goal was made. He may throw it from any point on or beyond the end line, or he may pass it to a team-mate on or behind the end line. Not more than five seconds shall be taken when throwing the ball in, the count starting the instant the ball is at the disposal of the first player out-of-bounds.

The Official should not handle the ball unless by so doing the game can be resumed more quickly. Opponents of the player who is to throw the ball in shall not touch the ball. Allowance may be made for touching the ball accidentally or instinctively, but if a player delays the game by interfering with the ball, it is a technical foul.

Exception. Following a technical foul charged against the Coach the ball shall be thrown in from out-of-bounds at mid-court, whether or not the last free throw is successful (see art. 78—penalty).

32. Decision of Game

A game shall be decided by the scoring of the greater number of points in the playing time.

33. Game to be Forfeited

A team shall forfeit the game if it refuses to play after being instructed to do so by the Referee. When during a game the number of players of a team on the court shall be less than two, the game shall end, and that team shall lose the game by forfeit. If the team to which the game is forfeited is ahead, the score at the time of forfeiture shall stand. If this team is not ahead, the score shall be recorded as 2–0 in its favour.

34. Tied Score and Extra Periods

If the score is a tie at the expiration of the second half, the game shall be continued for an extra period of five minutes or as many such periods of five minutes as may be necessary to break the tie. Before the first extra period the teams shall toss for baskets and shall change baskets at the beginning of each additional extra period. An interval of two minutes shall be allowed before each extra period. At the beginning of each extra period, the game shall be re-started with a jump-ball at the centre circle.

35. When Game is Terminated

The game shall terminate at the sounding of the Timekeeper's signal indicating the end of playing time.

When a foul is committed simultaneously with or just previous to the Timekeeper's signal ending a half or an extra period, time shall be allowed for the free throw or throws, if any are involved in the penalty.

When a shot (see art. 57) is taken near the end of playing time the goal, if made, shall count if the ball was in the air before time expired. All provisions contained in articles 29 and 30 shall apply until the ball touches the ring. If the ball strikes the ring, rebounds and then enters the basket, the goal shall count. If, after the ball has touched the ring, a player of either team touches the ball, it is a violation. If a defensive player commits such a violation, 2 points shall be awarded. If an offensive player commits such a violation, the ball becomes dead and the goal, if scored, shall not count. These provisions apply until it is apparent the shot will not be successful.

RULE 6

Timing Regulations

36. Game Clock Operations

The game clock shall be started:

(*a*) when the ball after having reached its highest point on a toss during a jump-ball is tapped by the first player,

(*b*) if a free throw is not successful and the ball is to continue in play, when the ball touches a player on the court,

(*c*) if the game is resumed by a throw-in from out-of-bounds, when the ball touches a player on the court.

The game clock shall be stopped at the end of each half and extra period, and when an Official blows his whistle for: (*a*) a violation, (*b*) a foul, (*c*) a held ball, (*d*) unusual delay in re-starting the game following a dead ball, (*e*) suspension of play for injury, or for removal of a player, such removal being ordered by an Official, (*f*) suspension of play for any reason, ordered by the Officials, (*g*) when the 30-seconds signal is sounded, or (*h*) when a field goal is scored against the team of a Coach who has requested a charged time-out.

37. Ball Goes into Play

The ball goes into play (is in play) when:

(*a*) the Official enters the circle to administer a jump-ball, or

(*b*) the Official enters the free throw lane to administer a free throw (see art. 72), or

(*c*) when in an out-of-bounds situation the ball is at the disposal of the player who is at the point of the throw-in.

38. Ball Becomes Alive

The ball becomes alive when:

(*a*) after having reached its highest point in a jump-ball it is tapped by the first player, or (*b*) when the Official places it at the disposal of a free throw shooter (see art. 72), or

(*c*) after a throw-in from out-of-bounds, it touches a player in the court.

39. Dead Ball

The ball becomes dead when:

(*a*) Any goal is made (see art. 28).

(*b*) Any violation occurs.

(*c*) A foul occurs while the ball is alive or in play.

(*d*) Held ball occurs or ball lodges on the basket support.

(*e*) It is apparent that the ball will not go into the basket; on a free throw for a technical foul by Coach, Assistant Coach, substitute or team follower, or a free throw which is to be followed by another free throw.

(*f*) Official's whistle is blown while the ball is alive or in play.

(*g*) The 30-seconds Operator's signal is sounded while the ball is alive.

(*h*) Time expires for a half or extra period.

(*i*) The ball already in flight on a shot for goal is touched by a player of either team after time has expired for a half or extra period, or after a foul has been called. The provisions of art. 29, 30 and 35 still apply.

Exceptions: The ball does not become dead at the time of the listed act and goal, if made, counts if:

(1) ball is in flight on a free throw or shot for goal when (*c*), (*f*), (*g*) or (*h*) occurs, or

(2) an opponent fouls while the ball is still in control of a player who is shooting for goal and who finished his shot with a continuous motion which started before the foul occurred (see art. 85).

40. Time-out

Time-out occurs and the Game Clock shall be stopped when an Official signals:

(*a*) A violation;

(*b*) A foul;

(*c*) A held-ball;

(*d*) Unusual delay in the game being resumed following a dead ball;

(*e*) Suspension of play for an injury, or for removal of a player, such removal being ordered by an Official;

(*f*) Suspension of play for any reason, ordered by the Officials;

(*g*) When the 30-seconds signal is sounded; or

(*h*) When a basket is scored against the team of a coach who has requested a charged time-out.

41. Charged Time-out

A Coach has the right to request time-out. He shall do so by going in person to the Scorer and asking clearly for a "time-out", making the proper conventional sign with his hands. Electrical devices enabling Coaches, if they so wish, to request a time-out without leaving their places may be used. Such devices may not, under any circumstances, be used to request a player substitution.

The Scorer shall indicate to the Officials that a request for charged time-out has been made by sounding his signal as soon as the ball is dead and the Game Clock is stopped *but before the ball is again in play* (see art. 37).

A Coach may also be granted a charged time-out if, after a request from him for a time-out, a field goal is scored by his opponents. In this case the Timekeeper shall immediately stop the Game Clock. The Scorer shall then sound his signal and indicate to the Officials that a charged time-out has been requested.

A charged time-out shall not be granted from the moment the ball is in play for the first or only free throw until the ball becomes dead after being alive again after the free throw or throws.

A time-out shall be charged to a team for each minute consumed under these provisions. If the team responsible for the time-out is ready to play before the end of the charged time-out the Referee is hereby given authority to start the game immediately.

Exceptions: No time-out is charged if an injured player is ready to play immediately or is substituted as soon as possible or if a disqualified player, or a player who has committed his fifth foul is replaced within one minute, or if an Official permits a delay.

42. Legal Charged Time-out

Two charged time-outs may be granted to each team during each half of playing time, and one charged time-out for each extra period. Unused time-outs may not be carried over to the next half or extra period.

43. Time-out in Case of Injury

The Officials may order time-out in case of injury to players or for any other reason. If the ball is alive when an injury occurs, the Officials shall withhold their whistles until the play has been completed, that is, the team in control of the ball has shot for goal, lost control of the ball, has withheld the ball from play, or the ball has become dead.

When necessary to protect an injured player, the Officials may suspend play immediately.

If the injured player cannot continue to play immediately, he must be substituted within one minute or as soon as possible, should the injury prevent an earlier substitution. If free throws have been awarded to the injured player, they must be attempted by his substitute. If this occurs, the provisions contained in the last paragraph of article 46, *Exception*, shall not apply. If an injured player is not substituted as set out in this article, his team shall be charged with a time-out except in the case of a team having to continue with fewer than five players. If his team has no charged time-outs left, a technical foul shall be charged against the Coach.

44. Time-in

After time has been out, the Game Clock shall be started:

(*a*) If the game is resumed by a jump-ball, when the ball after having reached its highest point is tapped by the first player.

(*b*) If a free throw is not successful and the ball is to continue in play, when the ball touches a player in the court.

(*c*) If play is resumed by a throw-in from out-of-bounds, when the ball touches a player on the court.

45. How Game is Resumed

After time-out or after the ball has become dead for any other reason the game is resumed as follows: (*a*) If a team had control of the ball, any player of that team shall throw it in from the point out-of-bounds at the side line nearest the point where the ball became dead. (*b*) If neither team had control, by a jump-ball in the circle nearest where the ball became dead. (*c*) After a foul, as provided in article 80. (*d*) After a held ball, or the ending of a half period; or a field goal or an out-of-bounds, or the ending of a free throw, or a violation; ball is put in play as prescribed in the relevant Rule.

RULE 7

Players' Regulations

46. Substitutions

A substitute before going on the court shall report to the Scorer and must be ready to play immediately. The Scorer shall sound his signal immediately if the ball is dead and the Game Clock stopped, or as soon as the ball becomes dead and the Game Clock is stopped, but before the ball is again in play (see art. 37), as the consequence of one of the following situations:

(*a*) a held ball has been called,

(*b*) a foul has been called,

(*c*) a charged time-out has been granted, or

(*d*) game has been stopped, to attend an injured player, or for any other reason, ordered by the Officials.

Following a violation, only the team who is to make the throw-in from out-of-bounds may effect a substitution. If such a situation occurs, the opponents may also effect a substitution.

The substitute shall remain outside the boundary line until an Official beckons him on, whereupon he shall enter the court immediately. Substitutions shall be completed as quickly as possible. If, in the opinion of the Official, there is an unreasonable delay, a time-out shall be charged against the offending team. A player involved in a jump-ball may not be substituted by another player. A substitution is not permitted from the moment that the ball is in play for the first or only free throw until the ball becomes dead after being alive again after the free throw or throws.

Exception: After a successful last free throw only the player who was attempting the free throw may be substituted provided such substitution was requested before the ball went into play for the first or only free throw, in which case the opponents may be granted one substitution provided the request is made before the ball goes into play for the last free throw.

47. Location of Player and Official

The location of a player is determined by where he is touching the floor. When he is in the air from a leap, he retains the same status as when he last touched the floor as far as the boundary lines, the centre line, the three-point line, the free throw line or the lines delimiting the free throw lanes are concerned (except as provided in article 69 (b)).

The location of an Official is determined in the same manner as that of a player. When the ball touches an Official it is the same as touching the floor at the Official's location.

48. How Ball is Played

In Basketball the ball is played with the hands. *It is a violation to run with the ball, kick it or strike it with the fist. For penalty see article 66.*

Kicking the ball, or blocking it with any part of a player's leg, is a violation only when it is done deliberately. To accidentally strike the ball with the foot or leg is not a violation.

49. Control of the Ball

A player is in control when he is holding or dribbling a live ball or in an out-of-bounds situation when the ball is at his disposal for a throw-in (see art. 37c). A team is in control when a player of that team is in control and also when the ball is being passed between team mates. Team control continues until an opponent secures control or the ball becomes dead or on a shot for goal when the ball is no longer in contact with the hand of the shooter.

50. Player Out-of-Bounds—Ball Out-of-Bounds

A player is out-of-bounds when he touches the floor on or outside of the boundary lines.

The ball is out-of-bounds when it touches a player who is out-of-bounds, or any other person, the floor or any object on or outside a boundary line, or the supports or back of the backboard.

51. How Ball Goes Out-of-Bounds

The ball is caused to go out-of-bounds by the last player to touch it before it goes out, even in the event of the ball going out-of-bounds by touching something other than a player. If a player deliberately throws or taps the ball on to an opponent, thus causing it to go out-of-bounds, the ball shall be awarded to the opponents, even though it was last touched by that team. An Official shall clearly indicate the team which shall take the throw-in from out-of-bounds. Out-of-bounds decisions should be clearly signalled by the Officials. If there is doubt about players understanding the decision, the Official should secure the ball and delay the throw-in until the decision has been made clear. (See art. 56.)

To cause the ball to go out-of-bounds is a violation. For penalty see article 66.

Officials should declare held-ball when they are in doubt as to which team caused the ball to go out-of-bounds (see art. 55).

52. Pivot

A pivot takes place when a player who is holding the ball steps once or more than once in any direction with the same foot, the other foot, called the pivot foot, being kept at its point of contact with the floor.

53. Dribbling

A dribble is made when a player, having gained control of the ball, gives impetus to it by throwing, tapping or rolling it, and touches it again before it touches another player. In a dribble the ball must come in contact with the floor. After giving impetus to the ball as described in the foregoing, the player completes his dribble the instant he touches the ball simultaneously with both hands, or permits the ball to come to rest in one or both hands. There is no limit to the number of steps a player may take when the ball is not in contact with his hand; he may take as many steps as he wishes between bounces of a dribble.

A player shall not dribble a second time after his first dribble has ended, unless it is after he has lost control because of (*a*) a shot for goal, (*b*) a tap by an opponent or (*c*) a pass or fumble that has then touched or been touched by another player.

A player who throws the ball against a backboard and touches it before it touches another player commits a violation unless in the opinion of the Official it was a shot.

Exception: The following are not dribbles: Successive shots for goal, fumbles, attempts to gain control of the ball by tapping it from the vicinity of other players striving for it, tapping it from the control of another player, blocking a pass and recovering the ball, or tossing the ball from hand(s) to hand(s) and permitting it to come to rest before touching the floor, provided he does not commit a progressing-with-the-ball violation.

To make a second dribble is a violation. For penalty see article 66.

54. Progressing with the Ball

A player may progress with the ball in any direction within the following limits:

ITEM 1. A player who receives the ball while standing still may pivot, using either foot as the pivot foot.

ITEM 2. A player who receives the ball while he is progressing or upon completion of a dribble may use a two-count rhythm in coming to a stop or in getting rid of the ball. The first count occurs:

(a) as he receives the ball if either foot is touching the floor at the time he receives it, or

(b) as either foot touches the floor or as both feet touch the floor simultaneously after he receives the ball if both feet are off the floor when he receives it.

The second count occurs when, after the count of one, either foot touches the floor or both feet touch the floor simultaneously.

A player who has come to a stop at the first count of the two-count rhythm, is not entitled to a new movement within the second-count.

When a player comes to a legal stop if one foot is in advance of the other he may pivot but the rear foot only may be used as the pivot foot. However, if neither foot is in advance of the other he may use either foot as the pivot foot.

ITEM 3. A player who receives the ball while standing still, or who comes to a legal stop while holding the ball, (a) may lift the pivot foot or jump when he throws for goal or passes, but the ball must leave his hands before one or both feet again touch the floor; (b) may not lift the pivot foot in starting a dribble before the ball leaves his hands.

To progress with the ball in excess of these limits is a violation. For penalty see article 66.

55. Held Ball

A held ball shall be declared when two or more players of opposing teams have one or both hands firmly on the ball.

Officials should not declare held ball too quickly, thereby interrupting the continuity of the game, and unjustly taking the ball from the player who gained or is about to gain possession. Under the first clause of this article, held ball should not be called until at least one player from each team has one or both hands firmly on the ball so that neither player could gain possession without undue roughness. A held ball decision is not warranted merely on the grounds that the defensive player gets his hands on the ball. Usually such a decision is unfair to the player who has firm possession of the ball. If a player is lying or sitting on the floor while in possession of the ball, he should have opportunity to play it.

When held ball is called, the ball shall be tossed up between the two contending players at the nearest circle. In case of doubt as to which is the nearest circle, the ball shall be tossed up at the centre. If there are more than two players involved, the ball shall be tossed up between two contending players of approximately the same height.

56. Held Ball in Special Situations

If the ball goes out-of-bounds and was last touched simultaneously by two opponents, or if the Official is in doubt as to who last touched the ball, or if the Officials disagree, the game shall be resumed by a jump-ball between the two involved players at the nearest circle.

Whenever the ball lodges on the basket support, the game shall be resumed by a jump-ball between any two opponents on the nearer free throw line. *Exception*: See art. 78.

57. Player in the Act of Shooting

A player is in the act of shooting when in the judgment of an Official he starts an attempt to score by throwing, dunking, or tapping the ball and it continues until the ball has left the player's hand(s).

Exception: Players who tap the ball towards the basket directly from a jump-ball are not considered to be in the act of shooting.

58. Three-seconds Rule

A player shall not remain for more than three seconds in that part of the opponents' restricted area, between the end line and the further edge of the free throw line, while the ball is in control of his team. The three-seconds restriction is in force in all out-of-bounds situations, and the count shall start at the moment the player throwing-in is out-of-bounds and has control of the ball.

The lines bounding the restricted area are part of it and a player touching one of these lines is in the area. The three-seconds restriction does not apply while the ball is in the air on a shot for goal, or while it is rebounding from the backboard or is dead, because the ball is not in control of either team at such times. Allowance may be made for a player who, having been in the restricted area for less than three seconds, dribbles in to shoot for goal.

An infraction of this rule is a violation. For penalty see article 66.

59. Five-seconds Rule

A violation shall be called when a closely guarded player who is holding the ball does not pass, shoot, roll or dribble the ball within five seconds. *For penalty, see art. 66.*

60. Ten-seconds Rule

When a team gains control of the ball in its back court, it must, within ten seconds, cause the ball to go into its front court.

The ball goes into a team's front court when it touches the court beyond the centre line or touches a player of that team who has part of his body in contact with the court beyond the centre line.

An infraction of this rule is a violation. For penalty see article 66.

61. Ball Returned to Back Court

A player whose team is in control of the ball in the front court may not cause the ball to go into his back court. It is caused to go into the back court by the last player of the team in control to touch it before it goes into the back court. This restriction applies to all situations occurring in a team's front court, including a throw-in from out-of-bounds. It does not apply, however, to jump-ball situations at the centre circle or to the situation described in article 78 (Penalty) and in article 89.

A player in his front court who gains control of the ball directly from a jump-ball at the centre circle, may pass the ball into his back court.

The ball goes into a team's back court when it touches a player of that team who has part of his body in contact with the centre line or with the court beyond the centre line, or is first touched by a player of that team after it has touched the back court.

Penalty. The ball is awarded to an opponent for a throw-in from the mid-point of a side line and having one foot either side of the extended centre line he shall be entitled to pass the ball to a player at any point on the playing court.

62. 30-seconds Rule

When a team gains control of a live ball on the court, a shot for goal must be made within 30 seconds. *Failure to do so is a violation of this rule. For penalty see article 66.*

A new 30-sec. period, however, does not begin following a throw-in from out-of-bounds at the side line when (*a*) the ball has gone out-of-bounds and the throw-in is taken by a player from the same team previously in control of the ball or (*b*) the Officials have suspended play to protect an injured player and the throw-in is taken by a player from the same team as the one injured. In such circumstances the 30-sec. Operator will re-start the device from the time it was stopped when team control is again established by the same team after the throw-in has been made.

All regulations concerning the end of playing time shall apply to violations of the 30-seconds rule.

RULE 8

Infractions and Penalties

63. Violations

A violation is an infraction of the Rules, the penalty for which is the loss of the ball.

64. Fouls

A foul is an infraction of the Rules involving personal contact with an opponent or unsportsmanlike conduct, charged against the offender and consequently penalised according to the provisions contained in the relevant article of these Rules.

65. How Game is Resumed following a Violation or Foul

After the ball has become dead following an infraction of the Rules, the ball is put in play (*a*) by a throw-in from out-of-bounds, or (*b*) by a jump-ball at one of the circles, or (*c*) by one or more free throws.

66. Procedure when a Violation is Called

When a violation is called the ball becomes dead. The ball is awarded to a nearby opponent for a throw-in from the side line at the point nearest that where the violation occurred. If the ball goes into a basket during the dead ball which follows such a violation, no point can be scored.

67. Procedure When Foul is Called

When a player foul is called the Official shall signal to the Scorer the number of the offender. The player thus indicated shall turn to face the Scorer's Table and shall immediately raise his hand above his head. For failure to do so, after having been warned once by the Official, a technical foul may be called against the offending player.

If the foul was committed on a player who was not in the act of shooting, the Official shall hand the ball to him or to one of his team-mates for a throw-in from the side line at a spot nearest the place of the foul (see also art. 91).

If the foul was committed on a player in the act of shooting, (*a*) if the goal is made it shall count and in addition one free throw shall be awarded, (*b*) if the goal is missed, the Official shall take the ball to the free throw line and shall put it at the disposal of the shooter to take the free-throws. *Exceptions*, see art. 83 and 89.

68. Throw-in from Out-of-Bounds

The player who is to throw the ball in from out-of-bounds shall stand out-of-bounds at the side line at a spot nearest the point where the ball left the court or the violation or foul was committed. Within five seconds from the time the ball is at his disposal, he shall throw, bounce or roll the ball to another player within the court. While the ball is being passed into the court, no other player shall have any part of his body over the boundary line. When the margin of out-of-bounds territory free from obstruction is less than 2 m, no player of either team shall be within 1 m of the player who is putting the ball in play.

Whenever the ball is awarded to a team for a throw-in from out-of-bounds at the side line in its front court, an Official must hand the ball to the player who is to put it in play. The purpose of this is to make the decision clear, and not to delay the game until the defensive team gets "set".

Whenever the ball is awarded to a team for a throw-in from out-of-bounds at the side line in its back court, the Official, if there is confusion as to the decision, shall hand the ball to the thrower-in at the side line closest to the violation.

69. Violation on Out-of-Bounds Play

A player shall not violate provisions governing a throw-in from out-of-bounds. These provisions:

(*a*) forbid a player who has been awarded the ball for a throw-in to touch it in the court before it has touched another player, or to step on the court whilst releasing the ball, or to consume more than five seconds in putting the ball in play;

(*b*) forbid any other player to have any part of his body over the boundary line before the ball has been thrown across the line, or to take the throw-in after the Official has awarded it to the other team. (*Penalty*: If infraction is of (*a*) see art. 66; if of (*b*) see art. 77.)

70. Free Throws

A free throw is a privilege given to a player to score one point from an unhindered shot for goal from a position directly behind the free throw line (see art. 72).

71. Player to Attempt Free Throw

When a personal foul is called, and a free throw penalty is awarded, the player upon whom the foul was committed shall be designated by the Official to attempt the free throws. If any other player attempts the throw, it shall not count if made, and whether made or missed the ball shall be awarded to an opponent for a throw-in from out-of-bounds at the side line opposite the free throw line. However, if the discovery of the substitution occurs after the ball is again alive following the last free throw, the whole matter shall be disregarded and the points scored shall be valid.

Should a player, by mistake, execute a free throw into his own basket, the free throw shall be annulled, whether successful or not, and a new try shall be granted at the other basket.

If the designated player must leave the game because of injury, his substitute must attempt the free throws. If the player who has been fouled is to leave the game because of a substitution, he shall attempt the free throws before leaving (see art. 46).

When there is no substitute available, the free throws may be attempted by the Captain or any player designated by him.

When a technical foul is called, the free throw or throws may be attempted by any player of the opposing team.

72. How a Free Throw is Attempted

The shot for goal shall be made within five seconds after the ball has been placed at the disposal of the free throw shooter at the free throw line. This shall apply to each free throw.

The free throw shooter shall take a position immediately behind the free throw line and may use any method to shoot for goal provided he does not touch the free throw line or the court beyond the line until the ball touches the ring.

Players may not attempt to disconcert the thrower by their actions. Neither Official shall stand in the free throw area (restricted area) or behind the backboard.

When a player is attempting a free throw, the other players shall be entitled to take the following position:

(a) two players from the opposing team the two places nearer the basket,

(b) the other players shall take alternate positions,

(c) all other players may take any other position, provided that:

(i) they neither disturb nor are in the way of the free throw shooter and of the Officials,

(ii) they do not move from their positions before the ball has touched the ring,

(iii) they do not occupy the places along the free throw lane next to the end line.

On free throws following technical fouls by Coach or substitutes, players shall not line up along the free throw lane (see art. 78—penalty).

73. Violation of Free Throw Provisions

After the ball has been placed at the disposal of the free throw shooter:

(*a*) he shall shoot for goal within five seconds, and in such a way that the ball enters the basket or touches the ring before it is touched by a player;

(*b*) neither he nor any other player shall touch the ball or basket while the ball is on its way to the basket or is on or within the basket;

(*c*) he shall not touch the floor on or across the free throw line and no other player of either team shall touch the free throw lane or disconcert the shooter. This restriction applies until the ball touches the ring or until it is apparent it will not touch it.

Penalty: (1) If the violation is by the free throw shooter only, no point can be scored. Ball becomes dead when violation occurs. Ball is awarded for a throw-in from out-of-bounds at the side line, to the free throw shooter's team at mid-court after a technical foul by Coach, Assistant Coach, substitute or team followers, and to the opponents opposite the free throw line after a player foul.

(2) If violation of (*b*) is by a team-mate of the free throw shooter, no point can be scored and violation shall be penalised as above. If violation (*b*) is by both teams, no point can be scored and play shall be resumed by a jump-ball on the free throw line. If violation of (*b*) is by the free throw shooter's opponents, violation is penalised as indicated in article 30.

(3) If violation of (*c*) is by a team-mate of the free throw shooter and the free throw is successful, the goal shall count and violation be disregarded. If the free throw is not successful, violation shall be penalised as above. However, if

the ball misses the ring and goes out-of-bounds or falls within bounds, then the violation is penalised as in (1).

(4) If violation of (c) is by the free throw shooter's opponents only, and if the shot is successful, the goal counts and violation is disregarded; if it is not successful, a substitute free throw shall be attempted by the free throw shooter.

(5) If there is a violation of (c) by both teams, and the free throw is successful, the goal shall count and violation be disregarded. If the free throw is not successful play shall be resumed by a jump-ball on the free throw line.

If more than one free throw is taken, the out-of-bounds and jump-ball provisions apply only to a violation during the last free throw.

74. Technical Foul before the Game or during an Interval of Play

If a technical foul is called before the game, during the half-time or during an interval before an extra period, the penalty shall be two free throws. The game shall be started or resumed by a jump-ball at centre after the throws have been attempted in accordance with art. 25.

75. Ball in Play if Free Throw is Unsuccessful

If the free throw is unsuccessful, play shall continue after the last free throw following a player foul. If the ball misses the ring, it is a violation (see art. 73) and the game shall be resumed by a throw-in from the side line at the point opposite the free throw line by the opposing team. In case of a free throw following a technical foul by Coach, Assistant Coach, substitute or team followers, see article 78 and the penalty.

RULE 9

Rules of Conduct

76. Definition

The proper conduct of the Game demands the full and loyal co-operation of members of both teams, including Coaches and substitutes, with the Officials and their assistants.

Both teams are entitled to do their best to secure victory, but this must be done in a spirit of sportsmanship and fair play.

An infringement of this co-operation or of this spirit, when deliberate or repeated, should be considered as a Technical Foul and penalised as provided in the following articles of these Rules.

77. Technical Foul by Player

A player shall not disregard admonitions by Officials or use unsportsmanlike tactics such as:

(*a*) disrespectfully addressing or contacting an Official,

(*b*) using language or gestures likely to give offence,

(*c*) baiting an opponent or obstructing his vision by waving hands near his eyes,

(*d*) delaying the game by preventing ball from being promptly put in play,

(*e*) not raising his hand properly when a foul is called on him (see art. 66),

(*f*) changing his playing number without reporting to Scorer and to Referee,

(*g*) entering the court as a substitute without reporting to Scorer, or without reporting promptly to an Official (unless between halves) or during a time-out after having withdrawn during the same time-out,

(*h*) grasping the ring; a player who violates this provision must be promptly penalised by a technical foul awarded against him.

Technical infractions which are obviously unintentional and have no effect on the game, or are of an administrative character, are not considered technical fouls unless there is a repetition of the same infraction after a warning by an Official to the offending player and to his Captain.

Technical infractions which are deliberate or are unsportsmanlike or give the offender an unfair advantage should be penalised promptly with a technical foul.

Penalty. A foul shall be charged and recorded for each offence and two free throws awarded the opponents and the Captain shall designate the free throw shooter. For flagrant or persistent infraction of this article, a player shall be disqualified and removed from the game.

If discovery of such a foul is after the ball is in play following the foul, penalty should be administered as if foul had occurred at the time of discovery. Whatever occurred in the interval between the foul and its discovery shall be valid.

78. Technical Foul by Coaches, Substitutes or Team Followers

The Coach, Assistant Coach, substitutes or team followers shall not enter the court unless by permission of an Official to attend an injured player, not leave their place to follow the action on the court from the boundary lines, nor disrespectfully address Officials (including Scorer, Timekeeper and 30-seconds Operator) or opponents.

A Coach may address players of his team during a charged time-out, provided he does not enter playing court and players do not cross boundary line, unless permission is first obtained from an Official. Substitutes may also listen-in provided they do not enter the playing court.

The distinction between unintentional and deliberate infractions (see art. 77) applies also to infractions committed by Coaches, Assistant Coaches, substitutes and team followers. A foul by a player who has committed his fifth foul is considered as a substitute's foul. It is therefore inscribed to the Coach and is penalised as a substitute's foul.

Penalty. A foul shall be charged and inscribed against the Coach and two free throws awarded. The opposing Captain shall designate the shooter. During the free throws players shall not line up along the free throw lanes. After the throws, the ball shall be thrown in by any player of the free thrower's team from out-of-bounds at mid-court on the side line, whether or not the free throws are successful (see art. 88). The player taking the throw-in, having one foot either side of the extended centre line, is entitled to pass the ball to a player at any point on the playing court.

Technical fouls may also be called before the game, during half-time or during the interval before an extra period (see art. 74). If called against the Coach, the assistant Coach or team follower, the penalty shall be two free throws and a foul inscribed against the Coach of that team. If called against a player or a substitute, a technical foul shall be charged against him and two free throws awarded to the opponents.

For a flagrant infraction of this article, or when a Coach is charged with three technical fouls as a result of unsportsman-like conduct by the Coach, Assistant Coach, substitute or team follower, the Coach shall be disqualified and banished from the vicinity of the court. He shall be replaced by the assistant Coach, or in the event of there not being an Assistant Coach, by the Captain.

B. PERSONAL CONTACT

79. Contact

Although Basketball is theoretically a "no-contact game", it is obvious that personal contact cannot be avoided entirely when ten players are moving with great rapidity over a limited space. For instance, the ball is free; two opponents start quickly for the ball and collide. The personal contact may be serious, yet, if both were in favourable positions from which to get the ball and were intent only upon getting it, an unavoidable accident, and not a foul, occurs. On the other hand, if one player is about to catch the ball and an opponent behind him, jumping in an attempt to get the ball, strikes him in the back, the opponent commits a foul even though he is "playing the ball". In this case, as in "guarding from the rear", the player behind is usually responsible for the contact because of his unfavourable position relative to the ball and to his opponent. In short, if personal contact results from a "bona fide" attempt to play the ball, if the players are in such positions that they could reasonably expect to gain the ball without contact and if they use due care to avoid contact, such contact may be classified as accidental and need not be penalised.

80. Personal Foul

A personal foul is a player foul which involves contact with an opponent whether the ball is in play, alive or dead.

A player shall not block, hold, push, charge, trip, impede the progress of an opponent by extending his arm, shoulder, hip or knee, or by bending his body into other than normal position, nor use any rough tactics.

Definitions:

Blocking is personal contact which impedes the progress of an opponent.

Holding is personal contact with an opponent that interferes with his freedom of movement.

Pushing is personal contact that takes place when a player forcibly moves or attempts to move an opponent. Contact caused with a player holding the ball by an opponent approaching from the rear may be a form of pushing.

Guarding from the rear which results in personal contact is a personal foul. Officials should give special attention to this type of infraction. The mere fact that the defensive player is attempting to play the ball does not justify him in making contact with an opponent who controls the ball.

Charging is personal contact which occurs when a player, with or without the ball, makes his way forcibly and contacts an opponent in his path.

Illegal use of hands occurs when a player contacts an opponent with his hand(s) unless such contact is only with the opponent's hand while it is on the ball and is incidental to an attempt to play the ball.

Screening is an attempt to prevent an opponent who does not control the ball from reaching a desired position.

A dribbler shall not charge into nor contact an opponent in his path nor attempt to dribble between opponents or between an opponent and a boundary line, unless there is a reasonable chance for him to go through without contact. If a dribbler, without causing contact, passes an opponent, sufficiently to have head an shoulders in advance of him, the greater responsibility for subsequent contact is on the opponent. If a dribbler has established a straight line path, he may not be forced out of that path but, if an opponent is able to establish a legal guarding position in that path, the dribbler must avoid contact by stopping or changing direction.

A player who screens has the greater responsibility if contact occurs: (*a*) if he takes a position so near an opponent that pushing or charging occurs when normal movements are made by him, or (*b*) if he takes a position so quickly in a moving opponent's path that pushing or charging cannot be avoided.

Penalty. A personal foul shall be charged to the offender in all cases. In addition:

(1) If a foul is committed on a player who is not in the act of shooting, the ball shall be put in play by the non-offending team from out-of-bounds on the side line nearest the place of the foul. As soon as the foul is called, the Official shall signal the Scorer the number of the offender and shall then hand the ball to the opponents for a throw-in from the side line (for exception, see art. 91, 92 and also art. 89 and 93).

(2) If a foul is committed on a player who is in the act of shooting, (i) if the goal is made, it shall count and in addition one free throw shall be awarded, (ii) if the goal is missed, two free throws shall be awarded (see art. 89 and 90). As soon as the foul is called, the Official shall signal the Scorer the number of the offender and shall then place the ball at the disposal of the free throw shooter (see also art. 89).

81. Intentional Foul

An intentional foul is a personal foul which in the opinion of the Official was committed deliberately by a player.

A player who deliberately disregards the ball and causes personal contact with an opponent who controls the ball commits an intentional foul. This is generally true also of fouls committed on a player who does not have the ball. A player who controls the ball may also commit an intentional foul if he deliberately contacts an opponent. A player who repeatedly commits intentional fouls may be disqualified.

Penalty. A personal foul shall be charged to the offender and in addition two free throws are awarded. However if the foul is committed on a player who is in the act of shooting and who scores, the basket shall count and in addition one free throw shall be awarded (see art. 67 and 80).

If the foul is committed on a player in the act of shooting who fails to score, two free throws shall be awarded (see art. 67, 80 and 89, according to the place from where the shot for goal was attempted).

82. Disqualifying Foul

Any flagrantly unsportsmanlike infractions of articles 77 and 80 is a disqualifying foul. A player who commits such a foul must be disqualified and removed immediately from the game and a foul shall be charged against him. *Penalty*: same as art. 78, 81.

83. Double Foul

A double foul is a situation in which two opponents commit fouls against each other at approximately the same time. *Penalty*:

In the case of a double foul, no free throws shall be awarded but a personal foul shall be charged against each offending player.

The game shall be resumed at the nearest circle by a jump-ball between the two players involved, unless a valid goal is scored at the same time, in which case the ball shall be put into play from the end line.

84. Multiple Foul

A multiple foul is a situation in which two or more team- mates commit personal fouls against the same opponent at approximately the same time.

Penalty: When two or more personal fouls are committed against a player by opponents, one foul shall be charged to each offending player and the offended player shall be awarded two free throws, irrespective of the number of fouls (see art. 88). If the fouls are committed on a player in the act of shooting, the goal if made shall count, and in addition one free throw shall be awarded.

85. Foul on a Player in the Act of Shooting

Whenever a foul is called on the opponent of a player who, as part of a continuous motion which started before the foul occurred, succeeds in making a field goal, the goal shall count even if the ball leaves the player's hands after the whistle blows, provided the whistle did not affect the action of the shooter. The player must be shooting for goal or starting an effort to shoot for goal when the whistle blows; the goal does not count if he makes an entirely new effort after the whistle blows.

C. GENERAL PROVISIONS

86. Basic Principle

Each Official has power to call fouls independently from the other, and this at any time during the game, whether the ball is in play, alive or dead.

Fouls committed during the dead ball period that follows a foul and until the moment when the ball is again in play (see art. 37) are considered as being committed at the time the ball became dead because of the first foul.

Any number of fouls may therefore be called at the same time against one or both teams.

Irrespective of the penalty, a foul shall be inscribed on the Score Sheet against the offender for each foul.

87. Double and Additional Foul

When a double foul and another foul are committed at the same time, the double foul shall be dealt with as in article 83, and the other foul dealt with according to the respective Rule. The game shall be resumed, after the fouls have been charged and the eventual penalty administered, as though the double foul had not occurred.

88. Fouls in Special Situations

Situations other than those foreseen in these Rules may occur when fouls are committed at approximately the same time or during the dead ball period that follows a foul, a double foul or a multiple foul. In such situations the following principles shall be applied:

(a) a foul shall be charged for each offence;

(*b*) fouls that involve penalties of about the same gravity against both teams shall not be penalised by awarding free throws, and the ball shall be put in play by a jump-ball at the nearest circle or, in case of doubt, at the centre;

(*c*) penalties that are not compensated by similar penalties against the other team shall be maintained and administered. This does not apply to a double foul situation, the penalty for which shall be administered according to art. 83. But under no circumstances shall a team be awarded more than two or three free throws as in art. 80, penalties, and possession of the ball for a throw-in from out-of-bounds at the midpoint of the side line.

89. Right of Option

A team that has been awarded two free throws (see also art. 89) shall have the option of either attempting the throws or of putting the ball in play from out-of-bounds at the midpoint of a side line.

The decision shall rest with the Captain of the team, who shall take the initiative to indicate immediately and clearly to the Official in charge that the ball is to be put in play from the side line. A delay by the Captain in using the right of option shall forfeit this right, and the two free throws shall be attempted.

The player who is to put the ball in play from out-of-bounds shall be entitled to pass the ball to a player at any point on the playing court.

The right of option shall not apply if a team has been awarded one or two free throws and possession of the ball (see art. 78 and 88*c*).

90. Disqualifying Foul

Any flagrantly unsportsmanlike infraction of articles 77 and 80 is a disqualifying foul. A player who commits such a foul must be disqualified and removed immediately from the game.

91. Five Fouls by Player

A player who has committed five fouls either personal or technical must automatically leave the game.

92. Seven Fouls by Team

After a team has committed seven player fouls, personal or technical, in a half (extra periods are considered to be part of the second half) all subsequent player fouls shall be penalised by two free throws (for exceptions, see art. 80, Penalty (2), art. 89 and 93).

93. Foul by Player whilst His Team is in Control of the Ball

A foul committed by a player whilst his team is in control of the ball shall aways be penalised by recording the foul against the offender and awarding the ball for a throw-in to an opponent at the nearest point out of bounds at a side-line (for exceptions, see art. 77 and 81). For definition of team in control of the ball, see art. 49.

Information on Wheelchair Basketball Rules may be obtained from: the International Stoke Mandeville Games Federation, Harvey Road, Aylesbury, Bucks.

The Laws of
Bowls

Bowls

DEFINITIONS

1. (*a*) "Controlling Body" means the body having immediate control of the conditions under which a match is played. The order shall be:

    (i) The International Bowling Board;

    (ii) The National Bowling Association;

    (iii) The State, Division, Local District or County Association;

    (iv) The Club on whose Green the Match is played.

(*b*) "Skip" means the Player, who, for the time being, is in charge of the head on behalf of the team.

(*c*) "Team" means either a four, triples or a pair.

(*d*) "Side" means any agreed number of Teams, whose combined scores determine the results of the match.

(*e*) "Four" means a team of four players whose positions in order of playing are named Lead, Second, Third, Skip.

(*f*) "Bowl in Course" means a bowl from the time of its delivery until it comes to rest.

(*g*) "End" means the playing of the Jack and all the bowls of all the opponents in the same direction on a rink.

(*h*) "Head" means the Jack and such bowls as have come to rest within the boundary of the rink and are not dead.

(*i*) "Mat Line" means the edge of the Mat which is nearest to the front ditch. From the centre of the Mat Line all necessary measurements to Jack or bowls shall be taken.

(*j*) "Master Bowl" means a bowl which has been approved by the I.B.B. as having the minimum bias required, as well as in all other respects complying with the Laws of the Game and is engraved with the words "Master Bowl".

    (i) A Standard Bowl of the same bias as the Master Bowl shall be kept in the custody of each National Association.

    (ii) A Standard Bowl shall be provided for the use of each official Licensed Tester.

(*k*) "Jack High" means that the nearest portion of the Bowl referred to is in line with and at the same distance from the Mat Line as the nearest portion of the Jack.

(*l*) "Pace of Green" means the number of seconds taken by a bowl from the time of its delivery to the moment it comes to rest, approximately 30 yd (27.43 m) from the Mat Line.

(*m*) "Displaced" as applied to a Jack or Bowl means "disturbed" by any agency that is not sanctioned by these laws.

THE GREEN

2. Area and Surface

The green should form a square of not less than 40 yd (36.58 m) and not more than 44 yd (40.23 m) a side. It shall have a suitable playing surface, which shall be level. It shall be provided with suitable boundaries in the form of a ditch and bank.

3. The Ditch

The green shall be surrounded by a ditch and shall have a bowling surface not injurious to bowls and be free from obstacles. The ditch shall be not less than 8 in (203 mm) nor more than 15 in (381 mm) wide and it shall be not less than 2 in (51 mm) nor more than 8 in (203 mm) below the level of the green.

4. Banks

The banks shall be not less than 9 in (229 mm) above the level of the green, preferably upright, or alternatively at an angle of not more than 35 degrees from the perpendicular. The surface of the face of the bank shall be non-injurious to bowls. No steps likely to interfere with play shall be cut in the banks.

5. Division of the Green

The green shall be divided into spaces called rinks, each not more than 19 ft (5.79 m) nor less than 18 ft (5.48 m) wide. They shall be numbered consecutively, the centre line of each rink being marked on the bank at each end by a wooden peg or other suitable device. The four corners of the rink shall be marked by pegs made of wood or other suitable material, painted white, and fixed to the face of the bank and flush therewith, or alternatively fixed on the bank not more than 4 in (102 mm) back from the face thereof. The corner pegs shall be connected by a green thread drawn tightly along the surface of the green, with sufficient loose thread to reach the corresponding pegs on the face or surface of the bank, in order to define the boundary of the rink.

White pegs or discs shall be fixed on the side banks to indicate a clear distance of 27 yd (24.89 m) from the ditch on the line of play. Under no circumstances shall the boundary thread be lifted while the bowl is in motion.

The boundary pegs of an outside rink shall be placed at least 2 ft (61 cm) from the side ditch.

6. Permissible Variations of Laws 2 and 5

(*a*) National Associations may admit Greens in the form of a square not longer than 44 yd (40.23 m) nor shorter than 33 yd (30.17 m), or of a rectangle of which the longer side should not be more than 44 yd and the shorter side not less than 33 yd.

(*b*) For domestic play the green may be divided into rinks not less than 14 ft (4.27 m) nor more than 19 ft (5.79 m) wide. National Associations may dispense with the use of boundary threads.

MAT, JACK, BOWLS, FOOTWEAR

7. Mat

The mat shall be of a definite size, namely 24 in (61 cm) long and 14 in (35.6 cm) wide.

8. Jack

The Jack shall be round and white, with a diameter of not less than $2\frac{15}{32}$ in (63 mm) nor more than $2\frac{17}{32}$ in (64 mm), and not less than 8 oz (227 gr) nor more than 10 oz (283 gr) in weight.

9. Bowls

    (*a*) (i) Bowls shall be made of wood, rubber or composition and shall be black or brown in colour. Each bowl of the set shall bear the member's individual and distinguishing mark on each side. The provision relating to the distinguishing mark on each side of the bowl need not apply other than in International Matches, World Bowls Championships and Commonwealth Games. Bowls made of wood (Lignum Vitae) shall have a maximum diameter of $5\frac{1}{4}$ in (133.35 mm) and a minimum diameter of $4\frac{5}{8}$ in (117 mm) and the weight shall not exceed 3 lb 8 oz (1.59 kg). Loading of bowls made of wood is strictly prohibited.

(ii) For all International and Commonwealth Games Matches a bowl made of rubber or composition shall have a maximum diameter of $5\frac{1}{8}$ in (130 mm) and a minimum diameter of $4\frac{5}{8}$ in (117 mm) and the weight shall not exceed 3 lb 8 oz (1.59 kg). Subject to bowls bearing a current stamp of the Board, and/or a current stamp of a Member National Authority, and/or the current stamp of the B.I.B.C. and provided they comply with the Board's Laws, they may be used in all matches controlled by the Board, or by any Member National Authority. Notwithstanding the aforegoing provisions, any Member National Authority may adopt a different scale of weights and sizes of bowls to be used in matches under its own control—such bowls may not be validly used in International Matches, World Championships, Commonwealth Games, or other matches controlled by the Board, if they differ from the Board's Laws, and unless stamped with a current stamp of the Board or any Member National Authority of the B.I.B.C.

(iii) The controlling body may, at its discretion, supply and require players to temporarily affix an adhesive marking to their bowls in any competition game. Any temporary marking under this Law shall be regarded as part of the bowl for all purposes under these Laws.

(*b*) *Bias of Bowls*. The master bowl shall have a bias approved by the International Bowling Board. A bowl shall have a bias not less than that of the master bowl and shall bear the imprint of the stamp of the International Bowling Board or that of its National Association. National Associations may adopt a standard which exceeds the bias of the master bowl. To ensure accuracy of bias and visibility of stamp, all bowls shall be re-tested and re-stamped at least once every 10 years, or earlier if the date of the stamp is not clearly legible. (*B.I.B.C. ruling for domestic play only. For 10 years read 15 years for all bowls stamped or re-stamped from 1.1.1977.*). *As from 1974 the date stamp on the bowl will show the year of expiry.*

(*c*) *Objection to Bowls.* A challenge or any intimation thereof shall not be lodged with any opposing player during the progress of a match. A challenge may be lodged with the Umpire at any time during a match, provided the Umpire is not a player in that or in any other match of the same competition.

If a challenge be lodged it shall be made not later than ten minutes after the completion of the final end in which the bowl was used. Once a challenge is lodged with the Umpire, it cannot be withdrawn.

The challenger shall immediately lodge a fee of £1 with the Umpire. The challenge shall be based on the grounds that the bowl does not comply with one or more of the requirements set out in Law 9(*a*) and 9(*b*).

The Umpire shall request the user of the bowl to surrender it to him for forwarding to the controlling body. If the owner of the challenged bowl refuses to surrender it to the Umpire, the match shall thereupon be forfeited to the opponent. The user or owner, or both, may be disqualified from playing in any match controlled or permitted by the controlling body, so long as the bowl remains untested by a licensed tester.

On receipt of the fee and the bowl, the Umpire shall take immediate steps to hand them to the Secretary of the controlling body, who shall arrange for a table test to be made as soon as practicable, and in the presence of a representative of the controlling body.

If a table test be not readily available, and any delay would unduly interfere with the progress of the competition, then, should an approved green testing device be available, it may be used to make an immediate test on the green. If a green test be made, it shall be done by, or in the presence of the Umpire, over a distance of not less than 25 yards (22.86 m). The comparison shall be between the challenged bowl and a standard bowl, or if it be not readily available then a recently stamped bowl of similar size, or nearly so, should be used.

The decision of the Umpire, as a result of the test, shall be final and binding for that match.

The result of the subsequent table test shall not invalidate the decision given by the Umpire on the green test.

If a challenged bowl, after an official table test, be found to comply with all the requirements of Law 9(*a*) and (*b*), it shall be returned to the user or owner and the fee paid by the challenger shall be forfeited to the controlling body.

If the challenged bowl be found not to comply with Law 9(*a*) and (*b*), the match in which it was played shall be forfeited to the opponent, and the fee paid by the challenger shall be returned to him.

If a bowl in the hands of a licensed tester has been declared as not complying with Law 9, (*a*) and (*b*), by an official representative of the controlling body, then, with the consent of the owner, and at his expense, it shall be altered so as to comply before being returned to him.

If the owner refuses his consent, and demands the return of his bowl, any current official stamp appearing thereon shall be cancelled prior to its return.

(*d*) *Alteration to Bias*. A player shall not alter, or cause to be altered other than by an official bowl tester, the bias of any bowl bearing the imprint of the official stamp of the Board, under penalty of suspension from playing for a period to be determined by the Council of the National Association of which his club is a member. Such suspension shall be subject to confirmation by the Board or a committee thereof appointed for that purpose and shall be operative among all Associations in membership with the Board.

10. Footwear

Players, umpires and markers shall wear white, brown or black smooth-soled, heel-less footwear while playing on the green, or acting as umpires or markers. (*E.B.A. Ruling: Brown footwear only will be worn.*)

ARRANGING A GAME

11. General Form and Duration

A game of bowls shall be played on one rink or on several rinks. It shall consist of a specified number of shots or ends, or shall be played for any period of time as previously arranged. The ends of the game shall be played alternatively in opposite directions excepting as provided in Laws 38, 42, 44, 46 and 47.

12. Selecting the Rinks for Play

When a match is to be played, the draw for the rinks to be played on shall be made by the Skips or their representatives.

In a match for a trophy or where competing Skips have previously been drawn, the draw to decide the numbers of the rinks to be played on shall be made by the visiting Skips or their representatives.

No player in a competition or match shall play on the same rink on the day of such competition or match before play commences, under penalty of disqualification.

This law shall not apply in the case of open tournaments.

13. Play Arrangements

Games shall be organised in the following play arrangements:
- (*a*) As a single game.
- (*b*) As a team game.
- (*c*) As a sides game.
- (*d*) As a series of single games, team games or side games.
- (*e*) As a special tournament of games.

14. A single game shall be played on one rink of a green as a single-handed game by two contending players, each playing two, three or four bowls singly and alternately.

15. A pairs game by two contending teams of two players called lead and Skip according to the order in which they play, and who at each end shall play four bowls, alternately, the leads first, then the Skips similarly. (For other than Internationals and Commonwealth Games, players in a pairs game may play two, three or four bowls each, as previously arranged by the controlling body.)

16. A triples game by two contending teams of three players, who shall play two or three bowls singly and in turn, the leads playing first.

17. A fours game by two contending teams of four players, each member playing two bowls singly and in turn.

18. A side game shall be played by two contending sides, each composed of an equal number of teams/players.

19. Games in series shall be arranged to be played on several and consecutive occasions, as:

(*a*) A series or sequence of games organised in the form of an eliminating competition and arranged as singles, pairs, triples, or fours.

(*b*) A series or sequence of side matches, organised in the form of a league competition, or an eliminating competition, or of inter-association matches.

20. A special tournament of games: Single games and team games may also be arranged in group form as a special tournament of games in which the contestants play each other in turn; or they may play as paired-off teams of players on one or several greens in accordance with a common time-table, success being adjudged by the number of games won, or by the highest net score in shots in accordance with the regulations governing the tournament.

21. For International Matches, World Bowls, and Commonwealth Games, in matches where played,

    (i) Singles shall be 21 shots up (shots in excess of 21 shall not count) four bowls each player, played alternately.

   (ii) Pairs shall be 21 ends, four bowls each player, played alternately.

  (iii) Triples shall be 18 ends, three bowls each player, played alternately.

  (iv) Fours shall be 21 ends, two bowls each player, played alternately.

Provided that pairs, triples and fours may be of a lesser number of ends, but in the case of pairs and fours there shall not be less than 18 ends, but in the case of triples not less than 15 ends, subject in all cases to the express approval of the Board as represented by its most senior officer present. If there be no officer of the Board present at the time, the decision shall rest with the "Controlling Body" as defined in Law 1. Any decision to curtail the number of ends to be played shall be made before the commencement of any game, and such decision shall only be made on the grounds of climatic conditions, inclement weather, or shortage of time to complete a programme.

22. Awards

Cancelled. See by-laws after Rule 73 under heading "Players' Status and Involvement".

STARTING THE GAME

23. (*a*) Trial Ends

Before start of play in any competition, match or game, or on the resumption of an unfinished competition, match or game on another day, not more than one trial end each way shall be played.

(*b*) Tossing for Opening Play

The captains in a side game or Skips in a team game shall toss to decide which side or team shall play first, but in all singles games the opponents shall toss, the winner of the toss to have the option of decision. In the event of a tied (no score) or a dead end, the first to play in the tied end or dead end shall again play first.

In all ends subsequent to the first the winner of the preceding score end shall play first.

24. Placing the Mat

At the beginning of the first end the player to play first shall place the mat lengthwise on the centre line of the rink, the front edge of the mat to be 6 ft (1.84 m) from the ditch.

Where ground sheets are in use, the mat at the first and every subsequent end shall be placed at the back edge of the sheet, the mat's front edge being 6 ft (1.84 m) from the ditch.

25. The Mat and its Replacement

After play has commenced in any end the mat shall not be

moved from its first position. If the mat be displaced during the progress of an end it shall be replaced as nearly as is practicable in the same position. If the mat be out of alignment with the centre line of the rink, it may be straightened at any time during the end.

After the last bowl in each end has come to rest in play, or has sooner become dead, the mat shall be lifted and placed wholly beyond the face of the rear bank. Should the mat be picked up by a player before the end has been completed, the opposing player shall have the right of replacing the mat in its original position.

26. The Mat in Subsequent Ends

(*a*) In all subsequent ends the front edge of the mat shall be not less than 6 ft (1.84 m) from the rear ditch, and the front edge not less than 27 yd (24.69 m) from the front ditch, and on the centre line of the rink of play.

(*b*) Should the Jack be improperly delivered under Law 30, the opposing player may then move the mat in the line of play, subject to clause (*a*) above, and deliver the Jack, but shall not play first. Should the Jack be improperly delivered twice by each player in any end, it shall not be delivered again in that end but shall be centred so that the front of the Jack is a distance of 6 ft (1.84 m) from the opposite ditch and the mat placed at the option of the first to play.

27. Stance on Mat

A player shall take his stance on the mat and, at the moment of delivering the Jack or his bowl, shall have one foot remaining entirely within the confines of the mat. The foot may be either in contact with or over the mat. Failure to observe this law constitutes foot-faulting.

28. Foot-faulting

Should a player infringe the law on foot-faulting, the Umpire may, after having given a warning, have the bowl stopped and declared dead. If the bowl has disturbed the head, the opponents shall have the option of either re-setting the head, leaving the head as altered, or declaring the end dead.

29. Delivering the Jack

The players to play first shall deliver the Jack. If the Jack in its original course comes to rest at a distance of less than 2 yd from the opposite ditch, it shall be moved out to that distance and be centred. If the Jack during its original course be obstructed or deflected by a neutral object or neutral person, or by a marker, opponent, or member of the opposing team, it shall be redelivered by the same player, but if it be obstructed or deflected by a member of his own team, it shall be redelivered by the lead of the opposing team.

30. Jack Improperly Delivered

Should the Jack in any end be not delivered from a proper stance on the mat, or if it ends its original course in the ditch or outside the side boundary of the rink or less than 25 yd (22.86 m) in a straight line of play from the front edge of the mat, it shall be returned and the opposing player shall deliver the Jack, but shall not play first.

The Jack shall be returned if it is improperly delivered, but the right of the player first delivering the Jack in that end, to play the first bowl of the end, shall not be affected.

No player shall be permitted to challenge the legality of the original length of the Jack after each player in a singles game, or the leads in a team game, have each bowled one bowl.

31. Variations to Laws 24, 26, 29 and 30

Notwithstanding anything contained in Laws 24, 26, 29 and 30, any National Authority may for domestic purposes, but not in any International Matches, World Bowls Championships or Commonwealth Games, vary any of the distances mentioned in these Laws.

MOVEMENT OF BOWLS

32. "Live" Bowl

A bowl which, in its original course on the green, comes to rest within the boundaries of the rink, and not less than 15 yd (13.71 m) from the front edge of the mat, shall be accounted as a "live" bowl and shall be in play.

33. "Touchers"

A bowl which, in its original course on the green, touches a Jack, even though such bowl passes into the ditch within the boundaries of the rink, shall be accounted as a live bowl, and shall be called a "toucher". If after having come to rest a bowl falls over and touches the Jack before the next succeeding bowl is delivered, or if in the case of the last bowl of an end it falls and touches the Jack within the period of half-minute invoked under Law 53, such bowl shall also be a "toucher". No bowl shall be accounted a "toucher" by playing on to, or by coming into contact with, the Jack while the Jack is in the ditch. If a "toucher" in the ditch cannot be seen from the mat, its position may be marked by a white or coloured peg about 2 in (51 mm) broad placed upright on the top of the bank and immediately in line with the place where the "toucher" rests.

34. Marking a "toucher"

A "toucher" shall be clearly marked with a chalk mark by a member of the player's team. If, in the opinion of either Skip, or opponent in singles, a "toucher" or a wrongly chalked bowl comes to rest in such a position that the act of making a chalk mark, or of erasing it, it likely to move the bowl or to alter the head, the bowl shall not be marked or have its mark erased but shall be "indicated" as a "toucher" or "non-toucher" as the case may be. If a bowl is not so marked or not so "indicated" before the succeeding bowl comes to rest, it ceases to be a "toucher". If both Skips or opponents agree that any subsequent movement of the bowl eliminates the necessity for continuation of the "indicated" provision, the bowl shall thereupon be marked or have the chalk mark erased as the case may be. Care should be taken to remove "toucher" marks from all bowls before they are played, but should a player fail to do so, and should the bowl not become a "toucher" in the end in play, the marks shall be removed by the opposing Skip or his deputy or marker immediately the bowl comes to rest, unless the bowl is "indicated" as a "non-toucher" in circumstances governed by earlier provisions of this Law.

35. Movement of "Touchers"

A "toucher" in play in the ditch may be moved by the impact of a Jack in play or of another "toucher" in play, and also by the impact of a "non-toucher" which remains in play after the impact, and any movement of the "toucher" by such incidents shall be valid. However, should the "non-toucher" enter the ditch at any time after the impact, it shall be dead, and the "toucher" shall be deemed to have been displaced by a dead bowl, and the provisions of Law 38 (*e*) shall apply.

36. Bowl Accounted "Dead"

(*a*) Without limiting the application of any other of these Laws, a bowl shall be accounted dead if it:
  (i) not being a "toucher", comes to rest in the ditch or rebounds on to the playing surface of the rink after contact with the bank or with the Jack or a "toucher" in the ditch, or
  (ii) after completing its original course, or after being moved as a result of play, it comes to rest wholly outside the boundaries of the playing surface of the rink, or within 15 yd (13.71 m) of the front of the mat, or
  (iii) in its original course, passes beyond a side boundary of the rink on a bias which would prevent its re-entering the rink. (A bowl is not rendered "dead" by a player carrying it whilst inspecting the head.)

(*b*) Skips, or opponents in singles, shall agree on the question as to whether or not a bowl is "dead", and having reached agreement, the question shall not later be subject to appeal to the Umpire. Any member of either team may request a decision from the Skips but no member shall remove any bowl prior to the agreement of the Skips. If Skips or opponents are unable to reach agreement as to whether or not a bowl is "dead" the matter shall be referred to the Umpire.

37. Bowl Rebounding

Only "touchers" rebounding from the face of the bank to the ditch or the rink shall remain in play.

38. Bowl Displacement

(*a*) Displacement by rebounding "non-toucher": A bowl displaced by a "non-toucher" rebounding from the bank shall be restored as near as possible to its original position, by a member of the opposing team.

(*b*) Displacement by participating player: If a bowl, while in motion or at rest on the green or a "toucher" in the ditch, be interfered with or displaced by one of the players, the opposing Skip shall have the option of:

- (i) Restoring the bowl as near as possible to its original position;
- (ii) Letting it remain where it rests;
- (iii) Declaring the bowl "dead"; or
- (iv) Declaring the end "dead".

(*c*) Displacement by a neutral object or neutral person— (other than as provided in Clause (*d*) hereof):

- (i) of a bowl in its original course: if such a bowl be displaced within the boundaries of the rink of play without having disturbed the head, it shall be replayed.

   If it be displaced and it has disturbed the head, the Skips, or the opponents in singles, shall reach agreement on the final position of the displaced bowl and on the replacement of the head, otherwise the end shall be "dead". These provisions shall also apply to a bowl in its original course displaced outside the boundaries of the rink of play provided such bowl was running on a bias which would have enabled it to re-enter the rink.

- (ii) of a bowl at rest, or in motion as a result of play after being at rest—if such a bowl be displaced the Skips, or opponents in singles, shall come to an agreement as to the position of the bowl and of the replacement of any part of the head disturbed by the displaced bowl, otherwise the end shall be "dead".

(*d*) Displacement inadvertently produced: If a bowl be moved at the time of its being marked or measured it shall be restored to its former position by an opponent. If such displacement is caused by a Marker or an Umpire, the Marker or Umpire shall replace the bowl.

(*e*) Displacement by a "dead" bowl: If a "toucher" in the

ditch be displaced by a "dead" bowl from the rink of play, it shall be restored to its original position by a player of the opposite team or by the Marker.

39. "Line bowls"

A bowl shall not be accounted as outside any circle or line unless it be entirely clear of it. This shall be ascertained by looking perpendicularly down upon the bowl or by placing a square on the green.

MOVEMENT OF JACK

40. A "live" Jack in the Ditch

A Jack moved by a bowl in play into the front ditch within the boundaries of the rink shall be deemed to be "live". It may be moved by the impact of a "toucher" in play and also by the impact of a "non-toucher" which remains in play after the impact; any movement of the Jack by such incidents shall be valid. However, should the "non-toucher" enter the ditch after impact, it shall be "dead" and the Jack shall be deemed to have been "displaced" by a "dead" bowl and the provisions of Law 48 shall apply. If the Jack in the ditch cannot be seen from the mat its position shall be marked by a white peg about 2 in (51 mm) broad and not more than 4 in (102 mm) in height, placed upright on top of the bank and immediately in line from the place where the Jack rests.

41. A Jack accounted "Dead"

Should the Jack be driven by a bowl in play and come to rest wholly beyond the boundary of the rink, i.e., over the bank or over the side boundary or into any opening or inequality of any kind in the bank or rebound to a distance less than 22 yd (20.12 m) in a direct line from the centre of the front edge of the mat to the Jack in its rebounded position, it shall be accounted "dead".

(National Associations have the option to vary the distance to which a Jack may rebound and still be playable for games other than International and Commonwealth Games.)

42. "Dead" End

When the Jack is "dead", the end shall be regarded as a "dead" end and shall not be accounted as a played end, even though all the bowls in that end have been played. All "dead" ends shall be played anew in the same direction unless both Skips or opponents in singles agree to play in the opposite direction.

43. Playing to a Boundary Jack

The Jack, if driven to the side boundary of the rink and not wholly beyond its limits, may be played to on either hand and if necessary a bowl may pass outside the side limits of the rink. A bowl so played which comes to rest within the boundaries of the rink shall not be accounted "dead".

If the Jack be driven to the side boundary line and come to rest partly within the limits of the rink, a bowl played outside the limits of the rink and coming to rest entirely outside the boundary line, even though it has made contact with the Jack, shall be accounted "dead" and shall be removed to the bank by a member of the player's team.

44. A Damaged Jack

In the event of a Jack being damaged, the Umpire shall decide if another Jack is necessary and, if so, the end shall be regarded as a "dead" end and another Jack shall be substituted and the end shall be replayed anew.

45. A Rebounding Jack

If the Jack be driven against the face of the bank and rebound on to the rink, or after being played into the ditch it be operated on by a "toucher" so as to find its way on to the rink, it shall be played to in the same manner as if it had never left the rink.

46. Jack Displacement

(*a*) By a player:

If the Jack be diverted from its course while in motion on the green or displaced while at rest on the green or in the ditch by any one of the players, the opposing Skip shall have the Jack restored to its former position, or allow it to remain where it rests and play the end to a finish, or declare the end "dead".

(*b*) Inadvertently produced:

If the Jack be moved at the time of measuring by a player it shall be restored to its former position by an opponent.

47. Jack Displaced by Non-player

(*a*) If the Jack, whether in motion or at rest on the rink or in the ditch, be displaced by a bowl from another rink or by any object or by any individual not a member of the team, the two Skips shall decide as to its original position, and if they are unable to agree, the end shall be declared "dead".

(*b*) If a Jack be displaced by a Marker or Umpire, it shall be restored by him to its original position, of which he shall be the sole judge.

48. Jack Displaced by "Non-toucher"

A Jack displaced in the rink of play by a "non-toucher" rebounding from the bank shall be restored, or as near as possible, to its original position by a player of the opposite team. Should a Jack however, after having been played into the ditch, be displaced by a "dead bowl", it shall be restored to its marked position by a player of the opposing team or by the Marker.

FOURS PLAY

The basis of the game of bowls is fours play.

49. The Rink and Fours Play

(*a*) Designation of players: A team shall consist of four players, named respectively lead, second, third and Skip, according to the order in which they play, each playing two bowls.

(*b*) Order of play: The leads shall play their two bowls alternately, and so on, each pair of players in succession to the end.

No one shall play until his opponent's bowl shall have come to rest.

Except under circumstances provided for in Law 63, the order of play shall not be changed after the first end has been played, under penalty of disqualification, such penalty involving the forfeiture of the match or game to the opposing team.

50. Possession of the Rink

Possession of the rink shall belong to the team whose bowl is being played.

The players in possession of the rink for the time being shall not be interfered with, annoyed or have their attention distracted in any way by their opponents.

As soon as each bowl shall have come to rest, possession of the rink shall be transferred to the other team, time being allowed for marking a "toucher".

51. Position of Players

Players of each team not in the act of playing or controlling play shall stand behind the Jack and away from the head or 1 yd (92 cm) behind the mat.

As soon as the bowl is delivered, the Skip or player directing, if in front of the Jack, shall retire behind it.

52. Players and their Duties

(*a*) The Skip shall have sole charge of his team and his instructions shall be observed by his players. With the opposing Skip he shall decide all disputed points and when both agree their decision shall be final.

If both Skips cannot agree, the point in dispute shall be referred to and considered by an Umpire, whose decision shall be final.

A Skip may at any time delegate his powers and any of his duties to other members of his team, provided that such delegation is notified to the opposing Skip.

(*b*) The third: The third player may have deputed to him the duty of measuring any and all disputed shots.

(*c*) The second: The second player shall keep a record of all shots scored for and against his team and shall at all times retain possession of the score card whilst play is in progress. He shall see that the names of all players are entered on the score card, shall compare his record of the game with that of the opposing second player as each end is declared, and at the close of the game shall hand his score card to his Skip.

(*d*) The lead: the lead shall place the mat and shall deliver the Jack, ensuring that the Jack is properly centred before playing his first bowl.

(*e*) In addition to the duties specified in the preceding clauses, any player may undertake such duties as may be assigned to him by the Skip in Clause 52(*a*) hereof.

RESULT OF END

53. "The Shot"

A shot or shots shall be adjudged by the bowl or bowls nearer to the Jack than any bowl played by the opposing player or players.

When the last bowl has come to rest, half a minute shall elapse, if either team desires, before the shots are counted.

Neither Jack nor bowls shall be moved until each Skip has agreed as to the number of shots, except in circumstances where a bowl has to be moved to allow the measuring of another bowl.

54. Measuring Conditions to be Observed

No measuring shall be allowed until the end has been completed.

All measurements shall be made to the nearest point of each object. If a bowl requiring to be measured is resting on another bowl which prevents its measurement, the best available means shall be taken to secure its position, whereupon the other bowl shall be removed. The same course shall be followed where more than two bowls are involved, or where, in the course of measuring, a single bowl is in danger of falling or otherwise changing its position. When it is necessary to measure to a bowl or Jack in the ditch, and another bowl or Jack on the green, the measurement shall be made with the ordinary flexible measure. Calipers may be used to determine the shot only when the bowls in question and the Jack are on the same plane.

55. "Tie"—no shot

When at the conclusion of play in any end the nearest bowl of each team is touching the Jack, or is deemed to be equidistant from the Jack, there shall be no score recorded. The end shall be declared "drawn" and shall be counted a played end.

56. Nothing in these Laws shall be deemed to make it mandatory for the last player to play his last bowl in any end, but he shall declare to his opponent or opposing Skip his intention to

refrain from playing it before the commencement of determining the result of the end and this declaration shall be
irrevocable.

GAME DECISIONS

57. Games Played on one Occasion

In the case of a single game or a team game or a side game
played on one occasion, or at any stage of an eliminating
competition, the victory decision shall be awarded to the player,
team or side of players producing at the end of the game the
higher total score of shots, or in the case of a "game of winning
ends", a majority of winning ends.

58. Tournament Games and Games in Series

In the case of tournament games or games in series, the victory
decision shall be awarded to the player, team or side of players
producing at the end of the tournament or series of contests
either the largest number of winning games or the highest net
score of shots in accordance with the regulations governing the
tournament or series of games. Points may be used to indicate
game successes. Where points are equal, the aggregate shots
scored against each team (or side) shall be divided into the
aggregate shots it has scored. The team (or side) with the
highest result shall be declared the winner.

59. Playing to a Finish and Possible drawn Games

If in an eliminating competition consisting of a stated or
agreed-upon number of ends, it be found, when all the ends
have been played, that the scores are equal, an extra end or
ends shall be played until a decision has been reached.

The captains or Skips shall toss and the winner shall have
the right to decide who shall play first. The extra end shall be
played from where the previous end was completed and the
mat shall be placed in accordance with Law 24.

DEFAULTS OF PLAYERS IN
FOURS PLAY

60. Absentee Players in any Team or Side

(*a*) In a single fours game, for a trophy, prize or other

competitive award, where a club is represented by only one four, each member of such four shall be a *bona-fide* member of the club. Unless all four players appear and are ready to play at the end of the maximum waiting period of 30 minutes, or should they introduce an ineligible player, then that team shall forfeit the match to the opposing team.

(*b*) In a domestic fours game: Where in a domestic fours game the number of players cannot be accommodated in full teams of four players, three players may play against three players, but shall suffer the deduction of one-fourth of the total score of each team. A smaller number of players than six shall be excluded from that game.

(*c*) In a side game: If, within a period of 30 minutes from the time fixed for the game, a single player is absent from one or both teams in a side game, whether a friendly club match or a match for a trophy, prize, or other award, the game shall proceed, but in the defaulting team, the number of bowls shall be made up by the lead and second players playing three bowls each, but one-fourth of the total shots scored by each "four" playing three men shall be deducted from their score at the end of the game. Fractions shall be taken into account.

(*d*) In a side game: Should such default take place where more fours than one are concerned, or where a four has been disqualified for some other infringement, and where the average score is to decide the contest, the scores of the non-defaulting fours only shall be counted, but such average shall, as a penalty in the case of the defaulting side, be arrived at by dividing the aggregate score of that side by the number of fours that should have been played and not, as in the case of the other side, by the number actually engaged in the game.

61. Play Irregularities

(*a*) Playing out of turn: When a player has played before his turn, the opposing Skip shall have the right to stop the bowl in its course and it shall be played in its proper turn, but, in the event of the bowl so played having moved or displaced the Jack or a bowl, the opposing Skip shall have the option of allowing the end to remain as it is after the bowl so played has come to rest, or of having the end declared "dead".

(*b*) Playing the wrong bowl: A bowl played by mistake shall be replaced by the player's own bowl.

(*c*) Changing bowls: A player shall not be allowed to change his bowls during the course of a game, or in a resumed game, unless they be objected to as provided in Law 9(*c*) or when a bowl has been so damaged in the course of play as, in the Umpire's opinion, to render the bowl (or bowls) unfit for play.

(*d*) *Omitting to play.* (i) If the result of an end has been agreed upon, or the head has been touched in the agreed process of determining the result, then a player who forfeits or has omitted to play a bowl, shall forfeit the right to play it.

(ii) A player who has neglected to play a bowl in the proper sequence shall forfeit the right to play such bowl, if a bowl has been played by each team before such mistake was discovered.

(iii) If before the mistake be noticed a bowl has been delivered in the reversed order and the head has not been disturbed, the opponent shall then play two successive bowls to restore the correct sequence. If the head has been disturbed, Law 61(*a*) shall apply.

62. Play Interruptions

(*a*) Game stoppages: When a game of any kind is stopped, either by mutual arrangement or by the Umpire after appeal to him on account of darkness or the condition of the weather, or any other valid reason, it shall be resumed with the scores as they were when the game was stopped. An end commenced, but not completed, shall be declared null.

(*b*) Substitutes in a resumed game: If in a resumed game any one of the four original players be not available, one substitute shall be permitted as stated in Law 63 below. Players, however, shall not be transferred from one team to another.

INFLUENCES AFFECTING PLAY

63. Leaving the Green

If during the course of a side, fours, triples or pairs game a player has to leave the green owing to illness, or other reasonable cause, his place shall be filled by a substitute, if in the opinion of both Skips (or failing agreement by them, then in the opinion of the Controlling Body) such substitution is necessary. Should the player affected be a Skip, his duties and position in a fours game shall be assumed by a third player and the substitute shall play either as lead, second or third. In the case of triples the substitute may play either as lead or second but not as Skip, and in the case of pairs the substitute shall play as lead only. Such substitute shall be a member of the club to which the team belongs. In domestic play National Associations may decide the position of any substitute.

If during the course of a single-handed game a player has to leave the green, owing to illness or other reasonable cause, the provisions of Law 62(*a*) shall be observed.

No player shall be allowed to delay the play by leaving the rink or team, unless with the consent of his opponent, and then only for a period not exceeding 10 minutes.

Contravention of this law shall entitle the opponent or opposing team to claim the game or match.

64. Objects on the Green

Under no circumstances, other than as provided in Laws 29, 33 and 40, shall any extraneous object to assist a player be placed on the green, or on the bank, or on the Jack, or on a bowl, or elsewhere.

65. Unforeseen Incidents

If during the course of play the position of the Jack or bowls be disturbed by wind, storm or by any neutral object, the end shall be declared "dead", unless the Skips are agreed as to the replacement of Jack or bowls.

DOMESTIC ARRANGEMENTS

66. In addition to any matters specifically mentioned in these Laws, National Associations may, in circumstances dictated by climate or other local conditions, make such other regulations as are deemed necessary and desirable. Such regulations must be submitted to the International Bowling Board for approval. For this purpose the Board shall appoint a committee, to be known as the Laws Committee, with powers to grant approval or otherwise to any proposal, such decision to be valid until the proposal is submitted to the Board for a final decision.

67. Local Arrangements

Constituent clubs of National Associations shall also, in making their domestic arrangements, make such regulations as are deemed necessary to govern their club competitions, but such regulations shall comply with the Laws of the Game and be approved by the Council of their National Association.

68. National Visiting Teams or Sides

No team or side of bowlers visiting overseas or the British Isles shall be recognised by the International Bowling Board unless it first be sanctioned and recommended by the National Association to which its members are affiliated.

69. Contracting Out

No club, club management committee or any individual shall have the right or power to contract out of any of the Laws of the Game as laid down by the International Bowling Board.

REGULATING SINGLE-HANDED, PAIRS AND TRIPLES GAMES

70. The foregoing Laws, where applicable, shall also apply to single-handed, pairs and triples games.

SPECTATORS

71. Persons not engaged in the game shall be situate clear of and beyond the limits of the rink of play and clear of verges. They shall preserve an attitude of strict neutrality, and neither by word nor act disturb or advise the players.

Betting or gambling in connection with any game or games shall not be permitted or engaged in within the grounds of any constituent club.

DUTIES OF MARKER

72. (*a*) The Marker shall control the game in accordance with the I.B.B. Basic Laws. He shall, before play commences, examine all bowls for the imprint of the I.B.B. stamp, or that of its National Association, such imprint to be clearly visible, and shall ascertain by measurement the width of the rink of play.

(*b*) He shall centre the Jack and shall place a full-length Jack 2 yd (1.84 m) from the ditch.

(*c*) He shall ensure that the Jack is not less than 25 yd (22.86 m) from the front edge of the mat after it has been centred.

(*d*) He shall stand at one side of the rink and to the rear of the Jack.

(*e*) He shall answer affirmatively or negatively a player's enquiry as to whether a bowl is Jack high. If requested he shall indicate the distance of any bowl from the Jack or from any other bowl, and also, if requested, indicate which bowl he thinks is shot and/or the relative position of any other bowl.

(*f*) Subject to contrary directions from either opponent under Law 34, he shall mark all "touchers" immediately they come to rest, and remove chalk marks from "non-touchers". With the agreement of both opponents he shall remove all dead bowls from the green and the ditch. He shall mark the positions of the Jack and "touchers" which are in the ditch (see Laws 33 and 40).

(*g*) He shall not move, or cause to be moved, either Jack or bowls until each player has agreed as to the number of shots.

(*h*) He shall measure carefully all doubtful shots when requested by either player. If unable to come to a decision satisfactory to the players, he shall call in an Umpire. If an official Umpire has not been appointed, the Marker shall select one. The decision of the Umpire shall be final.

(*i*) He shall enter the score at each end and shall intimate to the players the state of the game. When the game is finished, he shall see that the score card, containing the names of the players, is signed by the players and disposed of in accordance with the rules of the competition.

DUTIES OF UMPIRE

73. An Umpire shall be appointed by the Controlling Body of the Association, Club or Tournament Management Committee. His duties shall be as follows:

(*a*) He shall examine all bowls for the imprint of the I.B.B. stamp or that of its National Association, and ascertain by measurement the width of the rinks of play.

(*b*) He shall measure any shot or shots in dispute, and for this purpose shall use a suitable measure. His decision shall be final.

(*c*) He shall decide all questions as to the distance of the mat from the ditch and the Jack from the mat.

(*d*) He shall decide as to whether or not Jack and/or bowls are in play.

(*e*) He shall enforce the Laws of the Game.

(*f*) In World Bowls Championships and Commonwealth Games the Umpire's decision shall be final in respect of any breach of a Law, except that, upon questions relating to the meaning or interpretation of any Law, there shall be a right of appeal to the Controlling Body.

INTERNATIONAL BOWLING BOARD
BY-LAWS
PLAYERS' STATUS AND INVOLVEMENT

(**A**) Any player may participate in any event for reward in cash or kind.

An amateur player is one who plays the game wholly as a non-remunerative or non-profit-making sport or pastime.

To maintain his amateur status the recipient of such rewards may conduct his expenses as defined by the International Olympic Committee Constitution but must remit the balance to the Governing Body concerned. The I.O.C. Rules deal with the following: (*a*) assistance administered through his national association for: the costs of food and lodging; the costs of transport; pocket money to cover incidental expenses; the expenses for insurance cover in respect of accidents, illness, personal property and disability; the purchase of personal sports equipment and clothing; the cost of medical treatment, physiotherapy and authorised coaches. (*b*) compensation authorised by the National Authority concerned in case of necessity to cover financial loss resulting from his absence from work or basic occupation. In no circumstances shall payment made under this provision exceed the sum which the player would have earned in his work in the same periods. The compensation may be paid with the approval of the National Authority concerned.

(**B**) Each National Authority may introduce By-Laws to effectively ensure that a player who wishes to remain an amateur does not contravene the I.B.B. By-Laws.

These Laws, originally formulated by the Scottish Bowling Association and last revised in 1984, may not be published without the consent of the International Bowling Board.

The Laws of
Cricket

Cricket

1. THE PLAYERS

1. Number of Players and Captain

A match is played between two sides each of eleven Players, one of whom shall be Captain. In the event of the Captain not being available at any time a Deputy shall act for him.

2. Nomination of Players

Before the toss for innings, the Captain shall nominate his Players who may not thereafter be changed without the consent of the opposing Captain.

NOTES

(*a*) More or Less than Eleven Players a Side.

A match may be played by agreement between sides of more or less than eleven players but not more than eleven players may field.

2. SUBSTITUTES AND RUNNERS: BATSMAN OR FIELDSMAN LEAVING THE FIELD: BATSMAN RETIRING: BATSMAN COMMENCING INNINGS

1. Substitutes

Substitutes shall be allowed by right to field for any player who during the match is incapacitated by illness or injury. The consent of the opposing Captain must be obtained for the use of a Substitute if any player is prevented from fielding for any other reason.

2. Objection to Substitutes

The opposing Captain shall have no right of objection to any player acting as Substitute in the field, nor as to where he shall field, although he may object to the Substitute acting as Wicket-Keeper.

3. Substitute Not to Bat or Bowl

A Substitute shall not be allowed to bat or bowl.

4. A Player for whom a Substitute has acted

A player may bat, bowl or field even though a Substitute has acted for him.

5. Runner

A Runner shall be allowed for a Batsman who during the match is incapacitated by illness or injury. The player acting as Runner shall be a member of the batting side and shall, if possible, have already batted in that innings.

6. Runner's Equipment

The player acting as Runner for an injured Batsman shall wear batting gloves and pads if the injured Batsman is so equipped.

7. Transgression of the Laws by an Injured Batsman or Runner

An injured Batsman may be out should his Runner break any one of Laws 33 (Handled the Ball), 37 (Obstructing the Field) or 38 (Run Out). As Striker he remains himself subject to the Laws. Furthermore, should he be out of his ground for any purpose and the wicket at the Wicket-Keeper's end be put down he shall be out under Law 38 (Run Out) or Law 39 (Stumped) irrespective of the position of the other Batsman or the Runner and no runs shall be scored.

When not the Striker, the injured Batsman is out of the game and shall stand where he does not interfere with the play. Should he bring himself into the game in any way then he shall suffer the penalties that any transgression of the Laws demands.

8. Fieldsman Leaving the Field

No Fieldsman shall leave the field or return during a session of play without the consent of the Umpire at the Bowler's end. The Umpire's consent is also necessary if a Substitute is required for a Fieldsman, when his side returns to the field after an interval. If a member of the fielding side leaves the field or fails to return after an interval and is absent from the field for longer than 15 minutes, he shall not be permitted to bowl after his return until he has been on the field for at least that length of playing time for which he was absent. This restriction shall not apply at the start of a new day's play.

9. Batsman Leaving the Field or Retiring

A Batsman may leave the field or retire at any time owing to illness, injury or other unavoidable cause, having previously notified the Umpire at the Bowler's end. He may resume his innings at the fall of a wicket, which for the purposes of this Law shall include the retirement of another Batsman.

If he leaves the field or retires for any other reason he may only resume his innings with the consent of the opposing Captain.

When a Batsman has left the field or retired and is unable to return owing to illness, injury or other unavoidable cause, his innings is to be recorded as "retired, not out". Otherwise it is to be recorded as "retired, out".

10. Commencement of a Batsman's Innings

A Batsman shall be considered to have commenced his innings once he has stepped on to the field of play.

3. THE UMPIRES

1. Appointment

Before the toss for innings two Umpires shall be appointed, one for each end, to control the game with absolute impartiality as required by the Laws.

2. Change of Umpire

No Umpire shall be changed during a match without the consent of both Captains.

3. Special Conditions

Before the toss for innings, the Umpires shall agree with both Captains on any special conditions affecting the conduct of the match.

4. The Wickets

The Umpires shall satisfy themselves before the start of the match that the wickets are properly pitched.

5. Clock or Watch

The Umpires shall agree between themselves and inform both Captains before the start of the match on the watch or clock to be followed during the match.

6. Conduct and Implements

Before and during a match the Umpires shall ensure that the conduct of the game and the implements used are strictly in accordance with the Laws.

7. Fair and Unfair Play

The Umpires shall be the sole judges of fair and unfair play.

8. Fitness of Ground, Weather and Light

(*a*) The Umpires shall be the sole judges of the fitness of the ground, weather and light for play.

   (i) However, before deciding to suspend play or not to start play or not to resume play after an interval or stoppage, the Umpires shall establish whether both Captains (the Batsmen at the wicket may deputise for their Captain) wish to commence or to continue in the prevailing conditions; if so, their wishes shall be met.

   (ii) In addition, if during play, the Umpires decide that the light is unfit, only the batting side shall have the option of continuing play. After agreeing to continue to play in unfit light conditions, the Captain of the batting side (or a Batsman at the wicket) may appeal against the light to the Umpires, who shall uphold the appeal only if, in their opinion, the light has deteriorated since the agreement to continue was made.

(*b*) After any suspension of play, the Umpires, unaccompanied by any of the Players or Officials shall, on their own initiative, carry out an inspection immediately the conditions improve and shall continue to inspect at intervals. Immediately the Umpires decide that play is possible they shall call upon the Players to resume the game.

9. Exceptional Circumstances

In exceptional circumstances, other than those of weather, ground or light, the Umpires may decide to suspend or abandon play. Before making such a decision the Umpires shall establish, if the circumstances allow, whether both Captains (the Batsmen at the wicket may deputise for their Captain) wish to continue in the prevailing conditions: if so their wishes shall be met.

10. Position of Umpires

The Umpires shall stand where they can best see any act upon which their decision may be required.

Subject to this over-riding consideration the Umpire at the Bowler's end shall stand where he does not interfere with either the Bowler's run up or the Striker's view.

The Umpire at the Striker's end may elect to stand on the off instead of the leg side of the pitch, provided he informs the Captain of the fielding side and the Striker of his intention to do so.

11. Umpires Changing Ends

The Umpires shall change ends after each side has had one innings.

12. Disputes

All disputes shall be determined by the Umpires and if they disagree the actual state of things shall continue.

13. Signals

The following code of signals shall be used by Umpires who will wait until a signal has been answered by a Scorer before allowing the game to proceed.

Boundary	by waving the arm from side to side.
Boundary 6	by raising both arms above the head.
Bye	by raising an open hand above the head.
Dead Ball	by crossing and re-crossing the wrists below the waist.
Leg Bye	by touching a raised knee with the hand.
No Ball	by extending one arm horizontally.

Out	by raising the index finger above the head. If not out the Umpire shall call "not out".
Short Run	by bending the arm upwards and by touching the nearer shoulder with the tips of the fingers.
Wide	by extending both arms horizontally.

14. Correctness of Scores

The Umpires shall be responsible for satisfying themselves on the correctness of the scores throughout and at the conclusion of the match. See Law 21.6. (Correctness of Result).

4. THE SCORERS

1. Recording Runs

All runs scored shall be recorded by Scorers appointed for the purpose. Where there are two Scorers they shall frequently check to ensure that the score sheets agree.

2. Acknowledging Signals

The Scorers shall accept and immediately acknowledge all instructions and signals given to them by the Umpires.

5. THE BALL

1. Weight and Size

The ball, when new, shall weigh not less than $5\frac{1}{2}$ oz (155.9 g), nor more than $5\frac{3}{4}$ oz (163 g): and shall measure not less than $\frac{13}{16}$ in (22.4 cm), nor more than 9 in (22.9 cm) in circumference.

2. Approval of Balls

All balls used in matches shall be approved by the Umpires and Captains before the start of the match.

3. New Ball

Subject to agreement to the contrary, having been made before the toss, either Captain may demand a new ball at the start of each innings.

4. New Ball in Match of 3 or more Days Duration

In a match of 3 or more days' duration, the Captain of the fielding side may demand a new ball after the prescribed number of overs has been bowled with the old one. The Governing Body for cricket in the country concerned shall decide the number of overs applicable in that country which shall be not less than 75 six-ball overs (55 eight-ball overs).

5. Ball Lost or Becoming Unfit for Play

In the event of a ball during play being lost or, in the opinion of the Umpires, becoming unfit for play, the Umpires shall allow it to be replaced by one that in their opinion has had a similar amount of wear. If a ball is to be replaced, the Umpires shall inform the Batsmen.

6. THE BAT

1. Width and Length

The bat overall shall not be more than 38 in (96.5 cm) in length; the blade of the bat shall be made of wood and shall not exceed $4\frac{1}{4}$ in (10.8 cm) at the widest part.

7. THE PITCH

1. Area of Pitch

The pitch is the area between the bowling creases – see Law 9. (The Bowling, Popping and Return Creases). It shall measure 5 ft (1.52 m) in width on either side of a line joining the centre of the middle stumps of the wickets. (See Law 8: The Wickets.)

2. Selection and Preparation

Before the toss for innings, the Executive of the Ground shall be responsible for the selection and preparation of the pitch; thereafter the Umpires shall control its use and maintenance.

3. Changing Pitch

The pitch shall not be changed during a match unless it becomes unfit for play, and then only with the consent of both Captains.

4. Non-Turf Pitches

In the event of a non-turf pitch being used, the following shall apply:

(*a*) *Length:* That of the playing surface to a minimum of 58 ft (17.68 m).

(*b*) *Width:* That of the playing surface to a minimum of 6 ft (1.83 m).

8. THE WICKETS

1. Width and Pitching

Two sets of wickets, each 9 in (22.86 cm) wide, and consisting of three wooden stumps with two wooden bails upon the top, shall be pitched opposite and parallel to each other at a distance of 22 yd (20.12 m) between the centres of the two middle stumps.

2. Size of Stumps

The stumps shall be of equal and sufficient size to prevent the ball from passing between them. Their tops shall be 28 in (71.1 cm) above the ground, and shall be dome-shaped except for the bail grooves.

3. Size of Bails

The bails shall be each $4\frac{3}{8}$ in (11.1 cm) in length and when in position on the top of the stumps shall not project more than $\frac{1}{2}$ in (1.3 cm) above them.

9 THE BOWLING, POPPING AND RETURN CREASES

1. The Bowling Crease

The bowling crease shall be marked in line with the stumps at each end and shall be 8 ft 8 in (2.64 m) in length, with the stumps in the centre.

2. The Popping Crease

The popping crease, which is the back edge of the crease marking, shall be in front of and parallel with the bowling crease. It shall have the back edge of the crease marking 4 ft (1.22 m) from the centre of the stumps and shall extend to a minimum of 6 ft (1.83 m) on either side of the line of the wicket.

The popping crease shall be considered to be unlimited in length.

3. The Return Crease
The return crease marking, of which the inside edge is the crease, shall be at each end of the bowling crease and at right angles to it. The return crease shall be marked to a minimum of 4 ft (1.22 m) behind the wicket and shall be considered to be unlimited in length. A forward extension shall be marked to the popping crease.

10. ROLLING, SWEEPING, MOWING, WATERING THE PITCH AND RE-MARKING OF CREASES

1. Rolling
During the match the pitch may be rolled at the request of the Captain of the batting side, for a period of not more than 7 minutes before the start of each innings, other than the first innings of the match, and before the start of each day's play. In addition, if, after the toss and before the first innings of the match, the start is delayed, the Captain of the batting side shall have the right to have the pitch rolled for not more than 7 minutes.

The pitch shall not otherwise be rolled during the match.

The 7 minutes rolling permitted before the start of a day's play shall take place not earlier than half an hour before the start of play and the Captain of the batting side may delay such rolling until 10 minutes before the start of play should he so desire.

If a Captain declares an innings closed less than 15 minutes before the resumption of play, and the other Captain is thereby prevented from exercising his option of 7 minutes rolling or if he is so prevented for any other reason the time for rolling shall be taken out of the normal playing time.

2. Sweeping

Such sweeping of the pitch as is necessary during the match shall be done so that the 7 minutes allowed for rolling the pitch provided for in 1 above is not affected.

3. Mowing

(*a*) *Responsibilities of Ground Authority and of Umpires.* All mowings which are carried out before the toss for innings shall be the responsibility of the Ground Authority. Thereafter they shall be carried out under the supervision of the Umpires, see Law 7.2 (Selection and Preparation).

(*b*) *Initial Mowing.* The pitch shall be mown before play begins on the day the match is scheduled to start or in the case of a delayed start on the day the match is expected to start. See 3(a) above (Responsibilities of Ground Authority and of Umpires).

(*c*) *Subsequent Mowings in a Match of 2 or More Days' Duration.* In a match of two or more days' duration, the pitch shall be mown daily before play begins. Should this mowing not take place because of weather conditions, rest days or other reasons the pitch shall be mown on the first day on which the match is resumed.

(*d*) *Mowing of the Outfield in a Match of 2 or More Days' Duration.* In order to ensure that conditions are as similar as possible for both sides, the outfield shall normally be mown before the commencement of play on each day of the match, if ground and weather conditions allow.

4. Watering

The pitch shall not be watered during a match.

5. Re-Marking Creases

Whenever possible the creases shall be re-marked.

6. Maintenance of Foot Holes

In wet weather, the Umpires shall ensure that the holes made by the Bowlers and Batsmen are cleaned out and dried whenever necessary to facilitate play. In matches of 2 or more days' duration, the Umpires shall allow, if necessary, the re-turfing of foot holes made by the Bowler in his delivery stride, or the use of quick-setting fillings for the same purpose, before the start of each day's play.

7. Securing of Footholds and Maintenance of Pitch

During play, the Umpires shall allow either Batsman to beat the pitch with his bat and players to secure their footholds by the use of sawdust, provided that no damage to the pitch is so caused, and Law 42 (Unfair Play) is not contravened.

11. COVERING THE PITCH

1. Before the Start of a Match

Before the start of a match complete covering of the pitch shall be allowed.

2. During a Match

The pitch shall not be completely covered during a match unless prior arrangement or regulations so provide.

3. Covering Bowlers' Run-Up

Whenever possible, the Bowlers' run-up shall be covered, but the covers so used shall not extend further than 4 ft/1.22 m in front of the popping crease.

12. INNINGS

1. Number of Innings

A match shall be of one or two innings of each side according to agreement reached before the start of play.

2. Alternate Innings

In a two innings match each side shall take their innings alternately except in the case provided for in Law 13 (The Follow-On).

3. The Toss

The Captains shall toss for the choice of innings on the field of play not later than 15 minutes before the time scheduled for the match to start, or before the time agreed upon for play to start.

4. Choice of Innings

The winner of the toss shall notify his decision to bat or to field to the opposing Captain not later than 10 minutes before the time scheduled for the match to start, or before the time agreed upon for play to start. The decision shall not thereafter be altered.

5. Continuation After One Innings of Each Side

Despite the terms of 1 above, in a one innings match, when a result has been reached on the first innings the Captains may agree to the continuation of play if, in their opinion, there is a prospect of carrying the game to a further issue in the time left. See Law 21 (Result).

13. THE FOLLOW-ON

1. Lead on First Innings

In a two innings match the side which bats first and leads by 200 runs in a match of five days or more, by 150 runs in a three-day or four-day match, by 100 runs in a two-day match, or by 75 runs in a one-day match, shall have the option of requiring the other side to follow their innings.

2. Day's Play Lost

If no play takes place on the first day of a match of two or more days' duration, 1 above shall apply in accordance with the number of days' play remaining from the actual start of the match.

14. DECLARATIONS

1. Time of Declaration

The Captain of the batting side may declare an innings closed at any time during a match irrespective of its duration.

2. Forfeiture of Second Innings

A Captain may forfeit his second innings, provided his decision to do so is notified to the opposing Captain and Umpires in sufficient time to allow 7 minutes rolling of the pitch. See Law 10 (Rolling, Sweeping, Mowing, Watering the Pitch and Re-Marking of Creases). The normal 10 minute interval between innings shall be applied.

15. START OF PLAY

1. Call of Play

At the start of each innings and of each day's play and on the resumption of play after any interval or interruption the Umpire at the Bowlers' end shall call "play".

2. Practice on the Field

At no time on any day of the match shall there be any bowling or batting practice on the pitch.

No practice may take place on the field if, in the opinion of the Umpires, it could result in a waste of time.

3. Trial Run-Up

No Bowler shall have a trial run-up after "play" has been called in any session of play, except at the fall of a wicket when an Umpire may allow such a trial run-up if he is satisfied that it will not cause any waste of time.

16. INTERVALS

1. Length

The Umpire shall allow such intervals as have been agreed upon for meals, and 10 minutes between each innings.

2. Luncheon Interval—Innings Ending or Stoppage within 10 Minutes of Interval

If an innings ends or there is a stoppage caused by weather or bad light within 10 minutes of the agreed time for the luncheon interval, the interval shall be taken immediately.

The time remaining in the session of play shall be added to

the agreed length of the interval but no extra allowance shall be made for the 10 minutes interval between innings.

3. Tea Interval—Innings Ending or Stoppage within 30 Minutes of Interval

If an innings ends or there is a stoppage caused by weather or bad light within 30 minutes of the agreed time for the tea interval, the interval shall be taken immediately.

The interval shall be of the agreed length and, if applicable, shall include the 10 minute interval between innings.

4. Tea Interval—Continuation of Play

If at the agreed time for the tea interval, nine wickets are down, play shall continue for a period not exceeding 30 minutes or until the innings is concluded.

5. Tea Interval—Agreement to Forego

At any time during the match, the Captains may agree to forego a tea interval.

6. Intervals for Drinks

If both Captains agree before the start of a match that intervals for drinks may be taken, the option to take such intervals shall be available to either side. These intervals shall be restricted to one per session, shall be kept as short as possible, shall not be taken in the last hour of the match and in any case shall not exceed 5 minutes.

The agreed times for these intervals shall be strictly adhered to except that if a wicket falls within 5 minutes of the agreed time then drinks shall be taken out immediately.

If an innings ends or there is a stoppage caused by weather or bad light within 30 minutes of the agreed time for a drinks interval, there will be no interval for drinks in that session.

At any time during the match the Captains may agree to forgo any such drinks interval.

17. CESSATION OF PLAY

1. Call of Time

The Umpire at the Bowler's end shall call "time" on the cessation of play before any interval or interruption of play, at the end of each day's play, and at the conclusion of the match. See Law 27 (Appeals).

2. Removal of Bails

After the call of "time", the Umpires shall remove the bails from both wickets.

3. Starting a Last Over

The last over before an interval or the close of play shall be started provided the Umpire, after walking at his normal pace, has arrived at his position behind the stumps at the Bowler's end before time has been reached.

4. Completion of the Last Over of a Session

The last over before an interval or the close of play shall be completed unless a Batsman is out or retires during that over within 2 minutes of the interval or the close of play or unless the Players have occasion to leave the field.

5. Completion of the Last Over of a Match

An over in progress at the close of play on the final day of a match shall be completed at the request of either Captain even if a wicket falls after time has been reached.

If during the last over the Players have occasion to leave the field the Umpires shall call "time" and there shall be no resumption of play and the match shall be at an end.

6. Last Hour of Match—Number of Overs

The Umpires shall indicate when one hour of playing time of the match remains according to the agreed hours of play. The next over after that moment shall be the first of a minimum of 20 6-ball overs, (15 8-ball overs), provided a result is not reached earlier or there is no interval or interruption of play.

7. Last Hour of Match—Intervals Between Innings and Interruptions of Play

If, at the commencement of the last hour of the match, an interval or interruption of play is in progress or if, during the last hour there is an interval between innings or an interruption of play, the minimum number of overs to be bowled on the resumption of play shall be reduced in proportion to the duration, within the last hour of the match, of any such interval or interruption.

The minimum number of overs to be bowled after a resumption of play shall be calculated as follows:

(*a*) In the case of an interval or interruption of play being in progress at the commencement of the last hour of the match, or in the case of a first interval or interruption a deduction shall be made from the minimum of 20 6-ball overs (or 15 8-ball overs).

(*b*) If there is a later interval or interruption a further deduction shall be made from the minimum number of overs which should have been bowled following the last resumption of play.

(*c*) These deductions shall be based on the following factors:

  (i) the number of overs already bowled in the last hour of the match or, in the case of a later interval or interruption in the last session of play.

 (ii) the number of overs lost as a result of the interval or interruption allowing one 6-ball over for every full three minutes (or one 8-ball over for every full four minutes) of interval or interruption.

(iii) any over left uncompleted at the end of an innings to be excluded from these calculations.

(iv) any over left uncompleted at the start of an interruption of play to be completed when play is resumed and to count as one over bowled.

 (v) an interval to start with the end of an innings and to end 10 minutes later; an interruption to start on the call of "time" and to end on the call of "play".

(*d*) In the event of an innings being completed and a new innings commencing during the last hour of the match, the number of overs to be bowled in the new innings shall be calculated on the basis of one 6-ball over for every three minutes or part thereof remaining for play (or one 8-ball over for every four minutes or part thereof remaining for play); or alternatively on the basis that sufficient overs be bowled to enable the full minimum quota of overs to be completed under circumstances governed by (*a*), (*b*) and (*c*) above. In all such cases the alternative which allows the greater number of overs shall be employed.

8. Bowler Unable to Complete an Over During Last Hour of the Match

If, for any reason, a Bowler is unable to complete an over during the period of play referred to in 6 above, Law 22.7 (Bowler Incapacitated or Suspended during an Over) shall apply.

18. SCORING

1. A Run

The score shall be reckoned by runs. A run is scored:

(*a*) So often as the Batsmen, after a hit or at any time while the ball is in play, shall have crossed and made good their ground from end to end.

(*b*) When a boundary is scored. See Law 19 (Boundaries).

(*c*) When penalty runs are awarded. See 6 below.

2. Short Runs

(*a*) If either Batsman runs a short run, the Umpire shall call and signal "one short" as soon as the ball becomes dead and that run shall not be scored. A run is short if a Batsman fails to make good his ground on turning for a further run.

(*b*) Although a short run shortens the succeeding one, the latter, if completed shall count.

(*c*) If either or both Batsmen deliberately run short the Umpire shall, as soon as he sees that the fielding side have no chance of dismissing either Batsman, call and signal "dead ball" and disallow any runs attempted or previously scored. The Batsmen shall return to their original ends.

(*d*) If both Batsmen run short in one and the same run, only one run shall be deducted.

(*e*) Only if three or more runs are attempted can more than one be short and then, subject to (*c*) and (*d*) above, all runs so called shall be disallowed. If there has been more than one short run the Umpires shall instruct the Scorers as to the number of runs disallowed.

3. Striker Caught

If the Striker is Caught, no run shall be scored.

4. Batsman Run Out

If a Batsman is Run Out, only that run which was being attempted shall not be scored. If, however, an injured Striker himself is run out no runs shall be scored. See Law 2.7 (Transgression of the Laws by an Injured Batsman or Runner).

5. Batsman Obstructing the Field

If a Batsman is out Obstructing the Field, any runs completed before the obstruction occurs shall be scored unless such obstruction prevents a catch being made in which case no runs shall be scored.

6. Runs Scored for Penalties

Runs shall be scored for penalties under Laws 20 (Lost Ball), 24 (No Ball), 25 (Wide Ball), 41.1 (Fielding the Ball) and for boundary allowances under Law 19 (Boundaries).

7. Batsman Returning to Wicket he has Left

If, while the ball is in play, the Batsmen have crossed in running, neither shall return to the wicket he has left even though a short run has been called or no run has been scored as in the case of a catch. Batsmen, however, shall return to the wickets they originally left in the cases of a boundary and of any disallowance of runs and of an injured Batsman being, himself, run out. See Law 2.7 (Transgression of the Laws by an Injured Batsman or Runner).

19. BOUNDARIES

1. The Boundary of the Playing Area

Before the toss for innings, the Umpires shall agree with both Captains on the boundary of the playing area. The boundary shall, if possible, be marked by a white line, a rope laid on the ground, or a fence. If flags or posts only are used to mark a boundary, the imaginary line joining such points shall be regarded as the boundary. An obstacle, or person, within the playing area shall not be regarded as a boundary unless so decided by the Umpires before the toss for innings. Sightscreens within, or partially within, the playing area shall be regarded as the boundary and when the ball strikes or passes within or under or directly over any part of the screen, a boundary shall be scored.

2. Runs Scored for Boundaries

Before the toss for innings, the Umpires shall agree with both Captains the runs to be allowed for boundaries, and in deciding the allowance for them, the Umpires and Captains shall be guided by the prevailing custom of the ground. The allowance for a boundary shall normally be 4 runs, and 6 runs for all hits pitching over and clear of the boundary line or fence, even though the ball has been previously touched by a Fieldsman. 6 runs shall also be scored if a Fieldsman, after catching a ball, carries it over the boundary. 6 runs shall not be scored when a ball struck by the Striker hits a sightscreen full pitch if the screen is within, or partially within, the playing area, but if the ball is struck directly over a sightscreen so situated, 6 runs shall be scored.

3. A Boundary

A boundary shall be scored and signalled by the Umpire at the Bowler's end whenever, in his opinion:

(a) A ball in play touches or crosses the boundary, however marked.

(b) A Fieldsman with ball in hand touches or grounds any part of his person on or over a boundary line.

(c) A Fieldsman with ball in hand grounds any part of his

person over a boundary fence or board. This allows the Fieldsman to touch or lean on or over a boundary fence or board in preventing a boundary.

4. Runs Exceeding Boundary Allowance

The runs completed at the instant the ball reaches the boundary shall count if they exceed the boundary allowance.

5. Overthrows or Wilful Act of a Fieldsman

If the boundary results from an overthrow or from the wilful act of a Fieldsman, any runs already completed and the allowance shall be added to the score. The run in progress shall count provided that the Batsmen have crossed at the instant of the throw or act.

20. LOST BALL

1. Runs Scored

If a ball in play cannot be found or recovered any fieldsman may call "lost ball" when 6 runs shall be added to the score; but if more than 6 have been run before "lost ball" is called, as many runs as have been completed shall be scored. The run in progress shall count provided that the Batsmen have crossed at the instant of the call of "lost ball".

2. How Scored

The runs shall be added to the score of the Striker if the ball has been struck, but otherwise to the score of byes, leg-byes, no-balls or wides as the case may be.

21. THE RESULT

1. A Win—Two Innings Matches

The side which has scored a total of runs in excess of that scored by the opposing side in its two completed innings shall be the winners.

2. A Win—One Innings Matches

(a) One innings matches, unless played out as in 1 above, shall be decided on the first innings, but see Law 12.5 (Continuation After One Innings of Each Side).

(*b*) If the Captains agree to continue play after the completion of one innings of each side in accordance with Law 12.5 (Continuation After One Innings of Each Side) and a result is not achieved on the second innings, the first innings result shall stand.

3. Umpires Awarding a Match

(*a*) A match shall be lost by a side which, during the match,
   (i) refuses to play, or
   (ii) concedes defeat,
and the Umpires shall award the match to the other side.

(*b*) Should both Batsmen at the wickets or the fielding side leave the field at any time without the agreement of the Umpires, this shall constitute a refusal to play and, on appeal, the Umpires shall award the match to the other side in accordance with (*a*) above.

4. A Tie

The result of a match shall be a tie when the scores are equal at the conclusion of play, but only if the side batting last has completed its innings.

If the scores of the completed first innings of a one-day match are equal, it shall be a tie but only if the match has not been played out to a further conclusion.

5. A Draw

A match not determined in any of the ways as in 1, 2, 3 and 4 above shall count as a draw.

6. Correctness of Result

Any decision as to the correctness of the scores shall be the responsibility of the Umpires. See Law 3.14 (Correctness of Scores).

If, after the Umpires and Players have left the field, in the belief that the match has been concluded, the Umpires decide that a mistake in scoring has occurred, which affects the result, and provided time has not been reached, they shall order play to resume and to continue until the agreed finishing time unless a result is reached earlier.

If the Umpires decide that a mistake has occurred and time has been reached, the Umpires shall immediately inform both Captains of the necessary corrections to the scores and, if applicable, to the result.

7. Acceptance of Result

In accepting the scores as notified by the scorers and agreed by the Umpires, the Captains of both sides thereby accept the result.

22. THE OVER

1. Number of Balls

The ball shall be bowled from each wicket alternately in overs of either 6 or 8 balls according to agreement before the match.

2. Call of "Over"

When the agreed number of balls has been bowled, and as the ball becomes dead or when it becomes clear to the Umpire at the Bowler's end that both the fielding side and the Batsmen at the wicket have ceased to regard the ball as in play, the Umpire shall call "over" before leaving the wicket.

3. No Ball or Wide Ball

Neither a no ball nor a wide ball shall be reckoned as one of the over.

4. Umpire Miscounting

If an Umpire miscounts the number of balls, the over as counted by the Umpire shall stand.

5. Bowler Changing Ends

A Bowler shall be allowed to change ends as often as desired provided only that he does not bowl two overs consecutively in an innings.

6. The Bowler Finishing an Over

A Bowler shall finish an over in progress unless he be incapacitated or be suspended under Law 42.8. (The Bowling of Fast Short Pitched Balls), 42.9. (The Bowling of Fast High Full Pitches), 42.10. (Time Wasting) and 42.11. (Players Damaging the Pitch). If an over is left incomplete for any reason at the start of an interval or interruption of play, it shall be finished on the resumption of play.

7. Bowler Incapacitated or Suspended During an Over

If, for any reason, a Bowler is incapacitated while running up to bowl the first ball of an over, or is incapacitated or suspended during an over, the Umpire shall call and signal "dead ball" and another Bowler shall be allowed to bowl or complete the over from the same end, provided only that he shall not bowl two overs, or part thereof, consecutively in one innings.

8. Position of Non-Striker

The Batsman at the Bowler's end shall normally stand on the opposite side of the wicket to that from which the ball is being delivered, unless a request to do otherwise is granted by the Umpire.

23. DEAD BALL

1. The Ball Becomes Dead, when:—

(*a*) It is finally settled in the hands of the Wicket-Keeper or the Bowler.

(*b*) It reaches or pitches over the boundary.

(*c*) A Batsman is out.

(*d*) Whether played or not, it lodges in the clothing or equipment of a Batsman or the clothing of an Umpire.

(*e*) A ball lodges in a protective helmet worn by a member of the fielding side.

(*f*) A penalty is awarded under Law 20 (Lost Ball) or Law 41.1 (Fielding the Ball).

(*g*) The Umpire calls "over" or "time".

2. Either Umpire Shall Call and Signal "Dead Ball", when:

(*a*) He intervenes in a case of unfair play.

(*b*) A serious injury to a Player or Umpire occurs.

(*c*) He is satisfied that, for an adequate reason, the Striker is not ready to receive the ball and makes no attempt to play it.

(*d*) The Bowler drops the ball accidentally before delivery, or the ball does not leave his hand for any reason.

(*e*) One or both bails fall from the Striker's wicket before he receives delivery.

(*f*) He leaves his normal position for consultation.

(*g*) He is required to do so under Laws 26.3 (Disallowance of Leg-Byes), etc.

3. The Ball Ceases to be Dead, when:

(*a*) The Bowler starts his run up or bowling action.

4. The Ball is Not Dead, when:

(*a*) It strikes an Umpire (unless it lodges in his dress).

(*b*) The wicket is broken or struck down (unless a Batsman is out thereby).

(*c*) An unsuccessful appeal is made.

(*d*) The wicket is broken accidentally either by the Bowler during his delivery or by a Batsman in running.

(*e*) The Umpire has called "no ball" or "wide".

24. NO BALL

1. Mode of Delivery

The Umpire shall indicate to the Striker whether the Bowler intends to bowl over or round the wicket, overarm or under-arm, or right or left-handed. Failure on the part of the Bowler to indicate in advance a change in his mode of delivery is unfair and the Umpire shall call and signal "no ball".

2. Fair Delivery—The Arm

For a delivery to be fair the ball must be bowled not thrown. If either Umpire is not entirely satisfied with the absolute fairness of a delivery in this respect he shall call and signal "no ball" instantly upon delivery.

3. Fair Delivery—The Feet

The Umpire at the bowler's wicket shall call and signal "no ball" if he is not satisfied that in the delivery stride:

   (a) the Bowler's back foot has landed within and not touching the return crease or its forward extension, or

   (b) some part of the front foot whether grounded or raised was behind the popping crease.

4. Bowler Throwing at Striker's Wicket Before Delivery

If the Bowler, before delivering the ball, throws it at the Striker's wicket in an attempt to run him out, the Umpire shall call and signal "no ball". See Law 42.12 (Batsman Unfairly Stealing a Run) and Law 38 (Run Out).

5. Bowler Attempting to Run Out Non-Striker Before Delivery

If the Bowler, before delivering the ball, attempts to run out the non-Striker, any runs which result shall be allowed and shall be scored as no balls. Such an attempt shall not count as a ball in the over. The Umpire shall not call "no ball". See Law 42.12 (Batsman Unfairly Stealing a Run).

6. Infringement of Laws by a Wicket-Keeper or a Fieldsman

The Umpire shall call and signal "no ball" in the event of the Wicket-Keeper infringing Law 40.1 (Position of Wicket-Keeper) or a Fieldsman infringing Law 41.2 (Limitation of On-side Fieldsmen) or Law 41.3 (Position of Fieldsmen).

7. Revoking a Call

An Umpire shall revoke the call "no ball" if the ball does not leave the Bowler's hand for any reason. See Law 23.2 (Either Umpire Shall Call and Signal "Dead Ball").

8. Penalty

A penalty of one run for a no ball shall be scored if no runs are made otherwise.

9. Runs From a No Ball

The Striker may hit a no ball and whatever runs result shall be added to his score. Runs made otherwise from a no ball shall be scored no balls.

10. Out From a No Ball

The Striker shall be out from a no ball if he breaks Law 34 (Hit the Ball Twice) and either Batsman may be Run Out or shall be given out if either breaks Law 33 (Handled the Ball) or Law 37 (Obstructing the Field).

11. Batsman Given Out Off a No Ball

Should a Batsman be given out off a no ball the penalty for bowling it shall stand unless runs are otherwise scored.

25. WIDE BALL

1. Judging a Wide

If the Bowler bowls the ball so high over or so wide of the wicket that, in the opinion of the Umpire it passes out of reach of the Striker, standing in a normal guard position, the Umpire shall call and signal "wide ball" as soon as it has passed the line of the Striker's wicket.

The Umpire shall not adjudge a ball as being a wide if:

(*a*) The Striker, by moving from his guard position, causes the ball to pass out of his reach.

(*b*) The Striker moves and thus brings the ball within his reach.

2. Penalty

A penalty of one run for a wide shall be scored if no runs are made otherwise.

3. Ball Coming to Rest in Front of the Striker

If a ball which the Umpire considers to have been delivered comes to rest in front of the line of the Striker's wicket, "wide" shall not be called. The Striker has a right, without interference from the fielding side, to make one attempt to hit the ball. If the fielding side interfere, the Umpire shall replace the ball where it came to rest and shall order the Fieldsmen to resume the places they occupied in the field before the ball was delivered.

The Umpire shall call and signal "dead ball" as soon as it is clear that the Striker does not intend to hit the ball, or after the Striker has made one unsuccessful attempt to hit the ball.

4. Revoking a Call

The Umpire shall revoke the call if the Striker hits a ball which has been called "wide".

5. Ball Not Dead

The ball does not become dead on the call of "wide ball"—see Law 23.4 (The Ball is Not Dead).

6. Runs Resulting from a Wide

All runs which are run or result from a wide ball which is not a no ball shall be scored wide balls, or if no runs are made one shall be scored.

7. Out from a Wide

The Striker shall be out from a wide ball if he breaks Law 35 (Hit Wicket) or Law 39 (Stumped). Either Batsman may be Run Out and shall be out if he breaks Law 33 (Handled the Ball) or Law 37 (Obstructing the Field).

8. Batsman Given Out Off a Wide

Should a Batsman be given out off a wide, the penalty for bowling it shall stand unless runs are otherwise made.

26. BYE AND LEG-BYE

1. Byes

If the ball, not having been called "wide" or "no ball" passes the Striker without touching his bat or person, and any runs are obtained, the Umpire shall signal "bye" and the run or runs shall be credited as such to the batting side.

2. Leg-Byes

If the ball, not having been called "wide" or "no ball" is unintentionally deflected by the Striker's dress or person, except a hand holding the bat, and any runs are obtained the

Umpire shall signal "leg-bye" and the run or runs so scored shall be credited as such to the batting side.

Such leg-byes shall only be scored if, in the opinion of the Umpire, the Striker has:

(*a*) attempted to play the ball with his bat, or

(*b*) tried to avoid being hit by the ball.

3. Disallowance of Leg-Byes

In the case of a deflection by the Striker's person, other than in 2(*a*) and (*b*) above, the Umpire shall call and signal "dead ball" as soon as one run has been completed or when it is clear that a run is not being attempted or the ball has reached the boundary.

On the call and signal of "dead ball" the Batsmen shall return to their original ends and no runs shall be allowed.

27. APPEALS

1. Time of Appeals

The Umpires shall not give a Batsman out unless appealed to by the other side which shall be done prior to the Bowler beginning his run-up or bowling action to deliver the next ball. Under Law 23.1 (*g*) (The Ball Becomes Dead) the ball is dead on "over" being called; this does not, however, invalidate an appeal made prior to the first ball of the following over provided "time" has not been called. See Law 17.1 (Call of Time).

2. An Appeal "How's That?"

An appeal "How's That?" shall cover all ways of being out.

3. Answering Appeals

The Umpire at the Bowler's wicket shall answer appeals before the other Umpire in all cases except those arising out of Law 35 (Hit Wicket) or Law 39 (Stumped) or Law 38 (Run Out) when this occurs at the Striker's wicket.

When either Umpire has given a Batsman not out, the other Umpire shall, within his jurisdiction, answer the appeal or a further appeal, provided it is made in time in accordance with 1 (Time of Appeals) above.

4. Consultation by Umpires

An Umpire may consult with the other Umpire on a point of fact which the latter may have been in a better position to see and shall then give his decision. If, after consultation, there is still doubt remaining the decision shall be in favour of the Batsman.

5. Batsman Leaving his Wicket under a Misapprehension

The Umpires shall intervene if satisfied that a Batsman, not having been given out, has left his wicket under a misapprehension that he has been dismissed.

6. Umpire's Decision

The Umpire's decision is final. He may alter his decision, provided that such alteration is made promptly.

7. Withdrawal of an Appeal

In exceptional circumstances the Captain of the fielding side may seek permission of the Umpire to withdraw an appeal providing the outgoing Batsman has not left the playing area. If this is allowed, the Umpire shall cancel his decision.

28. THE WICKET IS DOWN

1. Wicket Down

The wicket is down if:

(*a*) Either the ball or the Striker's bat or person completely removes either bail from the top of the stumps. A disturbance of a bail, whether temporary or not, shall not constitute a complete removal, but the wicket is down if a bail in falling lodges between two of the stumps.

(*b*) Any player completely removes with his hand or arm a bail from the top of the stumps, providing that the ball is held in that hand or in the hand of the arm so used.

(*c*) When both bails are off, a stump is struck out of the ground by the ball, or a player strikes or pulls a stump out of the ground, providing that the ball is held in the hand(s) or in the hand of the arm so used.

2. One Bail Off

If one bail is off, it shall be sufficient for the purpose of putting the wicket down to remove the remaining bail, or to strike or pull any of the three stumps out of the ground in any of the ways stated in 1 above.

3. All the Stumps Out of the Ground

If all the stumps are out of the ground, the fielding side shall be allowed to put back one or more stumps in order to have an opportunity of putting the wicket down.

4. Dispensing with Bails

If owing to the strength of the wind, it has been agreed to dispense with the bails, the decision as to when the wicket is down is one for the Umpires to decide on the facts before them. In such circumstances and if the Umpires so decide the wicket shall be held to be down even though a stump has not been struck out of the ground.

29. BATSMAN OUT OF HIS GROUND

1. When out of his Ground

A Batsman shall be considered to be out of his ground unless some part of his bat in his hand or of his person is grounded behind the line of the popping crease.

30. BOWLED

1. Out Bowled

The Striker shall be out bowled if:

(*a*) His wicket is bowled down, even if the ball first touches his bat or person.

(*b*) He breaks his wicket by hitting or kicking the ball on to it before the completion of a stroke, or as a result of attempting to guard his wicket. See Law 34.1 (Out—Hit the Ball Twice).

31. TIMED OUT

1. Out Timed Out

An incoming Batsman shall be out Timed Out if he wilfully takes more than two minutes to come in—the two minutes being timed from the moment a wicket falls until the new batsman steps on to the field of play.

If this is not complied with and if the Umpire is satisfied that the delay was wilful and if an appeal is made, the new Batsman shall be given out by the Umpire at the Bowler's end.

2. Time to be Added

The time taken by the Umpires to investigate the cause of the delay shall be added at the normal close of play.

32. CAUGHT

1. Out Caught

The Striker shall be out Caught if the ball touches his bat or if it touches below the wrist his hand or glove, holding the bat, and is subsequently held by a Fieldsman before it touches the ground.

2. A Fair Catch

A catch shall be considered to have been fairly made if:

(*a*) The Fieldsman is within the field of play throughout the act of making the catch.

   (i) The act of making the catch shall start from the time when the Fieldsman first handles the ball and shall end when he both retains complete control over the further disposal of the ball and remains within the field of play.

   (ii) In order to be within the field of play, the Fieldsman may not touch or ground any part of his person on or over a boundary line. When the boundary is marked by a fence or board the Fieldsman may not ground any part of his person over the boundary fence or board, but may touch or lean over the boundary fence or board in completing the catch.

(*b*) The ball is hugged to the body of the catcher or accidentally lodges in his dress or, in the case of the Wicket-Keeper, in his pads. However, a Striker may not be caught if a ball lodges in a protective helmet worn by a Fieldsman, in which case the Umpire shall call and signal "dead ball". See Law 23 (Dead Ball).

(*c*) The ball does not touch the ground even though a hand holding it does so in effecting the catch.

(*d*) A Fieldsman catches the ball, after it has been lawfully played a second time by the Striker, but only if the ball has not touched the ground since being first struck.

(*e*) A Fieldsman catches the ball after it has touched an Umpire, another Fieldsman or the other Batsman. However a Striker may not be caught if a ball has touched a protective helmet worn by a Fieldsman.

(*f*) The ball is caught off an obstruction within the boundary provided it has not previously been agreed to regard the obstruction as a boundary.

3. Scoring of Runs

If a Striker is caught, no runs shall be scored.

33. HANDLED THE BALL

1. Out Handled the Ball

Either Batsman on appeal shall be out Handled the Ball if he wilfully touches the ball while in play with the hand not holding the bat unless he does so with the consent of the opposite side.

34. HIT THE BALL TWICE

1. Out Hit the Ball Twice

The Striker, on appeal, shall be out Hit the Ball Twice if, after the ball is struck or is stopped by any part of his person, he wilfully strikes it again with his bat or person except for the sole purpose of guarding his wicket: this he may do with his bat or any part of his person other than his hands, but see Law 37.2 (Obstructing a Ball From Being Caught).

For the purpose of this Law, a hand holding the bat shall be regarded as part of the bat.

2. Returning the Ball to a Fieldsman

The Striker, on appeal, shall be out under this Law, if, without the consent of the opposite side, he uses his bat or person to return the ball to any of the fielding side.

3. Runs from Ball Lawfully Struck Twice

No runs except those which result from an overthrow or penalty, see Law 41 (The Fieldsman), shall be scored from a ball lawfully struck twice.

35. HIT WICKET

1. Out Hit Wicket

The Striker shall be out Hit Wicket if, while the ball is in play:—

(*a*) His wicket is broken with any part of his person, dress, or equipment as a result of any action taken by him in preparing to receive or in receiving a delivery, or in setting off for his first run, immediately after playing, or playing at, the ball.

(*b*) He hits down his wicket whilst lawfully making a second stroke for the purpose of guarding his wicket within the provisions of Law 34.1 (Out Hit the Ball Twice).

36. LEG BEFORE WICKET

1. Out L.B.W.

The Striker shall be out L.B.W. in the circumstances set out below:

(*a*) *Striker Attempting to Play the Ball.* The Striker shall be out L.B.W. if he first intercepts with any part of his person, dress or equipment a fair ball which would have hit the wicket and which has not previously touched his bat or a hand holding the bat, provided that:

(i) The ball pitched in a straight line between wicket and wicket or on the off side of the Striker's wicket, or in the case of a ball intercepted full pitch would have pitched in a straight line between wicket and wicket.

and

    (ii) the point of impact is in a straight line between wicket and wicket, even if above the level of the bails.

   (*b*) *Striker Making No Attempt to Play the Ball.* The Striker shall be out L.B.W. even if the ball is intercepted outside the line of the off-stump, if, in the opinion of the Umpire, he has made no genuine attempt to play the ball with his bat, but has intercepted the ball with some part of his person and if the circumstances set out in (*a*) above apply.

37. OBSTRUCTING THE FIELD

1. Wilful Obstruction

Either Batsman, on appeal, shall be out Obstructing the Field if he wilfully obstructs the opposite side by word or action.

2. Obstructing a Ball from Being Caught

The Striker, on appeal, shall be out should wilful obstruction by either Batsman prevent a catch being made.

   This shall apply even though the Striker causes the obstruction in lawfully guarding his wicket under the provisions of Law 34. See Law 34.1 (Out Hit the Ball Twice).

38. RUN OUT

1. Out Run Out

Either Batsman shall be out Run Out if in running or at any time while the ball is in play—except in the circumstances described in Law 39 (Stumped)—he is out of his ground and his wicket is put down by the opposite side. If, however, a Batsman in running makes good his ground he shall not be out Run Out, if he subsequently leaves his ground, in order to avoid injury, and the wicket is put down.

2. "No Ball" Called

If a no ball has been called, the Striker shall not be given Run Out unless he attempts to run.

3. Which Batsman is Out

If the Batsmen have crossed in running, he who runs for the wicket which is put down shall be out; if they have not crossed, he who has left the wicket which is put down shall be out. If a Batsman remains in his ground or returns to his ground and the other Batsman joins him there, the latter shall be out if his wicket is put down.

4. Scoring of Runs

If a Batsman is run out, only that run which is being attempted shall not be scored. If however an injured Striker himself is run out, no runs shall be scored. See Law 2.7 (Transgression of the Laws by an Injured Batsman or Runner).

39. STUMPED

1. Out Stumped

The Striker shall be out Stumped if, in receiving a ball, not being a no-ball, he is out of his ground otherwise than in attempting a run and the wicket is put down by the Wicket-Keeper without the intervention of another Fieldsman.

2. Action by the Wicket-Keeper

The Wicket-Keeper may take the ball in front of the wicket in an attempt to Stump the Striker only if the ball has touched the bat or person of the Striker.

40. THE WICKET-KEEPER

1. Position of Wicket-Keeper

The Wicket-Keeper shall remain wholly behind the wicket until a ball delivered by the Bowler touches the bat or person of the Striker, or passes the wicket, or until the Striker attempts a run.

In the event of the Wicket-Keeper contravening this Law, the Umpire at the Striker's end shall call and signal "no ball" at the instant of delivery or as soon as possible thereafter.

2. Restriction on Actions of the Wicket-Keeper

If the Wicket-Keeper interferes with the Striker's right to play the ball and to guard his wicket, the Striker shall not be out, except under Laws 33 (Handled the Ball), 34 (Hit the Ball Twice), 37 (Obstructing the Field) and 38 (Run Out).

3. Interference with the Wicket-Keeper by the Striker

If in the legitimate defence of his wicket, the Striker interferes with the Wicket-Keeper, he shall not be out, except as provided for in Law 37.2 (Obstructing a Ball From Being Caught).

41. THE FIELDSMAN

1. Fielding the Ball

The Fieldsman may stop the ball with any part of his person, but if he wilfully stops it otherwise, 5 runs shall be added to the run or runs already scored; if no run has been scored 5 penalty runs shall be awarded. The run in progress shall count provided that the Batsmen have crossed at the instant of the act. If the ball has been struck, the penalty shall be added to the score of the Striker, but otherwise to the score of byes, leg-byes, no balls or wides as the case may be.

2. Limitation of On-Side Fieldsmen

The number of on-side Fieldsmen behind the popping crease at the instant of the Bowler's delivery shall not exceed two. In the event of infringement by the fielding side the Umpire at the Striker's end shall call and signal "no ball" at the instant of delivery or as soon as possible thereafter.

3. Position of Fieldsmen

Whilst the ball is in play and until the ball has made contact with the bat or the Striker's person or has passed his bat, no Fieldsman, other than the Bowler, may stand on or have any part of his person extended over the pitch [measuring 22 yd (20.12 m) × 10 ft (3.05 m)]. In the event of a Fieldsman contravening this Law, the Umpire at the bowler's end shall call and signal "no ball" at the instant of delivery or as soon as possible thereafter. See Law 40.1 (Position of Wicket-Keeper).

42. UNFAIR PLAY

1. Responsibility of Captains

The Captains are responsible at all times for ensuring that play is conducted within the spirit of the game as well as within the Laws.

2. Responsibility of Umpires

The Umpires are the sole judges of fair and unfair play.

3. Intervention by the Umpire

The Umpires shall intervene without appeal by calling and signalling "dead ball" in the case of unfair play, but should not otherwise interfere with the progress of the game except as required to do so by the Laws.

4. Lifting the Seam

A Player shall not lift the seam of the ball for any reason. Should this be done, the Umpires shall change the ball for one of similar condition to that in use prior to the contravention.

5. Changing the Condition of the Ball

Any member of the fielding side may polish the ball provided that such polishing wastes no time and that no artificial substance is used. No one shall rub the ball on the ground or use any artificial substance or take any other action to alter the condition of the ball.

In the event of a contravention of this Law, the Umpires, after consultation, shall change the ball for one of similar condition to that in use prior to the contravention.

This Law does not prevent a member of the fielding side from drying a wet ball, or removing mud from the ball.

6. Incommoding the Striker

An Umpire is justified in intervening under this Law and shall call and signal "dead ball" if, in his opinion, any Player of the fielding side incommodes the Striker by any noise or action while he is receiving a ball.

7. Obstruction of a Batsman in Running

It shall be considered unfair if any Fieldsman wilfully obstructs a Batsman in running. In these circumstances the Umpire shall call and signal "dead ball" and allow any completed runs and the run in progress or alternatively any boundary scored.

8. The Bowling of Fast Short Pitched Balls

The bowling of fast short-pitched balls is unfair if, in the opinion of the Umpire at the Bowler's end, it constitutes an attempt to intimidate the Striker.

Umpires shall consider intimidation to be the deliberate bowling of fast short-pitched balls which by their length, height and direction are intended or likely to inflict physical injury on the Striker. The relative skill of the Striker shall also be taken into consideration.

In the event of such unfair bowling, the Umpire at the Bowler's end shall adopt the following procedure:

(*a*) In the first instance the Umpire shall call and signal "no ball", caution the Bowler and inform the other Umpire, the Captain of the fielding side and the Batsmen of what has occurred.

(*b*) If this caution is ineffective, he shall repeat the above procedure and indicate to the Bowler that this is a final warning.

(*c*) Both the above caution and final warning shall continue to apply even though the Bowler may later change ends.

(*d*) Should the above warnings prove ineffective the Umpire at the Bowler's end shall:

   (i) At the first repetition call and signal "no ball" and when the ball is dead direct the Captain to take the Bowler off forthwith and to complete the over with another Bowler, provided that the Bowler does not bowl two overs or part thereof consecutively. See Law 22.7 (Bowler Incapacitated or Suspended during an Over).

   (ii) Not allow the Bowler, thus taken off, to bowl again in the same innings.

   (iii) Report the occurrence to the Captain of the batting side as soon as the Players leave the field for an interval.

   (iv) Report the occurrence to the Executive of the fielding

side and to any governing body responsible for the match who shall take any further action which is considered to be appropriate against the Bowler concerned.

9. The Bowling of Fast High Full Pitches

The bowling of fast high full pitches is unfair.

In the event of such unfair bowling the Umpire at the bowler's end shall adopt the procedures of caution, final warning, action against the Bowler and reporting as set out in 8, above.

10. Time Wasting

Any form of time wasting is unfair.

(a) In the event of the Captain of the fielding side wasting time or allowing any member of his side to waste time, the Umpire at the Bowler's end shall adopt the following procedure:

   (i) In the first instance he shall caution the Captain of the fielding side and inform the other Umpire of what has occurred.

  (ii) If this caution is ineffective he shall repeat the above procedure and indicate to the Captain that this is a final warning.

 (iii) The Umpire shall report the occurrence to the Captain of the batting side as soon as the Players leave the field for an interval.

 (iv) Should the above procedure prove ineffective the Umpire shall report the occurrence to the Executive of the fielding side and to any governing body responsible for that match who shall take appropriate action against the Captain and the Players concerned.

(b) In the event of a Bowler taking unnecessarily long to bowl an over the Umpire at the Bowler's end shall adopt the procedures, other than the calling of "no-ball", of caution, final warning, action against the Bowler and reporting.

(c) In the event of a Batsman wasting time other than in the manner described in Law 31 (Timed Out), the Umpire at the Bowler's end shall adopt the following procedure:

   (i) In the first instance he shall caution the Batsman and inform the other Umpire at once, and the Captain of the batting side, as soon as the Players leave the field for an interval, of what has occurred.

(ii) If this proves ineffective, he shall repeat the caution, indicate to the Batsman that this is a final warning and inform the other Umpire.

(iii) The Umpire shall report the occurrence to both Captains as soon as the Players leave the field for an interval.

(iv) Should the above procedure prove ineffective, the Umpire shall report the occurrence to the Executive of the batting side and to any governing body responsible for that match who shall take appropriate action against the Player concerned.

11. Players Damaging the Pitch

The Umpires shall intervene and prevent Players from causing damage to the pitch which may assist the Bowlers of either side.

(*a*) In the event of any member of the fielding side damaging the pitch the Umpire shall follow the procedure of caution, final warning and reporting as set out in 10(*a*) above.

(*b*) In the event of a Bowler contravening this Law by running down the pitch after delivering the ball, the Umpire at the Bowler's end shall first caution the Bowler. If this caution is ineffective the Umpire shall adopt the procedures as set out in 8, other than the calling and signalling of "no-ball".

(*c*) In the event of a Batsman damaging the pitch the Umpire at the Bowler's end shall follow the procedures of caution, final warning and reporting as set out in 10(*c*) above.

12. Batsman Unfairly Stealing a Run

Any attempt by the Batsman to steal a run during the Bowler's run-up is unfair. Unless the Bowler attempts to run out either Batsman—see Law 24.4 (Bowler Throwing at Striker's Wicket Before Delivery) and Law 24.5 (Bowler Attempting to Run Out Non-Striker Before Delivery)—the Umpire shall call and signal "dead ball" as soon as the Batsmen cross in any such attempt to run. The Batsmen shall then return to their original wickets.

13. Players' Conduct

In the event of a player failing to comply with the instructions of an Umpire, criticising his decisions by word or action, or showing dissent, or generally behaving in a manner which might bring the game into disrepute, the Umpire concerned shall, in the first place, report the matter to the other Umpire and to the Player's Captain requesting the latter to take action. If this proves ineffective, the Umpire shall report the incident as soon as possible to the Executive of the Player's team and to any Governing Body responsible for the match, who shall take any further action which is considered appropriate against the Player or Players concerned.

Printed by permission of the M.C.C. Copies of the current edition of the official Laws of Cricket with full notes and interpretations can be obtained from Lord's Cricket Ground.

The Laws of
Association
Croquet
and
Golf Croquet

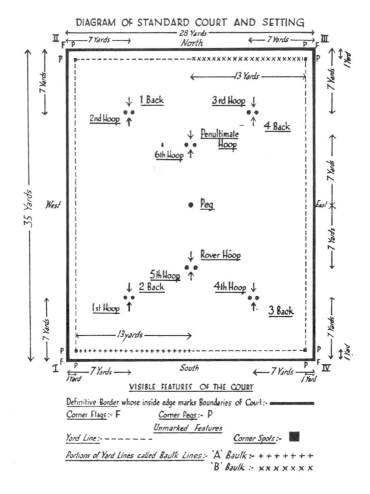

DIAGRAM OF STANDARD COURT AND SETTING

VISIBLE FEATURES OF THE COURT

Definitive Border whose inside edge marks Boundaries of Court:- ▬▬▬▬

Corner Flags:- F   Corner Pegs:- P

Unmarked Features

Yard Line:- - - - - - -   Corner Spots:- ▨

Portions of Yard Lines called Baulk Lines:- 'A' Baulk :- + + + + + + +

'B' Baulk :- × × × × × × ×

Association Croquet

I. THE STANDARD COURT AND EQUIPMENT

1. The Standard Court

(*a*) *The Standard Court*. The standard court is a rectangle measuring 35 by 28 yards. Its border must be marked out clearly, the inner edge of the definitive border being the actual boundary. Where more than one marking is visible, the most recent defines the true boundary.

(*b*) *Diagram 1*. This diagram depicts the setting for the standard court and together with its accompanying explanations is part of this law.

(*c*) *Court References*. The four boundaries are known as the south, west, north and east boundaries regardless of the actual orientation of the court. The corners of the court are known as corners 1, 2, 3 and 4.

(*d*) *Yard-line, Yard-line Area, Corner Spot, Corner Square*. The perimeter of an inner rectangle parallel to and distant one yard from the boundary is called the yard-line, its corners the corner spots and the space between the yard-line and the boundary the yard-line area. The square yard formed at each corner by the two corner pegs, the corner spot and the corner flag is called a corner square.

(*e*) *Baulk-lines*. The parts of the yard-line that extend from the corner spots at corners 1 and 3 and terminate on a line extended through the centres of hoops 5 and 6, and thus measure 13 yards, are known as the A and B baulk-lines respectively.

(*f*) *The Standard Setting*. The peg (see Law 2 (*a*)) is set in the centre of the court. There are six hoops (see Law 2 (*b*)) which are set parallel to the north and south boundaries; the centres of the two inner hoops are 7 yards to the north and south of the peg; the centres of the four outer hoops are 7 yards from the adjacent boundaries.

(*g*) *Permitted Tolerance.* All court dimensions of 7 yards or more in this law are subject to a tolerance of plus or minus 6 inches, provided that the peg lies on the lines joining the centres of hoops 1 and 3, 2 and 4, and 5 and 6, and that the baulk-lines still terminate on a line extended through the centres of hoops 5 and 6.

2. Equipment

(*a*) *The Peg.* The peg has two parts. The base has a uniform diameter of $1\frac{1}{2}$ inches and a height of 18 inches above the ground and is made of wood or metal. It must be vertical, firmly fixed and painted white to a height of at least 6 inches above the ground. The extension is about $\frac{1}{2}$ inch in diameter and 6 inches in length and is made of any suitable material. It is designed to hold clips (see Law 2 (*d*)) and is fixed detachably to the top of the base. The extension may be temporarily removed if it impedes the striker.

(*b*) *Hoops*
  (i) Each hoop is made of round metal of uniform diameter of $\frac{5}{8}$ inch above the ground and painted white. It is 12 inches in height above the ground measured to the top of the crown and must be vertical and firmly fixed. The crown must be straight and at right angles to the uprights, whose inner surfaces must be parallel and not less than $3\frac{3}{4}$ inches or more than 4 inches apart (but see Law 50 (*d*) for tournament play). Each hoop on a court must have the same dimensions within a tolerance of plus or minus $\frac{1}{32}$ inch. In addition, the crown of the first hoop (hoop 1) is painted blue and that of the last hoop (rover) is painted red.
  (ii) The jaws of a hoop are defined as the space enclosed by the inner surfaces of the uprights and the planes generated by raising a straight edge vertically against both sides of the hoop from the ground to the crown.

(*c*) *Balls.* There are four balls coloured blue, black, red and yellow. Alternative colours, namely green, brown, pink and white, are also permitted. A ball must be $3\frac{5}{8}$ inches, plus or minus $\frac{1}{32}$ inch, in diameter and must weigh 16 ounces, plus or minus $\frac{1}{4}$ ounce. When dropped from a height of 60 inches onto a steel plate 1 inch thick and set rigidly in concrete, a ball must rebound to a height of not less than 30 inches and not more than 45 inches. The rebound heights of a set of balls to be used in a game must not differ by more than 3 inches. Faulty or damaged balls may be changed at any time during a game.

(*d*) *Clips*. There are four clips made of plastic or metal, or any other suitable material, that must be the same colours as the balls used in a game. They are used to indicate the score (see Law 4 (*e*)) and may be temporarily removed if they impede the striker.

(*e*) *Mallets*. The end-faces of the head of a mallet may be made of wood or any other non-metallic material provided that no playing advantage is gained over wood. The end-faces must be parallel and identical in every respect. Bevelled edges are not part of the end-faces. A mallet may not be changed during a turn (see Law 4 (*d*)) unless it has suffered damage affecting use in that turn.

3. Court Accessories

The following accessories may be supplied for guidance, convenience and decoration but do not form part of the setting of the court. Accordingly, any accessories that impede the striker may be temporarily removed.

(*a*) *Corner Flags*. Flags coloured blue, red, black and yellow may be placed in corners 1, 2, 3 and 4 respectively. If used, the flags should be mounted on posts about 12 inches high that must touch the boundary but must not intrude into the court.

(*b*) *Corner Pegs*. Eight white corner pegs, measuring $\frac{3}{4}$ inch in diameter and 3 inches in height above the ground, may be placed on the boundary one yard from each corner flag, measured to the further side of the corner pegs (see Diagram 2). If used, the corner pegs must touch the boundary but must not intrude into the court.

(*c*) *Baulk-line Markers*. A mark or marker may be placed on the boundary to define the east end of the A baulk-line and the west end of the B baulk-line. If a marker is used, it must not intrude into the court.

(*d*) *Check-fence*. A check-fence just high enough to arrest the progress of the balls may be placed around the boundary and about 1 yard outside it.

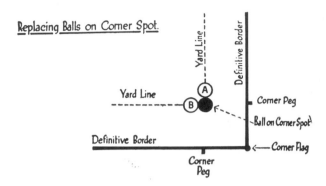

Replacing Balls on Corner Spot.

II. ORDINARY SINGLES PLAY

(A) AN OUTLINE OF THE GAME

4. An Outline of the Game

(*a*) *Scope of this Law*. This law gives a brief outline of the game and the laws of Association Croquet. Those provisions stated in general terms are subject to the detailed laws that follow.

(*b*) *The Object of the Game*. The game is played between two players, of whom one plays the blue and black and the other the red and yellow balls (or green and brown versus pink and white). The object of the game is for each player to make both his balls score 12 hoop points and a peg point, a total of 26 points, before his adversary. A ball scores a hoop point (see Law 14) by passing through the correct hoop in the order and in the direction shown in Diagram 1. This is also known as running a hoop in order. A ball which has scored all 12 hoop points is known as a rover. It may then score a peg point by hitting the peg and is then said to be pegged out (see Law 15 and, for handicap play, Law 39). A ball that is pegged out is removed from the game.

(*c*) *How the Game is Played*. The game is played by striking a ball with a mallet (see Laws 31 and 32). The player whose turn it is (see (*d*) below) is known as the striker, the ball that he strikes as the striker's ball and his other ball as the partner ball. The striker must never strike an adversary's ball and he may strike only one of his two balls during a turn (see Law 28 and, for doubles play, Law 40). By striking the striker's ball the striker may cause any other ball to move and to score a hoop point (see Law 14 (*e*)). When the striker's ball is a rover, it may cause another rover to score a peg point and thus be removed from the game (see Law 15).

(*d*) *The Turn*

(i) The players play alternate turns. A player may elect at the start of a turn to play that turn with either of his balls (see Law 8). He is initially entitled to play one stroke, after which the turn ends, unless in that stroke the striker's ball scores a hoop point for itself or hits another ball.

(ii) If the striker's ball scores a hoop point for itself, the striker becomes entitled to play one extra stroke which is known as a continuation stroke (see Laws 4 (*g*) and 21).

(iii) If the striker's ball hits another ball, it is said to have roqueted that other ball and the striker becomes entitled to play two extra strokes. The first extra stroke is known as a croquet stroke (see Laws 4 (*f*) and 20) and is played after placing the striker's ball in contact with the roqueted ball (see Law 19). In a croquet stroke the roqueted ball is known as the croqueted ball and the striker is said to take croquet from it. The second extra stroke is a continuation stroke (see Laws 4 (*g*) and 21).

(iv) At the start of a turn the striker's ball may roquet each of the other three balls once. However, every time the striker's ball scores a hoop point for itself it may roquet each of the other three balls again. It is therefore possible for the striker to become entitled to play a series of strokes in a turn in which he may cause the striker's ball to score one or more points for itself.

(*e*) *The Score*. The score is indicated by the correct position of the clips. At the start of every turn the hoop or peg next in order for each ball carries a clip of the same colour as the ball. When a ball runs such a hoop in order the striker must remove the clip and, at the end of the turn, place it on the appropriate hoop or the peg. For the first six hoops the clip is placed on the crown of the appropriate hoop and for the last six hoops on an upright. When a peg point is scored the clip is removed from the court.

(*f*) *Croquet Stroke*. In a croquet stroke the striker must move or shake the croqueted ball. Failure to do so constitutes a fault (see Law 32) and the turn ends. The turn also ends in a croquet stroke if the croqueted ball is sent off the court, unless it is pegged out in the stroke, or if the striker's ball is sent off the court without making a roquet or scoring a hoop point for itself (see Law 20 (*c*)).

(*g*) *Continuation Stroke*. A continuation stroke is an ordinary stroke in which, for example, a further roquet may be made or a point may be scored. Continuation strokes may not be accumulated; thus

(i) if the striker's ball scores a hoop point for itself and then makes a roquet in the same stroke, the striker takes croquet immediately;

(ii) if the striker's ball makes a roquet in a croquet stroke, the striker takes croquet immediately;

(iii) if the striker's ball scores two hoop points for itself in the same stroke, the striker plays only one continuation stroke;

(iv) if the striker's ball scores a hoop point for itself in a croquet stroke, the striker plays only one continuation stroke.

(*h*) *Double-banked Games*. Two games may be played simultaneously on the same court. The blue, black, red and yellow balls are used in one game and the green, brown, pink and white balls are used in the other game. The players and equipment of one game constitute outside agencies in relation to the other game (see Law 34 (*b*)(ii)). A guide to conduct in double-banked games is set out in Appendix 2.

(B) GENERAL LAWS OF PLAY

5. The Toss Before the Start of a Game

The winner of the toss decides whether he will take the choice of lead, which includes the right to play second, or the choice of balls. This is known as the right of choice. If he takes the choice of lead his adversary has the choice of balls and vice versa. When a match consists of more than one game the right of choice alternates after the first game.

6. The Start of a Game

At the start of a game, the player entitled to play first plays either of his balls into the game from any point on either baulk-line. At the end of that turn his adversary does likewise. In the third and fourth turns the remaining two balls are similarly played into the game (but see Law 36 (*d*) for advanced and semi-advanced play and Law 38 (*c*) for handicap play).

7. Ball in Play

A ball played under Law 6 may immediately score points and make roquets and is known as a ball in play. Except when it is a ball in hand (see Law 9), it continues to be a ball in play until the end of the stroke in which it is pegged out.

8. Option of Striker to Play Either Ball

(*a*) After all four balls have been played into the game under Law 6, the striker may elect at the start of any subsequent turn to play that turn with either of his balls (but see Law 38 (*a*) for handicap play). Subject to (*b*) below, this election is made by playing a stroke (see Law 31).

(*b*) If, at the start of a turn, the striker
(i) lifts a ball under Law 13 (or Law 36 in advanced or semi-advanced play), it becomes the striker's ball as soon as it is lifted; or
(ii) plays a ball in contact with another ball, it becomes the striker's ball as soon as it is moved before being placed for a croquet stroke.

In each case, the striker may not then play with his other ball. If he does so, Law 28 (*a*) applies.

9. Ball in Hand

(*a*) The striker's ball becomes a ball in hand and ceases to be a ball in play
  (i) when it goes off the court (see Law 10);
  (ii) at the end of a turn if it comes to rest in the yard-line area (see Law 11);
  (iii) when it is lifted under Law 13 (or Law 36 in advanced or semi-advanced play);
  (iv) at the end of a stroke in which it makes a roquet (see Law 18 (*a*)(iii);
  (v) when it is moved before being placed for a croquet stroke after a roquet is deemed to have been made (see Law 16 (*c*)).

(*b*) Any other ball becomes a ball in hand and ceases to be a ball in play
  (i) when it goes off the court (see Law 10);
  (ii) at the end of a stroke if it comes to rest in the yard-line area (see Law 11);
  (iii) when it is moved under Law 19 (*b*).

(*c*) A ball ceases to be a ball in hand and again becomes a ball in play when the next stroke is played (see Law 31).

10. Ball Off the Court

A ball goes off the court as soon as any part of it would touch a straight edge raised vertically from the boundary (see Law 1 (*a*)). It then becomes a ball in hand and an outside agency (see Law 34 (*b*) (ii)).

11. Ball in the Yard-line Area

At the end of each stroke any ball in the yard-line area other than the striker's ball, which is played from where it lies, becomes a ball in hand. Only at the end of a turn does the striker's ball in the yard-line area become a ball in hand.

12. Replacement of a Ball Off the Court or in the Yard-line Area

(*a*) Before the next stroke

(i) any ball off the court, other than the striker's ball entitled to take croquet, is replaced on the yard-line at the point nearest to that at which it went off the court; and

(ii) any ball in hand in the yard-line area, other than the striker's ball entitled to take croquet, is replaced on the yard-line at the point nearest to its position in the yard-line area.

A ball replaced on the yard-line is known as a yard-line. A ball replaced on a corner spot is also known as a corner ball.

(*b*) If a ball cannot be so replaced because of the presence of one or more yard-line balls, it is replaced on the yard-line in contact with that ball or one of them on either side at the striker's option. If one of two such yard-line balls is a corner ball, the ball to be replaced is replaced on the yard-line in contact with the corner ball on its unoccupied side.

(*c*) If a ball cannot be so replaced because of the presence of the striker's ball inside or any ball outside the yard-line area, it is replaced on the yard-line in contact with that other ball. If the ball to be replaced would otherwise be a corner ball it must in addition be replaced on the yard-line as near as possible to the corner spot.

(*d*) If two or more balls have to be so replaced and the replacement of one will interfere with the replacement of the other, the order of replacement is at the striker's option.

13. Wiring Lift

(*a*) The striker may lift one of his balls at the start of a turn and play it from any point on either baulk-line if

(i) it is wired from all other balls; and

(ii) the adversary is responsible for its position; and

(iii) it is not in contact with another ball.

(*b*) A ball ("the relevant ball") is wired from another ball ("the target ball") if

(i) any part of a hoop or the peg would impede the direct course of any part of the relevant ball towards any part of the target ball; or

(ii) any part of a hoop or the peg would impede the swing of the mallet prior to its impact with the relevant ball; or

(iii) any part of the relevant ball lies within the jaws of a hoop (see Law 2 (*b*)(ii)).

In (*b*)(ii) above, the swing is impeded if there is any part of the end-face of the mallet with which the striker cannot strike the centre of the relevant ball in order to drive it freely towards any part of the target ball. However, the swing is not impeded merely because a hoop or the peg interferes with the striker's stance.

(*c*) A player is responsible for the position of any ball moved or shaken as a consequence of his play, including a ball replaced after a fault (see Law 32), or which he is deemed to have played under Law 31 (*d*). He is not responsible for the position of any ball replaced after invalid play (see Laws 27, 28, 30 and 35) unless he would have been so responsible before such play or becomes so responsible thereafter.

14. Hoop Point

(*a*) Subject ot Law 18 (*a*)(i), a ball scores a hoop point by passing through the correct hoop in the order and in the direction shown in diagram 1. This is also known as running a hoop in order.

(*b*) The front of a hoop as it is approached by a ball about to run it in order is known as the playing side and the back as the non-playing side. The whole of the ball does not have to pass through the whole of the hoop to score a hoop point because

(i) a ball begins to run a hoop only when the front of the ball can be touched by a straight edge raised vertically against the non-playing side; and

(ii) a ball completes the running of a hoop if it comes to rest (see Law 22) in a position in which the back of the ball cannot be touched by a straight edge raised vertically against the playing side.

(*c*) A ball may complete the running of a hoop in two or more turns but, if it becomes a ball in hand, it must begin to run the hoop afresh.

(*d*) If a ball from which the striker is taking croquet lies within the jaws of the hoop next in order for the striker's ball, the striker's ball may run that hoop in the croquet stroke provided that it has not begun to run the hoop (see (*b*)(i) above) when placed in the actual position from which the striker will take croquet.

(*e*) If the striker's ball causes another ball to score a hoop point, that other ball is said to be peeled through the hoop.

15. Peg Point

(*a*) Subject to Law 18 (*a*)(i), a ball scores a peg point by hitting the peg in order. Only when the striker's ball has scored all 12 hoop points, and has thus become a rover, can it score a peg point (but see Law 39 for handicap play) or cause another rover to do so, whether directly or through the agency of another ball.

(*b*) If the striker's ball hits the peg in order and simultaneously makes a roquet, a peg point is scored unless the striker claims the roquet (but see Law 39 for handicap play).

(*c*) If, at the start of a turn, the striker plays a rover that is in contact with the peg, that ball is pegged out unless it is hit in a direction away from the peg (but see Law 39 for handicap play). Likewise, if the striker's ball is a rover and hits, or causes another ball to hit, another rover that is in contact with the peg, that other rover is pegged out unless it is hit in a direction away from the peg.

(*d*) A ball that has been pegged out in a stroke remains a ball in play throughout the stroke and may therefore cause other balls to score hoop or peg points; accordingly, it may only be picked up or arrested in its course to save time if the state of the game will not be affected thereby.

(*e*) If a ball is pegged out the striker must remove the ball and the corresponding clip from the court before the next stroke (see Law 30 (*d*)).

16. Roquet

(*a*) *When a Roquet May Be Made.* At the start of a turn the striker's ball may roquet each of the other three balls once. However, every time the striker's ball scores a hoop point for itself it may roquet each of the other three balls again.

(*b*) *When a Roquet Is Actually Made.* A roquet is actually made when the striker's ball hits a ball that may be roqueted, whether directly or after hitting a hoop or the peg or a ball that may not be roqueted. However,

    (i) if two or more balls that may be roqueted are hit in one stroke, a roquet is deemed only to be made on the ball first hit; if two or more such balls are hit simultaneously, a roquet is deemed only to be made on the ball that the striker nominates as the roqueted ball by taking croquet from it;

   (ii) if the striker's ball hits the peg in order and simultaneously makes a roquet, Law 15 (*b*) applies;

  (iii) if the striker's ball scores a hoop point for itself and thereafter in the same stroke hits a ball from which it started in contact, a roquet is deemed not to be made; however, if such balls come to rest in contact, a roquet is deemed to have been made under (*c*)(ii) below.

(*c*) *When a Roquet Is Deemed To Have Been Made.* Subject to (*d*) below, a roquet is deemed to have been made

    (i) at the start of a turn, if the striker plays a ball that is in contact with another ball (but see Law 36 for advanced or semi-advanced play); or

   (ii) during a turn that the striker is entitled to continue, if the striker's ball is in contact with a ball that may be roqueted.

(*d*) *Groups of Balls*

    (i) If the striker's ball is in contact with more than one ball that may be roqueted, a roquet is deemed only to have been made on the ball that the striker nominates as the roqueted ball by taking croquet from it.

   (ii) If the striker's ball forms part of a 3-ball or 4-ball group, a roquet may be deemed to have been made on any ball in the group that may be roqueted, but is deemed only to have been made on the ball that the striker nominates as the roqueted ball by taking croquet from it. A 3-ball group is formed by three balls, each of which is in contact with at least one other ball and at least one of which is a yard-line ball. A 4-ball group is formed by one ball in contact with a 3-ball group.

17. Hoop and Roquet in the Same Stroke

If, before completing the running of a hoop in order, the striker's ball hits a ball that is clear of the hoop on the non-playing side and finally completes the running of the hoop, as defined in Law 14 (*b*)(ii), it is deemed that a hoop point is scored and a roquet is then made. A ball is clear of a hoop if no part of it lies within the jaws of the hoop (see Law 2 (*b*)(ii)).

18. Consequences of a Roquet

(*a*) If the striker's ball makes a roquet under Laws 16 (*b*) or 17

(i) it cannot thereafter in the same stroke score a hoop point or a peg point for itself (except under Law 17);

(ii) it remains a ball in play throughout the stroke and may therefore cause other balls to score hoop or peg points; accordingly, it may only be picked up or arrested in its course to save time if the state of the game will not be affected thereby;

(iii) it becomes a ball in hand at the end of the stroke unless the striker's turn ends either under Law 20 (*c*) or because the roqueted ball is pegged out in the stroke; and

(iv) the striker takes croquet under Laws 19 and 20 unless the turn so ends.

(*b*) If a roquet is deemed to have been made under Law 16 (*c*) the striker takes croquet under Laws 19 and 20 forthwith.

19. Placing Balls for a Croquet Stroke

(*a*) To take croquet the striker must place the striker's ball on the ground in contact with the roqueted ball however he chooses provided that the striker's ball is not in contact with any other ball. Subject to (*b*) below, no other ball may be moved.

(*b*) If the striker is entitled to take croquet from a ball which will form part of a 3-ball or 4-ball group (see Law 16 (*d*)(ii)) when the striker's ball is placed in accordance with (*a*) above, all balls other than the roqueted ball, which may not be moved, become balls in hand immediately and are temporarily removed. They are replaced as follows.

(i) *3-Ball Groups*. The striker must place the striker's ball and the third ball on the ground in contact with the roqueted ball however he chooses provided that the striker's ball is only in contact with the roqueted ball.

(ii) *4-Ball Groups*. The striker must place the striker's ball and one of the remaining balls as in (i) above and must then place the fourth ball on the ground out of contact with the striker's ball but in contact with one or both of the other two balls.

(*c*) When placing the striker's ball for a croquet stroke, the striker may touch or steady the roqueted ball or apply such pressure to it by hand or foot, but not be mallet, as is reasonably necessary to make it hold its position, provided that its original position and rotational alignment are not finally disturbed.

20. Croquet Stroke

(*a*) In a croquet stroke the roqueted ball is known as the croqueted ball.

(*b*) The striker now plays a stroke with the balls placed in accordance with Law 19 and in so doing must play into the croqueted ball and move or shake it (see Law 32 (*a*)(xv)).

(*c*) In a croquet stroke the striker's turn ends if he sends off the court

(i) the croqueted ball, unless it is pegged out in the stroke; or

(ii) the striker's ball, unless it makes a roquet or scores a hoop point for itself in the stroke.

21. Continuation Stroke

After the striker's ball scores a hoop point for itself or after a croquet stroke the striker becomes entitled to play a continuation stroke (see Law 4 (*g*)) unless he is entitled to take croquet immediately or his turn ends under Law 20 (*c*).

(C) MISCELLANEOUS LAWS OF PLAY

22. Ball Moving Between Strokes

(*a*) A ball actually at rest or deemed to be at rest that

moves or apparently scores a point for itself between strokes is replaced immediately and any such point is not scored.

(b) A ball is deemed to be at rest if it appears to be at rest and

- (i) its position has been agreed upon by the striker and the adversary; or
- (ii) its position has been adjudicated upon by a referee; or
- (iii) the striker has taken his stance for the next stroke; or
- (iv) the striker has indicated that his turn has ended.

23. Imperfections on the Surface of the Court

(a) Loose impediments may be removed. Examples include worm casts, twigs, leaves, nuts, refuse and similar material.

(b) The striker may not move any ball on account of an inequality on the surface of the court unless the inequality constitutes special damage, namely a hole on a corner spot or an unrepaired or imperfectly repaired hole or scar. The normal hazards of an indifferent court are not special damage. However, subject to Law 45 (d), balls may be moved no more than is necessary to avoid special damage but never to the advantage of the striker.

(c) When any ball is so moved, the striker must also move any other ball likely to be affected by the next stroke so as to maintain their relative positions, provided that such a ball is not in a critical position. If such a ball is not affected by that stroke and two further strokes, it must be replaced.

(d) Examples of critical positions include positions in or near hoops, wired positions and some positions on or near the yard-line.

(e) Subject to Law 45 (d), the striker may wipe any ball at any time.

24. Interference with a Stroke

(a) Subject to Law 45 (d), if any fixed obstacle or change of level outside the court is likely to impede the playing of the next stroke, the striker may move the striker's ball no more than is necessary to allow a free swing of the mallet.

(b) When the striker's ball is so moved, the striker must

also move any other ball likely to be affected by the next stroke so as to maintain their relative positions, provided that such a ball is not in a critical position (see Law 23 (*d*)). If such a ball is not affected by that stroke and two further strokes, it must be replaced.

25. Local Laws

Clubs or persons controlling courts may submit local laws to suit particular needs to the appropriate Croquet Council for approval. If a local law is so approved, play must be in accordance therewith.

(D) ERRORS AND INTERFERENCE WITH PLAY

26. Definitions

(*a*) *Forestalling Play*. The adversary is said to forestall play when he observes that the striker has committed or is about to commit an error or is about to play a questionable stroke (see Law 45 (*c*)) and requests him to cease play until it can be corrected, investigated or watched. The adversary may forestall play by word or gesture. After play has been forestalled it must cease until the matter about to be raised is settled. If the striker continues to play nonetheless, Law 27 applies except that the striker's turn does not necessarily end.

(*b*) *Limit of Claims*. The limit of claims is the end of the period within which an error can be rectified under these laws. There may be a restricted remedy (see Laws 27 (*b*) and 28 (*c*)(ii)) if an error is discovered after the limit of claims but before the end of the game. Limits of claims are given in detail in the laws concerned and are summarised on page 61.

(*c*) *Condoning*. An error is condoned if it is not discovered before the limit of claims.

(*d*) *End of a Game*. A game ends when the players quit the court in the belief that it has ended or, in a match of more than one game, when they start the next game.

(*e*) *Compound Errors*. If the adversary forestalls play after the striker commits

    (i) more than one error in the same stroke, only the first of the applicable laws to appear below applies; or

(ii) a second error within the limit of claims of an earlier error, only the law applicable to the first error applies. However, in addition, if the striker commits an error under Law 30 (*a*), (*b*) or (*c*) in the same stroke as, or followed by, a fault under Law 32, the turn ends.

27. Playing when not entitled to do so

(*a*) If the striker plays a stroke when not entitled to play and the error is not condoned, that stroke and any subsequent strokes are invalid, no points may be scored for any ball thereby, the balls are replaced in their lawful positions before the first stroke in error and the turn ends. (See Law 38 (*h*)(i) for handicap play.)

(*b*) The error is condoned if it is not discovered before the first stroke of the adversary's next turn. In that event, the first stroke in error and any subsequent strokes are deemed to be valid and the balls are not replaced but only points scored in order are valid. (See Law 38 (*h*)(i) for handicap play.)

28. Playing a Wrong Ball

(*a*) *Playing the Partner Ball at the Start of a Turn*
(i) If the striker, having elected to play with one of the balls of his side under Law 8 (*b*), attempts to play with the partner ball and the error is not condoned, the partner ball is replaced in its lawful position if it has been moved and the striker continues his turn without penalty in accordance with Law 8 (*b*).
(ii) The error is condoned if it is not discovered before the first stroke of the striker's turn. In that event, the partner ball is deemed to be the striker's ball for that turn.

(*b*) *Playing an Adversary Ball That Is Not a Ball In Play*
(i) If the striker plays the first stroke of one of the first four turns of the game (see Law 38 (*c*) for handicap play) with an adversary ball that is not a ball in play and the error is not condoned, all play with that ball is deemed to be valid, the correct ball is interchanged with the adversary ball, any points scored by the

adversary ball for itself are deemed to be scored by the correct ball and the striker, if he is still in play, continues his turn without penalty.

(ii) The error is condoned if it is not discovered before the first stroke of the fifth turn of the game (see Law 38 (*c*) for handicap play). In that event, all play with the adversary ball is deemed to be valid, the balls are not interchanged and the clips are deemed to have been correctly placed at the end of the fourth turn of the game.

(*c*) *All Other Cases*

(i) In all other cases, if the striker plays a wrong ball and the error is not condoned, that stroke and any subsequent strokes are invalid, no points may be scored for any ball thereby, the balls are replaced in their lawful positions before the first stroke in error and the turn ends. If the first stroke in error should have been a croquet stroke, the striker's ball is then placed in any lawful position to take croquet provided that it is not within the yard-line area. If the error is committed in the first stroke of one of the first four turns of the game (see Law 38 (*c*) for handicap play), the correct ball is placed at any point on either baulk-line as the striker chooses. (See Law 38 (*h*)(ii) for handicap play.)

(ii) The error is condoned if it is not discovered before the first stroke of the adversary's next turn. In that event, the first stroke in error and any subsequent strokes are deemed to be valid and the balls are not replaced but the only points scored are

(1) when the striker plays any ball in error, points scored in order for any other ball by peeling; and

(2) when the striker plays the partner ball in error, points scored in order for it (but see Law 40 (*d*) for doubles play).

29. Playing When a Ball Is Misplaced—General Rule

Subject to Law 49 (*b*), if the adversary observes that the striker is about to play a stroke when any ball is misplaced, he must forestall play immediately. In the instances specified below this is his only remedy. If he fails to do so the stroke is deemed to be valid subject to Law 32. If a misplaced ball is not affected by the stroke it must be properly placed before the next stroke. The instances referred to above are

(*a*) playing without first replacing any ball irregularly moved after the end of the preceding stroke;

(*b*) playing the striker's ball when it has been wrongly brought onto the yard-line;

(*c*) playing when a ball has been wrongly left off the court or in the yard-line area;

(*d*) playing the striker's ball from some other position when it should be played from a baulk-line;

(*e*) playing a croquet stroke when the striker's ball is not touching the croqueted ball or is touching another ball; and

(*f*) all other cases except those dealt with in Law 30.

30. Playing When a Ball Is Misplaced—Exceptions

(*a*) *Taking Croquet From a Wrong Ball*

(i) If the striker, being entitled to take croquet, takes croquet from a wrong ball and the error is not condoned, the adversary may elect a replay. If he does so, the first stroke in error and any subsequent stroke are invalid, no points may be scored for any ball thereby, the balls are replaced in their lawful positions before the first stroke in error and the striker continues his turn without penalty by taking croquet from the correct ball. Otherwise, the first stroke in error and any subsequent stroke are deemed to be valid, the croqueted ball is interchanged with the correct ball and the striker continues his turn without penalty as if he had taken croquet from the correct ball.

(ii) The error is condoned if it is not discovered before the next stroke but one of the striker's turn. In that event, the first stroke in error and any subsequent stroke are deemed to be valid, the balls are not replaced or interchanged and play continues as if the roquet preceding the error had been made on the croqueted ball.

(*b*) *Taking Croquet When Not Entitled To Do So*

(i) If the striker takes croquet from a ball that has not been roqueted and the error is not condoned the first stroke in error and any subsequent stroke are invalid, no points may be scored for any ball thereby, the balls are replaced in their lawful positions before the first stroke in error and the striker continues his turn without penalty.

(ii) The error is condoned if it is not discovered before the next stroke but one of the striker's turn. In that event, the first stroke in error and any subsequent stroke are deemed to be valid, the balls are not replaced and play continues as if a roquet had been made on the croqueted ball.

(*c*) *Failing To Take Croquet When Entitled To Do So*

(i) If the striker, being entitled to take croquet, fails to do so and the error is not condoned, the first stroke in error and any subsequent stroke are invalid, no points may be scored for any ball thereby, the balls are replaced in their lawful positions before the first stroke in error and the striker continues his turn without penalty by taking croquet.

(ii) The error is condoned if it is not discovered before the next stroke but one of the striker's turn. In that event, the first stroke in error and any subsequent stroke are deemed to be valid, the balls are not replaced and play continues as if the roquet preceding the error had not been made but the striker had remained entitled to play.

(*d*) *Wrongly Removing or Failing To Remove a Ball From the Game*

(i) If a ball that has not been pegged out is removed from the court or if a ball that has been pegged out is left in play and the error is not condoned all subsequent play is invalid, no points may be scored for any ball thereby, the balls are replaced in their lawful positions before the first stroke in error and the player entitled to play when the error was committed continues his turn without penalty. (See Law 50 (*c*)(i) for tournament play.)

(ii) The error is condoned if it is not discovered before the end of the game (see Law 26 (*d*)).

31. Definition of a Stroke and the Striking Period

(*a*) Subject to (*b*) below, a stroke is any movement of the mallet made with intent to hit the ball or, after the striker has begun to strike, any contact between mallet and ball.

(*b*) A stroke and the striking period begin when the striker begins to swing the mallet with intent to hit the ball. But if the striker deliberately checks the mallet before

(i) there has occurred any contact between mallet and ball, or

(ii) a stroke is deemed to be played under (*d*)(i) below, or

(iii) a fault has been committed.

a stroke is deemed not to have been played and the stroke and the striking period do not begin again until the striker begins again to swing the mallet with intent to hit the ball.

(*c*) The striking period ends when the striker has quitted his stance under control. After this period no fault can be committed under Law 32. The stroke ends when all balls moved in consequence thereof have come to rest or have left the court.

(*d*) A stroke is deemed to be played if the striker

(i) misses the ball; or

(ii) announces his intention to leave it where it lies.

In each case, he thereby becomes responsible for its position for the purpose of Law 13 (*a*)(ii).

32. Faults

(*a*) A fault is committed during the striking period if the striker

(i) touches the head of the mallet with his hand;

(ii) causes or attempts to cause the mallet to strike the ball by kicking or hitting the mallet;

(iii) rests the shaft of the mallet or a hand or arm on the ground;

(iv) rests the shaft of the mallet or a hand or arm directly connected with the stroke against any part of his legs or feet;

(v) strikes the striker's ball with any part of the mallet other than an end-face (see Law 2 (*e*)); an accidental mis-hit in an unhampered stroke is not a fault under this sub-law;

Note: a stroke is hampered if it requires special care because of the proximity of a hoop or the peg or another ball.

(vi) plays a stroke without first striking the striker's ball audibly or distinctly;

(vii) in a croquet stroke, or in a continuation stroke when the balls start in contact, pushes or pulls the striker's ball after the balls have parted contact;

(viii) in a single ball stroke, pushes or pulls the striker's ball;

Note: in (vii) and (viii) above, pushing or pulling means maintaining contact between mallet and ball for an appreciable period or accelerating the mallet head if it has been checked after its initial contact with the ball.

(ix) strikes the striker's ball audibly or distinctly twice in the same stroke or maintains contact between mallet and ball after the striker's ball has hit another ball; a second hit or maintenance of contact caused by making a roquet or by interference by a ball pegged out in the stroke is not a fault under this sub-law;

(x) moves or shakes a ball at rest by hitting a hoop or the peg with the mallet or any part of his body or clothes;

(xi) strikes the striker's ball so as to cause it to touch a hoop or (unless the striker's ball is pegged out in the stroke) the peg when still in contact with the mallet;

(xii) strikes the striker's ball, when it lies in contact with a hoop or (unless the striker's ball is pegged out in the stroke) the peg, otherwise than in a direction away therefrom;

(xiii) touches a ball, other than the striker's ball, with the mallet or allows the striker's ball to re-touch the mallet;

(xiv) touches any ball with any part of his body or clothes;

(xv) in a croquet stroke, plays away from or fails to move or shake the croqueted ball;

(xvi) deliberately plays a stroke that is likely to cause and does cause substantial damage to the court or its equipment.

(*b*) If a fault is committed in a croquet stroke and the striker's turn would otherwise end under Law 20 (*c*), the adversary may waive the fault. In that event, the fault is deemed not to have been committed, any point scored for any ball in that stroke remain valid and the turn ends under Law 20 (*c*).

(*c*) If the striker commits a fault and it is not waived or condoned, the balls are replaced in their lawful positions before the stroke in which the fault was committed, no point may be scored for any ball in that stroke or any subsequent stroke and the turn ends.

(*d*) The fault is condoned if it is not discovered before the next stroke but one of the striker's turn. In that event, the fault is deemed not to have been committed.

33. Interference With a Ball Between Strokes

A ball at rest (see Law 22) that is moved between strokes is replaced without penalty.

34. Interference With a Ball During a Stroke

(*a*) *Interference by the Striker.* If the striker interferes with a ball after the end of the striking period but before the end of the stroke there is no penalty and (*c*) below applies.

(*b*) *Interference by the Adversary or an Outside Agency*
  (i) If the adversary or an outside agency other than weather interferes with a ball during a stroke and materially affects the outcome thereof, the stroke is replayed. In all other cases (*c*) below applies.
  (ii) An outside agency is any agency unconnected with the game. Examples include weather, animals, spectators, the players or equipment of another game, a ball off the court and other stray objects.

(*c*) *Replacement of Ball After Interference.* If the ball was at rest when interfered with, it is replaced. If it was moving, it is placed where it would otherwise have come to rest. After interference a ball cannot make a roquet, be roqueted or score a point or cause another ball to move or score a point.

(*d*) *Interference With a Pegged-out Ball or a Ball That Has Made A Roquet.* The provisions of Laws 15 (*d*) or 18 (*a*)(ii) apply respectively.

35. Playing When Misled

(a) (i) If the striker fails to place any clip correctly at the end of a turn, thereby leading the adversary into a line of play that he would not otherwise have adopted, and the error is not condoned, all play after the adversary was first misled is invalid, no points may be scored for any ball thereby, the balls are replaced in their lawful positions at that time and the adversary continues his turn accordingly. If the adversary was misled on the first stroke of the turn he may play with either of his balls in the replay. (See Law 38 (g) for handicap play and Law 40 (e) for doubles play.)

(ii) The error is condoned if it is not discovered before the second stroke of the offender's next turn. In that event, the clip is placed correctly and the striker continues his turn without penalty.

(b) If the striker plays any stroke or series of strokes in consequence of any false information concerning the state of the game supplied by the adversary, he is entitled to a replay in accordance with (a) above.

(c) If any player sees a misplaced clip he must immediately call attention to it and it must then be properly placed. It is the duty of both players to ensure that the clips are properly placed during the game.

III. OTHER FORMS OF PLAY

(A) ADVANCED SINGLES PLAY

When a game is played under the conditions of advanced singles play the laws of ordinary singles play apply subject to the following additional law.

36. Optional Life or Contact

(a) If the striker's ball scored 1-back or 4-back for itself in the preceding turn, the adversary may start his turn, subject to (c) below,

(i) by playing as the balls lie; or

(ii) by lifting either of his balls, even if it is in contact with one or more balls, and playing it from any point on either baulk-line.

(*b*) If the striker's ball scored 1-back and 4-back for itself in the preceding turn and its partner ball had not scored 1-back before that turn, the adversary may start his turn, subject to (*c*) below,

    (i) as in (*a*)(i) or (*a*)(ii) above; or

    (ii) by lifting either of his balls, even if it is in contact with one or more balls, placing it in contact with any ball and taking croquet forthwith.

(*c*) A player who has pegged out any ball during the game is not entitled to a lift or contact under this law.

(*d*) This law is subject to the provision of Law 6 which requires the partner balls to be played in the third and fourth turns of the game, but (*b*)(ii) above overrides the provision of Law 6 which requires such balls to be played from a baulk-line.

(B) SEMI-ADVANCED SINGLES PLAY

When a game is played under the conditions of semi-advanced singles play, the laws of ordinary singles play apply subject to the following additional law.

37. Optional Lift or Contact

Law 36 applies with the omission of the words "or 4-back" in (*a*) thereof.

(C) HANDICAP SINGLES PLAY

When a game is played under the conditions of handicap singles play, the laws of ordinary singles play apply subject to the following additional laws.

38. Bisques

(*a*) *Definition.* A bisque is an extra turn given in handicap play and can only be played by the striker with the striker's ball of the preceding turn. A half-bisque is a restricted extra turn in which no point can be scored for any ball.

(*b*) *Number To Be Given.* The number of bisques to be given by the lower-handicapped player to the higher is the difference between their handicaps. A bisque may not be split into two half-bisques.

(*c*) *When a Bisque May Be Played.* The player receiving a half-bisque or one or more bisques may play it or them at any time of the game whatsoever subject to Law 50 (*c*)(ii), and, if receiving more than one, in succession. This law overrides Law 6 but references in Law 28 to the first four turns of the game or the fifth turn of the game do not include half-bisques or bisques.

(*d*) *Indication of Intention To Play a Half-Bisque or Bisque*

(i) At the conclusion of a turn the striker must give a clear indication of his intention before playing a half-bisque or bisque. If he fails to do so but continues to play, Law 27 applies. Once the error has been rectified, the striker may then play a half-bisque or bisque.

(ii) If the striker is entitled to play either a half-bisque or a bisque and indicates an intention of playing one or the other, he may change his mind at any time before playing a stroke provided that he indicates his revised intention accordingly. If he indicates an intention of playing one or the other without specifying which, he is deemed to have indicated an intention of playing a bisque.

(iii) If the striker has played all the strokes to which he is entitled and indicates that he is not going to play a half-bisque or bisque, either by words or by quitting the court, he may not change his mind. The adversary must not start his turn until the striker has so indicated.

(*e*) *The Adversary's Duty.* The adversary must forestall play if he observes that the striker is about to play a half-bisque or bisque before he has played all the strokes that he is entitled to play. If the adversary fails to do so the striker is deemed to have played the half-bisque or bisque validly.

(*f*) *Playing a Wrong Ball.* Notwithstanding (*a*) above, if the striker plays a wrong ball under Law 28 (*c*) in the first stroke of a non-bisque turn and the error is not condoned, he may play with either of his balls if he then elects to play a half-bisque or bisque.

(*g*) *Playing when Misled*. The expression "line of play" in Law 35 (*a*)(i) includes a decision whether or not to play a half-bisque or bisque.

(*h*) *Restoration of Bisques After Certain Errors*

(i) *Law 27*. If the striker plays when not entitled to do so, any half-bisque or bisque played after the first stroke in error is restored if the error is discovered before the end of the game.

(ii) *Law 28* (*c*). If the striker plays a wrong ball, any half-bisque or bisque played after the first stroke in error is only restored if the error is discovered before the first stroke of the adversary's next turn.

39. Pegging Out

The striker may not peg out the striker's ball unless the partner ball is a rover or an adversary's ball has been pegged out. If he does so and removes the striker's ball from the court, Law 30 (*d*) applies.

(D) DOUBLES PLAY

40. General

(*a*) *An Outline of the Game*. The game is played between two sides, each of two players. One player of each side plays throughout with one ball of the side and his partner with the other.

(*b*) *Assistance to Partner*. A player may advise his partner and assist in the playing of a stroke by indicating the direction in which the mallet is to be swung and by placing the balls for a croquet stroke. However, when the stroke is actually played, he must stand well clear of the striker or any spot which might assist the striker in gauging the strength or direction of the stroke.

(*c*) *Modification of Terms*. In these laws "partner's ball" is substituted for "partner ball" and, where appropriate, including Law 34, the word "player" includes "side" and the word "striker" includes "the striker's partner".

(*d*) *Playing a Wrong Ball.* Laws 28 (*a*) and (*c*)(ii)(2) do not apply.

(*e*) *Playing when Misled.* If a side is entitled to replay from the start of a turn under Law 35, either player may play.

41. Ordinary Doubles Play

When a game is played under the conditions of ordinary doubles play, the laws of ordinary singles play apply subject to Law 40.

42. Advanced and Semi-Advanced Doubles Play

When a game is played under the conditions of advanced or semi-advanced doubles play, the laws of ordinary doubles play apply subject to Law 36 or 37 respectively.

43. Handicap Doubles Play

When a game is played under the conditions of handicap doubles play, the laws of ordinary doubles play apply subject to Laws 38 and 39 and the following additional laws.

(*a*) *Number of Bisques To Be Given.* Law 38 (*b*) does not apply. The number of bisques to be given by the lower-handicapped side to the higher is half the difference between their aggregate handicaps. A fraction of a bisque above a half is counted as one bisque, a fraction below a half as a half-bisque.

(*b*) *Playing a Wrong Ball.* Law 38 (*f*) does not apply. If the striker plays a wrong ball under Law 28 (*c*) in the first stroke of a non-bisque turn and the error is not condoned, either he or his partner may play a half-bisque thereafter.

(*c*) *Peels.* The striker may not peel his partner's ball through more than four hoops (see Law 55 (*b*) for modified games).

IV. CUSTOMS OF THE GAME

44. The State of the Game

A player is entitled to ask his adversary about the state of the game at all times. Questions concerning the correct positions of the balls or clips, whether an error has been committed, which player is responsible for the position of a ball, whether a ball has been hit or has run a hoop in order or is in a position to do so and any similar matters relate to the state of the game.

45. Referees of the Game

(a) *The Players as Joint Referees of the Game.* The players act as referees of the game in the absence of a referee in charge. However, the adversary is not obliged to watch the game and if he fails to do so the striker is the sole referee for that period. In doubles play, all four players act as referees of the game.

(b) *Certain Specified Duties of a Referee of the Game.* As a referee of the game the striker must immediately announce any error he believes or suspects he may have committed. Likewise, the adversary must immediately draw attention to any error he observes, subject to Law 49 (b), notwithstanding that it may be to his disadvantage. Further similar but not exhaustive examples are: if the adversary observes the striker about to leave the court wrongly believing that his turn has ended, he must inform him that he must complete his turn by playing another stroke or deeming it to have been played; in handicap play, if the striker announces his intention of playing a half-bisque or bisque before his previous turn has ended, the adversary must similarly inform him (see Law 38 (e)); a player must immediately call attention to a misplaced clip (see Law 35 (c)); a player must on request give the adversary any information concerning the state of the game (see Law 44).

(c) *Questionable Strokes.* If the striker suspects that either the fairness or the effect of his next stroke may be doubtful, that stroke is a questionable stroke. He must consult the adversary before playing and the stroke must then be specially watched, preferably by a referee or other independent person if available or, failing these, by the adversary. It is the striker's duty to take the initiative in this respect but if he fails to do so the adversary should forestall play, and Law 26 (a) then applies.

(d) *Consulting the Adversary.* The striker must not test whether a ball has run a hoop in order by placing an object against the hoop without first consulting the adversary. The test may then be carried out in his presence or, if either so desires, by a referee or other independent person if available. The same principle applies to testing whether a ball is in position to run a hoop in order; whether a ball is off the court; whether the striker is entitled to a wiring lift; whether a ball may be moved under Laws 23 or 24; or whether a ball may be wiped under Law 23 (*e*) if its position is critical.

(*e*) *The Striker as the Active Referee.* The adversary must not follow the striker around the court and should allow most decisions to be made by the striker without reference to himself, as the striker is usually in a better position to give a correct decision. If, however, a close decision has to be made and the adversary is in at least as good a position to give that decision, the striker must seek confirmation of his opinion before continuing to play.

(*f*) *When the Players' Opinions Differ.* If a ball has to be replaced because of the carelessness of a player, the offender should normally defer to the opinion of the other. When the question is whether a ball has been hit or has moved, the positive opinion is generally to be preferred to the negative opinion. If there are any reliable witnesses present the players should agree to consult them to resolve differences but no player may consult a witness without the express permission of the other.

46. Interruption of the Striker and Presence on Court

(*a*) The adversary must not interrupt the striker except to discharge his duty as a referee of the game.

(*b*) A player must not ordinarily remain on the court when his adversary is playing or move onto it until the turn has ended and, in handicap play, until his adversary has indicated that he does not intend to take a half-bisque or bisque.

47. Replacing Yard-line Balls

The striker must replace yard-line balls with his back to the court and take special care to ensure that such replacement is accurate.

48. Expedition in Play

(*a*) The striker must position the balls and play his strokes with reasonable despatch. In time-limited games the adversary should anticipate as far as possible with which ball he will play so that he may waste no time in approaching it at the start of his turn. In handicap play, the striker must indicate at the earliest opportunity whether or not he intends to play a half-bisque or bisque. In doubles play, time must not be wasted in prolonged discussion.

(*b*) The striker may not ask a referee to test whether or not one ball is wired from another unless he is claiming a wiring life in the turn about to be played. In the interests of expedition he must rely on an unaided ocular test.

49. Advice and Aids

(*a*) A player is not entitled to receive advice from anyone, except his partner in doubles play, and should not take advantage of unsolicited information or advice.

(*b*) The adversary must not warn the striker that he is about to run a wrong hoop or, unless Law 28 (*a*) or (*b*) will apply, that he is about to play a wrong ball. In a double-banked game, playing with a ball of the other game does not constitute playing a wrong ball and the adversary should forestall play.

(*c*) The striker may not make use of technical assistance from books or notes or artificial aids such as coins to assist him in placing a ball for a stroke, except in connection with its replacement under Laws 23 or 24.

(*d*) No mark or marker may be made or placed inside or outside the court to assist the striker in gauging the strength or direction of a stroke.

(*e*) During a game a ball may not be used as a trial ball for any purpose.

50. Tournament and Match Play

In tournaments and matches the following additional laws apply.

(*a*) *Questionable Strokes*. A referee must always be called before a questionable stroke is played and to decide all disputes. If both the striker and the adversary fail to call a referee before what the adversary should have recognised as a questionable stroke, the adversary may not appeal but should request the striker to take the initiative in calling a referee when another questionable stroke is about to be played.

(*b*) *Repeated Faults*. If the adversary believes that the striker is repeatedly committing faults in strokes that would not ordinarily require the presence of a referee, he should inform the striker and call a referee to watch a stroke or series of strokes or to take charge of the game temporarily. The striker has no justification for taking offence at this procedure as players may genuinely differ as to what is permitted under Law 32.

(*c*) *Time-Limited Games*
(i) *Law 30 (d)(i)*. If the provisions of Law 30 (*d*)(i) apply, any time lost is restored.
(ii) *Handicap Play*. Law 38 (*c*) applies subject to any restrictions in the Regulations for Tournaments (see Regulation 13 (*d*)).

(*d*) *Hoop Dimensions*. The distance between the inner surfaces of the uprights must be $3\frac{3}{4}$ inches plus or minus $\frac{1}{32}$ inch. However, in specially advertised events this dimension may be reduced to $3\frac{11}{16}$ inches with an upward tolerance of $\frac{1}{32}$ inch.

51. Emergency Law

Any infringement of these laws for which no penalty is prescribed or any situation that does not appear to be covered by these laws must be dealt with as best meets the justice of the case.

V. MODIFIED GAMES AND COURTS

52. Modified Games

The standard game of 26 points may be modified as follows.

(*a*) *22 Point Game*. The game is started with all the clips on hoop 3.

(*b*) *18 Point Game*. The following variations are permitted.

   (i) The game is started with all the clips on hoop 5

  (ii) The game is started with all the clips on hoop 1 and the peg point is the next point in order after 2-back.

 (iii) The standard setting is modified by removing the centre hoops; the game is started with all the clips on hoop 1, 1-back is the next point in order after hoop 4 and the peg point is the next point in order after 4-back.

 (iv) The game is started with all the clips on hoop 1 but as soon as one of the balls of a side runs or is peeled through hoop 1 in order, 3-back becomes the next hoop in order for its partner ball and the appropriate clip is placed on 3-back immediately. This variation is for singles play only.

    (*c*) *14 Point Game*. The game is started with all the clips on hoop 1 and the peg point is the next point in order after hoop 6.

53. Advanced Play in Modified Games

Law 36 applies with the omission of Law 36 (*b*). However, in certain of the variations set out in Law 52, the following hoops are substituted for 1-back and 4-back in Law 36 (*a*).

    (*a*) *18 Point Game*

        Law 52 (*b*)(ii). Hoop 4 and hoop 6;

        Law 52 (*b*)(iii). Hoop 4 and 2-back;

    (*b*) *14 Point Game*

        Law 52 (*c*). Hoop 4 only.

54. Semi-Advanced Play in Modified Games

Law 36 applies with the omission of Law 36 (*b*) and the words "or 4-back" in Law 36 (*a*). In addition, in the variations listed in Law 53, hoop 4 is substituted for 1-back.

55. Handicap Play in Modified Games

    (*a*) *Bisques*. The number of bisques to be given in a modified game is the number that would be given under Law 38 (*b*) in singles play or under Law 43 (*a*) in doubles play (before rounding) scaled down in accordance with Schedule 1 on page 60.

(*b*) *Peels*. In handicap doubles play, Law 43 (*c*) is modified as follows.

  (i) 22 or 18 point games: three hoops;

  (ii) 14 point games: two hoops.

56. Smaller Courts

  (*a*) *Smaller Courts of Standard Proportions*

  (i) *Dimensions*. The standard length unit is 7 yards. If the available area is too small to accommodate a standard court, a smaller court may be laid out in accordance with Part 1 of these laws by retaining the proportions of five length units by four length units and using a smaller length unit.

  (ii) *Baulk-lines*. Law 1 (*e*) applies with a reduced length for each baulk-line.

  (iii) *Permitted Tolerance*. The tolerance specified in Law 1 (*g*) for the standard court is retained for a modified court.

  (*b*) *Smaller Courts of Other Proportions*. The appropriate Croquet Council has power to approve other settings and dimensions for smaller courts.

APPENDIX 1

METRIC EQUIVALENTS OF STANDARD DIMENSIONS

Law	Subject	Imperial Units	Metric Equivalents
1	*The Standard Court*	35 yards	32.0 metres
		28 yards	25.6 metres
		13 yards	11.9 metres
		7 yards	6.4 metres
		1 yard	0.9 metres
2 (*a*)	*The Peg*	18 inches	450 millimetres
		6 inches	150 millimetres
		$1\frac{1}{2}$ inches	38 millimetres
2 (*b*)	*Hoops*	12 inches	300 millimetres
		4 inches	100 millimetres
		$3\frac{3}{4}$ inches	95 millimetres

Law	Subject	Imperial Units	Metric Equivalents
		$3\frac{11}{16}$ inches	93.5 millimetres
		$\frac{5}{8}$ inch	16 millimetres
		$\frac{1}{32}$ inch	0.8 millimetres
2 (c)	Balls	$3\frac{5}{8}$ inches	92 millimetres
		$\frac{1}{32}$ inch	0.8 millimetres
		16 ounces	454 grams
		$\frac{1}{4}$ ounce	7 grams
3 (a)	Corner Flags	12 inches	300 millimetres
3 (b)	Corner Pegs	3 inches	75 millimetres
		$\frac{3}{4}$ inch	19 millimetres

APPENDIX 2

GUIDE TO CONDUCT IN DOUBLE-BANKED GAMES

(A) CUSTOMS

1. General

The players of each game should be aware of course of play in the other game at all times, but especially when stepping onto the court. In particular, they should not cross another player's line of aim.

2. Expedition in Play (Law 48)

Players should be especially conscious of the need for expedition in play. In doubles play, mid-court conferences should be avoided if possible.

3. Precedence

(a) If one player is making a break, he should normally be given precedence.

(b) If two players are approaching the same hoop and both are making breaks, precedence should normally be given to the player who is most likely to get clear of the hoop first (subject to 4 (c) below).

(c) If two players are approaching the same hoop but neither is making a break, precedence should normally be given to the player who has made the first roquet towards the hoop.

4. Marking

(*a*) All players should carry ball markers (e.g. small coins).

(*b*) If a ball from the other game is not in a critical position and might interfere with a player's next stroke, its position may be marked and it may be removed temporarily with the permission of the players of the other game. Examples of critical positions include positions in or near hoops, wired positions and some positions on or near the yard-line.

(*c*) If a ball from the other game is in a critical position and might so interfere, the player should normally interrupt his turn until it has been removed in the normal course of play in the other game.

(B) LAWS

5. Interference by Balls or Players of the Other Game

(*a*) If a ball of one game has finally come to rest and is moved by a ball or player of the other game, it is replaced without penalty under Law 33.

(*b*) If a ball of one game is interfered with during a stroke by a ball or player of the other game, Law 34 (*b*) applies.

(C) MANAGEMENT

6. Start of Games

The manager may direct play in a second game to start as soon as the fifth turn has been played in the first game or after a specified length of time.

7. Timed Games

The manager may allow extra time for double-banked games under Regulation 12 (*f*)(ix).

APPENDIX 3

FULL BISQUE HANDICAP PLAY

When a game is played under the conditions of full bisque handicap play, the laws of handicap play apply subject to the following modifications.

1. The Base Handicap

The base handicap is scratch unless agreed or directed to be greater than scratch.

2. Singles Play

If both players have handicaps that are greater than the base handicap, the first sentence of Law 38 (*b*) does not apply and each player receives a number of bisques equal to the difference between his handicap and the base handicap.

3. Doubles Play

If both sides have aggregate handicaps that are greater than twice the base handicap, the second sentence of Law 43 (*a*) does not apply and each side receives a number of bisques equal to half the difference between its aggregate handicap and twice the base handicap. A player whose handicap is lower than the base handicap may play a half-bisque but may not play a bisque.

APPENDIX 4

ALTERNATE STROKE HANDICAP DOUBLES PLAY

When a handicap doubles game is played under the conditions of alternate stroke play, the laws of handicap doubles play apply subject to the following modifications.

1. Non-Application of Certain Laws

Laws 38 (*f*), 40 (*a*) and 43 (*b*) do not apply.

2. Alternate Stroke Play

Subject to Paragraph 3 below, the players of each side play

alternate strokes throughout the game and from turn to turn, whether such turns are ordinary turns, half-bisques or bisques. Thus the partner of the player who played the last stroke of a turn plays the first stroke of his side's next turn.

3. Errors

(*a*) *Playing Out of Sequence*

(i) If an adversary observes that the striker is about to play out of sequence, he must forestall play immediately.

(ii) If the striker plays out of sequence and the error is not condoned, that stroke and any subsequent stroke are invalid, no points can be scored thereby, the balls are replaced in their lawful positions before the first stroke in error, any half-bisque or bisque played after the error is restored and the correct player plays without penalty.

(iii) The error is condoned if it is not discovered before the offending side has played two further strokes or before the first stroke of the other side's next turn. In that event, the first stroke in error and any subsequent stroke are deemed to be valid, all points scored thereby remain valid and play continues according to the sequence thereby established.

(*b*) *Other Invalid Play*. If balls are replaced after invalid play (see Laws 27, 28, 30 and 35), the player who played the first stroke in error plays the first stroke of his side's next turn.

(*c*) *Faults*. If the balls are replaced after a fault, the partner of the player who committed the fault plays the first stroke of his side's next turn.

LAWS OF GOLF CROQUET

1. General

The Laws of Association Croquet relating to ordinary singles and doubles play and handicap singles and doubles play apply subject to the following modifications.

2. The Game

(*a*) All balls are always for the same hoop and a point is scored for the side whose ball first runs the hoop.

(*b*) A game is a contest for the best of either 13 or 19 points and ends as soon as one side has scored a majority of the points to be played. The score is kept by declaring a side to be one or more points up or down or all square as the case may be.

(*c*) Each turn consists of one stroke. Law 4 and the laws relating to wiring lifts (Law 13), peg points (Law 15), roquets (Laws 16 to 18), croquet strokes (Laws 19 and 20) and continuation strokes (Law 21) do not apply.

(*d*) Law 8 does not apply and the balls are played in the sequence blue, red, black, yellow (or green, pink, brown, white). Thus if yellow is played in one stroke, blue will be played in the following stroke.

3. The Course

(*a*) Law 6 does not apply and the balls are played into the game from the B baulk-line only.

(*b*) In a 13 point game the first 12 points are scored by contesting all the hoops in the same order as in Association Croquet. The final point is scored by contesting hoop 3 again.

(*c*) In a 19 point game the first 12 points are scored by contesting all the hoops in the same order as in Association Croquet. The next 6 points are scored by contesting 1-back to rover again. The final point is scored by contesting hoop 3 again.

4. Hoop Point

(*a*) Law 14 (*c*) does not apply and, subject to (*b*) below, a ball must complete the running of a hoop in order in one turn to score the point.

(*b*) If the striker causes an adversary ball partly to run a hoop in order that ball may score the point by completing the running of the hoop in a subsequent turn.

(*c*) If a ball runs two hoops in order in one stroke both points are scored.

5. Errors

(*a*) *Failing to Contest the Hoop in Order*

(i) The striker must always play to contest the hoop in order and must never play solely to gain an advantage for the next hoop in order. If he does do and the error is not condoned, the stroke is invalid, the balls are replaced in the positions they occupied before that stroke and the turn ends.

(ii) The error is condoned if it is not discovered before the next stroke is played. In that event the stroke in error is deemed to be valid.

(*b*) *Playing Out of Sequence*

(i) If a player plays out of sequence and the error is not condoned, the first stroke in error and all subsequent strokes are invalid, the balls are replaced in their lawful positions before the first stroke in error and the player entitled to play then plays.

(ii) The error is condoned if it is not discovered before the end of the game.

(*c*) *Playing a Wrong Ball*

(i) If the striker plays a wrong ball and the error is not condoned, the first stroke in error and all subsequent strokes are invalid, the balls are replaced in their lawful positions before the first stroke in error and the striker then plays with the correct ball.

(ii) The error is condoned if it is not discovered before the end of the game.

(*d*) *Jump Stroke*

(i) The striker must not play a deliberate jump stroke. If he does so and the error is not condoned, any point scored for his side thereby is invalid and all balls affected by the stroke may be replaced in their lawful positions at the option of the adversary.

(ii) The error is condoned if it is not discovered before the next stroke is played. In that event, the stroke in error is deemed to be valid.

6. Handicaps

Unless a player has been given a special Golf Croquet

handicap, his handicap shall be determined from his Association Croquet handicap in accordance with the following table.

Association Croquet Handicap	13 Point Game Handicap	19 Point Game Handicap
−5 to −1	0	0
−$\frac{1}{2}$ to 2	1	$1\frac{1}{2}$
$2\frac{1}{2}$ to 6	2	3
$6\frac{1}{2}$ to 9	3	$4\frac{1}{2}$
10 to 12	4	6
13 to 16	5	$7\frac{1}{2}$

The Laws of
Eton Fives

Eton Fives

DEFINITIONS

The Court is enclosed on three sides and open at the back. The "front wall" is the wall facing the player, and the "right-hand" and "left-hand" walls are the walls on his right hand and left hand respectively.

The "step" is a shallow step dividing the court into two portions, an " upper" or "top" and a "lower" or "bottom" "court" or "step". The vertical face of the "step" does not reckon as part of the floor of the court.

The "pepper-box" is a buttress projecting from the left-hand wall. With the "step", it encloses a small square portion of the floor called "Dead Man's Hole".

The "line" is the lower angle of the ledge running across the front wall, at the height of 4 ft 6in.

A vertical line is marked on the front wall at a distance of 3 ft 8 in from the right-hand wall.

1. The ball must in every case be hit up; i.e., it must be returned against the front wall on or above the line. Any ball which drops on the top of any of the walls or of the coping, or which hits any part of the roof or the sides of the court above the coping, or which touches the ground first outside the court, or touches any person or object outside the court before the first bound except in the case of a Blackguard (see Law 6 (*b*)) other than a Game Ball (see Law 11)), is out of court and counts against the striker. The sides and lower face of the coping shall be in.

2. The ball must be fairly hit with a single blow of the hand or hands or wrist, and must not touch any other part of the striker's person under penalty of losing the stroke. It must not be caught, carried, or held in any way, except to serve or to stop a ball as provided for in Law 6. A ball taken with both hands or with a cupped hand may often be technically held, in

which case the striker should declare a hold and allow the point to go against him.

Position of the Players

3. The game, is played by four persons, two against two. Thus, if A and B (with first service) play C and D, A, the server, should stand in the upper court and his side is said to be up. C should stand in the lower court ready to return the service, and his side is said to be down. B and D also stand in the lower court, B having choice of position.

Choice of First Service

4. The choice of first service shall be decided by one of the home side tossing a coin or placing the ball behind his back in one of his hands and one of the opposing side calling. The first server in each game also cuts first (see Law 6 for definition of, and rules for, the first cut) for his side after he and his partner have been sent down; thereafter the player who has the second hand of a service cuts first. If in the first game A serves first and C cuts, then in the second game C serves first and A cuts; in the third game B serves first and D cuts; in the fourth game D serves first and B cuts; and in the fifth game A again serves first and C cuts.

The Service

5. The ball when served must hit first the front wall above the line and then the right-hand wall, and must fall in the lower court. The player who is cutting need not return the first or any service until he gets one to his mind, and if he fails to return the service above the line no stroke is counted. A service which goes out of court carries no penalty and may be taken by the player making the first cut.

The First Cut

6. (a) Only the player who is cutting may return the service, and he may do so only between the first and second bounds. This return is called the "First Cut". He must return it so that it should hit either (1) first the right-hand wall and subsequently the front wall above the line; or (2) first the front wall above

the line between the right-hand wall and the vertical line marked on the front wall. In both cases the ball may afterwards hit any wall or walls and may fall anywhere in the upper or lower court.

(*b*) If the first cut is hit in such a way that it will probably fall out of court, the side which is down may, *without interference*, touch the ball so that it falls within the court, or catch it, provided that the player touching or catching the ball has one or both feet on the floor of the court, or, if he jumps for the purpose, alights on the floor of the court with the foot which first touches the ground. If the ball is caught, no stroke is counted; if only touched, one of the side which is up may, if he pleases, return the ball and neither of the opposing side may interfere with his shot; if he fails to return the ball up, no stroke is counted.

(*c*) If the first cut hits the front wall above the line but to the left of the vertical line marked on the front wall and without first touching the right-hand wall, this shot is called a "Blackguard". It may be returned before the second bound by either the server or his partner at their option, but if it is not returned above the line, no stroke is counted. The last sentence does not apply at Game Ball (see Law 11).

The Rally

7. After the service and the first cut the ball is returned alternately by either side. It may be returned by either of the partners before the first or second bound, and may or may not hit the side walls. A rally is lost to his side by the player who fails to return the ball above the line, or hits it out of court.

Lets

8. (*a*) A let may be *requested* when a player is in any way prevented from returning or impeded in his attempt to return the ball by one of the opposite side. A let may not be requested when the ball is returned above the line, whether or not it falls out of court, nor when a player is impeded by bystanders.

(*b*) A ball which would have hit the front wall above the line, but is prevented from doing so by one of the opposite side, counts as a let, unless it first strikes one of the opposite side, and thereafter the front wall above the line, in which case it counts as up; but if it first strikes one of the same side, it does not count as up, whether it goes up or not. A ball that was going to hit below the front line but first hits an opponent and then goes above the line shall be deemed to be up.

(c) If a ball after going up from a return by A or B strikes A or B before the second bound, it shall count as a let if C or D consider they could have returned it, if it had not hit A or B, except that if the ball clearly would have fallen out of court it shall count against A and B (subject to the provisions of Law 6 relating to a first cut). C or D may, however, elect to return the ball and continue the rally. If not returned up, it counts as a let. If returned above the line, a let may not be requested, whether or not it falls out of court.

(d) Where a ball becomes lodged on any ledge within the court before the second bound, it shall count as a let.

NOTE.—*If there is no umpire, a request for a let is generally allowed, except where this Law expressly provides that no let can be claimed.*

Scoring

9. A game is won by the side which first obtains twelve points, except as provided in Law 12. Matches generally consist of the best of five games. Only the side which is up may score points. When A is put out B takes his place. When B is out, the side is out and their opponents go up, the player who has been cutting being the first hand to go up, except as provided in Law 10. The result of each rally, except in the case of a let, is either to add one to the score of the side which is up, or to put one of them out, as the case may be.

Two Down

10. If C loses one point to the opposite side when he is cutting, he is said to be one down. If he loses a second point, he is said to be two down, and D takes his place; if D in turn loses two points, he is two down and C cuts again; and so on until both A and B are put out; provided that he who was two down first is then the first to go up; but if, through inadvertence or otherwise, he does not do so, the error cannot be corrected after

service has been returned. All balls which fall in the upper court belong to the player who is cutting. Failure to return a ball out of Dead Man's Hole does not count as one down against the player who is cutting. The player who is cutting cannot be two down at Game Ball.

Game Ball

11. When the side which is serving requires one point for game, this is called Game Ball and the following rules must be observed:

(*a*) The player serving must stand with at least one foot in the lower court, and he may not place both feet on the top step until the player who is cutting has hit the ball. If he forgets to stand thus, and serves the ball with both feet on the top step, the player who is cutting, or his partner, may try to catch the ball before it bounds. If they succeed in this, the side serving is out. If, however, they do not succeed in catching the ball, or if the player serving or his partner manage to touch the ball first, or if it hits the ground before being touched, it counts neither way. A player may remind his partner of this Law. Where the server places both feet on the top step after the first bound but before the player who is cutting has hit the ball a let may be claimed by the side cutting.

(*b*) When the ball is properly served, the player who is cutting may return the first cut against any part of the front wall above the line, with or without hitting the side walls.

(*c*) The side which is down may not touch or catch a game ball cut which is going out of Court (see Law 6 *(c)*).

Setting

12. If the score is at 10 all, the game may, at the option of the side which is cutting, be set to 5 or 3, or not at all; if 11 all, to 3 or not at all. If the game is set, Law 11 shall apply at 4 or 2 respectively. At 14 all or 12 all in the first case, or at 13 all in the second case, or at 11 all if the game is not set, the game shall be decided by "sudden death", Law 11 being observed on either side.

The Rules of
Rugby Fives

Rugby Fives

As approved by the Rugby Fives Association

DEFINITIONS

The game is played in a court enclosed by four walls. The "front" wall is distinguished by a board of wood running across it at an even height from the floor.

The wall opposite the front wall is the "back" wall, and the two adjoining walls, as the players stand facing the front wall, are respectively the "right" side wall and the "left" side wall.

The game may be played between two or four players i.e., as Singles or Doubles.

Server and Receiver. The player first hitting the ball is the "server" (who is said to be "out" or "down"), his opponent being known as the "receiver" (who is said to be "in" or "up").

"Up". The ball is said to be "up" when it is hit before the second bounce, strikes the front wall above the board, and does not leave the confines of the playing surface.

RULES OF THE SINGLES GAME

1.

At the commencement of a game a preliminary rally shall be played. The winner of this becomes the receiver, and the loser, the server.

2.

At the start of a rally the ball is thrown up so that it first strikes the front wall above the board and then one of the side walls, in such a manner as the server desires. The server may either throw up the ball for himself or request the receiver to do so. When the receiver is required to throw up the ball for the server, he shall not be required to do so in such a manner as to penalise himself in his attempt to return the service.

3.

The server may not serve unless the ball has been thrown up as described in Rule 2.

4. Service

The server shall serve in such a way that after the first bounce and before the second bounce the ball strikes first the side wall against which it has been thrown and then the front wall above the board.

5.

After the service and its return, the opponents shall alternately hit the ball, before the second bounce, on to the front wall above the board, either directly or after it has hit the side and/or back walls. No second attempt may be made to hit a ball after it has once been touched.

6. Blackguard

A service which hits the front wall above the board without having first touched the near side wall, but remains within the confines of the playing surface of the court, is called a "blackguard". The receiver may return a blackguard provided he calls out his intention to do before striking the ball. Such decision shall be irrevocable.

The server may not intentionally stop a blackguard. (See Rule 8(*b*) and (*d*).)

7. Scoring

The player who first scores 15 points (except as provided when the score reaches 14–14) wins the game.

Only the receiver can score points. When the receiver wins a rally, he scores one point. When the server wins a rally, he becomes receiver for the next rally.

Should each player score 14 points, the first player to reach 16 points wins the game.

8.

A rally is won by a player if:

(*a*) His opponent fails to hit the ball (except as provided under Rule 9(*d*)), or hits it after the second bounce, or hits it on to or below the board, or against the roof, or otherwise out of the confines of the playing surface, or on to the floor before hitting the front wall.

NOTE. — *When the receiver requires one point to win the game, the server is not penalised if he serves not more than twice incorrectly. The third service must be right or the server loses the point and game.*

(*b*) His opponent, being server, serves more than two consecutive untaken blackguards, or intentionally stops a blackguard.

(*c*) His opponent strikes him with a ball which would not have gone "up". (See Rule 9(*a*).)

(*d*) His opponent causes the ball, after it has hit the front wall, to strike himself before it has bounced. This also applies to blackguards.

(*e*) His opponent hits the ball otherwise than with the hand or forearm.

9. Lets

A let is allowed, and the rally shall not count if:

(*a*) A player strikes his opponent with a ball which would have gone "up".

(*b*) A player causes the ball, after it has hit the front wall, to strike himself after it has bounced.

(*c*) A player is prevented by his opponent from correctly returning the ball. Should a player, though impeded, hit the ball so that it go "up" he may claim a let at once; otherwise the rally shall continue.

(*d*) The Server, when about to serve, fails to hit the ball, or changes his mind and calls out "No" before hitting the ball, even if it accidentally goes "up".

10.

The umpire's decision is final.

RULES OF THE DOUBLES GAME

The Rules of the Singles Game shall apply to the Doubles Game, and wherever the words "server", "receiver", "opponent", or "player" are used in the Rules of the Singles Game, such words shall, whenever possible, be taken to include his partner in the Doubles Game. Thus, if the duration of the preliminary rally requires their participation, all four players shall take part.

1.

The receiver and his partner are known as "hands". The side winning the preliminary rally may choose whether to serve or receive and the side receiving shall have only one hand.

2.

The receiver remains "in" until his side loses a rally, whereupon his partner shall receive (except as provided for in Rule 1). When his side loses another rally, his opponents become receivers.

3.

The side that is "down" must change servers after every point scored by their opponents.

4.

If the wrong player serves or receives, the mistake must be pointed out before the start of the next rally, otherwise the rally counts; but at the next "hand", the players shall revert to their correct order.

5.

Only the receiver may return the service; either he or his partner may elect to take a blackguard. If either of them says "Yes" to a blackguard, the rally commences.

RULES OF MATCH PLAY

(*a*) For the preliminary rally (see Rule 1 of the Rules of Singles game) the receiver and server shall be decided by tossing—the winner to make his choice.

(*b*) A preliminary rally shall not be played at the beginning of the second and each subsequent game of a match and the winner of the previous game shall continue to receive. In doubles the winners shall have only one "hand".

(*c*) A new ball shall be taken before the start of each game if either side wishes it. A defective ball may be replaced at any time, if in the opinion of the umpire, a change is desirable. In selecting a replacement, the umpire shall take into account the time during which the defective ball has been in play.

(*d*) A let shall be allowed as in Rule 9(*a*), (*b*) and (*c*) only on a player's successful appeal to the umpire.

(*e*) A player shall not leave the court during a game, except with the permission of the umpire.

(*f*) A player shall not unreasonably delay between rallies. The umpire shall at once order the game to continue, if, in his opinion, such delay is occurring. If, after further warning by the umpire, a player is responsible for further delay or delays, the umpire may award the game (15 points or when appropriate 16 points) to the opponent or opponents of the defaulting player. In this event the losing side retains any points it may have scored.

(*g*) If a player, by reason of injury or ill-health, is, in the opinion of the umpire, unfit to continue a game, the umpire shall stop the game and award it to that player's opponent or opponents. Points shall be allotted as in Rule (*f*).

(*h*) In a match consisting of more than one game, not more than three minutes' interval shall be allowed between games.

The Laws of
Association Football

Association Football

1. THE FIELD OF PLAY

The Field of Play and appurtenances shall be as shown in the following plan:

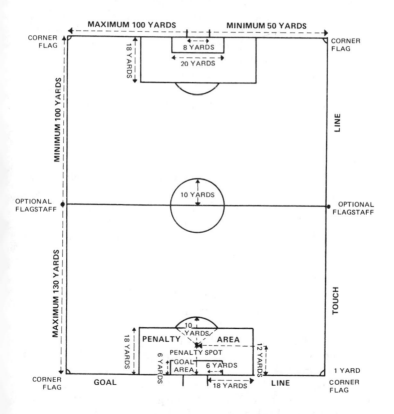

1. Dimensions

The field of play shall be rectangular, its length being not more than 130 yd nor less than 100 yd and its breadth not more than 100 yd nor less than 50 yd. (In International Matches the length shall be not more than 120 yd nor less than 110 yd and the breadth not more than 80 yd nor less than 70 yd.) The length shall in all cases exceed the breadth.

2. Marking

The field of play shall be marked with distinctive lines, not more than 5 in in width, not by a **V**-shaped rut, in accordance with the plan, the longer boundary lines being called the touch-lines and the shorter the goal-lines. A flag on a post not less than 5 ft high and having a non-pointed top, shall be placed at each corner; a similar flag-post may be placed opposite the halfway-line on each side of the field of play, not less than 1 yd outside the touch-line. A halfway-line shall be marked out across the field of play. The centre of the field of play shall be indicated by a suitable mark and a circle with a 10 yd radius shall be marked round it.

3. The Goal-Area

At each end of the field of play two lines shall be drawn at right angles to the goal-line, 6 yd from each goal-post. These shall extend into the field of play for a distance of 6 yd and shall be joined by a line drawn parallel with the goal-line. Each of the spaces enclosed by these lines and the goal-line shall be called the goal-area.

4. The Penalty-Area

At each end of the field of play two lines shall be drawn at right angles to the goal-line, 18 yd from each goal-post. These shall extend into the field of play for a distance of 18 yd and shall be joined by a line drawn parallel with the goal-line. Each of the spaces enclosed by these lines and the goal-line shall be called a penalty-area. A suitable mark shall be made within each penalty-area, 12 yd from the mid-point of the goal-line, measured along an undrawn line at right angles thereto. These shall be the penalty-kick marks. From each penalty-kick mark an arc of a circle, having a radius of 10 yd, shall be drawn outside the penalty-area.

5. The Corner-Area

From each corner-flag post a quarter circle, having a radius of 1 yd, shall be drawn inside the field of play.

6. The Goals

The goals shall be placed on the centre of each goal-line and shall consist of two upright posts, equidistant from the corner-flags and 8 yd apart (inside measurement), joined by a horizontal cross-bar, the lower edge of which shall be 8 ft from the ground. The width and depth of the goal-posts and the width and depth of the cross-bars shall not exceed 5 in (12 cm). The goal-posts and the cross-bars shall have the same width.

Nets may be attached to the posts, cross-bars and ground behind the goals. They should be appropriately supported and be so placed as to allow the goalkeeper ample room.

INTERNATIONAL BOARD DECISIONS

(1) In International Matches the dimensions of the field of play shall be: maximum 110 m × 75 m; minimum 100 m × 64 m.
(2) National Associations must adhere strictly to these dimensions. Each National Associations organizing an International Match must advise the Visiting Association, before the match, of the place and the dimensions of the field of play.
(3) The Board has approved this table of measurements for the Laws of the Game.

	Metres				*Metres*
130 yards ..	.. 120	1 yard	..	..	1
120 yards ..	.. 110	8 feet	..	..	2.44
110 yards ..	.. 100	5 feet	..	..	1.50
100 yards ..	.. 90	28 inches ..		..	0.71
80 yards ..	.. 75	27 inches ..		..	0.68
70 yards ..	.. 64	9 inches ..		..	0.22
50 yards ..	.. 45	5 inches ..		..	0.12
18 yards ..	.. 16.50	½ inch	..	..	12.7 mm
					See over

12 yards ..	.. 11	$\frac{3}{8}$ inch .. .. 10 mm
10 yards ..	.. 9.15	14 ozs. = 396 grams
8 yards ..	.. 7.32	16 ozs. = 453 grams
6 yards ..	.. 5.50	9 lb./sq. in. = 600 gr/cm²
		10.5 lb./sq. in. = 700 gr/cm²

(4) The goal-line shall be marked the same width as the depth of the goalposts and the cross-bar so that the goal-line and the goal-posts will conform in the same interior and exterior edges.

(5) The 6 yd (for the outline of the goal-area) and the 18 yd (for the outline of the penalty-area) which have to be measured along the goal-line, must start from the inner sides of the goal-posts.

(6) The space within the inside areas of the field of play includes the width of the lines marking these areas.

(7) All Associations shall provide standard equipment, particularly in International Matches, when the Laws of the Game must be complied with in every respect and especially with regard to the size of the ball and other equipment which must conform to the regulations. All cases of failure to provide standard equipment must be reported to F.I.F.A.

(8) In a match played under the rules of a competition if the cross-bar becomes displaced or broken play shall be stopped and the match abandoned unless the cross-bar has been repaired and replaced in position or a new one provided without such being a danger to the players. A rope is not considered to be a satisfactory substitute for a cross-bar.

In a friendly match, by mutual consent, play may be resumed without the cross-bar provided it has been removed and no longer constitutes a danger to the players. In these circumstances, a rope may be used as a substitute for a cross-bar. If a rope is not used and the ball crosses the goal-line at a point which in the opinion of the Referee is below where the cross-bar should have been he shall award a goal.

The game shall be restarted by the Referee dropping the ball at the place where it was when play was stopped.

(9) National Associations may specify such maximum and minimum dimensions for the cross-bars and goal-posts, within the limits laid down in Law 1, as they consider appropriate.

(10) Goal-posts and cross-bars must be made of wood, metal

or other approved material as decided from time to time by the International F.A. Board. They may be square, rectangular, round, half round, or elliptical in shape. Goal-posts and cross-bars made of other materials and other shapes are not permitted.

(11) "Curtain-raisers" to International Matches should only be played following agreement on the day of the match, and taking into account the condition of the field of play, between representatives of the two Associations and the Referee (of the International Match).

(12) National Associations, particularly in International Matches, should restrict the number of photographers around the field of play, have a line ("photographers" line) marked behind the goal-lines at least 3.5 metres behind the intersection of the goal-line with the line marking the goal area to a point situated at least six metres behind the goal-posts, prohibit photographers from passing over these lines and forbid the use of artificial lighting in the form of "flash-lights".

2. THE BALL

The ball shall be spherical; the outer casing shall be of leather or other approved materials. No material shall be used in its construction which might prove dangerous to the players. The circumference of the ball shall not be more than 28 in nor less than 27 in. The weight of the ball at the start of the game shall not be more than 16 oz nor less than 14 oz. *The pressure shall be equal to 0.6–1.1 atmosphere, which equals 600–1, 100 gr/ cm² at sea level.* The ball shall not be changed during the game unless authorised by the Referee.

INTERNATIONAL BOARD DECISIONS

(1) The ball used in any match shall be considered the property of the Association or Club on whose ground the match is played, and at the close of play it must be returned to the Referee.

(2) The International Board, from time to time, shall decide

what constitutes approved materials. Any approved material shall be certified as such by the International Board.

(3) The Board has approved these equivalents of the weights specified in the Law.

14 to 16 ounces = 396 to 453 grammes.

(4) If the ball bursts or becomes deflated during the course of a match, the game shall be stopped and restarted by dropping the new ball at the place where the first ball became defective, *unless it was within the goal area at that time, in which case it shall be dropped on that part of the goal area line which runs parallel to the goal-line, at the point nearest to where the ball was when play was stopped.*

(5) If this happens during a stoppage of the game (place-kick, goal-kick, corner-kick, free-kick, penalty-kick or throw-in) the game shall be restarted accordingly.

3. NUMBER OF PLAYERS

(1) A match shall be played by two teams, each consisting of not more than eleven players, one of whom shall be the goalkeeper.

(2) Substitutes may be used in any match played under the rules of an official competition at F.I.F.A., Confederation or National Association level, subject to the following conditions:

(*a*) that the authority of the International Association(s) or National Association(s) concerned, has been obtained:

(*b*) that, subject to the restriction contained in the following paragraph (*c*), the rules of a competition shall state how many, if any, substitutes may be used, and

(*c*) that a team shall not be permitted to use more than two substitutes in any match.

(3) Substitutes may be used in any other match provided that the two teams concerned reach agreement on a maximum number, not exceeding five, and that the terms of such agreement are intimated to the Referee, before the match. If the Referee is not informed, or if the teams fail to reach agreement, no more than 2 substitutes shall be permitted.

(4) Any of the other players may change places with the goalkeeper, provided that the Referee is informed before the change is made, and provided also, that the change is made during a stoppage in the game.

(5) When a goalkeeper or any other player is to be replaced by a substitute, the following conditions shall be observed:

(*a*) the Referee shall be informed of the proposed substitution, before it is made;

(*b*) the substitute shall not enter the field of play until the player he is replacing has left, and then only after having received a signal from the Referee;

(*c*) he shall enter the field during a stoppage in the game, and at the halfway-line;

(*d*) a player who has been replaced shall not take any further part in the game;

(*e*) a substitute shall be subject to the authority and jurisdiction of the Referee whether called upon to play or not;

(*f*) the substitution is completed when the substitute enters the field of play, from which moment he becomes a player and the player whom he is replacing ceases to be a player.

Punishment. (*a*) Play shall not be stopped for an infringement of para. 4. The players concerned shall be cautioned immediately the ball goes out of play.

(*b*) If a substitute enters the field of play without the authority of the Referee, play shall be stopped. The substitute shall be cautioned and removed from the field or sent off according to the circumstances. The game shall be restarted by the Referee dropping the ball at the place where it was when he stopped play.

(*c*) For any other infringement of this law, the player concerned shall be cautioned, and if the game is stopped by the Referee, to administer the caution, it shall be restarted by an indirect free-kick, to be taken by a player of the opposing team, from the place where the ball was when play was stopped. If the free-kick is awarded to a side within its own goal-area, it may be taken from any point within that half of the goal-area in which the ball was when play was stopped.

INTERNATIONAL BOARD DECISIONS

(1) The minimum number of players in a team is left to the discretion of National Associations.

(2) The Board is of the opinion that a match should not be considered valid if there are fewer than seven players in either of the teams.

(3) A competition may require that the Referee shall be informed, before the start of a match, of the names of not more than five players from whom the substitutes (if any) must be chosen.

(4) A player who has been ordered off before play begins may only be replaced by one of the named substitutes. The kick-off must not be delayed to allow the substitute to join his team.

A player who has been ordered off after play has started may not be replaced. A named substitute who has been ordered off, either before or after play has started, may not be replaced. (This decision only relates to players who are ordered off under Law 12. It does not apply to players who have infringed Law 4.)

4. PLAYERS' EQUIPMENT

A player shall not wear anything which is dangerous to another player. Footwear (boots or shoes) must conform to the following standard:

(*a*) Bars shall be made of leather or rubber and shall be transverse and flat, not less than half an inch in width and shall extend the total width of the sole and be rounded at the corners.

(*b*) Studs which are independently mounted on the sole and are replaceable shall be made of leather, rubber, aluminium, plastic or similar material and shall be solid. With the exception of that part of the stud forming the base, which shall not protrude from the sole more than one quarter of an inch, studs shall be round in plan and not less than half an inch in diameter. Where studs are tapered, the minimum diameter of any section of the stud must not be less than half an inch. Where metal seating for the screw type is used, this seating must be embedded in the sole of the footwear and any attachment screw shall be part of the stud. Other than the metal seating for the screw type of stud, no metal plates even though covered with leather or rubber shall be worn, neither studs which are threaded to allow them to be screwed on to a base screw that is fixed by nails or otherwise to the soles of footwear, nor studs which, apart from the base, have any form of protruding edge rim, or relief marking, or ornament, should be allowed.

(c) Studs which are moulded as an integral part of the sole and are not replaceable, shall be made of rubber, plastic, polyurethane or similar soft materials. Provided that there are no fewer than ten studs on the sole, they shall have a minimum diameter of $\frac{3}{8}$ in (10 mm). Additional supporting material to stabilise studs of soft materials, and ridges which shall not protrude more than 5 mm from the sole and moulded to strengthen it, shall be permitted provided that they are in no way dangerous to other players. In all other respects they shall conform to the general requirements of this law.

(d) Combined bars and studs may be worn, provided the whole conforms to the general requirements of this law. Neither bars nor studs on the soles shall project more than $\frac{3}{4}$ in. If nails are used they shall be driven in flush with the surface.

The goalkeeper shall wear colours which distinguish him from the other players and from the Referee.

Punishment. For any infringement of this Law, the player at fault shall be sent off the field of play to adjust his equipment and he shall not return without first reporting to the Referee, who shall satisfy himself that the player's equipment is in order; the player shall only re-enter the game at a moment when the ball has ceased to be in play.

INTERNATIONAL BOARD DECISIONS

(1) The usual equipment of a player is a jersey or shirt, shorts, stockings and footwear. In a match played under the rules of a competition, players need not wear boots or shoes, but shall wear jersey or shirts, shorts, or track suit or similar trousers, and stockings.

(2) The Law does not insist that boots or shoes must be worn. However, in competition matches Referees should not allow

one or a few players to play without footwear when all the other players are so equipped.

(3) In International Matches, International Competitions, International Club Competitions and friendly matches between clubs of different National Associations, the Referee, prior to the start of the match, shall inspect the players' footwear, and prevent any player whose footwear does not conform to the requirements of this Law from playing until such time as it does comply.

The rules of any competition may include a similar provision.

(4) If the Referee finds that a player is wearing articles not permitted by the Laws and which may constitute a danger to other players, he shall order him to take them off. If he fails to carry out the Referee's instruction, the player shall not take part in the match.

(5) A player who has been prevented from taking part in the game or a player who has been sent off the field for infringing Law 4 **must** report to the Referee during a stoppage of the game and may not enter or re-enter the field of play unless and until the Referee has satisfied himself that the player is no longer infringing Law 4.

(6) A player who has been prevented from taking part in a game or who has been sent off because of an infringement of Law 4, and who enters or re-enters the field of play to join or rejoin his team in breach of the conditions of Law 12, shall be cautioned.

If the Referee stops the game to administer the caution, the game shall be restarted by an indirect free-kick, taken by a player of the opposing side, from the place where the ball was when the Referee stopped the game. If the free-kick is awarded to a side within its own goal area, it may be taken from any point within that half of the goal area in which the ball was when play was stopped.

5. REFEREES

A Referee shall be appointed to officiate in each game. His authority and the exercise of the powers granted to him by the Laws of the Game commence as soon as he enters the field of play. His power of penalizing shall extend to offences committed when play has been temporarily suspended, or when the ball is out of play. His decision on points of fact connected with the play shall be final, so far as the result of the game is concerned.

He shall:

(a) Enforce the Laws.

(b) Refrain from penalising in cases where he is satisfied that, by doing so, he would be giving an advantage to the offending team.

(c) Keep a record of the game; act as time-keeper and allow the full or agreed time, adding thereto all time lost through accident or other cause.

(d) Have discretionary power to stop the game for any infringement of the Laws and to suspend or terminate the game whenever, by reason of the elements, interference by spectators or other cause, he deems such stoppage necessary. In such a case he shall submit a detailed report to the competent authority, within the stipulated time, and in accordance with the provisions set up by the National Association under whose jurisdiction the match was played. Reports will be deemed to be made when received in the ordinary course of post.

(e) From the time he enters the field of play, caution any player guilty of misconduct or ungentlemanly behaviour and, if he persists, suspend him from further participation in the game. In such cases the Referee shall send the name of the offender to the competent authority, within the stipulated time*, and in accordance with the provisions set up by the National Association under whose jurisdiction the match was played. Reports will be deemed to be made when received in the ordinary course of post.

(f) Allow no person other than the players and Linesmen to enter the field of play without his permission.

(g) Stop the game if, in his opinion, a player has been seriously injured; have the player removed as soon as possible from the field of play, and immediately resume the game. If a player is slightly injured the game shall not be

* In England, within two days, Sunday not included.

stopped until the ball has ceased to be in play. A player who is able to go to the touch- or goal-line for attention of any kind, shall not be treated on the field of play.

(*h*) Send off the field of play any player who in his opinion is guilty of violent conduct, serious foul play, or the use of foul or abusive language.

(*i*) Signal for recommencement of the game after all stoppages.

(*j*) Decide that the ball provided for a match meets with the requirements of Law 2.

INTERNATIONAL BOARD DECISIONS

(1) Referees in International Matches shall wear a blazer or blouse the colour of which is distinctive from the colours worn by the contesting teams.

(2) Referees for International Matches will be selected from a neutral country unless the countries concerned agree to appoint their own officials.

(3) The Referee must be chosen from the official list of International Referees. This need not apply to Amateur and Youth International matches.

(4) the Referee shall report to the appropriate authority misconduct or any misdemeanour on the part of spectators, officials, players, named substitutes or other persons which take place either on the field of play or in its vicinity at any time prior to, during, or after the match in question so that appropriate action can be taken by the authority concerned.

(5) Linesmen are assistants of the Referee. In no case shall the Referee consider the intervention of a Linesman if he himself has seen the incident and from his position on the field, is better able to judge. With this reserve, and the Linesmen neutral, the Referee can consider the intervention and if the information of the Linesman applies to that phase of the game immediately before the scoring of a goal, the Referee may act thereon and cancel the goal.

(6) The Referee, however, can only reverse his first decision so long as the game has not been restarted.

(7) If the Referee has decided to apply the advantage clause

and to let the game proceed, he cannot revoke his decision if the presumed advantage has not been realised, even though he has not, by any gesture, indicated his decision. This does not exempt the offending player from being dealt with by the Referee.

(8) The Laws of the Game are intended to provide that games should be played with as little interference as possible, and in this view it is the duty of Referees to penalise only deliberate breaches of the Law. Constant whistling for trifling and doubtful breaches produces bad feeling and loss of temper on the part of the players and spoils the pleasure of spectators.

(9) By para. (*d*) of Law 5 the Referee is empowered to terminate a match in the event of grave disorder, but he has no power or right to decide, in such event, that either team is disqualified and thereby the loser of the match. He must send a detailed report to the proper authority who alone has the power to deal further with this matter.

(10) If a player commits two infringements of a different nature at the same time, the Referee shall punish the more serious offence.

(11) It is the duty of the Referee to act upon the information of neutral Linesmen with regard to incidents that do not come under the personal notice of the Referee.

(12) The Referee shall not allow any person to enter the field until play has stopped, and only then, if he has given him a signal to do so, nor shall he allow coaching from the boundary lines.

6. LINESMEN

Two Linesmen shall be appointed whose duty (subject to the decision of the Referee) shall be to indicate: (*a*) when the ball is out of play, (*b*) which side is entitled to a corner-kick, goal-kick or throw-in, (*c*) when a substitution is desired. They shall also assist the Referee to control the game in accordance with the Laws. In the event of undue interference or improper conduct by a Linesman, the Referee shall dispense with his services and arrange for a substitute to be appointed. (The matter shall be reported by the Referee to the competent authority.) The Linesmen should be equipped with flags by the Club on whose ground the match is played.

INTERNATIONAL BOARD DECISIONS

(1) Linesmen where neutral shall draw the Referee's attention to any breach of the Laws of the Game of which they become aware if they consider that the Referee may not have seen it, but the Referee shall always be the judge of the decision to be taken.

(2) National Associations are advised to appoint official Referees of Neutral nationality to act as Linesmen in International Matches.

(3) In International Matches, Linesmen's flags shall be of a vivid colour – bright reds and yellows. Such flags are recommended for use in all other matches.

(4) A Linesman may be subject to disciplinary action only upon a report of the Referee for unjustified interference or insufficient assistance.

7. DURATION OF THE GAME

The duration of the game shall be two equal periods of 45 minutes, unless otherwise mutually agreed upon, subject to the following:

(*a*) Allowance shall be made in either period for all time lost through accident or other cause, the amount of which shall be a matter for the discretion of the Referee.

(*b*) Time shall be extended to permit of a penalty-kick being taken at or after the expiration of the normal period in either half.

At half-time the interval shall not exceed five minutes, except by the consent of the Referee.

INTERNATIONAL BOARD DECISION

(1) If a match has been stopped by the Referee, before the completion of the time specified in the rules, for any reason stated in Law 5 it must be replayed in full unless the rules of the

competition concerned provide for the result of the match at the time of such stoppage to stand.

(2) Players have a right to an interval at half-time.

8. THE START OF PLAY

(*a*) *At the beginning of the game* choice of ends and the kick-off shall be decided by the toss of a coin. The team winning the toss shall have the option of choice of ends or the kick-off.

The Referee having given a signal, the game shall be started by a player taking a place-kick (i.e., a kick at the ball while it is stationary on the ground in the centre of the field of play) into his opponents' half of the field of play. Every player shall be in his own half of the field and every player of the team opposing that of the kicker shall remain not less than 10 yd from the ball until it is kicked-off; it shall not be deemed in play until it has travelled the distance of its own circumference. The kicker shall not play the ball a second time until it has been played or touched by another player.

(*b*) *After a goal has been scored* the game shall be restarted in like manner by a player of the team losing the goal.

(*c*) *After half-time*; when restarting after half-time, ends shall be changed and the kick-off shall be taken by a player of the opposite team to that of the player who started the game.

Punishment. For any infringement of this Law, the kick-off shall be retaken, except in the case of the kicker playing the ball again before it has been touched or played by another player; for this offence, an indirect free-kick shall be taken by a player of the opposing team from the place where the infringement occurred, unless the offence is committed by a player in his opponents' goal-area, in which case the free-kick shall be taken from a point anywhere within that half of the goal-area in which the offence occurred. A goal shall not be scored direct from a kick-off.

(*d*) *After any other temporary suspension*; when restarting the game after a temporary suspension of play from any cause not mentioned elsewhere in these Laws, provided that immediately prior to the suspension the ball has not passed over the touch- or goal-lines, the Referee shall drop the ball at the place where it was when play was suspended and it shall be deemed in play when it has touched the ground; if, however, it goes over the touch- or goal-lines after it has been dropped by the Referee, but before it is touched by a player, the Referee shall again drop it. A player shall not play the ball until it has touched the ground. If this section of the Law is not complied with, the Referee shall again drop the ball.

INTERNATIONAL BOARD DECISIONS

(1) If, when the Referee drops the ball, a player infringes any of the Laws before the ball has touched the ground, the player concerned shall be cautioned or sent off the field according to the seriousness of the offence, but a free-kick cannot be awarded to the opposing team because the ball was not in play at the time of the offence. The ball shall therefore be again dropped by the Referee.

(2) Kicking-off by persons other than the players competing in a match is prohibited.

9. BALL IN AND OUT OF PLAY

The ball is out of play:

(a) When it has wholly crossed the goal-line or touch-line, whether on the ground or in the air.

(b) When the game has been stopped by the Referee.

The ball is in play at all other times from the start of the match to the finish, including:

(a) If it rebounds from a goal-post, cross-bar or corner-flag post into the field of play.

(b) If it rebounds off either the Referee or Linesmen when they are in the field of play.

(c) In the event of a supposed infringement of the Laws, until a decision is given.

INTERNATIONAL BOARD DECISIONS

(1) The lines belong to the areas of which they are the boun-

daries. In consequence, the touch-lines and the goal-lines belong to the field of play.

10. METHOD OF SCORING

Except as otherwise provided by these Laws, a goal is scored when the whole of the ball has passed over the goal-line, between the goal-posts and under the cross-bar, provided it has not been thrown, carried or propelled by hand or arm, by a player of the attacking side, except in the case of a goalkeeper, who is within his own penalty area.

The team scoring the greater number of goals during the game shall be the winner; if no goals or an equal number of goals are scored the game shall be termed a "draw".

INTERNATIONAL BOARD DECISIONS

(1) Law 10 defines the only method according to which a match is won or drawn; no variation whatsoever can be authorised.

(2) A goal cannot in any case be allowed if the ball has been prevented by some outside agency from passing over the goal-line. If this happens in the normal course of play, other than at the taking of a penalty-kick, the game must be stopped and restarted by the Referee dropping the ball at the place where the ball came into contact with the interference, *unless it was within the goal area at that time, in which case it shall be dropped on that part of the goal area line which runs parallel to the goal-line, at the point nearest to where the ball was when play was stopped.*

(3) If, when the ball is going into goal, a spectator enters the field before it passes wholly over the goal-line, and tries to prevent a score, a goal shall be allowed if the ball goes into goal, unless the spectator has made contact with the ball or has interfered with play, in which case the Referee shall stop the game and restart it by dropping the ball at the place where the contact or interference occurred.

11. OFF-SIDE

(1) A player is in an off-side position if he is nearer to his opponents' goal-line than the ball *unless*:

(*a*) He is in his own half of the field of play, or

(*b*) There are at least two of his opponents nearer to their own goal-line than he is.

(2) A player shall only be declared off-side and penalised for being in an off-side position, if, at the moment the ball touches, or is played by, one of his team, he is, in the opinion of the Referee

(*a*) interfering with play or with an opponent or

(*b*) seeking to gain an advantage by being in that position.

(3) A player shall not be declared off-side by the Referee

(*a*) merely because of his being in an off-side position, or

(*b*) if he receives the ball, direct, from a goal-kick, a corner-kick, a throw-in, or when it has been dropped by the Referee.

(4) If a player is declared off-side, the Referee shall award an indirect free-kick, which shall be taken by a player of the opposing team from the place where the infringement occurred, unless the offence is committed by a player in his opponents' goal-area, in which case, the free-kick shall be taken from a point anywhere within that half of the goal-area in which the offence occurred.

INTERNATIONAL BOARD DECISIONS

(1) Off-side shall not be judged at the moment the player in question receives the ball, but at the moment when the ball is passed to him by one of his own side. A player who is not in an off-side position when one of his colleagues passes the ball to him or takes a free-kick, does not therefore become off-side if he goes forward during the flight of the ball.

12. FOULS AND MISCONDUCT

A player who intentionally commits any of the following nine offences:

(*a*) Kicks or attempts to kick an opponent;

(*b*) Trips an opponent, i.e., throwing or attempting to throw him by the use of the legs or by stooping in front of or behind him;

(*c*) Jumps at an opponent;

(*d*) Charges an opponent in a violent or dangerous manner;

(*e*) Charges an opponent from behind unless the latter be obstructing;

(*f*) Strikes or attempts to strike an opponent;

(*g*) Holds an opponent;

(*h*) Pushes an opponent;

(*i*) Handles the ball, i.e., carries, strikes or propels the ball with his hand or arm. (This does not apply to the goalkeeper within his own penalty-area);

shall be penalised by the award of a *direct free-kick* to be taken by the opposing side from the place where the offence occurred, unless the offence is committed by a player in his opponents' goal-area, in which case the free-kick shall be taken from a point anywhere within that half of the goal-area in which the offence occurred.

Should a player of the defending side intentionally commit one of the above nine offences within the penalty-area he shall be penalised by a *penalty-kick*.

A penalty-kick can be awarded irrespective of the position of the ball, if in play, at the time an offence within the penalty-area is committed.

A player committing any of the five following offences:

1. Playing in a manner considered by the Referee to be dangerous, e.g., attempting to kick the ball while held by the goalkeeper;

2. Charging fairly, i.e., with the shoulder, when the ball is not within playing distance of the players concerned and they are definitely not trying to play it;

3. When not playing the ball, intentionally obstructing an opponent, i.e., running between the opponent and the ball, or interposing the body so as to form an obstacle to an opponent;

4. Charging the goalkeeper except when he:

(*a*) is holding the ball;

(*b*) is obstructing an opponent;

(*c*) has passed outside his goal-area;

5. *When playing as goalkeeper and within his own penalty-area, (a) from the moment he takes control of the ball with his hands, he takes more than four steps in any direction while holding, bouncing or throwing the ball in the air and catching it again without releasing it into play, or, having released it into play before, during or after the four steps, he touches it again with his hands, before it has been touched or played by another player, or (b)* indulges in tactics which, in the opinion of the Referee, are designed merely to hold up the game and thus waste time and so give an unfair advantage to his own team: *shall be penalised* by the award of an *indirect free-kick* to be taken by the opposing side from the place where the infringement occurred, unless the offence is committed by a player in his opponents' goal-area, in which case the free-kick shall be taken from a point anywhere within that half of the goal-area in which the offence occurred.

A player shall be *cautioned* if:

(*j*) He enters or re-enters the field of play to join or rejoin his team after the game has commenced or leaves the field of play during the progress of the game (except through accident) without, in either case, first having received a signal from the Referee showing him that he may do so. If the Referee stops the game to administer the caution it shall be restarted by an indirect free-kick taken by a player of the opposing team from the place where the ball was when the Referee stopped the game. If the free-kick is awarded to a side within its own goal-area, it may be taken from any point within the half of the goal-area in which the ball was when play was stopped. If, however, the offending player has committed a more serious offence he shall be penalised according to that section of the Law infringed.

(*k*) He persistently infringes the Laws of the Game.

(*l*) He shows, by word or action, dissent from any decision given by the Referee.

(*m*) He is guilty of ungentlemanly conduct.

For any of these last three offences, in addition to the caution, an *indirect free-kick* shall also be awarded to the opposing side from the place where the offence occurred, unless a more serious infringement of the Laws of the Game was committed. If the offence is committed by a player in his opponents' goal-area, a free-kick shall be taken from a point anywhere within that half of the goal-area in which the offence occurred.

A player shall be sent off the field of play if in the opinion of the Referee, he:

(*n*) *is guilty of violent conduct, or serious foul play;*

(*o*) *uses foul or abusive language;*

(*p*) *persists in misconduct after having received a caution.*

If play be stopped by reason of a player being ordered from the field for an offence without a separate breach of the Law having been committed, the game shall be resumed by an *indirect free-kick* awarded to the opposing side from the place where the infringement occurred, unless the offence is committed by a player in his opponents' goal-area, in which case the free-kick shall be taken from a point anywhere within that half of the goal-area in which the offence occurred.

INTERNATIONAL BOARD DECISIONS

(1) If the goalkeeper either intentionally strikes an opponent by throwing the ball vigorously at him, or pushes him with the ball while holding it, the Referee shall award a penalty-kick, if the offence took place within the penalty-area.

(2) If a player deliberately turns his back to an opponent when he is about to be tackled, he may be charged but not in a dangerous manner.

(3) In case of body-contact in the goal area between an attacking player and the opposing goalkeeper not in possession of the ball, the Referee, as sole judge of intention, shall stop the game if, in his opinion, the action of the attacking player was intentional, and award an indirect free-kick.

(4) If a player leans on the shoulders of another player of his own team in order to head the ball, the Referee shall stop the game, caution the player for ungentlemanly conduct and award an indirect free-kick to the opposing side.

(5) A player's obligation when joining or rejoining his team after the start of the match to "report to the Referee" must be interpreted as meaning to "draw the attention of the Referee

from the touch-line". The signal from the Referee shall be made by a definite gesture which makes the player understand that he may come into the field of play; it is not necessary for the Referee to wait until the game is stopped (this does not apply in respect of an infringement of Law 4), but the Referee is the sole judge of the moment in which he gives his signal of acknowledgement.

(6) The letter and spirit of Law 12 do not oblige the Referee to stop a game to administer a caution. He may, if he chooses, apply the advantage. If he does apply the advantage, he shall caution the player when play stops.

(7) If a player covers up the ball without touching it in an endeavour not to have it played by an opponent, he obstructs but does not infringe Law 12, para. 3, because he is already in possession of the ball and covers it for tactical reasons whilst the ball remains within playing distance. In fact, he is actually playing the ball and does not commit an infringement; in this case, the player may be charged because he is in fact playing the ball.

(8) If a player intentionally stretches his arms to obstruct an opponent and steps from one side to the other, moving his arms up and down to delay his opponent, forcing him to change course, but does not make "bodily contact" the Referee shall caution the player for ungentlemanly conduct and award an indirect free-kick.

(9) If a player intentionally obstructs the opposing goalkeeper, in an attempt to prevent him from putting the ball into play in accordance with Law 12, 5(a), the Referee shall award an indirect free-kick.

(10) If after a Referee has awarded a free-kick a player protests violently by using abusive or foul language and is sent off the field, the free kick should not be taken until the player has left the field.

(11) Any player, whether he is within or outside the field of play, whose conduct is ungentlemanly or violent, whether or not it is directed towards an opponent, a colleague, the Referee, a linesman or other person, or who uses foul or abusive language, is guilty of an offence, and shall be dealt with according to the nature of the offence committed.

(12) If in the opinion of the Referee a goalkeeper intentionally lies on the ball longer than is necessary, he shall be penalised for ungentlemanly conduct and

(a) be cautioned, and an indirect free-kick awarded to the opposing team;

(b) in case of repetition of the offence, be sent off the field.

(13) The offence of spitting at officials or other persons, or similar behaviour, shall be considered as violent conduct within the meaning of section (n) of Law 12.

(14) If, when a Referee is about to caution a player, and before he has done so, the player commits another offence which merits a caution, the player shall be sent off the field of play.

13. FREE-KICK

Free-kicks shall be classified under two heads:

"Direct" (from which a goal can be scored direct against the *offending side*), and "Indirect" (from which a goal cannot be scored unless the ball has been played or touched by a player other than the kicker before passing through the goal).

When a player is taking a direct or an indirect free-kick inside his own penalty-area, all of the opposing players shall be at least ten yards (9.15 m) from the ball and shall remain outside the penalty-area until the ball has been kicked out of the area. The ball shall be in play immediately it has travelled the distance of its own circumference and is beyond the penalty-area. The goalkeeper shall not receive the ball into his hands, in order that he may thereafter kick it into play. If the ball is not kicked direct into play, beyond the penalty-area, the kick shall be retaken.

When a player is taking a direct or an indirect free-kick outside his own penalty-area, all of the opposing players shall be at least ten yards from the ball, until it is in play, unless they are standing on their own goal-line, between the goal-posts. The ball shall be in play when it has travelled the distance of its own circumference.

If a player of the opposing side encroaches into the penalty-area, or within ten yards of the ball, as the case may be, before a free-kick is taken, the Referee shall delay the taking of the kick until the Law is complied with.

The ball must be stationary when a free-kick is taken, and the kicker shall not play the ball a second time, until it has been touched or played by another player.

Notwithstanding any other reference in these Laws to the point from which a free-kick is to be taken: 1. any free-kick awarded to the defending side, within its own goal-area, may be taken from any point within that half of the goal-area in which the free-kick has been awarded; 2. any indirect free-kick awarded to the attacking team within its opponent's goal-area shall be taken from the part of the goal-area line which runs parallel to the goal-line, at the point nearest to where the offence was committed.

Punishment. If the kicker, after taking the free-kick, plays the ball a second time before it has been touched or played by another player, an indirect free-kick shall be taken by a player of the opposing team from the spot where the infringement occurred, unless the offence is committed by a player in his opponents' goal-area, in which case the free-kick shall be taken from a point anywhere within that half of the goal-area in which the offence occurred.

INTERNATIONAL BOARD DECISIONS

(1) In order to distinguish between a direct and an indirect free-kick, the Referee, when he awards an indirect free-kick, shall indicate accordingly by raising an arm above his head. He shall keep his arm in that position until the kick has been taken and retain the signal until the ball has been played or touched by another player or goes out of play.

(2) Players who do not retire to the proper distance when a free-kick is taken must be cautioned and on any repetition be ordered off. It is particularly requested of Referees that attempts to delay the taking of a free-kick by encroaching should be treated as serious misconduct.

(3) If, when a free-kick is being taken, any of the players dance about or gesticulate in a way calculated to distract their opponents, it shall be deemed ungentlemanly conduct for which the offender(s) shall be cautioned.

14. PENALTY-KICK

A penalty-kick shall be taken from the penalty-mark and, when it is being taken, all players, with the exception of the player taking the kick, properly identified, and the opposing goalkeeper, shall be within the field of play, but outside the penalty-area, and at least 10 yd from the penalty-mark. The opposing goalkeeper must stand (without moving his feet) on his own goal-line, between the goal-posts, until the ball is kicked. The player taking the kick must kick the ball forward; he shall not play the ball a second time until it has been touched or played by another player. The ball shall be deemed in play directly it is kicked, i.e., travelled the distance of its circumference, and a goal may be scored direct from such a penalty-kick. If the ball touches the goalkeeper before passing between the posts, when a penalty-kick is being taken at or after the expiration of half-time or full-time, it does not nullify a goal. If necessary, time of play shall be extended at half-time or full-time to allow a penalty-kick to be taken.

Punishment. For any infringement of this Law: (*a*) by the defending team, the kick shall be retaken, if a goal has not resulted;

(*b*) by the attacking team, other than by the player taking the kick, if a goal is scored, the goal shall be disallowed and the kick retaken.

(*c*) by the player taking the penalty-kick, committed after the ball is in play, a player of the opposing team shall take an indirect free-kick from the spot where the infringement occurred.

If, in the case of paragraph (*c*), the offence is committed by the player in his opponents' goal area, the free-kick shall be taken from a point anywhere within that half of the goal-area in which the offence occurred.

INTERNATIONAL BOARD DECISIONS

(1) When the Referee has awarded a penalty-kick, he shall not signal for it to be taken, until the players have taken up position in accordance with the Law.

(2) (*a*) If, after the kick has been taken, the ball is stopped in its course towards goal, by an outside agent, the kick shall be retaken.

    (*b*) If, after the kick has been taken, the ball rebounds into play, from the goalkeeper, the cross-bar or a goal-post, and is then stopped in its course by an outside agent, the Referee shall stop play and restart it by dropping the ball at the place where it came into contact with the outside agent, *unless it was within the goal area at that time, in which case it shall be dropped on that part of the goal area line which runs parallel to the goal-line, at the point nearest to where the ball was when play was stopped.*

(3) (*a*) If, after having given the signal for a penalty-kick to be taken, the Referee sees that the goalkeeper is not in his right place on the goal-line, he shall, nevertheless, allow the kick to proceed. It shall be retaken, if a goal is not scored.

    (*b*) If, after the Referee has given the signal for the penalty-kick to be taken, and before the ball has been kicked, the goal-keeper moves his feet, the Referee shall, nevertheless, allow the kick to proceed. It shall be retaken, if a goal is not scored.

    (*c*) If, after the Referee has given the signal for a penalty-kick to be taken, and before the ball is in play, a player of the defending team encroaches into the penalty-area, or within ten yards of the penalty-mark, the Referee shall, nevertheless, allow the kick to proceed. It shall be retaken, if a goal is not scored.

    The player concerned shall be cautioned.

(4) (*a*) If, when a penalty-kick is being taken, the player taking the kick is guilty of ungentlemanly conduct, the kick, if already taken, shall be retaken, if a goal is scored.

    The player concerned shall be cautioned.

    (*b*) If, after the Referee has given the signal for a penalty-kick to be taken, and before the ball is in play, a colleague of the player taking the kick encroaches into the penalty-area or within ten yards of the penalty-mark, the Referee shall, nevertheless, allow the kick to proceed. If a goal is scored, it shall be disallowed, and the kick retaken.

The player concerned shall be cautioned.

(c) If, in the circumstances described in the foregoing paragraph, the ball rebounds into play from the goalkeeper, the cross-bar or a goal-post, the Referee shall stop the game, caution the player and award an indirect free-kick to the opposing team from the place where the infringement occurred.

(5) (a) If, after the Referee has given the signal for a penalty-kick to be taken, and before the ball is in play, the goalkeeper moves from his position on the goal-line, or moves his feet, and a colleague of the kicker encroaches into the penalty-area or within 10 yards of the penalty-mark, the kick, if taken, shall be retaken.

The colleague of the kicker shall be cautioned.

(b) If, after the Referee has given the signal for a penalty-kick to be taken, and before the ball is in play, a player of each team encroaches into the penalty-area, or within 10 yards of the penalty-mark, the kick, if taken, shall be retaken.

The players concerned shall be cautioned.

(6) When a match is extended, at half-time or full-time, to allow a penalty-kick to be taken or retaken, the extension shall last until the moment that the penalty-kick has been completed, i.e., until the Referee has decided whether or not a goal is scored.

A goal is scored when the ball passes wholly over the goal-line

(a) direct from the penalty kick,

(b) having rebounded from either goal-post or the cross-bar, or

(c) having touched or been played by the goalkeeper.

The game shall terminate immediately the Referee has made his decision.

(7) When a penalty-kick is being taken in extended time:—

(a) the provisions of all the foregoing paragraphs, except paragraphs 2 (b) and 4 (c) shall apply in the usual way, and (*b*) in the circumstances described in paragraphs 2 (*b*) and 4 (*c*) the game shall terminate immediately the ball rebounds from the goalkeeper, the cross-bar or the goal-post.

15. THROW-IN

When the whole of the ball passes over a touch-line, either on the ground or in the air, it shall be thrown in from the point where it crossed the line, in any direction, by a player of the team opposite to that of the player who last touched it. The thrower at the moment of delivering the ball must face the field of play and part of each foot shall be either on the touch-line or on the ground outside the touch-line. The thrower shall use both hands and shall deliver the ball from behind and over his head. The ball shall be in play immediately it enters the field of play, but the thrower shall not again play the ball until it has been touched or played by another player. A goal shall not be scored direct from a throw-in.

Punishment. (*a*) If the ball is improperly thrown in, the throw-in shall be taken by a player of the opposing team.

(*b*) If the thrower plays the ball a second time, before it has been touched or played by another player, an indirect free-kick shall be taken by a player of the opposing team from the place where the infringement occurred, unless the offence is committed by a player in his opponents' goal-area, in which case the free-kick shall be taken from a point anywhere within that half of the goal-area in which the offence occurred.

INTERNATIONAL BOARD DECISIONS

(1) If a player taking a throw-in, plays the ball a second time by handling it within the field of play before it has been touched or played by another player, the Referee shall award a direct free-kick.

(2) A player taking a throw-in must face the field of play with some part of his body.

(3) If, when a throw-in is being taken, any of the opposing

players dance about or gesticulate in a way calculated to distract or impede the thrower, it shall be deemed ungentlemanly conduct, for which the offender(s) shall be cautioned.

16. GOAL-KICK

When the whole of the ball passes over the goal-line, excluding that portion between the goal-posts, either in the air or on the ground, having last been played by one of the attacking team, it shall be kicked direct into play beyond the penalty-area, from a point within that half of the goal-area nearest to where it crossed the line, by a player of the defending team. A goal-keeper shall not receive the ball into his hands from a goal-kick in order that he may thereafter kick it into play. If the ball is not kicked beyond the penalty-area, i.e., direct into play, the kick shall be re-taken. The kicker shall not play the ball a second time until it has touched or been played by another player. A goal shall not be scored direct from such a kick. Players of the team opposing that of the player taking the goal-kick shall remain outside the penalty-area until the ball has been kicked out of the penalty-area.

Punishment. If a player taking a goal-kick plays the ball a second time after it has passed beyond the penalty-area, but before it has touched or been played by another player, an indirect free-kick shall be awarded to the opposing team, to be taken from the place where the infringement occurred, unless the offence is committed by a player in his opponents' goal-area, in which case the free-kick shall be taken from a point anywhere within that half of the goal-area in which the offence occurred.

INTERNATIONAL BOARD DECISIONS

(1) When a goal-kick has been taken and the player who has kicked the ball, touches it again before it has left the penalty-area, the kick has not been taken in accordance with the Law and must be retaken.

17. CORNER-KICK

When the whole of the ball passes over the goal-line, excluding that portion between the goal-posts, either in the air or on the ground, having last been played by one of the defending team, a member of the attacking team shall take a corner-kick, i.e. the whole of the ball shall be placed within the quarter circle at the nearest corner-flag post, which must not be moved, and it shall be kicked from that position.

A goal may be scored direct from such a kick. Players of the team opposing that of the player taking the corner-kick shall not approach within 10 yd of the ball until it is in play, i.e., it has travelled the distance of its own circumference, nor shall the kicker play the ball a second time until it has been touched or played by another player.

Punishment. (*a*) If the player who takes the kick plays the ball a second time before it has been touched or played by another player, the Referee shall award an indirect free-kick to the opposing team, to be taken from the place where the infringement occurred, unless the offence is committed by a player in his opponents' goal-area, in which case the free-kick shall be taken from a point anywhere within that half of the goal-area in which the offence occurred.

(*b*) For any other infringement the kick shall be retaken.

NOTES: *Provided the principles of these Laws be maintained they may be modified in their application:*

1. *To players of school age as follows:*

(*a*) *size of playing pitch;*

(*b*) *size, weight and material of ball;*

(*c*) *width between the goal-posts and height of the cross-bar from the ground;*

(*d*) *the duration of the periods of play.*

2. *For matches played by women as follows:*

(*a*) *size, weight and material of ball;*

(*b*) *duration of the periods of play;*

(*c*) *further modifications are only permissible with the consent of the International Board.*

The Rules of
British American
Football

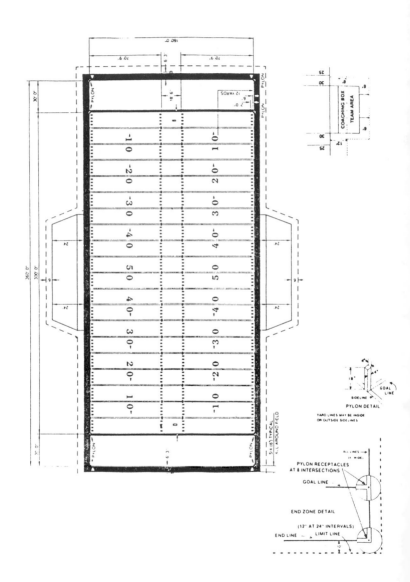

British American Football

THE FOOTBALL CODE

The British American Football League (BAFL) Code of Ethics states:

(a) The football code shall be an integral part of this code of ethics and should be carefully read and observed.

(b) To gain an advantage by circumvention or disregard for the rules brands a coach or player as unfit to be associated with football.

Football is and should be an aggressive, rugged, contact sport. However, there is no place in the game for unfair tactics, unsportsmanlike conduct or manoeuvres deliberately designed to inflict injury.

Through the years the rules committees has endeavored by rule and appropriate penalty to prohibit all forms of unnecessary roughness, unfair tactics and unsportsmanlike conduct. But rules alone cannot accomplish this end. Only the continued best efforts of coaches, players, officials and all friends of the game can preserve the high ethical standards that the public has a right to expect. Therefore, as a guide to players, coaches, officials and others responsible for the welfare of the game, the committee publishes the following code:

Coaching Ethics

Deliberately teaching players to violate the rules is indefensible. The coaching of intentional holding, beating the ball, illegal shifting, feigning injury, interference or illegal forward passing, such as the "forward fumble," will break down rather than aid in the building of the character of players. Teaching or condoning intentional "roughing," including the blind side blocking of an opponent below the waist anywhere on the field, is indefensible. Such instruction is not only unfair to one's opponents but is demoralising to the boys entrusted to a coach's care. It has no place in a game that is an essential part of an educational program. Changing numbers during the game to deceive opponents is an unethical act.

The football helmet is for the protection of the player and is not to be used as a weapon.

(*a*) The helmet shall not be used as the brunt of the contact in the teaching of blocking and tackling.

(*b*) Self-propelled mechanical apparatus shall not be used in the teaching of blocking and tackling.

(*c*) Greater emphasis by players, coaches and officials should be placed on eliminating spearing.

The use of nontherapeutic drugs in the game of football is not in keeping with the aims and purposes of amateur athletics and is prohibited.

Illegal Use of Hand or Arm

Indiscriminate use of hand or arm is unfair play, eliminates skill and does not belong in the game. The object of the game is to advance the ball by strategy, skill and speed without using illegal tactics.

Perhaps a good game could be invented, the object of which would be to advance the ball as far as possible with the assistance of holding, but it would not be football. It would probably become a team wrestling match of some kind.

"Beating the Ball"

"Beating the ball" by an unfair use of a starting signal is nothing less than deliberately stealing an advantage from the opponents. An honest starting signal is good football; but a signal that has for its purpose starting the team a fraction of a second before the ball is put in play, in the hope that it will not be detected by the officials, is nothing short of crookedness. It is the same as if a sprinter in a 100-yard dash had a secret arrangement with the starter to give him a tenth of a second warning before he fired the pistol.

Illegal Shifting

An honest shift is good football, but shaving the one-second pause, shifting in such manner as to simulate the start of a play or employing any other unfair tactic for the purpose of drawing one's opponents offside can be construed only as a deliberate attempt to gain an unmerited advantage. Such tactics cannot be tolerated in football.

Feigning injuries

An injured player must be given full protection under the rules. However, the feigning of an injury by an uninjured player for the purpose of gaining additional, undeserved time for his team is dishonest, unsportsmanlike and contrary to the spirit of the rules. Such tactics cannot be tolerated among sportsmen of integrity.

Talking to Your Opponents

Talking to opponents, if it falls short of being abusive or insulting, is not prohibited by the rules, but no good sportsman is ever guilty of cheap talk to his opponents.

Talking to Officials

When an official imposes a penalty or makes a decision, he is simply doing his duty as he sees it. He is on the field to uphold the integrity of the game of football, and his decisions are final and conclusive and should be accepted by players and coaches.

(*a*) On- and off-the-record criticism of officials to players or to the public shall be considered unethical.

(*b*) For a coach to address, or permit anyone on his bench to address, uncomplimentary remarks to any official during the progress of a game, or to indulge in conduct that might incite players or spectators against the officials, is a violation of the rules of the game and must likewise be considered conduct unworthy of a member of the coaching profession.

Sportsmanship

The football player who intentionally violates a rule is guilty of unfair play and unsportsmanlike conduct, and whether or not he escapes being penalised he brings discredit to the good name of the game, which it is his duty as a player to uphold.

RULE 1

THE GAME, FIELD, PLAYERS AND EQUIPMENT

1. GENERAL PROVISIONS

The Game

ARTICLE 1. (*a*) The game shall be played between two teams of no more than 11 players each, on a rectangular field and with an inflated ball having the shape of a prolate spheroid.

(*b*) A team legally may play with fewer than 11 players but is penalised if the following requirements are not met:
1. At least five men are within five yards of the restraining line when receiving a free kick (6-1-2).
2. At the snap, at least seven men are on the offensive scrimmage line, with not less than five numbered 50-79. (2-21-2) (7-1-3-b-1). (*Exception*: 1-4-2-b.)

Goal Lines

ARTICLE 2. Goal lines, one for each team, shall be established at opposite ends of the field, and each team shall be allowed opportunities to advance the ball across the other team's goal line by running, passing or kicking it.

Winning Team and Final Score

ARTICLE 3. (*a*) The teams shall be awarded points for scoring according to rule and, unless the game is forfeited, the team having the largest score at the end of the game, including extra periods, shall be the winning team.

(*b*) The game is ended and the score is final when the referee so declares.

(*c*) The score of a terminated-suspended game shall be the final score at the time of the suspension.

Supervision

ARTICLE 4. (*a*) The game may be played under the supervision of either three, four, five, six or seven officials: a referee, an umpire, a linesman, a field judge, a back judge, a line judge and a side judge. The use of a back judge, side judge and line judge is optional.

(*b*) The officials' jurisdiction begins with the scheduled coin toss at midfield and ends when the referee declares the score final.

Team Captains

ARTICLE 5. (*a*) Each team shall designate to the referee one or more players as its field captain(s) and one player at a time shall speak for his team in all dealings with the officials. A field captain's first announced choice of any options offered his team shall be irrevocable.

(*b*) Any player may request a team charged timeout.

Persons Subject to the Rules

ARTICLE 6. All players, substitutes, coaches, trainers, cheerleaders in uniform, band members in uniform, mascots in uniform and other persons affiliated with the teams are subject to the rules and shall be governed by the decisions of the officials. Affiliated persons are those authorised within the team area.

Member Institutions Subject to the Rules

ARTICLE 7. BAFL members shall conduct all contests under the official football playing rules of the BAFL. All economic or safety measures are to be solely authorised and approved in writing by the BAFL management committee.

2. THE FIELD

Dimensions

ARTICLE 1. The field shall be a rectangular area with dimensions, lines, zones, goals and pylons as indicated and titled in the field diagram.

(*a*) All field dimension lines shown must be marked four

inches in width with a white nontoxic material that is not injurious to the eyes or skin. (*Exception*: Sidelines and end lines may exceed four inches in width).

(*b*) Short yard-line extensions inside or outside the sidelines and at the in-bounds lines promote greater accuracy in progress and spotting of the ball and are recommended.

(*c*) All inside yard lines shal be four inches from the sideline.

(*d*) Contrasting decorative material is permissible in the end zones but it can be no closer than four feet to any lines. Contrasting decorative material is permissible outside the sidelines and end lines.

(*e*) If markings in the end zones are white or similar in colour to goal lines, they shall be no closer than four feet to the boundary lines or goal lines.

(*f*) Contrasting decorative material is permissible within the sidelines and between the goal lines, but shall not obliterate yard lines, goal lines or sidelines.

(*g*) Goal lines may be of contrasting colours.

(*h*) Commercial advertising is prohibited on the field.

(*i*) Field yard-line numbers measuring six feet in height and four feet in width nine yards from the in-bounds line are recommended.

Marking Boundary Areas

ARTICLE 2. Measurements shall be from the inside edges of the boundary markings. The area enclosed by the sidelines and end lines is "in bounds" and the area surrounding and including the sidelines and end lines is "out of bounds." The entire width of each goal line shall be in the end zone.

Limit Lines and Coaching Lines

ARTICLE 3. (*a*) Limit lines shall be marked with 12-inch lines and at 24-inch intervals 12 feet outside the sidelines and the end lines, except in stadiums where total field surface does not permit. In these stadiums, the limit lines shall not be less than six feet from the sidelines and end lines. Limit lines shall be four inches in width and may be yellow. No person outside the team area shall be within the limit lines. (see Rules 9-1-5-a, 9-2-1-b-1 and field diagram).

(*b*) It is recommended that the limit lines continue six feet from the team area around the side and back of the team area.

(*c*) A coaching line shall be marked with a solid line six feet outside the sideline between the 30-yard lines.

(*d*) A four-inch-by-four-inch mark at each five-yard line extended between the goal lines as an extension of the coaching line is recommended for yardage chain and down indicator six-foot reference points.

Team Area

ARTICLE 4. (*a*) On each side of the field, a team area back of the limit line and between the 25- or 30-yard lines shall be marked for the exclusive use of substitutes, trainers and other persons affiliated with the team. The area between the coaching line and the limit line between the 30-yard lines shall either be white throughout, contain white diagonal lines or be marked distinctly for use of coaches.

(*b*) The team area shall be limited to players in uniform and a maximum of 40 other individuals directly involved in the game. The 40 individuals not in uniform shall wear special identification.

(*c*) Coaches are permitted in the area between the limit line and coaching line between the 30-yard lines. This area is the coaching box.

(*d*) No media personnel, including journalists, radio and television personnel or their equipment, shall be in the team area or coaching box, and no media personnel may communicate in any way with persons in the team area or coaching box.

(*e*) Game management shall remove all persons not authorised by rule.

Goals

ARTICLE 5. Each goal shall consist of two uprights extending at least 20 feet above the ground with a connecting white horizontal crossbar, the top of which is 10 feet above the ground.

(*a*) Above the crossbar the uprights shall be white and 18′6″ apart inside to inside.

(*b*) The designated white posts and crossbar shall be free of decorative material. (*Exception:* 4-inch-by-42-inch orange wind directional streamers at the top of the uprights.)

(*c*) The height of the crossbar shall be measured from the top of each end of the crossbar to the ground directly below.

(*d*) "Offset uprights" may be used.

(*e*) The following procedure is recommended when one or both goals have been taken down and the original goals are not available for a try or field goal attempt:

A team is entitled to a kicking try and is not required to attempt a two-point play if the goals are not in position or complying with the dimensions required by Rule 1-2-5. A team is also entitled to a field goal attempt under the same conditions.

Kicking tries and field goal attempts must be made in the direction of the goal the team was attacking when they elected to make the kick.

The home team is responsible for the availability of a portable goal if original goals are removed during the game for any reason. The portable goal shall be erected or held in place for the kicks.

Pylons

ARTICLE 6. Soft flexible four-sided pylons 4″ × 4″ with an overall height of 18 inches, which may include a two-inch space between the bottom of the pylon and the ground, are required. They shall be red or orange in colour and placed at the inside corners of the eight intersections of the sidelines with the goal lines and end lines and at the intersections of the end lines and in-bounds lines extended.

Yardage Chain, Down Indicator

ARTICLE 7. The official yardage chain and down indicator shall be operated approximately six feet outside the sidelines opposite the press box except in stadiums where the total playing enclosure does not permit.

(*a*) The chain shall join two rods not less than five feet high, the rods being exactly 10 yards apart when the chain is fully extended.

(*b*) The down indicator shall be mounted on a rod not less than 5 ft high.

(*c*) An unofficial auxiliary down indicator and an unofficial line-to-gain indicator may be used six feet outside the other sideline.

(*d*) Unofficial red or orange nonslip line-to-gain ground markers may be positioned off the sidelines on both sides of the field. Markers are rectangular, weighted material 10 by 32 inches. A triangle with altitude of five inches is attached to the rectangle at the end toward the sideline.

(*e*) All yardage chains and down indicator rods shall have flat ends.

Markers or Obstructions

ARTICLE 8. All markers and obstructions within the playing enclosure shall be placed or constructed in such a manner as to avoid any possible hazard to players. This includes anything dangerous to anyone at the limit lines. The referee shall order removed any markers or obstructions constituting such a hazard.

Field Surface

ARTICLE 9. No material or device may be used to improve the playing surface and give one player or team an advantage. (*Exception:* Rules 2-15-4 a, b.)

3. THE BALL

Specifications

ARTICLE 1. The ball shall meet the following specifications:

(*a*) New or nearly new. (A nearly new ball is a ball that has not been altered and retains the properties and qualities of a new ball.)

(*b*) Cover consisting of four panels of pebble-grained leather without corrugations other than seams.

(*c*) One set of eight equally-spaced lacings.

(*d*) Natural tan colour.

(*e*) Two one-inch white stripes that are 3.00 to 3.25 inches from the end of the ball and located only on the two panels adjacent to the laces.

(*f*) Conforms to maximum and minimum dimensions and shape indicated in diagram.

(*g*) Inflated to the pressure of $12\frac{1}{2}$–$13\frac{1}{2}$ lb.

(*h*) Weight 14 to 15 oz.

(*i*) The ball may not be altered.

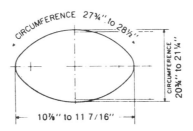

Diagram showing the longitudinal cross section of the standard ball. Maximum and minimum dimensions are used. This diagram is printed in order to secure uniformity in manufacture.

Administration and Enforcement

ARTICLE 2. (*a*) The referee shall test and be sole judge of no more than six balls offered for play by each team prior to and during the game. The referee may approve additional balls if warranted by conditions.

(*b*) Home management shall provide a pressure pump and measuring device.

(*c*) The home team is responsible for providing legal balls and should notify the opponent of the type to be used.

(*d*) During the entire game, either team may use a new or nearly new ball of its choice when it is in possession providing the ball meets the required specifications and has been measured and tested according to rule.

(*e*) The visiting team is responsible for providing the legal balls it wishes to use while it is in possession if the balls provided by the home team are not acceptable.

(*f*) All balls to be used must be presented to the referee for testing 60 minutes prior to the start of the game.

(*g*) When the ball becomes dead nearer the sidelines than the hash marks, is unfit for play, is subject to measurement in a side zone or is inaccessible, a replacement ball shall be obtained from the ball person.

(*h*) The referee or umpire shall determine the legality of each ball before it is put in play.

(*i*) The following procedures shall be used when measuring a ball:

1. All measurements shall be made after the ball is inflated to 13 lb.
2. The long circumference shall be measured around the ends of the ball but not over the laces.
3. The long diameter shall be measured with calipers from end to end but not in the nose indentation.
4. The short circumference shall be measured around the ball, over the valve, over the lace, but not over the cross lace.

4. PLAYERS AND PLAYING EQUIPMENT

Recommended Numbering

ARTICLE 1. It is strongly recommended that offensive players be numbered according to the following diagram that shows one of many offensive formations:

80-99	70-79	60-69	50-59	60-69	70-79	80-99
O	O	O	O	O	O	O
End	Tackle	Guard	Center	Guard	Tackle	End

O
Quarterback

O Halfback   Backs 1-49   O Halfback

O
Fullback

Mandatory Numbering

ARTICLE 2. (*a*) All players shall be numbered 1 through 99.

(*b*) On a scrimmage down, at least five offensive players on the scrimmage line shall be numbered 50 through 79. (*Exception:* During a scrimmage kick formation, a player who initially is an exception to the 50–79 mandatory numbering in a scrimmage kick formation remains an ineligible receiver continuously during the down, and he must be positioned on the line of scrimmage and between the end players on the line of scrimmage.)

(*c*) No two players of the same team shall participate in the same down wearing identical numbers.

(*d*) Numbers shall not be changed during the game to deceive opponents.

(*e*) Markings in the vicinity of the numbers are not permitted.

Penalty—5 yards from previous spot [S19].

Contrasting Colours

ARTICLE 3. (*a*) Players of the opposing teams shall wear jerseys of contrasting colours.

(*b*) National Conference teams must have both dark, and white jerseys available at each game. The home team shall have the choice of jersey.

(*c*) In the Anglo Conference the visiting team shall be responsible for ensuring that they have available jerseys of contrasting colours to that worn by the home team.

(*d*) Players of the same team shall:
 (i) wear jerseys of the same colour
 (ii) wear pants of the same colour
 (iii) wear helmets of the same colour.

Mandatory Equipment

ARTICLE 4. All players shall wear the following mandatory equipment, which shall be professionally manufactured and not altered to decrease protection:

(*a*) Soft knee pads at least a half-inch thick worn over the knees and covered by pants.

(*b*) Head protectors with a secured four-point chin strap. If chin strap is not secured, it is a violation. Officials should inform players when less than four snaps are secured without charging a timeout unless the player ignores the warning.

(*c*) Shoulder pads, hip pads with tailbone protector, thigh guards.

(*d*) An intra-oral mouthpiece that covers all upper jaw teeth.

(*e*) A jersey with sleeves that completely cover the shoulder pads that is not altered or designed to tear and conforms with Rule 1-4-4-f.

(*f*) Permanent Arabic block or Gothic numerals on the jersey at least eight and 10 inches in height front and back, respectively, of a colour in distinct contrast with the jersey, and each player shall have the same colour numbers. A solid colour border is permitted. The individual bars must be approximately one and one-half inches wide. Identical numbers shall be worn on front and back of each player's jersey.

(*g*) Sponsor's name or advertising shall be contained in an area not exceeding 32 sq. inches in total. Sponsor's logos or advertising may be worn on the sleeves but must be no more than 4 inches in diameter. Advertising must not be worn on the helmet.

Note: If a player is not wearing mandatory equipment in compliance in all respects with Rule 1-4-4, the team shall be charged a timeout. **Violation—See Rule 3-3-6 and 3-4-2-b-2 [S23, S3 or S21].**

NOCSAE:* All players shall wear head protectors that carry the manufacturer's or reconditioner's certification indicating satisfaction of NOCSAE test standards. All such reconditioned helmets shall show recertification to indicate satisfaction with the NOCSAE test standard.

[* National Operating Committee on Standards for Athletic Equipment (USA).]

Illegal Equipment

ARTICLE 5. No player wearing illegal equipment shall be permitted to play. Any question as to the legality of a player's equipment shall be decided by the umpire. Illegal equipment includes:

(*a*) Equipment worn by a player which, in the opinion of the umpire, would confuse his opponents or any equipment including artificial limbs that would endanger other players.

(*b*) Hard, abrasive or unyielding substances on the hand, wrist, forearm or elbow of any player unless covered on all sides with closed-cell, slow-recovery foam padding no less than one-half inch thick or an alternate material of the same minimum thickness and similar physical properties. Hard or unyielding substances are permitted only to protect an injury and hand and arm protectors (casts or splints) are permitted only to protect a fracture or dislocation.

(*c*) Hard or unyielding substances in thigh guards or shin guards unless such articles are covered on both sides and all of its edges overlapped with closed-cell, slow-recovery foam padding no less than one-half inch thick, or an alternate material of the same minimum thickness having similar physical properties. Therapeutic or preventive knee braces unless covered from direct external exposure.

(*d*) Projection of metal or other hard substance from a player's person or clothing.

(*e*) Shoe cleats—detachable:

1. More than one-half inch in length (measured from tip of cleat to the shoe). (*Exception*: If attached to only one 5/32 inch or less high platform that is wider than the base of the cleat and molded to the sole.)
2. Made of any material liable to chip or fracture;
3. Without an effective locking device;
4. With concave sides;
5. Conical cleats with flat free ends not parallel with their bases or less than three-eighths inch in diameter or with rounded free ends having arcs greater than seven-sixteenths inch in diameter;
6. Oblong cleats with free ends not parallel with bases or that measure less than one-quarter inch by three-quarters inch;
7. Circular or ring cleats without rounded edges and a wall less than three-sixteenths inch thick;
8. Steel tipped cleats without steel equivalent to SAE 1070 hardener and drawn to Rockwell C scale 42-45.

(*f*) Shoe cleats—nondetachable:
1. More than one-half inch in length (measured from tip of cleat to sole of shoe);
2. Made of any material that burrs, chips or fractures;
3. With abrasive surfaces;
4. Made of any metallic material.

(*g*) Tape or any bandage on a hand, wrist, forearm or elbow unless used to protect an injury and specifically sanctioned by the umpire.

(*h*) Head protectors, jerseys or attachments that tend to conceal the ball by closely resembling it in colour.

(*i*) Adhesive material, grease or any other slippery substance applied on an attachment, a playeres person or clothing that affects the ball or an opponent.

(*j*) Any face protector except those constructed of non-breakable material with rounded edges covered with resilient material designed to prevent chipping, burrs or an abrasiveness that would endanger players.

(*k*) Shoulder pads with the leading edge of the epaulet rounded with a radius more than one-half the thickness of the material used.

(*l*) Uniform attachments designating anything except player's numbers, player's name, school, game or memorial insignia. (This applies to towels or any other item attached to the uniform.)

(*m*) Gloves worn intentionally to closely resemble the opponent's jersey color or not in conformance with 1-4-5-b. *Note:* No player wearing illegal equipment shall be permitted to play. If illegal equipment is discovered by an official, the team shall be charged a team timeout.

Violation—See Rule 3-3-6 and 3-4-2-b-2 [S23, S3 or S21].

Exception: If equipment in Rule 1-4-5 becomes illegal through play, the player must leave the game but will not be charged a team timeout.

Mandatory and Illegal Equipment Enforcement

ARTICLE 6. Failure to wear mandatory equipment or the use of illegal equipment is enforced as follows:
(*a*) Each of the first three infractions for failure to wear

mandatory equipment or wearing illegal equipment requires a charged timeout. The fourth infraction in a half requires a five-yard penalty. The delay for the fourth timeout could be the first violation for not wearing mandatory equipment or wearing illegal equipment. The first three timeouts could have been taken by the team as charged team timeouts.

1. The timeouts are granted.
2. There is no offset for the first three violations when an opponent has fouled.
3. When timeouts are exhausted, the next violation is a dead-ball delay penalty at the succeeding spot.
4. A timeout is called, the offending team is indicated by the referee and the captain and coaches are notified through the officials nearest the sidelines.

(*b*) Officials should ascertain before the ready-for-play signal if players are not wearing mandatory equipment or wearing illegal equipment. Only in an emergency should the 25-second clock be interrupted.

(*c*) No jersey may be changed on the field of play and such changes must be made in the team area of the player making the change. When it is determined that a jersey does not comply with 1-4-4-e and/or f, a team timeout will be charged to that team at the succeeding spot. If the team has expended its three timeouts, a delay will be charged under 3-4-2-b-2. Players may change torn jerseys during team timeouts and return to play. A player may change a jersey and return during a delay penalty only if the game is not further delayed by that action.

(*d*) Tape may not cover or partially cover a glove. Tape may be used to secure glove fasteners.

Coaches' Certification

ARTICLE 7. The head coach or his designated representative shall certify to the umpire prior to the game that all players:

(*a*) Have been informed what equipment is mandatory by rule and what constitutes illegal equipment.

(*b*) Have been provided the equipment mandated by rule.

(*c*) Have been instructed to wear and how to wear mandatory equipment during the game.

(*d*) Have been instructed to notify the coaching staff when equipment becomes illegal through play during the game.

Prohibited Signal Devices

ARTICLE 8. Players are prohibited from being equipped with any electronic, mechanical or other signal devices for the purpose of communicating with any source. (*Exception:* A medically prescribed hearing aid of the sound amplifier type for hard-of-hearing players.)
Penalty—15 yards and disqualification of the player. Penalise as dead-ball foul at succeeding spot [S27 and S47].

Prohibited Field Equipment

ARTICLE 9. (*a*) Television replay or monitor equipment is prohibited at the sidelines, pressbox or other locations adjacent to the playing field for coaching purposes during the game.

(*b*) Motion pictures or any type of film for coaching purposes are prohibited any time during the game or between the periods.

(*c*) Media communicating equipment, including cameras, sound devices and microphones, is prohibited on the field or in the team area or coaching box.

(*d*) Microphones may be used only on referees for penalty or other game announcements, if controlled by the referee, and may not be open at other times. Microphones on other officials are prohibited.

(*e*) Microphones attached to coaches for media transmission are prohibited during the game.

RULE 2

DEFINITIONS

1. APPROVED RULING AND OFFICIALS' SIGNALS

ARTICLE 1. (*a*) An Approved Ruling (A.R.) is an official decision on a given statement of facts. It serves to illustrate the spirit and application of the rules. The relationship between the rules and an Approved Ruling is analogous to that between statutory law and a decision of the Supreme Court.

If there is a conflict between the official rules and approved rulings and examples, the rules take precedence.

(*b*) An official's signal [S] refers to the Official Football Signals 1 through 47.

2. THE BALL: LIVE, DEAD, LOOSE

Live Ball
ARTICLE 1. A live ball is a ball in play. A pass, kick or fumble that has not yet touched the ground is a live ball in flight.

Dead Ball
ARTICLE 2. A dead ball is a ball not in play.

Loose Ball
ARTICLE 3. A loose ball is a live ball not in player possession during:

(*a*) A running play.

(*b*) A scrimmage or free kick before possession is gained, regained or the ball is dead by rule.

(*c*) The interval after a legal forward pass is touched and before it becomes complete, incomplete or intercepted. *Note*—The interval is during a forward pass play and the ball may be batted in any direction.

(*d*) All players are eligible to touch or recover a ball that is loose from a fumble or a backward pass, but eligibility to touch a ball loose from a kick is governed by kick rules (Rule 6).

When Ball is Ready for Play
ARTICLE 4. A dead ball is ready for play when the referee:

(*a*) If time is in, sounds his whistle and signals ready for play.

(*b*) If time is out, sounds his whistle and signals either "start the clock" or "ball ready for play."

In Possession

ARTICLE 5. "In possession" is an abbreviation meaning the holding or controlling of a live ball or a ball to be free kicked.

(*a*) A player is "in possession" when he is holding or controlling the ball.

(*b*) A team is "in possession" when one of its players is "in possession" or attempting a punt, drop kick or place kick, while a forward pass thrown by one of its players is in flight or was last in possession during a loose ball.

Belongs To

ARTICLE 6. "Belongs to" as contrasted with "in possession" denotes temporary custody of a dead ball. Legality of such custody is immaterial because the ball must next be put in play in accordance with rules governing the existing situation.

Catch, Interception, Recovery

ARTICLE 7. A catch is an act of establishing player possession of a live ball in flight.

(*a*) A catch of an opponent's fumble or pass is an interception.

(*b*) Securing player possession of a live ball after it strikes the ground is "recovering it."

(*c*) To catch, intercept or recover a ball, a player who jumps to make a catch, interception or recovery must have the ball in his possession when he first returns to the ground in bounds or is so held that the dead ball provisions of 4-1-3-a apply.

1. If one foot first lands in bounds and the receiver has possession and control of the ball, it is a catch or interception even though a subsequent step or fall takes the receiver out of bounds.
2. A catch by any kneeling or prone in-bounds player is a completion or interception (7-3-1 and 2) (7-3-6 and 7).

Simultaneous Catch or Recovery

ARTICLE 8. A simultaneous catch or recovery is a catch or recovery in which there is joint possession of a live ball by opposing players in bounds.

3. BLOCKING

Legal Block

ARTICLE 1. Blocking is obstructing an opponent by legally contacting him with any part of the blocker's body.

Below Waist

ARTICLE 2. (*a*) Blocking below the waist is legally making the initial contact below the waist with any part of the blocker's body against an opponent, other than the runner, who has one or both feet on the ground.

(*b*) Blocking below the waist applies to the original contact by the blocker. A blocker who makes contact above the waist and then slides down below the waist has not fouled. If the blocker first contacts the opposing player's hands, it is a legal "above the waist" block.

(*c*) The position of the ball at the snap in the landmark that remains constant while Rule 9-1-2-e is in effect. Blocking toward the ball is always related to the position of the ball at the snap.

Chop Block

ARTICLE 3. A chop block is an illegal delayed block at the knee or below against an opponent who is in contact with a teammate of the blocker. A chop block is delayed if it occurs more than one second after a teammate contacts the opponent.

Frame (of the body)

ARTICLE 4. (*a*) The frame of the blocker's body is the front of the body at the shoulders or below.

(*b*) The frame of the opponent's body is at the shoulders or below other than the back (see Rule 9-3-3-a-1-c Exception).

4. CLIPPING

ARTICLE 1. Clipping is an illegal block against an opponent occurring when the force of the initial contact, except against the runner, is from behind. This includes running or diving into the back, or throwing or dropping the body across the back of the leg or legs of an opponent other than the runner.

(*a*) Position of the blocker's head or feet does not necessarily indicate the point of initial contact.

(*b*) It is not clipping if a player turns his back to a potential blocker who has committed himself in intent and direction of movement.

5. CRAWLING

ARTICLE 1. Crawling is an attempt by the runner to advance the ball after any part of his person, other than a hand or foot, has touched the ground (*Exception:* 4-1-3-b.)

6. DOWN AND BETWEEN DOWNS

ARTICLE 1. A down is a unit of the game that starts with a legal snap or legal free kick after the ball is ready for play and ends when the ball next becomes dead. Between downs is the interval during which the ball is dead.

7. FAIR CATCH

Fair Catch

ARTICLE 1 (*a*) A fair catch is a catch beyond the neutral zone by a player of Team B who has made a valid or valid illegal signal during a free kick or scrimmage kick that is untouched beyond the neutral zone.

(*b*) A valid, invalid or illegal fair catch signal deprives the receiving team of the opportunity to advance the ball and the ball is declared dead at the spot of the catch or recovery or at the spot of the foul if the catch precedes the signal.

(*c*) If the receiver shades his eyes from the sun, the ball is live and may be advanced.

Valid Signal

ARTICLE 2. A valid signal is a signal given by a player of Team B who has obviously signalled his intention by extending one hand only clearly above his head and waving the hand from side to side of the body more than once.

Illegal Signal

ARTICLE 3. (*a*) An illegal signal is a valid or invalid signal by a player of Team B beyond the neutral zone when a scrimmage kick is made and a fair catch is not permissible by rule.

(*b*) An illegal signal is a valid or invalid signal by a player of Team B when a free kick is made and a fair catch is not permissible by rule.

Invalid Signal

ARTICLE 4. An invalid signal is any signal by a player of Team B that does not meet the requirements of a valid signal.

8. FORWARD, BEYOND AND FORWARD PROGRESS

Forward, Beyond

ARTICLE 1. Forward, beyond or in advance of, as related to either team, denotes direction toward the opponent's end line. Converse terms are backward or behind.

Forward Progress

ARTICLE 2. Forward progress is a term indicating the end of advancement by the runner and applies to the position of the ball when it became dead.

9. FOUL AND VIOLATION

ARTICLE 1. A foul is a rule infraction for which a distance penalty is prescribed. A violation is a rule infraction for which no distance penalty is prescribed and that does not offset the penalty for a foul.

10. FUMBLE, MUFF, TOUCH, BAT

Fumble

ARTICLE 1. A fumble is loss of ball by a player in possession during his unsuccessful attempt to hold, hand, pass it backward or kick it.

Muff

ARTICLE 2. A muff is an unsuccessful attempt to catch or recover a ball that is touched in the attempt.

Batting

ARTICLE 3. Batting the ball is intentionally striking it or intentionally changing its direction with a hand or arm.

Touching

ARTICLE 4. Touching of a ball not in player possession denotes any contact with the ball. It may be intentional or unintentional and it always precedes possession and control. Touching of a loose ball by anyone or anything (other than a kick that scores a goal after touching goal posts) on a boundary line causes the ball to be out of bounds and dead at its most forward point in the field of play. (*Exception:* 6-1-4-a and b; 6-3-4-a and b.)

11. LINES

Goal lines

ARTICLE 1. Each goal line is a vertical plane separating an end zone from the field of play when a ball is touched or is in player possession. A team's goal line is that which it is defending.

Restraining Lines

ARTICLE 2. A restraining line is a vertical plane when a ball is touched or is in possession.

Yard Lines

ARTICLE 3. A yard line is any line in the field of play parallel to the end lines. A team's own yard lines, marked or unmarked, are numbered consecutively from its own goal line to the 50-yard line.

Inbounds Lines (Hash Marks)

ARTICLE 4. The two inbounds lines are 70′9″ inbounds from the sidelines and divide the field of play into three.

12. HANDING THE BALL

ARTICLE 1. (*a*) Handing the ball is transferring player possession from one teammate to another without throwing, fumbling or kicking it.

(*b*) Except when permitted by rule, handing the ball forward to a teammate is illegal.

(*c*) Loss of possession by unsuccess execution of attempted handing (muff by the recipient) is a fumble.

13. HUDDLE

ARTICLE 1. A huddle is two or more offensive players grouped together after the ball is ready for play before or after they have assumed a scrimmage formation prior to the snap.

14. HURDLING

ARTICLE 1. Hurdling is an attempt by a player to jump with one or both feet or knees foremost over an opponent who is still on his feet. "On his feet" means that no part of the opponent's body other than one or both feet is in contact with the ground.

15. KICKS

Legal and Illegal Kicks

ARTICLE 1. Kicking the ball is intentionally striking the ball with the knee, lower leg or foot.

(*a*) A legal kick is a punt, drop kick or place kick made according to the rules by a player of Team A before a change of team possession. Kicking the ball in any other manner is illegal.

(*b*) Any free kick or scrimmage kick continues to be a kick until it is caught or recovered by a player or becomes dead.

(*c*) A return kick is an illegal kick.

Punt

ARTICLE 2. A punt is a kick by a player who drops the ball and kicks it with his foot or leg before it strikes the ground.

Drop Kick

ARTICLE 3. A drop kick is a kick by a player who drops the ball and kicks it as it touches the ground.

Place Kick

ARTICLE 4. (*a*) A field goal place kick is a kick by a player of the team in possession while the ball is controlled on the ground or tee by a team-mate. If a tee is used, it may not elevate the ball's lowest point more than two inches above the ground.

(*b*) A free kick place kick is a kick by a player of the team in possession while the ball is positioned on a tee or the ground or controlled by a team-mate. If a tee is used, it may not elevate the ball's lowest point more than two inches above the ground.

Free Kick

ARTICLE 5. A free kick is a kick by a player of the team in possession made under restrictions that prohibit either team from advancing beyond or behind established restraining lines until the ball is kicked. A ball that falls from a tee and touches the ground may not be kicked.

Kickoff

ARTICLE 6. A kickoff is a free kick that starts each half and follows each try or field goal. It must be a place kick or a drop kick.

Scrimmage Kick

ARTICLE 7. A scrimmage kick is a kick by Team A during a scrimmage down before team possession changes. A scrimmage kick has crossed the neutral zone when it touches the ground, a player, an official or anything beyond the neutral zone.

Return Kick

ARTICLE 8. A return kick is a kick by a player of the team in possession after change of team possession during a down and is an illegal kick.

Field Goal Attempt

ARTICLE 9. A field goal attempt is any place kick or drop kick from scrimmage.

Scrimmage Kick Formation

ARTICLE 10. A scrimmage kick formation is a formation with at least one player seven yards or more behind the neutral zone and no player in position to receive a hand-to-hand snap from between the snapper's legs.

16. LOSS OF A DOWN

ARTICLE 1. "Loss of a down" is an abbreviation meaning: "loss of the right to repeat a down."

17. THE NEUTRAL ZONE

ARTICLE 1. The neutral zone is the space between the two lines of scrimmage and is established when the ball is ready for play.

18. ENCROACHMENT AND OFFSIDE

Encroachment

ARTICLE 1. Encroachment occurs when an offensive player is in or beyond the neutral zone after the snapper touches the ball and prior to the snap or offensive players are not behind the restraining line when the ball is free kicked. (*Exception:* The snapper or the kicker and holder of a place kick for a free kick are not encroaching when they are beyond their scrimmage line or restraining line when the ball is put in play.)

Offside

ARTICLE 2. Offside occurs when a defensive player is in or beyond the neutral zone when the ball is snapped, illegally contacts an opponent beyond and neutral zone before the ball is snapped or is not within the restraining lines when the ball is free kicked.

19. PASSES

Passing

ARTICLE 1. Passing the ball is throwing it. A pass continues to be a pass until it is caught, intercepted by a player or the ball becomes dead.

Forward and Backward Pass

ARTICLE 2 (*a*) An attempted backward pass is a live ball thrown toward or parallel to the passer's end-line; an attempted forward pass is a live ball thrown toward the opponents' end line. During a forward or backward pass, the point where the ball first strikes the ground, a player, an official or anything beyond or behind the spot of the pass, determines whether it is a forward or backward pass.

(*b*) When a Team A player is holding the ball to pass it forward toward the neutral zone, any intentional forward movement of his arm starts the forward pass. If a Team B player contacts the passer or ball after forward movement begins and the ball leaves the passer's hand, a forward pass is ruled regardless of where the ball strikes the ground or a player.

(*c*) When in question, the ball is a pass and not a fumble during an attempted forward pass.

Crosses Netural Zone

ARTICLE 3. (*a*) A legal forward pass has crossed the neutral zone when it first strikes the ground, a player, an official or anything beyond the neutral zone. It has not crossed the neutral zone when it first strikes the ground, a player, an official or anything in or behind the neutral zone.

(b) A passer has crossed the neutral zone when any part of his body is beyond the neutral zone.

Catchable Forward Pass

ARTICLE 4. A catchable forward pass is an untouched legal forward pass beyond the neutral zone and an eligible Team A player has a reasonable opportunity to catch the ball.

20. PENALTY

ARTICLE 1. A penalty is a yardage loss imposed by rule against a team that has committed a foul and may include a loss of down.

21. SCRIMMAGE

Scrimmage

ARTICLE 1. A scrimmage is the interplay of the two teams during a down in which play begins with a snap.

Scrimmage Line

ARTICLE 2. (a) The scrimmage line for each team is the yard line and its vertical plane that passes through the point of the ball nearest its own goal line.

(b) A player of Team A is "on his scrimmage line" at the snap when he faces his opponents' goal line with the line of his shoulders approximately parallel thereto and his head breaks the plane of the line drawn through the waistline of the snapper.

Backfield Line

ARTICLE 3. To be legally in the backfield, a Team A player's head must not break the plane of the line drawn through the rear-most part, other than the legs or feet, of the nearest Team A player (except the snapper) on the line of scrimmage.

22. SHIFT

ARTICLE 1. A shift is a simultaneous change of position by two or more offensive players after the ball is ready for play for a scrimmage and before the next snap.

23. SNAPPING THE BALL

ARTICLE 1. (*a*) Legally snapping the ball (a snap) is handing or passing it back from its position on the ground with a quick and continuous motion of the hand or hands, the ball actually leaving the hand or hands in this motion.

(*b*) If, during any backward motion of a legal snap, the ball slips from the snapper's hand, it is a snap and in play, provided the ball had been declared "ready" (4-1-1).

(*c*) While resting on the ground and prior to the snap, the long axis of the ball must be at right angles to the scrimmage line with neither end of the ball raised more than 45 degrees.

(*d*) Unless moved in a backward direction, the movement of the ball does not start a legal snap. It is not a legal snap if the ball is first moved forward or lifted.

(*e*) The snap need not be between the snapper's legs; but to be legal, it must be a quick and continuous backward motion.

(*f*) The ball must be snapped on or between the in bounds lines.

24. SPEARING

ARTICLE 1. Spearing is the intentional use of the helmet in an attempt to punish an opponent.

25. SPOTS

Enforcement Spot
ARTICLE 1. An enforcement spot is the point from which the penalty for a foul or violation is enforced.

Previous Spot
ARTICLE 2. The previous spot is the point from which the ball was last put in play.

Succeeding Spot

ARTICLE 3. The succeeding spot, as related to a foul, is the point at which the ball would next be put in play if that foul had not occurred. The try may not be the succeeding spot unless the ball has been declared ready for play on the try.

Dead-Ball Spot

ARTICLE 4. The dead-ball spot is the point at which the ball became dead.

Spot of the Foul

ARTICLE 5. The spot of the foul is the point at which that foul occurs. If out of bounds between the goal lines, it shall be the intersection of the nearer in-bounds line and the yard line extended through the spot of the foul.

Out-of-Bounds Spot

ARTICLE 6. The out-of-bounds spot is the point at which, according to the rule, the ball becomes dead because of going or being declared out of bounds.

In-Bounds Spot

ARTICLE 7. The in-bounds spot is the intersection of the nearer in-bounds line and the yard line passing through the dead-ball spot, or the spot where the ball is left in a side zone by a penalty.

Spot Where Run Ends

ARTICLE 8. The spot where the run ends is where the ball is declared dead or where player possession is lost during a running play. The spot where the run ends is at that point:
- (*a*) Where the ball is declared dead by rule.
- (*b*) Where player possession is lost on a fumble.
- (*c*) Where a legal (or illegal) handing of the ball occurs.
- (*d*) From where an illegal forward pass is thrown.
- (*e*) From where a backward pass is thrown.

Spot Where Kick Ends

ARTICLE 9. A scrimmage kick that crosses the neutral zone

ends at the spot where possession is gained or regained or the ball is declared dead by rule.

Exceptions:

1. Touchback—Basic enforcement spot: Team B's 20-yard line.
2. When the kick ends in Team B's end zone and is not a touchback—Basic enforcement spot: Team B's one-yard line.
3. Unsuccessful field goal attempt untouched by Team B beyond the neutral zone—Basic enforcement spot: previous spot. If the previous spot is between Team B's 20-yard line and the goal line, and the unsuccessful field goal attempt is untouched by Team B beyond the neutral zone, the spot where the kick ends is the 20-yard line.

Basic Spot

ARTICLE 10. The basic spot is the application of the "3 and 1" principle with enforcement of the penalty either from the spot where the run ends, the spot where the kick ends of the previous spot. Fouls by the team "in possession" behind the basic spot are spot fouls.

The following are the basic spots for enforcement on running plays, forward pass plays and legal kick plays utilizing the "3 and 1" principle:

(*a*) The basic spot on running plays when the run ends beyond the neutral zone is **the spot where the related run ends**, and fouls by the team "in possession" behind the basic spot are **spot fouls** (10-2-2-c-1) (*Exception* 9-3-3-a & b).

(*b*) The basic spot on running plays when the run ends behind the neutral zone is the previous spot and fouls by the team "in possession" behind the basic spot are spot fouls (10-2-2-c-2) (*Exception* 9-3-3-a & b).

(*c*) The basic spot on running plays that occur when there is no neutral zone (interception runbacks, kick runbacks, fumble advances, etc.) is **the spot where the related run ends** and fouls by the team "in possession" behind the basic spot are **spot fouls** (10-2-2-c-3).

(*d*) The basic spot on legal forward pass plays is the previous spot, and fouls by the team "in possession" behind the basic spot are spot fouls (10-2-2-d).

Exceptions:

1. Defensive pass interference may be a spot foul.
2. Illegal use of hands or holding by the offense behind the neutral zone during a legal forward pass play is not a spot foul and is penalised from the previous spot (9-3-3-a & b).

(*e*) The basic spot on legal kick plays before a change of possession is the previous spot, and fouls by the team in possession behind the basic spot are spot fouls (10-2-2-e *Exceptions*).

Postscrimmage Kick Spot

ARTICLE 11. The postscrimmage kick spot is the spot where the kick ends. Team B retains the ball after penalty enforcement from the postscrimmage kick spot. Fouls behind the basic spot are spot fouls (10-2-2-e-5).

26. TACKLING

ARTICLE 1. Tackling is grasping or encircling an opponent with a hand(s) or arm(s).

27. TEAM AND PLAYER DESIGNATIONS

Teams A and B

ARTICLE 1. Team A is the team that is designated to put the ball in play and it retains that designation until the ball is next declared ready for play; Team B designates the opponents.

Offensive Team

ARTICLE 2. The offensive team is the team in possession, or the team to which the ball belongs; the defensive team is the opposing team.

Kicker

ARTICLE 3. The kicker is any player who punts, drop kicks or place kicks according to rule. He remains the kicker until he has had a reasonable time to regain his balance.

Lineman and Back

ARTICLE 4. A lineman is any player legally on his scrimmage line when the ball is snapped; a back is any player whose head does not break the plane of the line drawn through the rear-most part, other than the legs or feet, of the nearest Team A player (except the snapper) on the line of scrimmage (*Exceptions* 7-1-3-b-1).

Passer

ARTICLE 5. The passer is the player who throws a legal forward pass. He is a passer from the time he releases the ball until it is complete, incomplete or intercepted.

Player

ARTICLE 6. A player is any one of the participants in the game and is subject to the rules when in bounds or out of bounds.

Runner

ARTICLE 7. The runner is a player in possession of a live ball or simulating possession of a live ball.

Snapper

ARTICLE 8. The snapper is the player who snaps the ball.

Substitute

ARTICLE 9. (*a*) A legal substitute is a replacement for a player or a player vacancy during the interval between downs.

(*b*) A legal incoming substitute becomes a player when he enters the field and communicates with a teammate or an official, enters the huddle, or participates in a play.

(*c*) The player he replaces becomes a replaced player when he leaves the field.

Replaced Player

ARTICLE 10. A replaced player is one who participated during the previous down and has been replaced by a substitute.

Player Vacancy

ARTICLE 11. A player vacancy occurs when a team has fewer than 11 players in the game.

Disqualified Player

ARTICLE 12. A disqualified player is one who is declared ineligible for further participation in the game.

28. TRIPPING

ARTICLE 1. Tripping is using the lower leg or foot to obstruct an opponent (except the runner) below the knees.

29. TIMING DEVICES

Game Clock

ARTICLE 1. Any device under the direction of the appropriate judge used to time the 60-minutes of the game.

25-Second Clock

ARTICLE 2. Any device under the direction of the appropriate official to time the 25 seconds between the ready for play and the ball being put in play. The type of device is determined by the game management.

30. PLAY CLASSIFICATION

Forward Pass Play

ARTICLE 1. A legal forward pass play is the interval between the snap and when a legal forward pass is complete, incomplete or intercepted.

Free Kick Play

ARTICLE 2. A free kick play is the interval from the time the ball is legally kicked until it comes into player possession or the ball is declared dead by rule.

Scrimmage Kick Play and Field Goal Play

ARTICLE 3. A scrimmage kick play or field goal play is the interval between the snap and when a scrimmage kick comes into player possession or the ball is declared dead by rule.

Running Play

ARTICLE 4. A running play is any live-ball action other than that which occurs before player possession is reestablished during a free kick play, a scrimmage kick play, or a legal forward pass play.

(*a*) A running play includes the spot where the run ends and the interval of any subsequent fumble or backward or illegal pass from the time the run ends until possession is gained, regained or the ball is declared dead by rule.

1. There may be more than one running play during a down if player possession is gained or regained beyond the neutral zone.
2. There may not be more than one running play behind the neutral zone if no change of team possession occurs, and the basic spot is the previous spot (see Rule 10-2-2-c-2).

(*b*) A run is that segment of a running play before player possession is lost.

31. FIELD AREAS

The Field

ARTICLE 1. The field is the area within the limit lines and includes the limit lines and team areas and the space above it (*Exception:* Enclosures over the field).

Field of Play

ARTICLE 2. The field of play is the area within the boundary lines other than the end zones.

End Zones

ARTICLE 3. The end zones are the 10-yard areas at both ends of the field between the end lines and the goal lines. The goal lines and goal line pylons are in the end zone and a team's end zone is the one they are defending.

Playing Surface

ARTICLE 4. The playing surface is the material or substance within the field.

Playing Enclosure

ARTICLE 5. The playing enclosure is that area bounded by the stadium, dome, stands, fences or other structures. (*Exception:* Scoreboards are not considered within the playing enclosure.)

RULE 3

PERIODS, TIME FACTORS AND SUBSTITUTIONS

1. START OF EACH PERIOD

First and Third Periods

ARTICLE 1. Each half shall start with a kickoff. Three minutes before the scheduled starting time the referee shall toss a coin at midfield in the presence of the field captains of the opposing teams, first designating which field captain shall call the fall of the coin.

During the coin toss, each team shall remain in the area between the sideline and in-bounds line nearest its team area or in the team area.

(*a*) The winner of the toss shall choose one of the following options for the first or second half at the beginning of the half selected.

1. To designate which team shall kick off.

2. To designate which goal line his team shall defend.

(*b*) The loser shall choose one of the above options for the half the winner of the toss did not select.

(*c*) The team not having the choice of options for a half shall exercise the option not chosen by the opponent.

(*d*) If the winner of the toss selects the second half option, the referee shall use [S10].

Second and Fourth Periods

ARTICLE 2. Between the first and second periods and also between the third and fourth periods, the teams shall defend opposite goal lines.

(*a*) The ball shall be relocated at a spot corresponding exactly, in relation to goal lines and sidelines, to its location at the end of the preceding period.

(*b*) Possession of the ball, the number of the down and the distance to be gained shall remain unchanged.

Extra Periods

ARTICLE 3. (*a*) When it is necessary to determine a champion, or a team's progress in post-season, extra periods of 15 minutes each shall be played to decide a tied game.

(*b*) The Referee shall toss a coin in the presence of field captains of both teams. The winner of the toss shall elect to:

(i) designate which team shall kick-off, OR

(ii) designate which goal-line his team will defend.

The loser of the toss shall elect one of the options the winner does not select.

(*c*) The game shall end when one team scores. That team shall be declared the winner.

(*d*) If the first score is a touchdown, no extra point attempt will be permitted.

2. PLAYING TIME AND INTERMISSIONS

Length of Periods and Intermissions

ARTICLE 1. The total playing time in a collegiate game shall be 60 minutes divided into four periods of 15 minutes each, with one-minute intermissions between the first and second periods (first half) and between the third and fourth periods (second half).

(*a*) No period shall end until the ball is dead.

(*b*) The intermission between halves shall be 20 minutes.

Timing Adjustments

ARTICLE 2. Before the game starts, playing time may be shortened by mutual agreement of the opposing field captains or may be arbitrarily shortened by the referee if he is of the opinion that darkness may interfere with the game. In either of such cases, the four periods must be of equal length.

(*a*) Anytime during the game, the playing time of any remaining period or periods may be shortened by mutual agreement of the opposing field captains and the referee.

(*b*) Timing errors on the game clock, or by an official, may be corrected by the referee.

Extensions of Periods

ARTICLE 3. A period shall be extended until a down free from live-ball fouls not penalised as dead-ball fouls has been played when:

(*a*) A penalty is accepted for a live-ball foul(s) not penalised as a dead-ball foul that occurs during a down in which time expires.

(*b*) An inadvertent whistle is sounded during a down in which time expires.

(*c*) A touchdown is scored during a down in which time expires. (*Exception:* If the winner of the game has been decided and both field captains agree to forego the try, the period is not extended.)

(*d*) Offsetting fouls occur during a down in which time expires.

Game Clock

ARTICLE 4. (*a*) Playing time shall be kept with a game clock that may be either a stop watch operated by the field judge, line judge or back judge or a game clock operated by an assistant under the direction of the appropriate judge.

(*b*) The 25 seconds between the ready for play and the ball being put in play shall be timed with a watch operated by the appropriate official or 25-second clocks at each end of the playing enclosure operated by an assistant under the direction of the appropriate official. The use of a 25-second clock shall be determined by the game management.

When Clock Starts

ARTICLE 5. Following a free kick the game clock shall be started when the ball is legally touched in the field of play or crosses the goal line after being legally touched by Team B in its end zone. On a scrimmage down, the game clock shall be started when the ball is snapped or on prior signal by the referee. The clock shall not run during a try or during an extension of a period.

(*a*) The referee signals, sounds his whistle and the game clock starts when the ball is ready for play, if it was stopped:

1. When Team A is awarded a first down (*Exception:* 3-2-5-b-2).
2. For a referee's timeout for an injured player or official.
3. At the referee's discretion (see Rule 3-4-3).
4. To complete a penalty (see Rule 3-2-5-e).
5. For an inadvertent whistle (except on a free kick).
6. For a head coach's conference.

(*b*) The referee does NOT signal and the game clock starts when the ball is put in play, if it was stopped:

1. By a charged team timeout, a score, a touchback, an incompleted forward pass, or a live ball going out of bounds.
2. To award a first down to Team B, or when after a kick Team A is awarded a first down. The referee shall not declare the ball ready for play until both teams have had reasonable opportunity to complete their substitutions.
3. To complete a penalty for an infraction by the defensive team with less than 25 seconds remaining in the second and fourth periods (*Exception:* Rule 3-4-3).
4. When a 7-1-3-a-4 fals start *Exception* occurs.
5. For a 3-4-2-a *Exception*.

(*c*) If incidents in (*a*), above, occur in conjunction with a charged team timeout or any other incident following which the clock would not start until the ball is put in play, it shall be started when the ball is put in play.

(*d*) If the clock has been stopped for incidents in (a), above, and then subsequently is stopped for a radio or TV timeout, the game clock shall start when the ball is ready for play.

(*e*) If the clock was stopped to complete a penalty, it shall be started when the ball is declared ready for play unless 3-4-3 or A.R. 4 is invoked. If the clock had been stopped otherwise by rule, it shall be started on the snap.

When Clock Stops

ARTICLE 6. The game clock shall be stopped when each period ends. Any official may signal timeout when the rules provide for stopping the clock or when a timeout is charged to a team or to the referee. (*Exception:* 3-3-4-e). Other officials should repeat timeout signals.

3. TIMEOUTS

How Charged

ARTICLE 1. (*a*) The referee shall declare a timeout when he suspends play for any reason. Each timeout shall be charged to one of the teams or designated as referee's timeout.

(*b*) When a team's timeouts are exhausted and it requests a timeout with the 25-second clock running, the official should not acknowledge the request, interrupt the 25-second count or stop the game clock.

(*c*) During a timeout, players shall not practice with a ball on the field of play. (*Exception:* During the halftime intermission.)

Timeout

ARTICLE 2. The referee shall declare a timeout:

(*a*) When a touchdown, field goal, touchback or safety is scored.

(*b*) When an injury timeout is allowed.

(*c*) When the clock is stopped to complete a penalty.

(*d*) When a live ball goes out of bounds or is declared out of bounds.

(*e*) When a forward pass becomes incomplete.

(*f*) When Team A or B is awarded a first down.

(*g*) When an inadvertent whistle is sounded.

(*h*) When a head coach's conference is requested.

(*i*) When a radio or TV timeout is allowed.

(*j*) When an unfair noise timeout is required.

(*k*) When there is a first-down measurement.

(*l*) When a delay is caused by both teams.

(*m*) When a charged timeout is requested.

Referee's Discretionary Timeout

ARTICLE 3. (*a*) The referee may temporarily suspend the game when conditions warrant such action. The referee may declare and charge himself with a timeout for any contingency not elsewhere covered by the rules.

(*b*) When the game is stopped by actions of a person(s) not subject to the rules or for any other reasons not in the rules and cannot continue, the referee shall:

1. Suspend play and direct the players to their team areas.
2. Refer the problem to those responsible for the game's management.
3. Resume the game when he determines conditions are satisfactory.

(*c*) If a game may not be resumed immediately after Rule 3-3-3-a & b suspensions, it shall be terminated or resumed at a later time only by mutual consent of both teams.

(*d*) A suspended game, if resumed, will begin with the same time remaining and under the identical conditions of down, distance and field position.

(*e*) The game is a no-contest if there is not mutual consent of both teams to resume or terminate the game. (*Exception:* Conference or league regulations.)

(*f*) The referee's discretionary timeout also applies to the following play situations:

1. When there is undue delay by officials in placing the ball for the next snap.
2. When there is a consultation with team captains.
3. When conditions warrant temporary suspension.
4. When the offensive team cannot hear its signals because of crowd noise or noise created by persons subject to the rules.

Administrative procedures for unfair noise:

(*a*) When unable to communicate signals to teammates

because of unfair noise, a quarterback may raise his hands and look to the referee to request a legal delay.

(*b*) The referee may charge himself with a timeout and the offensive team may huddle. The referee may deny the request by pointing toward the defensive team's goal line.

(*c*) When the offensive team returns to the line of scrimmage, the game clock will start on the snap. The referee shall declare the ball ready for play by sounding his whistle. The 25-second clock is not in operation.

(*d*) Should the quarterback, during the game, subsequently request a second legal delay by raising his hands and looking to the referee, the referee will again charge himself with a timeout if, in his opinion, the unfair noise makes it impossible to hear offensive signals.

(*e*) The referee will then request the defensive captain to ask the crowd/persons subject to the rules for quiet. This signals the public address announcer to request cooperation and courtesy to the offensive team. The announcer will state that the defensive team will be charged a timeout for the next noise infraction.

(*f*) When the offensive team returns to the line of scrimmage, the game clock will start on the snap. The referee shall declare the ball ready for play by sounding his whistle. The 25-second clock is not in operation.

(*g*) If the quarterback again, during the game, indicates by raising his hands and looking to the referee to request a legal delay because his signals are not audible and the referee agrees, a team timeout will be charged to the defensive team.

(*h*) Following this timeout, the defensive team will be charged an additional team timeout for each subsequent unsuccessful attempt to start play. Only one timeout may be charged during the interval between downs.

(*i*) If the 25-second clock has been stopped twice for unfair noise violations against the same team, any subsequent stopping of the 24-second clock because of unfair noise against the same team will result in a charged timeout, or a delay penalty, if all the offending team's timeouts have been used.

Charged Team Timeouts

ARTICLE 4. The referee shall allow a charged team timeout when requested by any player or when an obviously injured player is not replaced.

(*a*) Each team is entitled to three charged team timeouts during each half without penalty.

(*b*) Consecutive charged team timeouts during an interval between downs shall not be allowed the same team (*Exceptions:* 1-4-4, 1-4-5, 3-3-4-e, 3-3-5 and 9-1-5-a).

(*c*) After the ball is declared dead and before the snap, a legal substitute may request a timeout if he is within 15 yards of the ball.

(*d*) A player who participated during the previous down may request a timeout between the time of the ready for play and the snap without being within 15 yards of the ball.

(*e*) A player or incoming substitute may request a conference with the referee if the coach believes a rule has been improperly enforced. If the rule enforcement is not changed, the coach's team will be charged a timeout, or a delay penalty if all timeouts have been used.

1. Only the referee may stop the clock for a coach's conference.
2. A request for a conference must be requested before the ball is snapped or free-kicked for the next play and before the end of the second and fourth period.

Injury Timeout

ARTICLE 5. (*a*) In the event of an obviously injured player, the referee may charge himself with a timeout, provided the player for whom the timeout is taken is removed from the game for at least one down. Otherwise his team will be charged with a team timeout. After a team's charged timeouts have been exhausted, the injured player must leave for one down. The referee may charge himself with a timeout for an injured official.

(*b*) Any official may stop the clock for an injured player.

(*c*) To curtail a possible time-gaining advantage by feigning injuries, attention is directed to the strongly worded statement in "The Football Code" concerning the feigning of any injury.

(*d*) An injury timeout may follow a charged team timeout (3-3-5).

Violation Timeouts

ARTICLE 6. For noncompliance with 1-4-4, 1-4-5, 3-3-4-e or 9-1-5-a during a down, a timeout shall be charged to a team at the succeeding spot (see Rule 3-4-2-b).

Length of Timeouts

ARTICLE 7. (*a*) A charged team timeout requested by any player shall not exceed one minute and 30 seconds. Other timeouts shall be no longer than the referee deems necessary to fulfill the purpose for which they are declared including a radio or TV timeout, but any timeout may be extended by the referee for the benefit of a seriously injured player.

(*b*) If the team charged with a one-minute 30-second team timeout wishes to resume play before the expiration of one minute and its opponent indicates readiness, the referee will declare the ball ready for play.

(*c*) The length of a referee's timeouts depend on the circumstances of each timeout.

(*d*) The field captain must exercise his penalty option before he or a teammate consults with his coach on a sideline during a timeout.

Referee's Notification

ARTICLE 8. The referee shall notify both teams 30 seconds before a charged team timeout expires and five seconds later shall declare the ball ready for play.

(*a*) When a third timeout is charged to a team in either half, the referee shall notify the field captain and head coach of that team.

(*b*) Unless a game clock is the official timepiece, the referee also shall inform each field captain and head coach when approximately two minutes of playing time remain in each half. He may order the clock stopped for that purpose.

(*c*) If a visible game clock is not the official timing device during the last two minutes of each half, the referee or his representative shall notify each captain and head coach of the time remaining each time the clock is stopped by rule. Also, a representative may leave the team area along the limit line to relay timing information under these conditions.

4. DELAYS

Delaying the Start of a Half

ARTICLE 1 (*a*) Each team shall have its players on the field for the opening play at the scheduled time for the beginning of each half.
Penalty—15 yards [S7 and S21].
(*b*) The home management is responsible for clearing the field of play and end zones at the beginning of each half so the periods may start at the scheduled time. Bands, speeches, presentations, homecoming and similar activities are under the jurisdiction of home management and a prompt start of each half is mandatory.
Penalty—10 yards [S7 and S21].
Exception: The referee may waive the penalty for circumstances beyond the control of the home management.

Illegal Delay in the Game

ARTICLE 2. (*a*) The ball shall be declared ready for play consistently throughout game by the referee when the officials are in position. Consuming more than 25 seconds to put the ball in play after it is declared ready for play is an illegal delay. (*Exceptions:* When the 25-second count is interrupted by circumstances beyond the control of either team, or unfair noise situations occur, a new 25-second count shall be started and the game clock shall start on the snap.)
(*b*) Illegal delay also includes:
1. Crawling or deliberately advancing the ball after it is dead.
2. When a team has expended its three timeouts and commits a 1-4-4, 1-4-5, 3-3-4-e or 9-1-5-a infraction.
Penalty—5 yards [S7 and S21].

Unfair Game Clock Tactics

ARTICLE 3. The referee shall order the game clock started

or stopped whenever, in his opinion, either team is trying to conserve or consume playing time by tactics obviously unfair. This includes starting the clock on the snap if the foul is by the team ahead in the score and any illegal forward pass or illegal touching that conserves time for Team A.
Penalty—5 yards [S7 and S21].

5. SUBSTITUTIONS

Substitution Procedures
ARTICLE 1. Any number of legal substitutes for either team may enter the game between periods, after a score or try, or during the interval between downs only for the purpose of replacing a player(s).
Penalty—5 yards [S22].

Legal Substitutions
ARTICLE 2. A legal substitute may replace a player or fill a player vacancy provided none of the following restrictions is violated:

(*a*) No incoming substitute or replaced player shall be on the field while the ball is in play.

(*b*) An incoming legal substitute must enter the field directly from his team area and a substitute or player leaving must depart at the sideline nearest his team area. A replaced player must also leave at the sideline nearest his team area.

(*c*) Substitutes who become players must remain in the game for one play and replaced players must remain out of the game for one play except during the interval between periods, after a score, or when a timeout has been charged to a team, or to the referee.
Penalty—If ball is dead: 5 yards from succeeding spot; otherwise, 5 yards from previous spot [S22].

(*d*) Teams shall have no more than 3 American or Canadian players on the field at any one time (the field includes the players bench). These are defined as players who still hold American or Canadian nationality and/or passport. These players must be clearly identified by an A on the back of the Helmet no less than 4 inches in length and must be of a colour in complete contrast to the helmet so as to be clearly seen. If more than three of these players are discovered on the field, the offending club will be liable to disciplinary action by the league's disciplinary committee.

Regulations for Youth and Junior Teams

ARTICLE 3. Youth and Junior Teams may adopt more liberal substitution regulations when mutually agreed or when authorised by their association, league or federation.

RULE 4

BALL IN PLAY, DEAD BALL, OUT OF BOUNDS

1. BALL IN PLAY—DEAD BALL

Dead Ball Becomes Alive

ARTICLE 1. After a dead ball has been declared ready for play, it becomes a live ball when it is legally snapped, or free kicked legally. A ball snapped or free kicked before the ready for play shall be whistled by the official.

Live Ball Becomes Dead

ARTICLE 2. (*a*) A live ball becomes a dead ball as provided in the rules or when an official sounds his whistle (even though inadvertently), or otherwise declares the ball dead.

(*b*) An official sounds his whistle inadvertently during a down when:

1. A live ball in player possession or loose is in or behind the neutral zone and there has been no change of team possession—replay the down, if not in conflict with other rules.

2. A live ball is beyond the neutral zone and there has been no change of team possession:
   (a) Ball in player possession—Option: Team A may elect to put the ball in play where declared dead or replay the down, if not in conflict with other rules.

    (b) Loose following a fumble, backward pass or illegal forward pass—return to the spot where last possessed, if not in conflict with other rules.

3. Following a change of team possession, a live ball is:
    (a) In player possession—ball shall be put in play where declared dead, if not in conflict with other rules.
    (b) Loose following a fumble, backward pass or illegal forward pass—return to the spot where last possessed, if not in conflict with other rules.

4. During a legal forward pass or a free or scrimmage kick, the ball is returned to the previous spot and the down replayed, if not in conflict with other rules.

5. A live ball not in player possession touches anything in bounds other than the ground, a player or an official, the inadvertent whistle rule applies.

6. Anyone other than a player or an official interferes in any way other than with a live ball not in player possession, the inadvertent whistle rule applies.

Note: If a fouls occurs during any of the above downs, the penalty shall be administered as in any other play situation. Enforce postscrimmage kick fouls from the previous spot.

Ball Declared Dead

ARTICLE 3. A live ball becomes dead and an official shall sound his whistle or declare it dead:

(*a*) When it goes out of bounds, when a runner is out of bounds or when a runner is so held that his forward progress is stopped.

(*b*) When any part of the runner's body, except his hand or foot, touches the ground or when the runner is tackled or otherwise falls and loses possession of the ball as he contacts the ground with any part of his body, except his hand or foot. (*Exception:* The ball remains alive when an offensive player has simulated a kick or is in position to kick the ball held for a place kick by a teammate. The ball may be kicked, passed or advanced.)

(*c*) When a touchdown, touchback, safety, field goal, or successful try occurs, or when Team A completes an illegal forward pass in Team B's end zone, or Team A completes a forward pass to an ineligible player in Team B's end zone.

(*d*) When during a try, Team B obtains possession of the ball or when it becomes certain that a scrimmage kick on a try will not score the point.

(*e*) When a player of the kicking team catches or recovers any free kick or a scrimmage kick that is beyond the neutral zone; when a free kick or scrimmage kick comes to rest and no player attempts to secure it; when a free kick or scrimmage kick is caught or recovered by any player following a valid, invalid or illegal signal (any waving signal) for a fair catch beyond the neutral zone, or when a return kick is made.

(*f*) When a forward pass strikes the ground.

(*g*) When a live ball not in player possession touches anything in bounds other than a player, official or the ground.

(*h*) When a simultaneous catch or recovery of a live ball is made in bounds by opposing players.

(*i*) When the ball becomes illegal while in play, inadvertent whistle provisions apply.

Ball Ready For Play
ARTICLE 4. No player shall put the ball in play until it is declared ready for play.
Penalty—5 yards from the spot where the ball should have been put in play legally [S7 and S19].

25-Second Count
ARTICLE 5. The ball shall be put in play within 25 seconds after it is declared ready for play, unless, during that interval, play is suspended. If play is suspended, the 25-second count will start again (*Exception:* Unfair crowd noise situations.)
Penalty—5 yards [S7 and S21].

2. OUT OF BOUNDS

Player Out of Bounds
ARTICLE 1. A player is out of bounds when any part of his person touches anything, other than another player or game

official, on or outside a boundary line. A player who touches a pylon is out of bounds behind the goal line.

Held Ball Out of Bounds

ARTICLE 2. A ball in player possession is out of bounds when either the ball or any part of the runner touches the ground or anything else that is on or outside a boundary line except another player or game official.

Ball Out of Bounds

ARTICLE 3. A ball not in player possession, other than a kick that scores a goal, is out of bounds when it touches the ground, a player or anything else that is on or outside the boundary line. A ball that touches a pylon is out of bounds behind the goal line.

Out of Bounds at Crossing Point

ARTICLE 4. (*a*) If a live ball not in player possession crosses a boundary line and is then declared out of bounds, it is out of bounds at the crossing point.

(*b*) If the ball is in bounds when the runner is ruled out of bounds, the dead-ball spot is directly under the foremost part of the ball.

(*c*) If the ball is on or above the out-of-bounds territory when the runner is ruled out of bounds, the dead-ball spot is directly under the foremost part of the ball.

(*d*) A touchdown may be scored if the ball is in bounds and has broken the plane of the goal line before or simultaneously with the runner's going out of bounds.

(*e*) An eligible receiver who is in the opponent's end zone and contacting the ground is credited with a completion if he reaches over the sideline or end line and catches a legal pass.

Out of Bounds at Forward Point

ARTICLE 5. If a live ball is declared out of bounds and the ball does not cross a bondary line, it is out of bounds at the ball's most forward point when it was declared dead.

RULE 5

SERIES OF DOWNS, LINE TO GAIN

1. A SERIES: STARTED, BROKEN, RENEWED

When to Award Series

ARTICLE 1. (*a*) A series of four consecutive scrimmage downs shall be awarded to the team that is next to put the ball in play by a snap following a free kick, touchback, fair catch or change in team possession.

(*b*) A new series shall be awarded to Team A if it is in legal possession of the ball on or beyond its line to gain.

(*c*) A new series shall be awarded to Team B if, after fourth down, Team A has failed to earn a first down.

(*d*) A new series shall be awarded to Team B if A's scrimmage kick goes out of bounds or comes to rest and no player attempts to secure it.

(*e*) A new series shall be awarded to the team in legal possession:

1. If a change of team possession occurs during the down.
2. If a player of Team B first touches a scrimmage kick that has crossed the neutral zone. (*Exception:* When a penalty for a foul by either team is accepted and the down is replayed.)
3. If an accepted penalty awards the ball to the offended team.
4. If an accepted penalty mandates a first down.

Line to Gain

ARTICLE 2. The line to gain for a series shall be established 10 yards in advance of the most forward point of the ball; but if this line is in the opponents' end zone, the goal line becomes the line to gain.

Measurement of Distance

ARTICLE 3 (*a*) The most forward point of the ball when declared dead between the goal lines shall be the determining point in measuring distance gained or lost by either team during any down. The ball shall always be placed with its length axis parallel to the sideline before measuring.

(*b*) Unnecessary measurements to determine first downs shall not be requested, but any doubtful distance should be measured without request.

Continuity of Downs Broken

ARTICLE 4. The continuity of a series of downs is broken when:

(*a*) Team possession of the ball changes during a down.

(*b*) A player of Team B touches a scrimmage kick that has crossed the neutral zone.

(*c*) A kick goes out of bounds.

(*d*) A kick comes to rest and no player attempts to secure it.

(*e*) At the end of a down, Team A has earned a first down. Any down may be repeated if so provided by the rules.

(*f*) After fourth down, Team A has failed to earn a first down.

2. DOWN AND POSSESSION AFTER A PENALTY

Foul During Free Kick

ARTICLE 1. When a scrimmage follows the penalty for a foul committed during a free kick, the down and distance established by that penalty shall be first down with 10 yards to gain.

Penalty Resulting in First Down

ARTICLE 2. It is a first down with 10 yards to gain:

(*a*) After a penalty that leaves the ball in possession of Team A beyond its line to gain.

(*b*) After a pass interference penalty has awarded the ball to Team A between the goal lines.

(*c*) When a penalty stipulates a first down.

Foul Before Change of Team Possession

ARTICLE 3. After a distance penalty between the goal lines, incurred during a scrimmage down and before any change of team possession during that down, the ball belongs to Team A and the down shall be repeated unless the penalty also involves loss of a down, stipulates a first down, or leaves the ball on or beyond the line to gain (*Exception:* 10-2-2-e-5).

If the penalty involves loss of a down, the down shall count as one of the four in that series.

Foul After Change of Team Possession

ARTICLE 4. If a distance penalty is accepted for a foul incurred during a down after change of team possession, the ball belongs to the team in possession when the foul occurred. The down and distance established by any distance penalty incurred after change of team possession during that down shall be first down with 10 yards to gain. (*Exception:* Live-ball fouls penalised as dead-ball fouls).

Penalty Declined

ARTICLE 5. If a penalty is declined, the number of the next down shall be whatever it would have been if that foul had not occurred.

Foul Between Downs

ARTICLE 6. After a distance penalty incurred between downs, the number of the next down shall be the same as that established before the foul occurred unless enforcement for a foul by Team B leaves the ball on or beyond the line to gain or a foul requires a first down.

Foul Between Series

ARTICLE 7. A scrimmage following a penalty incurred after a series ends and before the next series begins shall be first down, but the line to gain shall be established before the penalty is enforced.

Fouls by Both Teams

ARTICLE 8. If offsetting fouls occur during a down, that down shall be repeated. (*Exceptions:* 10-1-4). If cancelling fouls occur between successive downs, the next down shall be the same as it would have been had no fouls occurred.

Fouls During a Loose Ball

ARTICLE 9. Fouls when the ball is loose shall be penalised from the basic or previous spot (10-2-2-c, d, e & f).

If a team had not fouled prior to gaining possession of a loose ball or forward pass, it may retain possession by refusing any penalty for a foul by an opponent.

Rule Decisions Final

ARTICLE 10. No rule decision may be changed after the ball is next legally snapped or legally free kicked.

RULE 6

KICKS

1. FREE KICKS

Restraining Lines

ARTICLE 1. For any free kick formation, the kicking team's restraining line shall be the yard line through the most forward point from which the ball shall be kicked, and the receiving team's restraining line shall be the yard line 10 yards beyond that point. Unless relocated by a penalty, the kicking team's restraining line on a kickoff shall be its 40-yard line and for a free kick after a safety, its 20-yard line.

Free Kick Formation

ARTICLE 2. A ball from a free kick formation must be kicked legally and from some point on Team A's restraining line and on or between the in-bounds lines. After the ball is ready for play and for any reason it falls from the tee, Team A shall not kick the ball and the official shall sound his whistle immediately. When the ball is kicked:

(*a*) All players of each team must be in bounds.

(*b*) Each Team A player except the holder and kicker of a place kick must be behind the ball. After a safety, when a punt or drop kick is used, the ball shall be kicked within one yard behind the kicking team's restraining line.

(*c*) All Team B players must be behind their restraining line.

(*d*) At least five Team B players must be within five yards of their restraining line.

(*e*) Team A substitutes may not touch a kick if they enter the field after the ball is declared ready for play.

(*f*) A Team A player who voluntarily goes out of bounds during the kick may not return in bounds during the down. **Penalty—5 yards from previous spot [S18 or S19]**

Free Kick Recovery

ARTICLE 3. A Team A player may touch a free kicked ball:

(*a*) After it touches a Team B player.

(*b*) After it breaks the plane of and remains beyond Team B's restraining line.

(*c*) After it touches any player, the ground or an official beyond Team B's restraining line.

Thereafter, all players of Team A become eligible to touch, recover or catch the kick (*Exception:* 6-1-2-e & f). Illegal touching of a free kick is a violation that, when the ball becomes dead, gives the receiving team the privilege of taking the ball at the spot of the violation. However, if a penalty incurred by either team before the ball becomes dead is accepted, this privilege is cancelled.

Forced Touching Disregarded

ARTICLE 4. (*a*) An in-bounds player pushed or blocked by an opponent into a free kick is not, while in bounds, deemed to have touched the kick.

(*b*) An in-bounds player touched by a ball batted by an opponent is not deemed to have touched the ball.

Free Kick at Rest

ARTICLE 5. If a free kick comes to rest in bounds and no player attempts to secure it, the ball becomes dead and belongs to the receiving team at the dead-ball spot.

Free Kick Caught or Recovered

ARTICLE 6. If a free kick is caught or recovered by a player of the receiving team, the ball continues in play

(*Exceptions:* 6-1-7, 6-5-1 and 2, and 4-1-3-e). If caught or recovered by a player of the kicking team, the ball becomes dead.

Touching Ground On or Beyond Goal Lines
ARTICLE 7. The ball becomes dead and belongs to the team defending its goal line when a free kick is untouched by Team B prior to touching the ground on or behind Team B's goal line.

2. FREE KICK OUT OF BOUNDS

Kicking Team
ARTICLE 1. A free kick out of bounds between the goal lines untouched in bounds by a player of Team B is a foul.
Penalty—Repeat kick 5 yards behind previous spot [S19].

Receiving Team
ARTICLE 2. When a free kick goes out of bounds between the goal lines, the ball belongs to the receiving team at the in-bounds spot. When a free kick goes out of bounds behind the goal line, the ball belongs to the team defending that goal line.

3. SCRIMMAGE KICKS

Fails to Cross Neutral Zone
ARTICLE 1. Except during a try, a scrimmage kick behind the neutral zone continues in play. All players may catch or recover the ball behind the neutral zone and advance it.

Crosses the Neutral Zone
ARTICLE 2. (*a*) No in-bounds player of the kicking team shall touch a scrimmage kick beyond the neutral zone before it touches an opponent. Such illegal touching is a violation that, when the ball becomes dead, gives the receiving team the privilege of taking the ball at the spot of the violation. However, if a penalty incurred by either team before the ball

becomes dead is accepted, this privilege is cancelled. (*Exceptions:* 2-25-11, 8-4-2-b and 10-2-2-e-5).

(*b*) Blocking of a kick that occurs in the vicinity of the neutral zone is ruled as having occurred within or behind that zone.

All Become Eligible

ARTICLE 3. When a scrimmage kick that has crossed the neutral zone touches a player of the receiving team who is in bounds, any player may catch or recover the ball.

Forced Touching Disregarded

ARTICLE 4. (*a*) A player pushed or blocked by an opponent into a scrimmage kick that has crossed the neutral zone, shall not, while in bounds, be deemed to have touched the kick.

(*b*) An in-bounds player touched by a ball batted by an opponent is not deemed to have touched the ball.

Catch or Recovery by Receiving Team

ARTICLE 5. If a scrimmage kick is caught or recovered by a player of the receiving team, the ball continues in play. (*Exception:* 6-3-9, 6-5-1 and 2, and 4-1-3-e).

Catch or Recovery by Kicking Team

ARTICLE 6. (*a*) If a player of the kicking team catches or recovers a scrimmage kick beyond the neutral zone, the ball becomes dead.

(*b*) When opposing players, each eligible to touch the ball, simultaneously recover a rolling kick or catch a scrimmage kick, this simultaneous possession makes the ball dead. A kick declared dead in joint possession of opposing players is awarded to the receiving team (2-2-8) (4-1-3-i).

Out of Bounds Between Goal Lines or at Rest

ARTICLE 7. If a scrimmage kick goes out of bounds between the goal lines, or comes to rest in bounds and no player attempts to secure it, the ball becomes dead and belongs to the receiving team at the dead-ball spot (*Exceptions:* 8-4-2-b).

Out of Bounds Behind Goal Line

ARTICLE 8. If a scrimmage kick (other than one that scores a field goal) goes out of bounds behind a goal line, the ball becomes dead and belongs to the team defending that goal line (*Exceptions:* 8-4-2-b).

Touching Ground On or Behind Goal

ARTICLE 9. The ball becomes dead and belongs to the team defending its goal line when a scrimmage kick is untouched by Team B beyond the neutral zone prior to touching the ground on or behind Team B's goal line (*Exception:* 8-4-2-b).

Legal Kick

ARTICLE 10. A legal scrimmage kick is a punt, drop kick or place kick made according to the rules. A return kick is an illegal kick and a live ball foul that causes the ball to become dead.
Penalty—For an illegal kick 5 yards [S31].

Loose Behind the Goal Line

ARTICLE 11. If a Team A player bats a loose ball behind Team B's goal line during a scrimmage kick, it is a live-ball foul (*Exception:* 8-4-2-b).
Penalty—Touchback [S7 and S31].

4. OPPORTUNITY TO CATCH A KICK

Interference with Opportunity

ARTICLE 1. A player of the receiving team who is within the boundary lines and is so located that he could have caught a free kick or a scrimmage kick that is beyond the neutral zone while such kick is in flight must be given an unmolested opportunity to catch the kick.

(*a*) No player of the kicking team may be within two yards of a player positioned to catch a free or scrimmage kick while the ball is in a downward flight.

(*b*) This protection terminates when the kick is touched by any player of Team B or the ground.

(*c*) If contact with a potential receiver is the result of a player being blocked or pushed by an opponent, it is not a foul.

(*d*) It is not a foul if a member of the kicking team is blocked to within two yards of the receiver when the ball is on its downward flight.

(*e*) It is a contact foul if the kicking team contacts the potential receiver prior to, or simultaneous with, his first touching of the ball.

Penalty—For foul between goal lines: receiving team's ball, first down, 15 yards beyond spot of foul for contact foul and 5 yards for noncontact foul. For foul behind goal line: award touchback and penalise from succeeding spot [S33]. Flagrant offenders shall be disqualified.

5. FAIR CATCH

Dead Where Caught

ARTICLE 1. (*a*) When a Team B player makes a fair catch, the ball becomes dead where caught and belongs to Team B at that spot.

(*b*) Rules pertaining to a fair catch apply only when a scrimmage kick crosses the neutral zone or during free kicks.

(*c*) The purpose of the fair catch provision is to protect the receiver who by his fair catch signal, agrees he or a team-mate will not advance after the catch.

(*d*) The ball shall be put in play by a snap by the receiving team at the spot of the catch, if the ball is caught.

No Advance

ARTICLE 2. No Team B player shall carry a caught or recovered ball more than two steps in any direction following a valid, invalid or illegal fair catch signal by any Team B player.

Penalty—5 yards from basic spot. Penalise as dead ball foul [S7 and S21].

Illegal Signals

ARTICLE 3 (*a*) During a down in which a kick is made, no

player of Team B shall make any illegal fair catch signal during a free kick or beyond the neutral zone during a scrimmage kick.

(*b*) A catch following a valid illegal signal is a fair catch. The ball is dead where caught unless the signal follows the catch.

(*c*) Fouls for illegal signals beyond the neutral zone apply only to Team B.

(*d*) An illegal signal beyond the neutral zone is possible only when the ball has crossed the neutral zone (2-15-7).

Penalty—Free kick: receiving team's ball 15 yards from spot of foul (10-2-2-e) [S32].

Scrimmage kick: receiving team's ball 15 yards from basic spot (10-2-2-e-5) [S32].

Illegal Block

ARTICLE 4. A player of Team B who has made a valid, invalid or illegal signal for a fair catch and does not touch the ball shall not block or foul an opponent during that down.

Penalty—Free kick: receiving team's ball 15 yards from spot of foul (10-2-2-e) [S38, S39 or S40].

Scrimmage kick: receiving team's ball 15 yards from basic spot (10-2-2-e-5) [S38, S39 or S40].

No Tackling

ARTICLE 5. No player of the kicking team shall tackle or block an opponent who has completed a fair catch. Only the player making a fair catch signal has this protection.

Penalty—Receiving team's ball 15 yards from succeeding spot [S7 and S38].

RULE 7

SNAPPING AND PASSING THE BALL

1. THE SCRIMMAGE

Starting with a Snap

ARTICLE 1. The ball shall be put in a legal snap unless the rules provide for a legal free kick.

Penalty—5 yards from previous spot. Penalise as dead-ball foul [S7 and S19].

Not in a Side Zone

ARTICLE 2. The ball may not be snapped in a side zone. If the starting point for any scrimmage down is in a side zone, it shall be transferred to the in-bounds spot.

Offensive Team Requirements

ARTICLE 3. The offensive requirments for a scrimmage are as follows:

(a) Before the ball is snapped:

1. The snapper, after assuming his position for the succeeding snap and adjusting the ball, may neither move nor change the position of the ball in a manner simulating the beginning of a play. An infraction of this provision may be penalised whether or not the ball is snapped and the penalty for any resultant offsides or contact foul by an opponent shall be cancelled. Excessive tilting is not a foul until the snap and is a live-ball foul [S7 and S19].

2. After the ball is ready for play and before the snap, each player or entering substitute of Team A must have been within 15 yards of the ball [S19].

3. No player of the offensive team shall make a false start including contacting an opponent after the ball is ready for play or be in or beyond the neutral zone after the snapper touches the ball and before the snap.

   (*Exceptions:* Does not apply to substitutes and replaced players or offensive players in a scrimmage kick formation who, after the snapper touches the ball, point at opponents and break the neutral zone with their hand(s).) A false start includes:

   (*a*) Feigning a charge.

   (*b*) A shift or movement that simulates the beginning of a play. This includes the snapper, who after assuming a position for the succeeding snap and touching the ball, moves to another position.

   (*c*) A lineman between the snapper and the player on the end of the line or a player other than the snapper wearing a number 50-79, after having placed a hand(s) on or near the ground, moves his hand(s), or makes any quick movement.

(*d*) An offensive player, neither legally in the backfield nor legally on the line of scrimmage after having placed a hand(s) on or near the ground, moves his hand(s) or makes any quick movement.

4. It is not a false start if any player on the line of scrimmage moves when threatened by a Team B player in the neutral zone. The threatened Team A player may not enter the neutral zone.

5. An official shall sound his whistle when:
   (*a*) There is a false start.
   (*b*) An offensive player is in or beyond the neutral zone after the snapper touches the ball.
   (*c*) A Team A player moves into the neutral zone when threatened by a Team B player in the neutral zone.
   (*d*) A 7-1-3-a-4 infraction occurs.

Note: An infraction of this rule may be penalised whether or not the ball is snapped and the penalty for any resultant offsides or contact foul other than unsportsmanlike or personal fouls by an opponent shall be cancelled [S18 or S19 and S7].

(b) When the ball is snapped:

The offensive team must be in a formation that meets these requirements:

1. At least seven players on their scrimmage line, not less than five of whom shall be numbered 50 through 79 (*Exceptions:* 1-4-2-b). The remaining players must be either on their scrimmage line or behind their backfield line, except as follows:

2. One player may be between his scrimmage line and his backfield line if in a position to receive a hand-to-hand snap from between the snapper's legs. When in such position, that player may receive the snap himself or it may go directly to any player legally in the backfield [S19].

3. The player on each side of and next to the snapper may lock legs with the snapper, but any other lineman of the team on offense must have both feet outside the outside foot of the player next to him when the ball is snapped [S19].

4. All players must be in bounds and only the snapper may be encroaching on the neutral zone, but no part of his person may be beyond the neutral zone and his feet must be stationary behind the ball [S18 or S19].

5. One offensive player may be in motion, but not in motion toward his opponents' goal line. If such player starts from his scrimmage line, he must be at least five yards behind that line when the ball is snapped. Other offensive players must be stationary in their positions without movement of the feet, body, head or arms [S20].

(c) After the ball is snapped:

1. No offensive lineman may receive a snap [S19].

Penalty—For foul before ball is snapped: 5 yards from succeeding spot. For foul as or after ball is snapped: 5 yards from previous spot [S18, S19 or S20].

Defensive Team Requirements

ARTICLE 4. The defensive team requirements are as follows:

(*a*) After the ball is ready for play and until it is snapped, no player on defense may touch the ball except when moved illegally as in 7-1-3-a-1 nor may any player contact an opponent or in any other way interfere with him [S7, S19]. An official shall sound his whistle immediately.

(*b*) No defensive player may be in or beyond the neutral zone at the snap [S18].

(*c*) No player of the team on defense shall use words or signals that disconcert opponents when they are preparing to put the ball in play. No player may call defensive signals that simulate the sound or cadence of (or otherwise interfere with) offensive starting signals. An official shall sound his whistle immediately [S7 and S19].

Penalty—For foul before ball is snapped: 5 yards from

succeeding spot. For fouls as or after ball is snapped: 5 yards from previous spot [S18 or S19].

Shift Plays

ARTICLE 5. (*a*) If a snap is preceded by a huddle or shift, all players of the offensive team must come to an absolute stop and remain stationary in their positions, without movement of the feet, body, head or arms, for at least one full second before the ball is snapped.

(*b*) It is not intended that Rule 7-1-3-a should prohibit smooth, rhythmical shifts if properly executed. A smooth, cadence shift or unhurried motion is not an infraction. However, it is the responsibility of an offensive player who moves before the snap to do so in a manner that in no way simulates the beginning of a play. After the ball is ready for play and all players are in scrimmage formation, no offensive player shall make a quick, jerky movement before the snap. Any such motion is an infraction of the rule. Although not intended to be all-inclusive, the following examples illustrate the type of movement prohibited before the snap:

1. A lineman moving his foot, shoulder, arm, body or head in a quick, jerky motion in any direction.
2. A centre shifting or moving the ball, or moving his thumb or fingers, or flexing elbows, jerking head or dipping shoulders or buttocks.
3. The quarterback "chucking" hands at centre, flexing elbows under centre or dropping shoulders quickly just before the snap.
4. A player starting in motion before the snap simulating receiving the ball by "chucking" his hands toward the centre or quarterback, or making any quick, jerky movement that simulates the beginning of a play.
5. After an interior offensive lineman or a player numbered 50 through 79, who is on the line of scrimmage, has assumed a position with hand or hands on or near the ground (below the knee) he is restricted in movement until the ball is snapped (7-1-3-a-3).

Penalty—5 yards from previous spot [S7 and S20].

Handling the Ball Forward

ARTICLE 6. No player may hand the ball forward except during a scrimmage down as follows:

(*a*) A Team A player who is behind his scrimmage line may hand the ball forward to a backfield teammate who is also behind that line.

(*b*) A Team A player who is behind his scrimmage line may hand the ball forward to a teammate who was on his scrimmage line when the ball was snapped, provided that teammate left his line position by a movement of both feet that faced him towards his own end line and was at least one yard behind his scrimmage line when he received the ball.

Penalty—5 yards from spot of foul also, loss of a down if by Team A before team possession changes during a scrimmage down [S35 and S9].

2. BACKWARD PASS AND FUMBLE

During Live Ball

ARTICLE 1 (*a*) A runner may hand or pass the ball backward at any time, except to throw the ball intentionally out of bounds to conserve time.

(*b*) A snap is a backward pass; however, it may not go directly to a lineman of Team A.

Penalty—5 yards from spot of foul also, loss of down if by Team A before team possession changes during a scrimmage down [S36 and S9].

Caught or Recovered

ARTICLE 2. A backward pass or fumble may be caught or recovered by any inbounds player (*Exception:* 7-2-1-b):

(*a*) If caught in flight in bounds, the ball continues in play unless the catch is made on or behind the opponent's goal line;

(*b*) If recovered by the fumbling or passing team, the ball continues in play;

(*c*) If recovered by the opponent of the fumbling or passing team, the ball becomes dead and belongs to his team where recovered;

(*d*) If a backward pass or fumble is caught or recovered simultaneously by opposing players, the ball becomes dead and belongs to the team last in possession.

Out of Bounds

ARTICLE 3. When a backward pass or fumble goes out of bounds between the goal lines, the ball belongs to the passing or fumbling team at the out-of-bounds spot; if out of bounds behind a goal line, it is a touchback or a safety (*Exception:* 9-4-2).

3. FORWARD PASS

Legal Forward Pass

ARTICLE 1. Team A may make one forward pass during each scrimmage down before team possession changes, provided the pass is thrown from a point in or behind the neutral zone.

Illegal Forward Pass

ARTICLE 2. A forward pass is illegal:

(*a*) If thrown by Team A when the passer is beyond the neutral zone.

(*b*) If thrown by Team B, or if thrown by Team A after team possession has changed during the down.

(*c*) If it is the second forward pass by Team A during the same down.

(*d*) If intentionally thrown into an area not occupied by an eligible Team A player to save loss of yardage or directly to the ground to conserve time.

Penalty—5 yards from spot of foul also, loss of a down if by Team A before team possession changes during a scrimmage down [S35 or S36 and S9].

Eligibility to Touch Legal Pass

ARTICLE 3. Eligibility rules apply only when a legal forward pass is thrown. All Team B players are eligible to touch or catch a pass. When the ball is snapped, the following Team A players are eligible:

(*a*) Each player who is in an end position on his scrimmage line and who is wearing a number other than 50 through 79.

(*b*) Each player who is legally in his backfield wearing a number other than 50 through 79.

(*c*) A player wearing a number other than 50 through 79, in position to receive a hand-to-hand snap from between the snapper's legs.

Eligibility Lost by Going Out of Bounds

ARTICLE 4. No eligible offensive player who goes out of bounds during a down shall touch a legal forward pass in the field of play or end zone until it has been touched by an opponent.

Exception: This does not apply to an eligible offensive player who attempts to return in bounds immediately after being blocked or pushed out of bounds by an opponent.

Penalty—Loss of down at previous spot [S31 and S9].

Eligibility Regained

ARTICLE 5. When a Team B player touches a legal forward pass all players become eligible.

Completed Pass

ARTICLE 6. Any forward pass is completed when caught by a player of the passing team who is in bounds, and the ball continues in play unless the completion results in a touchdown or the pass has been caught simultaneously by opposing players. If a forward pass is caught simultaneously by opposing players in bounds, the ball becomes dead and belongs to the passing team.

Incompleted Pass

ARTICLE 7. (*a*) Any forward pass is incomplete when the pass touches the ground or goes out of bounds. It is also incomplete when a player jumps and receives the pass but first lands on or outside a boundary line unless his forward progress has been stopped in the field of play (2–2–7–c).

(*b*) When a legal forward pass is incomplete, the ball belongs to the passing team at the previous spot.

(*c*) When an illegal forward pass is incomplete, the ball belongs to the passing team at the spot of the pass (*Exception:* if any illegal pass is thrown from the end zone, the offending team may accept a safety or decline the penalty and accept the result of the play.) (4-1-3-f).

Illegal Contact and Pass Interference

ARTICLE 8. (*a*) During a down in which a legal foreward pass crosses the neutral zone, illegal contact by Team A and Team B players is prohibited from the time the ball is snapped until it is touched by any player.

(*b*) Offensive pass interference by a Team A player beyond the neutral zone during a legal forward pass play in which a forward pass crosses the neutral zone is contact that interferes with a Team B eligible player. It is the responsibility of the offensive player to avoid the opponents. It is not offensive pass interference if it is the type that occurs:

1. When, immediately following the snap, a Team A player charges and contacts an opponent at a point not more than one yard beyond the neutral zone and does not continue the contact beyond three yards.
2. When two or more eligible players are making a simultaneous and bona fide attempt to reach, catch or bat the pass. Eligible players of either team have equal rights to the ball.

(*c*) Defensive pass interference is contact beyond the netural zone by a Team B player whose intent to impede an eligible opponent is obvious and it could prevent the opponent the opportunity of receiving a catchable forward pass. When in question, a legal forward pass is catchable. Defensive pass interference occurs only after a forward pass is thrown. It is not defensive pass interference if it is the type that occurs (9-3-4-c, d and e):

1. When, immediately following the snap, opposing players charge and establish contact with opponents at a point that is within one yard beyond the netural zone.
2. When two or more eligible players are making a simultaneous and bona fide attempt to reach, catch or

bat the pass, eligible players of either team have equal rights to the ball.

3. When a Team B player legally contacts an opponent before the pass is thrown (see Rule 9-3-4-c and d).

Penalty—Pass interference by Team A: 15 yards from previous spot plus loss of down [S33 and S9].

Pass interference by Team B: Team A's ball at spot of foul, first down. No penalty enforced from outside the two-yard line may place the ball inside the two-yard line.

If the previous spot was on or inside the two-yard line, first down half-way between the previous spot and the goal line [S33] (see Rule 10-2-3 Exception).

NOTE: When the ball is snapped between the Team B 17-yard line and the Team B two yard line and the spot of the foul is inside the two-yard line or in the end zone, the penalty shall place the ball at the two-yard line.

Contact Interference

ARTICLE 9. (*a*) Either A or B may legally interfere with opponents behind the neutral zone.

(*b*) Players of either team may legally interfere beyond the neutral zone after the pass has been touched.

(*c*) Defensive players may legally contact opponents who have crossed the neutral zone if the opponents are not in a position to receive a catchable forward pass.

1. Those infractions that occur during a down when a forward pass crosses the neutral zone are pass interference only if the receiver had the opportunity to receive a catchable forward pass.

2. Those infractions that occur during a down when a forward pass does not cross the neutral zone are 9-3-4 infractions and are penalised from the previous spot.

(*d*) Pass interference rules apply only during a down in which a legal forward pass crosses the neutral zone (A.R. 47) (2-19-3) (7-3-8-a and c).

(*e*) Contact by B with an eligible receiver that involves unnecessary roughness that interferes with a catchable pass is penalised as pass interference, but fouls occuring less than 15 yards beyond the neutral zone may be penalised 15 yards as personal fouls from the previous spot. Rule 7-3-8 is specific about contact during a pass. However, if the interference involves an act that would ordinarily result in disqualification, the fouling player must leave the game.

(*f*) Physical contact is required to establish interference.

(*g*) Each player has territorial rights and incidental contact is ruled under "attempt to reach . . . the pass" in 7-3-8. If opponents who are beyond the line collide while moving toward the pass, a foul by one or both players is indicated only if intent to impede the opponent is obvious. It is pass interference by Team B only if a catchable forward pass is involved.

(*h*) Pass interference rules do not apply after the pass has been touched anywhere in bounds by an in-bounds player. Players may tackle without waiting to determine possession and control, and players who are entitled to touch the pass may use his hand or arm to push opponents out of the way if there is a reasonable opportunity to reach the pass and if there is an actual attempt to reach it. If an opponent is fouled, the penalty is for the foul and not pass interference.

(*i*) After the pass has been touched, any player may execute a legal block during the remaining flight of the pass.

(*j*) Tackling or grasping a receiver or any other intentional contact before he touches the pass is evidence that the tackler is disregarding the ball and is therefore illegal.

(*k*) Tackling or running into a receiver when a forward pass is obviously underthrown or overthrown is disregarding the ball and is illegal. This is not pass interference but a violation of 9-1-2-f and is penalised 15 yards from the previous spot.

Ineligibles Downfield

ARTICLE 10. No ineligible player shall be or have been beyond the neutral zone until a legal forward pass that crosses the neutral zone has been thrown.

Exceptions:
  1. Immediately after the snap, offensive players may charge into opponents and drive them back no more than three yards from the neutral zone provided contact

is established at a point not more than one yard beyond the neutral zone.

2. When contact that has driven an opponent no more than three yards from the neutral zone is lost by a player who was ineligible at the snap, he must remain stationary at that spot until the pass is thrown.

Penalty—5 yards from previous spot plus loss of down [S37 and S9].

Illegal Touching

ARTICLE 11. No originally ineligible player while in bounds shall touch a legal forward pass until it has touched an opponent.

Penalty—5 yards from previous spot plus loss of a down [S31 and S9].

RULE 8

SCORING

1. VALUE OF SCORES

Scoring Plays

ARTICLE 1. The point value of scoring plays shall be:

Touchdown	....	6 Points
Field Goal	....	3 Points
Safety (points awarded to opponents)	....	2 Points
Successful Try — Touchdown	....	2 Points
Successful Try — Field Goal or Safety	....	1 Point

Forfeited Games

ARTICLE 2. The score of a forfeited game shall be: Offended Team—1, Opponent—0. If the offended team is ahead at time of forfeit, the score stands.

2. TOUCHDOWN

How Scored

ARTICLE 1. A touchdown shall be scored when a legal

forward pass is completed or a fumble or backward pass is caught on or behind the opponents' goal line or when a player is legally in possession of the ball while any part of it is on, above or behind his opponents' goal-line.

3. TRY

Opportunity to Score

ARTICLE 1. A try is an opportunity to score one or two additional points while the game clock is stopped and is a special interval in a game which, for purposes of penalty enforcement only, includes both a down and the "ready" period that precedes it.

(*a*) Opportunity shall be granted a team that has scored a touchdown.

(*b*) The try, which is a scrimmage down, begins when the ball is ready for play.

(*c*) The snap may be from any point on or between the inbounds lines on or behind the opponents' three-yard line and the ball may be relocated following a charged timeout to either team unless preceded by a Team A foul or offsetting penalties (8-3-3-a and 8-3-3-c-1).

(*d*) The opportunity ends if:
1. Team B gains possession of the ball or is entitled to possession after a foul;
2. If a penalty against Team A involves loss of a down;
3. If the accepted penalty results in a score.
4. If it is obvious a scrimmage kick is unsuccessful.

How Scored

ARTICLE 2. The point or points shall be scored if the try results in what would be a touchdown, safety or field goal under rules governing play at other times.

Foul During Try for Point

ARTICLE 3. **a. Offsetting fouls:** The down shall be replayed if offsetting fouls occur. Any replay after offsetting penalities must be from the previous spot.
b. Fouls by B on successful try:

1. Team A shall have the option of declining the score and repeating the try following enforcement, or accepting the score with enforcement of the penalty from the spot of the next kickoff.
2. A replay after a penalty against Team B may be from any point between the in-bounds lines on the yard line where the penalty leaves the ball.

c. Fouls by A on successful try:
1. After a foul by Team A, the ball shall be put in play at the spot where the penalty leaves it.

Next Play

ARTICLE 4. After a try the ball shall be put in play by a kickoff. The field captain of the team against which the touchdown was scored shall designate which team shall kick off.

4. FIELD GOAL

How Scored

ARTICLE 1. (*a*) A field goal shall be scored for the kicking team if a drop kick or place kick passes over the crossbar between the uprights of the receiving team's goal before it touches a player of the kicking team or the ground. The kick shall be a scrimmage kick but may not be a free kick.

(*b*) If a legal field goal attempt passes over the crossbar between the uprights and is grounded beyond the end lines or is blown back but does not return over the crossbar and is grounded anywhere, it shall score a field goal. The entire goal, crossbar, and uprights are treated as a **line** not a **plane** in determining forward progress of the ball.

Next Play

ARTICLE 2. (*a*) After a field goal is scored the ball shall be put in play by a kickoff. The field captain of the team scored against shall designate which team shall kick off.

(*b*) Following an unsuccessful field goal attempt that crosses the neutral zone, the ball, untouched by Team B beyond the neutral zone, will next be put in play at the previous spot. If the previous spot was between Team B's 20-yard line and goal line, the ball shall next be put in play at the 20-yard line. Otherwise, all rules pertaining to scrimmage kicks apply.

5. SAFETY AND TOUCHBACK

How Scored

ARTICLE 1. Touchback or safety.

(*a*) It is a touchback:

1. When the ball is out of bounds behind a goal line (except from an incompleted forward pass). If the attacking team is responsible for the ball being behind that goal line (*Exception:* 8-4-2-b).

2. When the ball becomes dead in possession of a player on, above or behind his own goal line and the attacking team is responsible for the ball being on, above or behind that goal line.

(*b*) It is a safety:

1. When the ball becomes dead in the possession of a player on, above or behind his own goal line and the defending team is responsible for the ball being on, above or behind the goal line.

2. When an accepted penalty for a foul or an illegal forward pass leaves the ball on or behind the offending team's goal line.

Exception: When a Team B player intercepts a forward pass or catches a scrimmage or free kick between his five-yard line and the goal line and his original momentum carries him into the end zone where the ball is declared dead in his team's possession or he goes out of bounds in the end zone, the ball belongs to Team B at the spot where the pass was intercepted or the kick caught.

Responsibility

ARTICLE 2. The team responsible for the ball being on, above or behind a goal line is the team whose player carried the ball or imparts an impetus to it that forces it on, above or across that goal line; or is responsible for a loose ball being on, above or behind the goal line.

Initial Impetus

ARTICLE 3. The impetus imparted by a player who kicks, passes, snaps or fumbles the ball shall be considered responsible for the ball's progress in any direction even though its course is deflected or reversed after striking the ground or after touching a player of either team. However, the initial impetus is considered expended and the responsibility for the progress of the ball is charged to a player: if he kicks a ball not in player possession or bats a loose ball after it strikes the ground; or if the ball comes to rest and he gives it new impetus by any contact with it.

Resulting From Foul

ARTICLE 4. If the penalty for a foul committed when the ball is loose leaves the ball behind the offender's goal line, it is a safety.

Kick After Safety

ARTICLE 5. When a safety is scored the ball belongs to the defending team at its own 20-yard line and that team shall put the ball in play between the in-bounds lines by a free kick that may be a punt, drop kick or place kick.

Snap After Touchback

ARTICLE 6. After a touchback is declared the ball shall belong to the defending team at its own 20-yard line and that team shall put the ball in play between the in-bounds lines by snap.

RULE 9

CONDUCT OF PLAYERS AND OTHERS SUBJECT TO RULES

1. CONTACT AND INTERFERENCE FOULS

Personal Fouls

ARTICLE 1. During the game and between periods, all

flagrant fouls require disqualification. Team B disqualification fouls may require first downs if not in conflict with other rules.

Player Restrictions

ARTICLE 2. No person subject to the rules shall commit a personal foul during the game or between the periods. Any act prohibited hereunder or any other act of unnecessary roughness is a personal foul.

(*a*) No player shall strike an opponent with the knee, or strike an opponent's head, neck or face or any part of the body with an extended forearm, elbow, locked hands, palm, fist or the heel, back or side of the open hand or gouge an opponent during the game or between the periods.

(*b*) No player shall strike an opponent with his foot or any part of his leg that is below the knee.

(*c*) There shall be no *tripping*.

(*d*) There shall be no *clipping*.

Exception: During a scrimmage down, only offensive players on the line of scrimmage at the snap within a rectangular area centred on the middle lineman of the offensive formation and extending five yards laterally in each direction and three yards longitudinally in each direction, may legally clip in the rectangular area. A player on the line of scrimmage within the legal clipping zone may not leave the zone and return and legally clip. The legal clipping zone exists until the ball is in player possession outside the legal clipping zone or has been muffed or fumbled outside the legal clipping zone.

(*e*) Blocking below the waist is permitted except as follows:

1. Offensive players at the snap positioned more than seven yards in any direction from the middle lineman of the offensive formation or in motion toward the ball at the snap are prohibited from blocking below the waist toward the ball until the ball has advanced beyond the neutral zone. The following formation sets are legal and the players are not restricted by 9-1-2-e when blocking toward the ball:

(A) An offensive end positioned less than two yards from the legal clipping zone.

(B) A wingback positioned one yard to the outside of an end who is flexed no more than one yard from the legal clipping zone.

(C) A wingback positioned no more than one yard outside the legal clipping zone and inside an end who is one yard outside the wingback.

2. During a scrimmage down, defensive players are prohibited from blocking an eligible Team A receiver below the waist beyond the legal clipping zone extended to the sideline unless attempting to get at the ball or runner. A Team A receiver remains eligible until a legal forward pass is no longer possible by rule.

3. During a down in which there is a free kick or scrimmage kick from a scrimmage kick formation, all players are prohibited from blocking below the waist except against the runner.

4. After any change of possession all players are prohibited from blocking below the waist except against the runner.

5. A Team A player behind the neutral zone and in position to receive a backward pass shall not be blocked below the waist.

(f) No player shall tackle or run into a receiver when a forward pass to him is obviously not catchable. This is not pass interference.

(g) There shall be no *piling* on, falling on, or throwing the body on an opponent after the ball becomes dead.

(h) No opponent shall tackle or block the runner *when he is clearly out of bounds* or throw him to the ground after the ball becomes dead.

(i) There shall be no *hurdling*.

(j) No player shall run into or *throw himself* against an opponent obviously out of the play either before or after the ball is dead.

(k) No player shall grasp the face mask or any helmet opening of an opponent. The open hand may be legally used on the mask.

Penalty—Defensive team 5 yards incidental grasping, 15 yards and first down against Team B for twisting, turning or pulling. Offensive team 15 yards. All dead-ball fouls 15 yards. Flagrant offenders shall be disqualified [S45].

(*l*) No player shall intentionally use his helmet to butt or ram an opponent.

(*m*) There shall be no *spearing*.

(*n*) No player shall intentionally strike a runner with the crown or the top of his helmet.

(*o*) No defensive player shall charge into a passer when it is obvious the ball has been thrown.

(*p*) The kicker of a free kick may not be blocked until he has advanced five yards beyond his restraining line or the kick has touched a player, an official or the ground.

(*q*) There shall be no chop blocking.

Penalty—15 yards and a first down for 9-1-2-a, b, g, h, j, l, m, n and o if Team B fouls and the first down is not in conflict with other rules [S34, S38, S39, S40, S41, S45 or S46]. Flagrant offenders shall be disqualified [S47].

Roughing or Running into Kicker or Holder

ARTICLE 3. (*a*) When it is obvious that a scrimmage kick will be made, no opponent shall run into or rough the kicker or the holder of a place kick.

1. Roughing is a personal foul that endangers the kicker or holder.
2. Running into the kicker or holder is a foul that occurs when the kicker or holder are displaced from their kicking or holding positions but are not roughed.
3. Incidental contact with a kicker or holder is not a foul.
4. The kicker and holder must be protected from injury but contact that occurs when or after a scrimmage kick has been touched is not roughing or running into the kicker.
5. The kicker of a scrimmage kick loses protection as a kicker when he has had a reasonable time to regain his balance.

Penalty—5 yards previous spot for running into kicker or holder. 15 yards previous spot and also first down for

roughing kicker or holder [S30]. Flagrant offenders shall be disqualified [S47].

(*b*) A kicker or holder simulating being roughed or run into by a defensive player commits an unfair act.
Penalty—15 yards previous spot [S27].

Illegal Interference

ARTICLE 4. (*a*) No substitute, coach, authorised attendant or any person subject to the rules other than a player or official, may interfere in any way with the ball or a player while the ball is in play.

(*b*) Participation by 12 or more players is illegal participation.
Penalty—15 yards from the spot most advantageous to the offended team. The referee may enforce any penalty he considers equitable, including awarding a score [S27, S28, S47].

Game Administration Interference

ARTICLE 5. (*a*) While the ball is in play, coaches, substitutes and authorised attendants in the team area may not be between the sidelines and coaching line.

(*b*) The procedure for enforcement of 9-1-5-a is as follows:
1. The head coach is informed by a game official that he is receiving a first or second warning because the area between the sideline and coaching line has been violated by coaches, players or persons authorised in the team area.
2. The official will record the time and period of each warning.
3. After a second warning, the official will notify the head coach that he has had two warnings and that the next infraction will result in a five-yard penalty.
4. After a five-yard penalty, the official will notify the head coach that he has had two warnings an a five-yard penalty and will receive a 15-yard penalty for the next infraction.
5. Warnings shall be given only when the clock is stopped.
Penalty—5 yards after two official warnings from a game

official and 15 yards for each additional foul. Penalise as a dead-ball foul [S29].

(c) Crowd noise, including bands and other persons subject to the rules, that prohibits a team from hearing its signals is an unfair act (3-3-3-f-4) **Violation 3-3-6 and 3-4-2-b. [S3 or S21].**

2. NONCONTACT FOULS

Unsportsmanlike Acts

ARTICLE 1. There shall be no unsportsmanlike conduct or any act that interferes with orderly game administration on the part of players, substitutes, coaches, authorised attendants or any other persons subject to the rules, either during the game or between periods.

a. Specifically prohibited acts and conduct include:
1. No player, substitute, coach, authorised attendant or other persons subject to the rules shall use abusive or insulting language to players or officials or indulge in any conduct that might incite players or spectators against officials.
2. If a player is injured, attendants may come in bounds to attend him but they must obtain recognition from an official.
3. No person subject to the rules, except players, officials and eligible substitutes, shall be on the field of play or end zones during any period without permission from the referee (*Exception:* 3-3-5).
4. After a score or any other play the player in possession must immediately return the ball to an official or leave it near the dead-ball spot. This prohibits:
   a. Taking a ball off the field of play or end zones.
   b. Kicking or throwing the ball any distance that requires an official to retrieve it.
   e. Throwing the ball high into the air.
   f. Any other unsportsmanlike act or actions that delay the game.
5. No player or substitute shall use language, gestures or engage in acts that provoke ill will including:

   a. Swinging a hand or arm and missing an opponent or kicking and missing an opponent.
   b. Pointing the ball at an opponent.
   c. Baiting an opponent verbally.
   d. Inciting an opponent in any other way.
6. No substitutes may enter the field of play or end zones for purposes other than replacing a player. This includes demonstrations after any play.

Penalty—15 yards [S7 and S27]. Succeeding spot. Penalise as a dead-ball foul. Flagrant offenders, if players or substitutes, shall be disqualified [S47].

b. Other prohibited acts include:
1. During the game, coaches, substitutes and authorised attendants in the team area shall not be on the field of play or outside the 25- or 30-yard lines without permission from the referee unless legally entering or leaving the field. (*Exception:* 3-3-8-c).
2. No disqualified player shall enter the field.

Penalty—15 yards [S7, S27]. Succeeding spot. Penalise as a dead-ball foul. Flagrant offenders, if players or substitutes, shall be disqualified [S47].

Unfair Tactics

ARTICLE 2. (*a*) No player shall conceal the ball beneath his clothing or substitute any other article for the ball.

(*b*) No simulated replacements or substitutions may be used to confuse opponents.

PENALTY—15 yards [S27]. Enforcement spot [10-2-2]. Penalise as a live-ball foul. Flagrant offenders shall be disqualified [S47].

Unfair Acts

ARTICLE 3. (*a*) The referee may enforce any penalty he considers equitable, including awarding a score:

1. If a team refuses to play within two minutes after ordered to do so by the referee.
2. If a team repeatedly commits fouls that can be penalised only by halving the distance to its goal line.

The referee shall, after one warning, forfeit the game to the opponents for 9-2-3-a-1 & 2 infractions.

(b) The referee may enforce any penalty he considers equitable, including awarding a score, if an obviously unfair act not specifically covered by the rules occurs during the game.

3. BLOCKING, USE OF HAND AND ARM

Who May Block

ARTICLE 1. Players of either team may block opponents provided it is not forward pass interference with opportunity to catch a kick, or a personal foul.

Interfering for or Helping the Runner

ARTICLE 2. (a) The runner or passer may use his hand or arm to ward off or push opponents.

(b) The runner shall not grasp a teammate, and no other player of his team shall grasp, push, lift or charge into him to assist him in forward progress.

(c) Teammates of the runner or passer may interfere for him by blocking but shall not use interlocked interference by grasping or encircling one another in any manner while contracting an opponent.

Penalty—5 yards [S44].

Use of Hand or Arm by Offense

ARTICLE 3. (a) A teammate of a runer or a passer may legally block with his shoulders, hands outer surface of his arms or any other part of his body under the following provisions.

1. The hand(s) shall be:
   (i) In advance of the elbow.
   (ii) Inside the frame of the blocker's body.
   (iii) Inside the frame of the opponent's body (*Exception:* When the opponent turns his back to the blocker).
   (iv) At or below the shoulder(s) of the blocker and the opponent.

2. The hand(s) shall be open with the palm(s) facing the frame of the opponent or closed or cupped with the palms not facing the opponent.

Penalty—5 yards basic spot. 5 yards previous spot when the foul is behind the netural zone [S43].

(*b*) Holding or illegal obstruction by a teammate of the runner or passer applies to 9-3-3-a:

1. The hand(s) and arm(s) shall not be used to grasp, pull or encircle in any way that illegally impedes or illegally obstructs an opponent.

2. The hand(s) or arm(s) shall not be used to hook, lock, clamp or otherwise illegally impede or illegally obstruct an opponent.

Penalty—10 yards basic spot. 10 yards previous spot when the foul is behind the neutral zone [S42].

(*c*) The following acts by a teammate of the runner or passer are illegal:

1. The hand(s) and arm(s) shall not be used to deliver a blow.

2. During no block shall the hands be locked.

Penalty—15 yards basic spot [S38]. Disqualification if flagrant [S47].

(*d*) A crab or cross-body block is legal if there is no illegal contact with the hand(s) or arm(s).

Penalty—5 yards [S43].

(*e*) A player on the kicking team may:

1. During a scrimmage kick play, use his hand(s) and/or arm(s) to ward off an opponent attempting to block him when he is beyond the neutral zone.

2. During a free kick play, use his hand(s) and/or arm(s) to ward off an opponent who is attempting to block him.

3. During a scrimmage kick play when he is eligible to touch the ball, legally use his hand(s) and/or arm(s) to push an opponent in an attempt to reach a loose ball.

4. During a free kick play when he is eligible to touch the ball, legally use his hand(s) and/or arm(s) to push an opponent obstructing his attempt to reach a loose ball.

(*f*) A player of the passing team may legally use his hand(s) and/or arm(s) to ward off or push an opponent in an attempt to reach a loose ball after a legal forward pass has been touched by any player.

Use of Hands or Arms by Defense

ARTICLE 4. (*a*) Defensive players may use hands and arms to push, pull, grasp, ward off or lift offensive players when attempting to reach the runner.

(*b*) Defensive players may not use hands and arms to tackle, hold or otherwise illegally obstruct an opponent other than a runner.

Penalty—10 yards basic spot [S42].

(*c*) Defensive players may use hands and arms to push, pull, grasp, ward off or lift offensive players obviously attempting to block them. Defensive players may ward off or push an eligible pass receiver until that player occupies the same yard line as the defender. Continuous contact is illegal or the opponent could possibly block him (7-3-8-c).

Penalty—5 yards basic spot [S43].

(*d*) When no attempt is being made to get at the ball or the runner, defensive players must comply with 9-3-3-a, b, c. (*Exception:* Pulling an offensive player out of the way to give a teammate the opportunity to block a kick or reach a runner is defensive holding only if the defensive man hangs on, or pulls the opponent to the ground with him.)

Penalty—5, 10 or 15 yard basic spot [S43, S42 or S38].

(*e*) When a legal forward pass crosses the neutral zone during a forward pass play and a contact foul that is not pass interference is committed, the enforcement spot is the previous spot. This includes Rule 9-3-4-c.

Penalty—5, 10 or 15 yards plus first down if foul occurred against an eligible receiver before the ball was thrown [S43, S42 or S38].

(*f*) A defensive player may legally use his hand or arm to ward off or push an opponent in an attempt to reach a loose ball:

1. During a backward pass, fumble or kick that he is eligible to touch.
2. During any forward pass that crossed the neutral zone and has been touched by any player.

Player Restrictions

ARTICLE 5. (*a*) No player may position himself with his feet on the back or shoulders of a teammate prior to the snap.
Penalty—Dead-ball foul 15 yards [S27].

(*b*) No defensive player, in an attempt to block a kick, may:
1. Step, jump or stand on a teammate or an opponent;
2. Place a hand(s) on a teammate to get leverage for additional height;
3. Be picked up by a teammate.

Penalty—15 yards basic spot [S27].

When Ball is Loose

ARTICLE 6. When the ball is loose, no player shall grasp, pull or tackle an opponent or commit a personal foul.
Penalty—10 or 15 yards from the basic or previous spot (10-2-2-c, d, e, f) [S38 or S42].

4. BATTING AND KICKING

Batting a Loose Ball

ARTICLE 1. (*a*) While a pass is in flight, any player eligible to touch the ball may bat it in any direction.

(*b*) Any player may block or partially block a scrimmage kick in the field of play or the end zone.

(*c*) No player shall bat other loose balls forward in the field of play or in any direction if they are in the end zone.
Penalty—15 yards from the basic or previous spot (10-2-2-c, d, e, f) [S31].

Batting a Backward Pass

ARTICLE 2. A backward pass in flight shall not be batted forward by the passing team in an attempt to gain yardage.
Penalty—15 yards from the basic or previous spot (10-2-2-c) [S31].

Batting Ball in Possession

ARTICLE 3. A ball in player possession may not be batted by a player of that team.

Penalty—15 yards from the basic or previous spot (10-2-2-c) [S31].

Illegally Kicking Ball

ARTICLE 4. A player shall not kick a loose ball, a forward pass or a ball being held for a place kick by an opponent. These illegal acts do not change the status of the loose ball or forward pass; but if the player holding the ball for a place kick loses possession during a scrimmage down, it is a fumble and a loose ball; if during a free kick, the ball remains dead. **Penalty—15 yards from the basic or previous spot, also loss of down (10-2-2-c, d, e, f) [S9 and S31].**

RULE 10

PENALTY ENFORCEMENT

1. PENALTIES COMPLETED

How and When Completed

ARTICLE 1. A penalty is completed when it is accepted, declined, cancelled according to rule, or when the most advantageous choice is obvious to the referee. Any penalty may be declined, but a disqualified player must leave the game. When a foul is committed at a time other than following a touchdown and before the ball is ready for play on a try, the penalty shall be completed before the ball is declared ready for play for any ensuing down (*Exception:* 10-2-2-g-2 Touchdown).

Simultaneous with Snap

ARTICLE 2. A foul that occurs simultaneously with a snap or free kick is considered as occurring during that down.

Live-Ball Fouls by the Same Team

ARTICLE 3. When two or more live-ball fouls by the same team are reported to the referee, the referee shall explain the alternative penalties to the field captain of the offended team who may then elect only one of these penalties (*Exception:*

When a foul (or fouls) for unsportsmanlike conduct (noncontact fouls) occurs, the penalty (or penalties) is administered from the succeeding spot as established by the acceptance or declination of the penalty for any other foul).

Offsetting Fouls

ARTICLE 4. If live-ball fouls by both teams are reported to the referee, each such foul is an offsetting foul and the penalties cancel each other and the down is replayed.
Exceptions:

1. When there is a change of team possession during a down or at the end of a down by rule, the team last gaining possession may decline offsetting fouls and thereby retain possession after completion of the penalty for its infraction if it had not fouled prior to its gaining possession.

2. When Team B's foul is postscrimmage kick enforcement, Team B may decline offsetting fouls and accept postscrimmage kick enforcement.

3. When a live-ball foul is administered as a dead-ball foul, it does not offset and is enforced in order of occurrence.

Dead-Ball Fouls

ARTICLE 5. Penalties for dead-ball fouls are administered separately and in order of occurrence.
Exception: When dead-ball fouls by both teams are reported and the order of occurrence cannot be determined, the fouls cancel, the number or type of down established before the fouls occurred is unaffected, and the penalties are disregarded, except that any disqualified player must leave the game (10-2-2-a) (5-2-6).

Live-Ball—Dead-Ball Fouls

ARTICLE 6. When a live-ball foul by one team is followed by one or more dead-ball fouls (or live-ball fouls penalised as dead-ball fouls) by an opponent or by the same team, the penalties are administered separately and in the order of occurrence.

Interval Fouls

ARTICLE 7. Fouls that occur in different down intervals between the scoring of a touchdown and the succeeding kickoff shall be enforced in the order of their occurrences.

2. ENFORCEMENT PROCEDURES

Spots

ARTICLE 1. The enforcement spots are: the previous spot, the spot of the foul, the succeeding spot, the spot where the kick ends and the spot where the run ends.

Procedures

ARTICLE 2. When no enforcement spot is specified in a rule penalty, the following procedures apply:

(*a*) Dead ball – The enforcement spot for a foul committed when the ball is dead is the succeeding spot.

(*b*) Snap or free kick – The enforcement spot for fouls occurring simultaneously with a snap or free kick is the previous spot.

(*c*) Running plays – The basic enforcement spots for fouls that occur during running plays in the field of play or end zone are as follows:
1. When the run ends beyond the neutral zone, the basic enforcement spot is the end of the related run (2-25-10-a) (*Exception:* 9-3-3-a and b).
2. When the run ends behind the neutral zone before a change of team possession, the basic enforcement spot is the previous spot (2-25-10-b) (*Exception:* 9-3-3-a and b).
3. When there is no neutral zone, the basic enforcement spot is the end of the related run (2-25-10-c).

(*d*) Pass plays – The basic enforcement spot for fouls during a legal forward pass play is the previous spot. (*Exceptions:* Team B pass interference spot fouls and 9-3-3-a, b fouls.)

(*e*) Kick plays – The basic enforcement spot for fouls that occur during a legal free or scrimmage kick play before possession is gained or regained or the ball is declared dead by rule is the previous spot.

Exceptions:

1. Interference with the opportunity to make a catch — spot foul (6-4-1).
2. Team A, during a scrimmage kick, bats a loose ball behind Team B's goal line—a live-ball foul and a touchback.
3. A block or foul after a valid, invalid or illegal signal for a fair catch by a Team B player who signalled for a fair catch during a free kick and had not touched the ball— spot foul (6-5-4).
4. Illegal fair catch signal during a free kick—spot foul (6-5-3).
5. Postscrimmage kick enforcement.
   The basic enforcement spot for Team B fouls during scrimmage kick plays, other than tries, that cross the neutral zone and occur beyond the legal clipping zone extended to the sideline and prior to player possession, is the spot where the kick ends (see Rule 2-25-9).
6. The enforcement spot for illegal participation during a free or scrimmage kick plays is the spot most advantageous to the offended team (see Rule 9-1-4).
7. 9-3-3-a and b fouls behind the neutral zone.

(*f*) Behind the goal line.

1. The enforcement spot is the goal line for fouls by the opponents of the team in possession after a change of team possession in the field of play when the run ends behind the goal line. Safety if no foul occurred (*Exception:* 8-5-1).
2. The basic enforcement spot is the 20-yard line for fouls that occur after a change of team possession in the end zone and the ball remains in the end zone where it is declared dead. These are live-ball fouls. Touchback if no foul occurred.

(*g*) Interval fouls—Succeding kickoff.

1. When a foul occurs after a touchdown and before the ball is ready for play for the try, the enforcement is at the spot of the succeeding kickoff.

2. Distance penalties for fouls by opponents of the team in possession during a down that ends in a touchdown, a field goal or a successful try are penalised at the succeeding kickoff. All defensive pass interference fouls are penalised 15 yards from the succeeding spot. However, the field goal or the successful try (8-3-3) may be declined and the penalty enforced according to rule (*Exceptions:* 10-2-2-e-5).

3. Fouls that occur in different down intervals between the scoring of a touchdown and the succeeding kickoff shall be enforced in the order of their occurrence.

4. Distance penalties for fouls by the receiving team may not extend the receiving team's restraining line behind their five-yard line. Fouls that place the restraining line of the receiving team behind their five-yard line are enforced from the succeeding spot.

Half-distance enforcement procedures

ARTICLE 3. No distance penalty shall exceed half the distance from the enforcement spot to the offending team's goal line. (*Exception:* Defensive pass interference penalties other than those from the two-yard line or closer to the goal line.)

Laws of
Rugby Union
Football

Plan of the Field (see Law 1)

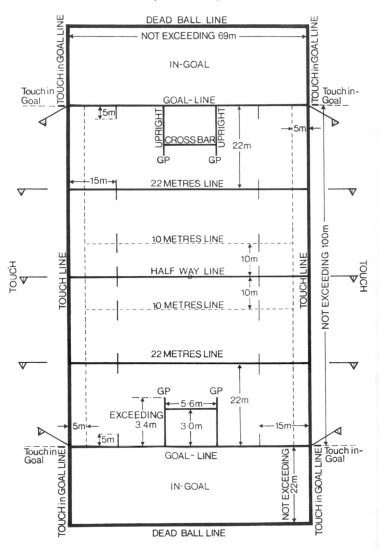

Rugby Union Football

The plan, including all words and figures thereon, is to take effect as part of these Laws.

The terms appearing on the plan are to bear their apparent meaning, and to be deemed part of the definitions as if separately included.

Notes: Length and breadth of field to be as near to dimensions indicated as possible. All areas to be rectangular.

— — — These broken lines indicate 10 m. distance from the halfway line and 5 m distance from the touch lines.

— These lines at the goal lines and intersecting the 22 m and 10 m lines and the halfway line are 15 m from the touch lines.

The lines at the goal lines extend 5 m into the field of play.

Goal dimensions: 3 m is taken from the ground to the top edge of the cross-bar, and 5.60 m inside to inside of the goal posts.

Where practicable the intersection of the dead-ball line and touch-in-goal lines should be indicated by a flag. A minimum height of 1.20 m above the ground is desirable for corner posts.

OBJECT OF THE GAME

The object of the game is that two teams of fifteen players each, observing fair play according to the Laws and a sporting spirit, should by carrying, passing, and kicking the ball score as many points as possible, the team scoring the greater number of points to be the winner of the match.

DECLARATION OF AMATEURISM

The game is an amateur game. No one is allowed to seek or to receive payment or other material reward for taking part in the game.

DEFINITIONS

The following terms have the meaning assigned to them:

Beyond or *Behind* or *In front* of any position implies "with both feet" except when unsuited to the context.

Dead means that the ball is for the time being out of play. This occurs when the Referee blows his whistle to indicate a stoppage of play or when an attempt to convert a try is unsuccessful.

Defending team means the team in whose half of the ground the stoppage to play occurs and the opponents of the defending team are referred to as "the attacking team".

Kick. A kick is made by propelling the ball with any part of the leg or foot (except the heel) from knee to toe inclusive. If the player is holding the ball, he must propel it out of his hands or, if it is on the ground, he must propel it a visible distance.

Drop kick. A drop kick is made by letting the ball fall from the hand (or hands) to the ground and kicking it at the first rebound as it rises.

Place kick. A place kick is made by kicking the ball after it has been placed on the ground for that purpose.

Punt. A punt is made by letting the ball fall from the hand (or hands) and kicking it before it touches the ground.

Mark. The mark is the place at which a free kick or penalty is awarded.

Line through the Mark (or Place). Except where specifically stated otherwise, the words "a line through the mark" or "a line through the place" always mean a line parallel to the touch line.

Union means the controlling body under whose jurisdiction the match is played and in the case of an International Match it means the International Rugby Football Board or a Committee thereof.

Other definitions are included in and have effect as part of the Laws.

LAWS

1. Ground

The field-of-play is the area shown on the plan, bounded by, but not including, the goal lines and touch lines. The playing area is the field-of-play and In-goal. The playing enclosure is the playing area and a reasonable area surrounding it.

(1) All lines shown on the Plan of the Field must be suitably marked out. The touch lines are in touch. The goal lines are In-goal. The dead-ball line is *not* In-goal. The touch-in-goal lines and corner posts are in touch-in-goal. The goal posts are to be erected in the goal lines.

(2) The game must be played on a ground of the area (maximum) shown on the plan and marked in accordance with the plan. The surface must be grass-covered or, where this is not available, clay or sand provided the surface is not of dangerous hardness.

(3) Any objection by the visiting team about the ground or the way it is marked out must be made to the referee before the first kick-off.

2. Ball

(1) The ball when new shall be oval in shape, of four panels, and of the following dimensions:

Length in line	280 to 300 mm
Circumference (end on)	760 to 790 mm
Circumference (in width)	580 to 620 mm
Weight	400 to 440 gm.

(2) The dimensions of the ball may be reduced only for younger schoolboys.

(3) Balls may be specially treated to make them resistant to mud and easier to grip. The casings need not be of leather.

3. Number of Players

(1) A match shall be played by not more than 15 players in each team.

(2) Replacement of players shall be allowed in recognised trial matches as determined by the Unions having jurisdiction over the match.

(3) In all other matches, a player may be replaced only on account of injury and subject to the following conditions:

(*a*) Not more than two players in each team may be replaced. *Exception:* In matches between teams of schoolboys or teams where all players are under the age of 19, up to six players may be replaced.

(*b*) A player who has been replaced must *NOT* resume playing in the match.

(4) (*a*) In matches in which a national representative team is playing, a player may be replaced *ONLY* when, in the opinion of a medical practitioner, the player is so injured that he should not continue playing in the match.

(*b*) For such competition and other domestic matches as a Union gives express permission, an injured player may be replaced on the advice of a medically trained person, or if a medically trained person is not present, with the approval of the referee.

(5) If the referee is advised by a doctor or other medically trained person or for any other reason considers that a player is so injured that it would be harmful for him to continue playing the referee shall require the player to leave the playing area.

(6) Any objection by either team as regards the number of players in a team may be made to the referee at any time but the objection shall not affect any score previously obtained.

4. Players' Dress

(1) A player must not wear dangerous projections such as buckles or rings.

(2) Shoulder pads of the "harness" type must not be worn. If the referee is satisfied that a player requires protection following an injury to a shoulder, the wearing of a pad of cotton-wool, sponge rubber or similar soft material may be permitted provided the pad is attached to the body or sewn on to the jersey.

(3) Studs of a player's boots must conform to the British Standard BS 6366: 1983. They must be circular, securely fastened to the boots and of the following dimensions:

Maximum length (measured from sole)	18 mm
Minimum diameter at base	13 mm
Minimum diameter at top	10 mm
Minimum diameter of washer (if separate from stud)	20 mm

The wearing of a single stud at the toe of a boot is prohibited.

(4) The referee has power to decide before or during the game that any part of a player's dress is dangerous. He must then order the player to remove the dangerous part and not

allow him to take further·part in the match until after it has been removed.

5. Toss, Time

No-side is the end of a match.

(1) Before a match begins the captains shall toss for the right to kick-off or the choice of ends.

(2) The duration of play in a match shall be such time not exceeding 80 minutes as shall be directed by the Union or, in the absence of such direction, as agreed upon by the teams or, if not agreed, as fixed by the referee. In International matches two periods of 40 minutes each shall be played.

(3) Play shall be divided into two halves. At half-time the teams shall change ends and there shall be an interval of not more than 5 minutes.

(4) A period not exceeding 1 minute shall be allowed for any other permitted delay. A longer period may be allowed only if the additional time is required for the removal of an injured player from the playing area.

Playing time lost as a result of any such permitted delay or of delay in taking a kick at goal shall be made up in that half of the match in which the delay occurred, subject to the power vested in the referee to declare no-side before time has expired.

6. Referee and Touch Judges

A. REFEREE

(1) There shall be a referee for every match. He shall be appointed by or under the authority of the Union or, in case no such authorised referee has been appointed, a referee may be mutually agreed upon between the teams or, failing such agreement, he shall be appointed by the home team.

(2) If the referee is unable to officiate for the whole period of a match a replacement shall be appointed either in such manner as may be directed by the Union, or in the absence of such direction, by the referee or, if he is unable to do so, by the home team.

(3) The referee shall keep the time and the score, and he must in every match apply fairly the Laws of the Game without any variation or omission, except only when the Union has

authorised the application of an experimental law approved by the International Board.

(4) He must not give any instruction or advice to either team prior to the match. During the match he must not consult with anyone except only

(*a*) either or both touch judges on a point of fact relevant to their functions, or

(*b*) in regard to time.

(5) The referee is the sole judge of fact and of law. All his decisions are binding on the players. He cannot alter a decision except when given before he observes that a touch judge's flag is raised or before he has received a report related to Law 26(3) from a touch judge.

(6) The referee must carry a whistle and must blow it

(*a*) to indicate the beginning of the match, half-time, resumption of play after half-time, no-side, a score or a touch-down, and

(*b*) to stop play because of infringement or otherwise as required by the Laws.

(7) During a match no person other than the players, the referee and the touch judges may be within the playing enclosure or the playing area unless with the permission of the referee which shall be given only for a special and temporary purpose.

(8) (*a*) All players must respect the authority of the referee and they must not dispute his decisions. They must (except in the case of a kick-off) stop playing at once when the referee has blown his whistle.

(*b*) A player must when so requested, whether before or during the match, allow the referee to inspect his dress.

(*c*) A player must not leave the playing enclosure without the referee's permission. If a player retires during a match because of injury or otherwise, he must not resume playing in that match until the referee has given him permission.

Penalty. Infringement by a player is subject to penalty as misconduct.

B. TOUCH JUDGES

(1) There shall be two touch judges for every match. Unless

touch judges have been appointed by or under the authority of the Union, it shall be the responsibility of each team to provide a touch judge.

(2) A touch judge is under the control of the referee who may instruct him as to his duties and may over-rule any of his decisions. The referee may request that an unsatisfactory touch judge be replaced and he has power to order off and report to the Union a touch judge who in his opinion is guilty of misconduct.

(3) Each touch judge shall carry a flag (or other suitable object) to signal his decisions. There shall be one touch judge on each side of the ground and he shall remain in touch except when judging a kick at goal.

(4) He must hold up his flag when the ball or a player carrying it has gone into touch and must indicate the place of throw in and which team is entitled to do so. He must also signal to the referee when the ball or a player carrying it has gone into touch-in-goal.

(5) The touch judge shall lower his flag when the ball has been thrown in except on the following occasions when he must keep it raised:

(*a*) when the player throwing in the ball puts any part of either foot in the field-of-play,

(*b*) when the ball has not been thrown in by the team entitled to do so,

(*c*) when, at a quick throw-in, the ball that went into touch is replaced by another or is handled by anyone other than the players.

It is for the referee to decide whether or not the ball has been thrown in from the correct place.

(6) In matches in which a national representative team is playing and in such domestic matches for which a Union gives express permission, and where referees recognised by the Union are appointed as touch judges, the touch judges may report incidents of foul play and misconduct under Law 26(3) to the referee for the match.

A touch judge may signal such an incident to the referee by raising his flag to a horizontal position pointing in the direction of the goal-line of the offending team. The touch judge must remain in touch and continue to carry out his other functions until the next stoppage in play when the referee shall consult him regarding the incident. The referee may then take whatever action he deems appropriate and any consequent penalties shall be in accordance with Law 26(3).

(7) When a kick at goal from a try, free kick or penalty kick is being taken both touch judges must assist the referee by signalling the result of the kick. One touch judge shall stand at or behind each of the goal posts and shall raise his flag if the ball goes over the cross bar.

7. Mode of Play

A match is started by a kick-off, after which any player who is on-side may at any time:

(*a*) catch or pick up the ball and run with it,

(*b*) pass, throw or knock the ball to another player,

(*c*) kick or otherwise propel the ball,

(*d*) tackle, push or shoulder an opponent holding the ball,

(*e*) fall on the ball,

(*f*) take part in scrummage, ruck, maul or line-out,

provided he does so in accordance with these Laws.

8. Advantage

The referee shall not whistle for an infringement during play which is followed by an advantage gained by the non-offending team. An advantage must be either territorial or such possession of the ball as constitutes an obvious tactical advantage. A more opportunity to gain advantage is not sufficient.

The *only* occasions when advantage does not apply are:

(*a*) when the ball or a player carrying it touches the referee (Law 9(1)).

(*b*) when the ball emerges from either end of the tunnel at a scrummage not having been played (Law 20).

(*c*) when a player is "accidentally" off-side (*Exception* (i) Law 24(A)(2)(*b*)).

When any irregularity of play not provided for in the Laws occurs, a scrummage shall be formed where the irregularity occurred. In deciding which team should put in the ball, the referee should apply Law 20 (7).

9. Ball or Player Touching Referee

(1) If the ball or a player carrying it touches the referee in the field-of-play, play shall continue unless the referee considers either team has gained an advantage in which case he shall order a scrummage. The team which last played the ball shall put it in.

(2) (*a*) If the ball in a player's possession or a player carrying it touches the referee in that player's In-goal, a touch-down shall be awarded.

(*b*) If a player carrying the ball in his opponent's In-goal touches the referee before grounding the ball, a try shall be awarded at that place.

10. Kick-off

Kick-off is (a) a place kick taken from the centre of the half-way line by the team which has the right to start the match or by the opposing team on the resumption of play after the half-time interval or by the defending team after a goal has been scored, or (b) a drop kick taken at or from behind the centre of the half-way line by the defending team after an unconverted try.

(1) The ball must be kicked from the correct place; otherwise it shall be kicked off again.

(2) The ball must reach the opponents' 10 m line, unless first played by an opponent; otherwise it shall be kicked off again, or a scrummage formed at the centre, at the opponents' option. If it reaches the 10 m line and is then blown back, play shall continue.

(3) If the ball pitches in touch, touch-in-goal or over or on the dead-ball line, the opposing team may accept the kick, have the ball kicked off again, or have a scrummage formed at the centre.

(4) The *kicker's team* must be behind the ball when kicked; otherwise a scrummage shall be formed at the centre.

(5) The *opposing team* must stand on or behind the 10 m line. If they are in front of that line or if they charge before the ball has been kicked, it shall be kicked off again.

11. Method of Scoring

Try. A try is scored by first grounding the ball in the opponents' In-goal.

A try shall be awarded if one would probably have been scored but for foul play by the opposing team.

Goal. A goal is scored by kicking the ball over the opponents' crossbar and between the goal posts from the field-of-play by any place kick or drop kick, except a kick-off, free kick or drop-out, without touching the ground or any player of the kicker's team.

A goal is scored if the ball has crossed the bar, even though it may have been blown backwards afterwards, and whether it has touched the cross-bar or either goal post or not.

A goal is scored if the ball has crossed the bar notwithstanding a prior offence of the opposing team.

A goal may be awarded if the ball is illegally touched by any player of the opposing team and if the referee considers that a goal would otherwise probably have been scored.

The *scoring values* are as follows:

A try	4 points
A goal scored after a try	2 points
A goal from a penalty kick	3 points
A dropped goal otherwise obtained	3 points

12. Try and Touch-down

Grounding the ball is the act of a player who

(*a*) *while holding the ball in his hand* (*or hands*) *or arm* (*or arms*) *brings the ball in contact with the ground, or*

(*b*) *while the ball is on the ground either* (i) *places his hand* (*or hands*) *or arm* (*or arms*) *on it with downward pressure, or* (ii) *falls upon it and the ball is anywhere under the front of his body from waist to neck inclusive.*

Picking up the ball from the ground is not grounding it.

A. TRY

(1) A player who is on-side scores a try when (*a*) he carries the ball into his opponents' In-goal, or (*b*) the ball is in his opponents' In-goal, and he first grounds it there.

(2) The scoring of a try includes the following cases:

(*a*) if a player carries, passes, knocks or kicks the ball into his In-goal and an opponent first grounds it,

(*b*) if, at a scrummage or ruck, a team is pushed over its goal line and before the ball has emerged it is first grounded in In-goal by an attacking player,

(c) if the momentum of a player, when tackled, carries him into his opponents' In-goal and he first there grounds the ball,

(d) if a player first grounds the ball on his opponents' goal line or if the ball is in contact with the ground and a goal post.

(3) If a player grounds the ball in his opponents' In-goal and picks it up again, a try is scored where it was first grounded.

(4) A try may be scored by a player who is in touch or in touch-in-goal provided he is not carrying the ball.

B. PENALTY TRY

A penalty try shall be awarded between the posts if but for foul play by the defending team,

(a) a try would probably have been scored, or

(b) it would probably have been scored in a more favourable position than that where the ball was grounded.

C. TOUCH-DOWN

(1) A touch-down occurs when a player first grounds the ball in his In-goal.

(2) After a touch-down, play shall be restarted either by a drop-out or a scrummage, as provided in Law 14.

D. SCRUMMAGE AFTER GROUNDING IN CASE OF DOUBT

Where there is doubt as to which team first grounded the ball in In-goal, a scrummage shall be formed 5 m from the goal line opposite the place where the ball was grounded. The attacking team shall put in the ball.

13. Kick at Goal after a Try

(1) After a try has been scored, the scoring team has the right to take a place kick or drop kick at goal, on a line through the place where the try was scored.

If the scoring team does not take the kick, play shall be restarted by a drop kick from the centre unless time has expired.

(2) If a kick is taken:

(a) it must be taken without undue delay;

(b) any player including the kicker may place the ball;

(c) the *kicker's team*, except a placer, must be behind the ball when kicked;

(*d*) if the kicker kicks the ball from a placer's hands without the ball being on the ground, the kick is void;

(*e*) the *opposing team* must be behind the goal line until the kicker begins his run or offers to kick when they may charge or jump with a view to preventing a goal.

(3) Neither the kicker nor a placer shall wilfully do anything which may lead the opposing team to charge prematurely. If either does so, the charge shall not be disallowed.

Penalty. For an infringement by the *kicker's team*—the kick shall be disallowed.

For an infringement by the *opposing team*—the charge shall be disallowed. If, however, the kick has been taken successfully, the goal shall stand. If it was unsuccessful, the kicker may take another kick under the original conditions without the charge and may change the type of kick.

14. In-Goal

In-goal is the area bounded by a goal line, touch-in-goal lines and dead-ball line. It includes the goal lines and goal posts but excludes touch-in-goal lines and dead-ball line.

Touch-in-goal occurs when the ball, or a player carrying it, touches a corner post, a touch-in-goal line or the ground or a person or object on or beyond it. The flag is not part of the corner post.

Five Metres Scrummage

(1) If a player carrying the ball in In-goal is so held that he cannot ground the ball, a scrummage shall be formed 5 m from the goal line opposite the place where he was held.

The attacking team shall put in the ball.

(2) (*a*) If a defending player heels, kicks, carries, passes or knocks the ball over his goal line and it there becomes dead except where

   (i) a try is scored, or
   (ii) he wilfully knocks or throws the ball from the field-of-play into touch-in-goal or over his dead-ball line, or

(*b*) if a defending player in In-goal has his kick charged down by an attacking player after he carried the ball back from the field-of-play, or a defending player put it into In-goal and the ball is then touched down or goes into touch-in-goal or over the dead-ball line, or

(c) if a defending player carrying the ball in the field-of-play is forced into his In-goal and he then touches down, or

(d) if, at a scrummage or ruck, a defending team with the ball in its possession is pushed over its goal line and before the ball has emerged first grounds it in In-goal:

a scrummage shall be formed 5 m from the goal line opposite the place where the ball or a player carrying it crossed the goal line. The attacking team shall put in the ball.

Drop-Out

(3) Except where the ball is knocked on or thrown forward or a try or goal is scored, if an attacking player kicks, carries, or passes the ball and it travels into his opponents' In-goal either directly or after having touched a defender who does not wilfully attempt to stop, catch or kick it, and it is there

(a) grounded by a player of *either team*, or

(b) goes into touch-in-goal or over the dead-ball line

a drop-out shall be awarded.

Penalties

(a) A penalty try shall be awarded when by foul play in In-goal the defending team has prevented a try which otherwise would *probably* have been scored.

(b) A try shall be disallowed and a drop-out awarded, if a try would *probably not* have been gained but for foul play by the attacking team.

(c) For foul play in In-goal while the ball is out of play the penalty kick shall be awarded at the place where play would otherwise have restarted and, in addition, the player shall either be ordered off or cautioned that he will be sent off if he repeats the offence.

(d) For wilfully charging or obstructing in In-goal a player who has just kicked the ball the penalty shall be a drop-out, or, at the option of the non-offending team, a penalty kick where the ball alights as provided for an infringement of Law 26(3)(d).

(e) for other infringements in In-goal, the penalty shall be:

(i) for an offence by the *attacking team*—a drop-out,

(ii) for an offence by the *defending team*—a scrummage 5 m from the goal line opposite the place of infringement.

15. Drop-out

A drop-out is a drop kick awarded to the defending team.

(1) The drop kick must be taken from anywhere on or behind the 25 yd (22 m) line; otherwise the ball shall be dropped out again.

(2) The ball must reach the 25 yd (22 m) line; otherwise the opposing team may have it dropped out again, or have a scrummage formed at the centre of the 25 yd (22 m) line. If it reaches the 25 yd (22 m) line and is then blown back, play shall continue.

(3) If the ball pitches directly into touch, the opposing team may accept the kick, have the ball dropped out again, or have a scrummage formed at the centre of the 25 yd (22 m) line.

(4) The *kicker's team* must be behind the ball when kicked; otherwise a scrummage shall be formed at the centre of the 25 yd (22 m) line.

(5) The *opposing team* must not charge over the 25 yd (22 m) line; otherwise the ball shall be dropped out again.

16. Fair-Catch (Mark)

(*a*) *A player makes a fair-catch when being stationary with both feet on the ground on his side of his 22 m line he cleanly catches the ball direct from a kick, knock-on or throw-forward by one of his opponents and, at the same time, he exclaims "Mark".*

A fair-catch may be obtained even though the ball on its way touches a goal post or cross-bar and can be made in In-goal.

(*b*) *A free kick is awarded for a fair-catch.*

(1) The kick shall be taken by the player making the fair-catch, unless he is injured in doing so. If he is unable to take the kick within 1 minute a scrummage shall be formed at the mark. His team shall put in the ball.

(2) If the mark is in In-goal, any resultant scrummage shall be 5 m from the goal line on a line through the mark.

17. Knock-on or Throw-forward

A knock-on occurs when the ball travels forward towards the direction of the opponents' dead-ball line after a player loses possession of it, or a player propels or strikes it with his hand or arm, or it strikes a player's hand or arm.

A throw-forward occurs when a player carrying the ball throws or passes it in the direction of his opponents' dead-ball line. A throw-in from touch is not a throw-forward. If the ball is not thrown or passed forward but it bounces forward after hitting a player or the ground, it is not a throw-forward.

(1) The knock-on or throw-forward must not be *intentional*. *Penalty*. Penalty kick at the place of infringement.

(2) If the knock-on or throw-forward is *unintentional*, a scrummage shall be formed either at the place of infringement or, if it occurs at a line-out, 15 m from the touch line along the line-of-touch unless:

(*a*) a fair catch has been allowed, or

(*b*) the ball is knocked on by a player who is in the act of charging down the kick of an opponent but is not attempting to catch the ball, or

(*c*) the ball is knocked on one or more times by a player who is in the act of catching or picking it up or losing possession of it and is recovered by that player before it has touched the ground or another player.

18. Tackle

A tackle occurs when a player carrying the ball in the field-of-play is held by one or more opponents so that while he is so held he is brought to the ground or the ball comes into contact with the ground. If the ball carrier is on one knee, or both knees, or is sitting on the ground or is on top of another player who is on the ground, the ball carrier is deemed to have been brought to the ground.

(1) A tackled player must play the ball immediately or, if unable to play it, must release it immediately and get up or move away from it. He must not play the ball again or interfere with it in any way until he is on his feet. Any other player must be on his feet before he can play the ball, not fall on or over a player lying on the ground with the ball in his

possession, not fall on or over players lying on the ground with the ball between them or in close proximity.

(2) It is illegal for any player:

(*a*) to prevent a tackled player from playing or releasing the ball, or getting up after he has played or released it, or

(*b*) to pull the ball from a tackled player's possession or attempt to pick up the ball before the tackled player has released it, or

(*c*) while lying on the ground after a tackle to play or interfere with the ball in any way or to tackle or attempt to tackle an opponent carrying the ball.

Penalty. Penalty kick at the place of infringement.

(3) If a player carrying the ball is thrown or knocked over but not tackled, he may pass the ball or get up and continue his run even though the ball has touched the ground.

(4) A try may be scored if the momentum of a player carries him into his opponents' In-goal even though he is tackled.

19. Lying with, on or Near the Ball

(1) A player who has not been tackled but who is lying on the ground and holding the ball must immediately pass or release the ball or roll away from it or get up on his feet.

(2) A player or players lying on the ground in close proximity to the ball must not prevent an opponent gaining possession of it.

(3) A player or players from either team must not *wilfully* fall on or over a player who is lying on the ground with the ball in his possession or in close proximity, or on players lying on the ground with the ball between them.

(4) A player must not fall on or over the ball emerging from a scrummage or ruck.

A player on one knee or both knees or sitting on the ground is deemed to be lying on the ground.

Penalty. Penalty kick at the place of infringement.

20. Scrummage

A scrummage, which can take place only in the field-of-play, is formed by players from each team closing up in readiness to allow the ball to be put on the ground between them but is not formed within five metres of the touchline.

The middle player in each front row is the hooker, and the player on either side of him are the props.

The middle line means an imaginary line on the ground directly beneath the line formed by the junction of the shoulders of the two front rows.

Forming a Scrummage

(1) A team must not wilfully delay the forming of a scrummage.

(2) Every scrummage shall be formed at the place of infringement or as near thereto as is practicable within the field-of-play. It must be stationary with the middle line parallel to the goal lines until the ball has been put in.

Before commencing engagement each front row must be in a crouched position with their heads and shoulders no lower than their hips and so that they are no more than one arm's length from their opponents' shoulders.

(3) It is dangerous play for a front row to form down some distance from its opponents and rush against them.

(4) A minimum of five players from each team shall be required to form a scrummage. Each front row shall have three players in it *at all times*. The head of a player in the front row shall not be next to the head of a player of the same team.

(5) While a scrummage is forming and is taking place, the shoulders of each player in the front row must not be lower than his hips. All players in each front row must adopt a normal stance. Both feet must be on the ground, and, until the ball has been correctly put in, must not be crossed. A hooker's foot must not be in front of the forward feet of his props.

Binding of Players

(6) (*a*) The players of each front row shall bind firmly and continuously while the scrummage is forming, while the ball is being put in and while it is in the scrummage.

(*b*) The hooker may bind either over or under the arms of his props but, in either case, he must bind firmly around their bodies at or below the level of the armpits. The props must bind the hooker similarly. The hooker must not be supported so that he is not carrying any weight on either foot.

(*c*) The outside (loose head) prop *must* either (i) bind his opposing (tight head) prop with his left arm inside the right arm of his opponent, or (ii) place his left hand or forearm on his left thigh. The tight head prop *must* bind with his right arm outside the left upper arm of his opposing loose head prop. He may grip the jersey of his opposing loose-head prop with his right hand but only to keep himself and the scrummage steady and he must not exert a downward pull.

(*d*) All players in a scrummage, other than those in a front row, must bind with at least one arm and hand around the body of another player of the same team.

(*e*) No outside player other than a prop may hold an opponent with his outer arm.

Putting the Ball into the Scrummage

(7) The team not responsible for the stoppage of play shall put in the ball. In the event of doubt as to responsibility, the ball shall be put in by the team which was moving forward prior to the stoppage or, if neither team was moving forward, by the attacking team.

(8) The ball shall be put in without delay as soon as the two front rows have closed together. A team must put in the ball when ordered to do so and on the side first chosen.

(9) The player putting in the ball shall:

(*a*) stand *one* m. from the scrummage and midway between the two front rows;

(*b*) hold the ball with both hands midway between the two front rows at a level midway between his knee and ankle;

(*c*) from that position put in the ball without any delay or without feint or backward movement, i.e. with a *single* forward movement and at a quick speed straight along the middle line so that it first touches the ground immediately beyond the width of the nearer prop's shoulders.

(10) Play in the scrummage begins when the ball leaves the hands of the player putting it in.

(11) If the ball is put in and it comes out at either end of the

tunnel, it shall be put in again, unless a free kick or penalty kick has been awarded. If the ball comes out otherwise than at either end of the tunnel and if a penalty kick has not been awarded play shall proceed.

Restrictions on Front Row Players

(12) All front row players must place their feet so as to allow a clear tunnel. A player must not prevent the ball from being put into the scrummage, or from touching the ground at the required place.

(13) No front row player may raise or advance a foot until the ball has touched the ground.

(14) When the ball has touched the ground, any foot of any player in either front row may be used in an attempt to gain possession of the ball, subject to the following:

Players in the front rows must not *at any time* during the scrummage:

(*a*) raise both feet off the ground at the same time, or

(*b*) wilfully adopt any position or wilfully take any action, by twisting or lowering the body or by pulling on an opponent's dress, which is likely to cause the scrummage to collapse, or

(*c*) wilfully kick the ball out of the tunnel in the direction from which it is put in.

Restrictions on Players

(15) Any player who is not in either front row must not play the ball while it is in the tunnel.

(16) A player must not:

(*a*) return the ball into the scrummage, or

(*b*) handle the ball in the scrummage except in the act of obtaining a "push over" try or touch-down, or

(*c*) pick up the ball in the scrummage by hand or legs, or

(*d*) wilfully collapse the scrummage, or

(*e*) wilfully fall or kneel in the scrummage, or

(*f*) attempt to gain possession of the ball in the scrummage with any part of the body except the foot or lower leg.

(17) The player putting in the ball and his immediate opponent must not kick the ball while it is in the scrummage.

Penalty. (*a*) for an infringement of paragraphs 2, 5, 8, 9, 12, 13 and 15, a free kick at the place of infringement; (*b*) for an infringement of paragraphs 1, 3, 4, 6, 14, 16 and 17, a penalty kick at the place of infringement.

For Off-side at Scrummage see Law 24B.

21. Ruck

A ruck, which can take place only in the field-of-play, is formed when the ball is on the ground and one or more players from each team are on their feet and in physical contact, closing around the ball between them.

(1) A player joining a ruck must have his head and shoulders no lower than his hips. He must bind with at least one arm around the body of a player of his team in the ruck.

(2) A player must not:

(*a*) return the ball into the ruck, or

(*b*) handle the ball in the ruck except in the act of securing a try or touch-down, or

(*c*) pick up the ball in the ruck by hand or legs, or

(*d*) wilfully collapse the ruck, or

(*e*) jump on top of other players in the ruck, or

(*f*) wilfully fall or kneel in the ruck, or

(*g*) while lying on the ground interfere in any way with the ball in or emerging from the ruck. He must do his best to roll away from it.

Penalty. Penalty kick at the place of infringement.

For Off-side at Ruck see Law 24C.

22. Maul

A maul, which can take place only in the field-of-play, is formed by one or more players from each team on their feet and in physical contact closing round a player who is carrying the ball.

A maul ends when the ball is on the ground or the ball or a player carrying it emerges from the maul or when a scrummage is ordered. A player joining a maul must have his head and shoulders no lower than his hips.

(1) A player is not in physical contact unless he is caught in or bound to the maul and not merely alongside it.

(2) A player must not (*a*) jump on top of other players in a maul or (*b*) wilfully collapse a maul, or (*c*) attempt to drag another player out of the maul.

Penalty. Penalty kick at the place of infringement.

(3) When the ball in a maul becomes unplayable a scrummage shall be ordered and the team which was moving forward immediately prior to the stoppage shall put in the ball, or if neither team was moving forward, the attacking team shall put it in.

For Off-side at Maul see Law 24C.

23. Touch and Line-out

A. TOUCH

(1) The ball is in touch (*a*) when it is not being carried by a player and it touches a touch line or the ground or a person or object beyond it, or (*b*) when it is being carried by a player and it or the player carrying it touches a touch line or the ground beyond it.

(2) If the ball is not in touch a player who is in touch may kick the ball or propel it with his hand but not hold it.

B. LINE-OUT

The line-of-touch is an imaginary line in the field-of-play at right angles to the touch line through the place where the ball is to be thrown in.

Formation of Line-Out

(1) A line-out is formed by at least two players from each team lining up in single lines parallel to the line-of-touch in readiness for the ball to be thrown in between them. The team throwing in the ball shall determine the maximum number of players from either team who so line up. Such players are those "in the line-out", unless excluded below.

(2) Until the ball is thrown in each player in the line-out must stand at least 1 m from the next player of his team in the line-out and avoid physical contact with any other player.

(3) The line-out stretches from 5 m from the touch line from which the ball is being thrown in to a position 15 m from that touch line.

(4) Any player of either team who is further than 15 m from the touch line when the line-out begins is *not* in the line-out.

(5) A clear space of 2 ft (500 mm) must be left between the two lines of players.

Throwing in the Ball

(6) When the ball is in touch the place at which it must be thrown in is as follows:

(*a*) when the ball goes into touch from a penalty kick, free kick, or from a kick within 25 yd (22 m) of the kicker's goal line, at the place where it touched or crossed the touch line;

(*b*) when the ball pitches directly into touch after having been kicked otherwise than as stated above, opposite the place from which the ball was kicked or at the place where it touched or crossed the touch line if that place be nearer to the kicker's goal line, or

(*c*) on all other occasions when the ball is in touch, at the place where it touched or crossed the touch line.

In each instance the place is where the ball last crossed the touch line before being in touch.

(7) The ball must be thrown in at the line-out by an opponent of the player whom it last touched, or by whom it was carried, before being in touch. In the event of doubt as to which team should throw in the ball, the attacking team shall do so.

(8) The ball must be thrown in without delay and without feint.

(9) A *quick throw in* from touch without waiting for the players to form a line-out is permissible provided the ball that went into touch is used, it has been handled only by the players and it is thrown in correctly.

(10) The ball may be brought into play by a quick throw-in or at a formed line-out. In either event the player must throw in the ball (*a*) at the place indicated, and (*b*) so that it first touches or is touched by a player at least 5 m from the touch line along the line-of-touch, and (*c*) while throwing in the ball, he must not put any part of either foot in the field-of-play.

If any of the foregoing is infringed, the opposing team shall have the right, at its option, to throw in the ball or to take a scrummage.

If on the second occasion the ball is not thrown in correctly a scrummage shall be formed and the ball shall be put in by the team which threw it in on the first occasion.

Beginning and End of Line-out

(11) The line-out begins when the ball leaves the hands of the player throwing it in.

(12) The line-out ends when (*a*) a ruck or maul is taking place and all feet of players in the ruck or maul have moved beyond the line-of-touch, or (*b*) a player carrying the ball leaves the line-out, or (*c*) the ball has been passed, knocked back or kicked from the line-out, or (*d*) the ball is thrown beyond a position 15 m from the touch line, or (*e*) the ball becomes unplayable.

Peeling Off

"*Peeling off*" *occurs when a player (or players) moves from his position in the line-out for the purpose of catching the ball when it has been passed or knocked back by another of his team in the line-out.*

(13) When the ball is in touch players who approach the line-of-touch must *always* be presumed to do so for the purpose of forming a line-out. Except in the peeling off movement such players must not leave the line-of-touch, or the line-out when formed, until the line-out has ended. A player must not begin to peel off until the ball has left the hands of the player throwing it in.

Exceptions. At a quick throw-in, when a player may come to the line-of-touch and retire from that position without penalty.

(14) In a peeling off movement a player must move parallel and close to the line-out. He must keep moving until a ruck or maul is formed and he joins it or the line-out ends.

Restrictions on Players in Line-out

(15) *Before* the ball has been thrown in and has touched the ground or has touched or been touched by a player, any player

in the line-out must not: (*a*) be off-side, or (*b*) push, charge, shoulder or bind with or in any way hold another player of *either* team, or (*c*) use any other player as a support to enable him to jump for the ball, or (*d*) stand within 5 m of the touch line or prevent the ball from being thrown 5 m.

(16) *After* the ball has touched the ground or touched or been touched by a player, any player in the line-out must not (*a*) be off-side, or (*b*) hold, push, shoulder or obstruct an opponent not holding the ball, or (*c*) charge an opponent except in an attempt to tackle him or to play the ball.

(17) Except when jumping for the ball, or peeling off, each player in the line-out must remain at least 1 m from the next player of his team until the ball has touched or has been touched by a player or has touched the ground.

(18) Except when jumping for the ball or peeling off, a clear space of 500 mm (2 ft) must be left between the two lines of players until the ball has touched or has been touched by a player or has touched the ground.

(19) A player in the line-out may move into the space between the touch line and the 5 m mark only when the ball has been thrown beyond him and, if he does so, he must not move towards his goal line before the line-out ends, except in a peeling off movement.

(20) Until the line-out ends, no player may move beyond a position 15 m from the touch line except as allowed when the ball is thrown beyond that position, in accordance with the *Exception* following Law 24D (1)(*d*).

Restrictions on Players not in Line-out

(21) Players of either team who are not in the line-out may not advance from behind the line-out and take the ball from the throw-in except only (*a*) a player at a quick throw-in or (*b*) a player advancing at a long throw-in, or (*c*) a player "participating in the line-out" (as defined in Section D of Law 24) who may run into a gap in the line-out and take the ball provided he does not charge or obstruct any player in the line-out.

Penalty. (*a*) For an infringement of paragraphs (1), (2), (3), (4), (5), (8), (13), (17), (18) or (19), a free kick 15 m from the touch line along the line-of-touch.

(*b*) For an infringement of paragraphs (14), (15), (16) or (20), a penalty kick 15 m from the touch line along the line-of-touch.

(*c*) For an infringement of paragraph (21) a penalty kick on the offending team's off-side line (as defined in Law 24D) opposite the place of infringement, but not less than 15 m from the touch line.

Place of Scrummage taken or ordered under this Law or as the result of any infringement in a line-out shall be formed 15 m from the touch line along the line-of-touch.

For off-side at Line-out see Law 24D.

24. Off-Side

Off-side means that a player is in a position in which he is out of the game and is liable to penalty.

In general play *the player is in an off-side position because he is in front of the ball when it has been last played by another player of his team.*

In play at scrummage, ruck, maul *or* line-out *the player is off-side because he remains or advances in front of the line or place stated in, or otherwise infringes, the relevant sections of this Law.*

A. OFF-SIDE IN GENERAL PLAY

(1) A player is in an off-side position if the ball has been kicked, or touched, or is being carried, by one of his team behind him.

(2) There is no penalty for being in an off-side position unless: (*a*) the player plays the ball or obstructs an opponent, or (*b*) he approaches or remains within 10 m of an opponent waiting to play the ball or the place where the ball pitches.

Where no opponent is waiting to play the ball but one arrives as the ball pitches, a player in an off-side position must not obstruct or interfere with him.

Exceptions.

  (i) When an off-side player cannot avoid being touched by the ball or by a player carrying it, he is "accidentally off-side". Play should be allowed to continue unless the infringing team obtains an advantage, in which case a scrummage shall be formed at that place.

(ii) A player who receives an unintentional throw-forward is not offside.

(iii) If, because of the speed of the game, an off-side player finds himself unavoidably within 10 m of an opponent waiting to play the ball or the place where the ball pitches, he shall not be penalised provided he retires without delay and without interfering with the opponent.

Penalty. Penalty kick at the place of infringement, or, at the option of the non-offending team, a scrummage at the place where the ball was last played by the offending team. If the latter place is In-goal, the scrummage shall be formed 5 m from the goal line on a line through the place.

B. OFF-SIDE AT SCRUMMAGE

The term "off-side line" means a line parallel to the goal lines through the hindmost foot of the player's team in the scrummage.

While a scrummage is forming or is taking place:

(1) A player is off-side if

(*a*) he joins it from his opponents' side, or,

(*b*) he, not being in the scrummage nor the player of either team who puts the ball in the scrummage, fails to retire behind the off-side line or to his goal line whichever is the nearer, or places either foot in front of the off-side line while the ball is in the scrummage.

A player behind the ball may leave a scrummage provided he retires immediately behind the off-side line. If he wishes to rejoin the scrummage, he must do so behind the ball. He may not play the ball as it emerges between the feet of his front row if he is in front of the off-side line.

Exception. The restrictions on leaving the scrummage in front of the off-side line do not apply to a player taking part in "wheeling" a scrummage providing he immediately plays the ball.

(2) A player is off-side if he, being the player on either team who puts the ball in the scrummage, remains, or places either foot, in front of the ball while it is in the scrummage, or if he is the immediate opponent of the player putting in the ball, takes

up position on the opposite side of the scrummage in front of the off-side line.

Penalty. Penalty kick at the place of infringement.

C. OFF-SIDE AT RUCK OR MAUL

The term "off-side line" means a line parallel to the goal lines through the hindmost foot of the player's team in the ruck or maul.

(1) *Ruck or maul otherwise than at line-out.*

While a ruck or maul is taking place (including one which continues after a line-out has ended), a player is off-side if he: (*a*) joins it from his opponents' side, or (*b*) joins it in front of the ball, or (*c*) does not join the ruck or maul but fails to retire behind the off-side line *without delay*, or (*d*) unbinds from the ruck or leaves the maul and does not *immediately* either rejoin it behind the ball or retire behind the off-side line, or (*e*) advances beyond the off-side line with either foot and does not join the ruck or maul.

Penalty. Penalty kick at the place of infringement.

(2) *Ruck or maul at line-out.*

The team "participating in the line-out" has the same meaning as in Section D of this Law. A player participating in the line-out is not obliged to join or remain in the ruck or maul and if he is not in the ruck or maul he continues to participate in the line-out, until it has ended.

While a line-out is in progress and a ruck or maul takes place, a player is off-side if he: (*a*) joins the ruck or maul from his opponents' side, or (*b*) joins it in front of the ball, or (*c*) being a player who is participating in the line-out and is not in the ruck or maul, does not retire to and remain at the off-side line defined in this Section.

Penalty. Penalty kick 15 m from the touch line along the line-of-touch.

(*d*) Or being a player who is not participating in the line-out, remains or advances with either foot in front of the off-side line defined in Section D of this Law.

Penalty. Penalty kick on the offending team's off-side line (as defined in Section D of this Law) opposite the place of infringement, but not less than 15 m from the touch line.

D. OFF-SIDE AT LINE-OUT

The term "participating in the line-out" refers exclusively to the following players: those players who are in the line-out, and the player who throws in the ball, and his immediate opponent who may have the option of throwing in the ball, and one other player of either team who takes up position to receive the ball if it is passed or knocked back from the line-out.

All other players are *not* participating in the line-out.

The term "off-side line" means a line 10 m behind the line-of-touch and parallel to the goal lines or, if the goal line be nearer than 10 m to the line-of-touch, the "off-side line" is the goal line.

Off-side while participating in line-out

(1) A participating player is off-side if: (*a*) *before* the ball has touched a player or the ground he wilfully remains or advances with either foot in front of the line-of-touch, unless he advances solely in the act of jumping for the ball, or (*b*) *after* the ball has touched a player or the ground, if he is not carrying the ball, he advances with either foot in front of the ball, unless he is lawfully tackling or attempting to tackle an opponent who is participating in the line-out. Such tackle or attempt to tackle must, however, start from his side of the ball.

(*c*) in a peeling off movement he fails to keep moving close to the line-out until a ruck or maul is formed and he joins it or the line-out ends, or (*d*) before the line-out ends he moves beyond a position of 15 m from the touch line.

Exception. Players of the team throwing in the ball may move beyond a position of 15 m from the touch line for a long throw-in to them. They may do so only when the ball leaves the hands of the player throwing it in and if they do so their opponents participating in the line-out may follow them. If players so move and the ball is not thrown to or beyond them they must be penalised for off-side.

Penalty. Penalty kick 15 m from the touch line along the line-of-touch.

(2) The player throwing in the ball and his immediate opponent must: (*a*) remain within 5 m of the touch line, or (*b*) retire to the off-side line, or (*c*) join the line-out after the ball

has been thrown in 5 m or (*d*) move into position to receive the ball if it is passed or knocked back from the line-out provided no other player is occupying that position at that line-out.

Off-side while not participating in line-out

(3) A player who is not participating is off-side if before the line-out has ended he advances or remains with either foot in front of the off-side line.

Exception. Players of the team throwing in the ball who are not participating in the line-out may advance for a long throw-in to them beyond the line-out. They may do so only when the ball leaves the hand of the player throwing in the ball and, if they do, their opponents may advance to meet them. If players so advance for a long throw-in to them and the ball is not thrown to them they must be penalised for off-side.

Players returning to "on-side" position

(4) A player is not obliged, before throwing in the ball, to wait until players of his team have returned to or behind the line-out but such players are off-side unless they return to an on-side position *without delay*.

Penalty. Penalty kick on the offending team's off-side line opposite the place of infringement, but not less than 15 m from the touch line.

25. On-side

On-side means that a player is in the Game and not liable to penalty for off-side.

Player made on-side by action of his team

(1) Any player who is off-side in general play, *including* an off-side player who is within 10 m of an opponent waiting to play the ball or where the ball pitches and is retiring as required, becomes on-side as a result of any of the following actions of his team:

(*a*) when the off-side player has retired behind the player of his team who last kicked, touched or carried the ball, or

(*b*) when one of his team carrying the ball has run in front of him; or (*c*) when one of his team has run in front of him after coming from the place or from behind the place where the ball was kicked. In order to put the off-side player on-side, this other player must be in the playing area. But he is not debarred from following up in touch or touch-in-goal.

Player made on-side by action of opposing team

(2) Any player who is off-side in general play, *except* an off-side player within 10 m of an opponent waiting to play the ball or where the ball pitches, becomes on-side as a result of any of the following actions: when an opponent carrying the ball has run 5 m or when an opponent kicks or passes the ball, or when an opponent *intentionally* touches the ball and does not catch or gather it.

An off-side player within 10 m of an opponent waiting to play the ball or where the ball pitches *cannot* be put on-side by *any* action of his opponents. Any *other* off-side player in general play is *always* put on-side when an opponent plays the ball.

Player retiring at scrummage, ruck, maul or line-out.

(3) A player who is in an off-side position when a scrummage, ruck, maul or line-out is forming or taking place and is retiring as required by Law 24 (Off-side) becomes on-side: when an opponent carrying the ball has run 5 m, or when an opponent has kicked the ball.

An off-side player in this situation is *not* put on-side when an opponent passes the ball.

26. Foul Play

Foul Play *is any action by a player which is contrary to the letter and spirit of the Game and includes obstruction, unfair play, misconduct, dangerous play, unsporting behaviour, retaliation and repeated infringements.*

OBSTRUCTION

(1) It is illegal for any player:

(*a*) who is running for the ball to charge or push an opponent also running for the ball, except shoulder to shoulder,

(*b*) who is in an off-side position wilfully to run or stand in front of another player of his team who is carrying the ball, thereby preventing an opponent from reaching the latter player,

(c) who is carrying the ball after it has come out of a scrummage, ruck, maul or line-out, to attempt to force his way through players of his team in front of him,

(d) who is an outside player in a scrummage or ruck, to prevent an opponent from advancing round the scrummage or ruck.

Penalty. Penalty kick at the place of infringement. A penalty try may be awarded.

UNFAIR PLAY, REPEATED INFRINGEMENTS

(2) It is illegal for any player:

(a) deliberately to play unfairly or wilfully infringe any Law of the Game,

(b) wilfully to waste time,

(c) wilfully to knock or throw the ball from the playing area into touch, touch-in-goal or over the dead-ball line.

(d) to infringe repeatedly any Law of the game.

Penalty. Penalty kick at the place of infringement. A penalty try may be awarded. For offences under (2)(c) occurring in In-goal, Law 14 penalty (e) applies. For offences under (2)(d) a player may be cautioned and, if he repeats the offence, must be ordered off.

MISCONDUCT, DANGEROUS PLAY

(3) It is illegal for any player:

(a) to strike an opponent,

(b) wilfully to hack or kick an opponent or trip him with the foot, or to trample on an opponent lying on the ground,

(c) to tackle early or late or dangerously, including the action known as "a stiff arm tackle",

(d) who is not running for the ball wilfully to charge or obstruct an opponent who has just kicked the ball,

(e) to hold, push, charge, obstruct or grasp an opponent not holding the ball, except in a scrummage, ruck or maul. (Except in a scrummage or ruck, the dragging away of a player lying close to the ball is permitted. Otherwise pulling any part of the clothing of an opponent is holding.)

(f) in the front row of a scrummage to form down some distance from the opponents and rush against them,

(g) wilfully to cause a scrummage or ruck or maul to collapse,

(h) while the ball is out of play to molest, obstruct or in any way interfere with an opponent or be guilty of any form of misconduct,

(i) to commit any misconduct on the playing area which is prejudicial to the spirit of good sportsmanship.

Penalty. A player guilty of misconduct and dangerous play shall either be ordered off or else cautioned that he will be sent off if he repeats the offence. For a similar offence after caution the player must be sent off.

In addition to a caution or ordering off, a penalty try or a penalty kick shall be awarded as follows:

(i) If the offence prevents a try which would otherwise *probably* have been scored, a penalty try shall be awarded.

(ii) The place for a penalty kick shall be: (**a**) For offences other than (d) and (h), at the place of infringement. (**b**) In the case of an infringement of (d) the non-offending team shall have the option of taking the kick at the place of infringement or where the ball alights, and if the ball alights in touch, the mark is 15 m from the touch line on a line parallel to the goal lines through the place where it went into touch. If the ball alights within 15 m from the touch line, the mark is 15 m from the touch line on a line parallel to the goal lines through the place where it alighted. If the ball alights in In-goal, touch-in-goal, or over or on the dead-ball line, the mark is 5 m from the goal line on a line parallel to the touch line through the place where it crossed the goal line or 15 m from the touch line, whichever is the greater. When the offence takes place in touch the "place of infringement" in the optional penalty award is 15 m from the touch line opposite to where the offence took place. If the offence takes place in touch-in-goal Law 14, Penalty (d) applies. (**c**) In the case of an offence against (h) the penalty kick may be taken at any place where the ball would next have been brought into play, if the offence had not occurred, or if that place is on or beyond the touch line, at a point 15 m from that place on a line parallel to the goal lines.

(iii) For an offence in In-goal, a penalty kick is to be awarded *only* for offences under Law 14, Penalty (*d*) and Law 26(3)(*h*).

(iv) For an offence under Law 26(3)(*h*), the penalty kick is to be taken at whichever is the place where play would restart, i.e. at the 25 yd (22 m) line (at any point the non-offending team may select), or at the centre of the half-way line, or, if a scrummage 5 m from the goal line would otherwise have been awarded, at that place or 15 m from the touch line on a line 5 m from and parallel to the goal line, whichever is the greater.

(v) For an offence which occurs outside the playing area while the ball is *still in play* and which is not otherwise covered in the foregoing, the penalty kick shall be awarded in the playing area 15 m from the touch line and opposite to where the offence took place.

(vi) For an offence reported by a Touch Judge under Law 6B(6) a penalty kick may be awarded where the offence occurred or at the place where play would restart.

Player Ordered Off

A player who is ordered off shall take no further part in the match. When a player is ordered off, the Referee shall, as soon as possible after the match, send to the Union or other disciplinary body having jurisdiction over the match, a report naming the player and describing the circumstances which necessitated the ordering off. Such report shall be considered by the Union or other disciplinary body having jurisdiction over the match who shall take such action and inflict such punishment as they see fit.

27. Penalty kick

A penalty kick is a kick awarded to the non-offending team as stated in the Laws. It may be taken by any player of the non-offending team and by any form of kick provided that the kicker, if holding the ball, must propel it out of his hands or, if the ball is on the ground, he must propel it a visible distance from the mark. He may keep his hands on the ball while kicking it.

(1) The non-offending team has the option of taking a scrummage at the mark and shall put in the ball.

(2) When a penalty kick is taken the following shall apply:

(*a*) The kick must be taken without undue delay.

(*b*) The kick must be taken at or behind the mark, on a line through the mark, and the kicker may place the ball for a place kick.

If the place prescribed by the Laws for the award of a penalty kick is within 5 m of the opponents' goal line, the mark for the penalty kick or a scrummage taken instead of it shall be 5 m from the goal line on a line through that place.

(*c*) The kicker may kick the ball in any direction and may play the ball again without restriction except that if the kicker has indicated to the referee that he intends to attempt a kick at goal, or has taken any action indicating such intention, he must not kick the ball in any other way. Any indication of intention is irrevocable.

(*d*) The kicker's team, except the placer for a place kick, must be behind the ball until it has been kicked.

(*e*) The opposing team must run *without delay* (and continue to do so while the kick is being taken and while the ball is being played by the kicker's team) to or behind a line parallel to the goal lines and 10 m from the mark, or to their own goal line if nearer to the mark, and there remain motionless with their hands by their sides until the kick has been taken. Retiring players will not be penalised if their failure to retire 10 m is due to the rapidity with which the kick has been taken, but they must not stop retiring and enter the game until an opponent carrying the ball has run 5 m.

(*f*) The opposing team must not prevent the kick or interfere with the kicker in any way. This applies to actions such as wilfully carrying, throwing or kicking the ball out of reach of the kicker.

Penalty. (i) For an infringement by the kicker's team—a scrummage at the mark.

(ii) For an infringement by the opposing team—a penalty kick 10 m in front of the mark or 5 m from the goal line, whichever is the nearer, on a line through the mark. Any player of the non-offending team may take the kick

28. Free Kick

A free kick is a kick awarded for a fair-catch, or to the non-offending team as stated in the Laws.

A goal shall not be scored by the kicker from a free kick unless the ball has first been played by another player.

For an infringement it may be taken by any player of the non-offending team.

It may be taken by any form of kick provided that the kicker, if holding the ball, must propel it out of his hands or, if the ball is on the ground, he must propel it a visible distance from the mark. He may keep his hand on the ball while kicking it.

(1) The team awarded a free kick has the option of taking a scrummage at the mark and shall put in the ball.

(2) When a kick is taken, it must be taken without undue delay.

(3) The kick must be taken at or behind the mark on a line through the mark and the kicker may place the ball for a place kick.

(4) If the place prescribed by the Laws for the award of a free kick is within 5 m of the opponents' goal line, the mark for the free kick, or the scrummage taken in place of it, shall be 5 m from the goal line on a line through that place.

(5) The kicker may kick the ball in any direction and he may play the ball again without restriction.

(6) The *kicker's team*, except a placer for a place kick, must be behind the ball until it has been kicked.

(7) The *opposing team* must not wilfully resort to any action which may delay the taking of a free kick. This includes actions such as wilfully carrying, throwing or kicking the ball away out of reach of the kicker.

(8) The *opposing team* must retire without delay to or behind a line parallel to the goal lines and 10 m from the mark or to their own goal line if nearer to the mark. Having so retired, players of the opposing team may charge with a view to preventing the kick, as soon as the kicker begins his run or offers to kick.

Retiring players will not be penalised if their failure to retire 10 m is due to the rapidity with which the kick has been taken, but they may not stop retiring and enter the game until an opponent carrying the ball has run 5 m.

(9) If having charged fairly, players of the opposing team prevent the kick from being taken, it is void.

(10) Neither the kicker nor the placer shall wilfully do anything which may lead the opposing team to charge prematurely. If either does so, the charge shall not be disallowed.

Penalty: For an infringement by the *kicker's team* or for a void kick—a scrummage at the mark and the *opposing team* shall put in the ball.

If the mark is in In-goal, the scrummage shall be awarded 5 m from the goal line on a line through the mark.

For an infringement by the *opposing team*—a penalty kick 10 m in front of the mark or 5 m from the goal-line whichever is nearer, on a line through the mark. Any player of the non-offending team may take the kick.

The Laws of
Rugby League
Football

SECTION 1
THE PLAYING FIELD

The PLAN and markings thereon and the Notes relating thereto are part of these Laws.

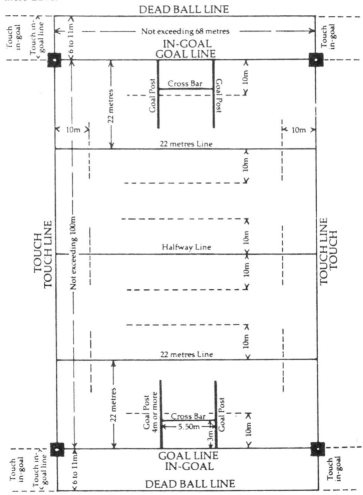

Laws of
Rugby League Football

1. THE FIELD OF PLAY

The plan (overleaf) and markings thereon and the Notes relating thereto are part of these Laws.

NOTES:

1. The Touch Lines are in Touch, the Touch-in-Goal lines are Touch-in-Goal, the Goal-Lines are in the In-Goal area and the Dead-Ball Line is beyond In-Goal.

2. ⊡ Indicates a corner-post (see Glossary) placed at the intersection of each goal-line and touch-line. A corner-post is in touch-in-goal. Touch-Judges should ensure that corner-posts are correctly positioned.

3. The goal-posts are considered to extend indefinitely upwards. It is recommended that the bottom 2 m of each upright be padded.

-shaped goal-posts are permissible provided the relevant dimensions are observed.

4. For adult games the dimensions should be as near maximum as possible. Minimum permissible dimensions should be laid down in the rules of the Competition in which a match is played.

5. The broken lines in the Plan shall consist of marks or dots on the ground not more than 2 m apart. It is of advantage for transverse broken lines to be marked across the full width of the field but if restricted as shown in the Plan then each shall be not less than 15 m long.

II GLOSSARY

The terms set out below shall have the meanings assigned to them:

Advantage

Allowing the advantage means allowing play to proceed if it is to the advantage of the side which has not committed an offence or infringement.

Attacking Team

The team which at the time has a territorial advantage. If a scrum is to be formed on the halfway line the team which last touched the ball before it went out of play is the attacking team.

Back

As applied to a player means one who is not taking part in the scrum.

Ball Back

Means to form a scrum where the ball was kicked after it has entered touch on the full.

Behind

When applied to a player means, unless otherwise stated, that both feet are behind the position in question. Similarly "in front" implies "with both feet".

When applied to a position on the field-of-play, "behind" means nearer to one's own goal-line than the point in question. Similarly "in front of" means nearer to one's opponents' goal-line.

Blind-side

Means the side of the scrum or of the play-the-ball nearer to touch (*cf.* Open Side).

Charging-down

Blocking the path of the ball with hands, arm or body as it rises from an opponent's kick.

Converting a Try

The act of kicking a goal following the scoring of a try.

Corner Post

A post surmounted by a flag placed at the intersection of each touch-line and goal-line. The post shall be of non-rigid material and shall be not less than 4 ft (1.25 m) high. The corner-posts are in touch-in-goal.

Dead Ball

Means that the ball is out of play.

Defending Team

The team opposing the attacking team (see p. 340).

Differential Penalty

Differs in one respect from a Penalty Kick in that a goal cannot be scored from it.

Drop Goal

Sometimes referred to as a Field Goal, is a goal scored by propelling the ball on the full, over the cross-bar by drop-kicking it.

Drop-kick

A kick whereby the ball is dropped from the hands (or hand) and is kicked immediately it rebounds from the ground.

Drop-out

Means a drop-kick from between the posts or from the centre of the "22 m" line when bringing the ball back into play.

Dummy

The pretence of passing or otherwise releasing the ball while still retaining possession of it.

Field-of-Play

The area bounded by, but not including, the touch-lines and goal-lines.

Forward

Means in a direction towards the opponents' dead-ball goal-line. As applied to a player it means one who is at the time packing down in the scrum.

Forward Pass

A throw towards the opponents' dead-ball line (see Section X).

Free Kick

Is the kick awarded to a team which kicks into touch from a penalty kick. The kick is taken 10 m in from touch opposite the point of entry into touch and the ball may be kicked in any manner in any direction but a goal cannot be scored from it, nor can ground be gained by kicking into touch on the full.

Full Time

Means the end of the game. Also referred to as No-side.

Goal

See Section VI.

Grounding the Ball

(*a*) Placing the ball on the ground with hand or hands, or

(*b*) Exerting a downward pressure on the ball with hand or arm, the ball itself being on the ground, or

(*c*) Dropping on the ball and covering it with the part of the body above the waist and below the neck, the ball itself being on the ground.

Half-time

Means the end of the first half of the game.

Handover

The surrendering of the ball to the opposition after a team has been tackled the statutory number of successive times (Section XI Law 7).

Heel

When a player propels the ball behind him with the sole or heel of his foot.

Hook

The act of the hooker when he strikes for the ball in the scrum.

In-Goal

See Plan (Section I).

In Possession

Means to be holding or carrying the ball.

Kick

Means imparting motion to the ball with any part of the leg (except the heel) from knee to toe inclusive.

Kick-off

See Section VIII.

Knock-on

Means to knock the ball towards the opponents' goal-line with hand or arm.

Loose Arm

An offence by the hooker if he packs with one arm loose in the scrum.

Loose Ball

When during play the ball is not held by a player and is not being scrummaged.

Loose Head

Refers to the front row forward in the scrum who is nearest to the referee.

Mark

The point at which a penalty kick is awarded or a scrum is formed.

Obstruction

The illegal act of impeding an opponent who does not have the ball.

Off-side

As applied to a player means that he is temporarily out of play and may be penalised if he joins in the game (see Section XIV).

On-side

Means that a player is not off-side.

Open-side

Means the side of the scrum or the play-the-ball further from touch (*cf*. Blind Side).

On the Full

Means the ball is kicked over a given line without first bouncing.

Pack

Refers collectively to the forwards of any one team. To pack down means to form a scrum.

Pass

A throw of the ball from one player to another.

Penalise

To award a penalty kick against an offending player.

Penalty Kick

See Section XIII.

Place Kick

To kick the ball after it has been placed on the ground for that purpose.

Playing Area

The area enclosed by the fence, or other such line of demarcation, which prevents the encroachment of spectators.

Playing Field

The area bounded by, but not including the touch-lines and dead-ball lines.

Play-the-Ball

The act of bringing the ball into play after a tackle. (See Section XI.)

Prop

The front-row forward in each team nearest to the scrum-half who is putting the ball into the scrum.

Punt

A kick whereby the ball is dropped from the hand or hands and is kicked before it touches the ground.

Put-In also known as Feeding the Scrum

The rolling of the ball into the scrum.

Scrum

Or Scrummage or Scrimmage. (See Section XII.)

Strike

As applied to the foot means to attempt to secure possession of the ball, usually by heeling it, in a scrum or at a play-the-ball.

Tackle

See Section XI.

Tap Kick

The placing of the ball on the ground and bringing it into play by playing it with the foot. The ball may be kicked in any direction and is not required to travel any specific distance. Any player, including the kicker, may pick up the ball after it has been tap-kicked.

Touch-down

The grounding of the ball by a defending player in his own in-goal.

Touch-in-Goal

See Section IX.

Try

See Section VI.

Upright Tackle

Where the player in possession is effectively tackled without being brought to the ground. (See Section XI).

Voluntary Tackle

Where the player in possession voluntarily stops play when not effectively tackled. (See Section XI.)

III. THE BALL

1. The game shall be played with an oval air-inflated ball the outer casing of which shall be of leather or other material approved by the International Board and nothing shall be used in its construction which might prove dangerous to the players.
2. The dimensions of the ball shall be:

	Desired Dimensions	*Permissible Min.*	*Permissible Max.*
Length	28 cm	27 cm	29 cm
Longest circumference	74 cm	73 cm	75 cm
Widest circumference	59 cm	58 cm	61 cm
Weight (clean and dry)	410 g	380 g	440 g

3. The Referee shall blow his whistle immediately he notices that the size and shape of the ball no longer comply with the Laws of the Game. Where a scrum is formed to re-start play the loose-head and put-in shall be awarded to the team last in contact with the ball in play.

IV. THE PLAYERS AND PLAYERS' EQUIPMENT

1. The game shall be played by two teams each consisting of not more than thirteen players.
2. Each team may replace up to two players at any time

provided that the names of the substitutes are made known to the referee before the commencement of the game. A player once replaced shall take no further part in the game.

A replacement must be sanctioned by the referee and can only be effected when the ball is out of play or play is stopped because of injury.

3. The numbers displayed on the backs of the jerseys worn by the players shall normally indicate the positions occupied by the players as set out hereunder.

Backs:	No.	1.	Full-back.
	No.	2.	Right Wing-threequarter.
	No.	3.	Right Centre-threequarter.
	No.	4.	Left Centre-threquarter.
	No.	5.	Left Wing-threequarter.
	No.	6.	Stand-off-half.
	No.	7.	Scrum-half.
Forwards:	No.	8.	Front Row Prop Forward.
	No.	9.	Hooker.
	No.	10.	Front Row Forward.
	No.	11.	Second Row Forward.
	No.	12.	Second Row Forward.
	No.	13.	Loose Forward.
Substitutes:	No.	14.	Reserve back.
	No.	15.	Reserve forward.

4. (*a*) A player shall not wear anything that might prove dangerous to other players.

(*b*) A player's normal gear shall consist of a jersey of distinctive colour and/or pattern (preferably numbered—see para. 3 above), a pair of shorts, stockings of distinctive colour and/or pattern and studded boots or shoes.

(*c*) Protective clothing may be worn provided it contains nothing of a rigid nature.

(*d*) The Referee shall order a player to remove any part of his equipment which might be considered dangerous and shall not allow the player to take any further part in the game until the order is obeyed. The player shall retire from the field-of-play to remove the offending item if the start or re-start of the game would otherwise be delayed.

(*e*) The colours of the jerseys worn by competing teams shall be easily distinguishable and, if, in the opinion of the referee similarity between the jerseys might affect the proper conduct of the game he may, at his discretion, order either team to change jerseys in accordance with the Rules governing the competition in which the game is played.

(*f*) Studs on boots or shoes shall be no less than $\frac{5}{16}$ in (8 mm) diameter at the apex and, if made of metal, shall have rounded edges.

V. MODE OF PLAY

1. The object of the game shall be to ground the ball in the opponents' in-goal to score tries and to kick the ball over the opponents' cross-bar to score goals (see Section VI).

2. The captains of the two teams shall toss for choice of ends in the presence of the referee. The team of the captain losing the toss shall kick-off to start the game.

3. Once play has started any player who is on-side or not out of play can run with the ball, kick it in any direction and throw or knock it in any direction other than towards his opponents' goal-line. (See Section X for Knock-on and Forward Pass.)

4. A player who during play is holding the ball may be tackled by an opposing player or players in order to prevent him from running with the ball or from kicking or passing it to one of his own side. (See Section XI for Tackle.)

5. A player who is not holding the ball shall not be tackled or obstructed. (See Section XV.)

VI. SCORING—TRIES AND GOALS

1. A try shall count four points. A conversion or penalty Goal shall count two points. A Drop Goal during play shall count one point.

2. The game shall be won by the side scoring the greater number of points. If both sides score equal number of points, or if both sides fail to score, then the game shall be drawn.

3. A try is scored when:

(*a*) a player first grounds the ball in his opponents' in-goal provided that he is not in touch or touch-in-goal or on or over the dead-ball line;

(*b*) opposing players simultaneously ground the ball in the in-goal area provided that the attacking player is not in touch or touch-in-goal or on or over the dead-ball line;

(*c*) a tackled player's momentum carries him into the opponents' in-goal where he grounds the ball even if the ball has first touched the ground in the field-of-play but provided that when the ball crosses the goal-line the player is not in touch or touch-in-goal or on or over the dead-ball line;

(*d*) the Referee awards a penalty try which he may do if, in his opinion, a try would have been scored but for the unfair play of the defending team. A penalty try is awarded between the goal-posts irrespective of where the offence occurred;

(*e*) an attacking player carrying the ball comes into contact with the Referee or a Touch-Judge or an encroaching spectator in the opponents' in-goal and play is thereby irregularly affected.

4. The Try is awarded:

(*a*) where grounded if scored as in 3(*a*) and 3(*b*) above;

(*b*) where it first crosses the goal-line if scored as in 3(*c*) above;

(*c*) between the posts if a penalty try;

(*d*) where contact took place if scored as in 3(*e*) above.

5. Only the Referee may award a try but he may take into consideration advice given by the Touch-Judges before arriving at his decision. He shall signal that a try has been scored by pointing to where the try has been awarded but should only do so after looking at the two Touch-Judges to ensure they are not reporting a prior incident.

6. A goal is scored if the whole of the ball at any time during its flight passes over the opponents' cross-bar towards the dead ball line after being kicked on the full by a player (and not being touched in flight by any other player) in any of these circumstances:

(*a*) by a place-kick after a try has been scored and counts two points;

(*b*) by a place-kick or a drop-kick when a penalty kick has been awarded and counts two points;

(*c*) by a drop-kick during play from any position in the field-of-play and counts one point.

7. A kick at goal after a try may be taken from any point on an imaginary line drawn parallel to the touch-line in the field-of-play and through the point where the try was awarded. A kick at goal from a penalty kick may be taken from the Mark or from any point on an imaginary line drawn from the Mark towards the kicker's own goal-line and parallel to the touch-line.

8. When a kick at goal is being taken following a try, the opposing players shall stand outside the field-of-play. Players of the kicker's side must be behind the ball.

When a kick at goal is being taken from a penalty kick, the opponents shall retire to their goal-line or not less than 10 m from the Mark. (See Section XIII.)

It is illegal to attempt to distract the attention of a player who is kicking a goal.

9. For the purpose of judging a kick-at-goal, the goal-posts are assumed to extend indefinitely upwards.

10. When a kick at goal is being taken, the Referee shall assign one Touch-Judge to each post. If a Touch-Judge is of the opinion that a goal has been scored he shall raise his flag above his head. If the kick is unsuccessful he shall wave his flag in front of him and below the waist. If there is no disagreement between the Touch-Judges their decision shall be accepted. In the event of disagreement, the Referee shall decide.

VII. TIME-KEEPING

1. The game shall normally be of 80 min duration.

At half-time there shall be an interval of 5 min but this may be extended or reduced by the Referee.

2. A team shall defend one in-goal for the first half of the game and then change ends for the second half.

3. If time expires in either half when the ball is out of play or a player in possession is tackled and has not risen to his feet, the Referee shall immediately blow his whistle to terminate play.

If the ball is in play when time expires, the Referee shall terminate play when next the ball goes out of play or a player in possession is tackled but time shall be extended to allow a penalty kick or a kick at goal to be taken in which case the half is terminated when next the ball goes out of play or a tackle is effected, unless a further penalty is awarded in which case time is again extended for the kick to be taken.

4. Extra time shall be added to each half to compensate for time wasted or lost from any cause. The Referee shall be the sole judge of extra time. He shall inform the respective captains how much extra time is to be played and shall keep a written record of same except where these duties have been delegated to a timekeeper.

5. If the continuance of play endangers an injured player the Referee may stop the game. If, when the game is stopped, a player is about to play-the-ball after a tackle, then the game shall be re-commenced by that player playing-the-ball. If the injured player was in possession and is unable to resume playing or the ball is loose when play is stopped, then play is re-started with a scrum the team in possession to have the loose-head and put-in.

VIII. THE KICK-OFF AND DROP-OUT

1. The kick-off is a place-kick from the centre of the half-way line. The team which loses the toss for choice of ends kicks-off to start the first half of the game and their opponents kick-off to start the second half.

When points have been scored, the team against which the points have been scored shall kick-off to re-start the game.

2. The game is re-started with a place-kick from the centre of the "25" (22 m) line if:

(*a*) an attacking player last touches the ball before it goes out of play over the dead-ball line or into touch-in-goal except after a penalty kick (see 3) or after a kick-off from the centre of the halfway line;

(*b*) an attacking player infringes in the in-goal area;

(*c*) an attacking player is tackled in the in-goal area before he grounds the ball.

The ball may be kicked in any direction and is immediately in play. Opposing players shall retire 10 yd from the "25" line and shall not advance until the ball has been kicked. Defending players shall not advance in front of the ball before it is kicked. Any deliberate offence by either side shall incur a penalty to be awarded at the centre of the "25" line.

3. If the ball goes dead after an unsuccessful penalty kick at goal the game is restarted with a drop-out by a defending player from the centre of the "25" line.

4. The game is restarted with drop-out by a defending player from the centre of his goal-line if:

(*a*) a defending player last touches the ball before it goes over the dead-ball line or into touch-in-goal;

(*b*) a defending player accidentally infringes in the in-goal area;

(*c*) a defending player touches down in the in-goal area;

(*d*) a defending player in possession is tackled in the in-goal area;

(*e*) a defending player kicks the ball into touch on the full from his own in-goal;

(*f*) the ball or a defending player carrying the ball touches the Referee, a Touch-Judge, or an encroaching spectator in the in-goal area and play is thereby irregularly affected.

5. A player who kicks-off or drops-out shall be penalised if he:

(*a*) advances in front of the appropriate line before kicking the ball;

(*b*) kicks the ball on the full over the touch-line, touch-in-goal line, or over the dead-ball line;

(*c*) kicks the ball so that it fails to travel at least 10 m forward in the field-of-play;

(*d*) kicks the ball other than in the prescribed manner.

6. Any other player shall be penalised if he:

(*a*) wilfully touches the ball after a kick-off or drop-out before it has travelled 10 m forward in the field-of-play;

(*b*) runs in front of one of his own side who is kicking-off or dropping-out;

(*c*) approaches nearer than 10 m to the line from which the kick is being taken when an opponent is kicking-off or dropping-out.

IX. TOUCH AND TOUCH-IN-GOAL

1. The ball is in touch when it or a player in contact with it touches the touch-line or the ground beyond the touch-line or any object on or outside the touch-line except when a player, tackled in in the field-of-play, steps into touch as he regains his feet, in which case he shall play-the-ball in the field-of-play.

The ball is in touch if a player jumps from touch and while off the ground touches the ball. The ball is not in touch if during flight it crosses the touch-line but is knocked back by a player who is off the ground after jumping from the field-of- play.

2. The ball is in touch-in-goal when it or a player in contact with it touches the touch-in-goal line, or any object on or outside the touch-in-goal lines.

3. When a ball has entered touch or touch-in-goal, the point of entry shall be taken as the point at which the ball first crossed the touch or touch-in-goal line.

4. If the ball is kicked by or bounces off a player in a forward direction (except from in-goal, Section VIII [4e]) and it goes into touch on the full, a scrum is formed where contact with the ball was made (but not nearer than 10 m to the touch-line or 5 m to the goal-line). (See Section XII.)

5. If the ball is kicked into touch from a penalty kick the game is restarted by placing the ball on the ground 10 m in field opposite the point of entry into touch. (See Section XIII.)

6. Other than as outlined in paras. 4 and 5 above, the game is restarted after the ball has gone into touch by forming a scrum 10 m in-field opposite the point of entry into touch but not nearer than 5 m to the goal-line. (See Section XII.)

X. KNOCK-ON AND FORWARD PASS

1. A player shall be penalised if he deliberately knocks-on or passes forward.

2. If, after knocking-on accidentally, the player knocking-on regains or kicks the ball before it touches the ground, a goal-post or a cross-bar, then play shall be allowed to proceed. Otherwise play shall stop and a scrum shall be formed.

3. To charge-down a kick is permissible and is not a knock-on.

XI. THE TACKLE AND PLAY-THE-BALL

1. A player in possession may be tackled by an opposing player or players. It is illegal to tackle or obstruct a player who is not in possession.

2. A player in possession is tackled:

(*a*) when he is held by one or more opposing players and the ball or the hand or arm holding the ball comes into contact with the ground;

(*b*) when he is held by one or more oposing players in such a manner that he can make no further progress and cannot part with the ball;

(*c*) when, being held by an opponent, the tackled player makes it evident that he has succumbed to the tackle and wishes to be released in order to play-the-ball;

(*d*) when he is lying on the ground and an opponent places a hand on him.

3. Once a player in possession has been tackled it is illegal for any player to move or try to move him from the point where the tackle is effected.

4. A player in possession shall not deliberately and unnecessarily allow himself to be tackled by voluntarily falling to the ground when not held by an opponent. If a player drops on a loose ball he shall not remain on the ground waiting to be tackled if he has time to regain his feet and continue play.

5. If a tackled player, because of his momentum, slides along the ground, the tackle is deemed to have been effected where his slide ends. (See Section VI, 3(c).)

6. If any doubt arises as to a tackle, the Referee should give a verbal instruction to "play on" or shout "held" as the case may be.

7. A team in possession shall be allowed five successive "play-the-balls" but if tackled a sixth time, the ball not having been touched by an opponent during this period, the tackled player shall immediately release the ball and place it

on the ground at the point where he was tackled. The ball shall then be brought into play by the opposing player nearest to this point playing the ball, which play-the-ball shall not be counted for the purposes of the tackle count. The play-the-ball shall operate as provided for in Law 10 of this Section.

8. A tackled player shall not intentionally part with the ball other than by bringing it into play in the prescribed manner. If, after being tackled, the accidentally loses possession, a scrum shall be formed.

9. Once a tackle has been completed, no player shall take or attempt to take the ball from the tackled player.

10. The play-the-ball shall operate as follows:

(*a*) the tackled player shall be *immediately* released and shall not be touched until the ball is in play;

(*b*) the tackled player shall *without delay* regain his feet where he was tackled, lift the ball clear of the ground, face his opponents' goal-line and drop or place the ball on the ground in front of his foremost foot;

(*c*) when the ball touches the ground it may be kicked or heeled in any direction by the foot of any player after which it is in play;

(*d*) one opponent may take up position immediately opposite the tackled player;

(*e*) neither the tackled player nor the player marking him shall raise a foot from the ground before the ball has been released;

(*f*) a player of each side, to be known as the acting half-back, may stand immediately and directly behind his own player taking part in the play-the-ball;

(*g*) players, other than the two taking part in the play-the-ball and the two acting half-backs, are out of play if they fail to retire 5 m or more behind their own player taking part in the play-the-ball or to their own goal-line. Having retired 5 m they may advance as soon as the ball has been dropped to the ground. A player who is out of play may again take part in the game when the advantage gained by not retiring has been lost.

11. The play-the-ball must be performed as quickly as possible. Any player who intentionally delays the bringing of the ball into play shall be penalised.

12. If part of the tackled player is on or over the goal-line but the ball is in the field of play the tackled player shall play the ball where it lies. If a player is tackled in an upright position bestriding the goal-line, play is re-started with a 5 m scrum, the team in possession of the ball being deemed the offending side.

XII. THE SCRUM

1. A scrum is formed to restart play whenever play is not being restarted with a kick-off, a drop-out (Section VIII), a penalty kick (Section XIII) or a play-the-ball (Section XI).
2. To form a scrum not more than three forwards of either side shall interlock arms and heads and create a clear tunnel at right angles to the touch-line. The forward in the centre of a front row (i.e. the hooker) shall bind with his arms over the shoulders of the two supporting forwards. Not more than two second-row forwards on each side shall pack behind their respective front rows by interlocking arms and placing their heads in the two spaces between the hooker and his prop forwards. The loose forward of each side shall pack behind his second-row forwards by placing his head in the space between them. All forwards must pack square, i.e. their bodies and legs must be at right angles to the tunnel and the upper parts of their bodies horizontal. Once the ball has been put in the scrum no other player can lend his weight to it.
3. No more than six players on each side shall assist in the formation of a scrum and when the ball is in the scrum no more than seven players of each side shall act as backs.
4. It is permissible for the forwards to push once the scrum has been correctly formed, but if it moves an appreciable distance to the disadvantage of any one side before the ball is put in, then the Referee shall order the scrum to re-form in its original position.
5. (*a*) At the scrum the non-offending team shall have the loose-head and the put-in, except that if the ball is kicked into touch otherwise than on the full or after the fifth tackle the attacking team shall have the loose-head and the defending team shall have the put-in at the ensuing scrum.

(*b*) In the case of a mutual infringement, the attacking team shall have the loose-head and the put-in.

6. (*a*) The ball shall be put into the scrum from the Referee's side by holding it in a horizontal position with a point in each hand and rolling it along the ground. It must be put into the centre of the tunnel formed by opposing front row forwards.

(*b*) The ball shall not be put in before the scrum has been correctly formed.

(*c*) There shall be no undue delay in putting the ball into the scrum.

(*d*) The player putting it in shall not hesitate or dummy and after putting it in he shall immediately retire behind his own pack of forwards.

7. All players outside the scrum (other than the scrum-half putting the ball in) shall take up positions behind their own forwards and shall remain so until the ball has emerged correctly from the scrum.

8. When the ball is in the scrum it can only be played with the foot.

The front-row forwards shall not advance their feet into the tunnel or have one foot raised before the ball is put in or strike for the ball before the hookers.

A hooker may strike for the ball with either foot but not until it first contacts the ground in the centre of the tunnel.

After the hookers have struck for the ball the other forwards in the scrum may kick or heel the ball.

No player shall wilfully collapse a scrum or wilfully have any part of him other than his feet in contact with the grounds.

A player shall not wilfully delay the correct formation of a scrum.

9. To be in play, the ball must emerge from between and behind the inner feet of the second row forwards.

If the ball does not emerge correctly and the fault cannot be attributed to any one side then it should be put into the scrum once again.

10. If a scrum is ordered it shall normally be formed where the breach of Laws occurs. If such breach is within 10 m of a touch-line or 5 m of a goal-line the scrum shall be brought in 10 m from the touch-line and 5 m from the goal-line.

11. If a penalty kick is awarded relating to a scrum offence and the scrum has wandered from its original position, the Mark is where the scrum was first formed.

12. If the ball emerges correctly from the scrum it is in play even though the scrum has wheeled. Any forward can detach himself from the scrum to gather or kick the ball. Any back can similarly play it provided he remained behind the scrum until the ball emerged.

XIII. PENALTY KICK

1. A Penalty Kick shall be awarded against any player who is guilty of misconduct (Section XV) provided that this is not to the disadvantage of the non-offending side. Unless otherwise stated, the Mark is where the offence occurs. If misconduct occurs in touch the Mark shall be 5 m from the touch-line in the field-of-play and opposite where the offence occurred or, in the case of obstruction, where the ball next bounces in the field-of-play, or 5 m opposite the point of entry if the ball enters touch on the full, or 5 m from the goal-line if the ball crosses the goal-line on the full, whichever is to the greater advantage of the non-offending side. If the offence is committed by a defender in his own in-goal or an attacker in his opponents' in-goal, the Mark is taken 5 m into the field-of-play opposite where the offence occurred. In the event of further misconduct by the offending side, the referee shall advance the Mark once only 10 m towards the offending team's goal-line.

2. A player may take a Penalty Kick by punting, drop-kicking, or place-kicking the ball from any point on or behind the Mark and equidistant from the touch-line. Other than when kicking for goal the ball may be kicked in any direction, after which it is in play.

3. Players of the kicker's side must be behind the ball when it is kicked.

Players of the side opposing the kicker shall retire to their own goal-line or 10 m or more from the Mark towards their own goal-line and shall not make any attempt to interfere with or distract the attention of the kicker. They may advance after the ball has been kicked.

4. If the ball is kicked into touch without touching any other player the kicking side shall restart play with a free-kick. Opposing players shall retire 10 m from the point of entry into touch or to their own goal-line.

5. No player shall deliberately take any action which is likely to delay the taking of a Penalty Kick.

6. If the kick is not taken as stated or if a player of the kicker's side infringes, a scrum shall be formed at the Mark.

7. If a player of the side opposing the kicker infringes, another Penalty Kick shall be awarded at the Mark or where the offence occurred, whichever is to the greater advantage to the non offending side.

8. When the Referee penalises a player he must explain the nature of the offence.

9. Where a penalty would normally be awarded in the in-goal area for an offence by the attacking team, play shall be restarted with a place-kick from the centre of the "25" line as described in Section VIII, para. 2.

For an in-goal offence by the defending team which incurs a penalty the Mark is in the field-of-play 5 yd from the goal-line and opposite where the offence occurred except where foul play is committed on a player who scores a try, in which case the Mark shall be the centre of the line 10 yd from the goal-line. This penalty kick shall take the form of a kick at goal only and shall be taken after the attempted conversion of the try.

10. The Differential Penalty will operate for technical offences at the scrum, the non-offending side being awarded a tap penalty to be taken at the Mark. The side may elect to kick for touch and follow this with a second phase tap but may *not* kick for goal.

XIV. OFFSIDE

1. A player is offside except when he is in his own in-goal if the ball is kicked, touched or held by one of his own side behind him.

2. An offside player shall not take any part in the game or attempt in any way to influence the course of the game. He shall not encroach within 5 m of an opponent who is waiting

for the ball and shall immediately retire 5 m from any opponent who first secures possession of the ball.

3. An offside player is placed onside if:

(*a*) an opponent moves 5 m or more with the ball;

(*b*) an opponent touches the ball without retaining it;

(*c*) one of his own side in possession of the ball runs in front of him;

(*d*) one of his own side kicks or knocks the ball forward and takes up a position in front of him in the field-of-play;

(*e*) he retires behind the point where the ball was last touched by one his own side.

XV. PLAYER'S MISCONDUCT

A player is guilty of misconduct if he:

(*a*) deliberately trips, kicks or strikes another player;

(*b*) unnecessarily attacks the head of an opponent when effecting a tackle;

(*c*) drops knees first on to an opponent who is on the ground;

(*d*) uses any dangerous throw when effecting a tackle;

(*e*) deliberately breaks the Laws of the Game;

(*f*) uses foul or obscene language;

(*g*) disputes a decision of the Referee or Touch-Judge;

(*h*) re-enters the field-of-play without the permission of the Referee or a Touch-Judge having previously temporarily retired from the game;

(*i*) behaves in any way contrary to the true spirit of the game;

(*j*) Deliberately obstructs an opponent who is not in possession.

XVI. DUTIES OF REFEREE AND TOUCH-JUDGES

1. In all matches a Referee and two Touch-Judges shall be appointed or mutually agreed upon by the contesting teams.

2. The Referee shall enforce the Laws of the Game and may impose penalties for any deliberate breach of the Laws. He

shall be the sole judge on matters of fact except those relating to Touch and Touch-in-Goal. (See para. 11.)

3. He shall record the tries and goals scored during the match.

4. He shall be the sole time-keeper except where this duty has been delegated to another person. (See Section VII.)

5. He may, at his discretion, temporarily suspend or prematurely terminate a match because of adverse weather, undue interference by spectators, misbehaviour by players, or any other cause which, in his opinion, interferes with his control of the game.

6. He shall not allow anyone apart from the players on to the playing area without his permission.

7. The players are under the control of the Referee from the time they enter the playing area until they leave it.

8. The Referee must carry a whistle which he shall blow to commence and terminate each half of the game. Except for these occasions the blowing of the whistle shall temporarily stop the play. The Referee shall blow the whistle:

(*a*) when a try or a goal has been scored;

(*b*) when the ball has gone out of play;

(*c*) when he detects a breach of the Laws of the Game, except when to stop the play would be to the disadvantage of the non-offending team;

(*d*) when play is irregularly affected by the ball or the player carrying the ball coming into contact with the Referee, a Touch-Judge, or with any person not taking part in the match or with any object which should not normally be on the playing field.

(*e*) when any irregularity, not provided for in these Laws, occurs and one team unjustifiably gains an advantage;

(*f*) when a stoppage is necessary in order to enforce the Laws or for any other reason.

9. If the Referee judges on a matter of fact, he shall not subsequently alter that judgement but he may cancel any decision made if facts of which he had no prior knowledge are reported to him by a Touch-Judge.

10. The Referee shall accept the decision of a neutral Touch-Judge relating to touch and touch-in-goal play and to kicks at goal.

11. A Touch-Judge shall indicate when and where the ball goes into touch by raising his flag and standing opposite the point of entry into touch except in the case of "ball back" (see Section IX, para. 4) when the Touch-Judge must indicate that no ground has been gained by waving his flag above his head accentuating the movements in the direction of the kicker's goal-line.

12. If the ball enters Touch-in-Goal the Touch-Judge shall wave his flag above his head and then point it towards the goal-posts if the ball last touched a defending player or towards the 22 m line if it was last touched by an attacking player.

13. Touch-Judges shall assist the Referee in judging kicks at goal. (See Section VI, para. 10.)

14. When a Penalty Kick is being taken, the nearer Touch-Judge shall take up a position near the touch-line 10 m beyond the Mark to act as a marker for the team which is required to retire. He shall wave his flag horizontally in front of him if any player fails to retire 10 m.

15. In cases where circumstances in connection with the match are likely to be made the subject of official investigation, the Referee and Touch-Judges shall report to the investigating authority only and shall refrain from expressing criticism or comment through other channels.

Printed by permission of the R.F.L. Full notes and interpretations of these Laws, and the referee's signals, can be found in the official Rugby Football League International Laws of the Game & Notes on the Laws.

The Rules of
Golf

Golf

As approved by the Royal and Ancient Golf Club of St. Andrews, Scotland, and the United States Golf Association. See Note on p. 527

SECTION I ETIQUETTE

COURTESY ON THE COURSE

Consideration for Other Players

The player who has the honour should be allowed to play before his opponent or fellow-competitor tees his ball.

No one should move, talk or stand close to or directly behind the ball or the hole when a player is addressing the ball or making a stroke.

In the interest of all, players should play without delay.

No player should play until the players in front are out of range.

Players searching for a ball should signal the players behind them to pass as soon as it becomes apparent that the ball will not easily be found. They should not search for five minutes before doing so. They should not continue play until the players following them have passed and are out of range.

When the play of a hole has been completed, players should immediately leave the putting green.

Priority on the Course

In the absence of special rules, two-ball matches should have precedence over and be entitled to pass any three- or four-ball match.

A single player has no standing and should give way to a match of any kind.

Any match playing a whole round is entitled to pass a match playing a shorter round.

If a match fails to keep its place on the course and loses more than one clear hole on the players in front, it should allow the match following to pass.

Care of the Course

Holes in Bunkers

Before leaving a bunker, a player should carefully fill up and smooth over all holes and footprints made by him.

Replace Divots; Repair Ball-Marks and Damage by Spikes

Through the green, a player should ensure that any turf cut or displaced by him is replaced at once and pressed down and that any damage to the putting green made by a ball is carefully repaired. Damage to the putting green caused by golf shoe spikes should be repaired on *completion of the hole*.

Damage to Green—Flagsticks, Bags, etc.

Players should ensure that, when putting down bags or the flagstick, no damage is done to the putting green and that neither they nor their caddies damage the hole by standing close to it, in handling the flagstick or in removing the ball from the hole. The flagstick should be properly replaced in the hole before the players leave the putting green. Players should not damage the putting green by leaning on their putters, particularly when removing the ball from the hole.

Golf Carts

Local notices regulating the movement of golf carts should be strictly observed.

Damage Through Practice Swings

In taking practice swings, players should avoid causing damage to the course, particularly the tees, by removing divots.

SECTION II DEFINITIONS

Addressing the Ball

A player has "addressed the ball" when he has taken his stance and has also grounded his club, except that in a hazard a player has addressed the ball when he has taken his stance.

Advice

"Advice" is any counsel or suggestion which could influence a player in determining his play, the choice of a club or the method of making a stroke.

Information on the Rules or on matters of public information, such as the position of hazards or the flagstick on the putting green, is not advice.

Ball Deemed to Move

See "Move or Moved".

Ball Holes

See "Holed".

Ball Lost

See "Lost Ball".

Ball in Play

A ball is "in play" as soon as the player has made a stroke on the teeing ground. It remains in play until holed out, except when it is out of bounds, lost or lifted, or another ball has been substituted under an applicable Rule; a ball so substituted becomes the ball in play.

Bunker

A "bunker" is a hazard consisting of a prepared area of ground, often a hollow, from which turf or soil has been removed and replaced with sand or the like. Grass-covered ground bordering or within a bunker is not part of the bunker.

Caddie

A "caddie" is one who carries or handles a player's clubs during play and otherwise assists him in accordance with the Rules.

When one caddie is employed by more than one player, he is always deemed to be the caddie of the player whose ball is involved, and equipment carried by him is deemed to be that player's equipment, except when the caddie acts upon specific directions of another player, in which case he is considered to be that other player's caddie.

Casual Water

"Casual water" is any temporary accumulation of water on the course which is visible before or after the player takes his stance and is not in a water hazard. Snow and ice are either casual water or loose impediments, at the option of the player. Dew is not casual water.

Committee

The "Committee" is the committee in charge of the competition or, if the matter does not arise in a competition, the committee in charge of the course.

Competitior

A "competitor" is a player in a stroke competition. A "fellow-competitor" is any person with whom the competitor plays. Neither is partner of the other.

In stroke play foursome and four-ball competitions, where the context so admits, the word "competitor" or "fellow-competitor" shall be held to include his partner.

Course

The "course" is the whole area within which play is permitted (see Rule 33-2).

Equipment

"Equipment" is anything used, worn or carried by or for the player except any ball he has played and any small object, such as a coin or a tee, when used to mark the position of a ball or the extent of an area in which a ball is to be dropped. Equipment includes a golf cart, whether or not motorised. If such a cart is shared by more than one player, its status under the Rules is the same as that of a caddie employed by more than one player. See "Caddie".

Fellow-Competitor

See "Competitor".

Flagstick

The "flagstick" is a movable straight indicator, with or without bunting or other material attached, centred in the hole to show its position. It shall be circular in cross-section.

Forecaddie

A "forecaddie" is one who is employed by the Committee to indicate to players the position of balls on the course, and is an outside agency.

Ground Under Repair

"Ground under repair" is any portion of the course so marked by order of the Committee or so declared by its authorised representative. It includes material piled for removal and a hole made by a greenkeeper, even if not so marked. Stakes and lines defining ground under repair are in such ground.

Note 1: Grass cuttings and other material left on the course which have been abandoned and are not intended to be removed are not ground under repair unless so marked.

Note 2: The Committee may make a Local Rule prohibiting play from ground under repair.

Hazards

A "hazard" is any bunker or water hazard.

Hole

The "hole" shall be 4¼ inches (108 mm) in diameter and at least 4 inches (100 mm) deep. If a lining is used, it shall be sunk at least 1 inch (25 mm) below the putting green surface unless the nature of the soil makes it impracticable to do so; its outer diameter shall not exceed 4¼ inches (108 mm).

Holed

A ball is "holed" when it is at rest within the circumference of the hole and all of it is below the level of the lip of the hole.

Honour

The side entitled to play first from the teeing ground is said to have the "honour".

Lateral Water Hazard

A "lateral water hazard" is a water hazard or that part of a water hazard so situated that it is not possible or is deemed by the Committee to be impracticable to drop a ball behind the water hazard and keep the spot at which the ball last crossed the margin of the water hazard between the player and the hole.

That part of a water hazard to be played as a lateral water hazard should be distinctively marked.

Note: Lateral water hazards should be defined by red stakes or lines.

Loose Impediments

"Loose impediments" are natural objects such as stones, leaves, twigs, branches and the like, dung, worms and insects and casts or heaps made by them, provided they are not fixed or growing, are not solidly embedded and do not adhere to the ball.

Sand and loose soil are loose impediments on the putting green, but not elsewhere.

Snow and ice are either casual water or loose impediments, at the option of the player.

Dew is not a loose impediment.

Lost Ball

A ball is "lost" if:

(*a*) It is not found or identified as his by the player within five minutes after the player's side or his or their caddies have begun to search for it; or

(*b*) The player has put another ball into play under the Rules, even though he may not have searched for the original ball; or

(*c*) The player has played any stroke with a provisional ball from the place where the original ball is likely to be or from a point nearer the hole than that place, whereupon the provisional ball becomes the ball in play.

Time spent in playing a wrong ball is not counted in the five-minute period allowed for search.

Marker

A "marker" is one who is appointed by the Committee to record a <u>competitor's</u> score in stroke play. He may be a <u>fellow-competitor</u>. He is not a <u>referee</u>.

A marker should not lift a ball or mark its position unless authorised to do so by the competitor and, unless he is a fellow-competitor, should not attend the flagstick or stand at the hole or mark its position.

Matches

See "Sides and Matches".

Move or Moved

A ball is deemed to have "moved" if it leaves its position and comes to rest in any other place.

Observer

An "observer" is one who is appointed by the Committee to assist a <u>referee</u> to decide questions of fact and to report to him any breach of a Rule. An observer should not attend the flagstick, stand at or mark the position of the hole, or lift the ball or mark its position.

Obstructions

An "obstruction" is anything artificial including the artificial surfaces and sides of roads and paths, except:

(*a*) Objects defining <u>out of bounds,</u> such as walls, fences, stakes and railings;

(*b*) Any part of an immovable artificial object which is out of bounds; and

(*c*) Any construction declared by the Committee to be an integral part of the course.

Out of Bounds

"Out of bounds" is ground on which play is prohibited.

When out of bounds is defined by reference to stakes or a fence or as being beyond stakes or a fence, the out of bounds line is determined by the nearest inside points of the stakes or fence posts at ground level excluding angled supports.

When out of bounds is defined by a line on the ground, the line itself is out of bounds.

The out of bounds line is deemed to extend vertically upwards and downwards.

A ball is out of bounds when all of it lies out of bounds.

A player may stand out of bounds to play a ball lying within bounds.

Outside Agency

An "outside agency" is any agency not part of the match or, in stroke play, not part of a competitor's side, and includes a referee, a marker, an observer or a forecaddie. Neither wind nor water is an outside agency.

Partner

A "partner" is a player associated with another player on the same side.

In a threesome, foursome or a four-ball match where the context so admits, the word "player" shall be held to include his partner.

Penalty Stroke

A "penalty stroke" is one added to the score of a player or side under certain Rules. In a threesome or foursome, penalty strokes do not affect the order of play.

Provisional Ball

A "provisional ball" is a ball played under Rule 27-2 for a ball which may be <u>lost</u> outside a <u>water hazard</u> or may be <u>out of bounds</u>. It ceases to be a provisional ball when the Rule provides either that the player continue play with it as the <u>ball in play</u> or that it be abandoned.

Putting Green

The "putting green" is all ground of the hole being played which is specially prepared for putting or otherwise defined as such by the Committee. A ball is on the putting green when any part of it touches the putting green.

Referee

A "referee" is one who is appointed by the Committee to accompany players to decide questions of fact and apply the Rules of Golf. He shall act on any breach of a Rule which he observes or is reported to him.

A referee should not attend the flagstick, stand at or mark the position of the hole, or lift the ball or mark its position.

Rub of the Green

A "rub of the green" occurs when a ball in motion is accidentally deflected or stopped by any outside agency (see Rule 19-1).

Rule

The term "Rule" includes Local Rules made by the Committee under Rule 33-8a.

Sides and Matches

Side: A player, or two or more players who are partners.

Single: A match in which one plays against another.

Threesome: A match in which one plays against two, and each side plays one ball.

Foursome: A match in which two play against two, and each side plays one ball.

Three-ball: A match in which three play against one another, each playing his own ball.

Best-ball: A match in which one plays against the better ball of two or the best ball of three players.

Four-ball: A match in which two play their better ball against the better ball of two other players.

Stance

Taking the "stance" consists in a player placing his feet in position for and preparatory to making a stroke.

Stipulated Round

The "stipulated round" consists of playing the holes of the course in their correct sequence unless otherwise authorised by the Committee. The number of holes in a stipulated round is

18 unless a small number is authorised by the Committee. As to extension of stipulated round in match play, see **Rule 2-4**.

Stroke

A "stroke" is the forward movement of the club made with the intention of fairly striking at and moving the ball.

Teeing Ground

The "teeing ground" is the starting place for the hole to be played. It is a rectangular area two club-lengths in depth, the front and the sides of which are defined by the outside limits of two tee-markers. A ball is outside the teeing ground when all of it lies outside the teeing ground.

Through the Green

"Through the green" is the whole area of the course except:

(*a*) The teeing ground and putting green of the hole being played; and

(*b*) All hazards on the course.

Water Hazard

A "water hazard" is any sea, lake, pond, river, ditch, surface drainage ditch or other open water course (whether or not containing water) and anything of a similar nature.

All ground or water within the margin of a water hazard is part of the water hazard. The margin of a water hazard is deemed to extend vertically upwards. Stakes and lines defining the margins of water hazards are in the hazards.

Note: Water hazards (other than lateral water hazards) should be defined by yellow stakes or lines.

Wrong Ball

A "wrong ball" is any ball other than:

(*a*) The ball in play,

(*b*) A provisional ball or

(*c*) In stroke play, a second ball played under Rule 3-3 or Rule 20-7b.

SECTION III THE RULES OF PLAY

THE GAME

Rule 1. The Game

1-1 General

The Game of Golf consists in playing a ball from the teeing ground into the hole by a stroke or successive strokes in accordance with the Rules.

PENALTY FOR BREACH OF RULE 1-1:
Match play—Loss of hole; Stroke play—Disqualification.

1-2 Exerting Influence on Ball

No player or caddie shall take any action to influence the position or the movement of a ball except in accordance with the Rules.

PENALTY FOR BREACH OF RULE 1-2:
Match play—Loss of hole; Stroke play—Two strokes.
Note: In the case of a serious breach of Rule 1-2, the Committee may impose a penalty of disqualification.

1-3 Agreement to Waive Rules

Players shall not agree to exclude the operation of any Rule or to waive any penalty incurred.

PENALTY FOR BREACH OF RULE 1-3:
Match play—Disqualification of both sides;
Stroke play—Disqualification of competitors concerned.

1-4 Points Not Covered by Rules

If any point in dispute is not covered by the Rules, the decision shall be made in accordance with equity.

Rule 2. Match Play

2-1 Winner of Hole

In match play the game is played by holes.

Except as otherwise provided in the Rules, a hole is won by the side which holes its ball in the fewer strokes. In a handicap match the lower net score wins the hole.

2-2 Halved Hole

A hole is halved if each side holes out in the same number of strokes.

When a player has holed out and his opponent has been left with a stroke for the half, if the player thereafter incurs a penalty, the hole is halved.

2-3 Reckoning of Holes

The reckoning of holes is kept by the terms: so many "holes up" or "all square", and so many "to play".

A side is "dormie" when it is as many holes up as there are holes remaining to be played.

2-4 Winner of Match

A match (which consists of a stipulated round, unless otherwise decreed by the Committee) is won by the side which is leading by a number of holes greater than the number of holes remaining to be played.

A side may concede a match at any time prior to the conclusion of the match.

The Committee may, for the purpose of settling a tie, extend the stipulated round to as many holes as are required for a match to be won.

2-5 Claims

In match play, if a doubt or dispute arises between the players and no duly authorised representative of the Committee is available within a reasonable time, the players shall continue the match without delay. Any claim, if it is to be considered by the Committee, must be made before any player in the match plays from the next teeing ground or, in the case of the last hole of the match, before all players in the match leave the putting green.

No later claim shall be considered unless it is based on facts previously unknown to the player making the claim and the player making the claim had been given wrong information (Rules 6-2a and 9) by an opponent. In any case, no later claim shall be considered after the result of the match has been officially announced, unless the Committee is satisfied that the opponent knew he was giving wrong information.

2-6 General Penalty

The penalty for a breach of a Rule in match play is loss of hole except when otherwise provided.

Rule 3. Stroke Play

3-1 Winner

The competitor who plays the <u>stipulated round</u> or rounds in the fewest strokes is the winner.

3-2 Failure to Hole Out

If a competitor fails to hole out at any hole before he has played a <u>stroke</u> from the next <u>teeing ground</u> or, in the case of the last hole of the round, before he has left the <u>putting green</u>, *he shall be disqualified.*

3-3 Doubt as to Procedure

In stroke play only, when during play of a hole a competitor is doubtful of his rights or procedure, he may, without penalty, play a second ball. After the doubtful situation has arisen and before taking further action, he should announce to his marker his decision to proceed under this Rule and which ball he will score with if the Rules permit.

On completing the round, the competitor shall report the facts immediately to the <u>Committee</u>; if he fails to do so, *he shall be disqualified.* If the Rules allow the procedure selected in advance by the competitor, the score with the ball selected shall be his score for the hole. If the competitor fails to announce in advance his procedure or selection, the ball with the higher score shall count if the Rules allow the procedure adopted for such ball.

Note: A second ball played under Rule 3-3 is not a provisional ball under Rule 27-2.

3-4 Refusal to Comply with a Rule

If a competitor refuses to comply with a Rule affecting the rights of another competitor, *he shall be disqualified.*

3-5 General Penalty

The penalty for a breach of a Rule in stroke play is two strokes except when otherwise provided.

CLUBS AND THE BALL

The Royal and Ancient Golf Club of St. Andrews and the United States Golf Association reserve the right to change the Rules and make and change the interpretations relating to clubs, balls and other implements at any time.

Rule 4. Clubs

If a manufacturer is in doubt as to whether a club which he proposes to manufacture conforms with Rule 4 and Appendix II, he should submit a sample to the Royal and Ancient Golf Club of St. Andrews for a ruling, such sample to become its property for reference purposes.

A player in doubt as to the conformity of a club should consult the Royal and Ancient Golf Club of St. Andrews.

4-1 Form and Make of Clubs

A club is an implement designed to be used for striking the ball.

A putter is a club designed primarily for use on the putting green.

The player's clubs shall conform with the provisions of this Rule and with the specifications and interpretations set forth in Appendix II.

a. General

The club shall be composed of a shaft and a head. All parts of the club shall be fixed so that the club is one unit. The club shall not be designed to be adjustable except for weight. The club shall not be substantially different from the traditional and customary form and make.

b. Shaft

The shaft shall be generally straight, with the same bending and twisting properties in any direction, and shall be attached to the clubhead at the heel either directly or through a single plain neck or socket. A putter shaft may be attached to any point in the head.

c. Grip

The grip consists of that part of the shaft designed to be held by the player and any material added to it for the purpose of obtaining a firm hold. The grip shall be substantially straight and plain in form and shall not be moulded for any part of the hands.

d. Clubhead

The length of the clubhead, from heel to toe, shall be greater than the breadth from face to back. The clubhead shall be generally plain in shape.

The clubhead shall have only one face designed for striking the ball, except that a putter may have two such faces if the loft of each is substantially the same and does not exceed ten degrees.

e. Club Face

The face shall not have any degree of concavity and, in relation to the ball, shall be hard and rigid. It shall be generally smooth except for such markings as are permitted by Appendix II. If the basic structural material of the head and face of a club, other than a putter, is metal, no inset or attachment is permitted.

f. Wear

A club which conforms to Rule 4-1 when new is deemed to conform after wear through normal use. Any part of a club which has been purposely altered is regarded as new and must conform, in the altered state, to the Rules.

g. Damage

A club which ceases to conform to Rule 4-1 because of damage sustained in the normal course of play may be used in its damaged state, but only for the remainder of the stipulated round during which such damage was sustained. A club which ceases to conform because of damage sustained other than in the normal course of play shall not be used unless it is repaired so as to conform to Rule 4-1.

4-2 Playing Characteristics Not to be Changed

During a stipulated round, the playing characteristics of a club shall not be purposely changed, except that damage occurring during such round may be repaired, provided play is not unduly delayed. Damage which occurred prior to the round may be repaired, provided the playing characteristics are not changed.

4-3 Foreign Material

No foreign material shall be applied to the club face for the purpose of influencing the movement of the ball.

PENALTY FOR BREACH OF RULE 4-1, -2 or -3:
Disqualification.

4-4 Maximum of Fourteen Clubs

a. Selection and Replacement of Clubs

The player shall start a stipulated round with not more than fourteen clubs. He is limited to the clubs thus selected for that round except that, without unduly delaying play, he may:

(i) if he started with fewer than fourteen, add as many as will bring his total to that number; and

(ii) replace, with any club, a club which becomes unfit for play in the normal course of play.

The addition of replacement of a club or clubs may not be made by borrowing from any other person playing on the course.

b. Partners May Share Clubs

Partners may share clubs, provided that the total number of clubs carried by the partners so sharing does not exceed fourteen.

PENALTY FOR BREACH OF RULE 4-4a or b,
REGARDLESS OF NUMBER OF EXCESS CLUBS CARRIED:

Match play—At the conclusion of the hole at which the breach is discovered, the state of the match shall be adjusted by deducting one hole or each hole at which a breach occurred. Maximum deduction per round: two holes.

Stroke play—Two strokes for each hole at which any breach occurred; maximum penalty per round: four strokes.

Bogey and par competitions—Penalties as in match play.
Stableford competitions—see Rule 32-1b.

c. Excess Club Declared Out of Play

Any club carried or used in breach of this Rule shall be declared out of play by the player immediately upon discovery that a breach has occurred and thereafter shall not be used by the player during the round *under penalty of disqualification.*

Rule 5. The Ball

5-1 General

The ball the player uses shall conform to specifications set forth in Appendix III on maximum weight, minimum size, spherical symmetry and initial velocity when tested under specified conditions.

Note :1 The Rules of the United States Golf Association specify a larger minimum size and also an Overall Distance Standard.

In international team competitions, the size of the ball shall not be less than 1.620 inches (41.15 mm) and the Overall Distance Standard shall not apply.

Note 2: In laying down the conditions under which a competition is to be played (Rule 33-1), the Committee may stipulate that the ball to be used shall be of certain specifications, provided these specifications are within the limits prescribed by Appendix III, and that it be of a size, brand and marking as detailed on the current List of Conforming Golf Balls issued by the Royal and Ancient Golf Club of St. Andrews.

5-2 Foreign Material Prohibited

No foreign material shall be applied to a ball for the purpose of changing its playing characteristics.

PENALTY FOR BREACH OF RULE 5-1 or 5-2:
Disqualification.

5-3 Ball Unfit for Play

A ball is unfit for play if it is visibly cut or out of shape or so cracked, pierced or otherwise damaged as to interfere with its true flight or true roll or its normal behaviour when struck. A ball is not unfit for play solely because mud or other materials adhere to it, its surface is scratched or its paint is damaged or discoloured.

If a player has reason to believe his ball has become unfit for play during play of the hole being played, he may during the play of such hole lift his ball without penalty to determine whether it is unfit, provided he announces his intention in advance to his opponent in match play or his marker or a fellow-competitor in stroke play and gives his opponent, marker or fellow-competitor an opportunity to examine the ball. If he lifts the ball without announcing his intention in advance or giving his opponent, marker or fellow-competitor an opportunity to examine the ball, *he shall incur a penalty of one stroke.*

If it is determined that the ball has become unfit for play during play of the hole being played, the player may substitute another ball, placing it on the spot where the original ball lay. Otherwise, the original ball shall be replaced.

If a ball breaks into pieces as a result of a stroke, the stroke shall be replayed without penalty (see Rule 20-5).

*PENALTY FOR BREACH OF RULE 5-3:

Match play—Loss of hole; Stroke play—Two strokes.

*If a player incurs the general penalty for breach of Rule 5-3, no additional penalty under the Rule shall be applied.

Note 1: The ball may not be cleaned to determine whether it is unfit for play—see Rule 21.

Note 2: If the opponent, marker or fellow-competitor wishes to dispute a claim of unfitness, he must do so before the player plays another ball.

PLAYER'S RESPONSIBILITIES

Rule 6. The player

Definition

A "marker" is one who is appointed by the Committee to record a competitor's score in stroke play. He may be a fellow-competitor. He is not a referee.

A marker should not lift a ball or mark its position unless

authorised to do so by the competitor and, unless he is a fellow-competitor, should not attend the flagstick or stand at the hole or mark its position.

6-1 Conditions of Competition

The player is responsible for knowing the conditions under which the competition is to be played (Rule 33-1).

6-2 Handicap

a. Match Play

Before starting a match in a handicap competition, the player shall declare to his opponent the handicap to which he is entitled under the conditions of the competition. If a player declares and begins the match with a higher handicap which would affect the number of strokes given or received, *he shall be disqualified*; otherwise, the player shall play off the declared handicap.

b. Stroke Play

In any round of a handicap competition, the competitor shall ensure that the handicap to which he is entitled under the conditions of the competition is recorded on his score card before it is returned to the Committee. If no handicap is recorded on his score card before it is returned, or if the recorded handicap is higher than that to which he is entitled and this affects the number of strokes received, *he shall be disqualified* from that round of the handicap competition; otherwise, the score shall stand.

Note: It is the player's responsibility to know the holes at which handicap strokes are to be given or received.

6-3 Time of Starting and Groups

a. Time of Starting

The player shall start at the time laid down by the Committee.

b. Groups

In stroke play, the competitor shall remain throughout the

round in the group arranged by the Committee unless the Committee authorises or ratifies a change.

PENALTY FOR BREACH OF RULE 6-3: *Disqualification.*
(Best-ball and four-ball play—see Rules 30-3a and 31-2.)

Note: The Committee may provide in the conditions of a competition (Rule 33-1) that, in the absence of circumstances which warrant waiving the penalty of disqualification as provided in Rule 33-7, if the player arrives at his starting point, ready to play, within five minutes of his starting time, the penalty for failure to start on time is *loss of the first hole to be played in match play or two strokes in stroke play* instead of disqualification.

6-4 Caddie

The player may have only one caddie at any one time, *under penalty of disqualification.*

For any breach of a Rule by his caddie, the player incurs the relative penalty.

6-5 Ball

The responsibility for playing the proper ball rests with the player. Each player should put an identification mark on his ball.

6-6 Scoring in Stroke Play

a. Recording Scores

After each hole the marker should check the score with the competitor. On completion of the round the marker shall sign the card and hand it to the competitor; if more than one marker record the scores, each shall sign for the part for which he is responsible.

b. Checking Scores

The competitor shall check his score for each hole, settle any doubtful points with the Committee, ensure that the marker has signed the card, countersign the card himself and return it to the Committee as soon as possible. The competitor is responsible for the correctness of the score recorded for each hole.

PENALTY FOR BREACH OF RULE 6-6b: *Disqualification.*
Note: As to the Committee's responsibility to add the scores and apply the recorded handicap, see Rule 33-5.

c. No Alteration of Scores
No alteration may be made on a card after the competitor has returned it to the Committee.

If the competitor returns a score for any hole lower than actually taken, *he shall be disqualified.* If he returns a score for any hole higher than actually taken, the score as returned shall stand.

Note: In four-ball stroke play, see also Rule 31-4 and -7a.

6-7 Under Delay
The player shall play without undue delay. Between completion of a hole and playing from the next teeing ground, the player shall not unduly delay play.
PENALTY FOR BREACH OF RULE 6-7:
Match play—Loss of hole; Stroke play—Two strokes.
For repeated offence—Disqualification.
If the player unduly delays play between holes, he is delaying the play of the next hole and the penalty applies to that hole.

6-8 Discontinuance of Play
a. When Permitted
The player shall not discontinue play unless:
  (i) the Committee has suspended play;
 (ii) he believes there is danger from lightning;
(iii) he is seeking a decision from the Committee on a doubtful or disputed point (see Rules 2-5 and 34-3); or
 (iv) there is some other good reason such as sudden illness.
Bad weather is not of itself a good reason for discontinuing play.

If the player discontinues play without specific permission from the Committee, he shall report to the Committee as soon as practicable. If he does so and the Committee considers his reason satisfactory, the player incurs no penalty. Otherwise, *the player shall be disqualified.*

Exception in match play: Players discontinuing match play

by agreement are not subject to disqualification unless by so doing the competition is delayed.

Note: Leaving the course does not of itself constitute discontinuance of play.

b. Procedure

When play is discontinued in accordance with the Rules, it should, if feasible, be discontinued after the completion of the play of a hole. If this is not feasible, the player should lift his ball. The ball may be cleaned when so lifted. If a ball has been so lifted, the player shall, when play is resumed, place a ball on the spot from which the original ball was lifted.

PENALTY FOR BREACH OF RULE 6-8b:
Match play—Loss of hole; Stroke play—Two strokes.

Rule 7. Practice

7-1 Before or Between Rounds

a. Match Play

On any day of a match play competition, a player may practise on the competition <u>course</u> before a round.

b. Stroke Play

On any day of a stroke competition or play-off, a competitor shall not practise on the competition <u>course</u> or test the surface of any putting green on the course before a round or play-off. When two or more rounds of a stroke competition are to be played over consecutive days, practice between those rounds on any competition course remaining to be played is prohibited.

Exception: Practice putting or chipping on or near the first <u>teeing ground</u> before starting a round or play-off is permitted.

PENALTY FOR BREACH OF RULE 7-1b: *Disqualification.*

Note: The Committee may in the conditions of a competition (Rule 33-1) prohibit practice on the competition course on any day of a match play competition or permit practice on the competition course or part of the course (Rule 33-2c) on any day of or between rounds of a stroke competition.

7-2 During Round

A player shall not play a practice <u>stroke</u> either during the play of a hole or between the play of two holes except that, between the play of two holes, the player may practise putting or chipping on or near the <u>putting green</u> of the hole last played, any practice putting green or the <u>teeing ground</u> of the next hole to be played in the round, provided such practice stroke is not played from a hazard and does not unduly delay play (Rule 6-7).

Exception: When·play has been suspended by the Committee, a player may, prior to resumption of play, practise (*a*) as provided in this Rule, (*b*) anywhere other than on the competition course and (*c*) as otherwise permitted by the Committee.

PENALTY FOR BREACH OF RULE 7-2:

Match play—Loss of hole; Stroke play—Two strokes.

In the event of a breach between the play of two holes, the penalty applies to the next hole.

Note 1: A practice swing is not a practice <u>stroke</u> and may be taken at any place, provided the player does not breach the Rules.

Note 2: The Committee may prohibit practice on or near the <u>putting green</u> of the hole last played.

Rule 8. Advice; Indicating Line of Play

Definition

"Advice" is any counsel or suggestion which could influence a player in determining his play, the choice of a club or the method of making a <u>stroke</u>.

Information on the <u>Rules</u> or on matters of public information, such as the position of hazards or the flagstick on the putting green, is not advice.

8-1 Advice

Except as provided in Rule 8-2, a player may give advice to, or ask for advice from, only his partner or either of their caddies.

Note: In a team competition without concurrent individual competition, the Committee may in the conditions of the competition (Rule 33-1) permit each team to appoint one person, e.g., team captain or coach, who may give <u>advice</u> to members of that team. Such person shall be identified to the Committee prior to the start of the competition.

8-2 Indicating Line of Play
a. Other Than on Putting Green

Except on the <u>putting green</u>, a player may have the line of play indicated to him by anyone, but no one shall stand on or close to the line while the <u>stroke</u> is being played. Any mark placed during the play of a hole by the player or with his knowledge to indicate the line shall be removed before the stroke is played.

Exception: Flagstick attended or held up—Rule 17-1.

b. On the Putting Green

When the player's ball is on the <u>putting green</u>, the player's caddie, his partner or his partner's caddie may, before the <u>stroke</u> is played, point out a line for putting, but in so doing the putting green shall not be touched in front of, to the side of, or behind the hole. No mark shall be placed anywhere on the putting green to indicate a line for putting.

PENALTY FOR BREACH OF RULE:
Match play—Loss of hole; Stroke play—Two strokes.

Rule 9. Information as to Strokes Taken

9-1 General

The number of strokes a player has taken shall include any penalty strokes incurred.

9-2 Match Play

A player who has incurred a penalty shall inform his opponent as soon as practicable. If he fails to do so, he shall be deemed to have given wrong information, even though he was not aware that he had incurred a penalty.

An opponent is entitled to ascertain from the player, during the play of a hole, the number of strokes he has taken and, after play of a hole, the number of strokes taken on the hole just completed.

If during the play of a hole the player gives or is deemed to give wrong information as to the number of strokes taken, he shall incur no penalty if he corrects the mistake before his opponent has played his next stroke. If after play of a hole the player gives or is deemed to give wrong information as to the number of strokes taken on the hole just completed, he shall incur no penalty if he corrects his mistake before any player plays from the next <u>teeing ground</u> or, in the case of the last hole of the match, before all players leave the <u>putting green</u>. If the player fails so to correct the wrong information, *he shall lose the hole*.

9-3 Stroke Play

A competitor who has incurred a penalty should inform his market as soon as practicable.

ORDER OF PLAY

Rule 10. Order of Play

10-1 Match Play

a. Teeing Ground

The side entitled to play first from the <u>teeing ground</u> is said to have the "honour".

The side which shall have the honour at the first teeing ground shall be determined by the order of the draw. In the absence of a draw, the honour should be decided by lot.

The side which wins a hole shall take the honour at the next teeing ground. If a hole has been halved, the side which had the honour at the previous teeing ground shall retain it.

b. Other Than on Teeing Ground

When the balls are in play, the ball farther from the hole shall be played first. If the balls are equidistant from the hole, the ball to be played first should be decided by lot.

Exception: Rule 30-3c (best-ball and four-ball match play).

c. Playing Out of Turn

If a player plays when his opponent should have played, the opponent may immediately require the player to abandon the ball so played and, without penalty, play a ball in correct order (see Rule 20-5).

10-2 Stroke Play

a. Teeing Ground

The competitor entitled to play first from the teeing ground is said to have the "honour".

The competitor who shall have the honour at the first teeing ground shall be determined by the order of the draw. In the absence of a draw, the honour should be decided by lot.

The competitor with the lowest score at a hole shall take the honour at the next teeing ground. The competitor with the second lowest score shall play next and so on. If two or more competitors have the same score at a hole, they shall play from the next teeing ground in the same order as at the previous teeing ground.

b. Other Than on Teeing Ground

When the balls are in play, the ball farthest from the hole shall be played first. If two or more balls are equidistant from the hole, the ball to be played first should be decided by lot.

Exceptions: Rules 22 (ball interfering with or assisting play) and 31-5 (four-ball stroke play).

c. Playing Out of Turn

If a competitor plays out of turn, no penalty shall be incurred and the ball shall be played as it lies. If, however, the Committee determines that competitors have agreed to play in an order other than that set forth in Clauses 2a and 2b of this Rule to give one of them an advantage, *they shall be disqualified.*
(Incorrect order of play in threesomes and foursomes stroke play—see Rule 29-3.)

10-3 Provisional Ball or Second Ball from Teeing Ground

If a player plays a provisional ball or a second ball from a teeing ground, he should do so after his opponent or fellow-competitor has played his first stroke. If a player plays a provisional ball or a second ball out of turn, Clauses 1c and 2c of this Rule shall apply.

10-4 Ball Moved in Measuring

If a ball is moved in measuring to determine which ball is farther from the hole, no penalty is incurred and the ball shall be replaced.

TEEING GROUND

Rule 11. Teeing Ground

Definition

The "teeing ground" is the starting place for the hole to be played. It is a rectangular area two club-lengths in depth, the front and the sides of which are defined by the outside limits of two tee-markers. A ball is outside the teeing ground when all of it lies outside the teeing ground.

11-1 Teeing

In teeing, the ball may be placed on the ground, on an irregularity of surface created by the player on the ground or on a tee, sand or other substance in order to raise it off the ground.

A player may stand outside the teeing ground to play a ball within it.

When the first stroke with any ball (including a provisional ball) is played from the teeing ground, the tee-markers are immovable obstructions (see Rule 24-2).

11-2 Ball Falling Off Tee

If a ball, when not in play, falls off a tee or is knocked off a tee by the player in addressing it, it may be re-teed without penalty, but if a stroke is made at the ball in these circumstances, whether the ball is moving or not, the stroke shall be counted but no penalty shall be incurred.

11-3 Playing Outside Teeing Ground

a. Match Play

If a player, when starting a hole, plays a ball from outside the teeing ground, the opponent may immediately require the player to replay the stroke from within the teeing ground, without penalty.

b. Stroke Play

If a competitor, when starting a hole, plays a ball from outside the teeing ground, *he shall be penalised two strokes* and shall then play a ball from within the teeing ground. Strokes played by a competitor from outside the teeing ground do not count in his score. If the competitor fails to rectify his mistake before making a stroke on the next teeing ground or, in the case of the last hole of the round, before leaving the putting green, *he shall be disqualified.*

PLAYING THE BALL

Rule 12. Searching for and Identifying Ball

Definitions

A "hazard" is any bunker or water hazard.

A "bunker" is a hazard consisting of a prepared area of ground, often a hollow, from which turf or soil has been removed and replaced with sand or the like. Grass-covered ground bordering or within a bunker is not part of the bunker.

A "water hazard" is any sea, lake, pond, river, ditch, surface drainage ditch or other open water course (whether or not containing water) and anything of a similar nature.

All ground or water within the margin of a water hazard is part of the water hazard. The margin of a water hazard is deemed to extend vertically upwards. Stakes and lines defining the margins of water hazards are in the hazards.

12-1 Searching for Ball; Seeing Ball

If a ball lies in long grass, rushes, bushes, whins, heather or the like, only so much thereof may be touched as will enable the player to find and identify his ball, except that nothing shall be done which improves its lie, the area of his intended swing or his line of play.

A player is not necessarily entitled to see his ball when playing a stroke.

In a hazard, if the ball is covered by loose impediments or sand, the player may remove only as much thereof as will enable him to see a part of the ball. If the ball is moved in such removal, no penalty is incurred and the ball shall be replaced. As to removal of loose impediments outside a hazard, see Rule 23.

If a ball lying in <u>casual water</u>, <u>ground under repair</u> or a hole, cast or runway made by a burrowing animal, a reptile or a bird is accidentally moved during search, no penalty is incurred; the ball shall be replaced, unless the player elects to proceed under Rule 25-1b.

If a ball is believed to be lying in water in a <u>water hazard</u>, the player may probe for it with a club or otherwise. If the ball is moved in so doing, no penalty shall be incurred; the ball shall be replaced, unless the player elects to proceed under Rule 26-1.

PENALTY FOR BREACH OF RULE 12-1:
Match play—Loss of hole; Stroke play—Two strokes.

12-2 Identifying Ball

The responsibility for playing the proper ball rests with the player. Each player should put an identification mark on his ball.

Except in a <u>hazard</u>, the player may, without penalty, lift a ball he believes to be his own for the purpose of identification and clean it to the extent necessary for identification. If the ball is the player's ball, he shall replace it on the spot from which it was lifted. Before the player lifts the ball, he shall announce his intention to his opponent in match play or his marker or a fellow-competitor in stroke play and give his opponent, marker or fellow-competitor an opportunity to observe the lifting and replacement. If he lifts the ball without announcing his intention in advance or giving his opponent, marker or fellow-competitor an opportunity to observe, or if he lifts his ball for identification in a hazard, *he shall incur a penalty of one stroke* and the ball shall be replaced.

If a player who is required to replace a ball fails to do so, *he shall incur the penalty* for a breach of Rule 20-3a, but no additional penalty under Rule 12-2 shall be applied.

Rule 13. Ball Played As It Lies; Lie, Area of Intended Swing and Line of Play; Stance

Definitions

A "hazard" is any bunker or water hazard.

A "bunker" is a hazard consisting of a prepared area of ground, often a hollow, from which turf or soil has been removed and replaced with sand or the like. Grass-covered ground bordering or within a bunker is not part of the bunker.

A "water hazard" is any sea, lake, pond, river, ditch, surface drainage ditch or other open water course (whether or not containing water) and anything of a similar nature.

All ground or water within the margin of a water hazard is part of the water hazard. The margin of a water hazard is deemed to extend vertically upwards. Stakes and lines defining the margins of water hazards are in the hazards.

13-1 Ball Played As It Lies

The ball shall be played as it lies, except as otherwise provided in the Rules. (Ball at rest moved—Rule 18.)

13-2 Improving Lie, Area of Intended Swing or Line of Play

Except as provided in the Rules, a player shall not improve or allow to be improved:

the position or lie of his ball,

the area of his intended swing or

his line of play

by any of the following actions:

moving, bending or breaking anything growing or fixed (including objects defining out of bounds) or

removing or pressing down sand, loose soil, replaced divots, other cut turf placed in position or other irregularities of surface

except as follows:

as may occur in fairly taking his stance,

in making a stroke or the backward movement of his club for a stroke,

on the teeing ground in creating or eliminating irregularities of surface, or on the <u>putting green</u> in removing sand and loose soil as provided in Rule 16-1a or in repairing damage as provided in Rule 16-1c.

The club may be grounded only lightly and shall not be pressed on the ground.

Exception: Ball lying in or touching hazard—Rule 13-4.

13-3 Building Stance

A player is entitled to place his feet firmly in taking his stance, but he shall not build a stance.

13-4 Ball Lying in or Touching Hazard

Except as provided in the Rules, before making a <u>stroke</u> at a ball which lies in or touches a <u>hazard</u> (whether a <u>bunker</u> or a <u>water hazard</u>), the player shall not:

(*a*) Test the condition of the hazard or any similar hazard,

(*b*) Touch the ground in the hazard or water in the water hazard with a club or otherwise, or

(*c*) Touch or move a <u>loose impediment</u> lying in or touching the hazard.

Exceptions:

1. At address or in the backward movement for the stroke, the club may touch any <u>obstruction</u> or any grass, bush, tree or other growing thing.

2. The player may place his clubs in a <u>hazard</u>, provided nothing is done which may constitute testing the soil or improving the lie of the ball.

3. The player after playing the stroke, or his <u>caddie</u> at any time without the authority of the player, may smooth sand or soil in the hazard, provided that, if the ball still lies in the hazard, nothing is done which improves the lie of the ball or assists the player in his subsequent play of the hole.

PENALTY FOR BREACH OF RULE:
Match play—Loss of hole; Stroke play—Two strokes.
(Searching for ball—Rule 12-1.)

Rule 14. Striking the Ball

Definition

A "stroke" is the forward movement of the club made with the intention of fairly striking at and moving the ball.

14-1 Ball to be Fairly Struck At

The ball shall be fairly struck at with the head of the club and must not be pushed, scraped or spooned.

14-2 Assistance

In making a stroke, a player shall not accept physical assistance or protection from the elements.

PENALTY FOR BREACH OF RULE 14-1 or -2:
Match play—Loss of hole; Stroke play—Two strokes.

14-3 Artificial Devices and Unusual Equipment

Except as provided in the Rules, during a stipulated round the player shall not use any artificial device or unusual equipment:

(*a*) For the purpose of gauging or measuring distance or conditions which might affect his play; or

(*b*) Which might assist him in gripping the club, in making a stroke or in his play, except that plain gloves may be worn, resin, tape or gauze may be applied to the grip (provided such application does not render the grip non-conforming under Rule 4-1c) and a towel or handkerchief may be wrapped around the grip.

PENALTY FOR BREACH OF RULE 14-3: *Disqualification.*

14-4 Striking the Ball More than Once

If a player's club strikes the ball more than once in the course of a stroke, the player shall count the stroke and *add a penalty stroke*, making two strokes in all.

14-5 Playing Moving Ball

A player shall not play while his ball is moving.
Exceptions:
Ball falling off tee—Rule 11-2.
Striking the ball more than once—Rule 14-4.

Ball moving in water—Rule 14-6.

When the ball begins to move only after the player has begun the stroke or the backward movement of his club for the stroke, he shall incur no penalty under this Rule for playing a moving ball, but he is not exempt from any penalty incurred under the following Rules:

Ball at rest moved by player—Rule 18-2a.

Ball at rest moving after address—Rule 18-2b.

Ball at rest moving after loose impediment touched—Rule 18-2c.

14-6 Ball Moving in Water

When a ball is moving in water in a water hazard, the player may, without penalty, make a stroke, but he must not delay making his stroke in order to allow the wind or current to improve the position of the ball. A ball moving in water in a water hazard may be lifted if the player elects to invoke Rule 26.

PENALTY FOR BREACH OF RULE 14-5 or -6:
Match play—Loss of hole; Stroke play—Two strokes.

Rule 15. Playing a Wrong Ball

Definition

A "wrong ball" is any ball other than:

(*a*) The ball in play,

(*b*) A provisional ball or

(*c*) In stroke play, a second ball played under Rule 3-3 or Rule 20-7b.

15-1 General

A player must hole out with the ball played from the teeing ground unless a Rule permits him to substitute another ball.

15-2 Match Play

If a player plays a stroke with a wrong ball except in a hazard, *he shall lose the hole.*

If a player plays any strokes in a hazard with a wrong ball, there is no penalty. Strokes played in a hazard with a wrong ball do not count in the player's score.

If the player and opponent exchange balls during the play of a hole, the first to play the wrong ball other than from a hazard shall lose the hole; when this cannot be determined, the hole shall be played out with the balls exchanged.

15-3 Stroke Play

If a competitor plays a stroke with a wrong ball except in a hazard, *he shall add two penalty strokes to his score* and shall then play the correct ball.

If a competitor plays any strokes in a hazard with a wrong ball, there is no penalty.

Strokes played with a wrong ball do not count in a competitor's score.

If a competitor holes out with a wrong ball, but has not made a stroke on the next teeing ground or, in the case of the last hole of the round, has not left the putting green, he may rectify his mistake by playing the correct ball, subject to the prescribed penalty. *The competitor shall be disqualified* if he does not so rectify his mistake.

Note: For procedure to be followed by owner of wrong ball, see Rule 18-1.

THE PUTTING GREEN

Rule 16. The Putting Green

Definitions

The "putting green" is all ground of the hole being played which is specially prepared for putting or otherwise defined as such by the Committee. A ball is on the putting green when any part of it touches the putting green.

A ball is "holed" when it is at rest within the circumference of the hole and all of it is below the level of the lip of the hole.

16-1 General

a. Touching Line of Putt

The line of putt must not be touched except:

(i) the player may move sand, loose soil and other loose

impediments by picking them up or by brushing them aside with his hand or a club without pressing anything down;

(ii) in addressing the ball, the player may place the club in front of the ball without pressing anything down;

(iii) in measuring—Rule 10-4;

(iv) in lifting the ball—Rule 16-1b;

(v) in repairing old hole plugs or ball marks—Rule 16-1c; and

(vi) in removing movable obstructions—Rule 24-1.

(Indicating line for putting on putting green—Rule 8-2b.)

b. Lifting Ball

A ball on the putting green may be lifted and, if desired, cleaned. A ball so lifted shall be replaced on the spot from which it was lifted.

c. Repair of Hole Plugs and Ball Marks

The player may repair an old hole plug or damage to the putting green caused by the impact of a ball, whether or not the player's ball lies on the putting green. If the ball is moved in the process of such repair, it shall be replaced, without penalty.

d. Testing Surface

During the play of a hole, a player shall not test the surface of the putting green by rolling a ball or roughening or scraping the surface.

e. Standing Astride or on Line of Putt

The player shall not make a stroke on the putting green from a stance astride, or with either foot touching, the line of the putt or an extension of that line behind the ball. For the purpose of this Clause only, the line or putt does not extend beyond the hole.

f. Position of Caddie or Partner

While making the stroke, the player shall not allow his caddie, his partner or his partner's caddie to position himself on or close to an extension of the line of putt behind the ball.

g. Other Ball to Be at Rest

A player shall not play a stroke or touch his ball in play while another ball is in motion after a stroke on the putting green.

h. Ball Overhanging Hole

When any part of the ball overhangs the edge of the hole, the player is allowed enough time to reach the hole without unreasonable delay and an additional ten seconds to determine whether the ball is at rest. If by then the ball has not fallen into the hole, it is deemed to be at rest.

PENALTY FOR BREACH OF RULE 16-1:
Match play—Loss of hole; Stroke play—Two strokes.

16-2 Conceding Opponent's Next Stroke

When the opponent's ball is at rest or is deemed to be at rest, the player may concede the opponent to have holed out with his next stroke and the ball may be removed by either side with a club or otherwise.

Rule 17. The Flagstick

17-1 Flagstick Attended, Removed or Held Up

Before and during the stroke, the player may have the flagstick attended, removed or held up to indicate the position of the hole. This may be done only on the authority of the player before he plays his stroke.

If the flagstick is attended or removed by an opponent, a fellow-competitor or the caddie of either with the player's knowledge and no objection is made, the player shall be deemed to have authorised it. If a player or a caddie attends or removes the flagstick or stands near the hole while a stroke is being played, he shall be deemed to attend the flagstick until the ball comes to rest.

If the flagstick is not attended before the stroke is played, it shall not be attended or removed while the ball is in motion.

17-2 Unauthorised Attendance

a. Match Play

In match play, an opponent or his caddie shall not attend or remove the flagstick without the player's knowledge or authority.

b. Stroke Play

In stroke play, if a fellow-competitor or his caddie attends or removes the flagstick without the competitor's knowledge or authority while the competitor is making a stroke or his ball is in motion, *the fellow-competitor shall incur the penalty* for breach of this Rule. In such circumstances, if the competitor's ball strikes the flagstick or the person attending it, the competitor incurs no penalty and the ball shall be played as it lies, except that, if the stroke was played from the putting green, the stroke shall be replayed.

PENALTY FOR BREACH OF RULE 17-1 or -2:
Match play—Loss of hole; Stroke play—Two strokes.

17-3 Ball Striking Flagstick or Attendant

The player's ball shall not strike:

a. The flagstick when attended or removed by the player, his partner or either of their caddies, or by another person with the player's knowledge or authority; or

b. The player's caddie, his partner or his partner's caddie when attending the flagstick, or another person attending the flagstick with the player's knowledge or authority, or equipment carried by any such person; or

c. The flagstick in the hole, unattended, when the ball has been played from the putting green.

PENALTY FOR BREACH OF RULE 17-3:
*Match play—Loss of hole; Stroke play—Two strokes,
and the ball shall be played as it lies.*

17-4 Ball Resting Against Flagstick

If the ball rests against the flagstick when it is in the hole, the player or someone authorised by him may move or remove the flagstick and if the ball falls into the hole, the player shall be deemed to have holed out at his last stroke; otherwise the ball, if moved, shall be placed on the lip of the hole, without penalty.

BALL MOVED, DEFLECTED OR STOPPED

Rule 18. Ball at Rest Moved

Definitions

A ball is deemed to have "moved" if it leaves its position and comes to rest in any other place.

An "outside agency" is any agency not part of the match or, in stroke play, not part of a competitor's side, and includes a referee, a marker, an observer or a forecaddie. Neither wind nor water is an outside agency.

"Equipment" is anything used, worn or carried by or for the player except any ball he has played and any small object, such as a coin or a tee, when used to mark the position of a ball or the extent of an area in which a ball is to be dropped. Equipment includes a golf cart, whether or not motorised. If such a cart is shared by more than one player, its status under the Rules is the same as that of a caddie employed by more than one player. See "Caddie".

A player has "addressed the ball" when he has taken his stance and has also grounded his club, except that in a hazard a player has addressed the ball when he has taken his stance.

Taking his "stance" consists in a player placing his feet in position for and preparatory to making a stroke.

18-1 By Outside Agency

If a ball at rest is moved by an outside agency, the player shall incur no penalty and the ball shall be replaced before the player plays another stroke. If the ball moved is not immediately recoverable, another ball may be substituted.

(Player's ball at rest moved by another ball—see Rule 18-5.)

18-2 By Player, Partner, Caddie or Equipment

a. General

When a player's ball is in play, if:

> (i) the player, his partner or either of their caddies lifts or moves it, touches it purposely (except with a club in the act of addressing it) or causes it to move except as permitted by a Rule, or

(ii) equipment of the player or his partner causes the ball to move,

the player shall incur a penalty stroke. The ball shall be replaced unless the movement of the ball occurs after the player has begun his swing and he does not discontinue his swing.

Under the Rules no penalty is incurred if a player accidentally causes his ball to move in the following circumstances:

In measuring to determine which ball farther from hole—Rule 10-4

In searching for covered ball in hazard or for ball in casual water, ground under repair, etc.—Rule 12-1

In the process of repairing hole plug or ball mark—Rule 16-1c

In the process of removing loose impediment on putting green—Rule 18-2c

In the process of lifting ball under a Rule—Rule 20-1

In the process of placing or replacing ball under a Rule—Rule 20-3a

In complying with Rule 22 relating to lifting ball interfering with or assisting play

In removal of movable obstruction—Rule 24-1.

b. Ball Moving After Address

If a ball in play moves after the player has addressed it other than as a result of a stroke, he shall be deemed to have moved the ball and *shall incur a penalty stroke*, and the ball shall be played as it lies.

c. Ball Moving After Loose Impediment Touched

Through the green, if the ball moves after any loose impediment lying within a club-length of it has been touched by the player, his partner or either of their caddies and before the player has addressed it, the player shall be deemed to have moved the ball and *shall incur a penalty stroke*. The player shall replace the ball unless the movement of the ball occurs after he has begun his swing and he does not discontinue his swing.

On the putting green, if the ball moves in the process of removing any loose impediment, it shall be replaced without penalty.

18-3 By Opponent, Caddie or Equipment in Match Play

a. During Search

If, during search for a player's ball, it is moved by an opponent, his caddie or his <u>equipment</u>, no penalty is incurred and the player shall replace the ball.

b. Other Than During Search

If, other than during search for a ball, the ball is touched or moved by an opponent, his caddie or his <u>equipment</u>, except as otherwise provided in the Rules, *the opponent shall incur a penalty stroke*. The player shall replace the ball.

(Ball moved in measuring to determine which ball farther from the hole—Rule 10-4.)

(Playing a wrong ball—Rule 15-2.)

(Ball moved in complying with Rule 22 relating to lifting ball interfering with or assisting play.)

18-4 By Fellow-Competitor, Caddie or Equipment in Stroke Play

If a competitor's ball is moved by a fellow-competitor, his caddie or his <u>equipment</u>, no penalty is incurred. The competitor shall replace his ball.

(Playing a wrong ball—Rule 15-3.)

18-5 By Another Ball

If a player's ball at rest is moved by another ball, the player's ball shall be replaced.

*PENALTY FOR BREACH OF RULE:

Match play—Loss of hole; Stroke play—Two strokes.

*If a player who is required to replace a ball fails to do so, he shall incur the general penalty for breach of Rule 18 but no additional penalty under Rule 18 shall be applied.

Note: If it is impossible to determine the spot on which a ball is to be placed, see Rule 20-3c.

Rule 19. Ball in Motion Deflected or Stopped

Definitions

An "outside agency" is any agency not part of the match or, in stroke play, not part of a competitor's side, and includes a referee, a marker, an observer or a forecaddie. Neither wind nor water is an outside agency.

"Equipment" is anything used, worn or carried by or for the player except any ball he has played and any small object, such as a coin or a tee, when used to mark the position of a ball or the extent of an area in which a ball is to be dropped. Equipment includes a golf cart, whether or not motorised. If such a cart is shared by more than one player, its status under the Rules is the same as that of a caddie employed by more than one player. See "Caddie".

19-1 By Outside Agency

If a ball in motion is accidentally deflected or stopped by any outside agency, it is a rub of the green, no penalty is incurred and the ball shall be played as it lies except:

a. If a ball in motion after a stroke other than on the putting green comes to rest in or on any moving or animate outside agency, the player shall, through the green or in a hazard, drop the ball, or on the putting green place the ball, as near as possible to the spot where the outside agency was when the ball came to rest in or on it, and

b. If a ball in motion after a stroke on the putting green is deflected or stopped by, or comes to rest in or on, any moving or animate outside agency, the stroke shall be cancelled and the ball shall be replaced.

If the ball is not immediately recoverable, another ball may be substituted.

(Player's ball deflected or stopped by another ball at rest— see Rule 19-5.)

Note: If the referee or the Committee determines that a ball has been deliberately deflected or stopped by an outside agency, including a fellow-competitor or his caddie, further procedure should be prescribed in equity under Rule 1-4.

19-2 By Player, Partner, Caddie or Equipment

a. Match Play

If a player's ball is deflected or stopped by himself, his partner or either of their caddies or equipment, *he shall lose the hole.*

b. Stroke Play

If a competitor's ball is deflected or stopped by himself, his partner or either of their caddies or <u>equipment</u>, *the competitor shall incur a penalty of two strokes.* The ball shall be played as it lies, except when it comes to rest in or on the competitor's, his partner's or either of their caddies' clothes or equipment, in which case the competitor shall <u>through the green</u> or in a <u>hazard</u> drop the ball, or on the <u>putting green</u> place the ball, as near as possible to where the article was when the ball came to rest in or on it.

Exception: Dropped Ball—see Rule 20-2a.

19-3 By Opponent, Caddie or Equipment in Match Play

a. Purposely

If a player's ball is purposely deflected or stopped by an opponent, his caddie or his <u>equipment</u>, *the opponent shall lose the hole.*

Note: In the case of a serious breach of Rule 19-3a, the Committee may impose a penalty of disqualification.

b. Accidentally

If a player's ball is accidentally deflected or stopped by an opponent, his caddie or his <u>equipment</u>, no penalty is incurred. The player may play the ball as it lies or, before another <u>stroke</u> is played by either side, cancel the stroke and replay the stroke (see Rule 20-5). If the ball has come to rest in or on the opponent's or his caddie's clothes or equipment, the player may <u>through the green</u> or in a <u>hazard</u> drop the ball, or on the <u>putting green</u> place the ball, as near as possible to where the article was when the ball came to rest in or on it.

Exception: Ball striking person attending flagstick—Rule 17-3b.

19-4 By Fellow-Competitor, Caddie or Equipment in Stroke Play

See Rule 19-1 regarding ball deflected by outside agency.

19-5 By a Ball at Rest

If a player's ball in motion is deflected or stopped by a ball at rest, the player shall play his ball as it lies. In stroke play, if both balls lay on the <u>putting green</u> prior to the stroke, *the player incurs a penalty of two strokes.* Otherwise, no penalty is incurred.

PENALTY FOR BREACH OF RULE
Match play—Loss of hole; Stroke play—Two strokes.

RELIEF SITUATIONS AND PROCEDURE

Rule 20. Lifting, Dropping and Placing; Playing from Wrong Place

20-1 Lifting

A ball to be lifted under the Rules may be lifted by the player, his partner or another person authorised by the player. In any such case, the player shall be responsible for any breach of the Rules.

The position of the ball shall be marked before it is lifted under a rule which requires it to be replaced. If it is not marked, *the player shall incur a penalty of one stroke* and the ball shall be replaced. If it is not replaced, *the player shall incur the general penalty* for breach of this Rule but no additional penalty under Rule 20-1 shall be applied.

If a ball is accidentally moved in the process of lifting it under a Rule, no penalty shall be incurred and the ball shall be replaced.

Note: The position of a lifted ball should be marked, if feasible, by placing a ball-marker or other small object immediately behind the ball. If the ball-marker interferes with the play, <u>stance</u> or <u>stroke</u> of another player, it should be placed one or more clubhead-lengths to one side.

20-2 Dropping and Re-dropping

a. By Whom and How

A ball to be dropped under the Rules shall be dropped by the player himself. He shall stand erect, hold the ball at shoulder height and arm's length and drop it. If a ball is dropped by any other person or in any other manner and the error is not corrected as provided in Rule 20-6, *the player shall incur a penalty stroke.*

If the ball touches the player, his partner, either of their caddies or their equipment, before or after it strikes the ground, the ball shall be redropped, without penalty.

(Taking action influence position or movement of ball—Rule 1-2.)

b. Where to Drop

When a ball is to be dropped, it shall be dropped as near as possible to the spot where the ball lay, but not nearer the hole, except when a Rule permits it to be dropped elsewhere. If a ball is to be dropped in a hazard, the ball shall be dropped in and come to rest in that hazard.

c. When to Re-Drop

A dropped ball shall be re-dropped without penalty if it:
- (i) rolls into a hazard;
- (ii) rolls out of a hazard;
- (iii) rolls onto a putting green;
- (iv) rolls out of bounds;
- (v) rolls back into the condition from which relief was taken under Rule 24-2 (immovable obstruction) or Rule 25 (abnormal ground conditions and wrong putting green);
- (vi) rolls and comes to rest more than two club-lengths from where it first struck the ground; or
- (vii) rolls and comes to rest nearer the hole than is permitted by the Rules.

If the ball again rolls into such position, it shall be placed as near as possible to the spot where it first struck the ground when re-dropped.

20-3 Placing and Replacing

a. By Whom and Where

A ball to be placed under the Rules shall be placed by the player or his partner. A ball to be replaced shall be replaced by the player, his partner or the person who lifted or moved it on the spot where the ball lay. In any such case, the player shall be responsible for any breach of the Rules.

If a ball is accidentally moved in the process of placing or replacing it under a Rule, no penalty shall be incurred and the ball shall be replaced.

b. Lie of Ball to Be Placed or Replaced Altered

Except in a bunker, if the original lie of a ball to be placed or replaced has been altered, the ball shall be placed in the nearest lie most similar to that which it originally occupied, not more than one club-length from the original lie and not nearer the hole. In a bunker, the original lie shall be recreated as nearly as possible and the ball shall be placed in that lie.

c. Spot Not Determinable

If it is impossible to determine the spot where the ball is to be placed, the ball shall through the green or in a hazard be dropped, or on the putting green be placed, as near as possible to the place where it lay but not nearer the hole.

d. Ball Fails to Remain on Spot

If a ball when placed fails to remain on the spot on which it was placed, it shall be replaced without penalty. If it still fails to remain on that spot, it shall be placed at the nearest spot not nearer the hole where it can be placed at rest.

PENALTY FOR BREACH OF RULE 20-1, -2 or -3:
Match play—Loss of hole; Stroke play—Two strokes.

20-4 Ball in Play When Dropped or Placed

A ball dropped or placed under a Rule governing the particular case is in play.

20-5 Playing Next Stroke from Where Previous Stroke Played

When, under the Rules, a player elects or is required to play his next stroke from where a previous stroke was played, he shall proceed as follows: If the stroke is to be played from the teeing ground, the ball to be played shall be played from anywhere within the teeing ground and may be teed; if the stroke is to be played from through the green or a hazard, it shall be dropped; if the stroke is to be played on the putting green, it shall be placed.

PENALTY FOR BREACH OF RULE 20-5:
Match play—Loss of hole; Stroke play—Two strokes.

20-6 Lifting Ball Wrongly Dropped or Placed

A ball dropped or placed in a wrong place or otherwise not in accordance with the Rules but not played may be lifted, without penalty, and the player shall then proceed correctly.

In match play, if, before the opponent plays his next stroke, the player fails to inform him that the ball has been lifted, *the player shall lose the hole*.

20-7 Playing from Wrong Place

For a ball played outside teeing ground, see Rule 11-3.

a. Match Play

If a player plays a stroke with a ball which has been dropped or placed under an applicable Rule but in a wrong place, *he shall lose the hole*.

b. Stroke Play

If a competitor plays a stroke with a ball which has been (i) dropped or placed under an applicable Rule but in a wrong place or (ii) moved and not replaced in a case where the Rules require replacement, *he shall incur the penalty prescribed by the relevant Rule* and play out the hole with the ball. If a serious breach of the relevant Rule is involved, *the competitor shall be disqualified*, unless the breach has been rectified as provided in the next paragraph.

If a serious breach may be involved and the competitor has not made a stroke on the next teeing ground or, in the case of the last hole of the round, has not left the putting green, the competitor may rectify any such serious breach by *adding two penalty strokes to his score*, dropping or placing a second ball in accordance with the Rules and playing out the hole. The competitor should play out the hole with both balls. On completion of the round the competitor shall report the facts immediately to the Committee; if he fails to do so, *he shall be disqualified*. The Committee shall determine, whether a serious breach of the Rule was involved and, accordingly, whether the score with the second ball shall count.

Note: Penalty strokes incurred by playing the ball ruled not to count and strokes subsequently taken with that ball shall be disregarded.

Rule 21. Cleaning Ball

A ball may be cleaned when lifted as follows:
>Upon suspension of play in accordance with Rule 6-8b;
>For identification under Rule 12-2, but the ball may be cleaned only to the extent necessary for identification;
>On the putting green under Rule 16-1b;
>For relief from an obstruction under Rule 24-1b or -2b;
>For relief from abnormal ground conditions or wrong putting green under Rules 25-1b, -2 and -3;
>For relief from a water hazard under Rule 26;
>For relief for an unplayable ball under Rule 28; or
>Under a Local Rule permitting cleaning the ball.

If the player cleans his ball during the play of a hole except as permitted under this Rule, *he shall incur a penalty of one stroke* and the ball, if lifted, shall be replaced.

If a player who is required to replace a ball fails to do so, *he shall incur the penalty* for breach of Rule 20-3a, but no additional penalty under Rule 21 shall be applied.

Rule 22. Ball Interfering with or Assisting Play

Any player may:

(*a*) Lift his ball if he considers that it might assist any other player or

(*b*) Have any other ball lifted if he considers that it might interfere with his play or assist the play of any other player. but this may not be done while another ball is in motion. In stroke play, a player required to lift his ball may play first rather than lift. A ball lifted under this Rule shall be replaced.

If a ball is accidentally moved in complying with this Rule, no penalty is incurred and the ball shall be replaced.

PENALTY FOR BREACH OF RULE:
Match play—Loss of hole; Stroke play—Two strokes.

Rule 23. Loose Impediments

Definition

"Loose impediments" are natural objects such as stones, leaves, twigs, branches and the like, dung, worms and insects and casts or heaps made by them, provided they are not fixed or growing, are not solidly embedded and do not adhere to the ball.

Sand and loose soil are loose impediments on the <u>putting green</u> but not elsewhere.

Snow and ice are either <u>casual water</u> or loose impediments, at the option of the player.

Dew is not a loose impediment.

23-1 Relief

Except when both the <u>loose impediment</u> and the ball lie in or touch a <u>hazard</u>, any loose impediment may be removed without penalty. If the ball moves, see Rule 18-2c.

When a player's ball is in motion, a loose impediment on his line of play shall not be removed.

PENALTY FOR BREACH OF RULE:

Match play—Loss of hole; Stroke play—Two Strokes.
(Searching for ball in hazard—Rule 12-1.)
(Touching line of putt—Rule 16-1a.)

Rule 24. Obstructions

Definition

An "obstruction" is anything artificial, including the artificial surfaces and sides of roads and paths, except:

(*a*) Objects defining <u>out of bounds</u>, such as walls, fences, stakes and railings;

(*b*) Any part of an immovable artificial object which is out of bounds; and

(*c*) Any construction declared by the Committee to be an integral part of the course.

24-1 Movable Obstruction

A player may obtain relief from a movable <u>obstruction</u> as follows:

(a) If the ball does not lie in or on the obstruction, the obstruction may be removed; if the ball moves, no penalty is incurred and the ball shall be replaced.

(*b*) If the ball lies in or on the obstruction, the ball may be lifted, without penalty, and the obstruction removed. The ball shall through the green or in a hazard be dropped, or on the putting green be placed, as near as possible to the spot directly under the place where the ball lay in or on the obstruction, but not nearer the hole.

The ball may be cleaned when lifted for relief under Rule 24-1b.

When a ball is in motion, an obstruction on the player's line of play other than an attended flagstick and equipment of the players shall not be removed.

24-2 Immovable Obstruction

a. Interference

Interference by an immovable obstruction occurs when a ball lies in or on the obstruction, or so close to the obstruction that the obstruction interferes with the player's stance or the area of his intended swing. If the player's ball lies on the putting green, interference also occurs if an immovable obstruction on the putting green intervenes on his line of putt. Otherwise, intervention on the line of play is not, of itself, interference under this Rule.

b. Relief

Except when the ball lies in or touches a water hazard or a lateral water hazard, a player may obtain relief from interference by an immovable obstruction, without penalty, as follows:

(i) **Through the Green:** If the ball lies through the green, the point on the course nearest to where the ball lies shall be determined (without crossing over, through or under the obstruction) which (*a*) is not nearer the hole, (*b*) avoids interference (as defined) and (*c*) is not in a hazard or on a putting green. The player shall lift the ball and drop it within one club-length of the point thus determined on ground which fulfils (*a*), (*b*) and (*c*) above.

Note: The prohibition against crossing over, through or under the obstruction does not apply to the artificial surfaces and sides of roads and paths or when the ball lies in or on the obstruction.

(ii) **In a Bunker:** If the ball lies in or touches a bunker, the player shall lift and drop the ball in accordance with Clause (i) above, except that the ball must be dropped in the bunker.

(iii) **On the Putting Green:** If the ball lies on the putting green, the player shall lift the ball and place it in the nearest position to where it lay which affords relief from interference, but not nearer the hole nor in a hazard.

The ball may be cleaned when lifted for relief under Rule 24-2b. (Ball rolling back into condition from which relief taken—see Rule 20-2c(v).)

Exception: A player may not obtain relief under Rule 24-2b if (*a*) it is clearly unreasonable for him to play a stroke because of interference by anything other than an immovable obstruction of (*b*) interference by an immovable obstruction would occur only through use of an unnecessarily abnormal stance, swing or direction of play.

Note: If a ball lies in or touches a water hazard (including a lateral water hazard), the player is not entitled to relief without penalty from interference by an immovable obstruction. The player shall play the ball as it lies or proceed under Rule 26-1.

PENALTY FOR BREACH OF RULE:
Match play—Loss of hole; Stroke play—Two strokes.

Rule 25. Abnormal Ground Conditions and Wrong Putting Green

Definitions

"Casual water" is any temporary accumulation of water on the course which is visible before or after the player takes his stance and is not in a water hazard. Snow and ice are either casual water or loose impediments, at the option of the player. Dew is not casual water.

"Ground under repair" is any portion of the course so marked by order of the Committee or so declared by its authorised representative. It includes material piled for removal and a hole made by a greenkeeper, even if not so marked. Stakes and lines defining ground under repair are in such ground.

Note 1: Grass cuttings and other material left on the course which have been abandoned and are not intended to be re-moved are not ground under repair unless so marked.

Note 2: The Committee may make a Local Rule prohibiting play from ground under repair.

25-1 Casual Water, Ground Under Repair and Certain Damage to Course

a. Interference

Interference by casual water, ground under repair or a hole, cast or runway made by a burrowing animal, a reptile or a bird occurs when a ball lies in or touches any of these conditions or when the condition interferes with the player's stance or the area of his intended swing.

If the player's ball lies on the putting green, interference also occurs if such condition on the putting green intervenes on his line of putt.

If interference exists, the player may either play the ball as it lies (unless prohibited by Local Rule) or take relief as provided in Clause b.

b. Relief

If the player elects to take relief, he shall proceed as follows:

(i) **Through the Green:** If the ball lies through the green, the point on the course nearest to where the ball lies shall be determined which (*a*) is not nearer the hole, (*b*) avoids interference by the condition, and (*c*) is not in a hazard or on a putting green. The player shall lift the ball and drop it without penalty within one club-length of the point thus determined on ground which fulfils (*a*), (*b*), and (*c*) above.

(ii) **In a Hazard:** If the ball lies in or touches a hazard, the player shall lift and drop the ball either:

(*a*) Without penalty, in the hazard, as near as possible to the spot where the ball lay, but not nearer the hole, on ground which affords maximum available relief from the condition;

or

(*b*) *Under penalty of one stroke,* outside the hazard, keeping the spot where the ball lay directly between himself and the hole.

Exception: If a ball lies in or touches a water hazard (including a lateral water hazard), the player is not entitled to relief without penalty from a hole, cast or runway made by a burrowing animal, a reptile or a bird. The player shall play the ball as it lies or proceed under Rule 26-1.

  (iii) **On the Putting Green:** If the ball lies on the putting green, the player shall lift the ball and place it without penalty in the nearest position to where it lay which affords maximum available relief from the condition, but not nearer the hole nor in a hazard.

The ball may be cleaned when lifted under Rule 25-1b.

(Ball rolling back into condition from which relief taken—see Rule 20-2c(v).)

Exception: A player may not obtain relief under Rule 25-1b if (*a*) it is clearly unreasonable for him to play a stroke because of interference by anything other than a condition covered by Rule 25-1a or (*b*) interference by such a condition would occur only through use of an unnecessarily abnormal stance, swing or direction of play.

c. Ball Lost Under Condition Covered by Rule 25-1

It is a question of fact whether a ball lost after having been struck toward a condition covered by Rule 25-1 is lost under such condition. In order to treat the ball as lost under such condition, there must be reasonable evidence to that effect. In the absence of such evidence, the ball must be treated as a lost ball and Rule 27 applies.

  (i) **Outside a Hazard**—If a ball is lost outside a hazard under a condition covered by Rule 25-1, the player may take relief as follows: the point on the course nearest to where the ball last crossed the margin of the area shall be determined which (*a*) is not nearer the hole than where the ball last crossed the margin, (*b*) avoids interference by the condition and (*c*) is not in a hazard or on a putting green. He shall drop a ball without penalty within one club-length of the point thus determined on ground which fulfils (*a*), (*b*) and (*c*) above.

  (ii) **In a Hazard**—If a ball is lost in a hazard under a condition covered by Rule 25-1, the player may drop a ball either:

(*a*) Without penalty, in the hazard as near as possible to the point at which the ball last crossed the margin of the area, but not nearer the hole, on ground which affords maximum available relief from the condition; or

(*b*) *Under penalty of one stroke*, outside the hazard, keeping the spot at which the ball last crossed the margin of the hazard directly between himself and the hole.

Exception: If a ball lies in a water hazard (including a lateral water hazard), the player is not entitled to relief without penalty for a ball lost in a hole, cast or runway made by a burrowing animal, a reptile or a bird. The player shall proceed under Rule 26-1.

25-2 Embedded Ball

A ball embedded in its own pitch-mark in any closely mown area through the green may be lifted, cleaned and dropped, without penalty, as near as possible to the spot where it lay but not nearer the hole. "Closely mown area" means any area of the course, including paths through the rough, cut to fairway height or less.

25-3 Wrong Putting Green

If a ball lies on a putting green other than that of the hole being played, the point on the course nearest to where the ball lies shall be determined which (*a*) is not nearer the hole and (*b*) is not in a hazard or on a putting green. The player shall lift the ball and drop it without penalty within one club-length of the point thus determined on ground which fulfils (*a*) and (*b*) above. The ball may be cleaned when so lifted.

Note: Unless otherwise prescribed by the Committee, the term "a putting green other than that of the hole being played" includes a practice putting green or pitching green on the course.

PENALTY FOR BREACH OF RULE:
Match play—Loss of hole; Stroke play—Two strokes.

Rule 26. Water Hazards
(including Lateral Water Hazards)

Definitions

A "water hazard" is any sea, lake, pond, river, ditch, surface drainage ditch or other open water course (whether or not containing water) and anything of a similar nature.

All ground or water within the margin of a water hazard is part of the water hazard. The margin of a water hazard is deemed to extend vertically upwards. Stakes and lines defining the margins of water hazards are in the hazards.

Note: Water hazards (other than lateral water hazards) should be defined by yellow stakes or lines.

A "lateral water hazard" is a water hazard or that part of a water hazard so situated that it is not possible or is deemed by the Committee to be impracticable to drop a ball behind the water hazard and keep the spot at which the ball last crossed the margin of the water hazard between the player and the hole.

That part of a water hazard to be played as a lateral water hazard should be distinctively marked.

Note: Lateral water hazards should be defined by red stakes or lines.

26-1 Ball in Water Hazard

It is a question of fact whether a ball lost after having been struck toward a water hazard is lost inside or outside the hazard. In order to treat the ball as lost in the hazard, there must be reasonable evidence that the ball lodged therein. In the absence of such evidence, the ball must be treated as a lost ball and Rule 27 applies.

If a ball lies in, touches or is lost in a water hazard (whether the ball lies in water or not), the player may *under penalty of one stroke*:

(*a*) Play his next stroke as nearly as possible at the spot from which the original ball was last played or moved by him (see Rule 20-5);

or

(*b*) Drop a ball behind the water hazard, keeping the point at which the original ball last crossed the margin of the water hazard directly between himself and the hole, with no limit to how far behind the water hazard the ball may be dropped; or

(c) *As additional options available only if the ball lies or is lost in a lateral water hazard*, drop a ball outside the water hazard within two club-lengths of (i) the point where the original ball last crossed the margin of the water hazard or (ii) a point on the opposite margin of the water hazard equidistant from the hole. The ball must be dropped and come to rest not nearer the hole than the point where the original ball last crossed the margin of the water hazard.

The ball may be cleaned when lifted under this Rule.

26-2 Ball Played Within Water Hazard
a. Ball Remains in Hazard
If a ball played from within a water hazard has not crossed any margin of the hazard, the player may:
  (i) proceed under Rule 26-1; or
  (ii) *under penalty of one stroke*, play his next stroke as nearly as possible at the spot from which the last stroke from outside the hazard was played (see Rule 20-5).

b. Ball Lost or Unplayable Outside Hazard or Out of Bounds
If a ball played from within a water hazard is lost or declared unplayable outside the hazard or is out of bounds, the player, after taking a stroke-and-distance penalty under Rule 27-1 or 28a, may:
  (i) play a ball as nearly as possible at the spot from which the original ball was last played by him (see Rule 20-5); or
  (ii) under the penalty prescribed therein, proceed under Rule 26-1 or, as additional options in the case of a lateral water hazard, under Rule 26-1c, using as the reference point the point where the ball last crossed the margin of the hazard before it came to rest in the hazard; or
  (iii) *under penalty of one stroke*, play his next stroke as nearly as possible at the spot from which the last stroke from outside the hazard was played (see Rule 20-5).

PENALTY FOR BREACH OF RULE:

Match play—Loss of hole; Stroke play—Two strokes.

Rule 27. Ball Lost or Out of Bounds; Provisional Ball

If the original ball is lost under a condition covered by Rule 25-1 (casual water, ground under repair and certain damage to the course), the player may proceed under that Rule. If the original ball is lost in a water hazard, the player shall proceed under Rule 26.

Such Rules may not be used unless there is reasonable evidence that the ball is lost under a condition covered by Rule 25-1 or in a water hazard.

Definitions

A ball is "lost" if:

(*a*) It is not found or identified as his by the player within five minutes after the player's side or his or their caddies have begun to search for it; or

(*b*) The player has put another ball into play under the Rules, even though he may not have searched for the original ball; or

(*c*) The player has played any stroke with provisional ball from the place where the original ball is likely to be or from a point nearer the hole than that place, whereupon the provision ball becomes the ball in play.

Time spent in playing a wrong ball is not counted in the five-minute period allowed for search.

"Out of bounds" is ground on which play is prohibited.

When out of bounds is defined by reference to stakes or a fence, or as being beyond stakes or a fence, the out of bounds line is determined by the nearest inside points of the stakes or fence posts at ground level excluding angled supports.

When out of bounds is defined by a line on the ground, the line itself is out of bounds.

The out of bounds line is deemed to extend vertically upwards and downwards.

A ball is out of bounds when all of it lies out of bounds.

A player may stand out of bounds to play a ball lying within bounds.

A "provisional ball" is a ball played under Rule 27-2 for a ball which may be <u>lost</u> outside a <u>water hazard</u> or may be <u>out of</u> <u>bounds</u>. It ceases to be a provisional ball when the Rule provides either that the player continue play with it as the ball in play or that it be abandoned.

27-1 Ball Lost or Out of Bounds

If a ball is <u>lost</u> outside a <u>water hazard</u> or is <u>out of bounds</u>, the player shall play a ball, *under penalty of one stroke*, as nearly as possible at the spot from which the original ball was last played or moved by him (see Rule 20-5).

27-2 Provisional Ball

a. Procedure

If a ball may be <u>lost</u> outside a <u>water hazard</u> or may be <u>out of</u> <u>bounds</u>, to save time the player may play another ball provisionally as nearly as possible at the spot from which the original ball was played (see Rule 20-5). The player shall inform his opponent in match play or his marker or a fellow competitor in stroke play that he intends to play a <u>provisional ball</u>, and he shall play it before he or his partner goes forward to search for the original ball. If he fails to do so and plays another ball, such ball is not a provisional ball and becomes the <u>ball in play</u> *under penalty of stroke and distance* (Rule 27-1); the original ball is deemed to be lost.

b. When Provisional Ball Becomes Ball in Play

The player may play a provisional ball until he reaches the place where the original ball is likely to be. If he plays a stroke with the provisional ball from the place where the original ball is likely to be or from a point nearer the hole than that place, the original ball is deemed to be <u>lost</u> and the provisional ball becomes the ball in play under *penalty of stroke and distance* (Rule 27-1).

If the original ball is lost outside a water hazard or is out of bounds, the provisional ball becomes the ball in play, *under penalty of stroke and distance* (Rule 27-1).

c. When Provisional Ball to Be Abandoned

If the original ball is neither lost outside a water hazard nor out of bounds, the player shall abandon the provisional ball and continue play with the original ball. If he fails to do so, any further strokes played with the provisional ball shall constitute playing a wrong ball and the provisions of Rule 15 shall apply.

Note: If the original ball lies in a water hazard, the player shall play the ball as it lies or proceed under Rule 26. If it is lost in a water hazard or unplayable, the player shall proceed under Rule 26 or 28, whichever is applicable.

PENALTY FOR BREACH OF RULE:
Match play—Loss of hole; Stroke play—Two strokes.

Rule 28. Ball Unplayable

At any place on the course except in a water hazard a player may declare his ball unplayable. The player is the sole judge as to whether his ball is unplayable.

If the player deems his ball to be unplayable, he shall, *under penalty of one stroke*:

(*a*) Play his next stroke as nearly as possible at the spot from which the original ball was last played or moved by him (see Rule 20-5);
or

(*b*) Drop a ball within two club-lengths of the spot where the ball lay, but not nearer the hole;
or

(*c*) Drop a ball behind the spot where the ball lay, keeping that spot directly between himself and the hole, with no limit to how far behind that spot the ball may be dropped.

If the unplayable ball lies in a bunker and the player elects to proceed under Clause b or c, a ball must be dropped in the bunker.

The ball may be cleaned when lifted under this Rule.

PENALTY FOR BREACH OF RULE:
Match play—Loss of hole; Stroke play—Two strokes.

OTHER FORMS OF PLAY
Rule 29. Threesomes and Foursomes

Definitions

Threesome: A match in which one plays against two, and each side plays one ball.

Foursome: A match in which two play against two, and each side plays one ball.

29-1 General

In a threesome or a foursome, during any stipulated round the partners shall play alternately from the teeing grounds and alternately during the play of each hole. Penalty strokes do not affect the order of play.

29-2 Match Play

If a player plays when his partner should have played, *his side shall lose the hole.*

29-3 Stroke Play

If the partners play a stroke or strokes in incorrect order, such stroke or strokes shall be cancelled and *the side shall be penalised two strokes.* A ball shall then be put in play as nearly as possible at the spot from which the side first played in incorrect order (see Rule 20-5) before a stroke has been played from the next teeing ground or, in the case of the last hole of the round, before the side has left the putting green. If this is not done, *the side shall be disqualified.*

Rule 30. Three-Ball, Best-Ball and Four-Ball Match Play

30-1 Rules of Golf Apply

The Rules of Golf, so far as they are not at variance with the following special Rules, shall apply to three-ball, best-ball and four-ball matches.

30-2 Three-Ball Match Play

In a three-ball match, each player is playing two distinct matches.

a. Ball at Rest Moved by an Opponent

Except as otherwise provided in the Rules, if the player's ball is touched or moved by an opponent, his <u>caddie</u> or <u>equipment</u> other than during search, Rule 18-3b applies. *That opponent shall incur a penalty stroke in his match with the player*, but not in his match with the other opponent.

b. Ball Deflected or Stopped by an Opponent Accidentally

If a player's ball is accidentally deflected or stopped by an opponent, his <u>caddie</u> or <u>equipment</u>, no penalty shall be incurred. In his match with that opponent the player may play the ball as it lies or, before another stroke is played by either side, he may cancel the stroke and replay the stroke (see Rule 20-5). In his match with the other opponent, the occurrence shall be treated as a rub of the green and the hole shall be played out with the original ball.

Exception: Ball striking person attending flagstick—Rule 17-3b.

(Ball purposely deflected or stopped by opponent—Rule 19-3a.)

30-3 Best-Ball and Four-Ball Match Play

a. Representation of Side

A side may be represented by one partner for all or any part of a match; all partners need not be present. An absent partner may join a match between holes, but not during play of a hole.

b. Maximum of Fourteen Clubs

The side shall be penalised for a breach of Rule 4-4 by any partner.

c. Order of Play

Balls belonging to the same side may be played in the order the side considers best.

d. Wrong Ball

If a player plays a stroke with a <u>wrong ball</u> except in a <u>hazard</u>, *he shall be disqualified for that hole*, but his partner incurs no penalty even if the wrong ball belongs to him. The owner of the ball shall replace it on the spot from which it was played, without penalty. If the ball is not immediately recoverable, another ball may be substituted.

e. Disqualification of Side

(i) *A side shall be disqualified* for a breach of any of the following by any partner:

Rule 1-3	Agreement to Waive Rules.
Rule 4-1, -2 or -3	Clubs.
Rule 5	The Ball.
Rule 6-2a	Handicap (playing off higher handicap).
Rule 6-4	Caddie.
Rule 6-7	Undue Delay (repeated offence).
Rule 14-3	Artificial Devices and Unusual Equipment.

(ii) *A side shall be disqualified* for a breach of any of the following by all partners:

Rule 6-3	Time of Starting and Groups.
Rule 6-8	Discontinuance of Play.

f. Effect of Other Penalties

If a player's breach of a Rule assists his partner's play or adversely affects an opponent's play, *the partner incurs the relative penalty in addition to any penalty incurred by the player.*

In all other cases where a player incurs a penalty for breach of a Rule, the penalty shall not apply to his partner. Where the penalty is stated to be loss of hole, the effect shall be to disqualify the player for that hole.

g. Another Form of Match Played Concurrently

In a best-ball or four-ball match when another form of match is played concurrently, the above special Rules shall apply.

Rule 31. Four-Ball Stroke Play

In four-ball stroke play two competitors play as partners, each playing his own ball. The lower score of the partners is the score for the hole. If one partner fails to complete the play of a hole, there is no penalty.

31-1 Rules of Golf Apply

The Rules of Golf, so far as they are not at variance with the following special Rules, shall apply to four-ball stroke play.

31-2 Representation of Side

A side may be represented by either partner for all or any part of a stipulated round; both partners need not be present. An absent competitor may join his partner between holes, but not during play of a hole.

31-3. Maximum of Fourteen Clubs

The side shall be penalised for a breach of Rule 4-4 by either partner.

31-4 Scoring

The marker is required to record for each hole only the gross score of whichever partner's score is to count. The gross scores to count must be individually identifiable; otherwise *the side shall be disqualified.* Only one of the partners need be responsible for complying with Rule 6-6a and b.

(Wrong score—Rule 31-7a.)

31-5 Order of Play

Balls belonging to the same side may be played in the order the side considers best.

31-6 Wrong Ball

If a competitor plays a stroke with a wrong ball except in a hazard, *he shall add two penalty strokes to his score for the hole* and shall then play the correct ball. His partner incurs no penalty even if the wrong ball belongs to him.

The owner of the ball shall replace it on the spot from which it was played, without penalty. If the ball is not immediately recoverable, another ball may be substituted.

31-7 Disqualification Penalties
a. Breach by One Partner
A side shall be disqualified from the competition for a breach of any of the following by either partner:

Rule 1-3	Agreement to Waive Rules.
Rule 3-4	Refusal to Comply with Rule.
Rule 4-1, -2 or -3	Clubs.
Rule 5	The Ball.

Rule 6-2b	Handicap (playing off higher handicap; failure to record handicap).
Rule 6-4	Caddie.
Rule 6-6b	Checking Scores.
Rule 6-6c	No Alteration of Scores, i.e. when the recorded lower score of the partners is lower than actually played. If the recorded lower score of the partners is higher than actually played, it must stand as returned.
Rule 6-7	Undue Delay (repeated offence).
Rule 7-1	Practice Before or Between Rounds.
Rule 14-3	Artificial Devices and Unusual Equipment.
Rule 31-4	Gross Scores to count Not Individually Identifiable.

b. Breach by Both Partners

A side shall be disqualified for a breach of any of the following by both partners:

| Rule 6-3 | Time of Starting and Groups. |
| Rule 6-8 | Discontinuance of Play. |

At the same hole, of a Rule or Rules, the penalty for which is disqualification either from the competition or for a hole.

c. For the Hole Only

In all other cases where a breach of a Rule would entail disqualification, *the competitor shall be disqualified only for the hole at which the breach occurred.*

31-8 Effect of Other Penalties

If a competitor's breach of a Rule assists his partner's play, *the partner incurs the relative penalty in addition to any penalty incurred by the competitor.*

In all other cases where a competitor incurs a penalty for breach of a Rule, the penalty shall not apply to his partner.

Rule 32. Bogey, Par and Stableford Competitions

32-1 Conditions

Bogey, par and Stableford competitons are forms of stroke competition in which play is against a fixed score at each hole. The Rules for stroke play, so far as they are not at variance with the following special Rules, apply.

a. Bogey and Par Competitions

The reckoning for bogey and par competitions is made as in match play. Any hole for which a competitor makes no return shall be regarded as a loss. The winner is the competitor who is most successful in the aggregate of holes.

The marker is responsible for marking only the gross number of strokes for each hole where the competitor makes a net score equal to or less than the fixed score.

Note: Maximum of 14 Clubs—Penalties as in match play—see Rule 4-4.

b. Stableford Competitions

The reckoning in Stableford competitions is made by points awarded in relation to a fixed score at each hole as follows:

Hole Played in	Points
More than one over fixed score	0
One over fixed score	1
Fixed score	2
One under fixed score	3
Two under fixed score	4
Three under fixed score	5

The winner is the competitor who scores the highest number of points.

The marker shall be responsible for marking only the gross number of strokes at each hole where the competitor's net score earns one or more points.

Note: Maximum of 14 Clubs (Rule 4-4)—Penalties applied as follows: From total points scored for the round, deduction of two points for each hole at which any breach occurred; maximum deduction per round: four points.

32-2 Disqualification Penalties

a. From the Competition

A competitor shall be disqualified from the competition for a breach of any of the following:

Rule 1-3	Agreement to Waive Rules.
Rule 3-4	Refusal to Comply with Rule.
Rule 4-1, -2 or -3	Clubs.
Rule 5	The Ball.
Rule 6-2b	Handicap (playing off higher handicap; failure to record handicap).
Rule 6-3	Time of Starting and Groups.
Rule 6-4	Caddie.
Rule 6-6b	Checking Scores.
Rule 6-6c	No alteration of scores, except that the competitor shall not be disqualified when a breach of this Rule does not affect the result of the hole.
Rule 6-7	Undue Delay (repeated offence).
Rule 6-8	Discontinuance of Play.
Rule 7-1	Practice Before or Between Rounds.
Rule 14-3	Artificial Devices and Unusual Equipment.

b. For a Hole

In all other cases where a breach of a Rule would entail disqualification, *the competitor shall be disqualified only for the hole at which the breach occurred.*

ADMINISTRATION
Rule 33. The Committee

33-1 Conditions

The Committee shall lay down the conditions under which a competition is to be played.

Certain special rules governing stroke play are so substantially different from those governing match play that combining the two forms of play is not practicable and is not permitted. The results of matches played and the scores returned in these circumstances shall not be accepted.

In stroke play the Committee may limit a referee's duties.

33-2 The Course

a. Defining Bounds and Margins

The Committee shall define accurately:

(i) the <u>course</u> and <u>out of bounds,</u>

(ii) the <u>margins</u> of <u>water hazards</u> and <u>lateral water hazards</u>,

(iii) <u>ground under repair</u>, and

(iv) <u>obstructions</u> and integral parts of the course.

b. New Holes

New holes should be made on the day on which a stroke competition begins and at such other times as the Committee considers necessary, provided all competitors in a single round play with each hole cut in the same position.

Exception: When it is impossible for a damaged hole to be repaired so that it conforms with the Definition, the Committee may make a new hole in a nearby similar position.

c. Practice Ground

Where there is no practice ground available outside the area of a competition <u>course</u>, the Committee should lay down the area on which players may practise on any day of a competition, if it is practicable to do so. On any day of a stroke competition, the Committee should not normally permit practice on or to a <u>putting green</u> or from a <u>hazard</u> of the competition course.

d. Course Unplayable

If the Committee or its authorised representative considers that for any reason the course is not in a playable condition or that there are circumstances which render the proper playing of the game impossible, it may, in match play or stroke play, order a temporary suspension of play or, in stroke play, declare play null and void and cancel all scores for the round in question. When play has been temporarily suspended, it shall be resumed from where it was discontinued, even though resumption occurs on a subsequent day. When a round is cancelled, all penalties incurred in that round are cancelled.

(Procedure in discontinuing play—Rule 6-8.)

33-3 Times of Starting and Groups

The Committee shall lay down the times of starting and, in stroke play, arrange the groups in which competitors shall play.

When a match play competition is played over an extended period, the Committee shall lay down the limit of time within which each round shall be completed. When players are allowed to arrange the date of their match with these limits, the Committee should announce that the match must be played at a stated time on the last day of the period unless the players agree to a prior date.

33-4 Handicap Stroke Table

The Committee shall publish a table indicating the order of holes at which handicap strokes are to be given or received.

33-5 Score Card

In stroke play, the Committee shall issue for each competitor a score card containing the date and the competitor's name.

The Committee is responsible for the addition of scores and application of the handicap recorded on the card.

In four-ball stroke play, the Committee is responsible for recording the better ball score for each hole, the addition and the application of the handicaps recorded on the card.

33-6 Decision of Ties

The Committee shall announce the manner, day and time for the decision of a halved match or of a tie, whether played on level terms or under handicap.

A halved match shall not be decided by stroke play. A tie in stroke play shall not be decided by a match.

33-7 Modification of Penalty

The Committee has no power to waive a Rule of Golf. A penalty of disqualification, however, may, in exceptional individual cases, be waived or be modified or be imposed if the Committee considers such action warranted.

33-8 Local Rules

a. Policy

The Committee may make and publish Local Rules for abnormal conditions if they are consistent with the policy of the Governing Authority for the country concerned as set forth in Appendix I to these Rules.

b. Waiving Penalty

A penalty imposed by a Rule of Golf shall not be waived by a Local Rule.

Rule 34. Disputes and Decisions

34-1 Claims and Penalties

a. Match Play

In match play if a claim is lodged with the Committee under Rule 2-5, a decision should be given as soon as possible so that the state of the match may, if necessary, be adjusted.

If a claim is not made within the time limit provided by Rule 2-5, it shall not be considered unless it is based on facts previously unknown to the player making the claim and the player making the claim had been given wrong information (Rules 6-2a and 9) by an opponent. In any case, no later claim shall be considered after the result of the match has been officially announced, unless the Committee is satisfied that the opponent knew he was giving wrong information.

b. Stroke Play

No penalty shall be imposed after the competition is closed unless the Committee is satisfied that the competitor has knowingly returned a score for any hole lower than actually taken (Rule 6-6c); no penalty shall be rescinded after the competition is closed. A competition is deemed to have closed when the result of the competition is officially announced or, in stroke play qualifying followed by match play, when the player has teed off in his first match.

34-2 Referee's Decision

If a referee has been appointed by the Committee, his decision shall be final.

34-3. Committee's Decision

In the absence of a referee, the players shall refer any dispute to the Committee , whose decision shall be final.

If the Committee cannot come to a decision, it shall refer the dispute to the Rules of Golf Committee of the Royal and Ancient Golf Club of St. Andrews, whose decision shall be final.

If the point in doubt or dispute has not been referred to the Rules of Golf Committee, the player or players have the right to refer an agreed statement through the Secretary of the Club to the Rules of Golf Committee for an opinion as to the correctness of the decision given. The reply will be sent to the Secretary of the Club or Clubs concerned.

If play is conducted other than in accordance with the Rules of Golf, the Rules of Golf Committee will not give a decision on any question.

NOTE. RULES OF GOLF (The Royal and Ancient Golf Club of St. Andrews) includes Appendices dealing in some detail with "Local Rules", "Design of Clubs" and "The Ball", "Rules of Amateur Status".

The Rules of
Hockey

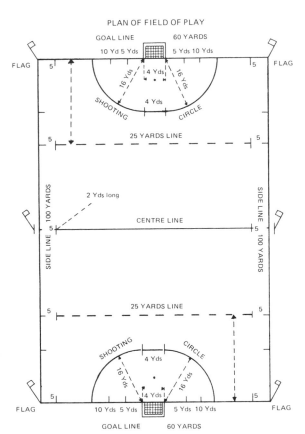

PLAN OF FIELD OF PLAY

The front of the goal-posts must be touching the outer edge of the goal-line. All lines must be 3 in wide.
A spot 6 in in diameter shall be marked 7 yd in front of the centre of each goal. All short indication marks must be inside the field only and shall be 12 in in length.

Hockey

Issued under the authority of the Hockey Rules Board

1. Teams and Duration of Play

(*a*) A game shall be played between two teams. Not more than eleven players of each team shall be on the field at the same time. Each team shall have one goalkeeper on the field or shall indicate a field player who has the privileges of a goalkeeper.

(*b*) Each team is permitted to substitute up to two players during the game. (This provision is not mandatory at any level.)

(*c*) No player once substituted shall be permitted on the field again, and no substitute shall be permitted for a suspended player during his suspension.

(*d*) (i) Substitution of players shall only take place with the prior permission of an umpire during any stoppage of play other than following the award of a penalty corner, or a penalty stroke subject to (ii). (ii) After the award of a penalty corner or penalty stroke any player who is injured and has to leave the field of play can be substituted subject to Rule (*c*). Rules 9 (*b*), 15 (*b*) (ii) and 16 (*b*) (i) shall apply.

(*e*) The duration of the game shall be two periods of thirty-five minutes each unless otherwise agreed before the game.

(*f*) At half-time the teams shall change ends, and the duration of the interval shall not exceed five minutes, unless otherwise agreed before the game, but it shall in no case exceed ten minutes.

(*g*) The game starts when the umpire blows his whistle for the opening pass-back. (See also Rule 10(*a*).)

2. Captains

Each team must have a captain on the field who may wear a distinctive arm-band and who shall:

(*a*) toss for choice of start. The winner of the toss shall have (i) the right to choose which end his team will attack in the first half *or* (ii) the right to have possession of the ball at the start of the game.

The winner of the toss having made his choice, the opposing side will automatically have the second option. The team not having started the game will have possession of the ball for restarting after half-time.

(*b*) before the start of play and on any change, indicate, if necessary, to each other and to the umpires, their respective goalkeepers subject to Rules 15 (*b*) (ii) and 16 (*b*) (i).

(*c*) In case he is substituted or suspended, indicate to the umpires the player who will replace him as captain.

3. Umpires and Timekeepers

(*a*) There shall be two umpires to control the game and to administer the rules. These umpires shall be the sole judges of fair and unfair play during the game.

(*b*) Unless otherwise provided, each team shall be responsible for providing one umpire.

(*c*) Each umpire shall be:
  (i) primarily responsible for decisions in his own half of the field, for the whole of the game without changing ends.
 (ii) solely responsible for decisions on the hit-in for the full length of his nearer side-line.
(iii) solely responsible for decisions on corners, penalty corners, penalty strokes and goals in his own half and free hits in his own circle.

(*d*) The umpires shall be responsible for keeping time for the duration of the game. It shall be permissible to have a timekeeper or timekeepers. Such timekeepers shall take over only those duties of the umpires which concern the keeping of time and the indication of the end of each half.

(*e*) Umpires shall allow the full or agreed time and shall keep a written record of the goals as they are scored.

(*f*) Time shall be allowed for all enforced stoppages and such time shall be added to that half in which the stoppage occurred.

(*g*) Umpires and timekeepers shall be debarred from coaching during a game and during the interval.

(*h*) Umpires shall only blow the whistle to:
  (i) start and end each half of the game,
  (ii) enforce a penalty or suspend the game for any other reason,
  (iii) start and end a penalty stroke,
  (iv) indicate, when necessary, that the ball has passed wholly outside the field of play,
  (v) signal a goal,
  (vi) re-start the game after a goal has been scored and after a suspension of play.

(*i*) Umpires shall satisfy themselves before the game that, as far as is practicable, Rules 4 to 9 inclusive are observed.

Umpires shall refrain from enforcing a penalty in cases where they are satisfied that by enforcing it an advantage would be given to the offending team.

4. Field of Play

(*a*) All lines used in the measurements of the field are to be 3-in. wide. The goal-lines and side-lines are part of the field of play.

(*b*) The field shall be rectangular, 100 yd long and 60 yd wide. Its boundaries shall be clearly marked out with lines in accordance with the Plan on page 436. The longer lines shall be called the side-lines and the shorter the goal-lines.

(*c*) The centre line shall be marked out, throughout its length. The 25-yd lines shall be marked with broken lines throughout their length. The broken line should consist of equal length lines and breaks in the line—these being 2 yd in length.

(*d*) To assist in the control of the hit-in, across the centre line and each 25-yd line, parallel to and 5 yd from the outer edge of the side-lines a mark 2 yd in length shall be made.

(*e*) A mark 12 in in length shall be placed inside the field of play on each side-line and parallel to the goal-line and 16 yd from its inner edge.

(*f*) For penalty corner hits, the field shall be marked inside the field of play on the goal-lines on both sides of the goal at

5 yd and 10 yd from the outer edge of the nearer goal-post such distance being to the further edge of those lines. For corner hits the field shall be marked inside the field of play on the goal- lines, 5 yd from the outer edge of the side-line. All these marks to be 12 in in length.

(g) A spot 6 in diameter shall be marked in front of the centre of each goal; the centre of the spot shall be 7 yd from the inner edge of the goal-line.

(h) No marks other than those shown on the plan on page 436 are permissible on the playing surface.

(i) Flag posts, at least 4 ft and not more than 5 ft high, shall be placed for the whole game at each corner of the field and at the centre; those at the centre shall be at 1 yd outside the side-lines.

5. Goals, Posts, etc.

(a) There shall be a goal at the centre of each back-line consisting of two perpendicular posts 4 yd (3.66 m) apart, joined together by a horizontal cross-bar 7 ft (2.14 m) from the ground (inside measurements). The front base of the goal- posts shall touch the outer edge of the back-line. The goal- posts shall not extend upwards beyond the cross-bar, nor the cross- bar sideways beyond the goal-posts.

(b) The goal-posts and cross-bar shall be rectangular and shall be 2 in (5 cm) wide and not more than 3 in (8 cm) deep, and shall be painted white.

(c) Nets shall be attached firmly at intervals of not more than 6 in (15 cm) to the goal-posts and the cross-bar and shall be attached firmly to the ground behind the goal.

(d) A back-board 4 yd long and 18 in (45 cm) high, shall be placed at the foot of and inside the goal-nets. Side- boards of a minimum length of 4 ft and 18 in high shall be placed at right angles to the goal-lines. The side-boards shall be fixed to the back of the goal-posts so that the width of the goal-post is not effectively increased.

(e) No chocks shall be placed inside the goal to support any of the boards.

6. Shooting Circles

In front of each goal shall be drawn a line, 4 yd (3.66 m) long, parallel to, and 16 yd (15 m) from, the back-line. The 16 yd shall be measured from the inside front corner of the goal-posts to the outer edge of that line. This line shall be continued each way to meet the back-lines by quarter circles having the inside front corners of the goal-posts as centres. The space enclosed by these lines, including the lines themselves, shall be called the shooting circle (hereinafter referred to as "the circle").

7. The Ball

(*a*) A ball of any material or any colour, sewn or seamless, but of the size and weight specified below, may be used, as agreed upon mutually before the game.

(*b*) The inner portion of the ball shall be composed of cork and twine.

(*c*) The weight of the ball shall be not more than $5\frac{3}{4}$ oz (165 gm) and not less than $5\frac{1}{2}$ oz (155 gm).

(*d*) The circumference of the ball shall be not more than $9\frac{1}{4}$ in (24 cm) and not less than $8\frac{13}{16}$ in (23 cm).

8. The Stick

(*a*) The stick shall have a flat face on its left-hand side only. The face of the stick is the whole of the flat side and that part of the handle for the whole of the length which is above the flat side.

(*b*) The head (i.e., the part below the lower end of the splice) shall be curved and shall be of wood. It shall not be edged with, nor have any insets or fittings of metal or any other substance, nor shall there be any sharp edges or dangerous splinters. The maximum length of the curved head of the stick, as measured from the lowest part of the flat face, shall not exceed 4 inches.

(*c*) The total weight of the stick shall not exceed 28 oz (795 gm), nor be less than 12 oz (340 gm), and the stick shall be of such a size (inclusive of any covering) that it can be passed through a ring with an interior diameter of 5.10 cm.

(*d*) Umpires shall forbid the use of any stick which does not comply with this Rule.

Penalty. For any breach of this Rule any player concerned shall not be allowed on the field of play until such time as he has complied with this Rule.

9. Players' Dress and Equipment

(*a*) Each player shall wear the dress approved by his Association or Club, unless varied to avoid confusion in a particular game. Goal-keepers shall wear a colour different from that of their own team and that of their opponents. Players shall not have dangerous spikes, studs or protruding nails in footwear, or wear anything that may be dangerous to other players.

(*b*) The following equipment is permitted for use by goalkeepers only: Body Protectors, Pads, Kickers, Gauntlet Gloves, Headgear, Facemasks and Elbow Pads.

Penalty. For any breach of this Rule any player concerned shall not be allowed on the field of play until such time as he has complied with this Rule.

10. To Start or Re-start the Game

(*a*) To start the game, re-start it after half-time and after each goal scored, a "pass-back" shall be played at the centre of the field. The pass-back for the start of the game shall be made by a player of the team which did not make a choice of ends (see Rule 2*a*), after half-time by a player of the opposing team and after a goal has been scored, by a player of the team against whom the goal has been awarded. The pass-back, which may be pushed or hit, must not be directed over the centre-line. At the moment when the pass-back is taken, no player of the opposing team shall be within 5 yd of the ball and all players of both teams other than the player making the pass-back must be in their own half of the field. If the striker hit at but miss the ball, the pass-back still has to be taken. After taking the pass-back, the striker shall not play the ball nor approach within playing distance until it has been touched or played by another player of either team. Timewasting shall not be permitted.

(*b*) (i) To re-start the game in accordance with Rule 12

III, Rule 12 Penalties 4(*a*) or Rule 18(*b*)(i) a bully shall be played on the spot where the incident occurred.

(ii) To bully, a player of each team shall stand squarely facing the side-lines, each with his own back-line on his right. The ball shall be placed on the ground between the two players. Each player shall tap with his stick first the ground between the ball and his own back-line and then, with the flat face of his stick, his opponent's stick over the ball three times alternately, after which one of these two players shall play the ball with his stick to put it into play.

(iii) Until the ball is in play, all other players shall be nearer to their own back-line than the ball is, and shall not stand within 5 yd (4.5 m) of the ball.

(iv) A bully in the circle shall not be played within 5 yd (4.5 m) of the back- or goal-line.

Penalties. 1. For a breach of Rule 10(*a*) a free hit shall be awarded to the opposing team.

2. For a breach of Rule 10(*b*)(ii) or (iii) the bully shall be played again.

3. For persistent breaches of Rule 10(*b*)(ii) and (iii), the umpire may award a free hit to the opposing team; or for such breaches in the circle by a defender, a penalty corner.

11. Scoring a Goal

(*a*) A goal is scored when the whole ball, having been hit or deflected by the stick of an attacker whilst in the circle and not having gone outside the circle, has passed completely over the goal-line between the goal-posts and under the cross-bar, except in circumstances detailed in Rule 15(*g*) and Rule 16. It is immaterial if the ball subsequently touch, or be played by one or more defenders. If, during the game, the goal-posts and/or the cross-bar become displaced, and the ball pass completely over the goal-line at a point which, in the umpire's opinion, be between where the goal-posts and/ or under where the cross-bar, respectively, should have been, a goal shall be awarded.

(*b*) The team scoring the greater number of goals shall be the winner.

12. Conduct of Play

I. A player shall not:

(*a*) play the ball with the rounded side of his stick,

(*b*) take part in or interfere with the game unless he has his own stick in his hand, or change his stick for the purpose of taking part in the game under Rules 14, 15, 16, and 17(*b*)(i) and (*c*).

"*Own stick*" *means the stick with which the player began to play, or any stick that he legitimately substitutes for it.*

(*c*) raise his stick in a manner that is dangerous, intimidating or hampering to another player when approaching, attempting to play, playing or stopping the ball. A ball above the height of a player's shoulder shall not be played or played at by any part of the stick.

(*d*) stop the ball with his hand or catch it. (For Goalkeepers, see Rule 12 II(*c*). *There is nothing in this Rule which prevents a player using his hand to protect himself from a dangerously raised ball.*

(*e*) hit wildly into an opponent or play or kick the ball in such a way as to be dangerous in itself, or likely to lead to dangerous play.

(*f*) stop or deflect the ball on the ground or in the air with any part of the body *to his or his team's advantage* (save as provided for in Rule 12 II(*c*)).

(*g*) use the foot or leg to support the stick in order to resist an opponent,

(*h*) pick up, kick, throw, carry or propel the ball in any manner or direction except with the stick (but see Rule 12 II(*c*)),

(*i*) hit, hook, hold, strike at or interfere with an opponent's stick,

(*j*) charge, kick, shove, trip, strike at or personally handle an opponent or his clothing,

(*k*) obstruct by running between an opponent and the ball or interpose himself or his stick as an obstruction.

II. A player may:

(*a*) play the ball only with the flat side of his stick, which includes that part of the handle above the flat side, (*b*) tackle from the left of an opponent provided that he play the ball without previous interference with the stick or person of his opponent (see Rule 12 I particularly (*i*), (*j*), (*k*).

(*c*) if he is goalkeeper, be allowed to kick the ball or stop it with any part of his body including his hand, but only when the ball is inside his own circle. If in stopping a shot at goal the ball, in the umpire's opinion, merely rebound off any part of the goal-keeper's body, no penalty shall be incurred.

III. If the ball become lodged in the pads of a goal-keeper (or in the clothing of any player or umpire) the umpire shall stop the game and restart it by a bully on the spot where the incident occurred (subject to Rule 10(*b*)(iv)). If the ball strike an umpire the game shall continue.

IV. *Misconduct. Rough or dangerous play, time-wasting or any other behaviour which in the Umpire's opinion amounts to misconduct shall not be permitted.*
Penalties.
1. *Outside the circle.*
A free hit shall be awarded to the opposing team. If the umpire be satisfied that the offence committed by any defender inside his own 25 yd (23 m) area was deliberate, he shall award a penalty corner.
2. *Inside the circle—by an attacker.*
A free hit shall be awarded to the defending team.
3. *Inside the circle—by a defender.*
A penalty corner or a penalty stroke shall be awarded to the attacking team.
4. *Inside and Outside the circle.*
For a simultaneous breach of this Rule by two opponents, the umpire shall order a bully to be played on the spot where the breach occurred (subject to Rule 10(*b*)(iv)).
5. *Inside and Outside the circle.*
For rough or dangerous play or misconduct, in addition to awarding the appropriate penalty, the umpire may:
   (i) warn the offending player(s) which may also be indicated by showing a green card,
   (ii) suspend him temporarily, for not less than five minutes (yellow card),

(iii) suspend him from further participation in the game (red card).

A temporarily suspended player shall remain behind his own goal or in such other places as designated before the game, until allowed by the umpire by whom he was suspended, to resume play; when necessary changing ends at the start of the second half of the game.

13. Off-side

(*a*) A player of the same team as the striker, or pusher-in, is in an off-side position if, *at any moment when the ball is hit or pushed-in*, he be nearer to this opponents' goal-line than the ball is, unless he is in his own half of the field or there are at least two opponents nearer to their own goal-line than he is.

For the purpose of this Rule, a player of either team shall be deemed to be on the field of play even though he be outside the side-line or behind the goal-line.

(*b*) A player who is in an off-side position shall not play or attempt to play the ball or gain any advantage for his team or influence the play of an opponent.

Penalty. A free hit to the defending team.

14. Free Hit

(*a*) A free hit shall be taken from the spot on which the breach occurred, except that (i) no free hit awarded to the attacking team shall be taken within 5 yd of the circle (ii) for a breach by an attacker within the circle, the free hit shall be taken either from any spot within that circle or from any spot within 16 yd (15 m) of the inner edge of the defending team's back-line or goal-line on a line drawn through the place where the breach occurred and parallel to the side-line (iii) for a breach by an attacker outside the circle but within 16 yd (15 m) of the defending team's back-line, it shall be taken from any spot within 16 yd (15 m) of the inner edge of the defending team's back-line on a line drawn through the place where the breach occurred and parallel to the side-line.

(*b*) The ball shall be stationary and the striker shall hit or push it. The ball must be moved and shall not be raised intentionally in such a way as to be dangerous in itself, or likely to lead to dangerous play.

(c) At the moment when the free hit is taken, no player of the opposing team shall remain within 5 yd (4.5 m) of the ball. Should, however, the umpire consider that a player is standing within 5 yd of the ball in order to gain time, the free hit shall not be delayed.

(d) If the striker hit at but miss the ball, provided that Rule 12 I (c) has not been contravened, the free hit still has to be taken.

(e) After taking the free hit, the striker shall not play the ball again nor remain or approach within playing distance until it has been touched or played by another player of either team.

Penalties.

1. *Inside the circle.* A penalty corner or a penalty stroke shall be awarded to the attacking team.

2. *Outside the circle.* A free hit shall be awarded to the opposing team. An umpire shall award a penalty corner for an offence by any defendeer in his own 25 yd area, when, in the umpire's opinion, the offence was deliberate.

15. Penalty Corner

(a) A player of the attacking team shall push or hit the ball from a spot on the back-line not less than 10 yd from the goal-post, on whichever side of the goal the attacking team prefers. The player concerned is not required to be wholly inside or outside the field of play when taking the corner. The ball shall not be raised intentionally but the hit shall not be penalised if the ball lifts off the ground without causing danger or appearing likely to lead to dangerous play.

(b) (i) At the moment when such hit or push is made, no other player shall be within 5 yd of the ball.

The rest of the attacking team shall be in the field of play with both sticks and feet outside the circle.

Not more than six of the defending team shall stand with both sticks and feet behind their own goal-line or back-line. The rest of the defending team shall be beyond the centre line.

(ii) In the event of a goalkeeper being incapacitated or suspended, the Captain of the defending team shall immediately nominate another goalkeeper. This goalkeeper shall be permitted to put on, without undue delay, protective equipment. Under the provisions of this Rule, a goalkeeper may also remove his headgear, face-mask and/or his gauntlet gloves (see Rule 9(*b*)).

(*c*) Until the ball be hit or pushed no attacker shall enter the circle, nor shall a defender cross the goal-line, back-line or the centre line.

(*d*) No shot at goal shall be made from a penalty corner until the ball be stopped on the ground or touch the stick or person of a defender.

(*e*) The player taking the penalty corner hit or push from the back-line shall not, after striking the ball, approach or remain within playing distance of the ball until it has been touched or played by another player of either team.

(*f*) If the striker of the penalty corner hit at or push at but miss the ball, the penalty corner still has to be taken.

(*g*) No goal shall be scored directly by the player taking the penalty corner hit or push from the back-line.

Penalties.

1. *For a breach of Rules* 15 (*b*)(i) *or* 15(*c*), *viz.*:

Attacker entering the circle or defenders crossing the goal-line or centre line too soon or coming within 5 yd of the ball too soon—the penalty corner may, at the discretion of the umpire, be taken again.

2. *For persistent breaches of Rules* 15(*b*)(i) *or* 15(*c*) *by the attackers*—The umpire may award a free hit.

3. *For persistent breaches of Rules* 15 (*b*)(i) *or* 15 (*c*) *by the defenders*—The umpire may award a penalty stroke.

4. *For any other breach of Rule* 15—A free hit shall be awarded to the defending team.

16. Penalty Stroke

(*a*) A penalty stroke shall be awarded to the opposing team if, in the opinion of the umpire:

(i) There has been an *intentional* breach of Rules 12 or 14 inside the circle, by a player of the defending team; or,

(ii) A goal would probably have been scored had an *unintentional* breach of Rule 12 inside the circle by a player of the defending team not occurred.

(*b*) (i) The penalty stroke shall be either a push, flick or scoop stroke taken from a spot 7 yd in front of the centre of the goal by a player of the attacking team and defended by the goalkeeper of the opposing team on the field at the time the breach occurred. In the event of the goalkeeper being incapacitated or suspended, the captain of the defending team shall immediately nominate another goalkeeper.

This goalkeeper shall be permitted to put on or remove without undue delay protective equipment. Under the provisions of this Rule, a goalkeeper may also remove his face mask, headgear and/or his gauntlet gloves (see Rule 9(*b*).

(ii) Whichever stroke is used, the ball may be raised to any height.

(iii) During the taking of a penalty stroke all the other players of both teams shall stand beyond the nearer 25-yd line and shall not influence or attempt to influence the conduct of the penalty stroke.

(*c*) (i) The attacking player shall not take the penalty stroke until the umpire, having satisfied himself that both defender and attacker are ready, has indicated that he may do so by blowing his whistle.

(ii) When taking the stroke the attacker shall stand close to and behind the ball and shall be permitted in making the stroke to take one stride forward. Dragging or lifting the rear foot is not a breach of this Rule provided that it does not pass the front foot before the ball is moved.

(iii) The attacker shall touch the ball once only and thereafter shall not approach either the ball or the goalkeeper.

(*d*) (i) The goalkeeper shall stand on the goal-line. After the player taking the stroke and the goalkeeper are in position and the umpire has blown his whistle, the goalkeeper may not leave the goal-line or move either of his feet until the ball has been played. (ii) The usual privileges of the goalkeeper shall be allowed to him but he shall not be allowed to delay the taking of the stroke by making unnecessary changes or modifications of clothing. He shall not be penalised, if, in stopping a shot at goal, the ball, in the opinion of the umpire, merely rebounds off his body or his hand. He may not touch the ball with any part of his stick when the ball is above the height of his shoulder. If the ball be caught and held by the goalkeeper, the penalty stroke is ended. (See also clause (*e*) (iii).)

(iii) If any deliberate action by the striker, prior to striking the ball, induce the goalkeeper to move either of his feet or, if the striker feint at striking the ball, the striker shall be penalised.

(*e*) If, as a result of the penalty stroke:

(i) The whole ball pass completely over the goal-line between the goal-posts and under the cross-bar, a goal is scored;

(ii) The ball should come to rest inside the circle, be lodged in the goalkeeper's pads, be caught by the goalkeeper or pass outside the circle, in all cases the penalty stroke is ended. Unless a goal has been scored or awarded, the game shall be re-started by a free hit to be taken by a defender from a spot in front of the centre of the goal and 16 yd from the inner edge of that line.

(*f*) All time taken between the award of a penalty stroke and resumption of play shall be added to the time of play.

Penalties.

1. For a breach of any rule by the goalkeeper which prevents a goal from being scored, a goal shall be awarded to the opposing team (see penalty 3).

2. For a breach of any rule by an attacker, the game shall be re-started with a free hit to be taken by a defender from a spot in front of the centre of the goal-line and 16 yd from the inner edge of that line.

3. For a breach of clause (*b*) (iii) or (*d*) (i), the umpire may order the stroke to be taken again.

17. Ball Outside Field of Play

When the whole ball passes completely over the back-line, and no goal is scored, or over the side-line, it is out of play and the game shall be re-started as in Rules 17 (i) and 17 (ii).

1. *Over side-line*

(*a*) When the whole ball passes completely over the side-line, it or another ball, shall be placed on the line at the spot at which it crossed the side-line. The ball shall be pushed or hit without undue delay by a player of the team opposed to the player who last touched it in play. This player is not required to be wholly inside or outside the side-line when making his push or hit.

(*b*) At the moment when the push or hit is taken, no other player of either team shall be within 5 yd of the ball. If any player of either team be within 5 yd of the ball, the umpire may require the push or hit to be taken again. If, however, in the umpire's opinion, any player remain within 5 yd of the ball to gain time, the push or hit shall not be delayed.

(*c*) If the striker hit at but miss the ball, provided that Rule 12 I (*c*) has not been contravened, the push or hit still has to be taken.

(*d*) After taking a push or hit the player shall not play the ball again, nor remain or approach within playing distance of the ball, until it has been touched or played by another player of either team.

2. *Over back-line*

(*a*) By an attacker.

When the whole ball passes completely over the opponents' back-line by or off one of the attacking team, and no goal is scored, it or another ball shall be placed on a spot opposite the place where it crossed the back-line and not more than 16 yd from the inner edge of that line. The ball shall be pushed or hit without undue delay by one of the defending team. Other than the striker, no player of either team shall be within 5 yd of the ball when the push or hit is taken. If the striker hit at but miss the ball, provided that Rule 12 I (*c*) has not been contravened, the push or hit still has to be taken. After taking the push or hit, the striker shall not play the ball again nor remain or approach within playing distance of the ball until it has been touched or played by another player of either team.

(*b*) By a defender.

(i) When the ball, in the umpire's opinion, is sent over the goal-line by or off one of the defending team who is within his own 25 yd area, a push or hit shall be taken by the attacking team, unless a goal has been scored. The player shall push or hit the ball from a spot on the goal-line within 5 yd of the corner flag nearer to the point where the ball crossed the back-line. Other than the striker, no player of either team shall be within 5 yd of the ball when the push or hit is taken. If the striker hit at but miss the ball, provided that Rule 12 I (*c*) has not been contravened, the push or hit still has to be taken. After taking the push or hit, the striker shall not play the ball again nor remain or approach within playing distance of the ball until it has been touched or played by another player of either team.

(ii) When the ball, in the umpire's opinion, is sent over the back- or goal-line by or off one of the defending team who is more than 25 yd from the goal line, the game shall be re-started by a push or hit by one of the defending team from a spot opposite the place where it crossed the goal-line and not more than 16 yd from the inner edge of that line. Other than the striker, no player of either team shall be within 5 yd of the ball when the push or hit is taken. If the striker hit at but miss the ball, provided that Rule 12 I (*c*) has not been contravened, the push or hit still has to be taken. After taking the push or hit, the striker shall not play the ball again nor remain or approach within playing distance of the ball until it has been touched or played by another player of either team.

(iii) No player may deliberately play or deflect the ball over his own back- or goal-line from an area enclosed by the 25 yd line. Penalty: a penalty corner to the opposing team.

Penalties. 1. For a breach of this Rule by an attacker, a free hit shall be awarded to the defending team.

2. For an unintentional breach of this Rule by a defender, a free hit shall be awarded to the attacking team.

3. For a ball raised dangerously from a free hit within the circle by a defender, a penalty corner shall be awarded.

18. Accidents

(*a*) If a player, or an umpire, be incapacitated, the umpire, or other umpire, shall suspend the game temporarily noting the time lost (see Rule 3 (*f*). In either case, if a goal be scored before the game be stopped it shall be allowed if, in the opinion of the umpire, it would have been scored had the accident not occurred.

(*b*) The umpire shall re-start the game as soon as possible, by:

(i) a bully (subject to Rule 10(*d*) (iv) on a spot to be chosen by the umpire in whose half of the ground the accident occurred, or (ii) the appropriate penalty when the accident was the result of a breach of the rules, or (iii) the implementation of a decision given before the game was stopped.

(*c*) If the umpire concerned cannot continue, the other umpire shall re-start the game.

The Rules of
Ice Hockey

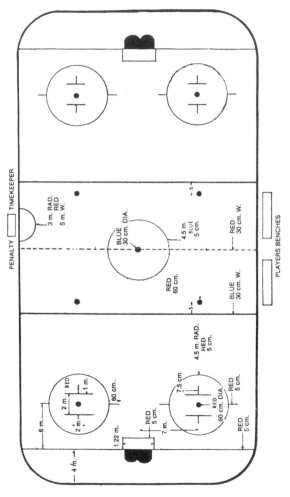

Refer to Rules 105, 106, 107 and 108.

Ice Hockey

I. THE RINK

101. Rink

The game of "Ice Hockey" shall be played on an ice surface known as a "RINK".

102. Dimensions of Rink

(*a*) The maximum size of the rink shall be 61 m. long and 30 m. wide with a minimum size of 56 m. long and 26 m. wide. The corners shall be rounded in the arc of a circle with a radius of 7 to 8.5 m.

NOTE 1*: *For the I.I.H.F. Championships the size of the rink shall be 60–61 m. long and 29–30 m. wide.*

NOTE 2: *In enclosed rinks, smoking shall be prohibited in the playing and spectator area.*

The rink shall be surrounded by a wooden or plastic wall or fence known as the "boards" which shall extend not less than 1.15 m. and not more than 1.22 m. in height above the level of the ice surface.

Except for the official markings provided for in these rules, the entire playing surface and the boards shall be white in colour.

(*b*)* The boards shall be constructed in such manner that the surface facing the ice shall be smooth and free of any obstruction or any object that could cause injury to players.

All doors giving access to the playing surface must swing away from the ice surface.

All protective screens and gear used to hold them in position shall be mounted on the boards on the side away from the playing surface.

It is recommended that above the boards of the rink there be:

* New or rule changes.

1. Protective glass 160–200 cm. in height on the ends between the goal lines and 80–100 cm. along the sides.
2. Nets at the ends behind the goals above the glass to protect the spectator.

For the I.I.H.F. Championships the protective glass is obligatory.

NOTE: *Under this rule, advertising may be placed on the boards provided specifications are approved and permission is given by the I.I.H.F. with regard to official international championships, and by the National Federations with regard to national games and international games in their territory.*

103. Goals

(*a*) 4.00 m. from each end of the rink and in the center of a red line 5 cm. wide drawn completely across the width of the ice and continued vertically up the side of the boards, regulation goal posts and nets shall be set in such manner as to remain stationary during the progress of a game.

(*b*) The goal posts shall be of approved design and material, extending vertically 1.22 m. above the surface of the ice and 1.83 m. apart, measured from the inside of the posts. A cross bar of the same material as the goal posts shall extend from the top of one post to the top of the other.

1. The inside measurement of the goal from the front of the goal line to the rear of the net, at its deepest point, shall not be more than 1 m. or less than 60 cm.
2. There shall be attached to the back of each goal frame a net which is constructed in such a manner as to keep the puck within the confines of the goal.

(*c*) The goal posts, cross bar and the exterior surface of other supporting framework for the goal shall be painted entirely in red. The surface of the base plate inside the goal and supports other than the goal posts shall be painted white.

(*d*) The red line, 5 cm. wide, between the goal posts on the ice and extended completely across the rink, shall be known as the "GOAL LINE".

(*e*) The goal area, enclosed by the goal line and the base of the goal, shall be painted white.

104. Goal Crease

(*a*) In front of each goal a "GOAL CREASE" area shall be marked by a red line 5 cm. in width.

(*b*) The goal crease shall be laid out as follows: 30 cm. from the outside of each goal post, lines 1.22 m. in length and 5 cm. in width shall be drawn at right angles to the goal line and the points of these lines farthest from the goal line shall be joined by another line, 5 cm. in width.

(*c*) The goal crease area shall include all the space outlined by the crease lines and extending vertically 1.22 m. to the level of the top of the goal frame.

105. Division of Ice Surface

(*a*) The ice area beteen the two goal lines shall be divided into three equal parts by lines 30 cm. in width and blue in colour, extending completely across the rink, parallel with the goal lines, and continuing vertically up the side of boards.

(*b*) That portion of the ice surface in which the goal is situated shall be called the "DEFENDING ZONE" of the team defending that goal; the central portions shall be known as the "NEUTRAL ZONE", and the portion farthest from the defending goal as the "ATTACKING ZONE". The zone line shall be considered part of the zone that the puck is in.

(*c*) There shall also be a line, known as the "CENTRE LINE", 30 cm. in width and red in colour, drawn completely across the rink in centre ice, parallel with the goal lines, continuing vertically up the side of the boards.

106. Centre Ice Spot and Circle

A circular blue spot, 30 cm. in diameter, shall be marked exactly in the centre of the rink; and with this spot as a centre, a circle of 4.5 m. radius shall be marked with a blue line 5 cm. in width.

107. Face-Off Spots in Neutral Zone

Two spots 60 cm. in diameter shall be marked with a red line 5 cm wide on the ice in the Neutral Zone 1.5 m. from each blue line, and the same distance from the boards as the end zone face-off spots. Within each face-off spot draw two parallel lines 7.5 cm. from the top and bottom of the spot. The area within the two lines shall be painted red, the remainder shall be painted white.

108. End Zones Face-Off Spots and Circles

(a)* Face-off spots and circles shall be marked on the ice in both end zones and on both sides of each goal. The face-off spots shall be 60 cm. in diameter and drawn with a red line 5 cm wide. Within each face-off spot draw two parallel lines 7.5 cm. from the top and bottom of the spot. The area within the two lines shall be painted red, the remainder shall be painted white. The circles shall have a radius of 4.5 m. from the centre of the face-off spots and marked with a red line 5 cm. wide. Extending from the outer edge of both sides of each face-off circle shall be two lines 5.5 m. and 6.5 m. from and parallel to the goal line, 60 cm. long and 5 cm. wide.

(b) The location of the face-off spots shall be fixed in the following manner.

Establish the imaginary point 6 m. directly in front of the centre of each goal. 7 m. on each side of this point, parallel to and 6 m. from the goal line, shall be the centre of the end zone face-off spots.

NOTE: *On open air rinks all the lines and spots fixed in Rules 105, 106, 107 and 108 may be marked by two lines or circles in the prescribed distance.*

109. Players' Benches

(a) Each rink shall be provided with seats or benches for the use of both teams, and the accommodations provided including benches and doors shall be uniform for both teams. Such seats or benches shall have accommodation for at least 14 persons of each team and shall be placed immediately alongside the ice, in the Neutral Zone, as near to the centre of the rink as possible, and convenient to the dressing rooms.

The players' benches should be on the same side of the playing surface opposite the penalty bench and should be separated by a substantial distance.

Where physically possible, each players' bench shall have two doors opening the the Neutral Zone, and all doors opening to the playing surface shall be constructed so that they swing inward.

(*b*) None but players in uniform, and not more than six team officials, shall be permitted to occupy the players bench area so provided.

(*c*) For the choice of players' benches, see Section B under Rule 632, Start of Game and Periods.

110. Penalty Bench

(*a*) Each rink must be provided with benches or seats to be known as the "PENALTY BENCH". It is preferable to have separate penalty benches for each team separated from each other and substantially separated from either players' bench. The penalty bench(es) must be situated opposite the Neutral Zone.

(*b*) A semi-circle, 3 m. in radius, to be known as the "REFEREES' CREASE", shall be marked on the ice by a line 5 cm. wide immediately in front of the Penalty Time keeper.

111. Signal and Timing Devices

(*a*) Each rink shall be provided with a siren, or other suitable sound device, for the use of Timekeepers.

(*b*) Each rink shall have some form of electrical clock for the purpose of keeping the specatators, players and game officials accurately informed as to all time elements at all stages of the game, including the time played in any period and the time remaining to be served by at least two penalised players on each team.

NOTE: *In the I.I.H.F. championships the time of the periods shall be counted up, from 0 to 20, and the time of the penalties down from the total minutes imposed to zero.*

(*c*) Behind each goal there shall be electrical lights for the use of the Goal Judges. A red light shall signify the scoring of a goal. Where automatic lights are available, a green light will signify the end of a period only.

NOTE: *The purpose of the green light is to enable the referee and linesmen to observe the goal and light in the same sight line and know exactly when the period ends.*

The red light shall be connected to the timing device in such a manner so that when the period has ended it will not be possible for the goal judge to put it on. However, the fact that the goal judge may not be able to put on the red light does not necessarily mean that the goal is not valid. The determining factor is whether or not the puck is completely over the goal line and in the goal before the period ends.

112. Dressing Rooms and Rink Lighting

(*a*) Each rink shall provide a suitable room, equipped with sanitary toilet and shower suitable for twenty-five persons with equipment, for the use of the visiting team.

(*b*) A separate dressing room equipped with sanitary toilet and shower shall be provided for the use of the Referees and Linesmen.

(*c*) No officer, Manager, player or employee of any team may enter into an acrimonious discussion with any Referee or Linesmen, during or after a game and no person, except as authorised by the Federation concerned, shall be allowed to enter the Referees' dressing room during the course of, or immediately following a game. For any infraction of this rule the matter shall be reported by the Referee to the Proper Authorities for further action.

(*d*) All rinks shall be sufficiently well lighted so that the players and spectators may conveniently follow play at all times.

NOTE: *If, in the opinion of the Referee, there is not sufficient light to continue the game, the Referee shall have the authority to postpone the remainder of the game or take time out pending the necessary improvement to the lights. If one team is being handicapped to a greater extent by failure of lights and in the opinion of the Referee the game should not be cancelled, he shall have the authority to alternate the teams so as each team will play the same amount of time in each end of the rink.*

II. TEAMS

201. Composition of Teams

(*a*) A team shall not have more than six players on the ice at any one time while the play is in progress. These six players shall be designated as follows: Goalkeeper, Right Defence, Left Defence, Centre, Right Wing and Left Wing.

(*b*) If at any time a team has more than six players on the ice, or the number to which they are entitled by reason of penalties, during the progress of play, they shall be assessed a bench minor penalty.

202. Captain of Team

(*a*) One captain shall be appointed by each team, and he alone shall have the privilege of discussing with the Referee any questions relating to interpretation of rules which may arise during the progress of a game. He shall wear the letter "C", approximately 8 cm. in height and in contrasting colour, in a conspicuous position on the front of his sweater. If the letter "C" is not worn, the privileges under this section will not be allowed.

If the Captain is not available due to injury or an imposed penalty, another player who was designated on the score sheet prior to the start of the game may act as Captain.

(*b*) The Referee and Official Scorer shall be advised prior to the start of each game, the name of the Captain of the team and the designated substitute (see (*a*) of this rule).

(*c*) No goalkeepers shall be entitled to exercise the privileges of Captain.

(*d*) Only the Captain shall have the privilege of discussing with the Referee any point relating to the interpretation of rules. Any other player who comes off the bench and makes any protest or intervention with the Officials for any purpose shall be assessed a misconduct penalty in addition to a minor penalty under Rule 601 (a), Abuse of Officials.

A complaint about a penalty is NOT a matter "relating to the interpretation of the rules" and a minor penalty under Rule 601 (a), Abuse of Officials, shall be imposed against any Captain or other player making such a complaint.

(*e*) No playing Coach or playing Manager shall be permitted to act as Captain.

203. Players in Uniform

(*a*) At the beginning of each game the Manager or Coach of each team shall list the players and goalkeepers who shall be eligible to play in the game. A maximum of eighteen players, plus two goalkeepers, shall be permitted.

(*b*) Each player shall wear an individual number at least 25 cm. in height on the back of his sweater.

All players of each team shall be dressed uniformly in colour of their helmet, sweaters, pants and stockings. Any player not complying with his provision shall not be permitted to participate in the game.

(*c*) A list of names and numbers of all eligible players and goalkeepers shall be handed to the Referee or Official Scorer before the game, and no change in the list or addition thereto shall be permitted after the commencement of the game.

(*d*) Each team shall be allowed one goalkeeper on the ice at one time. The goalkeeper may be removed and another "player" substituted. Such "player" substitute shall not be permitted the privileges of the goalkeeper.

(*e*) Each team shall have on its bench, or on a chair immediately beside the bench, a substitute goalkeeper who shall at all times be fully dressed and equipped ready to play.

Note*: *This rule may be modified by National Federations for games under their jurisdiction.*

The substitute goalkeeper may enter the game at any time following a stoppage of play, but no warm-up shall be permitted (scc Rule 205, Change of Players).

(*f*) Except when both goalkeepers are incapacitated, no player on the playing roster in that game shall be permitted to wear the equipment of the goalkeeper.

(*g*) In all games, where in the opinion of the Referee, the colours of the competing teams are so much alike that there is a possibility of a miscall by the Referee or Linesmen, it is the responsibility of the home team to change its sweaters if the Referee so orders.

204. Starting Line-up

(*a*) Prior to the start of the game, at the request of the Referee, the Manager or Coach of the visiting team is required to name the starting line-up to the Referee or the Official Scorer. At any time in the game, at the request of the Referee, made to the Captain, the visiting team must place a playing line-up on the ice and promptly commence play.

NOTE: *If in competition, the name of the home team has not been established, the competing teams will decide who is to be the home team by mutual agreement, that is, by the flip of a coin or some similar method.*

(*b*) Prior to the start of the game the Manager or Coach of the home team, having been advised by the Official Scorer or the Referee of the names of the starting line-up of the visiting team, shall name the starting line-up of the home team, which information shall be conveyed by the Official Scorer or the Referee to the Coach of the visiting team.

(*c*) No change in the starting line-up of either team, as given to the Referee or Official Scorer, or in the playing line-up on the ice, shall be made until the game is actually in progress. For an infraction of this rule, a bench minor penalty shall be imposed upon the offending team, provided such infraction is called to the attention of the Referee by the Captain of the opposing team before the second face-off in the first period takes place.

(*d*) Following a stoppage of play, the visiting team shall promptly place a line-up on the ice ready for play and no substitution shall be made from that time until play has been resumed. The home team may then make any desired substitution which does not result in the delay of the game.

If there is any undue delay by either team in changing lines, the Referee shall order the offending team or teams to take their positions immediately and not permit a line change.

NOTE: *In the application of this rule, the change of one or more player(s) shall constitute a line change.*

205. Change of Players

(*a*) Players may be changed at any time from the players'

bench, provided that the player or players leaving the ice shall always be at the players' bench and out of the play before any change is made.

A goalkeeper may be changed for another player at any time under the conditions set out in this section.

NOTE 1: *When a goalkeeper leaves his goal area and proceeds to his players' bench for the purpose of substituting another player, the rear Linesman shall be responsible to see that the substitution made is not by reason of the premature departure of the substitute from the bench (before the goalkeeper is within 3 m. of the bench). If the substitution is made prematurely, the Linesman shall stop the play immediately by blowing his whistle, unless the non-offending team has possession of the puck, in which event the stoppage will be delayed until the puck changes hands. There shall be no time penalty to the team making the premature substitution, but the resulting face-off will take place on the centre "face-off-spot".*

The Referee shall request that the public address announcer make the following announcement: "Play has been stopped due to premature entry of a player from the players' bench."

NOTE 2: *If, in the course of making a substitution, the player entering the game plays the puck with the stick, skates or hands or checks or makes any physical contact with an opposing player while the retiring player is actually on the ice, then the infraction of "too many men on the ice" will be called.*

If, in the course of a substitution, either the player entering the play or the player retiring is struck by the puck accidentally, the play will not be stopped and no penalty will be assessed.

(*b*) If, in the last two minutes of the game, a bench minor penalty is imposed for deliberate illegal substitution (too many men on the ice), a Penalty Shot shall be awarded against the offending team. The bench minor will not be served (see Rule 406 (d), Penalty Shot).

(*c*) A player serving a penalty on the penalty bench, who is to be changed after the penalty has been served, must proceed at once, by way of the ice, and be at his own players' bench before any change can be made.

For any violation of this rule, a bench minor penalty shall be imposed.

(*d*) When a substitution for the goalkeeper has been made during a stoppage of play, the goalkeeper who left the game may not reenter the game until the first stoppage of play thereafter.

There shall be no warm-up for any substitute goalkeeper. For violation of this rule a minor penalty shall be assessed to the goalkeeper returning to the game illegally.

206. Injured Players

(*a*) When a player, other than a goalkeeper, is injured or compelled to leave the ice during the game, he may retire from the game and be replaced by a substitute, but play must continue without the teams leaving the ice.

(*b*) If a goalkeeper sustains an injury or becomes ill, he must be ready to rcsume play immediately or be replaced by a substitute goalkeeper and no additional time shall be allowed by the Referees for the purpose of enabling the injured or ill goalkeeper to resume play (see also Section "d").

If both goalkeepers of the team are incapacitated and unable to play, the team shall have 10 minutes to prepare and dress another player in uniform to act as the goalkeeper. In this case, neither of the two regular goalkeepers may return to that game.

(*c*) The substitute goalkeeper shall be subject to the regular rules governing goalkeepers and shall be entitled to the same privileges.

(*d*) If a penalized player has been injured, he may proceed to the dressing room without the necessity of taking a seat on the penalty bench. If the injured player receives a minor, major or match penalty, the penalized team shall immediately put a substitute player on the penalty bench who shall serve the penalty without change. For violation of this rule, a bench minor penalty shall be imposed.

The penalized player who has been injured and been replaced on the penalty bench shall not be eligible to play until his penalty has expired.

(*e*) When a player is injured so that he cannot continue play or go to his bench, the play shall not be stopped until the injured player's team has secured possession of the puck. If the player's team is in possession of the puck at the time of injury, play shall be stopped immediately, unless his team is in a scoring position.

NOTE: *In the case where it is obvious that a player has sustained a serious injury, the Referee and/or Linesmen may stop the play immediately.*

III. EQUIPMENT

NOTE 1*: *Advertising or brand identification may be placed on the equipment provided specifications are approved and permission given by the I.I.H.F. for its Championships and the National Federations for their national and other international games.*

NOTE 2*: *Measurement of equipment. When a formal complaint is made by the Captain of a team against the dimensions of any equipment, the Referee shall make the necessary measurement immediately, except that no measurement shall be allowed during the stoppage of play following a goal being scored.*

If the complaint is not sustained, a bench minor penalty shall be imposed on the team requesting the measurement.

A request for measurement of any equipment covered by this section shall be limited to one request by each team during the course of any stoppage of play.

The Referee may, at his own discretion, measure any equipment.

301. Sticks

(*a*) The sticks shall be made of wood or other material approved by the I.I.H.F. such as aluminium or plastic and must not have any projections. Adhesive tape of any colour may be wrapped around the stick at any place.

(*b*) No stick shall exceed 147 cm. in length, from the heel to the end of the shaft, nor more than 32 cm. from the heel to the end of the blade.

The blade of the stick shall not be more than 7.5 cm. and less than 5 cm. in width at any point.

All edges of the blade shall bevelled.

The curvature of the blade of the stick shall be restricted in such a way that the distance of a perpendicular line measured from a straight line drawn from any point at the heel to the end of the blade to the point of maximum curvature shall not exceed 1.5 cm.

(*c*) The blade of the goalkeeper's stick shall not exceed 9 cm. in width at any point, except at the heel where it must not exceed 11.5 cm. in width, nor shall the goalkeeper's stick exceed 39 cm. in length from the heel to the end of the blade.

The widened portion of the goalkeeper's stick extending up the shaft from the blade shall not extend more than 71 cm. from the heel and shall not exceed 9 cm. in width.

(*d*) A minor penalty shall be imposed on any player or goalkeeper who uses a stick not conforming to the provisions of this rule.

NOTE: *A player who participates in the play while taking a replacement stick to his goalkeeper shall incur a minor penalty under this rule.*

(*e*)* A minor penalty plus a misconduct penalty shall be imposed on any player who refused to surrender his stick for measurement when requested to do so by the Referee.

302. Skates

(*a*) All skates (except goalkeepers) shall be equipped with safety heel tips.

When the Referee becomes aware that any person is wearing a skate on which the protective heel tip is missing or broken, he shall direct its replacement at the next intermission between periods. If such replacement is not carried out and the player re-enters the game, the Referee shall assess a minor penalty to the offending player.

(*b*) The use of speed skates or fancy skates or any skate so designed that it may cause injury is prohibited.

303. Goalkeeper's Equipment

(*a*) With the exception of skates and stick, all the

equipment worn by the goalkeeper must be constructed solely for the purpose of protection of head or body, and must not include any garment or contrivance which would give the goalkeeper undue assistance in keeping goal.

NOTE: *Cages on gloves and abdominal aprons extending down the front of the thighs on the outside of the pants are prohibited. A "Cage" shall mean any lacing, or webbing or other material in the goalkeeper's glove, joining the thumb and index fingers which is in excess of the minimum necessary to fill the gap when the goalkeeper's thumb and forefinger in the glove are fully extended and spread, and includes any pocket or pouch effect produced by excess lacing or webbing or other material between the thumb and forefinger when fully extended. Protective padding attached to the back or forming part of a goalkeeper's gloves shall not exceed 20.3 cm. in width nor more than 40.6 in length, at any point.*

(*b*) The leg guards worn by goalkeepers shall not exceed 25 cm. in extreme width when on the legs of the goalkeeper. No further expansion than one-tenth (2.5 cm.) shall be permitted for any leg guards used by goalkeepers.

(*c*) A minor penalty shall be imposed on a goalkeeper guilty of using or wearing illegal equipment.

304. Protective Equipment

(*a*) All protective equipment, except gloves, headgear or goalkeeper's leg guards, must be worn ENTIRELY under the uniform. For violation of this rule, after one warning by the Referee, a minor penalty shall be imposed on the offending player.

(*b*)* All players including goalkeepers, must wear a hockey helmet, with chin-strap properly fastened.

(*c*) All goalkeepers must wear a goalkeeper's full facemask.

(*d*)* Full face-masks shall be worn in all I.I.H.F. sanctioned games and tournaments in classifications of 20 years and younger. It is recommended that all senior players also wear full face-masks.

(*e*)* Full face-masks must be constructed in such a way that neither the puck nor the stick blade might get through it.

NOTE: *National Federations are authorised, at their discretion, to make the wearing of headgear compulsory for Referees and Linesmen.*

305. Dangerous Equipment

(*a*) The use of pads or protectors, made of metal or any other material likely to cause injury to a player, is prohibited.

NOTE*: *The Referee has the authority to prohibit a player from participating in the game while using or wearing any equipment that he considers dangerous to a player or game official.*

(*b*) A glove from which all or part of the palm has been intentionally removed or cut to permit the use of the bare hand shall be considered illegal equipment and if any player wears such a glove in play, a minor penalty shall be imposed.

306. Puck

The puck shall be made of vulcanized rubber or other approved material, 2.54 cm. thick and 7.62 cm. in diameter, and be primarily black in colour. The puck shall weigh not less than 156 gms. nor more than 170 gms.

IV. PENALTIES

401. Penalties

Penalties shall be actual playing time and shall be divided into the following classes:

(1) Minor Penalties
(2) Bench Minor Penalties
(3) Major Penalties
(4) Misconduct Penalties
(5) Match Penalties
(6) Penalty Shot

Where coincident penalties are imposed on players of both teams, the penalised players of the visiting team shall take their positions on the penalty bench first in the place designated for visiting players, or where there is no special designation, then on the bench farthest from the gate.

When penalties are imposed after the conclusion of any game and until the players have left the ice, such penalties shall be reported to the Proper Authorities by the Referees on the Official Game Report.

In cases when any rule states that the Manager or Coach shall designate a player to serve any penalty and if the Manager or Coach refuses to name a player, the Referee shall have the authority to name any player of the offending team that he desires to serve the penalty.

402. Minor Penalties

(*a*) For a "MINOR PENALTY", any player, other than a goalkeeper, shall be ruled off the ice for two minutes during which time no substitute shall be permitted.

(*b*) A "BENCH MINOR" penalty involves the removal from the ice of one player of the team against which the penalty is imposed for a period of two minutes. Any player, except the goalkeeper of the team, may be designated to serve the penalty by the Manager or the Coach, through the Captain, and such player shall take his place on the penalty bench promptly and serve the penalty as if it was a minor penalty imposed on him.

(*c*) If, while a team is "short-handed" by one or more minor or bench minor penalties, the opposing team scores a goal, one of such penalties shall automatically terminate.

NOTE 1: *"Short-handed" means that the team must be below the numerical strength of its opponents on the ice at the time the goal is scored. The minor or bench minor penalty which terminates automatically is the one which causes the team scored against to be "short-handed". Thus, an equal number of penalties to an equal number of players of both teams does not cause either team to be "short-handed".*

This rule shall also apply when a goal is scored on a penalty shot.

When the minor penalties of two players of the same team terminate at the same time, the Captain of that team shall designate to the Referee which of such players will return to the ice first and the Referee will instruct the Penalty Timekeeper accordingly.

When a player receives a major penalty and a minor penalty at the same time, the major penalty shall be served first by the penalised player.

NOTE 2: *This applies where BOTH penalties are imposed on the SAME player (see also Note to Rule 408, Delayed Penalties).*

403. Major Penalties

(*a*) For the first "MAJOR PENALTY" in any one game, except to the goalkeeper, the offender shall be ruled off the ice for five minutes, during which time no sbustitute shall be permitted.

(*b*) For the second major penalty in the same game, to the same player, he shall be ruled off the ice for the balance of the playing time, but a substitute shall be permitted to replace the player so suspended after five minutes shall have elapsed. (Major penalty plus game misconduct penalty.)

404. Misconduct Penalties

(*a*) A "MISCONDUCT PENALTY" to any player, except the goalkeepers, involves removal from the game for a period of ten minutes. A substitute player is permitted to replace, immediately, a player serving a misconduct penalty. A player whose misconduct penalty has expired shall remain in the penalty bench until the next stoppage of play.

When a player receives a minor or major penalty and a misconduct penalty at the same time, the penalized team shall immediately put a substitute player on the penalty bench and he shall serve the minor or major penalty without change.

Any player receiving two misconduct penalties in one game shall automatically be assessed a game misconduct.

(*b*) A "GAME MISCONDUCT" penalty involves removal for the balance of the game and the offender shall be ordered to the dressing room for the remainder of the game, but a substitute shall be permitted immediately.

NOTE: *A "game misconduct" penalty does not incur automatic suspension, except for that game, but such penalties shall be reported by the Referee to the proper authorities immediately following the game. This authority shall have the power to increase the suspension period.*

(*c*) A "GROSS MISCONDUCT" penalty involves the suspension of a player or team official for the balance of the game.

Any player or team official incurring a gross misconduct penalty shall be suspended from participating in any further games until his case has been dealt with by the proper authorities.

NOTE: *For game misconduct or gross misconduct penalties, regardless of when imposed, a total of ten minutes shall be charged in the records against the player.*

405. Match Penalties

(*a*) A "MATCH" penalty involves the suspension of a player for the balance of the game, and the offender shall be ordered to the dressing room immediately. A substitute player is permitted to replace the penalized player after five minutes playing time has elapsed.

For all match penalties, regardless of when imposed, a total of ten minutes shall be charged in the records against the offending player.

(*b*) A player incurring a match penalty shall be suspended from playing in any further games until his case has been dealt with by the proper authorities.

NOTE 1: *The Referee is required to report all match penalties and the surrounding circumstances to the proper authorities immediately following the game in which they occur.*

NOTE 2: *If any player is assessed a match or gross misconduct penalty in any I.I.H.F. sanctioned game or tournament, the Organizing Committee shall notify his National Federation immediately by telex or cable and forward the Referee's Report as quickly as possible.*

406. Penalty Shot

(*a*) When there is an infraction of the rules that calls for a penalty shot not involving a major, misconduct, game misconduct, or match penalty, the non-offending team shall be given the option of accepting the penalty shot or having a minor penalty assessed to the offending player. If, however, a major, misconduct, game misconduct, or match penalty is incurred with the penalty shot, the shot shall be awarded and the penalty for the prescribed infraction shall be assessed.

(b) Any infraction of the rules which calls for a "PENALTY SHOT" shall be taken as follows:

The Referee shall cause to be announced over the public address system the name of the player designated by him or selected by the team entitled to take the shot (as appropriate). He shall then place the puck on the centre face-off spot and the player taking the shot will on the instruction of the Referee, play the puck from there and shall attempt to score on the goalkeeper. Once the player taking the shot has possession of the puck, he may make one circle in his defensive zone after which he must proceed toward his opponent's goal line, and once the puck is shot, the play shall be considered complete. No goal can be scored by a second shot of any kind, and any time the puck crosses the goal line the shot shall be considered complete.

Only a player designated as a goalkeeper or alternate goalkeeper may defend against the penalty shot.

(c) The goalkeeper must remain in his crease until the player taking the penalty shot has touched the puck, and in the event of violation of this rule or any foul committed by the goalkeeper, the Referee shall allow the shot to be completed, signaling such violation by raising his arm, and if the shot fails, he shall permit the penalty shot to be taken over again.

The goalkeeper may attempt to stop the shot in any manner except by throwing his stick or any other object, in which case a goal shall be awarded.

NOTE: *See Rule 633, Throwing Stick*

(d) In cases where a penalty shot has been awarded under:

Rule 608 (c), Deliberately displacing the goal during a breakaway, or

Rule 617 (c) Hooking from behind or

Rule 619 (e) Interference or

Rule 623 (i) Illegal entry into the game or

Rule 633 (a) Throwin stick or

Rule 636 (b) Tripping from behind . . .

the Referee shall designate the player who has been fouled as the player who shall take the penalty shot. In cases where a penalty shot has been awarded under:

Rule 205 (*b*) Deliberate illegal substitution with 2 minutes or less remaining in the game or

Rule 608 (*c*) Deliberately displacing the goal in the last two minutes of the game or

Rule 611 (*c*) Falling on the puck in the crease or

Rule 614 (*d*) Picking up the puck from the crease . . .

the penalty shot shall be taken by a player selected by the Captain of the non-offending team from the players on the ice at the time when the foul was committed. Such selection shall be reported to the Referee and cannot be changed.

If, by reason of injury, the player designated by the Referee to take the penalty shot is unable to do so within a reasonable time, the shot may be taken by a player selected by the Captain of the non-offending team from the players on the ice when the foul was committed. Such selection shall be reported to the Referee and cannot be changed.

(*e*) Should the player, to whom a penalty shot has been awarded, himself commit a foul in connection with the same play or circumstances, either before or after the penalty shot penalty has been awarded, be designated to take the shot, he shall first be permitted to do so before being sent to the penalty bench to serve the penalty, except when such a penalty is for a game misconduct, gross misconduct, or match penalty, in which case the penalty shot shall be taken by a player selected by the Captain of the non-offending team from the players on the ice at the time when the foul was committed.

If, at the time, a penalty shot is awarded, the goalkeeper of the penalized team has been removed from the ice and substituted for by another player, including the substitute goalkeeper, the goalkeeper shall be permitted to return to the ice before the penalty shot is taken.

(*f*) While the penalty shot is being taken, players of both sides shall withdraw to the sides of the rink and behind the centre red line.

(*g*) If, while the penalty shot is being taken, any player of the opposing team shall have by some action interfered with or distracted the player taking the shot and, because of such action, the shot should have failed, a second attempt shall be permitted and the Referee shall impose a misconduct penalty on the player so interfering or distracting.

(*h*) If a goal is scored from a penalty shot, the puck shall be faced at centre ice in the usual way. If a goal is not scored, the puck shall be faced at either of the end face-off spots in the zone in which the penalty shot has been attempted.

(*i*) Should a goal be scored from a penalty shot, a further penalty to the offending player shall not be assessed unless the offense for which the penalty shot was awarded was such as to incur a major, misconduct, game misconduct, match or gross misconduct penalty, in which case the penalty pre-scribed for the particular offense shall be served.

If the offense for which the penalty shot was awarded was such as would normally incur a minor penalty then regardless of whether the penalty shot results in a goal or not, the minor penalty shall not be served.

(*j*) If the foul upon which the penalty shot is based occurs during actual playing time, the penalty shot shall be awarded and taken immediately in the usual manner, notwithstanding any delay occasioned by a slow whistle by the Referee to permit the play to be completed which delay results in the expiry of the regular playing time in any period.

The time required for the taking of a penalty shot shall not be included in the regular playing time or any overtime.

407. Goalkeeper's Penalties

(*a*) A goalkeeper shall not be sent to the penalty bench for an offense which results in a minor, major or misconduct penalty, but instead the penalty shall be served by another member of his own team who was on the ice when the offence was committed, said player to be designated by the Manager or Coach of the offending team, through the Captain, and such substitute shall not be changed.

(*b*) Should a goalkeeper incur two major penalties in one game, he shall also receive a game misconduct penalty.

(*c*) Should a goalkeeper incur a game misconduct penalty,

his place shall be taken by the substitute goalkeeper, if available, otherwise by a member of his team, who shall be permitted 10 minutes to dress in the goalkeeper's full equipment.

(*d*) Should a goalkeeper incur a match penalty, his place shall then be taken by the substitute goalkeeper, if available otherwise by a member of his team, and such player will be allowed the goalkeeper's equipment. However, any additional penalties as specifically called for by the individual rules covering match penalties will apply, and the offending team shall be penalized accordingly. Such additional penalty shall be served by another member of the team on the ice at the time the offence was committed, said player to be designated by the Manager or Coach of the offending team through the Captain.

(*e*) A minor penalty shall be imposed on a goalkeeper who leaves the immediate vicinity of his crease during an altercation.

NOTE: *All penalties imposed on a goalkeeper, regardless of who serves the penalty, shall be charged in the records against the goalkeeper.*

(*f*) If a goalkeeper participates in the play in any manner when he is beyond the centre red line, he shall be assessed a minor penalty.

408. Delayed Penalties

(*a*) If a third player of any team is penalized while two players of the same team are serving penalties, the penalty time of the third player shall not commence until the penalty time of one of the two players already penalized shall have elapsed. Nevertheless, the third player penalized shall at once proceed to the penalty bench, but may be replaced on the ice by a substitute, until such time as the penalty time of the penalized player shall commence.

(*b*) When any team has three or more players serving penalties at the same time and because of the delayed penalty rule, a substitute for the third offender on the ice, none of the three penalized players on the penalty bench may return to the ice until play has been stopped unless by reason of the expiration of penalties, the penalized team is entitled to have more than four players, including the goalkeeper, on the ice in which case the penalized player shall be permitted to return in the order of the expiry of their penalties. Otherwise, when play is stopped the player(s) whose penalty has expired may return to the game.

(*c*) If the penalties of two players of the same team will expire at the same time, the Captain of the team will designate to the Referee which of such players will return to the ice first and the Referee will instruct the Penalty Timekeeper accordingly.

(*d*) When a major and a minor penalty are imposed at the same time on two or more players of the same team, the Penalty Timekeeper shall record the minor as being the first of such penalties.

NOTE: *This applies to the case where the two penalties are imposed on* DIFFERENT *players of the same team. See also Note 2 to Rule 402, Minor Penalties.*

409. Calling of Penalties

(*a*) Should an infraction of the rules which would call for a penalty be committed by a player of the side in possession of the puck, the Referee shall immediately blow his whistle and assess the penalty to the offending player. The resulting face-off shall be made at the place where the play was stopped, unless the stoppage occurs in the Attacking Zone of the player penalized, in which case the face-off shall be made at the nearest face-off spot in the Neutral Zone.

(*b*) Should an infraction of the rules, which would call for a penalty, be committed by a player of team NOT in possession of the puck, the Referee shall signify the calling of a penalty by raising his arm and, upon completion of the play (as defined in Note 2 below) by the team in possession, will immediately blow his whistle and give the penalty to the offending player.

NOTE 1: *The subsequent face-off shall be made at the place where the play was stopped, unless during the period of a delayed whistle due to a foul by a player of the side* NOT *in possession, the side in possession ices the puck, shoots the puck from its defensive zone so that it goes out of bounds or is unplayable, then the face-off following the stoppage shall take place in the Neutral Zone near the Defending Blue line of the team shooting the puck.*

If the penalty or penalties to be imposed are minor penalties, and a goal is scored on the play by the non-offending team, the first minor penalty shall not be imposed, but all other minor, major or match penalties shall be imposed in the normal manner.

NOTE 2: *"Completion of the play by the team in possession" in this rule means that the puck must have come into the possession and control of or intentionally directed by an opposing player or goalkeeper, or has been "frozen". This does not mean a rebound off the goalkeeper, the goal or the boards, or any accidental contact with the body or equipment of an opposing player.*

NOTE 3: *If after the Referee has signalled a penalty, but before the whistle has been blown, the puck shall enter the goal of the non-offending team as the direct result of the action of a player of that team, the goal shall be allowed and the penalty signalled shall be imposed in the normal manner.*

If, when a team is "short-handed" by reason of one or more minor or bench minor penalties, the Referee signals a further minor penalty or penalties against the "short-handed" team a a goal is scored by the non-offending team before the whistle is blown, then the goal shall be allowed, the penalty signalled shall be waived and one of the minor penalties already being served shall automatically terminate under Rule 402, Minor Penalties.

(*c*) Should the same offending player commit other fouls on the same play, either before or after the Referee has blown his whistle, the offending player shall serve such penalties consecutively.

(*d*) If any fouls are committed after the play has been stopped, the offending players shall be penalized as though play were actually in progress.

410. Supplementary Discipline

In addition to the suspensions imposed under these rules, the proper disciplinary authority may, at any time after conclusion of the game, at their discretion investigate any incident that occurs in connection with any game, and may, if done before the next game of the offending team, assess additional suspensions for any offence committed during the course of a game or any aftermath thereof by a player or team official, whether or not such offence has been penalized by the Referee.

V. OFFICIALS

501. Appointment of Officials

For all International matches there shall be appointed one Referee and two Linesmen, one Game Timekeeper, one Penalty Timekeeper, one Official Scorer and two Goal Judges for each game.

National Federations have the authority to use the Two Referee system in games which are completely under their jurisdiction.

Rule 502. Referee

(*a*) The Referee shall have general supervision of the game, and shall have full control of game officials and players during the game, including stoppages; and in case of any dispute, his decision shall be final. The Referee shall remain on the ice at the conclusion of each period until all players have proceeded to their dressing rooms.

(*b*) All Referees and Linesmen shall be garbed in black trousers and official sweaters.

They shall be equipped with approved whistles and metal tape measures with minimum length of 2 m.

(*c*) The Referee shall order the teams on the ice at the appointed time for the beginning of a game, and at the commencement of each period. If for any reason there be more than fifteen minutes' delay in the commencement of the game or any undue delay in resuming play after the fifteen-minute interval between periods, the Referee shall state in his report to the proper authorities the cause of the delay and the team or teams which were at fault.

(*d*) The Referee may, at his own discretion, measure any equipment. The Referee shall check or measure the equipment worn by any player when requested to do so by the Captain of either team.

(*e*) The Referee shall, before starting the game, see that the appointed Game Timekeeper, Penalty Timekeeper, Official Scorer and Goal Judges are in their respective places, and satisfy himself that the timing and signalling equipment are in order.

(*f*) It shall be his duty to impose such penalties as are prescribed by the rules for infractions thereof, and to give the final decision in matters of disputed goals. The Referee, in matters of disputed goals, may consult with the Linesmen or Goal Judge before making his decision.

(*g*) The Referee shall announce to the Penalty Timekeeper all penalties, and for what such penalties are imposed. The infraction of the rules for which each penalty has been imposed will be announced correctly, as reported by the Referee, over the public address system. Where players of both teams are penalized on the same play, the penalty to the visiting player will be announced first.

(*h*) The Referee shall report to the Official Scorer the name or number of the goal scorer and any players entitled to assists. (In I.I.H.F. "A" Pool Championships, assists will be determined by the Official Scorer.)

NOTE: *The name of the scorer and any player entitled to an assist will be announced on the public address system.*

The Referee shall cause to be announced over the public address system the reason for not allowing a goal whenever the goal signal light is turned on in the course of play. This shall be done at the first stoppage of play regardless of any standard signal given by the Referee when the goal signal light was put on in error.

(*i*) The Referee shall see to it that players of opposing teams are separated on the penalty bench to prevent feuding.

(*j*) Should a Referee accidentally leave the ice or receive an injury which incapacitates him from discharging his duties while play is in progress, the game shall be stopped immediately by the Linesman, unless one of the teams has the puck in a scoring position, in which case the play shall be allowed to be completed. If it is obvious that the injury sustained is of a serious nature, play shall be stopped immediately.

(k) If, through misadventure or sickness, the Referees or Linesmen appointed are prevented from appearing, the team leaders of the two teams shall agree on a Referee or Linesmen. If they are unable to agree, the Proper Authorities shall appoint the Officials.

If the regularly appointed officials appear during the progress of the game, they shall at once replace the temporary officials.

(l) Should a Linesman appointed be unable to act at the last minute or through sickness or accident be unable to finish the game, the Refcree shall have the power to appoint a replacement, if he deems it necessary.

(m) If, owing to illness or accident, the Referee is unable to continue to officiate, one of the Linesmen shall perform such duties of the Referee during the balance of the game, the Linesman to be selected by the Referee, or, if necessary, by the team leaders of the competing teams.

(n) The Referee shall secure, from the Official Scorer, the Game Report immediately following each game. He shall sign and check this report and return same to the Official Scorer.

(o) The Referee is required to report on the Official Game Report all game misconducts, gross misconducts, and match penalties immediately following the game involved giving full details to the Proper Authorities concerned.

503. Linesman

(a) The duty of the Linesman is to determine any infractions of the rules concerning:

Off-side – Rule 624, Off-side

Off-side Pass – Rule 625, Passes

Icing – Rule 618, Icing the Puck

He shall stop the play when the puck

– goes out of playing area – Rule 626 (a), Puck Out of Bounds or Unplayable

- when it is interfered with by an ineligible person – Rule 620, Interference by Spectators
- when it is struck with the stick above the height of the shoulder – Rule 615 (*d*), High Sticks
- when the goal post has been displaced from its normal position – Rule 608, Delaying the Game

He shall stop the play
- for off-sides occuring on face-off circles – Rule 610, Face-Offs
- when there has been a premature substitution for a goalkeeper – Rule 205, Change of Players
- for injured player(s) – Rule 206, Injured Players
- interference by specatators – Rule 620, Interference by Spectators.

(*b*) He shall conduct the face-off at all times, except at the start of the game, at the beginning of each period and after a goal has been scored.

The Referee may call upon a linesman to conduct a face-off at any time.

(*c*) He shall, when requested to do so by the Referee, give his version of any incident that may have taken place during the playing of the game.

(*d*) He shall not stop play to impose any penalty except for violations of
- too many men on the ice – Rule 201 (*b*), Composition of Teams
- articles thrown on the ice from vicinity of the players' or penalty bench – Rule 601 (*j*), Abuse of Officials and other Misconduct
- stick thrown onto the ice from the players' or penalty bench – Rule 605, Broken Stick

and he shall report such violations to the Referee who shall impose a bench minor penalty against the offending team.

He shall report immediately to the Referee his version of the circumstances with respect to deliberately displacing the goal post from its normal position – Rule 608, Delaying the Game.

He shall report immediately to the Referee his version of any infraction of the rules constituting a bench minor penalty, a major or match foul, misconduct, game misconduct or gross misconduct penalty.

504. Two Referees

(*a*) The Referees shall have general supervision of the game, and shall have full control of all game officials and players during the game, including stoppages; and in case of any dispute, their decision shall be final. The Referees shall remain on the ice at the conclusion of each period until all players have proceeded to their dressing rooms.

(*b*) All Referees shall be garbed in black trousers and official sweaters.

They shall be equipped with approved whistles and metal tape measures with minimum length of 2 m.

(*c*) The Referees shall order the teams on the ice at the appointed time for the beginning of a game, and at the commencement of each period. If, for any reason, there be more than fifteen minutes' delay in the commencement of the game or any undue delay in resuming play after the 15-minute interval between periods, the Referees shall state in their report to the proper authorities the cause of the delay, and the team or teams which were at fault.

(*d*) The Referees may, at their own discretion, measure any equipment, the Referees shall check the equipment, worn by any player when requested to do by the Captain of either team.

(*e*) The Referees shall, before starting the game, see that the appointed Game Timekeeper, Penalty Timekeeper, Official Scorer and Goal Judges are in their respective places, and satisfy themselves that the timing and signalling equipment are in order.

(*f*) It shall be their duty to impose such penalties as are prescribed by the rules for infractions thereof, to stop play for any other infractions of the rules, and to give the final decision in matters of disputed goals. The Referees may, in matters of disputed goals, consult with the Goal Judge before making a decision.

(*g*) The Referees shall announce to the Penalty Timekeeper all penalties, and for what infractions such penalties are imposed.

The infraction of the rules for which each penalty has been imposed will be announced correctly, as reported by the Referees over the public address system. Where players of both teams are penalized at the same time, the penalty to the visiting player will be announced first.

(*h*) The Referees shall report to the Official Scorer the name or number of the goal scorer and any players entitled to assists.

NOTE: *The name of the scorer and any player entitled to an assist will be announced on the public address system.*

The Referees shall cause to be announced over the public address system the reason for not allowing a goal whenever the goal signal light is turned on in the course of play. This shall be done at the first stoppage of play regardless of any standard signal given by the Referees when the goal signal light was put on in error.

(*i*) The Referees shall see to it that players of opposing teams are separated on the penalty bench to prevent feuding.

(*j*) Should a Referee accidentally leave the ice or receive an injury which incapacitates him from discharging his duties while play is in progress the game shall be stopped immediately by the other Referee, unless one of the teams has the puck in a scoring position, in which case the play shall be allowed to be completed. If it is obvious that the injury sustained is of a serious nature, play shall be stopped immediately.

(*k*) If, through misadventure or sickness, both Referees appointed are prevented from appearing, the team leaders of the two clubs shall agree on Referees.

If they are unable to agree, the Proper Authorities shall appoint the Officials.

If the regularly appointed officials appear during the progress of the game, they shall at once replace the temporary officials.

(*l*) Should one of the appointed referees by unable to act at the last minute or through sickness or accident be unable to finish the game, the other Referee shall have no power to appoint a replacement, if he deems it necessary.

(*m*) The Referees shall secure from the Official Scorer the

Game Report immediately following each game. They shall sign and check this report and return it to the Official Scorer.

(*n*) The Referees are required to report on the Official Game Report all game misconducts, gross misconducts and match penalties immediately following the game involved, giving full details to the Proper Authorities concerned.

505. Goal Judges

(*a*) There shall be one Goal Judge at each goal. They shall not be members of either team engaged in the game, nor shall they be replaced during its progress, unless after the commencement of the game it becomes apparent that either Goal Judge, on account of partisanship or any other cause, is guilty of giving unjust decisions, in which case the Referee may appoint a replacement Goal Judge.

(*b*) Goal judges shall be stationed behind the goals, during the progress of play, in properly screened cages, so that there can be no interference with their activities. They shall not change goals during the game.

(*c*) The Goal Judge shall decide if the puck has passed between the goal posts and completely over the goal line and give the appropriate signal.

The Referee shall give the final decision in matters of a disputed goal. He may consult with the Goal Judge or Linesman before making his decision.

506. Penalty Timekeeper

(*a*) The Penalty Timekeeper shall keep, on the official forms provided, a correct record of all penalties imposed by the officials including the names of the players penalized, the infractions penalised, the duration of each penalty and the time at which each penalty was imposed. He shall report in the Penalty Record each penalty shot awarded, the name of the player taking the shot and the result of the shot.

(*b*) The Penalty Timekeeper shall check and ensure that the time served by all penalised players is correct. He shall be responsible for the correct posting of penalties on the scoreboard at all times and shall promptly call to the attention of the Referee any discrepancy between the time recorded on the clock and the official correct time, and he shall be responsible for making any adjustments ordered by the Referee.

He shall, upon request, give a penalised player correct information as to the unexpired time of his penalty.

NOTE 1: *The infraction of the rules for which each penalty has been imposed will be announced over the public address system, as reported by the Referee. Where players of both teams are penalized on the same day, the penalty to the visiting player will be announced first.*

NOTE 2: *Misconduct penalties should not be recorded on the timing device, but such penalized players should be alerted and released at the first stoppage of play following the expiration of their penalties.*

(*c*) The Penalty Timekeeper shall advise the Referee(s) when the same player has received his second major or misconduct penalty in the same game.

507. Official Scorer

(*a*) Before the start of the game, the Official Scorer shall obtain from the Manager or Coach of both teams a list of all eligible players and the starting line-up of each team, which information shall be made known to the opposing team Manager and Coach before the start of play, either personally or through the Referee.

(See Rule 203, Players in Uniform, and Rule 204, Starting Lineup.)

The Official Scorer shall secure the names of the Captain from the Manager or Coach at the time the line-ups are collected and will so indicate by placing the letter "C" opposite their names on the score sheet. This information shall be presented to the Referee for his signature at the completion of the game.

(*b*) The Official Scorer shall keep a record of the goals scored, the scorers, the players to whom assists have been credited, and shall indicate those players on the lists who have actually taken part in the game. He shall also record the time of entry into the game of any substitute goalkeeper. He shall record on the Official Score Sheet a notation where a goal is scored when the goalkeeper has been removed from the ice.

(c) The awards of points for goals and assists shall be announced over the public address system and all changes in such awards shall also be announced in the same manner.

NOTE: *In the "A" Pool I.I.H.F. World Championships, the Official Scorer shall determine the player or players entitled to receive "assists" on goals, and his decision shall be final.*

No request for changes in any award of points, shall be considered unless they are made at, or before, the conclusion of actual play in the game by the team Captain.

(d) The Official Scorer shall also prepare the Official Score Sheet for signature by the Referee and forward it to the Proper Authorities.

508. Game Timekeeper

(a) The Game Timekeeper shall record the time of the starting and finishing of each game and all actual playing time during the game.

(b) The Game Timekeeper shall signal the Referee(s) for the commencement of the game, for the start of second and third periods, and any overtime period or periods. He shall allow fifteen minutes intermission between each period after which Referee(s) shall start play. He shall also signal by ringing a gong, siren or by blowing a whistle, the ending of each period, any overtime period or periods and the ending of the game. This applies in rinks that are not provided with an automatic gong or siren, or if the automatic gong or siren should fail to operate.

(c) Where a public address system is used, the Game Time- keeper shall announce when only ONE MINUTE of actual playing time remains in the first and second period. and TWO MINUTES remain in the third period and overtime.

(d) In the event of any dispute regarding time, the Referee's decision shall be final.

509. Proper Authorities

The term "Proper Authorities" or "Proper Disciplinary

Authority" as applied under these rules is defined as the immediate governing body of the games involved.

VI. PLAYING RULES

601. Abuse of Officials and Other Misconducts

NOTE: *In the enforcement of this rule, the Referee has, in many instances, the option of imposing a "misconduct penalty" or a "bench minor penalty". In principal, the Referee is directed to impose a "bench minor penalty" in respect to the violations which occur on or in the immediate vicinity of the players' bench but off the playing surface, and in all cases affecting non-playing personnel or players. A "misconduct penalty" should be imposed for violations which occur on the playing surface or in the penalty bench area and where the penalised player is readily identifiable.*

(*a*) Any player who challenges or disputes the rulings of any official during the game shall be assessed a minor penalty for Unsportsmanlike Conduct. If the player persists in such a challenge or dispute, he shall be assessed a misconduct penalty, and any further dispute will result in a game misconduct penalty being assessed.

(*b*) If any play is guilty of any one of the following, his team shall be assessed a bench minor penalty:

1. After being penalised he does not proceed directly and immediately to the penalty bench and take his place on the penalty bench, or to the dressing room when so ordered by the Referee.
2. While off the playing surface, uses obscene, profane or abusive language to any person, or uses the name of any official coupled with any such remarks.
3. While off the playing surface, interferes in any manner with any game official, including the Referee, Linesmen, Timekeepers or Goal judges in the performance of their duties.

(*c*) Any player who is guilty of any one of the following shall be assessed a misconduct penalty:

1. Using obscene, profane or abusive language to any person on the ice or anywhere in the rink before, during

or after the game, except in the immediate vicinity of the players' bench (see (b) 2.).

2. Intentionally knocking or shooting the puck out of reach of an official who is retrieving it.

3. Deliberately throwing any equipment, except the stick (see Rule 633 (c), Throwing Stick) out of the playing area.

4. Banging the board with his stick or any other instrument at any time.

5. Failing to proceed directly and immediately to the penalty bench following a fight or other altercation in which he has been involved and which has been broken up, and for which he is penalized or causes any delay by retrieving his equipment. His gloves, stick, etc. shall be delivered to him at the penalty bench by a teammate (this misconduct penalty shall be in addition to any other penalties incurred).

6. After a warning by the Referee, persisting in any course of conduct (including threatening or abusive language or gestures or similar actions) designated to incite an opponent into incurring a penalty.

7. Entering or remaining in the Referee's crease while the Referee is reporting to, or consulting with, any game official, including Linesmen, Timekeeper, Penalty Timekeeper, Official Scorer or Announcer, except for the purpose of taking his place on the penalty bench.

(*d*) Any player who is guilty of any of the following shall, at the discretion of the Referee, be assessed a misconduct or game misconduct:

1. Touching or holding with his stick or hands, tripping or body checking a Referee, Linesman or any game official.

2. Throwing a stick out of the rink – Rule 633 (c), Throwing Stick.

3. Continuing or attempting to continue a fight or altercation after he has been ordered by the Referee to stop, or resisting a Linesman in the discharge of his duties.

(*e*) Any player who is guilty of any of the following shall be assessed a game misconduct.

1. Persisting in any course of conduct for which he has previously been assessed a misconduct penalty.
2. Using obscene gestures on the ice or anywhere in the rink before, during or after the game.

(*f*) Any player who is guilty of any of the following shall be assessed a gross misconduct penalty:

1. Any manner of behaviour which makes a travesty of, interferes with or is detrimental to the conducting of the game.
2. Attempts to injure or deliberately injures any game official.

(*g*) If any team official is guilty of any of the following, his team shall be assessed a bench minor penalty:

1. Banging the boards with a stick or other instrument at any time.
2. Using obscene, profane or abusive language to any person or uses the name of any official coupled with such remarks anywhere in the rink.
3. Interfering in any manner with any game official, including the Referee, Linesmen, Timekeepers or Goal Judges in the performance of their duties.

(*h*) Any team official who is guilty of any type of misconduct shall be assessed a game misconduct penalty.

(*i*) Any team official who is guilty of holding or striking an official, or any manner of behaviour which makes a travesty of or interferes with or is detrimental to the conducting of the game, shall be assessed a gross misconduct penalty.

(*j*)* Throwing anything onto the ice from anywhere in the rink is prohibited.

If this rule is violated by

1. A player – he shall be assessed a minor plus game misconduct penalty.
2. A team official – he shall be assessed a game misconduct and his team a bench minor penalty.
3. A unidentified person of the team in the vicinity of the players' bench – the team shall be assessed a bench minor penalty.

If the player or team is penalized under Rule 633, Throwing Stick, this rule shall not apply.

602. Adjustment of Equipment

(*a*) Play shall not be stopped nor the game delayed by reason of adjustments to clothing, equipment, shoes, skates or sticks.

(*b*) The onus of maintaining clothing and equipment in proper condition shall be upon the player. If adjustments are required, the player shall retire from the ice and play shall continue.

(*c*) No delay shall be permitted for the repair or adjustment of goalkeeper's equipment. If adjustments are required, the goalkeeper shall retire from the ice and his place shall be taken by the substitute goalkeeper immediately and no warm-up shall be permitted.

(*d*) For an infraction of this rule, a minor penalty shall be imposed.

603. Attempt to Injure or Deliberate Injury

(*a*) A match penalty shall be imposed on any player who attempts to injure or deliberately injures an opponent. The circumstances shall be reported to the proper authorities for further action. A substitute for the penalized player shall be permitted at the end of the fifth minute.

(*b*) A gross misconduct penalty shall be imposed on any player who attempts to injure or deliberately injures a team official.

604. Board Checking (Boarding)

A minor of major penalty, at the discretion of the Referee based upon the degree of violence of the impact with the boards, shall be imposed on any player who bodychecks, cross-checks, elbows, charges or trips an opponent in such manner that causes the opponent to be thrown violently into the boards.

NOTE: *Any unnecessary contact with a player playing the puck on an obvious "icing" or "off-side" play which results in that player being knocked into the boards is "boarding" and must be penalized as such. In other instances where there is no contact with the boards, it should be treated as "charging".*

"Rolling" an opponent (if he is the puck carrier) along the

boards where he is endeavouring to go through too small an opening is not boarding. However, if the opponent is not the puck carrier, then such action shall be penalized as boarding, charging, interference or if the arms or stick are employed it shall be called holding or hooking.

605. Broken Stick

(*a*) A player without a stick may participate in the game. A player whose stick is broken may participate in the game provided he drops the broken portion. A minor penalty shall be imposed for an infraction of this rule.

NOTE: *A broken stick is one which, in the opinion of the Referee, is unfit for normal play.*

(*b*) A goalkeeper may continue to play with a broken stick until stoppage of play or until he has been legally provided with a stick.

(*c*)* A player or goalkeeper whose stick is broken may not receive a stick thrown onto the ice from any part of the rink, but may receive a stick from a teammate without proceeding to his player's bench.

For an infraction of this rule penalties will be assessed under Rule 601 (*j*), Abuse of Officials and Other Misconducts.

(*d*) A goalkeeper whose stick is broken may not go to the players' bench during a stoppage of play for a replacement, but must receive his stick from a teammate.

For an infraction of this rule a minor penalty shall be imposed on the goalkeeper.

606. Charging

(*a*)* A minor or major penalty shall be imposed on a player who runs, jumps into or charges an opponent, or who body-checks or pushes an opponent from behind.

NOTE: *If more than two steps or strides are taken, it shall be considered "charging".*

(*b*) A double minor or major penalty shall be imposed on a player who commits any foul against a goalkeeper while the goalkeeper is within the goal crease.

A goalkeeper is NOT "fair game" just because he is outside

the goal crease area. A penalty for interference or charging (minor or major) should be called in every case where a opposing player makes unnecessary contact with a goalkeeper.

Likewise, Referees should be alert to penalize goalkeepers for tripping, slashing or spearing in the vicinity of the goal.

(*c*)* A minor or major penalty at the discretion of the Referee shall be imposed on a player who makes physical contact with an opponent after the whistle has been blown, if in the opinion of the Referee, the player has had sufficient time after the whistle to avoid such contact.

607. Cross-Checking

(*a*) A minor or major penalty, at the discretion of the Referee, shall be imposed on a player who "cross-checks" an opponent.

NOTE: *"Cross-check" shall mean a check delivered with both hands on the stick and no part of the stick on the ice.*

(*b*) A major penalty shall be imposed on any player who injures an opponent by "cross-checking".

608. Delaying the Game

(*a*) A minor penalty shall be imposed on any player or goalkeeper who deliberately shoots or bats with his hand or stick or throws the puck outside the playing area during or after a stoppage of play.

(*b*) A minor penalty shall be imposed on any player (including goalkeeper) who delays the game by deliberately displacing a goal post from its normal position. The Referee or Linesmen shall stop play immediately when a goal post has been displaced.

If the above mentioned delay is caused by any player or goalkeeper from the defending team in its defensive zone during the last two minutes of a game, or overtime, a penalty shot shall be awarded.

If the goal is deliberately displaced by a goalkeeper or player during the course of a "break-away" (see note), a penalty shot will be awarded to the non-offending team, and taken by the player last in possession of the puck. Should this violation occur after the goalkeeper has been removed for another player, a goal shall be awarded to the non-offending team.

NOTE: *A player with a "break-away" is defined as a player in control of the puck with no opposition between him and the opposing goal and with a reasonable scoring opportunity.*

(*c*) A bench minor penalty shall be imposed upon any team which, after warning by the Referee to its Captain to place the correct number of players on the ice and commence play, fails to comply with the Referee's direction and thereby causes any delay by making additional substitutions, by persisting in having players off-side, or in any other manner.

(*d*) The puck must be kept in motion at all times.

(*e*) Except to carry the puck behind its goal once, a team in possession of the puck in its own defence area shall advance the puck towards the opposing goal, except if it is prevented from so doing by players of the opposing team.

For the first infraction of this rule, play shall be stopped and a face-off shall be made at either end face-off spot adjacent to the goal of the team causing the stoppage, and the Referee shall warn the Captain of the offending team of the reason for the face-off. For a second violation by any player of the same team in the same period, a minor penalty shall be imposed on the player violating the rule.

(*f*) A minor penalty shall be imposed on any player including the goalkeeper who holds, freezes or plays the puck with his stick, skates or body along the boards in such a manner as to cause a stoppage of play unless he is actually being checked by an opponent.

(*g*) A player beyond his defensive zone shall not pass nor carry the puck backward into his defensive zone for the purpose of delaying the game, except when his team is below the numerical strength of the opponents on the ice.

(*h*) For an infringement of this rule, the face-off shall be at the nearest end face-off spot in the Defending Zone of the offending team.

609. Elbowing or Kneeling

(*a*) A minor or major penalty, at the discretion of the

Referee, shall be imposed on any player who uses his elbow or knee to foul an opponent.

(*b*) A major penalty shall be imposed on any player who injures an opponent as the result of a foul committed by using his elbow or knee.

610. Face-Offs

(*a*)* The puck shall be "faced-off" by the Referee or the Linesman by dropping the puck on the ice between the sticks of the players "facing-off". Players facing-off will stand squarely facing their opponents' end of the rink, approximately one stick length apart, with the blade of their sticks touching the ice.

When the face-off takes place at any of the end or Neutral Zone face-off spots, the players taking part shall take their positions so that they will stand squarely facing their opponent's end of the rink. The sticks of both players facing-off shall have the blade touching the ice in contact with the designated white area. The player of the attacking team in his attacking half of the rink shall place his stick within the designated white areas first.

No other players shall be alowed to enter the face-off circle or come within 4.5 m. of the players facing-off and must stand "on-side" on all face-offs.

If a violation of this sub-section of this rule occurs, the Referee or Linesman shall re-face the puck, UNLESS the non-offending team gained possession of the puck in which case the face-off will be considered valid and play shall be permitted to continue.

(*b*) If, after warning by the Referee or Linesman, either player fails to take his proper position for the face-off promptly, the official shall be entitled to face-off the puck notwithstanding such default.

(*c*) In the conduct of any face-off anywhere on the playing surface, no player facing-off shall make any physical contact with his opponent's body by means of his own body or by his stick, except in the course of playing the puck after the face-off has been completed.

For violation of this rule the Referee shall impose a minor

penalty or penalties on the player(s) whose action(s) caused the physical contact.

NOTE: *"Conduct of any face-off" commences when the Referee designates the place of the face-off and he (or the Linesman) takes his position to drop the puck.*

(*d*)* if a player facing-off fails to take his proper position immediately when directed by the Official, the Official may order him out of the face-off or the Referees may assess him a minor penalty. In the case where a player is ordered out of the face-off his team shall replace him with another player who is then on the ice.

No substitution of players shall be permitted until the face-off has been completed and play has been resumed, except when a penalty is imposed which will affect the on-ice strength of either team.

(*e*) When an infringement of a rule has been committed or a stoppage of play has been causes by any player of the attacking side in the Attacking Zone, the ensuing face-off shall be made in the Neutral Zone at the nearest face-off spot.

NOTE: *This includes stoppage of play caused by a player of the attacking side shooting the puck on the back of the defending team's goal without any intervening action by the defending team.*

(*f*) When an infringement of a rule has been committed by players of both teams the ensuing face-off will be made at the place where the puck was when the play was stopped.

(*g*) When stoppage occurs between the end face-off spots and the near end of the rink, the puck shall be faced-off at the end face-off spot, on the side where the stoppage occurs, unless otherwise expressly provided by these rules.

(*h*) No face-off shall be made within 6 m. of the goal or closer to the sideboards than the end zone and neutral zone face-off spots.

(*i*) When a goal is illegally scored as a result of a puck being deflected directly off or by an official, the resulting face-off shall be made at the end face-off spot in the defending zone.

(*j*) When the game is stopped for any reason not

specifically covered in the official rules, the puck shall be faced-off where it was last played.

(*k*) The whistle shall not be blown by the official to start play. Playing time shall commence from the instant the puck is faced-off and shall stop when the whistle is blown.

(*l*) Following a stoppage of play, should one or both defencemen, who are playing near their attacking blue line or any player coming from the bench of the attacking team enter into the attacking zone beyond the outer-edge of the corner face-off circle, the ensuing face-off shall take place at the nearest face-off spot in the neutral zone near the blue line of the defending team.

611. Falling on the Puck

(*a*) A minor penalty shall be imposed on a player other than the goalkeeper who deliberately falls on or gathers a puck into his body.

NOTE: *Any player who drops to his knees to block shots should not be penalized if the puck is shot under him or becomes lodged in his clothing or equipment, but any use of the hands to make the puck unplayable should be penalized promptly.*

(*b*) A minor penalty shall be imposed on a goalkeeper who deliberately falls on or gathers the puck into his body or who holds or places the puck against any part of the goal or against the boards which causes a stoppage of play unless an opposing player is near enough to play the puck.

(*c*) No defending player, except the goalkeeper, will be permitted to fall on the puck or hold the puck or gather the puck into his body or hands when the puck is within the goal creases.

For infringement of this rule, play shall immediately be stopped and a penalty shot shall be imposed against the offending team, but no other penalty shall be given.

NOTE: *This rule shall be interpreted so that a penalty shot will be awarded only when the puck is in the crease at the instant the offense occurs. However, in cases where the puck is outside the crease, Rule 611 (a) may still apply and a minor penalty may be imposed, even though no penalty shot is awarded.*

612. Fisticuffs or Roughing

(*a*) A match penalty shall be imposed on any player who starts fisticuffs.

(*b*) A minor penalty shall be imposed on a player who, having been struck, shall retaliate with a blow or attempted blow. However, at the discretion of the Referee, a double minor, major or match penalty may be imposed if such player continues the altercation.

NOTE 1: *It is the intent and purpose of this Rule that the Referee shall impose the match penalty in all cases when the instigator or retaliator of the fight is the aggressor.*

NOTE 2: *The Referee is provided very wide latitude in the penalties which he may impose under this rule. This is done intentionally to enable him to differentiate between the obvious degrees of responsibility of the participants, either for starting the fighting or persisting in continuing the fighting. The discretion provided should be exercised realistically.*

(*c*) At the discretion of the Referee a minor or double minor penalty may be imposed on any player deemed guilty of unnecessary roughness.

(*d*) A misconduct or game misconduct penalty shall be imposed on any player involved in fisticuffs off the playing surface. If one player is on the ice and one is off the ice, both shall be considered "on the ice" for the application of this rule (a) and (b) above.

(*e*) A game misconduct penalty shall be imposed on any player or goalkeeper who is the first to intervene in an altercation already in progress. This penalty is in addition to any other penalty incurred in the same incident.

NOTE: *For the purpose of application of this rule, it shall not be considered an altercation unless at least one penalty (minor or major) is assessed. However, the assessment of a penalty does not necessarily always constitute an "altercation", but shall be at the discretion of the Referee.*

613. Goal and Assist

NOTE: *It is the responsibility of the Referee to award goals and assists (except in I.I.H.F. "A Pool Championships") and his decision, in this respect, is final. Such awards shall be made or withheld strictly in accordance with the provisions of this rule. Therefore, it is essential that the Referee shall be thoroughly familiar with every aspect of this rule, be alert to observe all actions which could affect the making of an award and, above all, the awards must be made or withheld with absolute impartiality.*

In case of obvious error in awarding a goal or an assist which has been announced, it should be corrected promptly but changes shall not be made in the official scoring summary after the Referee has signed the Game Report.

(*a*) A goal shall be scored when the puck shall have been put between the goal posts below the cross bar, and entirely across the goal line by the stick of a player of the attacking side.

(*b*) A goal shall be scored if the puck is put into the goal in any way by a player of the defending side. The player of attacking side who last played the puck shall be credited with the goal but no assist shall be awarded.

(*c*) If an attacking player kicks the puck and it is deflected into the goal by any player or goalkeeper the goal shall not be allowed.

(*d*) If the puck shall have been deflected into the goal from the shot of an attacking player by striking any part of the person of a player of the same side, the goal shall be allowed. The player who deflected the puck shall be credited with the goal. The goal shall not be allowed if the puck has been kicked, thrown or otherwise deliberately directed into the goal by any means other than a stick.

(*e*) A goal shall not be allowed if the puck has been deflected directly into the goal off an official.

(*f*) Should a player legally propel a puck into the goal crease of the opposing team and the puck should become loose and available to another player of the attacking side, a goal scored on the play shall be valid.

(*g*) Unless the puck is in the goal crease area, a player of the attacking side may not stand on the goal crease line or in the goal crease or hold his stick in the goal crease area, and if the puck should enter the goal while such condition prevails (except as in "h" of this rule) a goal shall not be allowed, and the puck shall be faced in the neutral zone at the face-off spot nearest the attacking zone of the offending team.

(*h*) If a player of the attacking side has been physically interfered with by the action of any defending player so as to cause him to be in the goal crease, and the puck should enter the goal while the player so interfered with is still within the goal crease, the "goal" shall be allowed, unless, in the opinion of the Referee, he had sufficient time to get out of the crease, but stayed there of his own accord.

(*i*) Any goal scored, other than as covered by the official rules shall not be allowed.

(*j*) A "goal" shall be credited in the scoring records to a player who shall have propelled the puck into the opponents' goal. Each "goal" shall count one point in the player's record.

(*k*) When a player scores a goal, an "assist" shall be credited to the player or players taking part in the play immediately preceeding the goal, but not more than two assists can be given on any goal. Each "assist" so credited shall count one point in the player's record.

(*l*) Only on point can be credited to any one player on a goal.

614. Handling the Puck with the Hands

(*a*) A player, except the goalkeeper, shall not close his hand on the puck.

(*b*) A goalkeeper shall not:

1. Hold the puck in his hand(s) for longer than three (3) seconds or in any manner which in the opinion of the Referee causes a stoppage of play or
2. throw the puck forward towards his opponents goal which is first played by a teammate or
3. deliberately drop the puck into his pads or onto the goal net.

NOTE: *The object of this rule is to keep the puck in play continuously and any action by the goalkeeper which causes an unnecessary stoppage must be penalized without warning.*

(*c*) For a violation of this rule, the offending player shall be assessed a minor penalty.

(*d*) A defending player, other than the goalkeeper, shall not pick up the puck from the ice with his hands. For a violation of this rule, the player shall be assessed a minor penalty. However, if the puck was in the goal crease at the time of the violation, a penalty shot shall be awarded the opposing team.

(*e*) A player shall be permitted to stop or "bat" a puck in the air with his open hand, or push it along the ice with his hand, however the play shall be stopped if, in the opinion of the Referee, he has deliberately and intentionally directed the puck to a teammate, and the puck faced-off at the spot where the offense occurred. If this violation is committed by an attacking player in his attacking zone, the face-off shall take place at the nearest neutral zone face-off spot.

NOTE: *The object of this rule is to ensure continuous action and the Referees should NOT stop pay unless he is satisfied that the directing of the puck to a team-mate was in fact DELIBERATE AND INTENTIONAL.*

The goal shall be disallowed if the puck was batted with the hand by an attacking player and deflected off any player or goalkeeper into the goal.

615. High Sticks

(*a*) The carrying of sticks above the normal height of the shoulder is prohibited, and a minor penalty may be imposed on any player violating this rule, at the discretion of the Referee.

(*b*) A goal scored from a stick so carried except by a player of the defending team shall not be allowed.

(*c*) When a player carries or holds any part of his stick above the height of his shoulder so that injury to the face or head of an opposing player results, the Referee shall have no alternative but to impose a major penalty on the offending player.

(*d*) Batting the puck above the normal height of the shoulders with the stick is prohibited and when it occurs play shall be stopped and a face-off conducted at one of the end face-off spots adjacent to the goal of the team committing the high stick violation unless:

1. the puck is batted to an opponent, in which case the play shall continue, or
2. a player of the defending team bats the puck into his own goal, in which case the goal shall be allowed.

NOTE: *When a player bats the puck to an opponent under subsection 1, the Referee shall give the "washout" signal immediately. Otherwise he shall stop the play.*

616. Holding an Opponent

(*a*) A minor penalty shall be imposed on a player who holds an opponent with his hands or stick or in any other way.

(*b*)* A minor or major plus a misconduct penalty shall be imposed on a player who grabs or holds the face mask of an opponent with his hand.

617. Hooking

(*a*) A minor penalty shall be imposed on a player who impedes or seeks to impede the progress of an opponent by "hooking" with his stick.

(*b*) A major penalty shall be imposed on any player who injures an opponent by "hooking".

(*c*) When a player, in control of the puck on the opponent's side of the centre red line and having no opponent to pass other than the goalkeeper, is hooked or otherwise fouled from behind, thus preventing a reasonable scoring opportunity, a penalty shot shall be awarded to the non-offending team. The referee, however, shall not stop the play until the attacking team has lost possession of the puck to the defending team.

NOTE: *The intention of this rule is to restore a reasonable scoring opportunity which has been lost be reason of a foul from behind when the foul is committed on the opponent's side of the centre red line.*

By "control of the puck" is meant the act of propelling the puck with the stick. If, while it is being propelled, the puck is touched by another player or his equipment or hits the goal or goes free, the player shall no longer be considered to be "in control of the puck."

(*d*) If, when the opposing goalkeeper has been removed from the ice, a player in control of the puck is hooked or otherwise fouled with no opposition between him and the opposing goal, thus preventing a reasonable scoring opportunity, the Referee shall immediately stop the play and award a goal to the attacking team.

618. Icing the Puck

(*a*) For the purpose of this rule, the centre line will divide the ice into halves. Should any player of a team, equal or superior in numerical strength to the opposing team, shoot, bat, or deflect the puck from his own half of the ice, beyond the goal line of the opposing team, and it is first touched by a defending player other than the goalkeeper, play shall be stopped and the puck faced-off at the end face-off spot of the offending team nearest to where they last touched the puck, unless on the play the puck shall have entered the goal of the opposing team, in which case the goal shall be allowed.

For the purpose of this rule, the point of last contact with the puck by the team in possession shall be used to determine whether or not icing has occured.

NOTE 1: *If during the period of a delayed whistle due to a foul by a player of the side NOT in possession, the side in possession "ices" the puck, then the face-off following the stoppage of play shall take place in the Neutral Zone near the Defending Blue Line of the team "icing" the puck.*

NOTE 2: *When a team is "short-handed" as the result of a penalty and the penalty is about to expire, the decision as to whether there has been an "icing" shall be determined at the instant the penalty expires, and if the puck crosses the opponents' goal line after the penalty has expired it is "icing". The action of the penalized player remaining in the penalty box will not alter the ruling.*

NOTE 3*: *If in the action of the defending player touching the puck, it is knocked or deflected into the goal it is not a valid goal.*

NOTE 4: *When the puck is shot and rebounds from the body or stick of an opponent in his own half of the ice so as to cross the goal line of the player shooting, it shall not be considered as "icing".*

NOTE 5: *Notwithstanding the provisions of this section concerning "batting" the puck in respect to the "icing the puck" rule, the provisions of the final paragraph of Rule 614 (e), Handling the Puck with the Hands, apply and NO goal can be scored by batting the puck with the hand into the opponent's goal whether attended or not.*

NOTE 6: *If while the Linesman has signalled a slow whistle for a clean interception under Rule 624 (d), Offsides, the player intercepting shoots or bats the puck beyond the opponent's goal line in such a manner as to constitute "icing the puck", the Linesman's "slow whistle" shall be waived the instant the puck crosses the blue line and "icing" shall be called in the usual manner.*

(*b*) If a player of the team shooting the puck, who is "onside" and eligible to play the puck, is the first to touch it, the play shall continue and icing shall not be called.

(*c*) If the puck was so shot by a player of a side below the numerical strength of the opposing team, play shall continue and icing shall not be called.

(*d*) If, however, the puck shall go beyond the goal line in the opposite half of the ice directly from either of the players participating in a face-off, it shall not be considered a violation of this rule.

(*e*) If, in the opinion of the Linesman, a player of the opposing team except the goalkeeper, is able to play the puck before it passes his goal line, but has not done so, icing shall not be called and play shall continue. If, in the opinion of the Referee, the defending side intentionally abstains from playing the puck promptly when they are in a position to do so, he shall stop the play and order a face-off on the end-zone face-off spot nearest the goal of the offending team.

NOTE: *The purpose of this section is to enforce continuous action and both Referee and Linesman should interpret and apply the rule to produce this result.*

(*f*) If the puck shall touch any part of a player of the opposing side, or his skates or his stick, or if it passes through any part of the goal crease before it shall have reached the goal line, or shall have touched the goalkeeper, or his skates or his stick, before or after crossing the goal line, it shall not be considered as "icing the puck" and play shal continue.

NOTE: *If the goalkeeper takes any action to dislodge the puck from the back of the goal net icing shall not be called.*

(g) If the Linesman shall have erred in calling an "icing the puck" infraction (regardless of whether either team is short-handed) the puck shall be faced-off on the centre ice face-off spot.

619. Interference

(a) A minor penalty shall be imposed on a player who interferes with or impedes the progress of an opponent who is not in possession of the puck, or who deliberately knocks a stick out of an opponent's hand or who prevents a player who has dropped his stick or any other piece of equipment from regaining possession of it, or who knocks or shoots any abandoned or broken stick or illegal puck or other debris towards an opposing puck carrier in a manner that could cause him to be distracted (see also Rule 633 (a), Throwing Stick).

NOTE: *The last player to touch the puck – other than a goalkeeper – shall be considered the player in possession. In interpreting this rule the Referee should make sure which of the players is the one creating the interference – often it is the action and movement of the attacking player which causes the interference since the defending players are entitled to "stand their ground" or "shadow" the attacking players. Players of the side in possession shall not be allowed to "run" deliberate interference for the puck carrier.*

(b) A minor penalty shall be imposed on any player on the players' bench or on the penalty bench who by means of his stick or his body interferes with the movements of the puck or of any opponent on the ice during the progress of play.

(c) A minor penalty shall be imposed on a player who, by means of his stick or body, interferes with or impedes the movements of the goalkeeper while he is in his goal crease area, unless the puck is already in that area.

(*d*) If, when the goalkeeper has been removed from the ice, any member of his team (including the goalkeeper) not legally on the ice, including any team official, interferes by means of his body or stick or any other object with the movements of the puck or an opposing player, the Referee shall immediately award a goal to the non-offending team.

(*e*) When a player in control of the puck on the opponent's side of the centre red line, and having no opponent to pass other than the goalkeeper, is interfered with by a stick or part thereof or any other object thrown or shot by any member of the defending team including a team official, a penalty shot shall be awarded to the non-offending side.

NOTE: *The attention of Referees is directed particularly to three types of offensive interference which should be penalized:*

1. *When the defending team secures possession of the puck in its own end and the other players of that team run intereference for the puck carrier by forming a protective screen against forecheckers.*
2. *When a player facing-off obstructs his opponent after the face-off when the opponent is not in possession of the puck.*
3. *When the puck carrier makes a drop pass and follows through so as to make bodily contact with an opposing player.*

Defensive interference consists of bodily contact with an opposing player who is not in possession of the puck.

620. Interference by Spectators

(*a*) In the event of a player being held or interfered with by a spectator, play shall be stopped by the Referee or Linesman. If the team of the player interfered with is in possession of the puck at this time, the play shall be allowed to be completed before play is stopped. The puck shall be faced at the spot where last played at the time of the stoppage.

NOTE: *The Referee shall report to the proper authorities for disciplinary action all cases in which a player becomes involved in an altercation with a spectator.*

(*b*) Any player who physically interferes with a spectator shall, at the discretion of the Referee, be assessed a gross misconduct penalty and the Referee shall report all such infractions to the proper authorities.

(*c*) In the event that objects are thrown on to the ice which interfere with the progress of the game, the Referee shall stop the play and the puck shall be faced-off at the spot where play is stopped.

621. Kicking a Player

A match penalty shall be imposed on any player who kicks or attempts to kick another player.

622. Kicking the Puck

Kicking the puck shall be permitted in all zones, but a goal may not be scored by the kick of an attacking player. If an attacking player kicks the puck and it is deflected into the goal by any player or goalkeeper, the goal shall not be allowed.

623. Leaving the Players' or Penalty Bench

(*a*) No player may leave the players' bench or penalty bench at any time during the altercation. Substitutions made prior to the altercation shall be permitted provided the players so substituting do not enter the altercation.

(*b*) The first player to leave the players' or penalty bench during an altercation shall be assessed a double minor penalty and a game misconduct. If players of both teams leave their respective benches at the same time, the first identifiable player of each team to do so shall be penalized under this rule.

(*c*) Any other player or players (those not penalized under (*b*) above) who leave the players' bench during an altercation shall be assessed a misconduct penalty up to maximum of five misconducts per team as designated by the Referee.

(*d*) Any player or players (other than in (*b*) above) that leave the players' bench and incurs a minor, major or misconduct for his actions shall be automatically assessed a game misconduct.

NOTE 1: *Any game misconducts assessed under (b) or (d) above shall be considered as part of "five maximum" under (c).*

NOTE 2: *For the purpose of determining which player was the first to leave his players' bench during an altercation the Referee may consult with the Linesmen or off ice officials.*

(*e*) Except at the end of each period, or on expiration of a penalty, no player may, at any time leave the penalty bench.

(*f*) A penalized player who leaves the penalty bench, whether play is in progress or not, before his penalty time has expired shall be assessed

1. a minor penalty (except for (*g*) below) to be served at the expiration of his previous penalty.

2. If the violation occurred during a stoppage of play and an altercation was taking place, he shall also be assessed a game misconduct in addition to the minor penalty.

3. If the player is penalized under Rule 623 (*b*) above, as the first player off the players or penalty bench, he shall not be assessed any penalties under (f) Paragraph 1 and 2.

(*g*) If a player leaves the penalty bench before his penalty is fully served, the Penalty Timekeeper shall note the time and advise the Referee at the first stoppage of play.

If the player returned to the ice prematurely because of an error of the Penalty Timekeeper, he shall not be assessed an additional penalty but must serve the amount of time remaining in his penalty when he re-entered the game.

(*h*) If a player shall illegally enter the game from his own players' bench or from the penalty bench by his own error or the error of the Penalty Timekeeper, any goal scored by his own team while he is illegally on the ice shall be disallowed, but all penalties imposed against either team shall be served as regular penalties.

(*i*) If a player is in possession of the puck and in such a positions as to have no opposing player between himself and the opposing goalkeeper and he is interfered with by a player of the opposing team who has illegally entered the game, he shall be awarded a penalty shot.

(*j*) If, when the opposing goalkeeper has been removed from the ice, a player of the side attacking the unattended goal is interfered with by a player who shall have entered the play illegally, the Referee shall immediately award a goal to the non-offending team.

(*k*) Any team official who goes on the ice during any period, without permission of the Referees, shall be assessed a game misconduct.

624. Off-Sides

(*a*) Players of an attacking team may not precede the puck into the Attacking Zone.

(*b*) For a violation of this Rule, play shall be stopped and a face-off conducted.

If the puck was carried over the blue line at the time of the violation, the face-off shall take place at the nearest neutral zone face-off spot to where the puck crossed the line. If the puck was passed or shot over the blue line, the face-off shall take place where the pass or shot originated.

NOTE: *A player actually propelling and in control of the puck who shall cross the line ahead of the puck shall not be considered "off-side".*

(*c*) The position of the player's skates and not that of his stick shall be the determining factor in deciding an "off-side" violation. A player is off-side when both skates are completely over the blue line into his Attacking Zone.

NOTE 1: *A player is "on-side" when "either" of his skates are in contact with or on his own side of the line at the instant the puck completely crosses that line, regardless of the position of his stick.*

NOTE 2: *It should be noted that while the position of the player's skates is what determines whether a player is "off-side", nevertheless, the question of "off-side" never arises until the puck has completely crossed the line into the Attacking Zone, at which time the decision is to be made.*

(*d*) If, however, notwithstanding the fact that a member of the attacking team shall have preceded the puck into the Attacking Zone, the puck is intercepted by a member of the defending team at or near the blue line, and is carried or passed by them into the Neutral Zone the "off-side" shall be waived and play permitted to continue. Officials will carry out this rule by means of the "delayed whistle".

(*e*) If a player legally carries or passes the puck back into his own Defending Zone while a player of the opposing team is in such Defending Zone, the "off-side" shall be waived and play permitted to continue. (No "delayed whistle".)

(*f*) If, in the opinion of the Linesman, a player has intentionally caused an off-side play, the puck shall be faced-off at the end face-off spot in the defending zone of the offending team.

NOTE: *An intentional off-side is one which is made for the purpose of securing a stoppage of play, regardless of the reason, or where an off-side play is made under conditions where there is no possibility of completing a legal play.*

625. Passes

(*a*) The puck may be passed by any player to a teammate within any one of the three zones into which the ice is divided.

The puck, however, may not be passed by a player from his defensive zone to a teammate who is on the opposite side of the centre red line unless the puck preceded the receiving player across the centre line.

(*b*) For a violation of this Rule, play shall be stopped and a face-off shall take place at the place where the pass originated or the nearest face-off location.

NOTE 1: *The position of the puck (not the player's skates) shall be the determining factor in deciding from which zone the pass was made.*

NOTE 2: *If a receiving player is beyond the centre red line at the time the puck crosses it he may make himself eligible to play the puck by coming back and touching the centre red line with either skate. Thus, the puck being considered to have preceded him across the centre red line.*

NOTE 3: *If any part of either skate of a receiving player is touching the centre red line, he shall be considered on his defensive side of the centre line.*

NOTE 4: *If the player receiving the pass has his skates over the centre line, but plays the puck with his stick on his defensive side of the centre line, no violation of this Rule shall occur until the puck is carried or shot over the centre line by such player. The official, however, shall use a "delayed call" of this violation, and if the puck is intercepted by a player of the opposing team and carried or passed back over the centre line, the "off-side" pass shall not be called.*

If, in the same situation as above, the puck, having crossed the centre line, shall go directly over the goal line, and is first touched by a defending player, the "off-side pass" shall not be called but instead the icing violation shall be imposed.

(*c*) Should the puck having been passed, touch any player's body, stick or skates, between the passing players Defensive Zone and the centre red line, it shall nullify any violation of this rule.

(*d*) If the Linesman errors in calling an off-side pass infraction the puck shall be faced-off at the centre face-off spot.

626. Puck Out of Bounds or Unplayable

(*a*) When the puck goes outside the playing area at either end, or either side of the rink or strikes any obstacles above the playing surface other than the boards, glass or wire, it shall be faced off at the place from where it was shot or deflected, unless otherwise expressly provided in these rules.

(*b*) When the puck becomes lodged in the netting on the outside of either goal so as to make it unplayable, or if it is frozen against the goal between opposing players intentionally or otherwise, the Referee shall stop the play and face-off the puck at the nearest end-zone face-off spots unless, in the opinion of the Referee, the stoppage was caused by a player of the attacking team, in which case the resulting face-off shall be conducted in the Neutral Zone.

NOTE: *This includes the stoppage of play caused by a player of the attacking team shooting the puck on to the back of the defending team's goal without any intervening action by a defending player.*

The defending team and/or the attacking team may play the puck off the net at any time. However, should the puck remain on the net for longer than three seconds, play shall be stopped and the face-off shall take place at the nearest end-zone face-off spot except when the stoppage is caused by the attacking team, in which case the face-off shall take place on a face-off spot in the Neutral Zone.

(*c*) A minor penalty shall be imposed on a goalkeeper who deliberately drops the puck on the goal netting to cause a stoppage of play.

(*d*) If the puck comes to rest on top of the boards surrounding the playing area, it shall be considered to be "in play" and may be played legally by hand or stick.

627. Puck Out of Sight and Illegal Puck

(*a*) Should a scramble take place, or a player accidentally fall on the puck, and the puck is out of sight of the Referee, he shall immediately stop the play. The puck shall then be faced-off at the point where the play was stopped unless otherwise provided for in the rules.

(*b*) If, at any time while play is in progress, a puck other than the one legally in play shall appear on the playing surface, the play shall not be stopped, but shall continue with the legal puck until the play then in progress is completed by change of possession.

628. Puck Striking Official

Play shall not be stopped because the puck touches a Referee or Linesman anywhere on the rink, regardless of whether or not a team is short-handed, except when the puck has entered the goal in which case a face-off shall take place at the nearest end zone face-off spot.

629. Refusing to Start Play

(*a*) If, when both teams are on the ice, one team for any reason shall refuse to play when ordered to do so by the Referee, he shall warn the Captain and allow the team so refusing thirty seconds within which to begin the game or resume play. If at the end of that time, the team shall still refuse to play, the Referee shall impose a bench minor penalty on the offending team, and the case shall be reported to the proper authorities for further action.

Should there be a recurrence of the same incident, the Referee shall have no alternative but to declare that the game is forfeited to the non-offending team, and the case shall be reported to the proper authorities for further action.

(*b*) If a team, when ordered to do so by the Referee, through its Captain, Manager or Coach, fails to go on the ice and start play within two minutes, the game shall be forfeited, and the case shall be reported to the proper authorities for further action.

630. Slashing

(*a*) A minor or major penalty, at the discretion of the Referee, shall be imposed on any player who impedes or seeks to impede the progress of an opponent by "slashing" with his stick.

(*b*) A major penalty shall be imposed on any player who injures an opponent by slashing.

NOTE: *Referees should penalize as "slashing" any player who swings his stick at any opposing player (whether in or out of range) without actually striking him or where a player on the pretext of playing the puck makes a wild swing at the puck with the object of intimidating an opponent.*

(*c*) Any player who swings his stick at another player in the course of any altercation shall be subject to a major or match penalty.

NOTE: *The Referee shall impose the normal appropriate penalty provided in the other sections of this rule and shall, in addition, report the incident promptly to the proper authorities.*

631. Spearing or Butt Ending

(*a*) A minor or major penalty shall be imposed on a player who spears, attempts to spear, butt-ends, or attempts to butt-end an opponent. When a penalty is imposed under this Rule, the offending player shall automatically also be assessed a misconduct penalty.

NOTE 1: *"Spearing" shall mean stabbing an opponent with the point of the stick blade whether or not the stick is being carried with one or both hands.*

NOTE 2: *"Attempt to Spear"* shall include all cases where a spearing gesture is made whether or not contact is made.

NOTE 3: *"Attempting to butt-end"* shall include all cases where a butt-end gesture is made, whether or not actual contact is made.

(*b*) If any injury results from spearing or butt-ending, a match penalty shall be imposed.

632. Start of Game and Periods

(*a*) The game shall be commenced at the time scheduled by a "face-off" at the centre face-off spot and shall be renewed promptly at the conclusion of each intermission in the same manner.

(*b*) Home teams shall have the choice of goals to defend at the start of the game, except where both players' benches are on the same side of the rink, in which case the home team shall start the game, defending the goal nearest to its own players' bench. The teams shall change ends for each succeeding regular or overtime period.

(*c*) During the pre-game warm-up (which shall not exceed twenty minutes in duration) and before the commencement of play in any period, each team shall confine its activity to its own end of the rink so as to leave clear an area nine metres wide across the centre of the Neutral Zone.

NOTE: *Players shall not be permitted to come on the ice during a stoppage of play or at the end of the first and second periods for the purpose of warming-up. The Referee will report any violation of this rule to the proper authorities for disciplinary action.*

(*d*) Fifteen minutes before the time scheduled for the start of the game, both teams shall vacate the ice and proceed to their dressing rooms while the ice is being flooded. Both teams shall be signalled by the Game Timekeeper to return to the ice together in time for the scheduled start of the game.

633. Throwing a Stick

(*a*) When any player or goalkeeper or team official of the defending team deliberately throws or shoots a stick or any part thereof, or any other objects, in the direction of the puck in his Defending Zone, the Referee shall allow the play to be completed, and if a goal is not scored, a penalty shot shall be awarded to the non-offending team, which shot shall be taken by the player designated by the Referee as the player fouled.

NOTE 1: *If the Referee is unable to determine the person against whom the offence was made, the offended team, through the Captain shall designate a player on the ice at the time the offence was committed who will take the penalty shot.*

If, however, the goal being unattended and the attacking player having no defending player to pass and having a chance to score on an "open goal", a stick or part thereof or any other object, be thrown or shot by any member of the defending team, including a team official, thereby preventing a shot on the "open goal", a goal shall be awarded to the attacking team.

NOTE 2: *For the purpose of this rule, an open goal is defined as one from which a goalkeeper has been removed for an additional attacking player.*

(*b*) A major penalty shall be imposed on any player or goalkeeper on the ice who throws his stick or any part thereof, or any other object in the direction of the puck in any zone, except when such act has been penalized by the assessment of a penalty shot, the awarding of a goal or a goal is scored on the play by the non-offending team.

NOTE: *When a player or goalkeeper discards the broken portion of a stick by tossing it to the side of the ice (and not over the boards) in such a way as will not interfere with play or opposing player, no penalty will be imposed for so doing.*

(*c*) A misconduct or game misconduct penalty, at the discretion of the Referee, shall be imposed on a player or goalkeeper who throws his stick, or any part hereof within or outside the playing area, unless a penalty was imposed under 633 (*a*) or (*b*) above. If the offence is committed in protest of an official's decision, a minor penalty under Rule 601 (*a*), Abuse of Officials, plus a game misconduct shall be assessed to the offending player.

(*d*) If the goalkeeper intentionally leaves his stick or part thereof in front of his goal and if the puck hits the stick, while the goalkeeper is on or off the ice, the Referee shall stop play immediately and award a goal to the opposing team.

634. Time of Match

(*a*) The game shall consist of three twenty-minute periods of actual play with a rest intermission between periods. Play shall be resumed promptly following each intermission upon the expiry of fifteen minutes from the completion of play in the preceding period. A preliminary warning shall be given by the Game Timekeeper to the officials and to both teams three minutes prior to the resumption of play in each period and the final warning shall be given in sufficient time to enable the teams to resume play promptly.

In games played in outside or uncovered rinks, teams shall change ends at the mid-way period of the third period and overtime period. Goalkeepers shall not be permitted to go to the players' bench, except to be replaced. For a violation of this rule, a minor penalty shall be assessed.

NOTE: *For the purpose of keeping the spectators informed as to the time remaining during intermissions, the Game Timekeeper will use the electric clock to indicate the fifteen-minute intermission.*

(*b*) The team scoring the greatest number of goals during the three twenty-minute periods shall be the winner, and shall be credited with two points in the standings.

(*c*) In the intervals between periods, the ice surface shall be flooded unless mutually agree to by the teams to the contrary.

(*d*) If any unusual delay occurs within five minutes of the end of the first or second periods, the Referee may order the next regular intermission to be taken immediately and the balance of play with the teams defending the same goals, after which the teams will change ends and resume play of the ensuing period without delay.

(*e*) Each team shall be permitted to take one time out of thirty seconds duration during the course of regular time or over-time and which must be taken during a normal stoppage of play. Any player designated by the Coach will indicate to the Referee who will report the time-out to the Game Timekeeper who shall be responsible for signalling the termination of the time-out.

NOTE: *All players including goalkeepers on the ice at the time of the time-out will be allowed to go to their respective benches. Only one time-out per stoppage of play is allowed.*

635. Tied Game

Generally if, at the end of the three regular twenty-minutes periods, the score of both teams shall be equal, the game shall be called a "tie" with the points being shared equally between the two teams. This rule is subject to any Regulation of the I.I.H.F. or a National Federation.

636. Tripping

(*a*) A minor penalty shall be imposed on any player who shall place his stick, knee, foot, arm, hand or elbow in such a manner that it shall cause his opponent to trip or fall.

NOTE 1: *If, in the opinion of the Referee, a player is unquestionably hook-checking the puck and obtains possession of it, thereby tripping the puck carrier, no penalty shall be imposed.*

NOTE 2: *Accidental trips occurring simultaneously with, or after, stoppage of play will not be penalized.*

(*b*) When a player, in control of the puck in the opponent's side of the centre red line, and having no other opponent to pass than the goalkeeper, is tripped or otherwise fouled from behind, thus preventing a reasonable scoring opportunity, a penalty shot shall be awarded to the non-offending team. Nevertheless, the Referee shall not stop the play until the attacking team has lost possession of the puck to the defending team.

NOTE: *The intention of this rule is to restore a reasonable scoring opportunity which has been lost by reason of a foul from behind when the foul is committed in the opponent's side of the centre red line.*

By "control of the puck" is meant the act of propelling the puck with the stick. If, while it is being propelled, the puck is touched by another player or his equipment or hits the goal or goes free, the player shall no longer be considered to be "in control of the puck".

(c) If, when the opposing goalkeeper has been removed from the ice, a player in control of the puck is tripped or otherwise fouled with no opposition between him and opposing goal, thus preventing a reasonable scoring opportunity, the Referee shall immediately stop the play and award a goal to the attacking team.

The Rules of
Women's Lacrosse

POSITIONS IN THE FIELD
(as played in Great Britain)

| Goal |

1st Home	*Point*
2nd Home	*Cover Point*
3rd Home	*3rd Man*

Right Defence   *Left Defence*
Left Attack   Right Attack

Centre
Centre

Right Attack   *Left Attack*
Left Defence   Right Defence

3rd Man	*3rd Home*
Cover Point	*2nd Home*
Point	*1st Home*

| Goal |

This positioning is not compulsory

Women's Lacrosse

1. THE CROSSE

A. Construction

1. Basic materials: aluminium (handle only), fibre glass, gut, leather, nylon, plastic, rubber or wood. (Recessed metal screws may be used to affix the head to the handle.)

2. The head of the stick shall be triangular in concept and shall be affixed to the handle in such a way that it shall basically be in the same plane as the handle.

3. The pocket of the stick shall be strung traditionally i.e. four or five thongs with 8–12 stitches of cross lacing. (No mesh.)

4. The crosse shall be free of all sharp or protruding parts or edges and shall, in every way, provide for the safety of all players.

B. Dimensions

1. Overall length: 0.9 m (36 in) minimum, 1.1 m (44 in) maximum.

N.B. for young or small players a crosse shorter than 36 in will be permitted in order for it to fit comfortably along the full length of her arm.

2. Head: all width measurements as measured on a line perpendicular to the extension of the handle.

- (*a*) width overall 18 cm (7 in) minimum, 23 cm (9 in) maximum.
- (*b*) width when measured 2.5 cm (1 in) above the centre of the stop in a moulded crosse or 2.5 cm (1 in) above the bridge in a wooden crosse shall be 6.7 cm ($2\frac{5}{8}$ in) to 7.6 cm (3 in) inside and 7.6 cm (3 in) to 10.1 cm (4 in) outside.

(c) Length: as measured from the centre of the stop or bridge to the top of the head shall be 25.4 cm (10 in) minimum, 30.5 cm (12 in) maximum.

(d) Depth: The combined measurements of the pocket containing the ball with either a wood or plastic wall shall not exceed 6.3 cm (2.5 in) (the diameter of the ball).

3. Walls: wood or moulded crosse: 3.2 cm ($1\frac{1}{4}$ in) to 4.5 cm ($1\frac{3}{4}$ in) (measured at the highest point of the wall). Guard soft or woven 3.2 cm ($1\frac{1}{4}$ in) to 7.0 cm ($2\frac{3}{4}$ in) (measured at the highest point of the wall).

4. Weight: 20 oz (maximum).

C. A crosse is legal if:

1. It complies with the criteria in Rule 1A and 1B.

2. The top of the ball, when dropped into the pocket of a crosse held horizontally remains even with or above the top of the wooden or plastic walls.

3. The ball moves freely within all parts of the pocket, i.e. the ball cannot become wedged between the wood, guard and bridge of a wooden crosse or the stop of a moulded crosse.

4. It meets the manufacturer's specifications. All the equipment, including the crosses, that is to be used in the game must be checked and approved by the umpire prior to the game. At any time during the game, the umpire may, at her discretion, call time-out and re-check the equipment in use.

2. THE BALL

The ball is rubber of any solid colour, not less than 20 cm ($7\frac{3}{4}$ in) nor more than 20.3 cm (8 in) in circumference. It must weigh not less than 142 gm (5 oz) nor more than 149 gm ($5\frac{1}{4}$ oz). It must have a bounce of not less than 1.1 mm (44 in) nor more than 1.3 m (51 in) when dropped from 1.8 m (72 in) onto concrete at a temperature of approximately 18°C (65.F)–23°C (75°F). The ball must meet manufacturer's specifications.

3. THE PLAYING AREA

A. The playing area has no measured boundaries. An area of 110 × 60 m (120 × 70 yd) is desirable. The goals are 92 m

(100 yd) apart measured from goal line to goal line. There must be 9 m (10 yd) playing space behind each goal line running the width of the field. The minimum distance from goal line to goal line is 82 m (90 yd). There is a circle radius 9 m (10 yd) in the centre of the field and through the centre of this a line 3 m (3.3 yd) in length, parallel to the goal lines. Five marks 31 cm (1 ft) in length should be marked 8 m (8.8 yd) from the goal circle at 90° angles in front, 45° angles diagonally on a line from each goal post and parallel to the goal circle line. All lines are 5 cm (2 in) wide.

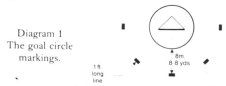

Diagram 1
The goal circle
markings.

B. The playing area must be flat and free of glass, stones and any protruding objects. The boundaries must be decided before the match by the captains and the umpires (see Rule 6-B). The lines marking the centre and goal circles are part of these areas. No marks may be added to or removed from the field.

4. THE GOALS

Each goal consists of two perpendicular posts or pipes, constructed of wood or metal, 1.83 m (6 ft) high and 1.83 m (6 ft) apart, joined at the top by a cross-bar 1.83 m (6 ft) from the ground (inside measurements). The goal posts (pipes) must not extend upwards beyond the goal posts nor the cross-bar sideways beyond the goal posts. The posts and cross-bar must be painted white and be 5 cm (2 in) square or 5 cm (2 in) in diameter. Pipe goals painted orange are acceptable. A line called the goal line must be drawn between the two posts, continuous with them and of the same width. The netting, not more than 4 cm (1.5 in) mesh, must be attached to the posts and cross-bar and to a point on the ground 1.83 m (6 ft) behind the centre of the goal line; it must be firmly pegged down. NB Goals with ground poles are legal but not recommended. If the side and bottom supports of the goal are exposed, they must be padded.

The Goal Circle

The goal circle is a circle, radius 2.6 m (8.5 ft) measured from the centre of the goal line to the outer edge of the goal circle line. The goal circle line shall be 5 cm (2 in) wide.

5. THE TEAMS

Twelve players constitute a full team one member of whom acts as captain. (See diagram: names of positions.)

6. CAPTAINS

The Captain's responsibilities are:
(*a*) To agree on the playing time with the umpire.
(*b*) To agree on the boundaries with the umpire.
(*c*) To indicate a substitute for an injured player.
(*d*) To designate an acting captain if the captain leaves the field.
(*e*) To confer with the umpires if the weather conditions make the continuation of play questionable, but the umpire's decision is final.
(*f*) To approach the umpire at half-time or after the game if a clarification of rules is needed (see Rule 20-A-5).

7. UNIFORM

A. Players must wear composition or rubber soled boots or shoes. No spikes are allowed. Plastic, leather or rubber cleats-studs may be worn.

B. The goalkeeper may wear leg pads, a body pad, a face mask and/or helmet, a throat protector and close fitting gloves with no webbing or excessive passing.

C. All players must wear numbers or positional letters differing from others on her team on the front and back of her uniform. Markings on the back must be at least 6 inches tall: markings on the front must be at least 3 inches tall.

D. Close-fitting gloves, noseguards, eye guards and mouth guards may be worn by all players. Players, with the exception of the goalkeeper, are not allowed to wear protective headgear or face masks. Further protective devices necessitated on genuine medical grounds may be used, providing that both captains and umpires agree that they do not endanger other players. All protective devices used should be close fitting, padded where necessary and not be of excessive weight.

E. Players may not wear earrings, necklaces, bracelets and watches on the field of play. Medical jewelry with information visible, soft jewelry and rings must be taped securely to the player or be removed entirely. Barrettes/hair slides are legal as long as they do not endanger other players. The umpire has the power to rule any decoration as dangerous and to remove it from the field of play.

F. The goalkeeper's colours must be the same corresponding colours as her teammates. The top must be the same colour; the bottom must be in agreement with the predominant colour.

G. No equipment including protective devices may be used unless it complies with the rules or manufacturer's specifications and is deemed not dangerous to the other players by the umpires.

8. DURATION OF PLAY

A. The playing time is 50 minutes (or such time agreed by the captains, see rule 6A). At half time, which may not exceed 10 minutes, the players must change ends. Time-out, which may not exceed 5 minutes per incident is taken for stoppage that occurs due to accident or injury.

B. In all games the clock is to be stopped on the umpire's whistle and arm signal after each goal during the entire game, and on every whistle in the last two minutes of each half. NB This rule is recommended for representative matches and is open to consultation at other levels of play.

C. Play should be continuous, but at the discretion of the umpire time-out is taken for unusual circumstances, e.g. a broken crosse, animal on the field, lost ball, a ball that has gone too far out-of-bounds, spectator interference, delay of game, to check a crosse, or to give warnings or suspensions.

D. If weather conditions make play dangerous, the umpire is authorised to suspend the game after consultation with the captain. The umpire's decision is final. A game is considered legal and complete if 80% of playing time has elapsed. If an interrupted game (one in which less than 80% of playing time has elapsed) is replayed, it must be played from the beginning.

E. The whistle is used only to stop play. Play is restarted verbally. The umpire will also give a visual arm signal by raising her arm above her head and moving it down to her side as she gives the verbal "play". The only exception to this is in the case of a "throw" where the arm signal to restart the clock is on the actual arm movement forward on the toss of the ball as she says the word "play".

9. SUBSTITUTION

A. Substitution during play takes place only when an accident, injury or illness occurs which, in the opinion of the umpire, prevents a player from taking further part in the game. If the player is incapacitated for longer than five minutes the game is restarted without her. She may return only with the umpire's permission and if no substitute has taken her place. Before a substitute enters the game she must report to the scorer's table and indicate the name and number of the player whom she is replacing. The umpire will beckon the substitute onto the field to the spot of the injured player. No substitution is permitted if a player is suspended due to misconduct. In no circumstances may a suspended player re-enter the game.

B. A limit of two substitutes is allowed at half-time.

C. Upon accident, injury or illness, re-entry is allowed only if no other substitute is available.

10. START OF THE GAME

The game is started and restarted after every goal and after every half-time by a draw on the centre line. All other players' feet must be outside the centre circle until after the words "ready draw".

The Draw

The opponents each stand with one foot toeing the centre line. The crosses are held in the air, above hip level, wood/

plastic to wood/plastic, angle to collar, parallel to and above the centre line and back to back, so that the players' crosses are between the ball and the goal they are defending. The ball is placed between the crosses by the umpire. On the words "ready draw" from the umpire, the two opponents must immediately draw their crosses up and away from one another.

The flight of the ball must attain a height higher than the heads of the players taking the draw. After one caution per game for an illegal draw by a specific player, the opponent is awarded a free position. A throw is awarded after one caution if both players draw illegally. For the free position the offending centre is placed 4 m (4.4 yd) away at an angle of 45° to the centre line towards the goal she is defending.

11. SCORING

A. The team scoring the greater number of goals is the winner. In the event of the scores being equal, the result is a draw/tie. A goal is scored by the whole ball passing completely over the goal line, between the posts, and under the cross-bar from in front, having been propelled by the crosse of an attacking player, or the crosse or person of a defending player.

B. A goal is not scored when:

1. The ball is put through the goal by a non-player.

2. The ball comes off the person of an attacking player.

3. The ball enters the goal after the whistle has been blown or the horn has been sounded.

4. The player shooting has followed through over the circle with any part of herself or her crosse, or any other attacking player has entered the circle.

5. The goalkeeper, while within the circle, is interfered with in any way by an attacking player.

6. The umpire has ruled that the shot is dangerous. (Rule 18–A–7).

NB to play off a tie, see "Special Recommendations".

12. STAND

The ball is "dead" when the umpire blows her whistle and no player except the goalkeeper within her circle or her deputy may move, unless directed by the umpire, until the game has been restarted. The umpire directs any player who moves to return to her original position.

13. OUT OF BOUNDS

When the ball goes out of bounds, the umpire blows her whistle and the players must "stand".

A. When one player is nearest the ball, she takes the ball in her crosse from the place where the ball went out of bounds, stands 4 m (4.4 yd) inside the agreed boundary and on the signal and word "play" the game proceeds.

B. When two opposing players are equally near the ball, a throw is taken (see Rule 14–B).

C. Each player involved maintains her same relationship relative to the other players at the time the whistle was blown.

D. Play must not be resumed within 8 mm (8.8 yd) of the goal circle.

14. THE THROW

The two players must stand with feet and crosse at least 1 m (1 yd) apart and each is nearer the goal she is defending and facing in towards the game. The umpire stands between the 4 m and 8 m (4.4 and 8.8 yd) from the players, and on the word "play", throws the ball with a short high throw so that the players take it as they move in towards the game. No player may be within 4 m (4.4 yd) of the players taking the throw. If the throw is inaccurate or is not touched by either player, the throw is taken again.

A throw is taken when:

(a) The ball goes into the goal off a non-player (see Rule 11-B-1) with the throw being taken to the side of the goal by two opposing field players nearest the goal.

(b) The ball goes out of bounds and two opposing players are equally near the ball (see Rule 13-B).

(c) There is an incident unrelated to the ball and players are equidistant from the ball (see Rule 15-A-2).

(d) A ball lodges in the clothing of a field player (see Rule

16-A) or cannot be dislodged from the crosse of a field
player (see Rule 16-B).

(*e*) Two players foul simultaneously (see Rule 19).

(*f*) The game is restarted after an incident related to the ball
when neither team had possession and two opposing
players are equally near the ball unless the accident has
been caused by a foul (see Rule 15).

(*g*) The game is stopped for any reason not specified in the
rules.

15. ACCIDENT, INTERFERENCE OR ANY OTHER INCIDENT

A. If the game has to be stopped due to an accident, injury,
illness, interference or an incident either related or unrelated to
the ball at the time the whistle is blown, the game is restarted in
one of the following ways:

1. If a foul has occurred, a free position is awarded on a spot
   determined by the umpire (see Rule 19).
2. If no foul is involved in the stoppage of play, the ball is
   given to the player who was in possession, or nearest to
   it, at the time play was stopped. If two players are equidistant from the ball, a throw is taken.

B. Time-out is called at the discretion of the umpire. No one
from the sideline may come onto the field without the permission of the umpire and no sideline personnel may come onto
the field for the purpose of coaching. No player may leave her
immediate area of the field without the permission of the umpire. If a player is incapacitated for longer than five minutes
the game is restarted without her or a substitute takes her place
(see Rule 9).

16. BALL LODGED IN CLOTHING OR CROSSE

When the ball lodges:

A. In the clothing of a player, a throw is taken with the
nearest opponent.

B. In the Crosse, the crosse must be struck on the ground

and the ball dislodged immediately, otherwise a throw is taken where the player caught the ball (Rule 14–D).

C. In the goal netting or in the clothing or pads of the goalkeeper while she is within the goal circle, she removes the ball, places it in her crosse and proceeds with the game. (Rule 17–B–3).

17. GOAL CIRCLE RULES

A. Only one player, either the goalkeeper or the person deputizing for her is allowed in the goal circle at any one time. No other player is allowed to enter or have any part of her body or crosse on or over the goal circle line at any time. A ball resting on the goal circle line is the goalkeeper's.

B. The goalkeeper or anyone deputizing for her while within the goal circle:
1. must clear the ball within ten seconds after it has entered the goal circle.
2. may stop the ball with either hand and/or body as well as her crosse; if she catches the ball with her hand she must put it in her crosse and proceed with the game.
3. must remove a ball lodged in her clothing or pads, place it in her crosse, and proceed with the game (see Rule 16–C).
4. may reach out her crosse and bring the ball back into the goal circle provided no part of her body is grounded outside the goal circle.

C. When the goalkeeper or anyone deputizing for her is outside the goal circle:
1. she loses all her goalkeeping privileges.
2. she may only re-enter the goal circle without the ball.
3. she may propel the ball into the goal circle and then follow it in.
4. she must return to the goal circle to play the ball if it is inside the circle.

D. The penalty for violation of Rule 17 is a free position no closer than 8 m (8.8 yd) out to either side level with the goal line.

18. FOULS

A. Major Field Fouls

A player must not:

1. Roughly or recklessly check/tackle another player's crosse. A crosse may be checked in a direction towards the body as long as the check/tackle is controlled. No player's crosse may hit or cause her opponent's crosse to hit her body. (Note: the attack player has a responsibility not to run her crosse into the defender's crosse). NB A crosse or ball within a crosse width of a player's head or neck is deemed potentially dangerous.

2. Hold her crosse within a crosse width around the face or throat of an opponent when she is level with or behind her.

3. Hold the head of her own crosse without cradling within a crosse width in front of the face or close to her body making a legal check impossible.

4. Reach around and across the body of an opponent to check the handle of her crosse with her feet behind her opponent.

5. Charge, block, barge, shoulder or back into an opponent, or push with the hand. Move into the path of an opponent without giving the player a chance to stop or change her direction. When a player is running to receive the ball a "blind side" defence player must give her enough time or space to change her direction.

6. Propel the ball or follow through with her crosse in a dangerous or uncontrolled manner at any time.

7. Shoot dangerously or without control.
   (*a*) A dangerous shot is judged on the basis of the combination of distance, force and placement.
   (*b*) A shot may not be directed at the goalkeeper's body, especially her head or neck. This would not apply if she moves into the path of the ball.
   (*c*) A shot may be uncontrolled even if it misses the goal.

8. With any part of her body guard the goal outside the goal circle so as to obstruct the *free space to goal* (see definition) between the ball and the goal circle which

denies the attack the opportunity to shoot safely and encourages shooting at an unprotected player.

 (*a*) This positioning applies only if initiated by the defender and not if she is drawn into the free space to goal by an attacking player.

 (*b*) The positioning applies to a defender not intentionally playing the player with the ball.

 9. Detain an opponent at any time by holding, tagging, pressing, or pushing against her body, clothing or crosse with an arm, leg, body or crosse.

10. Trip an opponent deliberately or otherwise.

B. Minor Field Fouls

A player must not:

11. Guard a ground ball with her foot or crosse or push an opponent off a ground ball.

12. Guard the crosse with an arm:

 (*a*) if one hand is removed from the crosse, the free hand may not be used to ward off an opponent deliberately or otherwise with or without contact.

 (*b*) elbows may not be used so as to protect the crosse.

13. Touch the ball with her hand, except as in Rules 16–C and 17–B.

14. Allow any part of her body, deliberately or otherwise, to impede, accelerate or change the direction of the ball to her team's distinct advantage. NOTE: Ball contact from an unexpected deflection should not be penalized.

15. Check/tackle an opponent's crosse when she is trying to get possession of the ball. This applies only if the opponent could have received the ball.

16. Throw her crosse in any circumstances.

17. Take part in the game if she is not holding her crosse.

18. Draw illegally after one "caution". Illegal draws occur when:

 (*a*) One player draws too soon.

 (*b*) No attempt is made to draw up and away.

 (*c*) The ball does not go above the heads of both centres.

19. Intentionally delay the game.

20. On a centre draw, step into the centre circle before the word "draw".
21. Play with an illegal crosse.

C. Goal Circle Fouls

1. A field player must not:
   enter or have any part of her body or crosse in the goal circle at any time, unless she is deputizing for the goalkeeper (see Rule 17–A).
2. The goalkeeper or her deputy must not:
   (a) When inside the goal circle, continue to hold the ball in her crosse, but must pass within 10 seconds (see Rule 17–B).
   (b) When inside the goal circle, may not reach beyond the goal circle to play the ball in the air or on the ground with her hand.
   (c) When any part of her is grounded outside the goal circle, draw the ball into her goal circle.
   (d) When outside the goal circle with the ball, step back into the goal circle until she no longer has the ball.
   (e) The goalkeeper, when outside the goal circle, throw any part of her equipment to her deputy.

D. Misconduct and Suspensions

1. A player must not:
   (a) conduct herself in a rough, dangerous, or unsportsmanlike manner.
   (b) Persistently cause infringement of the rules.
   (c) Deliberately endanger the safety of an opposing player.
   (d) Exhibit any type of behaviour which in the umpire's opinion amounts to misconduct.
2. The penalty for violation of Rule 18, Section D shall be: A free position for the opposing team with the offender placed 4m (4.4 yd) behind. In addition to awarding a free position, the umpire may also warn the offending player and then may, on further offence, suspend her from participation in the game. Time-out must be called to administer warnings and suspensions.

19. PENALTY FOR FOULS

The penalty for a foul is a "free position". In the event of two players fouling simultaneously a throw is taken. For a minor Field Foul the offending player is placed no closer than 4m (4.4yd) from the player taking the free position, in the direction from which she approached before committing the foul. For a Major Field Foul the offender will be placed 4m (4.4yd) behind the player taking the free position.

Free Position—Placement of Players

A. All players must "stand". The umpire indicates where the player taking the free position is to stand, and where the offending player is to stand.

1. No player is allowed within 4m (4.4yd) of the player taking the free position; if anyone is within this distance she must move to a position indicated by the umpire.
2. A free position must not be taken within 8m (8.8yd) of the goal circle. The free position will be taken on a line which passes from the centre of the goal line through the point where the foul occurred. The goalkeeper's free position is taken from within the goal circle unless she has been fouled outside the circle.
3. The penalty for a dangerous shot shall be taken by the goalkeeper within the goal circle.
4. If the foul prevented an almost certain goal, the umpire can order any player or players from between such free positions and the goal.
5. If any defence players are in the free space to goal with the implementation of a foul they should not be penalized unless, after the word "play" they make no effort to remove themselves to a legal position.

B. Resumption of Play

1. The player awarded the free position then takes the ball in her crosse and on the arm signal and the word "play" from the umpire, the game is restarted and the player may run, pass or shoot.

20. UMPIRES, SCORERS AND TIMERS

A. The umpire will:
1. Prior to the game inspect the grounds, goals, balls, crosses, clothing, boots/shoes, jewelry and protective equipment and see that they are in accord with the rules.
2. See that the timers and scorers understand their responsibilities.
3. Determine which umpire will be in charge of the game. The charge umpire will effect the toss for choice of ends and discuss ball colour with the captains.
4. Report goals to the scorer.
5. Be available for questions from captains or coaches during half time (see Rule 6–F).
6. Make the final decision, after consultation with captains on whether to continue a game due to weather conditions or any other extenuating circumstances (see Rule 6–E, 8–D)
7. Make the game official by signing the score book.
8. Umpire the game in accordance with the recommended procedures put forth by the IFWLA.
9. Umpire, at the same goal, both halves of the game.
   NOTE. The umpire's decision is final and without appeal.

B. HELD WHISTLE.
An umpire will refrain from enforcing any rule when it would penalize the non-offending team. If a player retains possession of the ball even though she has been fouled the umpire should indicate that she has seen the foul by an arm signal and by saying "advantage ——".

C. The Scorer will:
1. Record the line-ups of both teams and substitutes prior to the game.
2. Keep an accurate record of the goals scored and the time each was scored.
3. Record the name and number of a substitute.

D. The timer will:
1. Check with the umpires prior to the beginning of the game to see what the length of halves will be.

2. Stop the clock at the whistle and arm signal after each goal (see Rule 8–B).
3. Start the clock on the arm signal and verbal "ready draw" at each draw.
4. During the last two minutes of each half of the game, stop the clock on every whistle, then restart the clock on the umpire's verbal and arm signals (see Rule 8–E).
5. Indicate to the nearest umpire when there are 30 seconds remaining in each half.
6. Count out loud to the umpire the last 10 seconds of each half, sounding the horn when the time is up.
7. Stop the clock for any other circumstances only upon the time-out signal and whistle from the umpire.
8. Notify the umpire when there are two minutes remaining in each half of the game.
9. Let the umpire know when five and ten minutes have elapsed between halves.

Arm signals for Umpires:

Free position, held whistle, or possession of ball on out-of-bounds: indicates the direction with one arm raised horizontally towards the goal of the team in possession.

Goal: Arms are raised above the head and then turn and point both arms horizontally towards the centre of the field.

Goal circle foul: Point to goal circle and then indicate direction of free position.

No goal: With arms extended towards the ground, swing them out and in so that they cross each other.

Re-draw: Place arms fully extended horizontally in front of the body; begin with hands together and extend them up and out with a quick motion.

Substitution: Making a beckoning motion with one arm to entering player.

Time in: Hand open above the head with arm fully extended; then drop the arm in a chopping motion to start the clock.

Time out: Turn towards the timer and cross fully extended arms at the wrist above the head..

The foregoing are the International Women's Lacrosse Rules as adopted by the International Federation—slightly abbreviated for reasons of space.

The Laws of
Men's Lacrosse

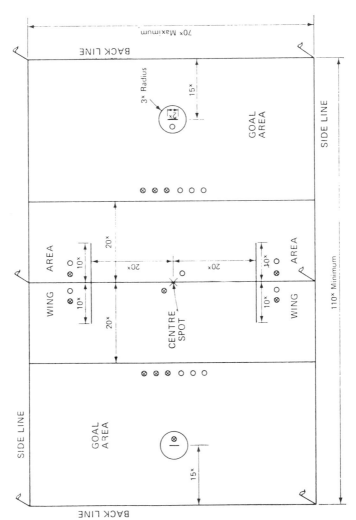

FIELD MARKINGS

Men's Lacrosse

THE RULES

These Rules have been approved by the English Lacrosse Union as the code for the playing of Men's Lacrosse in all games under its jurisdiction or under the auspices of affiliated Associations, Unions, Clubs or Bodies after 1 September 1985. The ultimate interpretation of the Rules shall be the sole prerogative of the Council of the English Lacrosse Union.

THE GAME

Lacrosse is played by two teams of ten players each. The purpose of each team is to score by causing the ball to enter the goal of its opponent and to prevent the other team from securing the ball and scoring. The ball is kept in play by being carried, thrown, or batted with the crosse, rolled or kicked in any direction subject to the restrictions laid down in the following rules. The ball may not be touched by the hands except by a goalkeeper while he is in the crease.

I. THE PLAYING FIELD

1. The Playing Field

The lacrosse playing field shall be wherever possible a rectangular field 110 yards (100 metres) long and 60 yards (55 metres) wide. The boundaries of the field shall be marked with white lines. A white line shall be marked through the centre of the field perpendicular to the side lines. This line shall be known as the 'centre line'. The boundary lines on the long sides of the field shall be designated 'side lines', those at each end shall be designated 'end lines'. Flag markers or pylons shall be placed at the four corners of the field and at the end of the centre line furthest from the Bench Area. Flag markers or pylons should be placed 2 yards (1.8 metres) either side of the end of the centre line, off the playing field, indicating the Bench Area. These flag markers or pylons must be made of flexible material so that they will bend a minimum of 90 degrees without breaking.

2. The Goals

Each goal shall consist of two vertical posts joined by a rigid top cross-bar. These posts shall be six feet (1.8 metres) apart and the top cross-bar shall be six feet (1.8 metres) from the ground (inside measurement). The goal posts shall be centred and shall be placed 80 yards (72 metres) apart and 15 yards (13.75 metres) from each end line. A line shall be drawn between the goal posts to indicate the plane of the goal, and it shall be designated as the 'goal-line'.

The vertical posts (known as 'goal posts') may be sunk in suitable sockets in the ground or they may be stood upon the ground by means of suitable angle-brackets and stays protruding directly behind each post and clamped securely to the ground. All the additional fixtures shall be contained inside the goal-net.

The vertical posts and the cross-bar shall be of wood or an approved metal or alloy and each shall be of not more than 3 ins (7.6 cm) square or equivalent circular cross section. The material used and the shape shall be such as to prevent injury resulting from collision with them.

A suitable bracket shall be attached near the top of each vertical post, and projected directly behind so that the net fastened to the cross-bar shall be supported to form a flat 'roof' of netting stretching between 9 in and 12 in (22.9 and 30.5 cm) behind the back face of the crossbar.

Where ground pipes are used they must have boards, 1 in × 3 in × 1½ in in length, securely fastened to the ground pipes directly behind the vertical posts at an angle of 45°.

3. Goal Crease

Around each goal there shall be plainly marked a circle known as the 'goal crease'. This circle shall be marked by using the mid-point of the goal-line as the centre and drawing a circle around that point with a radius of nine feet, (2.75 metres). The goal crease area is defined to be the circular ground territory about each goal within and including the goal crease.

4. Goal Nets

Each goal must be fitted with a pyramidal shaped cord netting which shall extend and be fastened on the ground at a point seven feet (2.1 metres) back from the centre of the goal. The mesh of the net shall not exceed one and one-half inches (3.8 cm) and shall be fastened to the goal posts, cross-bar and the ground so as to prevent the passage of the ball. Nets must be adjusted so the ball may pass completely through the imaginary plane of the goal at any place.

5. Goal Areas

At each end of the field a line shall be marked from side line to side line 20 yards (18 metres) from the centre line. The areas between these lines and the end lines and confined within the extremities of these lines are called the 'goal areas'.

6. Wing Areas

Lines parallel to the side lines shall be marked on each side of the field 20 yards (18 metres) from the centre of the field and extending 10 yards (9 metres) on each side of the centre line. The areas between these line segments and the side lines and confined within the extremities of these line segments shall be designated as 'wing areas'.

7. Centre of the Field

A point on the centre line equidistant from each side line shall be marked with an 'X' and shall be designated the 'Centre'.

8. Special Substitution and Penalty Area

Wherever possible there should be a special substitution and penalty area indicated by two lines marked on the side of the field. These lines shall be five feet (1.5 metres) in length extending from points on the side line five yards (4.5 metres) from the centre line at right angles to the side line. Where possible the penalty box should contain two seats for each team within the Bench Official's area.

9. Bench Areas

The bench areas are located off the playing field and between the imaginary extensions of the goal area lines away from the playing area. Where possible a dotted restraining line shall be placed 5 ft (1.5 metres) from the side line. It shall be parallel to the side line and extend the length of the bench area.

10. Lines

All lines called for by Rule 1 shall be a minimum of two inches (5.1 cm.) in width.

II. EQUIPMENT

1. The Ball

The ball shall be or white, yellow or orange rubber and between $7\frac{3}{4}$ and 8 inches (197 and 208 mm) in circumference, between 5 and $5\frac{1}{4}$ ounces (142 and 149 grammes) in weight, and shall bounce when dropped from a height of 72 inches (1.8 metres) upon a hard wood floor 45 to 49 inches (1.1 to 1.2 metres). Balls shall be supplied by the Home Team.

2. The Crosse

The crosse shall be of an overall length of between 40 and 72 inches (1.0 and 1.8 metres) (exception: goal keepers crosse may be any desired length). The head of the crosse shall measure between 4 and 10 inches (102 and 254 mm), inside measurement (*exception*: there may be one stick up to 15 inches (381 mm) inside measurement in the game at any time.)

The crosse shall be made of wood, laminated wood, or plastic with the head approximately perpendicular to the handle. The walls shall not be over two inches (5.1 cm) in height (*exception*: the gut wall). The centre line of the handle shall cross the head approximately two and a half inches (6.4 cm) from the wall. The head and sides of the crosse shall have holes bored in them to facilitate weaving of the stringing. The side wall opposite the wood shall be made by weaving gut lacing from the tip of the head to the handle, strung in such a manner as to prevent the tip from catching on an opponents crosse, or both walls may be of wood, laminated wood, or plastic. The guard stop at the throat of the stick must be a minimum of 10 inches (254 mm) from the outside edge of the head to the stop. The stop must be perpendicular to the handle of the stick and wide enough to permit the ball to rest loosely on the stop. The net of the crosse shall be constructed of gut, rawhide, clock cord, linen or nylon cord and shall be roughly triangular in shape.

3. Prohibitions Relating to Crosse

No player shall use a crosse which does not meet the specifications of Section 2 hereof or one in which the pocket has been permitted to sag to such a depth that it becomes unreasonably difficult for an opponent to dislodge the ball, or the construction or stringing at the throat of which is designed to hold the ball. Nor shall any player use a crosse of trick construction or stringing that tends to retard the normal and free dislodgement of the ball by an opponent. In general no stick may be tampered with in any way to give a player an advantage over his opponent.

NOTE: *The pocket shall be deemed to have sagged too deep within the prohibition of this rule, if the top surface of a lacrosse ball placed therein is below the bottom edge of the sidewalls when the crosse is held horizontally to the ground with the stringing or weaving to the bottom of the crosse. This prohibition does not apply to the crosse of the goalkeeper.*

4. Boots

Boots or shoes shall be of non-metalic construction except for the studs, but shall have no sharp edges or points which may injure other players.

NOTE: *This rule forbids inter alia, the use of boots or shoes containing nails and leather studs in any form.*

5. Personal Equipment

(*a*) Headgear and gloves are compulsory at League level and shall be of the approved Lacrosse pattern and style and shall not have any sharp points which might injure other players.

NOTE: *Play must be suspended immediately if a player loses any of the compulsory equipment in a scrimmage area. Otherwise the referee shall delay the sounding of his whistle in the same manner as set forth in Rule VI, Sec 13 A(1) and (2).*

(*b*) No protective clothing or gear shall be worn above the waist apart from approved headgear, arm guards, gauntlet gloves and in the case of the goalkeeper, the normal pad for the front of the body, and throat guards.

NOTE: *This rule forbids inter alia the wearing of any protection capable of producing a sharp edge or point which may injure other players. However shoulder protection manufactured from light weight foam may be worn.*

(*c*) No protective gear shall be worn on the legs apart from (1) shin guards and (2) the normal goalkeepers padding on his thighs.

NOTE: *The wearing of track suit trousers for all players is permitted, provided a uniform colour is used throughout the team.*

(*d*) No protective gear or clothing, other than headgear and gloves shall be visible.

(*e*) The normal dress shall be the team's registered jersey or shirt, shorts and stockings. Where shirts have short sleeves arm pads must be covered, unless the arm pads are manufactured from soft foam material. Jersey's should have no less than a six inch (15.1 cm) number on the front and an eight inch (20.3 cm) number on the back.

The colour of these numbers shall be contrasting with the colour of the jerseys. No duplicate numbers shall be permitted on the same team.

NOTE: *The visiting team shall notify the home team of the colour of the jerseys they are going to wear in the game and the home team must wear jerseys of a contrasting colour.*

III. THE TEAMS

1. Number and Designation of Players

Ten players shall constitute a full team.

They shall be, a goalkeeper, 3 defence players, 3 midfield and 3 attack players one of whom must be nominated 'In home'.

NOTE 1: *Before the commencement of the game the captain shall nominate to the referee the defenceman to serve the goalkeeper's penalty time.*

NOTE 2: *If because of injuries or men out on expulsion fouls, a team cannot keep 10 players in the game, it may continue the game with less than ten players but no exceptions will be made to the regular rules for this situation.*

2. Substitutes

The number of substitutes a team may have shall be up to three (3) in all.

3. Captains

Each team shall designate a captain who shall act as the sole representative of his team on the field of play during the game. The privilege of the captain to act as the sole representative of his team on the field does not grant him the right to enter into argument with or criticise any decision of an official. Should the captain leave the field of play, either he or his coach should designate to the nearest official the name and number of the replacing captain. In the event that a team should be without a designated captain at any time during the play of the game, either official may designate an acting captain.

NOTE: *Where a team has co-captains, one of them shall be designated as the official representative of that team on the field.*

4. Coaches

There is no limit on the number of coaches a team may have, but one shall be designated the head coach by each team and he shall be responsible for making all decisions for his team not specifically delegated to his game captain. He shall at all times conduct himself like a gentleman and shall endeavour in every way to have his players and substitutes also conduct themselves like gentlemen. He or the Captain shall also be in control of and responsible for the actions of all non-playing members of his squad also any and all persons officially connected with either side. He or the Captain shall assist the officials to keep the game under control at all times. It shall be their duty upon the request of an official to effectively control actions of spectators not in conformity with good sportsmanship. It shall be the responsibility of the home coach or Captain to see that the playing field is in proper condition for play; that the players and substitutes are properly equipped to play; that balls are provided; that Bench Officials are on hand with all equipment necessary to carry out their respective functions.

IV. CONTROL OF THE GAME

1. The Officials

The game of lacrosse shall be controlled by up to three officials (unless otherwise agreed upon by the teams in accordance with No. 1 hereto), 2 Referees and an Umpire.

Their duties shall be equal in all respects except that in the settlement of all disputes, the decision of the senior referee shall supersede that of the umpire and shall be final. The officials shall have authority over the play of the game, with control and jurisdiction over the appointed bench officials, players, substitutes, coaches, anyone officially connected with a team and spectators. Their authority shall begin with their arrival at the ground and terminate at a reasonable time after the end of the match.

By the sounding of his whistle either official may suspend the play of the game for any reason which he deems necessary for the proper enforcement of the rules or conduct of the game. The officials shall keep a record of the number of goals scored by each team and the number of the player scoring the goal.

One official shall keep an accurate record of the time played in each quarter.

NOTE 1: *Where both teams and the official agree, one official may be used, subject to the Bench official carrying out the offside duties.*

NOTE 2: *The officials uniform should be vertical black and white striped shirt with white shorts and black and white socks.*

2. Bench Official

A Bench Official shall be appointed and his duties shall be as follows:

(*a*) To supervise over and to hold complete jurisdiction over the coaches, substitutes and any other officials within the bench areas.

(*b*) To have in his possession a warning device distinctive from the whistles of the officials.

(*c*) To check the substitution of players going on and off the field of play and to sound a warning and subsequently advise the nearest official of any infringement relating to substitution, the number of players on the field of play, or any illegal action on the part of a coach or official member of either squad.

(*d*) To acknowledge to the officials, by raising one arm above his head, receipt and understanding of their signals relating to penalties, penalty periods or any other matters relating to the play of the game.

(*e*) To advise coaches, if so requested, as to the decisions of the officials.

(*f*) To keep a record of the name and number of each player upon whom a personal penalty is inflicted.

(*g*) To be equipped with time-pieces that can be stopped and record time in seconds, and time the period of any penalty imposed by the officials. To audibly count down the last ten seconds of that penalty time to the player concerned and to advise him that he may return to the field of play upon the expiration of the penalty time.

(*h*) To notify the nearest official of any player who has incurred five personal fouls.

NOTE 1: *See Rule IV, Section 1, Note 1.*

NOTE 2: *In the event of the failure of the Home team to so provide this competent fully conversant official, the Referee shall instruct the Captain of the Home team to select one substitute or player who is capable in undertaking the duties, to act as official. The player selected shall take no further part in the playing of the game.*

3. Mistakes of the Bench Official

Where the Bench Official or an Official makes a mistake which would result in a team or player being penalised, and where an official becomes aware that a mistake is being made, he shall promptly correct the mistake. If goals are scored during the mistake by the above mentioned officials and it is brought to the attention of the referee before the next live ball, after the player in question has participated in the game, then the referee must allow or disallow the goal depending upon the circumstances.

NOTE: *The Official's horn or whistle in itself, never stops the game, only the referee's whistle when appropriate, can stop the game. On hearing the horn the referee may operate the slow whistle depending on the circumstances at that time. (Refers to all of Rule IV).*

V. LENGTH OF THE GAME

1. Time of Match

The playing time shall be four quarters of 20 minutes each, in all matches whenever possible. If less time has to be played through failure of daylight or from any other cause then the curtailment of playing time shall be at the discretion of the Referee, who shall, if possible, arrange that all four quarters shall be of equal duration. If in any match it is not possible to play at least one hour in all, then such a match shall not count in any competition and shall be replayed.

2. Time Off

'Time off' incurred in each quarter shall be added to the agreed playing time of that quarter.

3. Interval between Quarters

At the conclusion of the 1st, 2nd and 3rd quarters the team shall change ends. The first quarter interval shall be of two minutes duration. At half time an interval of 10 minutes is permitted and both teams may leave the playing field. At three quarter time an interval of three minutes shall be allowed but players shall on leaving the playing field assemble in the bench area only, but to go beyond this area they must have the permission of the referee. By mutual agreement the Captains and referee may shorten the quarter time intervals.

NOTE: *The referee shall give a warning signal one minute prior to the commencement of all four periods.*

4. Defaulted Game

(*a*) If any team fails to fulfil an engagement without, in the opinion of the League Committee, giving adequate cause or reason, the Committee shall either disqualify the defaulting Team for that Match and award its opponents a win, or shall disqualify the Team for the remainder of the Competitions. In the former case the Committee may also deduct one point from the defaulting Team's total points, and in the latter case no points scored for and against the disqualified Teams shall count in the aggregates.

VI. PLAY OF THE GAME

1. Actions Prior to the Game

The following preliminaries to the game shall take place.

(*a*) TOSS FOR GOALS

The Captains of each team shall be called together at the centre of the field by the officials approximately five minutes before game time, and a coin shall be tossed by the referee to determine choice of goals. At this time any special ground rules shall be agreed upon. The visiting team Captain shall call the toss of the coin.

(*b*) LINE-UP

The referee shall draw up the players in lines facing each

other at the centre of the field with their left sides towards the goal they are defending, inspect equipment and explain any special ground rules.

2. Facing at the Centre

Play shall be started at the beginning of each period and after each goal has been scored by facing the ball at the centre of the field. The players facing shall stand on the same side of the centre line of the field as the goal each is defending with their crosses resting on the ground along the centre line. They must have both hands on the handle of their own crosse and not touching any strings, the feet shall not touch the crosse and both gloved hands must be on the ground; no portion of either crosse may touch and the walls must be approximately one inch apart and the ball must never be touching the ground. Both hands and both feet must be to the left of the throat of the crosse. Hands must be at least 18 inches apart at the beginning of the draw. The official shall place the ball between, in the centre, and resting on the walls of the reverse surfaces of the crosses of the players facing. When the official sounds his whistle to start play each player may attempt to direct the course of the ball by movement of his crosse in any manner he desires. Kicking or stepping on an opponent's crosse on a face-off is illegal. The following rules shall apply when the ball is faced at the centre of the field:

NOTE: *If after a centre face-off, and before possession is called by an official, an official mistakenly blows his whistle thinking an infringement of the rules has occurred, the ball shall be refaced at the centre of the field, with the same restrictions as in paragraphs (a) and (b) following.*

(*a*) Except under the conditions stated in paragraph (*b*) hereof, each team shall confine the goalkeeper and three other players in the defence goal area, three players in the attack goal area and one player in each of the wing areas. When the whistle sounds to start play, the players in the wing areas shall be released. All other players are confined to their areas until any player of either team has gained possession of the ball, the ball goes out-of-bounds or the ball crosses either goal area line.

(*b*) If a team has one or more players out of the game on penalty, that team shall be exempt from confining its players in the goal and wing areas to the extent of its players in the penalty box. It shall also have the right to choose in which confining area or areas it shall exercise its exemption.

NOTE: *A team that is short of players due to penalties may select the restraining areas that they desire to leave vacant, however they must obey the off-side rule.*

3. Facing in Other Parts of the Field

The following rules pertain when the facing occurs other than as provided for in Section 2 hereof.

(*a*) The crosses of the players shall be placed at right angles to an imaginary line running from the ball to the nearer goal. The defending player shall stand between his crosse and his own goal, so as to face away from his own goal. The attacking player shall face towards the goal and shall stand on the opposite side of his crosse. Conditions of Section 2 hereof apply as to method of facing.

(*b*) In no case shall the ball be faced closer to the goal than 20 yards in any direction.

(*c*) In all cases where the ball is faced, no player shall be allowed within 10 yards of those facing the ball until the official sounds his whistle to commence play.

(*d*) At no time shall a ball be faced closer than 20 feet from a boundary line.

(*e*) Whenever the goalkeeper would be the player to participate in a face-off, a player of his team may be substituted for him.

4. Free Play

When a player has been awarded the ball for any reason, no opposing player may take a position closer to him than 9 feet.

5. Scoring

A goal counts one point, and is scored when a loose ball passes from the front completely through the imaginary plane formed by the rear edges of the goal line as a base, the cross-bar of the goal as the top, and the goal posts as the two sides. Should the ball be caused to pass through the plane of the goal by one of the defending players it counts as a goal for the attacking team. Under the following conditions, however, a goal does not count:

(*a*) When the ball passes through the plane of the goal after the Referee's whistle sounds indicating the end of a quarter.

(*b*) When the ball passes through the plane of the goal when any part of the body of a player of the attacking team is in the goal crease area.

(*c*) When the ball passes through the plane of the goal when the attacking team has more than 10 men (including men in the penalty box) on the field of play at the time.

(*d*) When the ball passes through the plane of the goal when the attacking team or both teams are offside at the time.

(*e*) When the ball passes through the plane of the goal after one of the officials has sounded his whistle for any reason even though the sounding of the whistle was inadvertent.

6. Possession of Ball

In all situations possession of the ball shall be defined as follows:

(*a*) *Player possession.* A player shall be considered in possession of the ball when he has control of it and could perform any of the normal functions of play such as carrying, cradling, passing or shooting.

(*b*) *Team possession.* A team shall have possession of the ball only when a player on that team has possession of the ball as defined in paragraph (*a*) hereof.

(*c*) *Loose ball.* A ball not in player or team's possession is a loose ball.

7. Ball Out-of-Bounds

Play shall be suspended at any time when the ball is out-of-bounds.

(*a*) When a player with the ball in his possession steps on or beyond a boundary line or any part of his body or crosse touches the ground on or beyond a boundary line, the ball is out-of-bounds, and the player shall lose possession thereof. The ball shall be awarded to any player of the opposing team who is ready immediately to make the free play, at the point where the ball was declared out-of-bounds.

(b) When a loose ball touches a boundary line or the ground outside of a boundary line, or when it touches anything on the boundary line or outside of the boundary line, it is out-of-bounds, and the following rules shall apply:

1. Except on a shot or deflected shot at the goal provided for in paragraph 3 hereof, the ball shall be awarded at the point where it was declared out-of-bounds to any player on the opposing team to that of the player who last touched it, ready immediately to make the free play.

2. Should the ball go out-of-bounds on a face off, it shall be faced again at the same place where the previous face occurred, subject to the same restrictions as the original face off.

3. When the loose ball goes out-of-bounds as a result of a shot or deflected shot at the goal, it shall be awarded to the team one of whose inbound players was nearest to the ball when it became an out-of-bounds ball, at the point where the ball was declared out-of-bounds. If two inbounds players of opposite teams are equidistant to the ball when it goes out-of-bounds, the ball shall be faced by two players under the conditions of Rule VI, Section 3.

NOTE: *Deflected shot remains a shot until the ball comes to rest on the field of play; a team gains possession of the ball; the ball goes-out-of-bounds; or a player deliberately causes the ball to go out-of-bounds.*

8. Off-Side

Except as provided in paragraph (b) hereof, a team is considered off-side when:

1. It has less than three men in its attack half of the field between the centre line and the end line.

2. It has less than four men in its defensive half of the field between the centre line and the end line.

The offside rules must be observed at all times unless a goal has been scored or during an official or team time out.

(*a*) The following rules apply when play has been suspended as a result of off-side:

1. When only one team is off-side, a technical penalty shall be inflicted in accordance with the provisions of Rule XI, Sec. (*k*) the single exception being provided for in paragraph 4 hereof.
2. When both teams are off-side and one of the teams has possession of the ball, the men shall be placed on side and play resumed with the team in possession of the ball retaining possession, the single exception being provided for in paragraph 4 hereof.
3. When both teams are off-side and neither team has possession of the ball, the men shall be placed on side and the ball faced by the players on opposite teams closest to the ball when play was suspended subject to Rule VI. Sect. (*f*).
4. When the attacking team is off-side at the time a goal is made, the score shall not count, and the ball shall be awarded to the goalkeeper of the defensive team behind the goal. If the defensive team is offside the goal scores and no penalty shall be inflicted. If both teams are offside the score shall not count, and the ball shall be faced 20 feet from the end line directly behind the goal by players on opposite teams nearest the ball when the whistle blows.

(*b*) The following exception shall apply:

When four men or more are in the penalty box on the same team, that team is required to have three men in the attacking half of the field and the remainder of its players in the defensive half of the field at all times. Under such conditions no penalty shall result from the failure of the team to have the required number of players in the defensive half of the field.

9. Bodychecking

Bodychecking of an opponent in possession of the ball or within 9 ft. of a loose ball is permitted.

NOTE 1: *A bodycheck shall be considered to be the placing of the body in the way of and facing an approaching opponent, so that the latter is simply impeded.*

NOTE 2: *When a player uses his spread arm or arms in a bodycheck, they must be kept below the shoulders of the opponent throughout and both hands must remain in contact with the crosse.*

10. Shoulder Charge

A player may use a shoulder to shoulder charge against an opponent with whom he is engaged or about to be engaged in a ground scuffle.

11. Checking with Crosse

A player may check his opponent's crosse with his own crosse when said opponent has possession of the ball, is within 9 feet of a loose ball or the ball is in flight within 9 feet of the player. (See Rule IX, Sec. 2(*b*), for description of illegal checking with crosse.)

12. Holding

A player may hold off an opponent in possession of the ball (or within three yards of a loose ball) with either closed gloved hand on the handle of his crosse or either forearm. Both hands of the player must be on his crosse. The holding off must be merely the exerting of equal pressure.

13. Offensive Screening

Stationary and motionless offensive screening of an opponent is permitted. (See Rule XI. Sect 2(*b*) for description of illegal offensive screening).

14. Time Outs

Time outs are of two varieties, those called by the officials and those called by the teams.

(*a*) *Official Time Outs.* Either official may suspend play at his discretion. When a player is injured and in the judgement of the official the injury is serious, play shall be suspended immediately. Otherwise, the official shall delay the sounding of his whistle as follows:

1. If the attacking team is in possession of the ball in the attack half of the field and in the opinion of the official a scoring play is imminent, the official shall delay the sounding of his whistle in the same manner as under the 'slow whistle procedure' under Rule XIII, Sec. 3.

2. If the ball is not in the possession of either team, the official shall delay the sounding of his whistle until possession is secured and the play completed, if a scoring play is imminent, in the same manner as under the 'slow whistle procedure' under Rule XIII, Sec. 3. The signal flag is not dropped under these conditions.

(*b*) *Team Time Outs.* When the ball is dead the coach or the captain of either team may request an official to call a time-out for a period not to exceed 90 seconds. When the ball is in the possession of the offensive team in their attacking half of the field, the coach or captain of the offensive team may request a time-out. A team shall be limited to one time-out a half. Any suspension of play because of an injured player, shall not be charged as a team time-out, if such a player is removed from the field as soon as possible. A substitute for this man must report immediately, if available.

VII. SUBSTITUTION

1. Substitution

Maximum substitution may take place at any time during the match, subject to the following.

2. Method of Substitution

(*a*) The substituting player must wait in the substitution area for the player he is replacing to leave the field of play via the substitution area and only then may he enter the field of play. i.e. He may enter the field from either side of the centre line providing the Off-side Rule concerning the number of players in each half of the field is observed at all times as per Rule VI. Section 8, parts (1) and (2).

(*b*) If the player leaving the field of play is one of the players bound to his playing area by the off-side rule the provisions of the off-side rule will be deemed to be observed if the substituting player steps out of the substitution area onto the field of play at the same time as the player leaving the field steps into the substitution area.

(*c*) The player being replaced must leave the field of play through the substitution area otherwise a foul is committed by his team.

NOTES: *The following exceptions apply:*

1. On the scoring of a goal, substitution may be effected from the side line at any point and need not necessarily be through the substitution area. It will be necessary for the substituting player to remain on the side line until his counterpart leaves the playing field but the substitution must be completed before the referee is ready to recommence play.

2. Upon the calling of time out by an official for an injured player, if unable to continue, the injured player shall be removed from the field as soon as possible to the nearest boundary.

VIII. GOAL CREASE AND GOALKEEPER

1. Privileges of Goalkeeper

While within his own goal crease area, the designated goalkeeper shall have the following privileges and protections:

(*a*) He may stop or block the ball in any manner with his crosse or body, and he may block the ball or bat it away with his hand, but he may not catch the ball with his hand. He or any player of the defending team may receive a pass while in the crease area.

(*b*) No opposing player may initiate contact with the goalkeeper or his crosse while the goalkeeper is within the goal crease area whether he has the ball in his possession or not. An attacking player may reach within the crease area to play a loose ball so long as he does not initiate contact with the goalkeeper or his crosse.

NOTE: *When not in possession of the ball, the goalkeeper's crosse may be checked when it is extended outside an imaginary crease cylinder subject to being checked under the same circumstances as the crose of any other player.*

(*c*) Should the ball become mired in the mud within the crease area, time shall be suspended by the officials and the ball shall be faced no closer to goal than 20 yards laterally.

(*d*) Should the ball become ensnared in the goal netting, time shall be suspended by the official and the ball awarded to the goalkeeper at the end line directly behind the goal.

2. Prohibitions Relating to Goal Crease Area

The following rules relating to the goal crease area shall apply:

(*a*) An attacking player shall not be in the opponent's goal crease area at any time while the ball is in the attacking half of the field.

(*b*) A defending player with the ball in his possession may not enter the goal crease area.

(*c*) Any player with the ball in his possession may not re-enter the goal crease area. Nor may he remain within the goal crease area in possession of the ball longer than is necessary to step out of the crease.

NOTE: *A reasonable (necessary) length of time is four seconds, counted by the official 1001, 1002, 1003 and 1004.*

(*d*) A player is considered to have entered the goal crease area when any part of his body touches the goal crease area.

(*e*) The goalkeeper is considered to be outside the goal crease area for the purpose of paragraph C. hereof when no part of his body touches the goal crease area and part of his body is touching an area outside the goal crease area.

(*f*) Any player who tries to circumvent the four second rule of the crease by dropping the ball and then picking it up again will be assessed a technical foul.

IX. PERSONAL FOULS

1. Penalty for Personal Fouls

For personal fouls the penalty shall be suspension from the game for one to three minutes (depending upon the officials' diagnosis of the severity and intention of the violation).

2. Description of Personal Fouls

Personal fouls are those of the more serious kind, listed and defined as follows:

(*a*) *Illegal Bodycheck*. Any bodycheck of an opponent in possession of the ball or 9 ft. from a loose ball, where the body has not been placed in the way of and facing an approaching opponent so that the latter is simply impeded is illegal.

NOTE: *Any form of a 'Take Out' is illegal.*

(*b*) *Slashing*. Under no circumstances shall a player swing his crosse at an opponent's crosse with deliberate viciousness or reckless abandon, and a foul is committed by so doing whether or not the opponent's crosse or body is struck. Nor shall a player strike an opponent in an attempt to dislodge the ball from his crosse. However, a check shall not be declared illegal if, in an attempt to protect his crosse the offensive player uses some part of his body other than his head to ward off the thrust of the defensive player's crosse and as a result the defensive player's crosse strikes some part of the attacking player's body other than his head. Any strike on the head by the crosse of an opponent is illegal, except when done by a man in the act of passing or shooting.

NOTE 1: *For the purpose of all rules, the gloved hand on the crosse of a player is considered as part of his crosse.*

NOTE 2: *For the purpose of this rule, mere contact is not a "strike". The contact must be a definite blow and not merely a brush.*

(*c*) *Cross Check*. A player may not check his opponent with his crosse in a cross-check position, – that is, check him with that part of the handle of his crosse which is between his hands, either by thrusting it away from his body or by holding it extended from his body.

(*d*) *Tripping*. A player shall not trip an opponent with any part of his body or crosse.

NOTE: *Tripping is obstructing an opponent below the knees with the crosse, hands, arms, feet or legs, by any positive primary action if the obstructing player is on his feet, and by any positive secondary action if the obstructing player is not on his feet.*

(e) Unnecessary Roughness.

1. An excessively violent infraction of the rules against holding and pushing is a personal foul, designated unnecessary roughness. See elements of fouls of holding and pushing under Rule XI, Sect. 2(*c*).

2. A deliberate and excessively violent contact made by a defensive player against an offensive player, who has established a screening position and not committed a foul (see Rule XI, Sec. 2(*b*)) in so doing, shall be designated unnecessary roughness.

3. Any avoidable act on the part of a player which is deliberate and excessively violent shall be designated unnecessary roughness, whether it be with the body or stick.

(f) Unsportsmanlike Conduct. No player, substitute, non-playing member of a squad, coach or anyone officially connected with a competing team shall:

1. Enter into argument with an official as to any decision he has made, or in any way attempt to influence the decision of an official.

2. Use threatening, profane or obscene language at any time during the game.

3. Use a stick, with trick stringing, that is designed to hold the ball, and tends to retard the normal and free dislodgement of the ball by an opponent. This stick shall be placed in the custody of the bench official for the remainder of the game and the player using said stick shall be given a three minute penalty, which he shall serve regardless of goals scored etc.

4. Commit any act considered unsportsmanlike by the officials.

5. For repeated abuse of Rule VI, Sect. 2(*a*) the penalty shall be suspension from the game for one minute.

X. EXPULSION FOULS

1. Penalty for Expulsion Fouls

The penalty for expulsion fouls shall be suspension for the remainder of the game. In such cases the ball shall be given into the possession of the opposite team from that on which the expulsion foul was called, or faced if the foul occurs prior to the start of the game or after the whistle has blown denoting the scoring of a goal or the end of a period. In the case of an expulsion foul against a player, including a substitute, a substitute may be made after the lapse of three minutes. In the case of an expulsion foul against a coach, non-playing member of a squad or someone officially connected with a team, the inhome of the offending team shall be suspended from the game for three minutes, and he must remain in the penalty box for the entire three minutes. In any event, he cannot return to the game until the lapse of the penalty time.

2. Description of Expulsion Fouls

The act of deliberately striking or attempting to strike an opponent, non-playing member of an opponent's squad, coach or anyone controlling the play of the game, with the hand, crosse, ball or otherwise, by a player, substitute, non-playing member of a squad, coach or anyone officially connected with a team may be an expulsion foul.

Refusal to accept the authority of officials, of the use of foul or abusive language, may result in an expulsion foul.

3. Reporting of Expulsion Fouls

Players are reminded that should any player receive a direct expulsion foul, he shall be referred to the disciplinary committee immediately. After the game the referee shall immediately and in writing fully report the facts of any direct expulsion foul to the Secretary of the Referees Committee of the Regional Association in whose area the game was played, and the secretary shall immediately refer the case to the Association Disciplinary Committee for attention.

4. Player Committing Five Personal Fouls

Any player who commits five personal fouls shall be expelled from the game. A substitute for that player may enter the game at such time as the expelled player would have been permitted to re-enter the game had he not committed five personal fouls.

XI. TECHNICAL FOULS

1. Penalty for Technical Fouls

For technical fouls the penalty shall be either suspension from the game for 30 seconds if the offending team does not have possession of the ball at the time the foul is committed, or simply loss of the ball if the offending team does have possession of the ball or the ball is not in the possession of either team at the time the foul is committed. In the event that the foul occurs prior to the start of the game or after the whistle has blown denoting the scoring of a goal or the end of a period, the player is suspended from the game and the ball is faced. In the event that the foul occurs at some other time during the course of the game but while play is suspended, the general rule rather than the exception shall apply.

2. Description of Technical Fouls

Technical fouls are those of less serious kind. Any breach of the rules of play as set forth herein shall be a technical foul unless said breach is specifically listed as an expulsion or personal foul in Rule IX or Rule X hereof. Some of the technical fouls requiring definition are hereinafter listed, but this specific description of certain technical fouls is not intended to be comprehensive and all inclusive.

(*a*) *Interference*. A player may not interfere in any manner with an opponent in an attempt to keep him from a loose ball except when both are within 9 feet of the ball. Nor, may a player interfere, by the use of his body or crosse, in any manner with a player in pursuit of an opponent. Nor, may a player guard an opponent so closely as to prevent his free movement when that player is not in possession of the ball.

NOTE 1: *Nothing in this rule is intended to prohibit a legal offensive screen.*

NOTE 2: *This rule does prohibit a player from deliberately stepping on or kicking the crosse of an opponent.*

(*b*) *Illegal Offensive Screening*. No offensive player shall move into and make contact with a defensive player with the purpose of blocking a defensive player from the man he is playing:

NOTE: *Offensive player must be stationary and motionless before contact is made by the defensive player.*

(*c*) *Holding.* A player shall not hold an opponent or his crosse except as follows

NOTE 1: *This rule does not prohibit the player in possession of the ball from protecting his crosse with his hand, arm or other part of his body when his opponent makes a play to check his crosse. The hand, arm or other part of his body may be used to stop the check only, and must not be used to hold, push or control the checkers crosse.*

NOTE 2: *A player may hold off an opponent in possession of the ball (or within three yards of a loose ball) with either closed gloved hand on the handle of his crosse or either forearm. Both hands of the player must be on his crosse. The holding off must be merely the exerting of equal pressure.*

(*d*) *Touching the Ball.* A player shall not touch the ball with his hands while it is in play, excepting the goalkeeper as provided for in Rule VIII, Sec. 1(*a*).

(*e*) *Withholding the Ball from Play.*

1. A player shall not lie on a loose ball on the ground or trap it with his stick longer than is necessary for him to control the ball and pick it up in one continuous motion or withhold the ball from play in any manner.
2. A player shall not hold his stick in close proximity to his body with the express purpose of preventing an opponent from the opportunity of dislodging the ball.

(*f*) *Illegal Actions with Crosse.* A player shall not:

1. Throw his crosse under any circumstances.
2. Take part in the play of the game in any manner without his crosse.
3. During the play of the game, exchange his crosse for another except to replace a broken crosse.

NOTE: *This rule does not prohibit the interchange of crosses by players legally on the playing field.*

4. Should a player lose his crosse in any legal way so that repossession of the crosse would cause him to violate a rule, the slow whistle technique Rule XIII, Sect. 3. shall be employed by an official, except as in Rule VI. Should the crosse be in the crease so as to possibly

interfere with the goalkeepers play of an attempted shot at the goal, play shall be suspended immediately.

(*g*) *Illegal actions on the part of persons officially connected with a team.* A coach, trainer or other person officially connected with a team shall not:

1. Enter the field of play without the permission of an official, except when there is a team time-out or between periods.
2. Use artificial aids in communicating with players on the field of play.
3. Leave the area on his bench side of the field, between the centre line and the restraining line.

NOTE: *This rule does not prohibit a coach from communicating with a player out of the game on a penalty or from his bench area.*

(*h*) *Illegal procedure.* Any action on the part of players or substitutes of a technical nature not in conformity with the rules and regulations governing the play of the game shall be termed illegal procedure. Following are examples of illegal procedure:

1. Entering the game from the penalty box before authorised to do so by bench official is a foul, and the player shall be returned to the penalty box to serve out his original time plus 30 seconds.

    The exception being at the end of a quarter where he may leave the penalty area but must return at the commencement of the following quarter to complete suspension.

    If the ball is loose or in possession of the player's own team, it shall be awarded to the opposing team.

NOTE: *In the event that a goal is scored by his opponents the unexpired penalty time is nullified, but he must serve 30 seconds for illegal entry into the game.*

2. Delaying the game is a foul, and the penalty, therefore, shall be assigned to the inhome. Delaying the game shall be consuming of more than 30 seconds in such instances as:

(*a*) At the start of the game or a period
(*b*) After the expiration of a time out

(c) After a goal has been scored

(d) After a penalty has been inflicted

(e) After an out-of-bounds ball

(f) Adjusting of equipment

NOTE: *Thirty seconds begins for (a)* when the official blows his whistle to summon the players to position;

1. 30 seconds prior to the official game time;

2. after one and a half minutes have elapsed between the first and second quarters.

3. after $9\frac{1}{2}$ minutes have elapsed between the second and third quarters.

4. after $2\frac{1}{2}$ minutes have elapsed between the third and fourth quarters.

For (b) when the official blows his whistle to summon the players to position:

1. after one minute of a team charged time out has elapsed or after an injured player has been removed from the game;

2. whenever play is ready to be resumed after an officials' suspension of play.

For (c) when either official has the ball in his possession.

For (d) when the official inflicting the penalty has notified the Chief Bench Official.

For (e) when the ball is in possession of a player or official at the out-of-bounds spot.

For (f) when adjusting equipment.

3. Participation in the play of the game by a player out-of-bounds is a foul.

4. Any player not in his restraining area at the time the whistle is blown to start play at time of centre face-off is in violation of the centre face-off rule.

5. Failing to remain 10 yards from a face-off, or failure to remain 9 feet from an opponent having a free play is a foul.

6. Any breach of the provisions for substituting players as provided for under Rule VII is a foul.

7. Any breach of the provisions relating to the goal crease as provided for under Rule VIII, Sec. 2 is a foul.

8. Any breach of the provisions for time-outs under Rule VI, Sec 14 is a foul.

9. Any deliberate action on the part of a team in possession of the ball to maintain possession thereof outside the attack goal area by holding or passing the ball without reasonable effort to attack its opponents goal is a foul known as "stalling". In view of the fact that stalling is generally an obvious manoeuvre and harmful to the game of lacrosse, officials should strictly enforce the rule against stalling, after a verbal warning of 'Play On'.

NOTE 1: *This rule shall not be interpreted as preventing a team from employing a careful passing game for the purpose of manoeuvring the opposing team out of position.*

NOTE 2: *A team playing with fewer players than the opposing team due to penalties cannot be guilty of stalling.*

NOTE 3: *A team may not be called for stalling if they have possession in their attack goal area.*

10. Having more than 10 men in the game at any time (including man or men in the penalty box) is a foul.

11. Violation of Rule VI, Sec. 2(*a*) is a foul.

(*i*) *Illegal Crosse.* Should it come to the attention of an official that a player is using an illegal crosse, other than trick stringing, within the provisions of Rule II, Secs 2 and 3, the official shall demand that the player adjust the crosse to conform to specifications or else exchange it for another. For a second violation against the same player, the official shall inflict a technical foul and place the illegal crosse in the custody of the bench official for the remainder of the game.

(*j*) *Illegal Equipment.* Should it come to the attention of an official that a player is wearing illegal equipment within the provisions of Rule II, Secs 4 and 5 the official shall demand that the player conform to specifications. Should the player fail to do so, he shall be compelled to withdraw from the game until such time as he has complied with the regulations covering equipment, a substitute being allowed for him immediately. For a second violation against the same player, the official shall inflict a technical foul and compel the player to withdraw from the contest until such time as he has complied with the regulations.

(*k*) *Off-side.* Any breach of the provisions of Rule VI, Sec 8 is a technical foul. Enforcement shall be in accordance with the provisions of said rule and section.

(*l*) *Thrusting Crosse at Face of Opponent.* A player shall not push at, thrust, or 'flick' his crosse in the face of an opponent.

(*m*) *Avoidable Lateness of a Team.* When a team fails to appear on the field ready to play at the appointed time for the start of a contest and this tardiness is avoidable, a technical foul has been committed by that team, and the inhome of the offending team shall be charged with the technical foul.

XII. PLAYER COMMITTING FOUL

1. Procedures for Player Committing Foul

A player who has committed a violation of the rules must raise his stick at full arms length above his head, and on being sent out of the game by an official shall:

(*a*) Report immediately to the bench official and remain in the penalty area until informed by him that his penalty time has elapsed. He may then re-enter the game or, if being substituted, may then return to the players bench.

(*b*) When re-entering the game, enter the field of play at the off-side line.

(*c*) Where a "time" penalty is expressed, this refers to the time off the field, out of play, and to be served in the "Penalty Area" by the offending player.

(*d*) For Technical and Personal Fouls the timing of the penalties commences from the time when the offending player(s) steps within the penalty area or when the game is resumed, whichever is the later.

(*e*) Penalty time will be served only during normal playing time. Only stoppages in play for time-outs and at the end of a quarter will interrupt penalty time. Any unserved penalty time at the end of a quarter must be served out at the beginning of the next quarter.

(*f*) Penalty time will end when the time of the penalty has expired except that the scoring of a goal against a team having one or more players serving penalty time for technical fouls, shall release the player or players from serving the balance of their penalty time but not such players serving penalty time for personal fouls.

(*g*) In the event of a goalkeeper offending against the crease rules, the penalty shall be a free play awarded to the opposing team to be taken from the end line directly behind the goal, by the nearest player of the opposing team to that point when the offence occurred.

(*h*) Should a goalkeeper commit a technical or personal foul of a non-violent or non-abusive nature, a defence player will serve the penalty time incurred to reduce the chance of injury to an inadequately protected deputy. Should a goalkeeper commit a foul of a violent or abusive nature, the goalkeeper shall serve the penalty time incurred.

Where the designated goalkeeper is sent off for a time serving penalty whoever replaces the goalkeeper, by the exchanging of crosses, shall be afforded all the rights of the designated goalkeeper, until such time as the crosses are re-exchanged.

NOTE: *Before commencement of the game the captains shall nominate to the referee the defenceman to serve the goalkeepers penalty time. For disciplinary purposes such penalties will not be credited to the defence player but to the goalkeeper.*

XIII. EXECUTION OF PENALTIES BY OFFICIALS

1. Beginning of Play after Penalty

In all cases where a penalty has been called in the offended team's offensive half of the field, the ball shall be put in play by the closest player of the team awarded the ball at the point on the field where the ball was when play was suspended, the only exception being where the ball is within a 20 yard radius of the goal. In this case the ball shall (1) be given to the player nearest to the ball when play was suspended, and then (2) this player shall be moved to a position laterally across the field 20 yards from the gaol.

When a penalty occurs in the offended teams defensive half of the field where penalty time is to be served, the ball shall be awarded to any player of the offended team on the offensive side of the midfield line.

Exception: Where the ball is to be awarded to the goalkeeper as a result of a crease infraction, (loss of the ball only), instead of being moved 20 yards from the goal laterally, he shall be awarded the ball at the end line directly behind the goal.

2. Special Situations

The following rules shall pertain to the special situations listed below:

(*a*) Where an official is called upon to inflict a penalty against a team where no definite player is involved or where the penalty is against someone other than a player in the game, he shall select the inhome and inflict the suspension. If multiple fouls of this type occur, he shall inflict the suspension against additional attack players. Where the person committing the foul is a substitute, the foul shall be assessed against him insofar as the record is concerned and he may only re-enter the game subject to the same restrictions as though he were a player at the time the foul was committed.

(*b*) When simultaneous fouls have been committed, the following rules shall be applied by the officials:

When a simultaneous foul occurs and as a result one team incurs more penalty time, or times, than its opponent, the team with the lesser penalty time shall be awarded the ball. In the event the penalty time, or times, are equal the team in possession of the ball retains possession. If neither team has possession, the ball shall be faced where it was at the time the whistle blew, subject to Rule VI, Sec 3.

Both fouls being technical and the ball being in the possession of one team, the fouls cancel and the team in possession retains possession where the ball was at the time the whistle sounded. If there is no team in possession the fouls cancel and the ball is faced subject to Rule VI, Sec 3.

(*c*) When any foul occurs prior to the start of the game or after the official's whistle has sounded marking suspension of play, the penalty shall be inflicted the same as if it had occurred during the play of the game. (See Rule XI, Sec. 1 as to Technical Fouls.)

3. Slow Whistle Technique

If a defending player commits a foul against an attacking player and the ball is in the attacking half of the field, and an attack player has possession of the ball at the time this foul occurs and in the opinion of the official, a scoring play is imminent, and the act of fouling does not cause the player in possession of the ball to lose possession thereof, the official must drop a signal flag and withhold his whistle until such time as the scoring play has been completed.

The scoring play shall be considered to have been completed when the attacking team has lost control of the ball, has clearly lost the opportunity of scoring a goal on the original play; or has taken a shot or the ball has been passed more than once behind the goal and forward again. The slow whistle technique shall be used whether the foul is committed against the man in possession of the ball or some other member of the attacking team.

NOTE 1: *A pass is a movement of a ball caused by a player in control throwing or bouncing a ball to a team mate.*

NOTE 2: *During a slow whistle situation, a shot remains a shot until (1) it is clearly obvious a goal will not be scored. (2) No added impetus is given the ball by any member of the attacking team. (3) When possession is gained by any member of the defensive team. (4) After hitting goalkeeper post or posts, ball shall be declared dead as soon as it is touched by any player of either team.*

4. Enforcement

A player, or substitute, committing a personal foul shall always be suspended from the game for the designated penalty time regardless of whether or not a goal is scored. The only exception to this being a foul committed by the designated goalkeeper, when Rule XIII, Sec. I.H. may apply. If a goal is scored following a slow whistle technique on a technical foul, no penalty is given; if a goal is not scored following a slow whistle technique on a technical foul (or fouls) the penalty is always suspension from the game for 30 seconds for each foul. In all cases where a goal is not scored, the ball is awarded to the team fouled (the attacking team) at the spot where the ball is when play is suspended. Section 1 of this Rule being followed.

5. Procedure When Ball Caught in Crosse or Equipment

In the event that the ball shall become caught in a player's crosse, the official shall count 1001, 1002, 1003, 1004, and, if at the end of those four seconds the ball has not been dislodged, the official shall stop play and the ball shall be faced between the player in whose crosse the ball was caught and his nearest opponent. In the event that the ball shall become caught in a player's uniform or equipment other than his stick, play shall be suspended immediately and the ball faced between him and his nearest opponent subject to Rule VI, Sec. 3. In neither of these situations shall this general rule apply to a designated goalkeeper when he is within his goal crease area. In that event he shall be awarded the ball at the end line directly behind the goal.

The Rules of
Netball

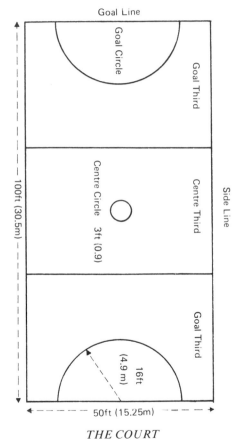

THE COURT

*All lines are part of the court and shall not be
more than 2 in (50 mm) wide.*

Netball

THE GAME

Netball is an International Sport. It is played by two teams of
seven players and is based on throwing and catching. Goals are
scored from within a defined area by throwing the ball into a
ring attached to a 3.05 m (10 feet) high post.

SECTION I—ORGANISATION OF THE GAME

Rule 1: Equipment

1.1 *Court*

1.1.1 The Court shall have a firm surface and shall be 30.5 m
(100 ft) long and 15.25 m (50 ft) wide. The longer sides
shall be called Side Lines and the shorter sides Goal
Lines.

1.1.2 The Court shall be divided into three equal parts—a
Centre Third and two Goal Thirds—by two transverse
lines drawn parallel to the Goal Lines.

1.1.3 A semi-circle with a radius of 4.9 m (16 ft) and with its
centre at the mid-point of the Goal Line, shall be drawn
in each Goal Third. This shall be called the Goal Circle.

1.1.4 A circle, 0.9 m (3 ft) in diameter shall mark the centre of
the Court. This shall be called the Centre Circle.

1.1.5 All lines are part of the Court, and shall be not more
than 50 mm (2 in) wide.

1.2 *Goalposts*

1.2.1 A Goalpost 3.05 m (10 ft) high shall be placed at the
mid-point of each Goal Line. A metal ring 380 mm (15 in)
in diameter shall project horizontally 150 mm (6 in) from
the top of the post, the attachment to allow 150 mm (6 in)
between the post and the near side of the ring. The ring
shall be of steel rod 15 mm ($\frac{5}{8}$ in) in diameter, fitted with
a net clearly visible and open at both ends. Both ring and net

are considered to be part of the Goalpost. If padding is used on the Goalpost it shall not be more than 25 mm (1 in) thick.

1.2.2 The post which shall be 65 mm (2.5 in) — 100 mm (4 in) in diameter or up to 100 mm (4 in) square may be inserted in a socket in the ground or may be supported by a metal base which shall not project on the Court.

1.3 *Ball*

The ball shall be a Netball or an Association Football size 5, and shall measure between 690 mm (27 in) and 710 mm (28 in) in circumference and weigh between 400 grams (14 ounces) and 450 grams (16 ounces). The ball may be of leather, rubber or similar material.

1.4 *Players*

1.4.1 Shoes or boots may be worn. They shall be of lightweight material. Spiked soles are not allowed.

1.4.2 Registered playing uniforms, which shall include initials of playing positions, shall be worn at all times. Playing initials shall be worn both front and back above the waist and shall be 200 mm (8 in) high.

1.4.3 No sharp adornment or item of jewellery except a wedding ring, shall be worn. If a wedding ring is worn, it shall be taped.

1.4.4 Fingernails shall be cut short.

Rule 2: Duration of Game

2.1 The game shall consist of four quarters of 15 minutes each, with an interval of 3 minutes between the first-second and third-fourth quarters and with a maximum of 10 minutes at half-time. The mean average time as requested by the respective teams shall determine the length of the interval at half time. An interval may be extended by the Umpires to deal with any emergency. Teams shall change ends each quarter.

2.2 Where any one team plays two or more matches in one day, or where time is limited, the game shall consist of two halves of 20 minutes each with a maximum of 5 minutes interval at half-time. The mean average time as requested by the respective teams shall determine the length of the interval at half-time. Teams shall change ends at half-time.

2.3 Playing time lost for an accident or any other cause must be noted and added to that quarter or half of the game. In no case shall extra time be allowed except to take a Penalty Shot.

2.4 In certain climatic conditions the duration of the game shall be predetermined by the countries concerned.

Rule 3: Officials

The Officials are:

Umpires, Scorers, Timekeepers.

The Team Officials are:

Coach, Manager, Captain.

All Umpires, Official Scorers and Official Timekeepers at International Matches shall be women.

3.1 *Umpires*

3.1.1 There shall be two Umpires who shall have control of the game and give decisions. They shall umpire according to the rules and decide on any matter not covered by the rules. The decision of the Umpire shall be final and shall be given without appeal.

3.1.2 The Umpire's whistle shall start and stop the game. Starting or re-starting the game after an interval, shall be controlled by the Umpire into whose half the play is to be directed.

3.1.3 After the players have taken their positions on the Court, the Umpires shall toss for goal end. The Umpire winning the toss shall control that half of the Court designated the northern half.

3.1.4 Umpires shall wear clothes distinct from those of the players and preferably white or cream in colour. Suitable shoes shall be worn.

3.1.5 Each Umpire shall:

(i) control and give decisions only in one half of the Court unless appealed to by the other Umpire for a decision in the other half and be ready for such an appeal at all times. For this purpose the length of the court is divided in half across the centre from Side Line to Side Line;

(ii) umpire in the same half of the Court throughout the game;

(iii) re-start the game after all goals scored in the half being controlled;

(iv) give decisions for the Throw In for one Goal Line and for the whole of one Side Line and shall call "play" when all other players are on the court. The Umpire responsible for the Side Line is responsible for making decisions related to infringements by the player throwing in and the defending opponents;

(v) keep outside the Court except when it is necessary to enter it to secure a clear view of play, or to indicate the point from which a penalty must be taken, or to take a Toss Up. If the ball strikes the Umpire during play, or if an Umpire interferes with the movements of the players, play does not cease unless one team has been unduly penalised in which case a Free Pass shall be awarded to that team;

(vi) when a Toss Up has been awarded, appeal where necessary to the other Umpire to take the Toss Up and that Umpire shall control points listed in SECTION IV—18.4: TOSS-UP 18.4.2—18.4.6;

(vii) move along the Side Line and behind the Goal Line to see play and make decisions;

(viii) refrain from blowing the whistle to penalise an infringement when by so doing the non-offending team would be placed at a disadvantage. An Umpire *may* call "advantage" to indicate an infringement has been observed and not penalised. Having blown the whistle for an infringement the penalty must be taken;

(ix) not criticise or coach any team while a match is in progress;

(x) Check that during a stoppage for injury or illness, other players remain on Court. During this stoppage coaching is not permitted;

(xi) state the infringement and penalty and *may* use hand signals to clarify decisions. (Guidelines for appropriate signals are listed for some of the Rules in Appendix 1).

3.2 *Scorers*

3.2.1 There shall be two Scorers who shall:

(i) keep a written record of the score together with a record of the Centre Pass;

(ii) record each goal as it is scored unless notified to the contrary by the Umpire. This constitutes the official score of the game;

(iii) keep a record of all unsuccessful shots;

(iv) call the Centre Pass if appealed to by the Umpire, and inform the Umpire immediately if the incorrect Centre Pass is indicated.

3.2.2 If the Umpires disagree with the Scorers they call for time to be taken while both Umpires and Scorers consult the Score sheet.

3.3 *Timekeepers*

3.3.1 There shall be a Timekeeper who shall:

(i) take time when the game is started by the Umpire's whistle and shall signal the end of each quarter or half to the Umpire;

(ii) take time when instructed by the Umpire who shall blow the whistle to stop play. To restart play the Umpire shall signal to the Timekeeper and blow the whistle for play to be resumed;

(iii) ensure that when instructed by the Umpire time lost for a stoppage is played in the quarter or half in which this occurs.

3.4 *Captains*

3.4.1 The Captains shall:

(i) toss for choice of goal or first Centre Pass and notify the Umpires of the results;

    (ii) during an interval or after stoppage for injury or illness notify the Umpires and the opposing Captain that they have changed the position of players whether or not a substitute is involved.

3.4.2 They have the right to approach an Umpire during an interval or after the game for clarification of any rule.

3.4.3 During an interval appeal to the Umpire for extra time to deal with an emergency affecting a member of the team and if the appeal is granted notify the opposing Captain of the amount of time that is to be added to the Interval.

Penalty for 3.4.1 (ii)

A Free Pass shall be awarded the first time a player enters an area which was offside in relation to that player's previous playing area.

    This pass shall be taken:

    (i) from the place in the offside area where the infringement occurred;

    (ii) by a player allowed in that area;

    (iii) after time has been allowed for the captain of the other team to rearrange playing positions if so wished.

The player concerned shall be permitted to remain in the position now being played.

Rule 4: The Team

4.1   The game is designed for single sex competition.

4.2   A team shall consist of seven players whose playing positions shall be:

        Goal Shooter (G.S.)
        Goal Attack (G.A.)
        Wing Attack (W.A.)
        Centre (C)
        Wing Defence (W.D.)
        Goal Defence (G.D.)
        Goal Keeper (G.K.)

4.3   Three substitutes only are permitted in any one game. These may be used to replace players on Court in the event of injury, illness, or during an interval.

4.4   No team may take the Court with fewer than five players.

Rule 5: Late Arrivals

5.1 No player arriving after play has started is allowed to replace a player who has filled the position of the late-comer.

5.2 Late arrivals may not enter the game while play is in progress, but after notifying the Umpires may take the court:
(i) after a goal has been scored. In this case the player must play in a position left vacant in the team;
(ii) immediately following an interval;
(iii) after a stoppage for injury or illness.

Penalty for 5.2(i) and 5.2(ii)

A Free Pass to the opposing team where the infringer was standing, and the infringer shall leave the Court until the next goal is scored or until after the next interval.

Rule 6: Substitution

6.1 Substitution on court is allowed for up to 3 players in any one game in the event of injury, illness, or during an interval. At the time a substitution is made playing positions may be changed.

6.2 It is the responsibility of the team Captain to notify the Umpire and the opposing Captain if substitutions and/ or changes in playing positions are made.

6.3 Sufficient time shall be allowed for the opposing team to make subsitutions and/or changes in playing positions if desired.

6.4 If a substitute is played the original player may take no further part in the game.

Penalty for 6.2

A Free Pass shall be awarded the first time a player enters an area which was offside in relation to that player's previous playing area.
This pass shall be taken:
(i) from the place in the offside area where the infringement occurred;
(ii) by a player allowed in that area;

(iii) after time has been allowed for the Captain of the other team to re-arrange playing positions if so wished.

The player concerned shall be permitted to remain in the position now being played.

Rule 7: Stoppages

7.1 Play may be stopped for injury or illness. When a player is injured or ill a stoppage of up to five minutes is allowed from when time is called to decide whether the injured or ill player is fit to continue play. The decision shall be left to the team's Officials.

7.2 Play may be stopped by an Umpire for any emergency relating to:
  (i) the equipment, court, weather or interference by outside agencies;
  (ii) a player's person or clothing;
  (iii) Officials officiating for the match.

7.3 To stop play the Umpire shall blow the whistle and instruct the Timekeeper to take time. The Umpire shall decide the length of time for the stoppage and shall ensure that play is re-started as soon as possible.

7.4 To re-start play the Umpire shall signal to the Timekeeper and blow the whistle for play to be resumed.

7.5 The game is continued from the spot where the ball was when play stopped other than when:
  (i) the ball is out of Court, in which case a Throw In is taken;
  (ii) the Umpire is unable to say who was in possession of the ball or the ball was on the ground when play was stopped, in which case a Toss Up is taken between any two opposing players allowed in that area, as near as possible to the spot where the ball was when play ceased;
  (iii) the stoppage is due to Obstruction or Contact, in which case the infringement is penalised where it occurred and play continues.

7.6 During a stoppage for injury or illness, other players remain on Court. During this stoppage coaching is not permitted.

7.7 After injury or illness when no substitution is made for a player unable to resume play the injured or sick player may return to the vacant position after notifying an Umpire of her intention to return to the game.

SECTION II—AREAS OF PLAY

Rule 8: Players areas

8.1 The playing area for each player is listed below:

Goal Shooter — 1, 2
Goal Attack — 1, 2, 3
Wing Attack — 2, 3
Centre — 2, 3, 4
Wing Defence — 3, 4
Goal Defence — 3, 4, 5
Goal Keeper — 4, 5

Lines bounding each area are included as part of that area.

8.2 Positions of players may be changed only:
(i) during an interval;
(ii) after stoppage caused by an injury or illness.

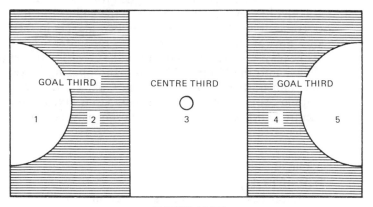

PLAYING AREAS

Penalty
See Penalty for 3.4.1 (ii).

Rule 9: Offside

9.1 *One Player Offside*

9.1.1 A player with or without the ball shall be offside if any area other than the playing area for that designated position is entered.

9.1.2 A player may reach over and take the ball from an offside area or may lean on the ball provided no body contact is made with the ground.

Penalty

A Free Pass to the opposing team where the infringement occurred.

9.2 *Simultaneous Offside*

When any two opposing players go offside at the same moment:

(i) if neither makes any contact with the ball, they are not penalised and play continues;

(ii) if one of them is in possession of the ball or touches it, a Toss Up is taken between those two players in their own area of play except as provided for under 9.2 (iv);

(iii) if both of them are in possession of the ball or touch it, a Toss Up is taken between those two players in their own area of play except as provided for under 9.2 (iv);

(iv) if one player who is allowed only in the Goal Third goes offside into the Centre Third, and an opposing player simultaneously goes offside into the Goal Third, one or both in contact with the ball, a Toss Up is taken in the Centre Third between any two opposing players allowed in that area.

Rule 10: Out of Court

10.1 THE BALL is out of Court when:

(i) it touches the ground outside the court;

(ii) it touches an object or person in contact with the ground outside the Court;

(iii) it is held by a player in contact with the ground, an object or a person outside the Court;

Penalty for 10.1

A Throw In to the team opposing the one who last had contact with the ball, to be taken where the ball crossed the line.

10.2 A BALL which hits any part of the Goalpost and rebounds into play is not out of Court.

10.3 A PLAYER IN CONTACT WITH THE BALL is out of Court when:

(i) the ground outside the Court is touched;

(ii) any object or person outside the Court is touched.

10.4 A PLAYER HAVING NO CONTACT WITH THE BALL may stand or move out of Court, but before playing the ball the player must re-enter the Court and no longer have contact with the ground out of Court.

Penalty for 10.3 and 10.4

A Throw In to the opposing team where the ball crossed the line.

10.5 Defending actions may only be attempted by players standing on Court or jumping from Court.

Penalty for 10.5

Penalty Pass or Penalty Pass or Shot opposite the spot where the infringer attempted to defend.

10.6 If the ball is caught simultaneously by two opposing players one of whom lands out of Court, a Toss Up is taken on Court between those two players opposite to the point where the player was out of Court.

10.7 A player who has left the Court to retrieve a ball or to take a Throw In must be permitted to re-enter the Court directly.

Penalty for 10.7

Penalty Pass or Penalty Pass or Shot to the opposing team where the infringement occurred.

SECTION III—CONDUCT OF THE GAME

Rule 11: Positioning of Players for Start of Play

11.1   The Centre in possession of the ball shall stand with both feet within the Centre Circle. The line is considered part of the Centre Circle.

11.2   The opposing Centre shall be in the Centre Third and free to move.

11.3   All other players shall be in the Goal Third which is part of their playing area and free to move. It is the responsibility of the Umpire to check the players' positions before blowing the whistle.

11.4   No other player is allowed in the Centre Third until the whistle has been blown to start the game.

Penalty

1. If one player enters the Centre Third before the whistle is blown, a Free Pass to the opposing team where the infringement occurred.

2. When any two opposing players simultaneously enter the Centre Third before the whistle has been blown:
   (i) if neither makes contact with the ball, they are not penalised and play continues;
   (ii) if one of them touches or catches the ball, a Toss Up is taken between those two players near to where the infringement occurred.

Rule 12: Start of Play

12.1   *Organisation for the Start of Play*

12.1.1 The Umpire shall blow the whistle to start and restart play.

12.1.2 The pass made by a Centre in response to the Umpire's whistle at the start and restart of play shall be designated a Centre Pass.

12.1.3 Play shall be started and restarted after every goal scored and after each interval, by a Centre Pass taken alternately by the two Centres throughout the game.

12.1.4 If, at a Centre Pass, the ball is still in the Centre's hands when the Umpire's whistle is blown to signal the end of a quarter or half, that team will take the pass after the interval.

12.2   *Controlling the Centre Pass*

12.2.1 When the whistle is blown the Centre in possession of the ball shall throw it within three seconds and shall obey the Footwork Rule.

12.2.2 The Centre Pass shall be caught or touched by a member of the attacking team who is standing or who lands within the Centre Third. A player who lands with the first foot, or on both feet simultaneously, wholly within the Centre Third, is judged to have received the ball in that third. That player's subsequent throw shall be considered to have been made from the Centre Third. A player who lands on both feet simultaneously, with one foot wholly within the Centre Third and the other wholly within the Goal Third, is judged to have received the ball in the Goal Third.

12.2.3 If a member of the team taking the Centre Pass catches the ball in the Goal Third without having touched it in the Centre Third, a Free Pass shall be awarded to the opposing team, to be taken in the Goal Third close to the point where the ball crossed the line.

12.2.4 If a member of the opposing team touches or catches the Centre Pass in the Centre Third, or in the Goal Third, or with feet astride the transverse line, the Advantage Rule shall apply.

12.2.5 If the ball from the Centre Pass goes untouched over the Side Line bounding the Centre Third, a Throw In is awarded to the opposing team where the ball crossed the line.

Rule 13: Playing the Ball

13.1   A Player may:
          (i) catch the ball with one or both hands;
          (ii) gain or regain control of the ball if it rebounds from the Goalpost;
          (iii) bat or bounce the ball to another player without first having possession of it;

     (iv) tip the ball in an uncontrolled manner once or more than once and then;
        (a) catch the ball; or
        (b) direct the ball to another player;
     (v) having batted the ball once, either catch the ball or direct the ball to another player;
     (vi) having bounced the ball once, either catch the ball or direct the ball to another player;
     (vii) roll the ball to oneself to gain possession;
     (viii) fall while holding the ball but must regain footing and throw within three seconds of receiving the ball;
     (ix) lean on the ball to prevent going offside;
     (x) lean on the ball on court to gain balance;
     (xi) jump from a position in contact with the Court and play the ball outside the Court, provided that neither the player nor the ball make contact with the ground, or any object or person outside the Court while the ball is being played.

13.2   A player may not:
     (i) deliberately kick the ball (if a ball which is thrown accidentally hits the leg of a player it is not a kick);
     (ii) strike the ball with a fist;
     (iii) deliberately fall on the ball to get it;
     (iv) attempt to gain possession of the ball while lying, sitting or kneeling on the ground;
     (v) throw the ball while lying, sitting or kneeling on the ground;
     (vi) use the Goalpost as a support in recovering the ball going out of court;
     (vii) use the Goalpost as a means of regaining balance, or in any other way for any other purpose.

Penalty

Free Pass to the opposing team where the infringement occurred.

13.3   A Player who has caught or held the ball shall play it or shoot for goal within three seconds. To play the ball a player may:

    (i) throw it in any manner and in any direction to another player;

    (ii) bounce it with one or both hands in any direction to another player.

13.4   A Player who has caught or held the ball may not:

    (i) roll the ball to another player;

    (ii) throw the ball and play it before it has been touched by another player;

    (iii) toss the ball into the air and replay it;

    (iv) drop the ball and replay it;

    (v) bounce the ball and replay it;

    (vi) replay the ball after an unsuccessful shot at goal unless it has touched some part of the Goalpost.

Penalty

Free Pass to the opposing team where the infringement occurred.

13.5   *Passing Distances*

13.5.1   *Short Pass*

    (i) On the Court: at the moment the ball is passed there must be room for a third player to move between THE HANDS of the thrower and those of the receiver.

    (ii) At the Throw In: at the moment the ball is passed there must be room on the Court between THE HANDS of the thrower and those of the receiver for a third player to attempt an interception.

Penalty

Free Pass to the opposing team where the ball was caught.

13.5.2   *Over a Third*

    (i) The ball may not be thrown over a complete Third without being touched or caught by a player who, at the time of touching or catching the ball, is wholly within that Third or who landed in that Third.

    (ii) The player who lands with the first foot wholly within the correct Third is judged to have received

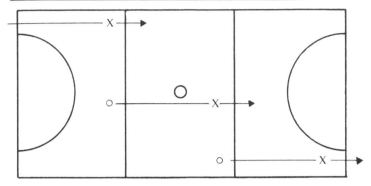

DIAGRAM OF THROWING OVER COMPLETED THIRD.

Arrow shows flight of ball.
X where the free pass is taken — just inside the second line that the ball has crossed

the ball in that Third. The subsequent throw shall be considered to have been made from the Third in which the player first landed.

(iii) The player who lands on both feet simultaneously with one foot wholly within the correct Third and the other in the incorrect Third, shall be penalised.

Penalty

Free Pass to the opposing team taken just beyond the second line that the ball has crossed, except where the ball thrown from the Centre Third passes out of Court over the Goal Line, when a Throw In shall be taken.

Rule 14: Footwork

14.1 A player may receive the ball with one foot grounded or jump to catch and land on one foot and then:

(i) step with the other foot in any direction, lift the landing foot and throw or shoot before this foot is regrounded;

(ii) step with the other foot in any direction any number of times, pivoting on the landing foot. The pivoting foot may be lifted but the player must throw or shoot before regrounding it;

(iii) jump from the landing foot onto the other foot and jump again but must throw the ball or shoot before regrounding either foot;

(iv) step with the other foot and jump but must throw the ball or shoot before regrounding either foot.

14.2 A player may receive the ball while both feet are grounded, or jump to catch and land on both feet simultaneously and then:

(i) step with either foot in any direction, lift the other foot and throw or shoot before this foot is regrounded;

(ii) step with either foot in any direction any number of times pivoting on the other. The pivoting foot may be lifted but the player must throw or shoot before regrounding it;

(iii) jump from both feet onto either foot, but must throw or shoot before regrounding the other foot;

(iv) step with either foot and jump but must throw the ball or shoot before regrounding either foot.

13.3 A player in possession of the ball may not:

(i) drag or slide the landing foot;

(ii) hop on either foot;

(iii) jump from both feet and land on both feet unless the ball has been released before landing.

Penalty

A Free Pass to the opposing team where the infringement occurred.

Rule 15: Scoring a Goal

15.1 A goal is scored when the ball is thrown or batted over and completely through the ring by Goal Shooter or Goal Attack from any point within the Goal Circle including the lines bounding the Goal Circle:

(i) If another player throws the ball through the ring no goal is scored and play continues.

(ii) If a defending player deflects a shot for goal and

the ball then passes over and completely through the ring a goal is scored.

(iii) Goal Shooter or Goal Attack may shoot for goal or pass if the ball is won at a Toss Up in the Goal Circle.

(iv) If the whistle for an interval or "time" is blown before the ball has passed completely through the ring, no goal is scored.

(v) if the whistle for an interval or "time" is blown *after* a Penalty Pass or Shot has been awarded to Goal Shooter or Goal Attack in the Goal Circle, a Penalty Shot shall be completed.

15.2 In taking a shot for goal a player shall:

(i) have no contact with the ground outside the Goal Circle either during the catching of the ball or whilst holding it. It is not contact with the ground to lean on the ball, but if this happens behind the Goal Line the ball is considered to be out of Court;

(ii) shoot within three seconds of catching or holding the ball;

(iii) obey the Footwork Rule.

Penalty

A Free Pass to the opposing team in the Goal Circle where the infringement occurred.

15.3 A defending player may not cause the Goalpost to move so as to interfere with the shot at goal.

Penalty

Penalty Pass or Shot to the opposing team to be taken:

(i) from where the infringer was standing unless this places the non-offending team at a disadvantage;

(ii) if the infringer was out of Court, on Court near where the infringer was standing.

Rule 16: Obstruction

16.1 An attempt to intercept or defend the ball *may* be made by a defending player if the distance on the ground is not less than 0.9 m (3 ft) from a player in possession of the ball. When the ball is received, this distance is measured as follows:

  (i) if the player's landing, grounded or pivoting foot remains on the ground, the distance is measured from that foot to the nearer foot of the defending player;

  (ii) if the player's landing, grounded or pivoting foot is lifted, the distance is measured from the spot on the ground from which the foot was lifted, to the nearer foot of the defending player;

  (iii) if the player is standing or lands on both feet simultaneously and remains grounded on both feet, the distance is measured from whichever is the nearer foot of that player to the nearer foot of the defending player;

  (iv) if the player is standing or lands on both feet simultaneously and either foot is lifted, the other foot is considered to be the grounded foot from which the 0.9 m (3 ft) distance is measured.

16.2   From the correct distance, a defending player *may* attempt to intercept or defend the ball:

  (i) by jumping towards the player with the ball, but if the landing is within 0.9 m (3 ft) of that player and interferes with the throwing or shooting motion, obstruction occurs;

  (ii) if the player with the ball steps forward to lessen the distance of 0.9 m (3 ft) between them.

16.3   A player *may* be within 0.9 m (3 ft) of an opponent in possession of the ball providing no effort is made to defend and there is no interference with that opponent's throwing or shooting action.

16.4   From the correct distance, a defending player *may not* attempt to intercept or defend the ball by stepping towards an opponent with the ball.

16.5 *Obstruction of a player not in possession of the ball*

16.5.1   A player is obstructing if within a distance of 0.9 m (3 ft) (measured on the ground) from an opponent without the ball, any movements are employed by that player (whether attacking or defending) which take the arms away from the body, other than those involved in natural body balance. Within this distance a player is not obstructing if the arms are outstretched:—

(i) to catch, deflect or intercept a pass or feint pass;
(ii) to obtain a rebound from an unsuccessful shot at goal;
(iii) momentarily to signal for a pass, or to indicate the intended direction of movement.

16.6 *Obstruction by intimidation*

When a player with or without the ball intimidates an opponent it is obstruction.

Penalty for 16.1 to 16.6

Penalty Pass or Penalty Pass or Shot where the infringer is standing except where this places the non-offending team at a disadvantage, when the penalty shall be taken where the obstructed player was standing.

16.7 *Defending a player who is out of Court*

16.7.1   A player may defend an opponent who has chosen to go out of Court provided that the defending player does not leave the Court or own playing area in order to defend.

Penalty

A Penalty Pass or Penalty Pass or Shot from the point where the infringing player leaves the Court.

16.7.2   A player who goes out of Court to collect a ball, to take a Throw In, or for any other valid reason must be allowed back into the area of play near to the point at which the player left the Court or took the Throw In. Any opponent attempting to defend is penalised.

Penalty

A Penalty Pass or Penalty Pass or Shot on Court immediately opposite the point where the obstruction occurred.

16.8 *Obstruction by a player from out of Court*

16.8.1 A player who is standing out of Court may not attempt to defend a player who is on the Court.

Penalty

A Penalty Pass or Penalty Pass or Shot on the Court opposite the point where the defending player is standing.

Rule 17: Contact

17.1 *Personal Contact*

17.1.1 No player shall come into personal contact with an opponent in such a manner as to interfere with the opponent's play either accidentally or deliberately.

17.1.2 In an effort to get free a player:
(i) shall not push an opponent in any way;
(ii) trip or knock an opponent in any way.

17.1.3 In an effort to contact the ball a player shall not bump or rush into an opponent.

17.1.4 In an effort to defend, a player shall not:
(i) keep an elbow against an opponent;
(ii) hold an opponent; this includes feeling to keep near an opponent;
(iii) push an opponent;
(iv) charge an opponent; that is, when jumping bump against a player.

17.1.5 Whether attempting to get free, or to defend, a player is responsible for any personal contact:
(i) if taking up a position so near an opponent that contact is inevitable;
(ii) if moving so quickly into the path of a moving player that contact cannot be avoided.

17.1.6 A player shall not contact another on any other occasion or in any other way in such a manner as to interfere with the opponent's play.

17.2 *Contact with the ball*

17.2.1 A player, while holding the ball, shall not touch or push an opposing player with it in such a manner as to interfere with that opponent's play.

17.2.2 A player shall not either accidentally or deliberately, place a hand or hands on, or remove from an opponent's possession, a ball held by an opposing player.

17.2.3 Where 17.2.1 and 17.2.2 occur simultaneously a Toss Up is taken between those two players.

Penalty for 17.1 to 17.2.2

Penalty Pass or Penalty Pass or Shot where the infringer is standing except where this places the non-offending team at a disadvantage, when the penalty shall be taken where the contacted player was standing.

SECTION IV—CONDUCTING PENALTIES

The penalties awarded for the breaking of the rules are:

Free Pass
Penalty Pass or Shot
Throw In
Toss Up

Rule 18: General Rules

for the taking of penalties are:

(i) A penalty for an infringement on Court is taken where the infringement occurred except:

(*a*) where THE ADVANTAGE RULE applies i.e. the Umpire shall refrain from blowing the whistle to penalise an infringement when by so doing the non-offending team would be placed at a disadvantage;

(*b*) as provided for under Penalty for Rules 16 and 17, Obstruction and Contact.

(ii) The Umpire indicates the correct place.

(iii) The penalties, with the exception of the Toss Up, are awarded to a team. Any member of the opposing team may take the penalty if allowed in the area where the penalty is awarded.

(iv) The player taking the penalty must throw the ball within three seconds after taking up a position at the correct place and being in possession of the ball.

(v) In the taking of a Free Pass, Penalty Pass or Shot or

Throw In, the Footwork Rule applies as though the
foot placed at the point indicated were equivalent to the
landing foot in a one foot landing or to receiving the
ball with one foot grounded.

(vi) If the player taking a Free Pass, or Penalty Pass or
Shot, infringes (iii) to (v) above, a Free Pass is awarded
to the opposing team.

(vii) If a player taking a Throw In infringes (iii) to (v) above,
a Throw In is awarded to the opposing team.

18.1 *Free Pass*

18.1.1　A Free Pass is awarded for infringements of the rules
on the Court with the exception of the Rules of Obstruction, Contact, simultaneous offences by two opposing players and interference with the Goalpost.

18.1.2　When a Free Pass is awarded, the ball may be thrown
by any player in the opposing team allowed in that
area, but the ball may not be thrown over a complete
third of the Court without being touched or caught by
a player.

18.2 *Penalty Pass or Shot*

18.2.1　A Penalty Pass or a Penalty Pass or Shot is awarded
for infringement of the Rules of Obstruction and Contact.

18.2.2　A player penalised for Obstruction and Contact must
stand beside and away from the thrower taking the
penalty and must make no attempt to take part in the
play until the ball has left the thrower's hands. If the
infringer moves before the ball has left the thrower's
hands the penalty shall be retaken unless the pass or
shot is successful.

18.2.3　The penalty shall be taken from where the infringer
was standing except where this puts the non-offending
team at a disadvantage, when the penalty shall be
taken where the obstructed or contacted player was
standing.

18.2.4　Any player allowed in the area may take the penalty.

18.2.5　(i) An attempt to intercept the Penalty Pass or Shot

may be made by any opposing player other than the offender.

(ii) If an opponent obstructs or contacts the thrower during the taking of the Penalty Pass or Shot, a Penalty Pass or Shot shall be awarded at the spot where the second infringer was standing unless this places the non-offending team at a disadvantage.

(iii) Both the original and second offenders must stand beside and away from the thrower taking the penalty and make no attempt to take part in the play until the ball has left the thrower's hands.

18.2.6   When two members of a team simultaneously obstruct or contact a member of the opposing team, each offender shall stand beside and away from the thrower taking the penalty. They must make no attempt to take part in the play until the ball has left the thrower's hands.

18.2.7   A Goal Shooter or Goal Attack taking a Penalty Pass in the Goal Circle, may either pass or shoot for goal.

18.3 *Throw In*

18.3.1   When the ball goes out of Court, it shall be put into play by a member of the team opposing either:

(i) the player on court who last had contact with the ball;

(ii) the player who received the ball with any part of her touching the ground outside the Court.

18.3.2   The player throwing the ball in shall:

(i) stand outside the Court and place one foot up to but not on the line at the point where the Umpire indicates that the ball has crossed the line;

(ii) wait for the Umpire to say "play" when all other players are on the Court;

(iii) throw within three seconds of the Umpire calling "play";

(iv) not enter the Court until the ball has been thrown;

(v) throw into the nearest third of the Court from

behind a Goal Line, or the nearest or adjacent third from behind a Side Line;

(vi) throw only from behind a line bounding her own playing area. If using the Footwork Rule the player must remain behind this area until she has released the ball;

(vii) apply the Footwork Rule as in SECTION IV: CONDUCTING PENALTIES—RULE 18: GENERAL RULES (v).

Penalties for infringement occurring at the Throw In

1. By the thrower—a Throw In is awarded to the opposing team at the spot where the infringement occurred except under (v) above when the penalty for breaking the "over a third" rule applies.

2. When a player obstructs or contacts during a Throw In, a Penalty Pass or Penalty Pass or Shot is awarded on Court.

3. If the ball fails to enter the Court the penalty Throw In shall be taken by the opposing team from the original Throw In point.

4. When the ball from a Throw In goes out of Court without being touched, a Throw In shall be taken by the opposing team from behind the point where the ball last went out.

5. If the ball is sent out of Court simultaneously by two players in opposing teams or the Umpire cannot decide who touched the ball last, there shall be a Toss Up opposite the point where the ball went out (Refer Rule 18.4.7 (iii)).

18.4 *Toss Up*

18.4.1 A Toss Up puts the ball into play when:

(i) opposing players gain simultaneous possession of the ball with either or both hands;

(ii) opposing players simultaneously knock the ball out of Court;

(iii) opposing players are involved and the Umpire is unable to determine the last player to touch the ball before it goes out of Court;

(iv) opposing players are simultaneously offside one in possession of or touching the ball;

(v) opposing players make simultaneous contact which interferes with play;

(vi) after an accident the Umpires are unable to say who had the ball, or the ball was on the ground when play stopped.

18.4.2 The Toss Up is taken on Court between the two opposing players concerned as near as possible to the place where the incident occurred.

18.4.3 The two players shall stand facing each other and their own goal ends with arms straight and hands to sides, but feet in any position. There shall be a distance of 0.9 m (3 ft) between the nearer foot of one player and that of her opponent. They shall not move from that position until the whistle is blown. If one player moves too soon, a Free Pass is awarded to the opposing team.

18.4.4 The Umpire shall release the ball midway between the two players from just below the shoulder level of the shorter player's normal standing position.

Momentarily, the Umpire shall be stationary and shall hold the ball in the palm of one hand and shall flick it vertically not more than 600 mm (2 ft) in the air as the whistle is blown.

18.4.5 The ball may be caught, or it may be batted in any direction except directly at the opposing player. All other players may stand or move anywhere within their playing area as long as they do not interfere with the Toss Up.

18.4.6 Goal Shooter or Goal Attack may shoot for goal or pass if the ball is won at a Toss Up in the Goal Circle.

18.4.7 When the Toss Up cannot be taken where the incident occurred because of the boundaries involved, the following applies:

(i) where the incident involves two opposing players across a line dividing areas one of which is common to both players, the Toss Up is taken between those two players in the common area.

(ii) where the incident involves two opposing players from adjoining playing areas across a transverse line and no area is common to both, the Toss Up

is taken in the Centre Third between any two
opposing players allowed in that area;

(iii) when two opposing players simultaneously knock
the ball out of Court over a line bounding an area
which is not common to both, the Toss Up is
taken between any two opposing players allowed
in that area, on Court opposite the point where
the ball crossed the line.

SECTION V—DISCIPLINE

1. The breaking of rules and/or the employment of any action
not covered by the wording of the rules, in a manner contrary to the spirit of the game, is not permitted. This includes:

(i) the breaking of rules:

(*a*) between the scoring of a goal and the restart of
play;

(*b*) between a ball going out of Court and the Throw
In;

(*c*) between the awarding and taking of any penalty on
Court.

Penalty for (*i*)

Immediately the play restarts, the Umpire shall penalise the
infringement unless the non-offending team is placed at a
disadvantage.

(ii) the deliberate delaying of play.

Penalty for (*ii*)

Free Pass unless the non-offending team is placed at a disadvantage.

(iii) deliberate action to prevent a player from re-entering
the Court after throwing in or retrieving a ball.

Penalty for (*iii*)

Penalty Pass or Penalty Pass or Shot where the infringer was
standing.

An Umpire may:

(i) Order a player to leave the Court, but only when sure

that the ordinary penalty is insufficient and, except in extreme cases, only after a warning;

(ii) stand a player off the Court for a specified part of the game, e.g. until the next goal is scored, until the next interval or for the rest of the game.

When a player is suspended, that player may not be replaced.

In the event of a Centre being suspended, that team may move only ONE player to allow play to continue.

That player shall continue to play as Centre until the next interval. At the end of the suspension period the suspended player must return to the vacant position.

2. During playing time an Umpire has the right to warn against any coaching from the sidelines and if coaching persists, after due warning may penalise the team which may benefit.

APPENDIX 1

Hand signals may be used to clarify decisions (Rule 3.1 Umpire: Clause 3.1.5(x)).

Guidelines for appropriate signals are given for some of the Rules as follows:

Stepping	— Rolling hands
Distance in	— Hands apart in front of body
Obstruction	—
Personal Contact	— One hand hits the other
Held ball	— Fingers apart held up
Direction of pass	— Arm pointed towards one Goal Line
Toss Up	— Palm of hand moved vertically upwards
Take time	— Make a T with the fingers of one hand against the palm of the other

The Laws of
Real Tennis and Rackets

The Laws of Real Tennis

1. Definitions

In these laws the following words have the following meanings:

Back Walls. The walls between the floor and the penthouse adjoining the main wall.

Bandeau. The strip of wall immediately below a penthouse, usually made of the same material as the penthouse.

Better. One chase is better than another if it is made on the same side of the court and further from the net (Rule 9). In marking chases, better means that the ball makes a chase

   (*a*) further from the net than the line mentioned, and

   (*b*) nearer to that line than to any other yard or gallery line (Rule 9b).

Bisque. One stroke in a set conceded to an opponent (Rule 22).

Chase. A chase is made whenever the ball falls in the hazard court, or anywhere on the service side, or enters a gallery, except the winning gallery (Rule 9).

   ... *attacking a*—When a chase is being played for, the opponent of the player who made the chase is said to be attacking the chase (Rules 11 and 12).

   ... *calling a*—The marker calls a chase when he states the chase that is to be played for.

   ... *defending a*—When a chase is being played for, the player who made the chase is said to be defending the chase (Rules 11 and 12).

   ... *lines*—The lines marked on the floor to enable the marker to mark chases are called chase lines or chases (Rule 8).

   ... *marking a*—The marker marks a chase when that chase is made.

   ... *off*—See rule 12b.

   ... *the line*—See Line, Chase the.

Court. The enclosure in which the game is played. The court is divided into two sides, the service side and the hazard side (*q.v.*).

Dead. A ball is said to be dead when it ceases to be in play.

Dedans. The opening at the back of the service side.

Double. If the ball falls before it is struck it is a double.

Drop. A ball is said to drop when, after passing the net, it first touches the floor, or enters an opening without having previously touched the floor.

Enter a Gallery or an Opening. See Opening, Entering an.

Fall. A ball is said to fall when, after having dropped, it touches the floor again, or enters an opening.

Fault Line. The line on the floor nearest the grille and extending from the service line to the grille wall.

Gallery. An opening below the penthouse opposite to the main wall.

The starting galleries are named as follows, starting from the net:

(*a*) on the service side, the line, the first gallery, the door, the second gallery, the last gallery;

(*b*) on the hazard side, the line, the first gallery, the door, the second gallery, the winning gallery.

Gallery Post. The post between two galleries is considered to be part of the gallery nearer the net.

The part of the gallery net that is attached to and surrounds a gallery post is part of that post.

Good Return. See Return.

Grille. The opening in the grille wall.

Grille Wall. The back wall on the hazard side.

Half-Court Line. The line that bisects the floor, between the main wall and the side wall.

Hazard Chase or Hazard Side Chase. A chase made on the hazard side of the court.

Hazard Court. The floor on the hazard side from the net up to, but not including, the service line.

Hazard Side. The side of the court on the left of the net when facing the main wall.

In Play. A ball served is in play until—

(*a*) the service becomes a fault, or

(*b*) either player fails to make a good return.

Ledge. The horizontal surface of a wall that forms an opening.

Line, Chase the, is chase at the line of the net.

On the floor it is the area between the net and worse than the first gallery.

The line gallery is that between the net post and the post next to it.

Main Wall. The wall that has no penthouse.

Net Post. The post supporting the net under the penthouse.

Nick. The junction of the wall and the floor, or a return when the ball, as it drops or falls, touches the wall and floor simultaneously.

Opening. Any gallery or winning opening.

Opening, Entering an. A ball enters an opening when a good return or service—

(*a*) touches the post (see Gallery Post), net, or tray or that opening, or

(*b*) touches anything lying in that opening (if an article is lying in an opening any part of it, even outside, is considered to be in that opening), or

(*c*) comes to rest in or on the ledge of that opening, or

(*d*) in the case of the grille, touches the woodwork at the back of the framing of the grille.

Out of Court. A ball is out of court if it touches any part of

(*a*) the walls above the area prepared for play, or

(*b*) the roof or roof beams or girders, or passes over any of these beams or girders, or

(*c*) the lighting equipment.

Passing the Net. The ball passes the net when it crosses it between the net post and the main wall, or when it crosses the line bisecting the side penthouse.

Rest. A stroke or series of strokes, commencing when the ball is served and terminating when the ball is dead.

Return, or Return of the Ball in Play. The return of the ball is good if—

(*a*) it is struck before it falls, and

(*b*) it is struck so that it passes the net without having previously touched the floor or anything lying on the floor, or the net post, or without having entered an opening, and

(*c*) it has not touched the player or anything he wears or carries except his racket in the act of striking the ball, and

(*d*) it does not go out of court, and

(*e*) it is struck definitely and only once, and

(*f*) it is not on the side of the net opposed to the player when he strikes it, and

(*g*) in courts where there is a wing net between the net post and the net, it does not touch the wing net before crossing the net.

Except that such a return is not good if—

(*h*) the player touches the net before striking the ball or

(*i*) the player touches the net after the ball and before the ball is dead, or

(*j*) the ball, after passing the net, comes back and drops on the side from which it was played (even if it touches the net before so dropping the return is not good).

Service. The method of starting a rest.

Service Court. The part of the floor on the hazard side that lies between the side wall, the grille wall, the fault line and the service line (including those two lines).

Service Line or Winning Gallery Line. The line which is nearest and parallel to the grille wall.

Service Penthouse. That part of the side penthouse which is on the hazard side of the court including the line that bisects the side penthouse.

Service Side. The side of the court on the right of the net when facing the main wall.

Service Wall. The wall above the side penthouse.

Side Penthouse. The penthouse above the galleries, up to its junction with the other penthouses.

Side Wall. The wall below the side penthouse.

Striker. The player who last struck the ball.

Striker-Out. The player who is to take the service.

Tray. The inner part of the bottom of an opening behind the ledge, usually made of wood.

Uneven Odds. When points given and/or received are not the same in each game, and/or when one or more bisques or half-bisques are given.

Winning Gallery. The last gallery on the hazard side.

Winning Openings. The dedans, the grille, and the winning gallery.

Worse. One chase is worse than another if it is made on the same side of the court and nearer to the net (Rule 9).

In marking chases, worse means that the ball makes a chase

(*a*) nearer to the net than the line mentioned, and

(*b*) nearer to that line than to any other yard or gallery line (Rule 9b).

2. Net

The height of the net above the level of the floor shall be—

(*a*) at the centre, 3 ft, and

(*b*) at the main wall and below the edge of the penthouse, 5 ft.

3. Balls

The balls shall be not less than $2\frac{7}{16}$ in and not more than $2\frac{9}{16}$ in in diameter.

They shall not be less than $2\frac{1}{2}$ oz and not more than $2\frac{3}{4}$ oz in weight.

4. Rackets

There are no restrictions as to the shape or size of rackets.

5. Sides

(*a*) The choice of sides at the beginning of a match is decided by spin of a racket.

(*b*) Subsequently the players change sides only when two chases have been scored or when one player is at 40 or advantage and one chase has been scored.

(*c*) If the players change sides before they should have done so, or do not change sides when they should, any strokes so played on the wrong side shall be scored and play shall continue as if no mistake had been made, except that any chase scored (Rule 10) in excess of the proper number shall be annulled if the mistake is discovered before that chase has been played for (Rule 11).

6. Service

The service is always given by the player who is on the service side.

A service is good if it is not a fault.

A service is a fault:

(a) if the server stands on or beyond the second gallery line, or

(b) if the server misses the ball or does not definitely strike it or strikes it more than once, or

(c) if the ball served, before touching the side penthouse, touches anything except the service wall (if the ball touches the edge of the penthouse before touching anything else it is a fault), or

(d) if the ball served does not touch the service penthouse (if the ball, after striking the service wall, in dropping touches the edge of the service penthouse, it is considered to have touched the penthouse), or

(e) if the ball served goes out of court, or

(f) if the ball served strikes the main wall before dropping, or

(g) if the ball served drops anywhere except in the service court or in the winning gallery.

A service that has become a fault may not be returned but one that would otherwise become a fault may be volleyed.

If striker-out is not ready for a service and does not attempt to take it, a let (Rule 17) shall be allowed.

8. Chase Lines, How Marked

Chase lines are marked on the floor as follows:

Service Side—

Half-a-yard,

One yard,

One and two,

Two,

and so on up to six, then

Half-a-yard worse than six,

The last gallery,

Half-a-yard worse than the last gallery,

A yard worse then the last gallery,

The second gallery,

The door, and

The first gallery.

Hazard Side. The same as on the service side, except that all chases between two and the second gallery are omitted and the last or winning gallery line is called the service line.

9. Chases, How Made

(*a*) When the ball enters a gallery (except the winning gallery) or falls on the floor (unless it falls in the service court) it makes a chase at the gallery it enters or at the line on which it falls.

(*b*) When it falls between two lines it makes a chase better or worse than the yard line or the gallery line nearest to the spot where it fell, except that—

(1) it makes chase better than half a yard when it so falls, and

(2) when it falls better or worse than the line "a yard worse than the last gallery" the chase is called "nearly a yard" or "more than a yard worse than the last gallery", and

(3) when it falls nearer to the net than to the first gallery line it makes chase the line, and

(4) when it drops or falls in the net on the side opposed to the striker or drops on the side opposed to the striker and then falls on the side from which it was struck it makes chase the line on the side opposed to the striker, and

(5) when it drops or falls on another ball on the floor it makes a chase as if it had fallen where that other ball was lying.

10. Chase, How and When Scored

(*a*) When no chase is being played for, a chase is scored when made in accordance with Rule 9.

(*b*) When a chase is scored, the score in strokes is unaltered.

11. Chases, When Played For

When two chases have been scored, or when one player is at 40 or advantage and one chase has been scored, the players change sides and the chase or chases in the order in which they were made are immediately played for.

A chase is played for once only, unless there is a let (Rule 17).

12. Chases, How Won or Lost

When a chase is being played for,

(*a*) the player attacking the chase loses it if—
  (1) he serves two consecutive faults, or
  (2) he does not make a good return, or
  (3) he makes a chase worse than the one being played for;

(*b*) it is a chase off when the player attacking the chase makes a chase equal to the one being played for;
  (when it is chase off the chase is annulled and the score is unaltered).

(*c*) the player attacking the chase wins it if—
  (1) his opponent serves two consecutive faults, or
  (2) his opponent does not make a good return (unless the player attacking the chase makes a chase worse than or equal to the one being played for, in which case paragraph (*a*) or (*b*) of this rule applies) or
  (3) he makes a chase better than the one being played for.

13. Errors Regarding Chases

(*a*) Either player may appeal regarding the marking of a chase (Rule 18*a*).

(*b*) If the chase to be played for is wrongly called by the marker, the server may appeal before delivering the service, and the striker-out before attempting to take it.

If there is no such appeal, the chase played for shall be that called by the marker immediately before the service is delivered, notwithstanding that this may be different from that marked when the chase was scored.

(*c*) If there has been any misunderstanding as to what chase the marker called, the rest as played shall stand or a let (Rule 17) may be allowed, whichever the marker (or referee if appealed to) considers equitable in view of all the circumstances.

(*d*) If, through any mistake, at the end of the game there is a chase that has been scored and not played for, that chase is annulled.

(*e*) If the players change sides when too few or too many chases have been made, see Rule 5.

14. Strokes, How Won

A player wins a stroke—
- (a) if he wins a chase (Rule 12c), or
- (b) if his opponent loses a chase (Rule 12a), or
- (c) if a return or a good service played by him enters a winning opening or falls on the service line or between the service line and grille wall or
- (d) if when no chase is being played for and provided that no chase is made his opponent does not make a good return, or
- (e) if his opponent serves two consecutive faults (Rule 6).

15. Strokes and Games, How Scored

In each game, when either player wins his first stroke his score is called 15; when he wins his second stroke, 30; when he wins his third stroke, 40; and when he wins his fourth stroke, he wins the game, except as below.

When both players have won three strokes, the score is called deuce, and it is called advantage to the player who then wins the next stroke.

If the player who is at advantage wins the next stroke, he wins the game; if he loses it, the score is again called deuce, and so on until the player who is at advantage wins a stroke and the game.

16. Sets, How Won

The player who first wins 6 games in a set wins it except that advantage sets are played—
- (a) if uneven odds are given and/or received, or
- (b) if the players agree.

In advantage sets, if the score is 5 games all, the set continues until either player has won two games more than his opponent.

17. Let

In the case of a let—
- (a) the rest to which it refers counts for nothing, and
- (b) if a chase was being played for, it is then played for again, and
- (c) if there was a previous fault, it is not annulled.

18. Referee

(*a*) Either player may appeal to the referee (whose decision is final) about any point subject to the following:

    (1) the server shall not, after delivering a service, appeal about any point prior to that service, and

    (2) the striker-out shall not, after attempting to take a service, appeal about any point prior to that service.

(*b*) When the marker calls "not up" or in any way indicates that a rest has terminated, the ball is dead.

If the referee's decision is that the rest should not then have been terminated, a let (Rule 17) shall be allowed.

(*c*) In all cases of doubt the referee may—

    (1) ask the opinion of one or more spectators who were in a better position to see, or

    (2) allow a let (Rule 17), or

    (3) accept the marker's decision.

(*d*) The referee may appoint someone, in a better position to judge the hazard side, to assist him in appeals as to where the ball dropped or fell on the hazard side.

(*e*) The referee shall not, without an appeal, correct any decisions of the marker but he should—

    (1) see that the players change sides at the right time and

    (2) correct errors in the calling of the score or of chases when such calls are not in accordance with the decision given when the stroke or chase was scored.

19. Marker

(*a*) In the absence of an appeal, the marker's decision is final.

(*b*) In cases of doubt the marker may appeal to the referee, or, if there is no referee, to one or more spectators.

(*c*) A fault-caller may be appointed to assist the marker.

If either the marker or the fault-caller calls fault, the service (subject to appeal) is a fault.

If the call of fault is reversed on appeal, that fault is annulled.

20. Three or Four-handed Games (also called Doubles)

(*a*) Before commencing each set the players on the service side select the partner who is to serve. He is then the server and striker-out for his side throughout that game and for alternate games throughout the set, his partner serving and striking out in the other games.

Similarly the players on the hazard side then decide who is to be striker-out and server.

(*b*) A return of service is not good if made by striker-out's partner, unless the ball served has dropped in the service court between the half-court line and the fault line (including those two lines).

(*c*) Apart from the above, the laws for Singles apply to Doubles and a player and his partner are in all cases subject to the same laws as a player in Singles.

HANDICAPS

21. Half Odds

(*a*) When half odds are given, one stroke less than the full odds is given in the first and every odd game of the set, and the full odds are given in every game (*e.g.*, $\frac{1}{2}$–30 means 15 in the first, third, etc., game and 30 in the second, fourth, etc., game).

(*b*) When half odds are owed, the full odds are owed in the odd games and one stroke less in the even games.

22. Bisque

The player receiving the bisque may take it to win one stroke in each set at any time subject to the following:

(*a*) he may not take it during a rest, and

(*b*) if server, he may not take it after serving one fault, and

(*c*) if he takes it to win or to defend a chase, he may not do so before the time comes to change sides. Then, if there is only one chase, he may take it and need not change sides, or he may take it after changing sides but, after he has passed the net, he may not go back again.

If there are two chases the players must change sides before he takes it to win or to defend either of them.

23. Half-bisque

The player receiving a half-bisque may take it—

(*a*) to call chase-off and so to annul a chase about to be played for, or (*b*) to annul a fault served by him, or

   (*c*) to add a second fault to one served by his opponent, or

   (*d*) the handicapper may give a half-bisque as being one bisque in every alternate set, in which case the bisque must be taken in the odd sets.

Apart from (*b*) the conditions regarding taking a bisque (Rule 22) apply equally to a half-bisque.

24. Cramped Odds

Unless specifically stated the limiting conditions of cramped odds do not apply to service.

Cramped odds may be such as are fixed by the handicapper but the more usual forms are as follows:

   (*a*) *Bar the Openings*. The giver of the odds loses a stroke whenever a ball returned by him enters an opening.

   (*b*) *Bar the Winning Openings*. The giver of the odds loses a stroke whenever a ball returned by him enters the dedans, the grille, or the winning gallery.

   (*c*) *Chase*. When a player gives a specified chase this applies only to a chase on the service side.

      Any chase made by the giver of the odds worse than the one specified loses him a stroke.

      Any chase made by the receiver of the odds worse than the one specified is considered equal to the one specified.

   (*d*) *Half-Court*. The players shall agree or the handicapper decide to which half-court, on each side of the net, the giver of the odds shall play. He loses a stroke if a ball returned by him drops in the other half-court or in an opening or in half the dedans in the other half-court.

      A ball that drops on the half-court line does not lose him a stroke.

      After the ball has dropped the ordinary rules apply.

   (*e*) *Round Services*. The striker-out may refuse to take any service that does not touch the grille penthouse. If he attempts to take such a service that service becomes good if not otherwise a fault.

      A service otherwise good, that does not touch the service penthouse, is not counted a fault.

   (*f*) *Touch No Side Walls*. The giver of the odds loses a stroke if a ball in play returned by him touches the side wall, the service wall, or the main wall, or enters a gallery.

(g) *Touch No Walls*. The giver of the odds loses a stroke whenever a ball in play returned by him touches any wall, or enters an opening.

A ball that falls in a nick is not considered to have touched the wall.

A penthouse is not a wall.

A bandeau is part of a wall.

The above odds are also given in the form that the ball must drop before touching a wall, etc., but after dropping it may touch them without penalty. In this form it is usually called "Touch no walls full pitch".

DIRECTIONS TO THE MARKER

It is the duty of the marker—

to see that the net is at the correct height and that it remains correct;

to call faults;

to call the strokes when won or when asked to do so;

to mark the chases when scored;

to direct the players to change sides;

to call the chase or chases as the players change sides and to call each chase before it is played for but not otherwise to repeat the chases;

when there is a referee not to call "not up" in doubtful cases but to allow the rest to be finished;

not to call "play" in the course of a rest;

to remove balls lying on the floor;

to keep the ball troughs replenished.

GLOSSARY OF TENNIS TERMS

(*See also the definitions contained in Rule 1 of the Laws*)

Advantage. See rule 15.
Advantage Set. See rule 16.
All the Walls, also called Touch No Walls, see rule 24 (g).
Attack. See rule 1. Chase, attacking a.

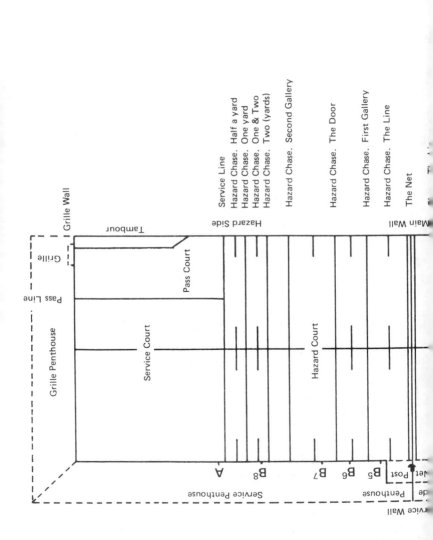

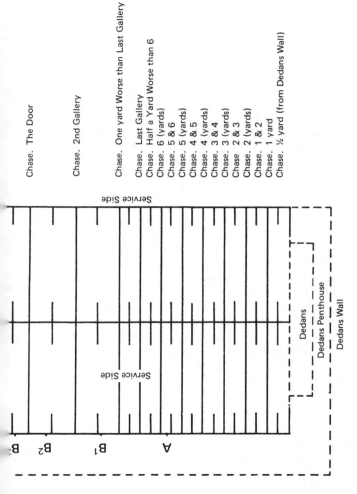

Chase. The Door

Chase. 2nd Gallery

Chase. One yard Worse than Last Gallery

Chase. Last Gallery
Chase. Half a Yard Worse than 6
Chase. 6 (yards)
Chase. 5 & 6
Chase. 5 (yards)
Chase. 4 & 5
Chase. 4 (yards)
Chase. 3 & 4
Chase. 3 (yards)
Chase 2 & 3
Chase. 2 (yards)
Chase. 1 & 2
Chase. 1 yard
Chase. ½ yard (from Dedans Wall)

A A Points where Galleries begin

B¹ to B³ Gallery Posts

Back Wall. See rule 1.

Bandeau. See rule 1.

Bar the Openings. See rule 24 (*a*).

Bar the Winning Openings. See rule 24 (*b*).

Batteries. The portions of wall between the openings and the floor.

Better. See rules 1 and 9.

Bisque. See rules 1 and 22.

Boast. A return that is struck against the main wall (presumably derived from *Bosse*). Originally the word appears to have been used only when it was intended that the ball should enter the dedans, but it is now used more widely to include returns struck against walls other than the main wall.

Boasted Force. A boast that drops in a winning opening. The term is usually employed only for a force to the dedans.

Chase. See rule 1.

Coup de Brèche. A straight force that drops in the dedans near to one of its outer edges.

Coup de Cabasse. A return that drops in the dedans after first striking the wall between the last gallery and the dedans wall (called after a French professional of that name who played this difficult stroke).

Coups de Chandelle. A lofted return that drops or (more usually) falls in the dedans.

Coup d'Orléans. A return that is struck against the service wall and drops in the dedans direct (called after Philippe Egalité, Duc d'Orleans, who invented or practised this stroke).

Coup de Temps. The stroke usually attempted off the back wall when the ball is too near to the wall and floor for an ordinary return to be made. The stroke is commenced before the ball reaches the wall so that immediately it leaves it the stroke can be completed with the minimum amount of further movement and acceleration of the racket.

Court. See rule 1.

Cramped Odds. Handicaps that prohibit certain strokes or services. See rule 24.

Dead. See rule 1.

Dedans. See rule 1.

Defend. See rule 1. Chase, defending a.

Deuce. See rule 15.

Door. See rules 1 (Gallery) and 8.

Double. See rule 1.

Doubles. See rule 20.

Drop. See rule 1.

Drop Service. A high service, delivered from near the main wall, that should drop near to the grille wall.

Du Tout. The score of a player who requires one stroke to win the set (cf. game-ball).

Enter a Gallery or an Opening. See rule 1.

Fall. See rule 1.

Fault. See rule 6.

Fault-Caller. See rule 19 (*c*).

Fifteen. See rule 15.

First Gallery. See rules 1 (Gallery) and 8.

First Stroke. The return of the service.

Fly Net. Not used in modern courts. In some old courts there was a fly net high up in each of the four corners. A ball striking the fly net was not out of court.

Force. A stroke that drops into an opening, usually a winning opening. The term is not used for a slow lofted return.

Forty. See rule 15. Originally this score was 45, but was subsequently called 40 for the sake of brevity.

Four-handed Game. See rule 20.

Gallery. See rule 1.

Gallery Lines. Chase lines that correspond to galleries (see rules 8 and 9 (*a*)).

Gallery Net. The net attached to a gallery post to separate a gallery from the one next to it.

Gallery Post. See rule 1.

Game. See rule 15.

Giraffe Service. A high underhand service delivered from near the side penthouse. (After dropping on the service penthouse the ball should drop on the floor near to the fault line and to the grille wall.)

Good Return. See rule 1 (Return).

Good Service. See rule 6.

Grille. See rule 1.

Grille Penthouse. The Penthouse above the grille wall.

Grille Wall. See rule 1.

Half a yard. See rule 8.

Half-Bisque. See rule 23.

Half Court. See rule 1.

Half Odds. See rule 21.

Hazard Chase. See rule 1.

Hazard Court. See rule 1.

Hazard Side. See rule 1.

Joues. The inner vertical walls of the dedans, grille, winning gallery and last gallery. A ball in touching a joue is not thereby deemed to have entered an opening (see rule 1).

Last Gallery. See rules 1 (Gallery) and 8.

Ledge. See rule 1.

Let. See rule 17.

Line. The cord that supports the net.

Line, Chase the. See rule 1.

Love. The score of a player who has not yet won a stroke in the game or a game in the set in question.

Love Game. A game won by a player in which his opponent does not score a stroke.

Love Set. A set won by a player by winning six successive games, or in the case of an advantage set, seven successive games.

Lune. A winning opening that was found in some old courts. There was no standard size, shape or position for lunes, but they were usually placed above the dedans and grille penthouses.

Net Post. See rule 1.

Nick. See rule 1.

Odds. Any form of handicap is called odds. See rules 21 to 24.

Opening. Entering an. See rule 1.

Out of Court. See rule 1.

Pass. See rule 7.

Pass Court. See rule 1.

Pass Line. See rule 1.

Passing the Net. See rule 1.

Penthouse is the sloping roof of the dedans, galleries and grille, extending along three sides of the court.

Piqué Service. The server stands near to the main wall and to the 2nd gallery line. He serves overhead on to the service penthouse and as near as possible to the service line. After striking the service wall the ball should drop near to the grille wall and the fault line.

Play Line. The line painted on the walls to mark the upper limits of the area prepared for play (see rule 1, Out of Court).

Post. See Net Post and Gallery Post, rule 1.

Railroad Service. An overhead service delivered by the server standing near the wall between the last gallery and the dedans wall. (The ball may touch the penthouse once or more times. On leaving the penthouse the ball, unless volleyed, should strike the grille wall with a twist on it that brings it back towards the side wall. A less common form of railroad service has the opposite twist on the ball so that it tends to go in the direction of the tambour after dropping.)

Referee. See rule 18.

Rest. See rule 1.

Rough. The side of the racket on which the knots are.

Second Gallery. See rules 1 (Gallery) and 8.

Service. See rule 1.

Service Court. See rule 1.

Service Line. See rule 1.

Service Penthouse. See rule 1.

Service Side. See rule 1.

Service Wall. See rule 1.

Set. See rule 16. A match is won by the player who wins an agreed number of sets. Each set is a separate unit and no game won in one set has any effect on another set. The method of scoring by sets appears to have been adopted in the 16th century. Prior to that games only were scored. At first 2 games won a set. At later periods, 3, 4, 6 and 8 game sets were usual.

Side Penthouse. See rule 1.

Side Wall. See rule 1.

Side Wall Service. Delivered from near the side penthouse. The ball usually touches the service wall before the service penthouse but need not do so. The twist on it should be such that it clings to the grille wall after dropping.

Smooth. The side of the racket on which is the gut with no knots.

Striker. See rule 1.

Striker-Out. See rule 1.

Stroke. See rules 14 and 15.

Tambour. The projection on the main wall near the grille. The whole of the projection should be called the tambour though the term is more commonly applied only to that part of it that is at an angle to the main wall.

Thirty. See rule 15.

Three-handed Game. See rule 20.

Touch No Walls. See rule 24 (*g*).

Touch No Side Walls. See rule 24 (*f*).

Twist Service. An underhand service delivered from near the side penthouse. The ball does not usually touch the service wall. The twist on it should be that, after striking the grille wall, it comes back towards the side wall.

Tray. See rule 1.

Uneven Odds. See rule 1.

Wing Net. A net put up in some courts for the protection of the marker in front of the net or post and attached to the underside of the service penthouse.

Winning Gallery. See rule 1.

Winning Openings. See rule 1.

Worse. See rule 1.

Yard. See rule 8.

Revised by the Tennis and Rackets Association, 1966.

THE LAWS OF RACKETS

The Single Game

1. The game is 15 up, that is, the player who first scores 15 aces wins the game excepting that:

(*a*) On the score being called 13 all for the first time in any game, hand-out may, before the next service has been delivered, set the game to 5; or to 3, i.e., the player winning 5 (or 3) aces first wins the game;

(*b*) similarly at 14 all hand-out may set the game to 3.

NOTE. *When hand-in requires one more ace to win the game, the Marker shall call his score "Game Ball".*

2. When the player fails to serve, or to return the ball, in accordance with the Rules of the game, his opponent wins the stroke. A stroke won by hand-in scores an ace. A stroke won by hand-out makes him hand-in.

3. The ball after being served, whether the service is good or not, is in play until it is a Double, or until after being properly returned it has failed to hit the front wall above the board, or until it has touched a player, or until it has gone out of court.

4. The right to serve first in a rubber shall be decided by the spin of a racket.

5. At the beginning of each game and of each hand the server may serve from either box, but after scoring an ace he shall then serve from the other, and so on alternately as long as he remains hand-in, or until the end of the game.

If the server serves from the wrong box there shall be no penalty and the service shall count as if served from the right box, except that the hand-out may, if he does not attempt to take the service, demand that it be served from the other box.

6. The hand-in serves his hand-out and loses the stroke

    (*a*) If the ball is served on to or below the board, or out of court, or against any part of the court before the front wall;

    (*b*) If he fails to strike the ball, or strikes the ball more than once;

    (*c*) If he serves two consecutive faults.

NOTE. *The ball is Out of Court when it touches the front, sides or back of the Court above the area prepared for play, or when it touches, or passes over, cross bars or other part of the roof or electric light fittings of the court.*

7. A service is a fault (except as provided by Rule 6)

    (*a*) If the player fails to stand with one foot at least on the floor within, and not touching, the one surrounding the Service Box (called a foot fault);

    (*b*) If the ball is served on to, or below, the Cut Line (called the Cut);

    (*c*) If the ball served touches the floor on its first bounce on, or in front of, the Short Line (called a Short);

    (*d*) If the ball served touches the floor, on its first bounce, in the wrong court, or on the Half Court Line. (The wrong court is the Left for a service from the Left-Hand Box, and Right from the Right-Hand Box.)

8. Hand-out may take a fault. If he attempts to do so, the service thereupon becomes good.

9. A player wins a stroke
    (*a*) Under Rule 6;
    (*b*) If his opponent fails to make a good return of the ball in play;
    (*c*) If the ball in play touches his opponent, or anything he wears or carries (other than his racket when in the act of striking), except
        (i) as is otherwise provided by Rules 11, 12 and 14;
        (ii) in the case of a fault which hand-out does not attempt to take.

10. A return is good if the striker returns the ball above the board without previously touching the floor, or the back wall, or any part of the striker's body or clothing, and before it has become a Double, and if he does not hit the ball twice, or out of court.

11. If the ball, after being struck and before reaching the front wall, hits the striker's opponent or his racket, or anything he wears or carries, a Let on appeal shall be allowed, if the return would have been good. If the return would not have been good the striker shall lose the stroke.

NOTE. *Play shall cease even if the ball goes up.*

12. Notwithstanding anything contained in these Rules, a Let *may* be allowed, on appeal by either player, in the following circumstances—
    (*a*) If the player is prevented from obtaining a fair view of the ball, or from reaching the ball, or from striking at the ball;
    (*b*) If, owing to the position of the striker, his opponent is unable to avoid being touched by the ball;
    (*c*) If the ball in play touches any other ball in the court;
    (*d*) If the player refrains from hitting the ball owing to a reasonable fear of injuring his opponent;

(*e*) If the player in the act of striking touches his opponent.

NOTE. *No Let shall be allowed:*

(i) *In respect of any stroke, which a player attempts to make, unless, in making the stroke, he touches an opponent;*

(ii) *Unless the striker could have made a good return.*

13. An appeal may be made against any decision to the Marker provided that with regard to service, the following Rules shall apply:

(*a*) A Let shall be allowed, if the hand-out is not ready and does not attempt to take the service;

(*b*) No appeal shall be made with respect to foot faults;

(*c*) When hand-out attempts to take a first serve no appeal shall be made, but when he does not attempt to take it (i) if he appeals against the marker's call of play and the appeal is allowed the service becomes a fault and (ii) if the server appeals against a call of fault and the marker's decision is reversed, a let shall be allowed.

(*d*) When the marker calls fault to a second serve, hand-out shall not attempt to take it.

If the marker's decision is reversed on appeal a Let shall be allowed.

(*e*) When the marker calls play to a second service hand-out may appeal even though he has taken it. If the appeal is allowed, hand-out becomes hand-in.

14. If the player strikes at and misses a ball, he may make further attempts to return it, but the following provisions shall apply:

(*a*) Notwithstanding that the ball accidentally touches his opponent the player shall lose the stroke, unless he could have made a good return;

(*b*) If the ball touches his opponent, a Let may be allowed, if the player could have made a good return.

In all other respects the Rules shall apply as if the player had not struck at the ball.

15. If in the course of play the Marker calls "not up" or

"out", the rally shall cease from that moment. If the Marker's decision is reversed on appeal, a Let shall be allowed.

16. If a Let be allowed, the service or rally shall not count, and the server shall serve again from the same service box. A Let shall not annul a previous fault.

17. After the first service is delivered, play shall be continuous, so far as is practical, providing that at any time play may be suspended, owing to bad light, or other circumstances beyond the control of the players, for such period as the Referee shall decide.

In the event of play being suspended for the day, the match shall start afresh, unless both players agree to the contrary.

18. After the delivery of a service, no appeal shall be made for anything that occurred before that service was delivered.

19. A new ball may only be claimed by a player when he is out of hand, but not between the delivery of the first and second service. The server may appeal to the Referee who may condemn the ball if he considers it unfit for play. If only one ball has been used throughout a game, there shall be a new ball to begin the next game.

20. If the Referee is unable to decide an appeal, he may allow a Let.

21. The Referee has power to order
    (a) A player, who has left the court, to play on;
    (b) A player to leave the court for any reason whatsoever, and may award the rubber to his opponent.

22. The Referee shall call foot faults, or must appoint a deputy.

23. Each player must get out of the way as much as possible. After making a stroke he must do all he can to:
    (a) Give his opponent a good view of the ball;
    (b) Avoid interfering with him in getting to, and striking at the ball;
    (c) Leave him, as far as the striker's position allows him, free to play the ball to any part of the front wall, or to either side wall near the front wall.

When a player fails to do any of these things, the Referee may on appeal allow a Let, or a stroke to his opponent, if in his opinion such is a fair decision considering all the circumstances, and in accordance with what would probably have happened had there been no such interference.

24. There may be a Referee and two Umpires, who shall decide all appeals.

If the Umpires are unanimous, the Referee shall give their decision; otherwise he shall give his own. In the absence of Umpires, the Referee shall decide all appeals.

In the absence of a Referee, the Marker shall act as Referee.

The Referee or Umpires shall give no decision unless an appeal is made, except for the purpose of preventing an accident, or correcting a mistake in the score.

The Four-Handed Game

1. The Rules of the Single Game shall apply to the Double Game and wherever the words server, hand-in, hand-out, striker, opponent or player are used in the Rules of the Single Game, such words (wherever applicable) shall be taken to include his partner in the Double Game.

2. Only one of a pair shall serve in the first hand of a game.

3. The order of serving may be changed at the beginning of any game. The player, however, who is serving when a game is won, must continue to serve in the following game, but need not serve first thereafter in that game.

4. If the player, who should serve second, serves first, hand-out may object, provided that he does so before an ace has been scored or an attempt has been made to take the first service. If no such objection is made, the server shall finish his hand and his partner shall then serve, but in subsequent hands the pair shall revert to their original order.

5. If in any hand a player serves again, after he has ceased to be hand-in, no aces so scored shall be counted, provided that the mistake is discovered before either of his opponents has served.

6. If a player does not serve when he should do so and one of his opponents serves instead, the player loses his right of service, unless it is claimed before he, or his partner, has attempted to take a service, or before an ace has been scored.

7. On each side one player shall receive the service served to the right court and one to the left. This order of receiving the

service may only be changed the first time the side is hand-out in any game.

8. Hand-in scores an ace, if the player in the right court strikes a service to the left court, and vice versa.

9. While the service is being delivered, the player who is to take the service may stand where he pleases. His partner shall stand behind the server. The server's partner shall stand near the back wall, and in the court into which the service is not being delivered.

NOTE. *In these Rules the expression:*

Board means: The Board across the lower part of the front wall.

Court means: The whole building in which the game is played, the back of the Court is divided by a Half Court Line into two halves, called the Right (or Fore-Hand) Court, and the Left (or Backhand) Court.

Cut Line or Service Line means: The line drawn on the front wall.

Double means: The ball after it has touched the floor a second time.

Half-Court Line means: The line on the floor, drawn from the Short Line to the Back Wall.

Hand-in means: The player who serves.

Hand-out means: The player who receives the service.

To Serve means: To start the ball in play by striking at it with a racket.

Service Box means: The small squares on each side of the Court from which the service is delivered.

Short Line means: The line drawn across the floor parallel to the front wall.

Striker means: The player whose turn it is to play after the ball in play has hit the front wall.

Drawn up by Major Spens, 1890. Revised by the Tennis, Rackets and Fives Association, 1911. Revised by the Tennis and Rackets Association, 1923, 1950, 1966 and 1980.

The Rules of
Rounders

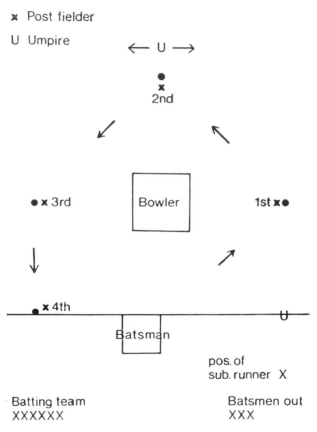

x Post fielder

U Umpire

← U →

● **x** 2nd

Bowler

● **x** 3rd   1st **x** ●

● **x** 4th

Batsman

U

pos. of sub. runner X

Batting team
XXXXXX

Batsmen out
XXX

Diagram of Pitch showing suggested positions of Umpires,
Post Fielders and Batsmen.

Rounders

I. THE PITCH

(*a*) *Running Track*
The running track shall be the area used by the batsman when running, as shown in the diagram facing, and will extend 2 m beyond 4th post.

(*b*) *Bowling Square*
The bowling area shall be 2.5 m square. All lines shall be considered as part of the square.

(*c*) *Batting Square*
The batting area shall be 2 m square. The front line shall be parallel with and 7.5 m away from the front line of the bowling square. All lines shall be considered as part of the square.

(*d*) *Forward Area and Backward Area*
   (i) The front line of the batting square shall be extended in both directions by solid lines measuring at least 12 m in length.
  (ii) This line and the area in front of it and the imaginary continuation of it, shall be called the "Forward Area".
 (iii) The area behind this line and the imaginary continuation of it, shall be called the "Backward Area".
 (iv) At least 5 m behind the backward/forward area line, and 9 m either side of the front right-hand corner of the batting square, lines shall be drawn to mark the positions for waiting batsmen and batsmen out.

II. EQUIPMENT

All equipment should be manufactured for the purpose and approved by the N.R.A.

(*a*) *Posts*
Each of the four posts shall be vertical and 1.2 m above the ground. The four posts shall be supported in a base and not fixed in the ground.

(*b*) *The Ball*

The ball shall weigh a minimum of 70 gm and a maximum of 85 gm and shall measure a minimum of 17 cm and a maximum of 19 cm in circumference.

(*c*) *The Bat*

The bat shall be round, and shall not measure more than 17 cm round the thickest part, nor more than 46 cm in length; it shall weigh not more than 370 gm.

(*d*) *Clothing*

Spiked footwear is prohibited. N.B. studs are allowed providing they measure more 30 mm in circumference at the base and are not larger than 12 mm in length.

III. TEAMS

(*a*) *The Game*

The game shall be played between two teams each consisting of 9 players, viz. bowler, backstop, first post, second post, third post, fourth post, three deep fielders (these positions are given as a suggestion and not as a rule).

(*b*) *Substitutes*

One player may be substituted from two substitutes nominated prior to the match. At any dead ball situation the substitute may take the field provided that the Umpires and the other team are first informed. In a mixed team the substitute shall be of the same sex as the player leaving the field.

IV. INNINGS

(*a*) An innings shall start at the time the first ball is bowled, after the Umpire has called play, and terminate when all the batsmen shall be declared out.

(*b*) The captains shall toss a coin for the choice of innings.

(*c*) A team shall keep the same batting order throughout an innings.

Penalty. As for batsmen overtaking on the track (see Rule 7(f)—OUT).

(*d*) A match shall consist of two innings for each team.

(e) A team leading by five or more rounders in the first innings shall have the option of requiring the other team to follow on.

V. BATTING

A batsman:

(a) while waiting for his turn to bat shall be in the backward area, well away from the 4th post and batting square; suggested position shown on the Diagram.

(b) shall have only one good ball bowled to him;

(c) shall stand with both feet within the square until the ball has left the bowler's hand, and shall not cross the front or back line until he has hit the ball or it has passed him;

(d) may, at his own discretion, take a no-ball and score in the usual way: he shall have been considered to have taken the ball if he made contact with or passed first post;

(e) must run to the first post after having hit, attempted to hit, or let pass the first good ball delivered by the bowler;

(f) who hits a ball so that it pitches in the backward area shall have made a "Backward hit". (This does not refer to balls that drop in the forward area and go afterwards behind);

(g) shall be entitled, if he is the only man left in on entering the square:

  (i) to have the option of 3 good balls but shall forfeit the right to any remaining balls if he is caught or takes the ball. (He shall be considered to have taken the ball if he has made contact with or passed first post.) He can then be put out in any of the usual ways or when the ball has been thrown full pitch or placed in the batting square.

  (ii) to a rest of one minute after each rounder he may score.

VI. PROCEDURE OF GAME

Whilst waiting at a post a member of the batting team shall have the advantage of running on if a no-ball is bowled and not taken by the batsman. He can, at his discretion, continue to run round the track in the normal way. Similarly a runner need not run on for every ball bowled unless the next batsman immediately behind him is obliged to run. More than one batsman may be put out between the delivery of consecutive balls.

A bowler can leave his square to field the ball and can be changed only after the delivery of a good ball. During the change the ball is dead.

A dummy throw or bowl is not allowed. A player losing contact through this dummy ball will be allowed to return to his original position.

VII. RUNNING ROUND THE TRACK

A batsman:

(*a*) shall run round the track (carrying his bat) to reach 4th post, having passed outside or halted at the previous posts in the order 1st, 2nd and 3rd. On reaching 4th post he shall rejoin the waiting batsmen.

Penalty. The Umpire shall declare the player out if he runs deliberately inside a post or deliberately drops his bat. (When trying to make contact with a post, a batsman who goes inside the post owing to obstruction by a fielder is not out.)

(*b*) shall not wait between posts.

Penalty. The Umpire shall order him to continue to the next post.

(*c*) stopping (even temporarily) within reach of a post shall make and maintain contact with it using his hand or bat, except that he may run on whenever the bowler is not in possession of the ball and is in his square.

Penalty. (1) If he does not make contact the Umpire shall order him to do so, and if he does not shall declare him out.

(2) If he loses contact or runs at any time when the bowler has the ball and is in his square (except an overrun—see 7(*d*))or unless ordered to do so by an Umpire (see 7(*e*)) or during the bowler's action but before he releases the ball, the Umpire shall declare him out.

(*d*) shall *continue* his run to the next post if he is between posts when the bowler becomes in possession of the ball and in his square, but may not run past the post.

Penalty. The Umpire shall order the player back to the post he passed.

(*e*) may not remain at the same post as another batsman.

Penalty. The Umpire shall order the player who batted first to run on and he may be put out in the usual ways.

(*f*) when completing the track, shall not overtake any batsman who is running ahead.

Penalty. The Umpire shall declare the batsman who overtakes to be out.

(*g*) shall not run beyond the first post after a backward hit until the ball returns or has been returned to the forward area.

Penalty. The Umpire shall order him back to the first post.

(*h*) must touch 4th post with his hand or bat.

Penalty. The Umpire shall declare him out if 4th post is touched with the ball by the fielding side provided that another ball has not been bowled.

(*i*) shall not return to a post unless he is ordered to do so by the Umpire, or unless in the Umpire's opinion he has over-run a post.

Penalty. The Umpire shall order him on to the next post and he may be put out in the usual ways. A batsman may return to 4th post to make contact before the next ball is bowled.

VIII. OBSTRUCTION

Fielding side

A fielder shall be considered to have obstructed if he impedes, in any way, a batsman during his hitting action or when he is on the running track or is attempting to make contact, whether or not the fielder is holding the ball. He shall also be considered to have obstructed if he verbally misleads the other team.

Penalty. The Umpire shall award half a rounder to the batting team and the batsman shall be allowed to make contact with the post to which he is running.

Batting side

(*a*) While waiting to bat shall stand behind the marked line in the backward area out of the way of backstop and 4th post fielders.

Penalty. The Umpire shall award half a rounder to the fielding side, in the event of obstruction.

 (b) A batsman shall be considered to have obstructed if he:

 (i) impedes the player who is fielding the ball by deviating from the running track;

 (ii) intentionally deflects the course of the ball;

 (iii) verbally misleads the other team.

Penalty. The Umpire shall declare the batsman out.

 (c) Whilst running round the track within the Rules, a batsman shall have the right of way.

 (d) A non-striking batsman causing obstruction and a rounder being scored by the striking batsman on this ball, the rounder would be declared void, but the striking batsman would remain in. (The obstructing batsman would be declared out.)

IX. SCORING

The Winning Team
The team scoring the greater number of rounders shall win the game.

 If a batsman stops within reach of a post, the fielders may prevent him from scoring by touching the next post with the ball or the hand holding the ball (see 9*(b)* (iii)). This does not prevent the batsman from continuing his run.

One Rounder
 (a) One rounder only may be scored from any one hit. In the case of a no-ball which is hit and caught, the batsman may still score in the usual way. See Rule 10*(b)*.

 (b) One rounder shall be scored if, after having hit the ball, the batsman succeeds in running round the track and touches the 4th post, or from 1st post when the ball returns or has been returned by a fielder to the forward area after a backward hit, provided that:

 (i) he has not overtaken any other batsman; see Rule 7 *(f)*.

 (ii) the bowler has not delivered another ball;

 (iii) if he has stopped at a post, the post *immediately ahead* has not been touched by a fielder with the ball or the hand holding the ball.

Half a Rounder
Half a rounder shall be scored by the batsman if he completes the track fulfilling the same conditions as for one rounder but without hitting the ball.

A Penalty Half Rounder
A penalty half rounder shall be awarded to the batting team when:

(*a*) the bowler delivers three consecutive no-balls to the same batsman; or

(*b*) a fielder obstructs a batsman. See Rule 8, Obstruction.

A penalty half rounder shall be awarded to the fielding team when waiting batsmen obstruct the fielders. See Rule 8, Obstruction.

One Rounder and Penalty Half Rounders
It should be noted that the rounder may be scored with the addition of the award:

(*a*) one penalty half rounder if the ball that is hit is the third consecutive no-ball to that batsman;

(*b*) one penalty half rounder if the batsman is obstructed;

(*c*) two penalty half rounders if the ball that is hit is the third consecutive no-ball to that batsman and the batsman is obstructed.

X. BATSMEN OUT

(*a*) A Batsman shall be declared out on a good ball:
  (i) if the ball be caught from bat or hand;
  (ii) if his foot projects over the front or back line of the batting square before he has hit the ball or it has passed him;
  (iii) if he runs to the inside of a post, unless prevented from reaching it by an obstructing fielder (see Penalty, Rule 7 (*a*));
  (iv) if a fielder touched the post immediately ahead with the ball or with the hand holding the ball, *while the batsman is running to that post* (N.B. if the post is separated from the base, the base is touched);
  (v) if he obstructs a fielder or intentionally deflects the course of the ball; see Rule 8, Obstruction;

(vi) if he overtakes another batsman;

(vii) if he loses contact or runs at any time when the bowler has the ball and is in his square (except an over-run—see 7(*d*)) or unless ordered to do so by an Umpire (see 7(*e*)) or during the bowler's action but before he releases the ball;

(viii) if after having been ordered to make contact with a post a batsman has not done so.

(*b*) Rule 10(*a*) shall apply to a No-ball excepting Section (i). Section (iv) shall apply only after the batsman has left the first post.

(*c*) Side Out. Where there is no batsman awaiting his turn to bat, all the batsmen on the running track can be put out simultaneously, by the ball being thrown full pitch or placed by any fielder into the batting square before any one of them has reached 4th post.

XI. NO-BALL

Decisions on height and direction are based on the position of the batsman when the bowler releases the ball.

A no-ball is one that:

(*a*) is not delivered with a continuous and smooth underarm action (this does not prevent spin).

(*b*) is bowled when the bowler fails to keep both feet within the square until the ball is released (the lines of the square are considered to be part of the square and the bowler should be penalised *only* when any part of his foot projects over the line).

(*c*) is on the non-hitting side of the batsman or wide when it reaches the batsman.

(*d*) is higher than the top of the head or lower than the knee when it reaches the batsman.

(*e*) would hit the batsman.

(*f*) hits the ground on the way to the batsman.

UMPIRES

There shall be two Umpires, the Batsman's Umpire, who shall stand on a level with the batsman in the batting square and in a position to see the first post without turning his head, and the Bowler's Umpire, who shall stand in such a position that he can see all the infringements of rules for which he is responsible. This may necessitate a change of position to facilitate his view of a left-handed batsman.

The Umpire's decisions on any aspect of the game shall be final but they should appeal to each other on any point that is doubtful.

The Umpires should both keep a record of the score.

The Umpires should exchange positions after the first innings of both sides have been completed.

Players may also appeal.

The Umpire has the right to order a player off the pitch for unsportsmanlike conduct, with no substitution being possible.

Duties of Batsman's Umpire

   (i) Call "Rounder" or "Half Rounder" and give the score of both sides, after a rounder or half rounder is scored or awarded.

  (ii) Call "No Ball" for balls that are not delivered with a continuous and smooth underarm action or for any balls that are too high or too low.

 (iii) Call "No Ball" if the bowler puts his foot over the front line of the bowling square. See Rule 11 (*b*).

 (iv) Give decisions concerning the batting square, 1st and 4th posts, backward hits and all catches.

Duties of Bowler's Umpire

   (i) Call "Play" at beginning of each innings.

  (ii) Call "No Ball" for wides, for balls straight at or on the non-hitting side of the batsman.

 (iii) Give decisions concerning 2nd and 3rd posts.

 (iv) Call "No Ball" if the bowler projects his foot over the back or side lines of the bowling square. See Rule 11 (*b*).

A SIMPLE METHOD OF MARKING A ROUNDERS PITCH

The Pitch

The simplest way of marking the pitch is by using lengths of string. Put a peg into the ground where the right-hand front corner of the batting square is to be, and directly opposite that another peg at a distance of 17 m. This gives the position of the second post.

Take a length of string measuring 24 m and tie a knot in the

Plan for marking pitch

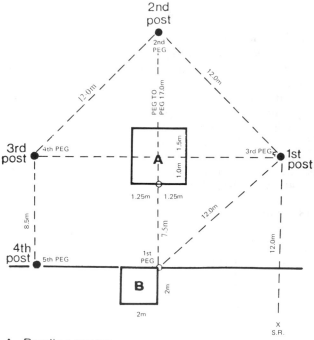

A – Bowling square

B – Batting square

Darker lines are compulsory markings

centre (each half 12 m). Tie one end of the string to each peg and carry the centre knot out to the right until the string is taut. At the knot put in another peg. This gives the position of the first post. Then carry the centre knot to the left, pull the string taut, put in a peg. This gives the position of the third post.

Take a length of string 17 m long with a centre knot (each half 8.5 m) and tie one end to the peg at third post and the other to the peg first put in at the corner of the batting square. Carry the knot to the left. This gives the position of the fourth post.

The Bowling Square (2.5 m by 2.5 m)

To locate the centre of the front line of the square, stretch the 17 m string from the first peg to the second post, then measure a distance of 7.5 m along the string. The front line of the bowling square can then be marked, 1.25 m either side of the string and parallel to the front line of the batting square. The other three sides of the square can then be marked. It will be found that if the string is stretched between the first and third posts it cuts the side lines of the square one m from the front line.

The Batting Square (2 m by 2 m)

The front line is made by marking a line extending 2 m from the first peg towards and in a direct line with fourth post and parallel to the front line of the bowling square. The remaining three sides of the square can then be marked.

The front line of the batting square is extended in both directions for at least 12 m by solid lines.

N.R.A. TOURNAMENTS

(*a*) A minimum boundary of 35 m and a maximum of 55 m.

(*b*) On N.R.A. official tournaments with limited balls, the end of the innings (often the last good ball) will be signified by the ball being placed in the square (batting).

(*c*) All N.R.A. tournaments to use leather balls unless both teams agree to polypropylene balls.

(*d*) Players to be numbered at tournaments—players batting out of given order will be declared out.

The Rules of
Squash Rackets

COURT MARKINGS

ALL COURT LINES ARE 50 mm WIDE AND ARE PAINTED RED

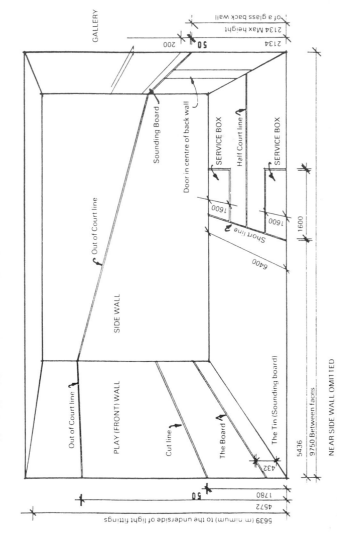

GALLERY

'of a glass back wall'

2134 Max height

2134

200

50

Sounding Board

Door in centre of back wall

SERVICE BOX

Half Court line

SERVICE BOX

1600

1600

Short line

6400

Out of Court line

SIDE WALL

Out of Court line

PLAY (FRONT) WALL

Cut line

The Board

The Tin (Sounding board)

432

5436

9750 Between faces

NEAR SIDE WALL OMITTED

50

1780

4572

5639 (minimum) to the underside of light fittings

SQUASH COURT DIMENSIONS

Squash Rackets

1. The Game, How Played

The game of squash rackets is played between two players, each using a standard racket, with a standard ball and in a court constructed to ISRF standard dimensions.

2. The Score

A match shall consist of the best of 3 or 5 games at the option of the organisers of the competition. Each game is to 9 points, in that the player who scores 9 points wins the game except that, on the score being called 8 all for the first time, the receiver shall choose, before the next service is delivered, to continue that game either to 9 points (known as "no set") or to 10 points (known as "set two"), in which latter case the player who scores 2 more points wins the game. The receiver shall in either case clearly indicate his choice to the marker, referee and his opponent.

The marker shall call either "no set" or "set two" as applicable before play continues.

3. Points, How Scored

Points can be scored only be the server. When the server wins a stroke, he scores a point; when the receiver wins a stroke, he becomes the server.

4. The Service

4.1 The right to serve first is decided by the spin of a racket. Thereafter the server continues to serve until he loses a stroke, whereupon his opponent becomes the server, and this procedure continues throughout the match. At the commencement of the second and each subsequent game, the winner of the previous game serves first.

4.2 At the beginning of each game and each hand, the server has the choice of either box and thereafter shall serve from alternate boxes while remaining the server. However if he serves a fault which the receiver does not attempt to return, or a rally ends in a let, he shall serve again from the same box. If the server does serve from the wrong box, play shall continue and the service shall count as if served from the correct box, except that the receiver may, if he does not attempt to return the service, require that it be served from the correct box.

Note to Markers. If it appears that the server intends to serve from the wrong box, or either player appears undecided as to which is the correct box, the marker shall indicate to the server the correct box.

4.3   For a service to be good, there must be no foot-fault and the ball, before being struck, shall be dropped or thrown in the air and shall not hit the walls, floor, ceiling or any objects suspended from the walls or ceiling; it must be served direct onto the front wall between the cut line and the outline, so that on its return, unless volleyed, it reaches the floor within the back quarter of the court opposite to the server's box. Should a player, having dropped or thrown the ball in the air, make no attempt to strike it, it shall be dropped or thrown again for that service. A player with the use of only one arm may utilise his racket to propel the ball into the air before striking it.

4.4   A service is good when it is not a fault (Rule 4.5) or does not result in the server serving his hand out (Rule 4.6). If the server serves one fault, which the receiver does not attempt to return, he shall serve again. The receiver may attempt to return a fault on the first service and, if he does so, that service becomes good, is no longer a fault and the ball continues in play. A second service fault cannot be played by the receiver.

Note to Referees. The referee shall decide what is an attempt to play the ball.

4.5   A service is a fault:

4.5.1   If at the time of striking the ball the server fails to have part of one foot in contact with the floor within the service box and no part of that foot touching the service box line (called a 'foot-fault'). Part of the foot may project over this line provided that it does not touch the line.

4.5.2 If the ball is served onto or below the cut line but above the board.

4.5.3 If the first bounce of the ball, unless volleyed, is on the floor on or outside the short or half-court lines delineating the back quarter of the court opposite to the server's box.

Any combination of types of faults in the one service counts as only one fault.

4.6 The server serves his hand out and loses the stroke:

4.6.1 If he serves two consecutive faults.

4.6.2 If the ball touches the walls, floor, ceiling or any object(s) suspended from the walls or ceiling before being served.

4.6.3 If the server makes an attempt but fails to strike the ball.

4.6.4 If, in the opinion of the referee, the ball is not struck correctly.

4.6.5 If the ball is served onto or below the board, or out, or against any part of the court before the front wall.

4.6.6 If the ball, before it has bounced more than once on the floor or before it has been struck at by the receiver, touches the server or anything he wears or carries, whether the service was otherwise good or a fault.

4.7 The server shall not serve until the marker has completed calling the score.

Note to Officials. The marker must not delay play by the calling of the score. However, if the server serves, or attempts to serve, prior to the calling of the score, the referee shall stop play and require the server to wait until the calling of the score has been completed.

5. The Play

After a good service has been delivered the players return the ball alternately until one fails to make a good return. The ball otherwise ceases to be in play in accordance with the rules, or on a call by the marker or referee.

6. Good Return

A return is good if the ball, before it has bounced more than once upon the floor, is returned correctly by the striker onto the front wall above the board, without first touching the floor or any part of the striker's body or clothing, or the opponent's racket, body or clothing, provided the ball is not hit out.

Note to Referees. It shall not be considered a good return if the ball touches the board before or after it hits the front wall, or if the racket is not in the player's hand at the time the ball is struck, or if the ball is carried on the racket.

7. Let

A let is an undecided stroke, and the service or rally in respect of which a let is allowed shall not count and the server shall serve again from the same box.

A let shall not cancel a previous fault.

8. Strokes, How Won

A player wins a stroke:
- 8.1 Under Rule 4.6, when the player is the receiver.
- 8.2 If the opponent fails to make a good return of the ball, unless a let is allowed or a stroke is awarded to the opponent.
- 8.3 If the ball touches his opponent or anything he wears or carries when the opponent is the non-striker, except as is otherwise provided by Rules 6, 9, 10 and 13.1.1.
- 8.4 If a stroke is awarded to him by the referee as provided for in the Rules.

9. Hitting an Opponent with the Ball

If the ball, before reaching the front wall, hits the striker's opponent or his racket, or anything he wears or carries, the ball shall cease to be in play and:
- 9.1 If the ball would have made a good return and would have struck the front wall without first touching any other wall, the striker shall win the stroke except if the

ball, after rebounding from the front wall, strikes a side wall and the striker follows the ball round and so turns, or without so turning, allows the ball to pass around his body, in either case taking the ball on the hand opposite to that of the side wall from which the ball rebounded, then a let shall be allowed.

Notes to Referees

(*a*) This includes the case where the striker plays the ball behind his back or between his legs.

(*b*) If the striker, having turned, or allowed the ball to pass around his body, chooses not to continue the rally due to the possibility of striking his opponent and, in the opinion of the referee, is able to make a good return, then a let shall be allowed.

9.2 If the ball either had struck or would have struck any other wall and would have made a good return, a let shall be allowed unless, in the opinion of the referee, a winning stroke has been intercepted, in which case the striker shall win the stroke.

Note to Referees. Where the striker has turned or allowed the ball to pass around his body, a let shall be allowed.

9.3 If the ball would not have made a good return, the striker shall lose the stroke.

Notes to Officials. When a player has been struck by the ball as described in Rule 9, the marker shall call "down".

The referee shall assess the trajectory of the ball and make all further decisions.

10. Further Attempts to Hit the Ball

If the striker strikes at and misses the ball, he may make further attempts to strike it. If, after being missed, the ball touches his opponent or his racket, or anything he wears or carries, then if, in the referee's opinion:

10.1 The striker could otherwise have made a good return, a let shall be allowed, or

10.2 The striker could not have made a good return, he loses the stroke.

If any such further attempt is successful resulting in a good return being prevented from reaching the front wall by hitting the striker's opponent or anything he wears or carries, a let shall be allowed in all circumstances. If any such further attempt would not have made a good return, then the striker shall lose the strike.

11. Appeals

Appeals to the referee under Rule 11 should be made with the words "appeal please".

In all cases under Rule 12 where a let or a stroke is desired, an appeal should be made to the referee with the words "let please".

Play shall then cease until the referee has given his decision. If an appeal under Rule 11 is disallowed, the marker's decision shall stand. If the referee is uncertain he shall allow a let except where provided for in note to referees on Rule 11.2.2. Appeals upheld are dealt with in each specific situation below.

Note to Referees. Players making a pointing gesture during a rally should be advised that such action is not a recognised form of appeal.

    11.1 Appeals on service.

        11.1.1 An appeal may be made against any decision of the marker except for a call of "fault" or "foot-fault" to the first service.

        11.1.2 If the marker fails to call "fault" or "foot-fault" to the first service, the receiver may appeal provided he makes no attempt to play the ball. If the appeal is upheld the service shall be a fault.

        11.1.3 If the marker calls "fault" or "foot-fault" to the second service, the server may appeal. If the appeal is upheld, a "let" shall be allowed, with "one fault" standing.

        11.1.4 If the marker fails to call "fault" or "foot-fault" to the second service the receiver may appeal, either immediately or at the end of the rally if he has played the ball. If the appeal is upheld, the receiver shall win the stroke.

11.1.5 If the marker calls "out", "not up" or "down" to either first or second service the server may appeal. If the appeal is upheld, a let shall be allowed.

11.1.6 If the marker fails to call "out", "nor up" or "down" to either first or second service the receiver may appeal, either immediately or at the end of the rally if he has played the ball. If the appeal is upheld, the receiver shall win the stroke.

Note to Referees. If the marker has not called "one fault" prior to the delivery of a second service and that service is a fault the receiver, if not awarded the stroke, may appeal that the service was a second service, either immediately or at the end of the rally if he has played the ball. If the appeal is upheld, the receiver shall win the stroke.

11.2 Appeals on play, other than service:

11.2.1 An appeal may be made against any decision of the marker.

11.2.2 If the marker has called the ball "out", "nor up" or "down" following a player's return, the player may appeal. If the appeal is upheld, a let shall be allowed, except that if in the opinion of the referee:

– The marker's call has interrupted that player's winning return, he shall award the stroke to the player.

– The marker's call has interrupted or prevented a winning return by the opponent, he shall award the stroke to the opponent.

Note to Referees. In the latter case the referee shall also award a stroke to the opponent if he is unsure whether the marker's call was correct.

11.2.3 When the marker has failed to call the ball "out", "not up" or "down" following a player's return, the opponent may appeal either immediately or at the end of the rally if he has played the ball. If the appeal is upheld, the referees shall award the stroke to the opponent.

Notes to Referees

(*a*) No appeal under Rule 11 may be made after the delivery of a service for anything that occurred before that service.

(*b*) Where there is more than one appeal in a rally, the referee shall consider each appeal in the order in which the situations occurred.

(*c*) If a return is called "not up" by the marker and subsequently goes "down" or "out", the referee, on appeal, if he reverses the marker's call, or is unsure, shall then rule on the subsequent occurrence.

12. Interference

12.1 After playing a ball, a player must make every effort to get out of his opponent's way. That is:

12.1.1 A player must make every effort to give his opponent a fair view of the ball.

12.1.2 A player must make every effort not to obstruct the opponent in the latter's direct movement to the ball. At the same time the opponent must make every effort to get to, and where possible play the ball.

12.1.3 A player must make every effort to allow his opponent freedom to play the ball.

Note to Referees. The freedom to play the ball must include a reasonable backswing, strike at the ball and a reasonable follow-through.

12.1.4 A player must make every effort to allow his opponent, as far as the latter's position permits, freedom to return the ball directly to the front wall, or to either side wall to within approximately one metre of the front wall.

If a player fails to fulfil one of the requirements of Rule 12.1 (1 to 4) above, whether or not he has made every effort to do so, then interference will have occurred.

12.2 If any such form of interference has occurred, and in the opinion of the referee, the player has not made every effort to avoid causing it, the referee shall on appeal, or on stopping play without waiting for an appeal, award the stroke to his opponent, provided the opponent was in a position to make a good return.

Note to Referees. In the case of Rule 12.1 the appeal must be immediate.

12.3 However, if interference has occurred but in the opinion of the referee the player has made every effort to avoid causing it, and the opponent could have made a good return, the referee shall on appeal, or on stopping play without waiting for an appeal, allow a let, except that, if his opponent is prevented from making a winning return by such interference from the player, the referee shall award the stroke to the opponent.

Notes to Referees

(*a*) A player who plays on despite interference forfeits the right of appeal concerning that interference.

(*b*) Where a player's opponent creates his own interference, the referee shall rule that interference has not occurred unless the player has contributed to it.

12.4 When, in the opinion of the referee, a player refrains from playing the ball which, if played, would clearly have won the rally under the terms of Rule 9.1 or 9.2, he shall be awarded the stroke.

12.5 If either player makes unnecessary physical contact with his opponent, the referee may stop play, if it has not already stopped, and award the stroke accordingly.

Notes to Referees

(*a*) The practice of impeding an opponent in his efforts to play the ball by crowding or obscuring his view is highly detrimental to the game. Unnecessary physical contact is also detrimental as well as being dangerous. Referees should have no hesitation in enforcing Rule 12.2 and 12.5.

(*b*) The words 'not to obstruct' in Rule 12.1.2 must be interpreted to include the case of an opponent having to wait for an excessive follow-through of the player's racket.

(*c*) A player's excessive backswing may create interference when his opponent has made every effort to avoid such interference. In this case if the player appeals for a let he shall not be awarded the stroke.

(*d*) When, in the opinion of the referee, a player's swing is excessive and is considered to be dangerous, the referee shall apply Rule 17.

13. Let, When Allowed

13.1 A let may be allowed:

   13.1.1 If, owing to the position of the striker, the opponent is unable to avoid being touched by the ball before the return is made.

Note to Referees. This rule shall be construed to include the cases where the striker's position is in front of his opponent and makes it difficult for the latter to see the ball, or where the striker shapes as if to play the ball but changes his mind at the last moment, preferring to take the ball off the back wall, and the ball in either case hits his opponent, who is between the striker and the back wall. This is not, however, to be taken as conflicting in any way with the duties of the referee under Rule 12.

   13.1.2 If the ball in play touches any articles lying on the floor.

Note to Referees. Referees must ensure that no articles are placed on the floor by the players.

   13.1.3 If the striker refrains from hitting the ball owing to a reasonable fear of injuring his opponent.

Note to Referees. This rule shall be construed to include the case of the striker wishing to play the ball onto the back wall.

   13.1.4 As provided for in Rule 12.

   13.1.5 If, in the opinion of the referee, either player is distracted by an occurrence on or off the court.

Note to Referees. This shall include the case of an obvious late call on the first service by the marker.

   13.1.6 If, in the opinion of the referee, court conditions have affected the result of the rally.

13.2 A let shall be allowed:

  13.2.1 If the receiver is not ready, and does not attempt to return the service.

  13.2.2 If the ball breaks during play.

  13.2.3 If the referee is asked to decide an appeal and is unable to do so.

  13.2.4 If an otherwise good return has been made, but the ball goes out of court on its first bounce.

  13.2.5 As provided for in Rules 9, 10, 11, 16.1, 17 and 19.5.

    In order for a let to be allowed in any of the Rules 13.1 (2 to 6) and 13.2.5 above, the striker must have been able to make a good return.

13.3 No let shall be allowed when the player has made an attempt to play the ball except where the rules definitely provide for a let, namely Rules 9, 10, 11, 13, 16.1, 17 and 19.5.

13.4 Unless an appeal is made by one of the players, no let shall be allowed except where the rules definitely provide for a let, namely Rules 9, 10, 12, 13, 16.1, 17 and 19.5.

14. The Ball

14.1 If the ball breaks during play, it shall be replaced promptly by another ball.

Note to Referees. The referee shall decide whether or not a ball is broken.

14.2 At any time, when the ball is not in actual play, another ball may be substituted by mutual consent of the players or, on appeal by either player, at the discretion of the referee.

Note to Referees. Either player or the referee may examine the ball at any time it is not in actual play, to check its condition.

14.3 If a ball has broken but this has not been established during play, a let for the rally in which the ball broke shall not be allowed once either the receiver has attempted to return the next service or the server has served his hand out with that service.

14.4 Where a player wishes to appeal about a broken ball, the appeal must be made before the next service is returned by the receiver or, if it is the final rally of the game, immediately after the rally.

14.5 If a player stops play during a rally to appeal that the ball is broken only to find subsequently that the ball is not broken, then that player shall lose the stroke.

15. Warm Up

15.1 Immediately preceding the start of play, the referee shall allow on the court of play a period of 5 minutes to the two players together for the purpose of warming up the ball to be used for the match.

With $2\frac{1}{2}$ minutes of the warm up remaining, the referees shall advise the players that they have used half their warm up time with the call "half-time" and ensure that they change sides unless they mutually agree otherwise. The referee shall also advise when the warm up period is complete with the call of "time".

In the event of a player electing to warm up separately on the court of play, the referee shall allow the first player a period of $3\frac{1}{2}$ minutes and his opponent $2\frac{1}{2}$ minutes. In the case of a separate warm up, the choice of warming up first or second shall be decided by the spin of a racket.

15.2 Where a ball has been substituted under Rule 14 or when the match is being resumed after considerable delay, the referee shall allow the ball to be warmed up to playing condition. Play shall resume on the direction of the referee, or upon mutual consent of the players, whichever is the earlier.

Note to Referees. The referee must ensure that both players warm up the ball fairly (Rule 15.1 and 15.2). An unfair warm up shall be dealt with under the provisions of Rule 17.

15.3 Between games the ball shall remain on the floor of the court in view and shall not be hit by either player except by mutual consent of the players.

16. Continuity of Play

After the first service is delivered, play shall be continuous so far as is practical, provided that:

16.1 At any time play may be suspended, owing to bad light or other circumstances beyond the control of the players, for such period as the referee shall decide. The score shall stand.

If another suitable court is available when the court originally in use remains unsuitable, the match may be transferred to it if both players agree, or as directed by the referee.

In the event of play being suspended for the day, the score shall stand unless both players disagree in which case the match will start again.

16.2 An interval of one minute shall be permitted between games and of two minutes between the fourth and fifth games of a five-game match. A player may leave the court during such intervals but shall be ready to resume play by the end of the stated time. When fifteen seconds of the interval permitted between games are left, the referee shall call "fifteen seconds" to warn the players to be ready to resume play. At the end of the interval between games the referee shall call "time".

It is the responsibility of the players to be within earshot of the court to hear the calls of "fifteen seconds" and "time".

Notes to Referees

(*a*) Should one player fail to be ready to resume play when "time" is called, the referee shall apply the provisions of Rule 17.

(*b*) Should neither player be ready to resume play when "time' is called, the referee shall apply the provisions of Rule 17 for both players.

16.3 If a player satisfies the referee that a change of equipment, clothing or footwear is necessary, the referee may allow the player to effect the change as quickly as possible with a maximum allowance of 2 minutes. If the player fails to return within the allotted time, the referee shall apply the provisions of Rule 17.

16.4 In the event of an injury to a player, the referee shall decide if it was:

16.4.1 Self-inflicted.

16.4.2 Contributed to accidentally by his opponent, or

16.4.3 Caused by the opponent's deliberate or dangerous play or action.

Notes to Referees.

(*a*) In 16.4.2 and 16.4.3 above, the referee must determine that the injury is genuine.

(*b*) The referee must not interpret the words 'contributed to accidentally by his opponent' to include the situation where the injury to the player is as a result of that player occupying an unnecessarily close position to his opponent.

In Rule 16.4.1 above the referee shall require the player to continue play; or concede the game, accept the minute interval and then continue to play; or concede the match.

In Rule 16.4.2 above the referee shall allow reasonable time for the injured player to recover having regard to the time schedule of the competition.

In Rule 16.4.3 above the referee shall award the match to the injured player.

16.5 The referee shall award a stroke, game or match to the opponent of a player, who, in his opinion persists, after due warning, in delaying the play unreasonably. Such delay may be caused by:

16.5.1 Unduly slow preparation to serve or receive service.

16.5.2 Prolonged discussion with the referee, or

16.5.3 Delay in returning to the court having left under terms of Rules 16.2 and 16.3.

17. Conduct on Court

If the referee considers that the behaviour of a player on court could be intimidating or offensive to an opponent, official or spectator, or could in any other way bring the game into disrepute the player shall be penalised.

Where a player commits any of the offences listed in the Rules 12.5, 15.2 and 15.3, 16.2, 16.3 or the I.S.R.F. Code of Conduct (Appendix VI), the following penalty provisions may be applied:

Warning by the referee

Stroke awarded to opponent

Game awarded to opponent, or

Match awarded to opponent

Notes to Referees

(*a*) If the referee stops play to give a warning, a let shall be allowed.

(*b*) If the referee awards a game, that game shall be the one in progress or the next game if one is not in progress. The offending player shall retain any points already scored in the game awarded.

18. Control of a Match

A match is normally controlled by a referee, assisted by a marker. One person may be appointed to carry out the functions of both referee and marker. When a decision has been made by the referee, he shall announce it to the players and the marker shall repeat it with the subsequent score.

Notes to Officials

(*a*) Having only one official to carry out roles of both marker and referee is undesirable.

(*b*) Up to 30 minutes before the commencement of a match either player may request a referee and/or marker other than appointed, and this request may be considered and a substitute appointed.

(*c*) Players are not permitted to request any such change(s) after the commencement of a match, unless both agree to do so. In either case the decision as to whether or not an official is to be replaced must remain in the hands of the tournament referee or adjudicator where applicable.

19. Duties of a Marker

19.1 The marker calls the play followed by the score, with the server's score first. He shall call "fault", "foot-fault", "out", "not up", or "down" as appropriate, and shall repeat the referee's decisions.

19.2 If in the course of play the marker calls "not up", "out", or "down", or in the case of a second service, "fault" or "foot-fault", the rally shall cease.

Note to Markers. If the marker is unsighted or uncertain he shall make no call.

19.3 Any service or return shall be considered good unless otherwise called.

19.4 After the server has served a fault, which has not been accepted for play, the marker shall repeat the score and the words 'ONE FAULT', before the server serves again. This call shall be repeated when the subsequent rally ends one or more times in a let, until the stroke is finally decided.

19.5 If play ceases, and the marker is unsighted or uncertain, he shall advise the players and shall call on the referee to make the relevant decision; if the referee is unable to do so, a let shall be allowed.

Note to Markers. Markers must use recognised marker's calls including when the rally has ceased (Appendix 1.2).

20. Duties of a Referee

20.1 The referee shall allow lets and award strokes; make decisions where called for by the rules, including when a player is struck by the ball and for injuries; and shall decide all appeal, including those against the marker's calls. The decision of the referee shall be final.

20.2 The referee shall not intervene in the marker's calling except:

20.2.1 Upon appeal by one of the players.

20.2.2 As provided for in Rules 12 and 17, or

20.2.3 When it is evident that the score has been called incorrectly, in which case he shall have the marker call the correct score.

Note to Officials. It is recommended that both marker and referee record the score.

20.2.4 If he is certain that the marker has made an

error in stopping play or allowing play to continue, he shall immediately rule accordingly.

20.3 The referee is responsible for ensuring that all times laid down in the rules are strictly adhered to.

20.4 The referee is responsible for ensuring that court conditions are appropriate for play.

20.5 In exceptional cases the referee may award a stroke, a game or the match to the opponent of a player whose conduct is in his opinion detrimental to the match in progress and the game of squash in general. The referee may also order:

20.5.1 A match to be awarded to a player whose opponent fails to be present on court ready to play, within 10 minutes of the advertised time of play.

20.5.2 Play to be stopped in order to warn that the conduct of one or both of the players is leading to an infringement of the rules.

Note to Referees. A referee should avail himself of this rule as early as possible when either player is showing a tendency to break the provisions of Rules 12, 16.5 or Rule 17.

APPENDIX I

I.1 DEFINITIONS

Adjudicator

Responsible for the conduct of players and officials throughout the Tournament.

Appeal

A player's request to the referee to consider an on or off court situation. "Appeal" is used throughout the rules in two contexts:

(*a*) where the player requests the referee to consider varying a marker's decision and,

(*b*) where the player requests the referee to allow a let.

Board

The Board is the lower horizontal line marking on the front wall, with the "tin" beneath it for the full width of the court.

Box (Service)

A square delineated area in each quarter court, bounded by part of the short line, part of the side wall and by two other lines and from within which the server serves.

Competition

A championship, tournament, league or other competitive match.

Correctly

The ball being hit by the racket (held in the hand) not more than once nor with prolonged contact on the racket.

Cut Line

A line upon the front wall, the top edge of which is 1.83 metres (6 feet) above the floor and extending the full width of the court.

Down

The expression used to indicate that an otherwise good return has struck the board or has failed to reach the front wall. ("Down" is used as a marker's call.)

Game

Part of a match, commencing with a service by server and concluding when one player has scored or been awarded 9 or 10 points (in accordance with the rules).

Game Ball

The state of the score when server requires one point to win the game in progress. ("Game ball" is also used as a marker's call.)

Half-Court Line

A line set upon the floor parallel to the side walls, dividing the back of the court into 2 equal parts, meeting the 'Short line' at its midpoint, forming the T.

Half-Time
The midpoint of the warm up (also used as a referee's call).

Hand
(As referred to in Rule 9.1.)

A player's racket hand position in regard to its approximate location on one side or the other of his body at the moment of ball contact with the racket, a hand on the right side of his body (if facing the front wall) being right and on the left side, left.

Hand-In
The period from the time a player becomes server until he becomes receiver.

Hand-Out
Condition when change of server occurs. ("Hand-out" is also used as a marker's call to indicate that a change of hand has occurred.)

Match
The complete contest between two players commencing with the warm up and concluding when both players have left the court at the end of the final rally. (Covers broken ball rule.)

Match Ball
The state of the score when the server requires one point to win the match. ("Match ball" is also used as a marker's call.)

Not Up
The expression used to indicate that a ball has not been struck in accordance with the rules. "not up" covers all returns which are not good and are neither "down" nor "out" – with the exception of "faults" and "foot-faults". ("Not up" is also used as a marker's call.)

Out

The expression used to indicate that a ball has struck the out line or a wall above such line or the roof, or has passed over any part of the roof (e.g. cross bars). ("Out" is also used as a marker's call.)

Out Line

A continuous line comprising the front wall line, both side wall lines and the back wall line and marking the top boundaries of the court.

Note. When a court is constructed without provision of such a line i.e. the walls comprise only the area used for play, or without the provision of part of such a line (e.g. a glass back wall), and the ball in play strikes part of the horizontal top surface of such a wall and deflects back into court, such a ball is out. Because of the difficulty in ascertaining just where the ball strikes the wall, the decision as to whether such a ball is out should be made by observing the deflection back into court – an abnormal deflection indicating that the ball is out. This decision should be made in the normal manner by the marker, subject to appeal to the referee.

Point

A unit of the scoring system. One point is added to a player's score when he is server and wins a stroke.

Quarter (Court)

One half of the back part of the court which has been divided into two equal parts by the half court line.

Rally

Series of returns of the ball, comprising one or more such returns. A rally commences with a service and concludes when the ball ceases to be in play.

Reasonable Backswing

The initial action used by a player in moving his racket away from his body as preparation prior to racket movement forward towards the ball for contact. A backswing is reasonable if it is not excessive. An excessive backswing is one in which the player's racket arm is extended towards a straight arm position and/or the racket is extended with the shaft approximately horizontal. The referee's decision on what constitutes a reasonable as distinct from excessive backswing is final.

Reasonable Follow-Through

The action used by a player in continuing the movement of his racket after it has contacted the ball. A follow-through is reasonable if it is not excessive. An excessive follow-through is one in which the player's racket arm is extended towards a straight arm position with the racket also extended with the shaft horizontal – particularly when the extended position is maintained for other than a momentary period of time. An excessive swing is also one in which the arm extended towards a straight position takes a wider arc than the continued line of flight of the ball, even though the racket shaft is in the correct vertical position. The referee's decision on what constitutes a reasonable versus excessive follow-through is final.

Referee (Tournament)

Tournament referee is given overall responsibility for all marking and refereeing matters throughout the tournament including the appointment of officials to matches.

Service

The method by which the ball is put into play by the server to commence a rally.

Short Line

A line set out upon the floor parallel to and 5.49 metres (18 feet) from the front wall and extending the full width of the court.

Standard

The description given to balls, rackets and courts that meet existing I.S.R.F. specifications.

Stop

Expression used by the referee to stop play.

Striker

The player whose turn it is to hit the ball after it has rebounded from the front wall, or who is in the process of hitting the ball, or who, up to the point of his return reaching the front wall, has just hit the ball.

Stroke

The gain achieved by the player who wins a rally either in the normal course of play or on award by the referee and which results in either the scoring of a point or a change of hand.

Time

The expression used by the referee to indicate that a period of time prescribed in the rules has elapsed.

Tin

Between the board and the floor for the full width of the court, the tin shall be constructed in such a manner as to make a distinctive noise when struck by the ball.

General Note 1

The use of the word "shall" in the rules indicates compulsion and the lack of any alternative. The word "must" indicates a required course of action with considerations to be taken into account if the action is not carried out. The word "may" indicates the option of carrying out or not carrying out the action.

General Note 2

When the words "he" or "him" are used in the rules, they shall be taken to mean "she" and "her" as appropriate.

I.2 MARKER'S CALLS

Fault

See Rule 4.5.2 and 4.5.3. The expression used to denote the service is a 'Fault'.

Foot-Fault

See Rule 4.5.1. The expression used to denote the service is a 'Foot-fault'.

Not Up

The expression used to denote that a ball has not been served or returned above the board in accordance with the rules.

Down

The expression used to indicate that a ball has been struck against the tin or board.

One Fault

The expression used to indicate the server is serving the second service.

Out

The ball is out when it touches the front, sides or back of the court above the area prepared for play or passes over any cross bars or other part of the roof of the court. The lines delimiting such area, the lighting equipment and the roof are out.

I.3 REFEREE'S CALLS

Stop

Expression used by referee to stop play.

Time

Expression used by referee to start play.

Half-time

Expression used by referee when $2\frac{1}{2}$ minutes of the warm up have passed.

Yes Let

Call made by referee when answering an appeal.

No Let

Call made by referee when answering an appeal.

Stroke to A

Call made by referee when answering an appeal.

Stroke to B

Call made by referee when answering an appeal.

APPENDIX II

DIMENSIONS OF A SINGLES COURT

Length	9.75 m	(32 ft)
Breadth	6.40 m	(21 ft)
Height to upper edge of cut line on front wall	1.83 m	(6 ft)
Height to lower edge of front wall line	4.57 m	(15 ft)
Height to lower edge of back wall line	2.13 m	(7 ft)
Distance to nearest edge of short line from back wall	4.26 m	(13 ft 10 in)
Height to upper edge of board from ground	0.48 m	(19 in)
Thickness of board (flat or rounded at top)	12.5 mm	($\frac{1}{2}$ in)
	to 25.0 mm	(1 in)

Height of side wall line: the diagonal line joining the front wall and back wall lines.

The service boxes shall be entirely closed on three sides within the court by lines, the short line forming the side nearest to the front wall, the side wall bounding the fourth side.

The internal dimensions of the service boxes shall be	1.60 m	(5 ft 3 in)

All dimensions in the court shall be measured from junction of the floor and front wall – 1 metre above the finished floor level.

All lines shall be 50 mm (2 in) in width. All lines shall be coloured red. In respect of the outer boundary lines on the walls, it is suggested that the plaster should be so shaped as to produce a concave channel along such lines.

APPENDIX III

DIMENSIONS OF A RACKET

1. Dimensions

(a) Maximum length .... 685 mm   (27 in)

(b) Internal stringing:

    Maximum length .... 215 mm   (8.5 in)

    Maximum breadth .... 184 mm   (7.25 in)

(c) Framework of head:

    Maximum width across the face   14 mm   (0.56 in)

    Minimum width across the face   9 mm   (0.36 in)

    Maximum depth across the face   20 mm   (0.81 in)

    Minimum depth across the face   12 mm   (0.47 in)

(d) Shaft:

    Minimum thickness ....   9 mm   (0.36 in)

(e) Maximum weight

    (including stringing and   bumper strip) .... 255 gms   (9 oz)

2. Construction

At all times, the head or shaft shall not contain outside edges with a radius of curvature less than 2 mm. String and string ends must be recessed within the racket head or, in cases where such recessing is impractical because of the racket material, or design, must be protected by a non-marking and securely attached bumper strip made of a flexible material which cannot crease into sharp edges following abrasive contact with floors and walls.

Strings shall be gut, nylon or a substitute material, providing metal is not used. Only two layers of string shall be allowed and these shall be alternately interlaced to form an orthogonal array.

Note to referees on degradation

Rackets which have suffered damage so as to cause a potential hazard must not be used for play, unless the damaged region is repaired adhesively or by wound overlays, such that the damaged region becomes stronger than the material on either side of the damaged zone and has a smooth surface.

Manufacturers were given two years from 1 November 1983, to allow rackets made of wood, but which do not meet the new specification to clear the market. As from 1 November 1985, *all* rackets must meet the above specification.

APPENDIX IV

SPECIFICATION FOR SQUASH RACKET BALLS

The ball must conform to the following:
1. It must weight not less than 23.3 grammes and not more than 24.6 grammes (approximately 360–380 grains).
2. Its diameter must be not less than 39.5 mm and not more than 41.5 mm (approximately 1.56 to 1.63 in).
3. It must have a surface finish which guarantees continuing correct rebound.
4. It must be of a type specifically approved for championship play by the I.S.R.F.
5. Compression specification:
    (i) The ball is mounted in an apparatus and a load of 0.5 kg is applied which deforms the ball slightly. Subsequent deformation in the test is measured from this datum.
   (ii) An additional load of 2.4 kg is applied and this deforms the ball further. The deformation from the datum position is recorded.
  (iii) The deformation obtained in (ii) should be between 3 and 7 mm for balls of playing properties acceptable to the I.S.R.F.

APPENDIX V

COLOUR OF PLAYERS' CLOTHING

Organisers may specify regulations concerning players' clothing which must be complied with in their particular tournament or tournaments.

S.R.A. Note. For all events under the control of the

S.R.A., players are required to wear white and/or light matching pastel clothing during the course of play. A coloured trim with a maximum width of 50 mm (2 in) is permissible. Shoes should be predominantly white with only 20% of colour trim inclusive of sole, which must be non marking. The maximum area for advertising is 50 mm^2 (2 sq in). Member countries of the I.S.R.F. have a limited discretion to allow advertising of a greater size to be worn for any other other events under their control. The referee's decision on compliance shall be final.

Note. Footwear is deemed clothing.

APPENDIX VI

CODE OF CONDUCT

6. The following offences may be subject to penalties under Rule 17 and/or disciplinary action:

   6.1 A player who verbally or physically abuses his opponent, the marker, referee, officials, spectators or the sponsors.

   6.2 A player who shows dissent to the marker, referee or officials, including foul or profane language and obscene or offensive gestures.

   6.3 A player who abuses playing equipment or the court.

   6.4 A player who fails to comply with the conditions of entry of a tournament including any rules with regard to clothing or advertising.

   6.5 A player who, having entered a tournament or accepted an invitation to play, withdraws from the event or fails to attend.

   6.6 A player who fails to complete a match.

   6.7 A player who defaults from a tournament or event. The Disciplinary Committee may require evidence or proof of 'bona fide' injury, illness or other emergency situation.

   6.8 A player who fails to make himself available to meet reasonable requests for interviews by the media.

6.9 A player who does not comply with the rules or spirit of the game.

6.10 A player guilty of any other unreasonable conduct which brings the game into disrepute.

The Rules of
Tennis

PLAN OF THE COURTS
(See Rules 1 and 32)

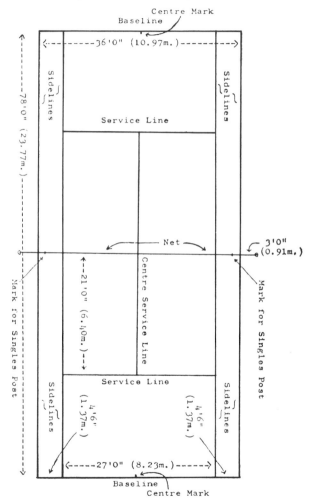

Tennis

THE SINGLES GAME

1. The Court shall be a rectangle, 78 ft (23.77 m) long and 27 ft (8.23 m) wide. It shall be divided across the middle by a net, suspended from a cord or metal cable of a maximum diameter of one-third of an inch (0.8 cm), the ends of which shall be attached to, or pass over, the tops of two posts, which shall be not more than 6 in (15 cm) square or 6 in (15 cm) in diameter. These posts shall not be higher than 1 inch (2.3 cm) above the top of the net cord. The centres of the posts shall be 3 ft (0.914 m) outside the court on each side and the height of the posts shall be such that the top of the cord or metal cable shall be 3 ft 6 in (1.07 m) above the ground.

When a combined doubles (see Rule 34) and singles court with a doubles net is used for singles, the net must be supported to a height of 3 ft 6 in (1.07 m) by means of two posts, called "singles sticks", which shall be not more than 3 in (7.5 cm) square or 3 in (7.5 cm) in diameter. The centres of the singles sticks shall be 3 ft (0.914 m) outside the singles court on each side. The net shall be extended fully so that it fills completely the space between the two posts and shall be of sufficiently small mesh to prevent the ball passing through. The height of the net shall be 3 ft (0.914 m) at the centre, where it shall be held down taut by a strap not more than 2 in (5 cm) wide and completely white in colour. There shall be a band covering the cord or metal cable and the top of the net of not less than 2 in (5 cm) nor more than 2½ in (6.3 cm) in depth on each side and completely white in colour. There shall be no advertisement on the net, strap, band or singles sticks. The lines bounding the ends and sides of the Court shall respectively be called the Base-lines and the Side-lines. On each side of the net, at a distance of 21 ft (6.40 m) from it and parallel with it, shall be drawn the Service-lines. The space on each side of the net between the service-line and the side-lines shall be divided into two equal parts called the service-courts by the centre service-line, which must be 2 in (5 cm) in width, drawn half-way between, and parallel with, the side-lines. Each base-line shall be bisected by an imaginary continuation of the centre service-line to a line 4 in (10 cm) in length and 2 in (5 cm) in width called the centre mark drawn inside the Court, at right angles to and in contact with such base-lines. All other lines shall be not less than 1 in (2.5 cm) nor more than 2 in (5 cm) in width, except the base-line, which may be 4 in (10 cm) in width, and all measurements shall be made to the outside of the lines. All lines shall be of uniform colour.

If advertising or any other material is placed at the back of the court, it may not contain white or yellow. A light colour may only be used if this does not interfere with the vision of the players. If advertisements are placed on the chairs of the linesmen sitting at the back of the Court, they may not contain white or yellow.

NOTE. *In the case of the International Tennis Championship (Davis Cup) or other Official Championships of the International Federation, there shall be a space behind each base-line of not less than 21 ft (6.4 m) and at the sides of not less than 12 ft (3.66 m).*

2. The Permanent Fixtures of the Court shall include not only the net, posts, singles sticks, cord or metal cable, strap and band, but also, where there are any such, the back and side stops, the stands, fixed or movable seats and chairs round the Court, and their occupants, all other fixtures around and above the Court, and the Umpire, Net-cord Judge, Foot-fault Judge, Linesmen and Ball Boys when in their respective places.

NOTE. *For the purpose of this Rule, the word "Umpire" comprehends the Umpire, the persons entitled to a seat on the Court, and all those persons designated to assist the Umpire in the conduct of a* match.

3. The Ball shall have a uniform outer surface and shall be white or yellow in colour. If there are any seams they shall be stitchless. The ball shall be more than $2\frac{1}{2}$ in (6.35 cm) and less than $2\frac{5}{8}$ in (6.67 cm) in diameter, and more than 2 oz (56.7 gm) and less than $2\frac{1}{16}$ oz (58.5 gm) in weight. The ball shall have a bound of more than 53 in (135 cm) and less than 58 in (147 cm) when dropped 100 in (254 cm) upon a concrete base. The ball shall have a forward deformation of more than 0.22 in (0.56 cm) and less than 0.29 in (0.74 cm) and a return deformation of more than 0.35 in (0.89 cm) and less than 0.425 in (1.08 cm) at 18 lb (8.165 kg) load. The two deformation figures shall be the averages of three individual readings along three axes of the ball and no two individual readings shall differ by more than 0.03 in (0.08 cm) in each case.

4. The Racket. Rackets failing to comply with the following specifications are not approved for play under the Rules of Tennis.

(a) The hitting surface of the racket shall be flat and consist of a pattern of crossed strings connected to a frame and alternately interlaced or bonded where they cross; and the stringing pattern shall be generally uniform, and in particular not less dense in the centre than in any other area. The strings shall be free of attached objects and protrusions other than those utilised solely and specifically to limit or prevent wear and tear or vibration, and which are reasonable in size and placement for such purposes.

(b) The frame of the racket shall not exceed 32 in (81.28 cm) in overall length, including the handle, and $12\frac{1}{2}$ in (31.75 cm) in overall width. The strung surface shall not exceed $15\frac{1}{2}$ in (39.37 cm) in overall length, and $11\frac{1}{2}$ in (29.21 cm) in overall width.

(c) The frame, including the handle, shall be free of attached objects and devices, other than those utilised solely and specifically to limit or prevent wear and tear or vibration, or to distribute weight. Any objects and devices must be reasonable in size and placement for such purposes.

(d) The frame, including the handle, and the strings, shall be free of any device which makes it possible to change materially the shape of the racket, or to change the weight distribution, during the playing of a point.

The International Tennis Federation shall rule on the question of whether any racket or prototype complies with the above specifications or is otherwise approved, or not approved, for play. Such ruling may be undertaken on its own initiative, or upon application by any party with a bona fide interest therein, including any player, equipment manufacturer or National Association or members thereof. Such rulings and applications shall be made in accordance with the applicable Review and Hearing Procedures of the I.T.F., copies of which may be obtained from the office of the Secretary.

5. Server and Receiver. The players shall stand on opposite sides of the net; the player who first delivers the ball shall be called the Server, and the other the Receiver.

6. Choice of Ends and Service and the right to be Server or Receiver in the first game shall be decided by toss. The player winning the toss may choose or require his opponent to choose:

(a) The right to be Server or Receiver, in which case the other player shall choose the end; or

(b) The end, in which case the other player shall choose the right to be Server or Receiver.

7. The Service shall be delivered in the following manner. Immediately before commencing to serve, the Server shall stand with both feet at rest behind (i.e. further from the net than) the base-line, and within the imaginary continuations of the centre-mark and side-line. The Server shall then project the ball by hand into the air in any direction and before it hits the ground strike it with his racket, and the delivery shall be deemed to have been completed at the moment of the impact of the racket and ball. A player with the use of only one arm may utilise his racket for the projection.

8. Foot Fault. The Server shall throughout the delivery of the service:

(i) Not change his position by walking or running.

(ii) Not touch, with either foot, any area other than that behind the base-line within the imaginary extension of the centre mark and side-line.

NOTE. *The following interpretation of Rule 8 was approved by the International Federation on 9th July, 1958: (a) The Server shall not, by slight movements of the feet which do not materially affect the location originally taken up by him, be deemed "to change his position by walking or running". (b) The word "foot" means the extremity of the leg below the ankle.*

9. *(a)* **In Delivering the Service,** the Server shall stand alternately behind the right and left Courts, beginning from the right in every game. If service from a wrong half of the court occurs and is undetected, all play resulting from such wrong service or services shall stand, but the inaccuracy of station shall be corrected immediately it is discovered.

(b) The ball served shall pass over the net and hit the ground within the Service Court which is diagonally opposite, or upon any line bounding such Court, before the Receiver returns it.

10. The Service is a Fault:

(a) If the Server commits any breach of Rules 7, 8 or 9;

(b) If he misses the ball in attempting to strike it;

(c) If the ball served touches a permanent fixture (other than the net, strap or band) before it hits the ground.

11. After a Fault (if it is the first fault) the Server shall serve again from behind the same half of the Court from which he served that fault, unless the service was from the wrong half, when, in accordance with Rule 9, the Server shall be entitled to one service only from behind the other half. A fault may not be claimed after the next service has been delivered.

12. When to serve. The Server shall not serve until the Receiver is ready. If the latter attempt to return the service, he shall be deemed ready. If, however, the Receiver signify that he is not ready, he may not claim a fault because the ball does not hit the ground within the limits fixed for the service.

13. The let. In all cases where a let has to be called under the rules, or to provide for an interruption to play, it shall have the following interpretations:

(a) When called solely in respect of a service that one service only shall be replayed.

(b) When called under any other circumstance, the point shall be replayed.

14. The Service is a Let:

(a) If the ball served touches the net, strap or band, and is otherwise good, or, after touching the net, strap or band, touches the Receiver or anything which he wears or carries before hitting the ground.

(b) If a service or fault is delivered when the Receiver is not ready (see Rule 12). In case of a let, that particular service shall not count, and the Server shall serve again, but a service let does not annul a previous fault.

15. Order of Service. At the end of the first game the Receiver shall become Server, and the Server Receiver; and so on alternately in all the subsequent games of a match. If a player serves out of turn, the player who ought to have served shall serve as soon as the mistake is discovered, but all points scored before such discovery shall be reckoned. A fault served before such discovery shall not be reckoned. If a game shall have been completed before such discovery, the order of service remains as altered.

16. The Players Shall Change Ends at the end of the first, third and every subsequent alternate game of each set, and at the end of each set unless the total number of games in such set is even, in which case the change is not made until the end of the first game of the next set.

If a mistake is made and the correct sequence is not followed the players must take up their correct station as soon as the discovery is made and follow their original sequence.

17. A Ball is in Play from the moment at which it is delivered in service. Unless a fault or a let be called it remains in play until the point is decided.

18. The Server Wins the Point:

(a) If the ball served, not being a let under Rule 14, touches the Receiver or anything which he wears or carries, before it hits the ground;

(b) If the Receiver otherwise loses the point as provided by Rule 20.

19. The Receiver Wins the Point:

(a) If the Server serves two consecutive faults;

(b) If the Server otherwise loses the point as provided by Rule 20.

20. A Player Loses the Point if:

(a) He fails, before the ball in play has hit the ground twice consecutively, to return it directly over the net (except as provided in Rule 24 *(a)* or *(c)*); or

(b) He returns the ball in play so that it hits the ground, a permanent fixture, or other object, outside any of the lines which bound his opponent's Court (except as provided in Rule 24 *(a)* and *(c)*); or

(c) He volleys the ball and fails to make a good return even when standing outside the Court; or

(d) In playing the ball he deliberately carries or catches it on his racket or deliberately touches it with the racket more than once: or

(e) He or his racket (in his hand or otherwise) or anything which he wears or carries touches the net, post, singles sticks, cord or metal cable, strap or band, or the ground within his opponent's Court at any time while the ball is in play; or

(f) He volleys the ball before it passed the net; or

(g) The ball in play touches him or anything that he wears or carries, except his racket in his hand or hands; or

(h) He throws his racket at and hits the ball.

(i) He deliberately and materially changes the shape of his racket during the playing of the point.

21. If a Player Commits Any Act which hinders his opponent in making a stroke, then, if this is deliberate, he shall lose the point or, if involuntary the point shall be replayed.

22. A Ball Falling on a Line is regarded as falling in the Court bounded by that line.

23. If the Ball in Play Touches a Permanent Fixture (other than the net, posts, singles sticks, cord or metal cable, strap or band) after it has hit the ground, the player who struck it wins the point; if before it hits the ground his opponent wins the point.

24. It is a Good Return:

(a) If the ball touches the net, posts, singles sticks, cord or metal cable, strap or band, provided that it passes over any of them and hits the ground within the Court; or

(b) If the ball, served or returned, hits the ground within the proper Court and rebounds or is blown back over the net, and the player whose turn it is to strike reaches over the net and plays the ball, provided that neither he nor any part of his clothes or racket touches the net, posts, singles sticks, cord or metal cable, strap or band or the ground within his opponent's Court, and that the stroke be otherwise good; or

(c) If the ball be returned outside the posts, or singles sticks, either above or below the level of the top of the net,

even though it touch the posts or singles sticks, provided that it hits the ground within the proper Court; or

(d) If a player's racket passes over the net after he has returned the ball, provided the ball passes the net before being played and be properly returned; or

(e) If a player succeeds in returning the ball, served or in play, which strikes a ball lying in the Court.

NOTE TO RULE 24. *In a singles match, if, for the sake of convenience, a doubles Court be equipped with singles sticks for the purpose of a singles game, then the doubles posts and those portions of the net, cord or metal cable and band outside such singles sticks shall at all times be permanent fixtures, and are not regarded as posts or parts of the net of a singles game.*

A return that passes under the net cord between the singles stick and adjacent doubles post without touching either net cord, net or doubles post and falls within the area of play, is a good return.

25. In Case a Player is Hindered in making a stroke by anything not within his control, except a permanent fixture of the Court, or except as provided for in Rule 21, a let shall be called.

26. Score in a Game. If a player wins his first point, the score is called 15 for that player; on winning his second point, the score is called 30 for that player; on winning his third point, the score is called 40 for that player, and the fourth point won by a player is scored game for that player except as below:

If both players have won three points, the score is called deuce; and the next point won by a player is scored advantage for that player. If the same player wins the next point, he wins the game; if the other player wins the next point the score is again called deuce; and so on, until a player wins the two points immediately following the score at deuce, when the game is scored for that player.

27. Score in a Set. *(a)* A player (or players) who first wins six games wins a set; except that he must win by a margin of two games over his opponent and where necessary a set shall be extended until this margin be achieved.

(b) See Appendix: (Tie-break)

28. The Maximum Number of Sets in a match shall be five, or, where women take part, three.

29. Role of Court Officials. In matches where an Umpire is appointed, his decision shall be final; but where a Referee is appointed, an appeal shall lie to him from the decision of an Umpire on a question of law, and in all such cases the decision of the Referee shall be final. In matches where assistants to the Umpire are appointed (linesmen, net-cord judges, foot fault judges) their decisions shall be final on questions of fact except that if in the opinion of an Umpire a clear mistake has been made he shall have the right to change the decision of an assistant or order a let to be played. When such an assistant is unable to give a decision he shall indicate this immediately to the Umpire who shall give a decision. When an Umpire is unable to give a decision on a question of fact he shall order a let to be played. In Davis Cup matches or other team competitions where a Referee is on Court, any decision can be changed by the Referee, who may also authorise an Umpire to order a let to be played.

The Referee, in his discretion, may at any time postpone a match on account of darkness or the condition of the ground or the weather. In any case of postponement the previous score and previous occupancy of Courts shall hold good, unless the Referee and the players unanimously agree otherwise.

30. Continuous Play and Rest Periods. Play shall be continuous from the first service until the match is concluded, in accordance with the following provisions:

(*a*) If the first service is a fault, the second service must be struck by the Server without delay.

The Receiver must play to the reasonable pace of the Server and must be ready to receive when the Server is ready to serve.

When changing ends a maximum of one minute thirty seconds shall elapse from the moment the ball goes out of play at the end of the game to the time the ball is struck for the first point of the next game.

The Umpire shall use his discretion when there is interference which makes it impractical for play to be continuous.

The organisers of international circuits and team events recognised by the ITF may determine the time allowed between points, which shall not at any time exceed 30 seconds.

(*b*) Play shall never be suspended, delayed or interfered with for the purpose of enabling a player to recover his strength, breath, or physical condition. However, in the case of accidental injury, the Umpire may allow a one-time three minute suspension for that injury.

The organisers of international circuits and team events recognised by the ITF may extend the one-time suspension period from three minutes to five minutes.

(*c*) If, through circumstances outside the control of the player, his clothing, footwear or equipment (excluding racket) becomes out of adjustment in such a way that it is impossible or undesirable for him to play on, the Umpire may suspend play while the maladjustment is rectified.

(*d*) The Umpire may suspend or delay play at any time as may be necessary and appropriate.

(*e*) After the third set, or when women take part the second set, either player is entitled to a rest, which shall not exceed 10 minutes, or in countries situated between latitude 15 degrees north and latitude 15 degrees south, 45 minutes and furthermore, when necessitated by circumstances not within the control of the players, the Umpire may suspend play for such a period as he may consider necessary. If play is suspended and is not resumed until a later day the rest may be taken only after the third set (or when women take part the second set) of play on such a later day, completion of an unfinished set being counted as one set.

If play is suspended and is not resumed until 10 minutes have elapsed in the same day the rest may be taken only after three consecutive sets have been played without interruption (or when women take part two sets), completion of an unfinished set being counted as one set.

Any nation and/or committee organising a tournament, match or competition, other than the International Tennis Championships (Davis Cup and Federation Cup), is at liberty to modify this provision or omit it from its regulations provided this is announced before the event commences.

(*f*) A tournament committee has the discretion to decide the time allowed for a warm-up period prior to a match but this may not exceed five minutes and must be announced before the event commences.

(*g*) When approved point penalty and non-accumulative point penalty systems are in operation, the Umpire shall make his decisions within the terms of those systems.

(*h*) Upon violation of the principle that play shall be continuous the Umpire may, after giving due warning, disqualify the offender.

31. Coaching. During the playing of a match in a team competition, a player may receive coaching from a captain who is sitting on the court only when he changes ends at the end of a game, but not when he changes ends during a tie-break game. A player may not receive coaching during the playing of any other match. The provisions of this rule must be strictly construed. After due warning an offending player may be disqualified. When an approved point penalty system is in operation the Umpire shall impose penalties according to that system.

32. Changing Balls. In cases where balls are changed after an agreed number of games, if the balls are not changed in the correct sequence the mistake shall be corrected when the player, or pair in the case of doubles, who should have served with the new balls is next due to serve. Thereafter the balls shall be changed so that the number of games between changes shall be that originally agreed.

THE DOUBLES GAME

33. The above Rules shall apply to the Doubles Game except as below.

34. The Doubles Court. For the Doubles Game, the Court shall be 36 ft (10.97 m) in width, i.e. 4½ ft (1.37 m) wider on each side than the Court for the Singles Game, and those portions of the singles side-lines which lie between the two service-lines shall be called the service side-lines. In other respects, the Court shall be similar to that described in Rule 1, but the portions of the singles side-lines between the base-line and service-line on each side of the net may be omitted if desired.

35. The Order of Service shall be decided at the beginning of each set as follows:

The pair who have to serve in the first game of each set shall decide which partner shall do so and the opposing pair shall decide similarly for the second game. The partner of the player who served in the first game shall serve in the third; the partner of the player who served in the second game shall serve in the fourth, and so on in the same order in all the subsequent games of a set.

36. The Order of Receiving the service shall be decided at the beginning of each set as follows:

The pair who have to receive the service in the first game shall decide which partner shall receive the first service, and that partner shall continue to receive the first service in every odd game throughout that set. The opposing pair shall likewise decide which partner shall receive the first service in the second game and that partner shall continue to receive the first service in every even game throughout that set. Partners shall receive the service alternately throughout each game.

37. Service Out of Turn in Doubles Services. If a partner serve out of his turn, the partner who ought to have served shall serve as soon as the mistake is discovered, but all points scored, and any faults served before such discovery, shall be reckoned. If a game shall have been completed before such discovery, the order of service remains as altered.

38. Error in Order of Receiving in Doubles. If during a game the order of receiving the service is changed by the receivers it shall remain as altered until the end of the game in which the mistake is discovered, but the partners shall resume their original order of receiving in the next game of that set in which they are receivers of the service.

39. Service Fault in Doubles. The service is a fault as provided for by Rule 10, or if the ball touches the Server's partner or anything which he wears or carries; but if the ball served touches the partner of the Receiver, or anything which he wears or carries, not being a let under Rule 14(*a*) before it hits the ground, the server wins the point.

40. Playing the Ball in Doubles. The ball shall be struck alternately by one or other player of the opposing pairs, and if a player touches the ball in play with his racket in contravention of this Rule, his opponents win the point.

NOTE: *Except where otherwise stated, every reference in these Rules to the masculine includes the feminine gender.*

APPENDIX

I.T.F. Approved Tie-Break Scoring System

27. (*b*) The tie-break system of scoring may be adopted as an alternative to the advantage set system in paragraph (*a*) of this Rule provided the decision is announced in advance of the match.

In this case, the following Rules shall be effective:

The tie-break shall operate when the score reaches six games all in any set except in the third or fifth set of a three-set or five-set match respectively, when an ordinary advantage set shall be played, unless otherwise decided and announced in advance of the match.

Procedure

The following system shall be used in a tie-break game:

Singles

(i) A player who first wins seven points shall win the game and the set provided he leads by a margin of two points. If the score reaches six points all, the game shall be extended until this margin has been achieved. Numerical scoring shall be used throughout the tie-break game.

(ii) The player whose turn it is to serve shall be the server for the first point. His opponent shall be the server for the second and third points and thereafter each player shall serve alternately for two consecutive points until the winner of the game and set has been decided.

(iii) From the first point, each service shall be delivered alternately from the right and left courts, beginning from the right court. If service from a wrong half of the court occurs and is undetected, all play resulting from such wrong service shall stand, but the inaccuracy of station shall be corrected immediately it is discovered.

(iv) Players shall change ends after every six points and at the conclusion of the tie-break game.

(v) The tie-break game shall count as one game for the ball change, except that, if the balls are due to be changed at the beginning of the tie-break, the change shall be delayed until the second game of the following set.

Doubles
In doubles, the procedure for singles shall apply. The player whose turn it is to serve shall be the server for the first point. Thereafter each player shall serve in rotation for two points, in the same order as previously in that set, until the winners of the game and set have been decided.

Rotation of Service
The player (or pair in the case of doubles) who served first in the tie-break game shall receive service in the first game of the following set.

These Rules are officially approved by the International Tennis Federation.

The Laws of
Table Tennis

Table Tennis

As adopted by the International Table Tennis Federation and approved by
the English Table Tennis Association

3.1 The Table

3.1.1 The upper surface of the table, known as the "playing surface", shall be rectangular, 2.74 m long and 1.525 m wide, and shall lie in a horizontal plane 76 cm above the floor.

3.1.2 The playing surface shall include the top edges of the table but not the sides of the table top below the edges.

3.1.3 The playing surface may be of any material and shall yield a uniform bounce of about 23 cm when a standard ball is dropped on to it from a height of 30 cm.

3.1.4 The playing surface shall be uniformly dark coloured and matt, with a white line 2 cm wide along each edge.

3.1.4.1 The lines along the 2.74 m edges shall be known as "side-lines".

3.1.4.2 The lines along the 1.525 m edges shall be known as "end lines".

3.1.5 The playing surface shall be divided into two equal "courts" by a vertical net running parallel with the end lines, and shall be continuous over the whole area of each court.

3.1.6 For doubles, . . .

3.1.6.1 . . . each court shall be divided into two equal "half-courts" by a white lines 3 mm wide, known as the "centre line", running parallel with the side lines;

3.1.6.2 . . . the centre line shall be regarded as part of the server's right half of the court and of the receiver's right half court.

3.2 The Net Assembly

3.2.1 The net assembly shall consist of the net, its suspension and the supporting posts.

3.2.2 The net shall be suspended by a cord attached at each end to an upright post 15.25 cm high, the outside limits of the post being 15.25 cm outside the side line.

3.2.3 The top of the net, along its whole length, shall be 15.25 cm above the playing surface.

3.2.4 The bottom of the net, along its whole length, shall be as close as possible to the playing surface and the ends of the net shall be as close as possible to the supporting posts.

3.3 The Ball

3.3.1 The ball shall be spherical, with a diameter of 38 mm.

3.3.2 The ball shall weigh 2.5 gm.

3.3.3 The ball shall be made of celluloid or similar plastics material and shall be white or yellow, and matt.

3.4 The Racket

3.4.1 The racket may be of any size, shape or weight but the blade shall be flat and rigid and shall be made of wood.

3.4.1.1 At least 85% of the blade by thickness shall be of natural wood.

3.4.1.2 An adhesive layer within the blade may be reinforced with fibrous material such as carbon fibre, glass fibre or compressed paper, but shall not be thicker than 7.5% of the total thickness or 0.35 mm, whichever is the smaller.

3.4.2 A side of the blade used for striking the ball shall be covered with either ordinary pimpled rubber with pimples outward having a total thickness including adhesive of not more than 2 mm, or sandwich rubber with pimples inwards or outwards having a total thickness including adhesive of not more than 4 mm.

3.4.2.1 "Ordinary pimpled rubber" is a single layer of non-cellular rubber, natural or synthetic, with pimples evenly distributed over its surface at a density of not less than 10/sq cm and not more than 50/sq cm.

3.4.2.2 "Sandwich rubber" is a single layer of cellular rubber covered with a single outer layer of ordinary pimpled rubber, the thickness of the pimpled rubber not being more than 2 mm.

3.4.3 The covering material shall extend up to but not

beyond the limits of the blade, except that the part nearest the handle and gripped by the fingers may be left uncovered or covered with any material and may be considered part of the handle.

3.4.4 The blade, any layer within the blade and any layer of covering material or adhesive shall be continuous and of even thickness.

3.4.5 The surface of the covering material on a side of the blade, or of a side of the blade if it is left uncovered, shall be uniformly dark-coloured and matt; any trimming round the edge of the blade shall be matt and no part of it shall be white.

3.4.6 Slight deviations from continuity of surface or uniformity of colour due to accidental damage, wear or fading may be allowed provided that they do not significantly change the characteristics of the surface.

3.4.7 At the start of a match and whenever he changes his racket during a match a player shall show his opponent and the umpire the racket he is about to use and shall allow them to examine it.

3.5 Definitions

3.5.1 A "rally" is the period during which the ball is in play.

3.5.2 A "let" is a rally of which the result is not scored.

3.5.3 A "point" is a rally of which the result is scored.

3.5.4 The "racket hand" is the hand carrying the racket.

3.5.5 The "free hand" is the hand not carrying the racket.

3.5.6 A player "strikes" the ball if he touches it with his racket, held in the hand, or with his racket-hand below the wrist.

3.5.7 A player "volleys" the ball if he strikes it in play when it has not touched his court since last being struck by his opponent.

3.5.8 A player "obstructs" the ball if he, or anything he wears or carries, touches it in play when it has not passed over his court or an imaginary extension of his end line, not having touched his court since last being struck by his opponent.

3.5.9 The "server" is the player due to strike the ball first in a rally.

3.5.10 The "receiver" is the player due to strike the ball second in a rally.

3.5.11 The "umpire" is the person appointed to decide the result of each rally.

3.5.12 Anything that a player "wears or carries" includes anything that he was wearing or carrying at the start of the rally.

3.5.13 The ball shall be regarded as passing "over or around" the net if it passes under or outside the projection of the net assembly outside the table or if, in a return, it is struck after it has bounced back over the net.

3.6 A Good Service

3.6.1 Service shall begin with the ball resting on the palm of the free hand, which shall be stationary, open and flat, with the fingers together and the thumb free.

3.6.2 The free hand, while in contact with the ball in service, shall at all times be above the level of the playing surface.

3.6.3 The whole of the racket shall be above the level of the playing surface from the last moment at which the ball is stationary on the palm of the free hand until the ball is struck in service.

3.6.4 The server shall then project the ball upwards, by hand only and without imparting spin, so that it rises from the palm of the hand within 45° of the vertical.

3.6.5 As the ball is falling from the highest point of its trajectory the server shall strike it so that:

3.6.5.1 In singles, it touches first his own court and then, passing directly over or around the net assembly, touches the receiver's court.

3.6.5.2 In doubles, touches first his right half-court and then, passing directly over or around the net assembly, touches the receiver's right half-court.

3.6.5.3 If, in attempting to serve, a player fails to strike the ball before it goes out of play, he shall lose a point.

3.6.6 When the ball is struck in service, it shall be behind the end line of the server's court or an imaginary extension thereof, but not farther back than the part of the server's body, other than his arm, head or leg, which is farthest from the net.

3.6.7 It is the responsibility of the player to serve so that the umpire or assistant umpire can see that he complies with the requirements for a good service.

3.6.7.1 Except when an assistant umpire has been appointed, the umpire may, on the first occasion in a match at which he has a doubt about the correctness of a player's service, interrupt play and warn the server without awarding a point.

3.6.7.2 On any subsequent occasion in the same match at which the same player's service action is of doubtful correctness, for the same or for any other reason, the player shall not be given the benefit of the doubt and shall lose a point.

3.6.7.3 Whenever there is a clear failure by the server to comply with the requirements for a good service no warning shall be given and he shall lose a point, on the first as on any other occasion.

3.6.8 Exceptionally, strict observance of any particular requirement for a good service may be waived where the umpire is notified, before play begins, that compliance with that requirement is prevented by physical disability.

3.7 A Good Return

3.7.1 The ball, having been served or returned, shall be struck so that it passes over or around the net assembly and touches the opponent's court, either directly or after touching the net assembly.

3.8 The Order of Play

3.8.1 In singles, the server shall first make a good service, the receiver shall then make a good return and thereafter server and receiver alternately shall each make a good return.

3.8.2 In doubles the server shall first make a good service, the receiver shall then make a good return, the partner of the server shall then make a good return, the partner of the receiver shall then make a good return and thereafter each player in turn in that sequence shall make a good return.

3.9 In Play

3.9.1 The ball shall be in play from the last moment at which it is stationary before being projected in service until

3.9.1.1 it touches anything other than the playing surface, the net assembly, the racket held in the hand or the racket hand below the wrist, or

3.9.1.2 the rally is otherwise decided as a let or a point.

3.10 A Let

3.10.1 The rally shall be a let

3.10.1.1 if in service the ball, in passing over or around the net assembly, touches it, provided the service is otherwise good or is volleyed or obstructed by the receiver or his partner;

3.10.1.2 if the service is delivered when, in the opinion of the umpire, the receiving player or pair is not ready, provided that neither the receiver nor his partner attempts to strike the ball;

3.10.1.3 if, in the opinion of the umpire, failure to make a good service or a good return or otherwise to comply with the Laws is due to a disturbance outside the control of the player;

3.10.1.4 if it is interrupted to correct an error in the order of serving, receiving or ends;

3.10.1.5 if it is interrupted to introduce the expedite system;

3.10.1.6 if it is interrupted to warn a player that his service is of doubtful correctness or that he has failed to notify a change of racket;

3.10.1.7 if the conditions of play are disturbed in a way which, in the opinion of the umpire, is likely to affect the outcome of the rally.

3.11 A Point

3.11.1 Unless the rally is a let, a player shall lose a point

3.11.1.1 if he fails to make a good service;

3.11.1.2 if he fails to make a good return;

3.11.1.3 if he volleys or obstructs the ball, except as provided in 3.10.1.1;

3.11.1.4 if he strikes the ball twice successively;

3.11.1.5 if the ball touches his court twice successively;

3.11.1.6 if he strikes the ball with a side of the racket blade whose surface does not comply with the requirements of 3.4.2;

3.11.1.7 if he, or anything he wears or carries, moves the playing surface while the ball is in play;

3.11.1.8 if his free hand touches the playing surface while the ball is in play;

3.11.1.9 if he, or anything he wears or carries, touches the net assembly while the ball is in play;

3.11.1.10 if, as he serves, he or his partner stamps his foot;

3.11.1.11 if, in doubles, he strikes the ball out of the scqucncc cstablished by the server and receiver;

3.11.1.12 if, under the expedite system, he serves and the receiving player or pair makes thirteen successive good returns.

3.12 A Game

3.12.1 A game shall be won by the player or pair first scoring 21 points unless both players or pairs score 20 points, when the game shall be won by the player or pair first scoring subsequently 2 points more than the opposing player or pair.

3.13 A Match

3.13.1 A match shall consist of the best of three games or the best of five games.

3.13.2 Play shall be continuous throughout a match except that any player shall be entitled to claim an interval of not more than five minutes between the third and fourth games of a match and not more than one minute between any other successive games of a match.

3.14 The Choice of Serving, Receiving and Ends

3.14.1 The right to make first choice shall be decided by lot.

3.14.2 The player or pair winning this right may

3.14.2.1 choose to serve or to receive first, when the loser shall have the choice of ends;

3.14.2.2 choose an end, when the loser shall have the choice of serving or receiving first;

3.14.2.3 require the loser to make the first choice, when the winner shall have whichever choice is not made by the loser.

3.14.3 In doubles the pair having the right to serve first in each game shall decide which of them will do so.

3.14.3.1 In the first game of a match, the opposing pair shall then decide which of them will receive first;

3.14.3.2 In subsequent games of the match, the first receiver will be determined by the choice of server, as provided in 3.15.5.

3.15 The Order of Serving, Receiving and Ends

3.15.1 After 5 points have been scored the receiving player or pair shall become the serving player or pair and so on until the end of the game, or until each player or pair has scored 20 points or until the introduction of the expedite system.

3.15.2 In doubles,

3.15.2.1 the first server shall be the selected player of the pair having the right to serve first and the first receiver shall be the appropriate player of the opposing pair;

3.15.2.2 the second server shall be the player who was the first receiver and the second receiver shall be the partner of the first server;

3.15.2.3 the third server shall be the partner of the first server and the third receiver shall be the partner of the first receiver;

3.15.2.4 the fourth server shall be the partner of the first receiver and the fourth receiver shall be the first server;

3.15.2.5 the fifth server shall be the player who was the first server and the players shall thereafter serve in the same sequence until the end of the game.

3.15.3 If both players or pairs have scored 20 points or if the expedite system is in operation the sequence of serving and receiving shall be the same but each player shall serve for only one point in turn until the end of the game.

3.15.4 The player or pair who served first in a game shall receive first in the immediate subsequent game of the match.

3.15.5 In each game of a doubles match after the first, the first server having been chosen, the first receiver shall be the player who served to him in the immediately preceding game.

3.15.6 In the last possible game of a doubles match the pair due next to receive shall change the order of receiving when first either pair scores 10 points.

3.15.7 The player or pair starting at one end in a game shall start at the other end in the immediately subsequent game of the match.

3.15.8 In the last possible game of a match the players shall change ends when first either player or pair scores 10 points.

3.16 Out of Order of Serving, Receiving and Ends

3.16.1 If the players have not changed ends when they should have done so, play shall be interrupted by the umpire as soon as the error is discovered and shall resume with the players at the ends at which they should be at the score that has been reached, according to the sequence established at the beginning of the match.

3.16.2 If a player serves or receives out of turn, play shall be interrupted as soon as the error is discovered and shall resume with those players serving and receiving who should be server and receiver respectively at the score that has been reached, according to the sequence established at the beginning of the match, and, in doubles, to the order of serving chosen by the pair having the right to serve first in the game during which the error is discovered.

3.16.3 In any circumstances, all points scored before the discovery of an error shall be reckoned.

3.17 The Expedite System

3.17.1 The expedite system shall come into operation if a game is unfinished after fifteen minutes' play, or at any earlier time at the request of both players or pairs.

3.17.1.1 If the ball is in play when the time limit is reached, play shall stop and shall resume with service by the player who served in the rally that was interrupted.

3.17.1.2 If the ball is not in play when the time limit is reached, play shall resume with the service by the player who received in the immediately preceding rally of the game.

3.17.2 Thereafter, each player shall serve for one point in turn, in accordance with 3.15.3, and if the rally is not decided before the receiving player or pair makes thirteen good returns the server shall lose a point.

3.17.3 Once introduced, the expedite system shall remain in operation for the remainder of the match.

The Rules of
Volleyball

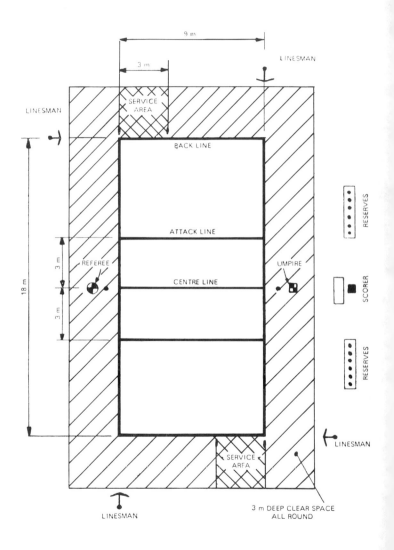

Volleyball

THE GAME

In brief, volleyball is a sport played by two teams of six players on a court measuring 18 m × 9 m and divided into two equal areas by a centre line. Above this line a net, 1 m wide and 9.50 m long, is placed at a height of 2.43 m for men, 2.24 m for women.

The aim of the players is, within the rules of the game, to send the ball with one hand or arm over the net to the ground on the opponents' court.

The first team to score 15 points (or more, with an advantage of 2 points) wins a set; a team winning 3 sets wins the match.

FACILITIES AND EQUIPMENT
RULE 1
PLAYING COURT

1.1 Dimensions

1.1.1 The playing court is a rectangle measuring 18 m × 9 m surrounded by a free zone of at least 2 m (at least 3 m in open air courts) and with a space free from any obstructions to a height of at least 7 m from the playing surface.

1.1.2 For official international competitions, the free zone shall measure at least 5 m from the side lines and 8 m from the end lines, the free space shall measure at least 12.5 m in height from the playing surface.

1.2 Playing Surface

1.2.1 The surface must be flat, horizontal and uniform.

1.2.2 For official international competitions, only a wooden or synthetic surface is allowed. Any surface must be previously approved by the F.I.V.B.

1.2.3 The playing surface must not present any danger of

injury to the players. It is forbidden to play on rough, wet, or slippery surfaces, for example: cement, sand, grass, etc.

1.2.4 On indoor courts, the surface of the playing court must be of one colour, light and bright.

For official international competitions, different colours for the lines, the playing court and the free zone, are required.

1.2.5 On outdoor courts a slope of 5 mm per metre is allowed for drainage.

Court lines made of solid materials are forbidden.

1.3 Boundary Lines

1.3.1 All lines are 5 cm. in width. The lines must be light, and of a different colour from the floor.

1.3.2 Two side lines and two end lines shall mark the playing court.

Both side and end lines are included in the 18 m × 9 m playing court.

1.4 Centre Line

The axis of the centre line divides the playing court into two courts measuring 9 m × 9 m. each. The centre line extends under the net from side line to side line.

1.5 Zone Lines

1.5 Attack lines and front zones: In each court the front zone is limited by the attack line (its width included) 3 m parallel to the axis of the centre line. Beyond the side lines, both attack lines and front zones are considered to extend indefinitely.

1.5.2 Service lines and service zones: Two lines, each 15 cm long, mark indefinitely the side limits of the service zone at the end of each court. They shall be drawn inside the service zone, 20 cm behind and perpendicular to the end line. One is drawn as an extension of each right side line and the other is 3 m to the left.

1.5.3 Substitution zone. The fringe of the free zone, limited by the imaginary extension of both attack lines up to both sides of the score table, is considered as the substitution zone.

1.6 Temperature

The minimum temperature shall not be below 10°C (50°F).

1.7 Lighting

Lighting in a hall should be from 500 to 1500 lux, measured from 1 m above the playing surface.

RULE 2

NET AND POSTS

2.1 Net

The net is a mesh, 1 m wide and 9.50 m long, vertically placed over the axis of the centre line, to divide the playing area into two parts. The net shall be made of 10 cm square mesh, with a double fold of white canvas, 10 cm wide; each 5 cm fold is sewn along the full length of the top of the net and a flexible cable stretched through to keep the top of the net taut. A cord sewn along the bottom edge keeps the lower part of the net taut.

2.2 Vertical Side Bands

Two tapes of white material 5 cm wide and 1 m long, shall be fastened, one on each side of the net, perpendicular to the intersection of the respective side line and to the axis of the centre line. Both side bands shall be considered as part of the net.

2.3 Antennae

The antennae are two flexible rods made of fibreglass or similar material 1.80 m long and 10 mm in diameter. The antennae shall be marked with 10 cm bands of contrasting colours preferably red and white. Each is fastened on the outer edge of each vertical sideband and extends 80 cm above the top of the net and on opposite sides of the net. They are considered part of the net and mark its side limits.

2.4 Height of the Net

2.4.1 The height of the net shall be 2.43 m for men, and 2.24 m for women.

2.4.2 The height of the net shall be measured from the centre of the playing court with a measuring rod. The two ends of the net (over the side lines) must be at the same height from the playing surface and may not exceed the regulation height by more than 2 cm.

2.5 Posts

2.5.1 Two posts, preferably adjustable, round, and smooth, with a height of 2.55 m, support the net, one at each end.

2.5.2 They must be fixed to the playing surface at a distance of between 0.50 and 1.00 m from each side line. Fixing the posts to the floor by means of wires is prohibited. All dangerous arrangements must be eliminated.

2.6 Additional Equipment

All additional equipment is determined by F.I.V.B. Administrative regulations.

RULE 3

BALL

3.1 Characteristics

The ball shall be spherical, made of a flexible leather case, with a bladder inside made of rubber or a similar material.

—Colour: it shall be uniform and light.
—Circumference: 65–67 cm.
—Wight: 260–280 g.
—Pressure: 0.40–0.45 Kg/cm².

3.2 Uniformity of Balls

All balls used during a match must have the same characteristics regarding circumfcrcncc, wcight, pressure, type, etc.

International matches must be played with F.I.V.B. approved balls.

3.3 Use of Three Balls

In official international matches, three balls shall be used. In this case six ball retrievers shall be stationed one at each corner of the free zone and one behind each referee.

PARTICIPANTS: THEIR RESPONSIBILITIES AND RIGHTS

RULE 4

TEAMS

4.1 Composition and Registration

4.1.1 A team consists of a maximum of 12 players, one coach, one assistant coach and one doctor or trainer.

4.1.2 Only the players recorded on the scoresheet may participate in the match.

4.1.3 Once the team captain and the coach have signed the scoresheet, the recorded players cannot be changed.

4.2 Appointment of Captain

4.2.1 One of the players recorded on the scoresheet will be appointed as team captain.

4.2.2 The team captain is identified with a ribbon or strip 8 cm by 2 cm of a different colour to the jersey and placed on the left side of the player's chest.

4.2.3 When the team captain is substituted and leaves the court, the coach or the captain himself will designate another player to act as game captain.

RULE 5

PLAYERS

5.1 Players' Equipment

5.1.1 A player's equipment consists of a jersey and shorts. It must be uniform, clean and of the same colour.

5.1.2 Shoes must be light and pliable, rubber or leather soles without heels.

5.1.3 Players' jerseys may be numbered from 1 to 15 (preferably from 1 to 12).

5.1.4 The numbers must be of a different contrasting colour to the jerseys and a minimum of 10 cm high on the chest and 15 cm high on the back. The strip forming the numbers shall be 2 cm minimum.

5.2 Authorised Changes

5.2.1 If both teams arrive at a match dressed in the same colour uniforms, the home team must change. If a neutral venue is involved, the team listed first on the scoresheet must change uniforms.

5.2.2 The first referee may authorise one or more players:

(*a*) to play barefoot,

(*b*) to change wet jerseys between sets or after substitution, provided the new jersey is the same colour and number as the wet one.

5.2.3 In cold weather the first referee may authorise the teams to play in training suits, provided that they are of the same colour, same design, and legally numbered.

5.3 Forbidden Objects and Uniforms

5.3.1 It is forbidden to wear jewelry, pins, bracelets, or a plaster cast.

5.3.2 It is forbidden to wear uniforms without legal numbers, or of an obviously different colour.

RULE 6

RIGHTS AND RESPONSIBILITIES OF PARTICIPANTS

6.1 Basic Responsibilities

6.1.1 Participants must know the rules of the game and abide by them.

6.1.2 Participants must accept the referees' decisions with sportsmanlike behaviour. In case of doubt, clarification may be requested through the game captain.

6.1.3 The conduct of participants must be in accordance with the spirit of fair play and the following principles;

6.1.4 The participants must show respectful and courteous attitude toward officials and opponents.

6.1.5 The participants must avoid actions and attitudes intended to influence the decisions of the referees or to cover up faults committed by their teams (e.g. applause or shouting at service reception, etc.).

6.1.6. The participants must avoid actions and attitudes aimed at prolonging stoppages or considered deliberate delays of the game.

6.1.7 If out of the game the participants must not give instructions to players on court.

6.1.8 The participants cannot dispute, protest against nor request clarifications of the referees' decisions.

6.1.9 Both the team captain and coach are responsible for the conduct and discipline of all the team players.

6.2 Rights and Responsibilities of the Team Captain

6.2.1 Prior to the match, the team captain:

(*a*) will sign the scoresheet,

(*b*) will represent his team during the toss.

6.2.2 During the match, the team captain will function as game captain while on the court:

(*a*) he may ask authorisation from the referees to change uniforms or equipment,

(*b*) he submits to the referee involved, the requests or questions properly submitted by his teammates during interuptions,

(*c*) he is the only person authorised to ask for an explanation on the application or interpretation of the rules. If the explanation or interpretation does not satisfy him, he must immediately protest to the referee and his protest is to be registered on the scoresheet at the end of the match,

(*d*) he is the only person who shall ask the first referee to check the net, the floor, the ball, or to verify the positions of the opponents, etc.

(*e*) he has the right to request legal interruptions in the game.

6.2.3 At the end of the match, the team captain:

(*a*) thanks the referees and signs the scoresheet to ratify the outcome,

(*b*) if he previously submitted a protest to the first referee, may have it confirmed in writing on the scoresheet (6.2.2*c*).

6.3 Responsibilities of the Coach

6.3.1 Prior to the game, he must register, check the names and numbers of his players on the scoresheet and place his signature on it.

6.3.2 Prior to each set he must give the scorer or the second referee the line-up sheet fully completed and signed.

6.3.3 He may direct warm-up sessions of his players on the playing court prior to the match.

6.3.4 During the match he must sit on the players' bench, nearest the scorer.

6.3.5 Only during time-outs and intervals between sets may the coach give instructions. These instructions must be given without entering the court or delaying the game.

6.4 Responsibilities of the Assistant Coach

6.4.1 He sits on the players' bench, but has no rights.

6.4.2 In the event of the coach having to leave his team, the assistant coach may assume his responsibilities with the authorisation of the first referee, at the request of the team captain.

PREPARATION AND DEVELOPMENT OF THE MATCH

RULE 7

TOSS-UP AND WARMING UP AT THE NET

7.1 Toss-up

7.1.1 Before entering the playing court the first referee carries out a toss-up in the presence of the two team captains. The winner of the toss chooses the court or the right to serve first.

7.1.2 in the event of a deciding set being necessary, the first referee will make another toss to decide the choice of court or service.

7.2 Teams warming up

7.2.1 Prior to the match each team will have a 3 minute warm-up period at the net, if they previously had another playing court at their disposal; if not, they have have 5 minutes each.

7.2.2 If both captains ask to warm up at the same time, both teams may use the net for 6 or 10 minutes according to 7.2.1.

7.2.3 In the event of consecutive warm-ups, the team winning the right to serve takes the first turn at the net.

RULE 8

TEAM LINE-UPS, POSITION OF PARTICIPANTS

8.1 Team Line-ups

8.1.1 Before the start of a set, each coach must present his starting line-up sheet to the scorer or the second referee.

8.1.2 The six players beginning a set compose the starting line-up of a team. The number of six players may not be reduced.

8.1.3 The six players on the court make up the game line-up.

8.2 Position of Substitutes and Coaches

8.2.1 The players not registered in the starting line-up of a set are the substitutes for that set.

8.2.2 The substitutes and coaches must sit on the bench located on the side of their own court.

8.2.3 The substitutes may actively warm up outside the free zone of the playing court, providing they do not use a ball, and return to their bench after warm-up.

8.2.4 The substitutes may cheer and applaud their teammates but not give them instructions.

RULE 9

PLAYERS' POSITIONS AND ROTATION

9.1 Game position

9.1.1 At the time the ball is hit by the server (who is exempt) each team must be within its own court in two lines of three players. These lines may be broken.

9.1.2 The three players along the net are the front line players and occupy positions 4 (the left), 3 (the centre), and 2 (the right); the other three players are the back line players and each one must be placed further from the net than his corresponding front line player, occupying positions 5 (the left), 6 (the centre), and 1 (the right).

9.1.3 Once the starting line-up has been given to the scorer, no change of line-up is authorised, unless there has been an error or omission by the scorer. Any discrepancy between the line-up sheet and the actual line-up of the players on the court must be corrected before the start of the game according to the line-up sheet without penalty. However, if one or more players on the court are not identified on the line-up sheet, the team is requested to correct the mistake without penalty. But if the coach of the team wishes to keep the player on court, he must request the substitution of the player. In this case, this team will be charged the necessary substitution.

9.1.4 The position of players is determined and controlled by the position of their feet contacting the ground as follows:

(a) At least a part of one foot of each front line player must be closer to the centre line than the feet of his corresponding back line teammate.

(b) At least part of one foot of each right or left player (either front or back line player) must always be closer to the respective side line than the feet of the centre player belonging to the same line of players.

9.1.5 Once the ball has been served, the players may move about and occupy any position in their own court and free zone.

9.2 Rotation of Players

9.2.1 When the team receiving the serve wins the exchange of play or the opponents commit a fault, it wins the right to serve (side-out) and its players must rotate one position clockwise.

9.2.2 The rotation order as recorded on the scoresheet at the beginning of each set must remain the same throughout that set.

9.2.3 A different rotation order for each new set may be used by the teams and any player recorded on the scoresheet may be registered in the new starting line-up.

9.3 Positional Fault

The players of a team commit a fault if they are not in their regulation positions (9.1.4.) at the moment the ball is hit by the server.

9.4 Consequences of a Positional Fault

9.4.1 If the server commits a serving fault at the moment he hits the ball, his fault shall be considered prior to the positional fault and thus penalised.

9.4.2 If the serve becomes a fault, after the ball is hit, such a fault shall be considered second to the positional fault and therefore the positional fault is the one penalised.

9.4.3 A positional fault is penalised as follows:

(a) The players must return to their proper positions immediately.

(b) The scorer must determine exactly when the error was committed in order to cancel all points scored by the team at fault. The opponents' points remain valid.

(c) If the points scored while the players were out of position or out of service order cannot be determined, the team at fault is sanctioned by a penalty only.

9.5 Rotational Fault

A fault in rotation is committed when the service is not made according to the rotation order. This represents an absolute positional fault for which the game must be suspended until the error is corrected and the team at fault penalised as in the case of a positional fault (9.4.3).

RULE 10

GAME INTERRUPTIONS

10.1 Definition of Legal Interruption

The legal interruptions of the game are time-outs and substitutions. They are only granted by the referees, when the ball is dead, at the request of either the coach or the game captain.

10.2 Number of Interruptions Allowed

A maximum of two time-outs and six substitutions per team per set are permitted.

10.3 Authorisation and Time Limit for Interruptions

10.3.1 An interruption will be granted only upon request by the game captain or the coach through the use of the respective official signal (manual or electric).

10.3.2 An interruption for substitution shall last only the time necessary to register the change and allow the entry and exit of the players.

10.3.3 Each time-out has a time limit of 30 seconds.

10.3.4 The team requesting the time-out has the right to shorten its time limit and the game should be resumed immediately.

10.3.5 A time-out will be charged to the team that prolongs an interruption after the referee's signal to resume the game.

10.4 Successive Requests for Interruption

10.4.1 One or two time-outs may be followed or preceded by a substitution, requested by either team, during the same interruption with no need to resume the game.

10.4.2 The same team is not allowed to request two consecutive game interruptions for substitution unless the game has been resumed, but two or more players may be substituted at the same time.

10.5 Use of the Time-out

10.5.1 The players may approach the side line but may not leave their court.

10.5.2 The first coach may also approach the side line and speak with his players, but may not enter the court.

10.5.3 Another member of the team may provide towels or soft drinks to players, but he may not speak to them.

10.5.4 at the request of the game captain, the first referee may authorise medical assistance to the players on court.

10.6 Improper Requests

The referees must reject as improper any request when:

10.6.1 The request is made during an exchange of play, at or after the whistle for service. If the second referee whistles the interruption by mistake, the request is rejected and the service is repeated.

10.6.2 A second interruption for substitution is requested by the same team before the game has resumed.

10.6.3 The request is made by an unauthorised team member.

10.6.4 A team requests any legal interruption after its allowable number has been exhausted. In this case the team will receive a warning.

10.7 Interruption due to Team Members

10.7.1 If a serious accident occurs whilst the ball is in play, the referee must stop the game and direct a replay.

(a) If a player is injured and cannot continue to play, he must be legally substituted.

(b) If a legal substitution is not possible, the first referee shall authorise an exceptionally illegal substitution for the injured player.

(c) If no substitution is possible, the first referee will give three minutes to the injured player.

(d) If the injured player does not recover after the three minutes, the team is declared incomplete (13.2 and 13.2.2).

10.7.2 If a player is expelled, the referee must stop the match for the player to be substituted.

If a legal substitution is not possible, the referee shall declare the team incomplete for that set (13.2.2).

10.7.3 If the coach is expelled, his responsibilities may be assigned to the assistant coach, at the request of the game captain.

10.8 Interruption Faults

A team commits a fault when:

10.8.1 It prolongs its second time-out after being called to resume the game.

10.8.2 It requests a third time-out for the second time.

10.8.3 It delays a substitution of player(s) after the use of two time-outs.

10.8.4 It is not ready to start a set after having been charged with two consecutive time-outs. The team may be declared in default (13.3.3).

10.9 Prolonged Interruptions During a Match

If any unforeseen circumstances prevent a match from continuing, the first referee, the organisers, and the jury if present, shall decide the measures to be taken to re-establish normal conditions.

The following procedure shall apply:

10.9.1 If one or several interruptions occur not exceeding four hours in all:

(a) If the match is resumed on the same playing court, the set shall continue, with the same score, players, and game positions.

Scores from the previous sets shall be retained.

(b) If the match is resumed on another playing court, the interrupted set will be cancelled and replayed with the same starting line-ups, game positions, etc.

The sets that have been completed will keep the same scores.

10.9.2 If one or several interruptions occur exceeding four hours in all, the match shall be replayed.

RULE 11

SUBSTITUTION OF PLAYERS

11.1 Definition

A substitution is considered the act by which the referees authorise a player to leave the court and another player to occupy his position on the court.

11.1.1 A maximum of six substitutions shall be permitted per team per set. These substitutions may be made all at once or during different legal interruptions.

11.1.2 A substitution may be legal, compulsory, or exceptionally illegal.

able substitutions, the team must use an exceptionally illegal substitution (107.1b).

11.5 Illegal Substitution

11.5.1 A substitution is illegal when it does not fulfil the conditions provided in 11.2.3.

11.5.2 The request must be refused and a time-out granted instead to the team at fault. An exception is a substitution for an injured player (11.4.2).

11.6 Substitution Faults

A team commits a substitution fault when:

11.6.1 The substitute is not in the substitution zone or he is not ready to enter when the referee authorises the substitution and the team has already exhausted its 2 allowable time-outs.

11.6.2 It requests a substitution declared as illegal and has already used its 2 time-outs.

11.6.3 It makes an illegal substitution. In this case, the referee must penalise the fault, rectify the substitution and cancel the points scored by the team at fault. The opposing team keeps the points it has scored.

RULE 12

INTERVALS BETWEEN SETS AND CHANGES OF COURT

12.1 Intervals Between Sets

12.1.1 Two minutes is the interval time limit allowed between sets. During this time limit, change of court and registration of starting line-ups on the scoresheet are made (8.1.2).

Five minutes is the interval between the 4th and 5th sets.

12.1.2 The teams must be formed-up on their end lines at the moment they are called by the first referee to resume the match.

If team players fail to report when the referee calls them to start, they will be penalised according to 10.8.4 and 13.3.3.

12.2 Changes of Court

12.2.1 After each set the teams change courts to play the following one, unless it is the deciding set (7.1.2). Substitute players and other team members change benches.

12.2.2 In the deciding set once a team reaches 8 points, the courts are changed, with no delay, no instructions by coaches and no change of positions. The player that served last prior to the change will continue to serve. If the change is not made at the proper time it will take place as soon as the error is noted.

The score at the time the change is made remains the same.

RULE 13

GAME RESULTS

13.1 Team Scoring a Point

Only the team that serves scores a point, if it wins the exchange of play, either because of its playing action, or because the opponents commit a fault penalised by the referee.

13.2 Winner of a Set

13.2.1 The winner of a set is the team that first scores 15 points with a minimum advantage of two points or, in the event of a tie (14–14), the winner is the team that obtains the advantage of two points (16–14, 17–15, etc).

13.2.2 If a team is declared incomplete by the referee, the opposing team will be given the points it needs to win the set. The incomplete team keeps its points.

13.3 Winner of a Match

13.3.1 The winner of a match is the team that wins 3 sets in accordance with Rule 13.2.

13.3.2 If a team becomes incomplete for the rest of the match the opposing team will be given the points and sets it needs to win the match, (the incomplete team keeps its points and sets).

13.3.3 If, after receiving a warning from the first referee, a team refuses to play it is declared in default and the opposing team is given, by default, the score of 15-0 for each set, and 3-0 for the match.

13.3.4 A team that, for no justifiable reason, does not appear on the playing court in due time is in default and the opposing team is given the same scores, 15-0 per set, and 3-0 for the match.

PLAYING ACTIONS AND FAULTS
RULE 14
14 SERVICE

14.1 Definition

The service is the act of putting the ball into play by the right back-line player, placed in the service zone, who hits the ball with one hand (open or closed), or any part of the arm to begin an exchange of play.

14.2 First Service

14.2.1 The first service of sets 1 and 5 will be given to the team choosing the right to do so after the toss.

14.2.2 The other sets will start with the service of the team that did not serve first in the previous set.

14.3 Principles of Service Order

The players follow the service order provided by each team on the line-up sheet.

During the game the player to serve is determined as follows:

14.3.1 When the serving team wins the exchange of play, the same player who served before, serves again.

14.3.2 When the serving team commits a fault, or the opposing team wins the exchange of play, the latter must rotate (9.2) and the player who moves from right forward to right back position will serve.

14.4 Conditions for Service

14.4.1 The server must be in the service zone.

He may freely move or jump as long as he does not touch the end line or the free zone outside the service lines at the moment he hits the ball (1.5.2). Once he has hit the ball, the server may land within the court or the free zone.

14.4.2 The server must hit the ball within 5 seconds after the first referee whistles for service.

14.4.3 Service made before the referee's whistle, is cancelled and must be repeated.

14.4.4 After being thrown or released the ball must be cleanly hit with one hand, or with any part of the arm, before it hits the playing surface.

14.5 Conditions for Directing the Service

The first referee authorises the service after having checked that:

14.5.1 The server of the team with the right to serve has taken possession of the ball in the service zone.

14.5.2 Both teams are in position, ready to play.

14.6 Service Attempt

14.6.1 When the ball lands after it has been thrown or released by the server, this is considered a service attempt, provided that the ball did not touch the server nor the server touches the ball before it lands.

14.6.2 After a service attempt, the referee should again authorise the service and the server must execute it within the next 5 seconds.

14.6.3 No other attempt will be authorised.

14.7 Screening

The players of the serving team must not, by screening, prevent their opponents watching the server or the trajectory of the ball.

14.7.1 Any player on the serving team, who waves his arms to distract his opponents, jumps or moves sideways, etc., while the serve is being effected, makes an individual screen.

14.7.2 A team makes a group screen when the server is hidden behind a group of two or more teammates and serves the ball over them in the direction of an opponent.

14.8 Serving Faults

The referee must call a change of service if the server or his team commits one of the following faults (even if the opposing team is out of position):

14.8.1 If he does not serve in accordance with the service order (14.3).

14.8.2 If he does not serve in accordance with the conditions for service (14.4).

14.8.3 If he did not accomplish the conditions for a service attempt (14.6).

14.9 Serving Faults After the Ball is Hit

After the ball has been properly hit the service becomes a fault (unless a player is out of position), if the ball:

14.9.1 Touches any object or a player of the serving team, or fails to cross the vertical plane of the net.

14.9.2 Touches the net or an antenna or fails to pass through the crossing space.

14.9.3 Lands outside the boundary lines of the opponents' court without having been touched first by an opponent.

14.9.4. If the team is carrying out an individual or group screen (14.7).

RULE 15

BALL CONTACT

15.1 Ball in Play

The ball is in play from the service hit to the moment the referee blows his whistle.

15.2 Number of Contacts per Team

Each team is entitled to a maximum of three contacts (in addition to the block contact, 19.4.1) to return the ball over the net to the opponents' court.

15.2.1 Each time a player touches the ball, or is touched by the ball, it counts as a contact for the team.

15.2.2 A player may not touch the ball twice consecutively. (*Exception*: blocking 19.4.)

15.3 Characteristics of the Contact

15.3.1 The ball may be contacted by any part of the body above and including the waist.

15.3.2 The ball may contact various parts of the body provided the contacts are made simultaneously, the hit is correct and the bounce is clear. During the first team contact (15.2), if the ball is not played overhand with the fingers, it may contact consecutively various parts of the body.

15.3.3 The ball must be cleanly hit and not come to rest (lifted, pushed, carried or thrown).

It may rebound in any direction.

15.3.4 When judging contact with the ball, neither the movements of players before or after contact, nor the sound produced, shall be taken into consideration.

15.4 Simultaneous Contacts

Two or more players may contact the ball at the same time and not commit a fault.

15.4.1 If the simultaneous contact by two opponents occurs over the net and the ball remains in play, the receiving team is entitled to another three contacts.

If the ball falls to the ground outside the playing court, the team on the opposite side of the net is at fault.

15.4.2 Simultaneous contact by teammates.

When two teammates contact the ball simultaneously, this shall be considered as two contacts for the team, except during blocking.

If only one of them makes contact, this shall be considered as one contact.

15.5 Physical Contact

15.5.1 A player may hold or stop a teammate who is about to commit a fault (contacting the net, entering the opponent's court, etc).

15.5.2 A player may also run into or push a teammate in order to contact the ball.

15.6 Fault in Ball Contact

15.6.1 If a player does not cleanly contact the ball, or lets it come to a momentary rest, he commits the fault: 'HELD BALL' (15.3.3).

15.6.2 If a player visibly contacts the ball more than once in succession without any other player having touched it between these contacts, he commits the fault: "DOUBLE CONTACT" (15.2.2. *Exception:* 19.4.2).

15.6.3 If a player contacts the ball with any part of the body below the waist, he commits the fault: "ILLEGAL CONTACT" (15.3.1).

15.6.4 If two opponents hold the ball simultaneously over the net, both commit the fault: "DOUBLE FAULT". A replay shall be ordered (20.2.3).

15.6.5 If a team contacts the ball four times, it commits the fault: "FOUR CONTACTS' (15.2. *Exception:* 19.4.1).

RULE 16

BALL AT THE NET

16.1 Ball Crossing the Net

16.1.1 The ball sent into the opponents' court must cross the vertical plane of the net within the crossing space.

16.1.2 The crossing space is the free space in the vertical plane of the net limited by the upper edge of the net and on the sides by the antennae and their imaginary extension.

16.2 Ball Touching the Net

16.2.1 Except on service, a ball sent to the opponents' court may touch the net, if it passes through the crossing space.

16.3 Ball in the Net (Other than the service ball)

16.3.1 A ball driven into the net may be recovered, provided it neither touches the floor, nor is contacted a fourth time.

16.3.2 If the ball rips the mesh of the net or brings the net down, the play is cancelled and there will be a replay.

16.4 Faults when the Ball Crosses the Vertical Plane of the Net

The team that sends the ball into the opponents' court commits the fault: 'BALL OUT' when:

16.4.1 The ball touches any other person or foreign object outside the court boundaries, the ceiling or outside parts of the net (antennae, ropes, posts, etc.).

16.4.2 The ball crosses, completely, the vertical plane outside the crossing space.

16.4.3 The ball crosses, completely, the vertical plane under the net.

RULE 17

PENETRATION INTO THE OPPONENTS' SPACE AND COURT

Each team must play within its own court and related playing space, except in the following cases:

17.1 Hands crossing the vertical plane of the net

17.1.1 During the block, it is permissible to contact the ball above the net within the opponent's space, providing the player does not interfere before or during the opponent's play.

17.1.2 After the attack-hit it is permissible to cross the hand over the net if the contact was made in its own playing space.

17.1.3 A ball in play that is heading toward the opponent's court, through the external space or the space below the net, may be returned by a teammate providing it has not yet completely crossed the vertical plane of the net or its imaginary extension when such contact is made.

17.2 Contact with the Net

17.2.1 It is forbidden to contact the net, all along its length including the antennae.

17.2.2 Once he has hit the ball, a player may touch the poles, ropes or any other object outside the 9.50 m length of the net, as it does not influence the play.

17.2.3 When a ball is driven into the net and causes the net to contact an opposing player, no fault is committed.

17.3 Penetration under the Net

17.3.1 The penetration of any part of the body into the

opponent's space from beneath the net, is permissible provided an opponent is not touched or interfered with.

17.3.2 The penetration into the opponent's court is forbidden. *Except* 17.4.2.

17.4 Contact with the Opponent's Court

17.4.1 With the exception of the feet, it is forbidden for a player to contact any part of his body beyond the centre line within the opponent's court, while in play.

17.4.2 To touch the opponent's court with a foot or feet is allowed, providing that some part of the encroaching foot or feet remain in contact with or above the centre line.

17.4.3 A player may contact the free zone surrounding the opponent's court, as long as he does not bother or interfere with an opponent in play.

17.4.4 A player may enter into the opponent's court after the referee has whistled to finish the exchange of play.

17.5 Penetration Faults

A penetration fault is committed when a player:

17.5.1 Touches a ball into the opponent's space before or during the opponent's attack-hit.

17.5.2 Interferes with any other ball contact in the opponents' space.

17.5.3 Penetrates into the opponent's space, from beneath the net and touches, bothers or interferes with an opponent.

17.5.4 Enters into the opponent's court, while the ball is in play (17.4).

17.5.5 Touches the net or an antenna because of his action.

RULE 18

ATTACK HIT

18.1 Definition

18.1.1 The attack hit is the action of a player who directs the ball to the opponents' court.

18.1.2 The attack-hit is considered as completed at the moment the ball completely crosses the vertical plane of the net or is contacted by the blocker.

18.2 Front Line Players' Attack-hit

The front-line players may carry out any type of attack-hit from their own court and at any height, providing the ball, at the time of the contact, is partially or entirely within their own playing space.

18.3 Back-line Players' Attack-hit

18.3.1 A back-line player may carry out any type of attack-hit from any height, if at the time of his take-off his foot has neither touched nor crossed over the attack-line. After the attack hit, he may land within the front zone.

18.3.2 A back line player may carry out any type of attack-hit from the front zone if he touches the ball when any part of it is below the horizontal plane of the top of the net.

18.4 Attack-hit Faults

A player commits an attack-hit fault when:

18.4.1 He hits the ball within the playing space of the opposing team.

18.4.2 He plays a ball that touches an object or lands completely outside the boundary lines of the opponents' court, without being previously touched by an opponent.

18.4.3 As a back-line player, he is in the front zone or touching the attack-line or its extension and hits the ball completely above the horizontal plane of the top of the net, and if the ball crosses, directly and completely, the vertical plane of the net or is contacted by a blocker (18.1.2).

RULE 19

BLOCK

19.1 Definition

Blocking is the action close to the net made by one or more front-line players (blockers) to intercept the ball coming from the opponents' court.

This action may be considered as:

19.1.1 An attempt to block: if a player, close to the net,

places one or both hands above the top of the net without touching the ball.

19.1.2 A block: if the ball is touched by a player, even if the ball contacts simultaneously the player and the upper edge of the net or if the ball bounces on the net and then touches the player.

19.1.3 Collective block: if it is carried out by 2 or 3 front-line players positioned close to each other.

19.2 Blocking Contact

19.2.1 Consecutive contacts (quick, continuous contacts) may be made by one or more blockers, provided the contacts are made during one action.

19.2.2 In blocking, the ball may be contacted with the hands or arms and touch the head or another part of the body above the waist.

19.3 Blocking within the Opponents' Space

19.3.1 One or more blockers may make an attempt to block, or block, by passing their hands and arms over the net, as long as this action does not interfere with the play of an opponent.

19.3.2 The block is permissible if the ball is blocked after the opponent has executed an attack-hit.

19.4 Contact Subsequent to the Block

19.4.1 The block does not count as one of the three permitted contacts.

After blocking, a team is entitled to three more contacts in order to send the ball to the opponents' court.

19.4.2 The first contact after the block may be made by any player, even if he had touched the ball during the block.

19.4.3 If a player makes an attempt to block separately and at a distance from an individual block or a collective block, and touches the ball blocked before, he makes the first team contact.

19.5 Blocking Faults

A blocker commits a fault when:

19.5.1 He blocks outside the antennae and touches the ball in the opponents' space.

19.5.2 He interferes with the play of an opponent within the opponents' space, either before or during the action. (17.1.1).

19.5.3 As a back-line player he effects or participates in a block.

19.5.4 He blocks the opponents' service.

RULE 20

FAULTS AND SANCTIONS

During the game, when participants commit faults due to actions contrary to the rules or due to misconduct, the first referee judges the faults and determines the sanction applicable, in accordance with the following principles:

20.1 Game Faults

These are individual actions or team movements contrary to the rules of the game and consist of:

20.1.1 Not sending the ball correctly over the net into the opponents' court.

20.1.2 Carrying out an action stipulated in the rules as a fault.

20.2 Consequences of a Fault

20.2.1 There is always a penalty for a fault.

20.2.2 Depending upon the case, a penalty means that the opponents of the team committing the fault gain a point or the right to serve.

20.2.3 If two opponents commit a fault simultaneously the penalties cancel each other out and a replay is called.

20.3 Misconduct

Behaviour towards officials, opponents, spectators or team mates may be incorrect, and, depending upon the degree of the offence, conduct must be sanctioned as:

20.3.1 Unsportsmanlike conduct: If a participant delays the game, coaches the team when it is forbidden to do so, shouts, intimidates the opponents, or argues with the players, officials or spectators.

20.3.2 Rude conduct: If the participant acts contrary to

good manners or moral principles, or if his action is the expression of contempt towards the officials, opponents, or spectators.

20.3.3 Offensive conduct: If any aggressive action is made by means of insulting words or gestures to an official, an opponent, or a spectator.

20.3.4 Aggression: If an actual physical attack or an intended physical aggression against officials, opponents, or spectators is made.

20.4 Sanctions for Misconduct

Depending on the degree of the incorrect conduct according to the judgement of the first referee, the sanctions to be applied are:

20.4.1 Warning, for unsportsmanlike conduct. No penalty is given, but it warns the player or team concerned against a second misconduct for the remainder of the set.

20.4.2 Penalty, for rude behaviour. It must be registered on the scoresheet and the opponents' team will gain a point or the service.

20.4.3 Expulsion and disqualification. Offensive conduct is sanctioned by expulsion which means that the player is not allowed to play for the remainder of the set.

Agression is sanctioned by disqualification, which means that the player must leave the playing area for the remainder of the match.

20.5 Sanctions Scale (Diagram 9)

20.5.1 The repetition of a misconduct by the same member of the team during the same set calls for the gradual application of sanctions, according to the misconduct sanctions scale. [See p. 693.]

20.5.2 Disqualification due to aggression does not call for any previous sanction.

Degree of Misconduct	Number of times	Sanction	Cards shown	Consequence
1. Unsportsmanlike Conduct	First	Warning	Yellow	Warning
	Second	Penalty	Red	Lose point or service
2. Rude Conduct	First	Penalty	Red	Lose point or service
	Second	Expulsion	Red and yellow together	Leave court for set
3. Offensive Conduct	First	Expulsion	Red and yellow together	Leave court
	Second	Disqualification	Red and yellow separately	Leave playing area for match
4. Agression	First	Disqualification	Red and yellow separately	Leave playing area for match

The Rules of
Water Polo

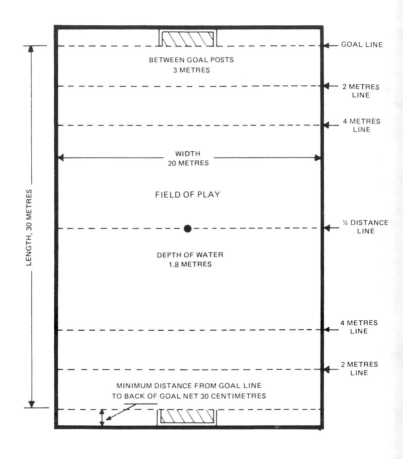

Water Polo

RULE 1

1. The promoting Club or Organisation shall be responsible for correct measurements and markings of the field of play and must provide all stipulated fixtures and equipment.

RULE 2
Field of Play and Measurements

2. (See diagram opposite.)

3. The uniform distance between the respective goal lines is 30 m. The uniform width of the field of play is 20 m. The depth of water must nowhere be less than 1.80 m. For matches in Olympic Games, World Championships and International Competitions the field of play shall be of full measurements as above.

4. For matches played by women, the maximum measurements are 25 × 17 m.

5. Distinctive marks must be provided on both sides of the field of play to denote the goal line, lines 2 m and 4 m from that line, and half distance between the goal lines. These markings must be clearly visible throughout the game. As uniform colours the following are recommended for these markings: goal line and half distance line white, 2 m from goal line red, 4 m from goal line yellow. A red or any other visible coloured sign shall be placed on the goal line, 2 m from the corner of the field of play on the side of the goal judge (or on the side opposite the timekeeper if there are no goal judges). The boundary of the field of play at both ends is 0.30 m behind the goal line.

6. Sufficient space must be provided to enable the referees to have free way from end to end of the field of play. Space must also be provided at the goal lines for the goal judges.

RULE 3
Goals

7. The goal posts and crossbar must be of wood, metal or synthetic (plastic), with rectangular sections of 0.075 m, square with the goal line and painted white. The goal posts must be fixed, rigid and perpendicular at each end of the playing space, equal distances from the sides and at least 0.30 m in front of the ends of the field of play or of any obstruction. Any standing or resting place for the goal-keeper, other than the floor of the bath, is not permitted.

8. The inner sides of the goal posts must be 3 m apart.

9. The underside of the crossbar must be 0.90 m above water surface when the water is 1.50 m or more in depth, and 0.40 m from the bottom of the bath when the depth of the water is less than 1.50 m.

10. Limp nets must be attached to the goal fixtures to enclose the entire goal space, securely fastened to the goal posts and crossbar and allowing not less than 0.30 m clear space behind the goal line everywhere within the goal area.

RULE 4
The Ball

11. The ball must be round and fully inflated and with an air chamber with a self-closing valve. The pressure in the ball shall be 13–14 lb atmospheres.

12. The circumference must not be less than 0.68 m nor more than 0.71 m.

13. It must be waterproof, without external strappings and without a covering of grease or similar substance.

14. The weight of the ball must not be less than 400 nor more than 450 g.

RULE 5
Flags

15. The referee must be provided with a stick 70 cm long, fitted with a white flag on one end and a blue flag on the other, each flag to be 35 × 20 cm.

16. Each goal judge must be provided with a red flag and a white flag, each 35 × 20 cm, mounted on separate sticks 50 cm long. One of the secretaries must be provided with a white flag and a blue one, to signal re-entrance of excluded players, and the other with a red flag with which to signal third Personal Faults (Rule 19/122). These flags also shall be of the dimensions prescribed above.

RULE 6
Caps

17. One team must wear dark blue and the other white caps, except goalkeepers, who must wear red caps. Caps must be tied with tapes under the chin. If a player loses his cap, it must be replaced at the next stoppage of the game. For Olympic Games and World Championships, caps must be fitted with malleable ear protectors and it is recommended that they be used for all other competitions. The malleable ear protectors of the goalkeepers must be of the same colour as that of the team's field players' caps.

18. Caps must be numbered on both sides, numbers being 0.10 m in height.

19. The goalkeeper shall wear cap No. 1 and the other caps shall be numbered 2 to 13. A substitute goalkeeper shall wear the goalkeeper's cap. No player is allowed to change his cap number without a referee's permission.

RULE 7
Teams

20. Each team shall consist of 7 players, one of whom will be the goalkeeper and wear the goalkeeper's cap, and no more than 6 reserves who may be used as substitutes. Prior to taking part in a match, the players must discard all articles likely to cause injury. The referee shall satisfy himself that the players observe this condition. A player failing to comply must be dismissed from the game. Players must wear trunks with separate drawers or slips underneath. When a player is dismissed from the game in accordance with this paragraph a reserve player may immediately take his place.

21. Players shall not be allowed to have grease, oil or any similar composition on the body. If the referee ascertains before starting the game that such substance has been used he must order the offending substance to be removed immediately. Should this offence be detected after the game has started, the player concerned must be ordered from the water for the whole game, and a substitute may enter immediately within 2 m from the corner of the field of play at his own goal line at the point nearest the goal-judge (or on the side opposite the time-keeper if there are no goal-judges).

22. The Captains must be playing members and be responsible for the good conduct and discipline of their respective teams.

23. Prior to the commencement of the game the Captains must, in the presence of the referee, toss for choice of ends or colours. The winner to have the choice of ends or colours.

RULE 8
Officials

24. 1. For Olympic Games and World Championships, the officials shall consist of two referees, two goal-judges, time-keepers and secretaries.

2. For all other competitions there must be at least a secretary, a time-keeper and either (a) two referees, or (b) one referee, and two goal-judges. However, it is recommended that two referees be used for all competitions. Each time-keeper and secretary may have assistants as needed.

3. The officials shall have powers and duties as specified below except that if a competition is held with two referees without goal-judges, the referees shall assume the duties specified for goal-judges in Rule 8 paras. 38–41 inclusive except that it shall not be necessary for them to make any of the flag signals specified in those rules.

Referees

25. The referees are in absolute control of the game. Their authority over the players is effective during the whole of the

time that they and the players are within the precincts of the bath.

26. Each must be provided with a shrill whistle with which to start and re-start the game and to declare goals, goal throws, corner throws (whether signalled by the goal-judge or not) and infringements of the rules.

27. All decisions of the referees on questions of fact are final and their interpretation of the rules must be obeyed during the game.

28. 1. A referee may refrain from declaring a foul if, in his opinion, such declaration would be an advantage to the offending team.

2. NOTE. *It is important that the referees shall apply this principle to the full extent. For example: to declare a foul in favour of a player who is in possession of the ball and making progress towards his opponents' goal, or whose team is in possession of the ball, is considered to give an advantage to the offender's team.*

29. He may alter his decision providing he does so before the ball is again in play.

30. He has power to order any player from the water in accordance with the appropriate Rules, and should a player refuse to leave the water when so ordered, the game must be stopped.

31. He may stop the game at any time if, in his opinion, the behaviour of the players or spectators or other circumstances prevent it being brought to a proper conclusion.

32. If the game has to be stopped, the referee must report his actions to the competent authority.

Time-keepers

33. The time-keepers must be fully acquainted with the Rules and each must be provided with a Water-Polo Stop-Watch and a shrill whistle.

34. 1. The duties of the time-keepers shall be (*a*) to record on the watch the exact periods of actual play and the intervals between the periods, as provided by these Rules, (*b*) to record the respective periods of exclusion of any player or players who may be ordered from the water in accordance

with these Rules, and (*c*) to record the periods of continuous possession of the ball by each team (Rule 16/93).

2. NOTE. *The time keeper recording the 35 seconds shall reset the clock when the ball leaves the hand of the player shooting at the goal. He shall again recommence the time when a team gains control of the ball—or if it goes out of the field of play, when the ball is put into play.*

35. All signals to stop play must be by whistle. Play is resumed when the ball leaves the hand of the player taking a free throw, goal throw, corner throw or penalty throw, or when the referee throws the ball in for a neutral throw.

36. 1. A time-keeper must signal by whistle the end of each period, independently of the referee. His signal takes immediate effect except as stated in Rule 20/133. The last minute of any game and of any extra time shall be audibly announced.

2. NOTE. *It is acceptable for the time-keeper to give this signal other than by whistle, provided that his signal shall be distinctive, acoustically efficient and readily understood.*

37. The time-keeper must be near to a referee.

Goal-judges

38. The goal-judges must take up position opposite a referee and they must mutually agree upon ends. They must stand directly level with the goal line and stay there for the whole game.

39. Their duties are to signal with the white flag for a goal throw (see Rule 13), with a red flag for a corner throw (see Rule 14), with both flags for a goal (see Rule 12) and with a red flag for an improper re-entry of an excluded player (see Rule 8/119.2 and 121.2.1).

Their further duty is to throw in a new ball when the original ball goes outside the field of play. Goal-judges shall each have a supply of balls (see Rule 4).

When the original ball goes out of the field of play in a manner resulting in a goal throw or corner throw, the goal-judge shall give a new ball immediately to the goalkeeper for each goal throw or to the nearest member of the attacking team for each corner throw.

40. Goal-judges shall be responsible to the referee for the correct score of each team at their respective ends.

41. Goal-judges should exhibit the red flag to indicate to the referee that players are correctly positioned on their respective goal lines, according to Rule 11/53.1, but the referee's whistle to start or re-start the game takes immediate effect.

Secretaries

42. The duties of the secretaries shall be (1) to maintain a record of all players, the score, all Major Fouls (time, colour and cap number) and to signal the award of a third Personal Fault (Rule 19/122) to any player by a signal with the red flag and a whistle immediately upon such award; (2) to control the periods of exclusion of players and to signal permission for re-entry upon expiration of their respective periods of exclusion by raising the flag corresponding with the colour of the player's cap; (3) to signal any improper entry (including after a flag signal by a goal-judge of an improper re-entry), which signal stops play immediately.

RULE 9
Time

43. The duration of the game shall be four periods of 7 minutes each, actual play. The teams shall change ends before commencing a new period. There shall be a 2-minute interval between periods. Time starts when a player touches the ball at the start of any period of the game. At all signals for stoppages the recording watch must be stopped until play is resumed.

RULE 10
Goalkeepers

44. While within the 4 m area, the goalkeeper is exempt from the following clauses of Rule 16, viz: Standing and walking; striking at the ball with clenched fist; jumping from the floor; touching the ball with both hands at the same time.

45. He must not go or touch the ball beyond the half-distance line. The penalty for his doing so is a free throw to the nearest opponent to be taken from where the offence occurred.

46. The goalkeeper may shoot at his opponent's goal as long as he is still within his half of the field of play.

47. [Deleted]

48. When a goalkeeper is penalised for holding or pushing off from the bar, rail or trough at the end of the bath, the free throw must be taken from the 2-m line opposite the point at which the foul occurred.

49. If a goalkeeper, taking a free throw or goal throw, releases the ball and, before any other player has touched it, regains possession and allows it to pass through his own goal, a corner throw must be awarded. If in the same circumstances he releases the ball, and after another player has touched it regains possession and allows it to pass through his own goal, a goal must be awarded.

50. Should a goalkeeper retire from a game through accident, illness or injury, Rule 22/140 shall apply.

51. [Deleted]

52. A goalkeeper who has been replaced by a substitute may, if he returns to the game, play anywhere.

RULE 11
Starting

53. 1. At the commencement of each period of play, the players must take up positions on their respective goal lines about 1 m apart and at least 1 m from either goal post. More than two players are not allowed between the goal posts. When he has ascertained that the teams are ready, the referee shall give the starting signal by a blast on his whistle and immediately afterwards release or throw the ball into the centre of the field of play.

2. NOTE. *If the ball is thrown giving one team a definite advantage, the referee should call for the ball and declare a neutral throw between the two players. Time shall commence when one player touches the ball.*

After a Goal

54. After a goal has been scored, players must take up positions anywhere within their respective halves of the field of play, behind the half-distance line, when a player of the team not having last scored shall re-start the game from the centre of the field of play. Upon the referee signalling by one blast of the whistle, the ball must be put into play promptly by passing it to another player of his team who must be behind the half-distance line when he receives it.

55. Ruling: Actual play is resumed when the ball leaves the hand of the player making the re-start.

56. A re-start made improperly must be retaken.

57. Ruling: When the start or re-start is from the goal line, no portion of a player's body, at water level, may be beyond the goal line; and when the re-start is from the centre, no part of a player's body may be beyond the half-distance line.

RULE 12
Scoring

58. A goal is scored by the ball passing fully over the goal line between the goal posts and subject to the following conditions:

59. A goal may be scored by any part of the body, except the clenched fist, provided that at the start or re-start of the game the ball has been played by two or more players. The team to which they belong or the place in the field of play from where the goal is scored is immaterial.

60. Any attempt by the goalkeeper to stop the ball before it has been played in this way does not constitute "playing" and should the ball cross the goal line or hit the goal post or goalkeeper, the goalkeeper must be awarded a goal throw.

61. Dribbling the ball through the goal posts is permissible.

62. Should a foul occur before the foregoing conditions have been complied with, Rules 16, 17, 18, 19, 20 and 21 operate.

RULE 13
Goal Throw

63. The referee must signal by whistle immediately the ball crosses the goal line.

64. When the entire ball passes over the goal line, excluding that portion between the goal posts, having last been touched by one of the attacking team, a goal throw is awarded to the defending goalkeeper, to be taken from any place within the 2 m area. (See also Rules 16 (94) and 17 (107).)

65. A goal throw taken improperly must be re-taken, except as provided by Rule 96.

66. Ruling: In the event of a goalkeeper being out of the water, another player must take the throw from any place within the 2 m area.

RULE 14
Corner Throw

67. The referee must signal by whistle immediately the ball crosses the goal line.

68. When the entire ball passes over the goal line, excluding that portion between the goal posts, having last been touched by one of the defending team, a corner throw is awarded to the opposing team, to be taken at the 2 m mark on the side where the ball goes out.

69. The throw is taken from the 2 m mark.

70. When a corner throw is taken, no player (except the defending goalkeeper) may be within the 2 m line.

71. Ruling: Should a defending goalkeeper be out of the water when a corner throw is awarded, another player of his team may take up a position on the goal line, but without the limitations and privileges of a goalkeeper.

72. If a goalkeeper, taking a free throw or goal throw, releases the ball and before any other player has touched it, regains possession and allows it to pass through his own goal, a corner throw must be awarded.

73. A corner throw taken improperly must be re-taken.

74. Ruling: If a corner throw is taken before the players

have left the 2 m area, the throw must be re-taken.

75. If a player taking a free throw passes the ball towards his own goalkeeper, and before any other player has touched it, the ball crosses the goal line or enters the net, a corner throw must be awarded. An attempt by the goalkeeper to stop the ball is not regarded as "touching" for the purposes of this rule.

RULE 15
Neutral Throw

76. 1. When one or more players of each team commit a foul at the same moment which makes it impossible for the referee to distinguish which player offended first, he must take the ball and throw it into the water in such a manner that the players of both teams have an equal opportunity to reach the ball after it has touched the water.

Clauses 105, 106 and 107 must be applied.

2. All neutral throws awarded within the 2 m area are to be taken on the 2 m line opposite the point at which the incident took place.

77. Ruling: If from a neutral throw the referee is of the opinion that the ball has fallen into a position to the advantage of one team, he must take the throw again.

RULE 16
Ordinary Fouls

78. It is a foul (for goalkeepers' exceptions see Rule 10):

79. To advance beyond the goal line at the start or re-start of the game, before the referee has given the signal.

80. To assist a player at the start or re-start or during a game.

81. To hold on to, or push off from, the goal posts or their fixtures. To hold on to the rails, except at start or re-start. To hold on to, or push off from, the sides or ends during actual play.

82. To take any active part in the game when standing on the floor of the bath; to walk when play is in progress.

83. To take or hold the ball under water when tackled.

84. To strike at the ball with clenched fist.

85. To simulate being fouled.

86. To touch the ball before it reaches the water when thrown in by the referee.

87. To jump from the floor of the bath to play the ball or tackle an opponent.

88. Deliberately to impede, or prevent the free movement of, an opponent unless he is holding the ball. Swimming on the shoulders, back or legs of an opponent constitutes impeding. "Holding" is lifting, carrying, or touching the ball. Dribbling the ball is not considered to be "holding".

89. To touch the ball with both hands at the same time.

90. To push, or push off from, an opponent.

91. 1. To be within 2 m of the opponents' goal line or to remain there except when behind the line of the ball.

2. Ruling: It is not an offence if the player taking the ball into the 2 m area passes the ball to his associate who is behind the line of the ball and who shoots at the goal immediately before the first player can leave the 2 m area.

92. To waste time.

93. Ruling: 1. For a team to retain possession of the ball for more than 35 seconds without shooting at their opponents' goal, is deemed to be wasting time, and a free throw shall be awarded against the player who last touched the ball before this foul is signalled.

2. Should a team shoot at goal as above and regain possession upon the ball rebounding or being in any other manner kept in play the measurement of 35 seconds shall immediately recommence from 35.

3. Time recommences from 35 when the ball comes into the possession of the opposing team or immediately the ball is put into play after a major foul.

(Ruling: The ball does not leave the possession of the holding team merely by being touched in flight by an opponent player, provided that it is not deflected into the possession of the opponent team.)

4. Time recommences when the ball comes into the possession of a team as the result of a "neutral throw".

5. [Deleted]

6. At expiration of the 35 seconds the free throw shall be taken by the opposing player nearest the point at which the game is stopped and undue delay by any member of the penalised team shall be punished as a Major Foul.

7. It is always permissible for the referee to penalise a foul under 16/92 before the period of 35 seconds has expired.

94. For the goalkeeper to go or touch the ball outside his own half of the field of play.

95. To take a penalty throw otherwise than in the prescribed manner.

96. To delay unduly when taking a free throw, goal throw or corner throw.

97. Ruling: The time allowed for a player to take a free throw is left to the discretion of the referee. It must be reasonable and without undue delay but does not have to be immediate.

98. Except as provided by Rule 10 (48) or 17 (100), the punishment for an ordinary foul shall be a free throw to the opposing team to be taken by any one of their players.

RULE 17
Free Throws

99. The referee must blow his whistle to declare fouls and exhibit the flag corresponding in colour to the caps worn by the team to which the free throw is awarded.

100. A free throw by a defending player awarded for a foul committed within the 2 m area must be taken from the 2 m line opposite the point at which the foul occurred. With this exception, and the exception in Rule 21.134.2, free throws are to be taken from the point at which the foul occurred. Should the game be stopped through illness or accident or other unforeseen reason, the team in possession of the ball at the time is awarded a free throw at that point when time is resumed.

101. Ruling: The responsibility for returning the ball to the player who is to take the free throw is primarily that of the side to which the free throw is awarded. The opponents have

no duty to do this, but no player may deliberately throw the ball away to prevent the normal progress of the game. (See also Rule 18/118).

102. Ruling: *A goalkeeper awarded a free throw must take the throw himself and the throw is subject to the limitations and privileges of a goalkeeper.*

103. The throw must be made to enable other players to observe the ball leaving the hand of the thrower. It is permitted to dribble the ball before passing to another player.

104. As soon as the ball leaves the hand of a player taking a free throw, it is in play. In the meantime all players are allowed to change position.

105. Except as provided by Rule 10/49, in all cases of a free throw, corner throw, or neutral throw, at least two players (excluding the defending goalkeeper) must play or touch the ball before a goal can be scored.

106. Ruling: To touch the ball means to touch intentionally.

107. Except as provided by Rule 10/49, an attempt by the goalkeeper to stop the ball from an attacking player, before it has been touched or played by a second player, is not regarded as touching and should the ball cross the goal line or hit the goal posts or the goalkeeper, the goalkeeper must be awarded a goal throw.

108. If, before a goal throw, corner throw, free throw, penalty throw or neutral throw is taken, an offence against Rule 16/85, 16/88, 16/90 or Rule 18 is committed by a member of the team not in possession of the ball, the offender shall be ordered from the water for a period of 45 seconds actual play, or until a goal has been scored, whichever period is the shorter, and the original throw maintained. If a member of the team in possession of the ball commits the offence a free throw shall be awarded to the opponent team and a Personal Fault shall be recorded against the player committing the offence. (See Rule 19/122).

2. NOTE. *If simultaneous fouls are committed by players from opposing teams, both players shall be evicted from the water for 45 seconds actual play, or until a goal has been scored, and the original throw shall be maintained.*

3. Ruling: In the special circumstances described in this paragraph, an offence against Rule 16/85, 16/88 or 16/90 shall be deemed to be a Major Foul and a Personal Fault shall be recorded against the player committing the offence.

109. A free throw taken improperly must be re-taken, except as provided by Rule 96.

RULE 18
Major Fouls

110. It is a Major Foul for a player:

111. To hold, sink or pull back an opponent not holding the ball.

112. To kick or strike an opponent or make disproportionate movements with that intent.

113. 1. To commit any foul, within the 4 m area, but for which a goal would probably have resulted.

2. NOTE: *In addition to other offences it is a Major Foul within the meaning of this paragraph to pull down the goal, or to play with the ball with clenched fist or with both hands in the 4 m area with the object of preventing a goal from being scored. A penalty throw must be awarded.*

3. Ruling: When the goalkeeper or any other player pulls over the goal completely with the object of preventing a goal, the player has shown disrespect and must be excluded from the remainder of the game (Rule 18 (115)). A substitute may enter the game within 2 m from the corner of the field of play on the side of the goal-judge (or on the side opposite the time-keeper if there be no goal-judges), under his goal line after the expiration of 35 seconds of actual play or when a goal has been scored, whichever period is the shorter. The eviction of the offending player is in addition to awarding the Penalty Throw.

114. To intentionally splash in the face of an opponent.

115. To refuse obedience to, or show disrespect for, the officials. The offending player shall be excluded from the remainder of the game and a substitute may enter the game at his own goal line at the point nearest the goal-judge after expiration of 35 seconds actual play, when a goal is scored, or

when an attacking team loses possession of the ball, whichever period is the shortest.

116. 1. To commit an act of brutality against another player or an official. A free throw *must* be awarded to the opponent's team and the offending player *must* be excluded from the remainder of the game and *must not be substituted*.

2. NOTE. *"Brutality" includes deliberately striking or kicking, or attempting deliberately to strike or kick.*

3. This rule (with the exception of a free throw) is also applicable if this happens during the interval between two periods of play.

117. To be guilty of misconduct. Misconduct is violence, the use of foul language, persistent foul play, etc. This is deemed to be an offence against Rule 115.

118. 1. To interfere with the taking of a free throw, penalty throw, corner throw or goal throw. 2. "Interference" includes (i) deliberately to throw the ball away to prevent the normal progress of the game, and (ii) any attempt to play the ball before it leaves the hand of the thrower.

119. 1. For an excluded player to re-enter or a substitute to enter the water improperly.

2. NOTES: (1) *Improper entry is to enter or re-enter:* (a) *without permission of the Secretary,* (b) *by jumping or pushing off from the side or wall of the bath or field of play,* (c) *from any place other than prescribed by Rule 121/2(a);*

(2) When this offence occurs during the last minute of the final quarter of any game, or during the last minute of any of the two periods of extra time (Rule 23), the offender shall be excluded for the remainder of the game without substitution and a Penalty Throw shall be awarded to the opponent team.

3. Ruling: Entry at any time of a player not entitled under the rules to participate at that time (except for a player awaiting the passage of a 35 second exclusion period to be entitled to participate and except in the situation described in Rule 121 (*c*)) shall cause such player to be excluded from the remainder of the game with immediate substitution when appropriate, and one penalty throw will be awarded to the opposing team.

4. Ruling: At any time when a player awaiting the passage

of an expulsion period enters illegally with the object of preventing a goal, it is deemed to constitute a violation of Rule 18/113, and after the player has left the water to complete the original exclusion period, a penalty throw shall be awarded to the opposing team. This penalty takes precedence over the penalty otherwise provided under Rule 11/119 (expulsion or penalty throw).

120. Except as otherwise expressly provided in these Rules the punishment for a Major Foul is:

121. 1. The offending player *must* be ordered from the field of play for a period of 35 seconds actual play, when a goal is scored or when the attacking team loses possession of the ball, whichever period is the shortest, and a free throw to be taken by a player of the opponent's team after the excluded player has commenced to leave the field of play and the referee has signalled the free throw to be taken. The penalty period will start upon the taking of the free throw. If the player leaving the field of play intentionally interferes with the play, it shall constitute an additional major foul and a penalty throw shall be awarded. Upon a change of possession, all players excluded for 35 seconds re-enter immediately.

2.1. After the expiration time the excluded player himself must re-enter within 2 m from the corner of the field of play on the side of the goal-judge, under his goal line, and without affecting the alignment of the goals.

2.2. In cases of simultaneous fouls by members of both teams the offending players shall be excluded as above and a neutral throw be taken. Both excluded players will return on signal of the referee after a period of 35 seconds actual play, when a goal has been scored, or when the attacking team loses possession of the ball, whichever period is the shortest.

2.3. If a player is excluded and there are not 3 Personal Faults recorded against him, and at the end of his exclusion period a substitute player enters in his place, this is deemed to be an offence against Rule 18/115.

RULE 19
Personal Faults

122. 1. A player committing a Major Foul anywhere in the field of play shall be awarded a Personal Fault, and upon being awarded a third such Personal Fault in any one game he shall be excluded from the remainder of the game and a substitute may enter at his own goal line at the point nearest to the goal judge after expiration of the exclusion time under the Rules.

2. If such third Personal Fault results from a foul requiring the award of a Penalty Throw, the entry of the substitute shall be immediate and before the Penalty Throw is taken. If such third Personal Fault results from a violation of Rule 17/108 by a member of the team in possession of the ball, the offending player continues in the game until the next interruption of the referees. The entry of the substitute shall be after this interruption.

RULE 20
Penalty Throw

123. Should a player be fouled within his opponents' 4 m area according to Rule 18/112 or 18/116 or commit a foul according to Rule 18/113, 18/119–2 or 18/121, a Penalty Throw *must* be awarded against the offender's team. The referee must announce the offender's number to the secretary.

124. When a Penalty Throw is awarded, the offending player shall be ordered from the water only if the offence is so serious as to justify ordering from the water for the remainder of the game. (Rule 18/116, 18/119–2 and 19/122.)

125. A penalty throw may be executed by any player of the team to which it is awarded, except the goalkeeper, and the player taking the throw may elect to do so from any point on his opponents' 4 m line.

126. 1. The player taking the throw must await the signal of the referee which shall be given by whistle and by simultaneously lowering the respective flag from a vertical to a horizontal position. The player must have possession of the

ball and immediately throw it with an uninterrupted movement directly at the goal (see Rule 16/95). Should the ball rebound from the goal posts or crossbar it remains in play. It is not necessary for the ball to be played by any other player before a goal can be scored.

2. Ruling: A Penalty Throw may commence by lifting the ball from the water or with the ball held in the raised hand. It is permissible for the ball to be taken backwards from the direction of the goal in preparation for the forward throw at the goal, but the throw shall commence immediately upon the signal, and continuity of the movement shall not be broken before the ball leaves the thrower's hand.

127. All players, except the defending goalkeeper, or the other player according to Rule 20/130, must leave the 4 m area until the throw is taken, and no player may be within 2 m of the player taking the penalty throw.

128. The goalkeeper must take up a position anywhere on the goal line, and the referee will withhold the signal to throw until satisfied on this point.

129. Ruling: No portion of the goalkeeper's body, at water level, may be beyond the goal line.

130. Ruling: Should the defending goalkeeper be ordered from the water before or after the award of a penalty throw, another player of his team may take a position on the goal line before the throw is taken, but without the privileges and limitations of a goalkeeper.

131. A player must take a penalty throw as described. The penalty for not complying shall be a free throw to the player's nearest opponent.

132. If the taking of a penalty throw is interfered with, or Rules 20/127 and 20/128 are not complied with, the offender or offenders must be punished in accordance with Rule 18/115 and the throw must be re-taken.

133. If at precisely the same time as the referee awards a penalty throw or before a penalty throw is completed, the time-keeper whistles for an interval or full-time, the shot at goal must be allowed and should the ball rebound into the field of play from the goal post, crossbar or goalkeeper, it is dead.

NOTE: *When a penalty throw is to be taken in accordance with this paragraph all players except the defending goalkeeper and the player taking the penalty throw shall leave the water.*

RULE 21
Out of Play

134. 1. Should a player send the ball out of the field of play at either side, a free throw is awarded to the opposing team, to be taken nearest the place where the ball left the field of play.

2. Should the ball go out of the field of play between the goal line and the 2 m line the free throw must be taken from the 2 m mark on the side where the ball went out.

135. Should the ball strike or lodge in an overhead obstruction, it must be considered out of play, and the referee must stop the game and conduct a neutral throw. In that case, the ball may not be played until it has touched the water. Should the ball rebound from the goal posts or crossbar or from the side of the field of play at water level, it remains in play, except as provided by Rules 12/60 and 17/107. If the ball rebounds from the side of the field of play above water level, it is considered to be out of play.

RULE 22
Leaving the Water and Substitutes

136. A player must not leave the water or sit or stand on the steps or sides of the bath during a game except: (*a*) during an interval; (*b*) in case of illness or accident; or (*c*) by permission of the referee.

137. A player infringing this rule must be deemed guilty of misconduct. A player having left the water legitimately may re-enter at his own goal line by permission of the referee.

138. In the case of accident or illness, the referee may, at his discretion, suspend the game for not more than three minutes. It shall be the duty of a referee to instruct the time-keeper where any 3 minute stoppage for injury shall commence.

139. [Deleted]

140. In the event of a player retiring from the game through any medical reason, the referee may permit his immediate substitution by a reserve. The referee shall refuse such permission only if he considers the request unjustified. The player so retiring shall not be allowed at any time to re-enter the game. Otherwise a player may be substituted only: (*a*) In accordance with provisions of Rules 7/20, 7/21, 18/115 or 19/122, (*b*) during the interval between periods of play, (*c*) after a goal has been scored or (*d*) prior to the commencement of extra time. Note: During extra time the provisions of (*a*), (*b*) and (*c*) above shall apply.

141. A substitute shall not be allowed for a player who has been ordered from the water according to rule 18/116 and 18/119–2.2.

142. A substitute must be ready to replace a player without delay; if he is not ready the referee may re-start the game without him, in which case he may not take part in the match until the next stoppage.

143. Ruling: In case of accident, illness or injury, a substitute takes his position in the water where the accident occurred and will take the free throw or corner throw which may have been awarded the injured player, but should there be no substitute, another player shall take the throw.

144. The Captain, coach or team manager must notify the referee of substitutions.

RULE 23
Extra Time

145. Should there be level scores at full time (Rule 9) in any game for which a definite result is required, any continuation into extra time must be after 5 minute interval. There shall then be played two periods of 3 minutes each actual play, with an interval of 1 minute for changing ends.

146. This system of extra time shall be continued until a decision has been reached.

147. A player who has been ordered from the water by the referee—but not for the rest of the game—shall resume with

his team for extra time only when his penalty time has expired or a goal has been scored.

The A.S.A. Water Polo Referees' Handbook, *which contains the Rules together with notes, comments and instructions for referees, is available from the Amateur Swimming Association, Harold Fern House, Derby Square, Loughborough, Leicestershire.*